D0195791

'08

ANTHONY HAM

MADRID

CITY GUIDE

INTRODUCING MADRID

A monument to Felipe III keeps watch over life day and night on the Plaza Mayor (p61)

No city on earth is more alive than Madrid, a beguiling place whose sheer energy carries a simple message: this is one city which really knows how to live.

If Madrid were a woman, she'd be a cross between Penélope Cruz (beautiful and quintessentially Spanish) and Madonna (sassy, getting better with age). If it were a man, it would have to be Javier Bardem (not the world's most handsome but with that special, irresistible something). And if you could distil the city to its essence, it would be this: Madrid is a rebellious ex-convent schoolgirl who grew up, got sophisticated but never forgot how to have a good time.

Madrid is a city that becomes truly great once you get to know its unique barrios. There you'll discover that Madrid is an idea, a diverse city whose contradictory impulses are legion. Spain's capital is a wonderful city year-round, but you'll especially appreciate being here when the weather's warm and the kaleidoscopic variety of life Madrid-style courses through the streets or takes up residence in the city's plazas.

Madrid's calling cards are many: astonishing art galleries, relentless nightlife, its transformation into Spain's premier style city, an exceptional live music scene, a feast of fine restaurants and tapas bars, and a population that's mastered the art of living the good life. It's not that other cities don't have some of these things. It's just that Madrid has all of them in bucketloads.

CITY LIFE

It's often said that Madrid is the most Spanish of Spain's cities. Very few madrileños come from here originally, a vast number having moved here from elsewhere in Spain and other parts of the world. Consequently, this may just be Europe's most open and welcoming capital. If this can be summed up in a single phrase, it's the oft-heard, 'If you're in Madrid, you're from Madrid'. It's not that madrileños will knock you over with the warmth of their welcome. Rather, you'll find yourself in a bar or lost somewhere and in need of directions, and you'll suddenly be made to feel like one of their own. Just as suddenly, without knowing exactly when it happened, you'll realise that you never want to leave.

This is a city on the upswing and there's a real feeling on the streets that Madrid's time is now. Having spent a decade in the shadow of Barcelona, Madrid is rapidly reclaiming the title of Spain's most exciting city. All things Spanish may be taking the world by storm, but it's here in Madrid that you'll find the laboratory of Spanish innovation, whether in the world of fashion, food or, increasingly, architecture. Dare we say it, Madrid long ago became the new Barcelona.

Further changes to the city include a marked rise in the number of newly arrived madrileños. In 1999 immigrants amounted to just 2% of the city's population. That figure now stands closer to 15% – the country received as many immigrants in five years as France did in four decades. This massive demographic shift is unsettling for some, but Madrid is still defined by its tolerance.

There are challenges though. As Spain's economy slows, madrileños are casting an uncertain eye on the future. Salaries in Madrid may be higher than in the rest of Spain, but they're pitiful by European standards and prices are rising to match those elsewhere on the continent. With a large proportion of the city's population mortgaged to the hilt, the question of how to pay the bills is one of the few issues guaranteed to keep madrileños awake at night for reasons other than revelry. They also worry that the country's politicians are trying to turn Spaniards into, as they themselves say, 'good Europeans', whether it's stricter antismoking laws or the slow death of the siesta. 'Leave us alone to be who we are' is a typical madrileño response.

How Madrid – which has always been a window on the soul of the Spanish heartland – reacts to these challenges will most likely determine the direction of Spain's future.

Get a taste for the local speciality cocido a la madrileña (meat and chickpea stew) at Malacatín (p164)

HIGHLIGHTS

LOS AUSTRIAS, SOL & CENTRO

From the grand monuments of old Madrid to the clamour of a city converging on its busiest crossroads, Los Austrias, Sol and Centro are at once Madrid in microcosm and the city writ large.

❶ Plaza Mayor
Watch the passing parade amid stunning
architecture (p61).

❷ Chocolatería San Ginés
Partake of *chocolate con churros* (Spanish donuts
with chocolate) at 3am (p186).

❸ Plaza de Oriente
Relax in one of the city's most beautiful plazas
(p63).

❹ Palacio Real
Marvel at the excess in the Royal Palace (p67).

❺ Plaza de la Puerta del Sol
Take Madrid's pulse at its beating heart (p68).

❻ Restaurante Sobrino de Botín
Eat suckling pig in the world's oldest restaurant
(p160).

❶ El Rastro
Treasure-hunt on Sunday morning in Europe's largest flea market (p74).

❷ Tapas on Calle de la Cava Baja
Eat Madrid's best tapas along this emblematic street (p163).

❸ Basílica de San Francisco El Grande
Search for St Francis of Assisi in this grand basilica (p74).

LA LATINA & LAVAPIÉS

La Latina sits on the cusp of downtown Madrid, awash with restaurants and bars where the art of taking tapas has never been more fun amid the medieval architecture of Madrid's origins. Just down the hill, Lavapiés is gritty and multicultural.

HUERTAS & ATOCHA

Huertas is best known for its nightlife, for streets that come to life after dark and capture the essence of a city that never seems to rest. The narrow lanes of the Barrio de las Letras yield to the sublime Centro de Arte Reina Sofía in Atocha.

1 Centro de Arte Reina Sofía
Admire Picasso's *Guernica*, as well as works by Dalí and Miró (p82).

2 Plaza de Santa Ana
Take up residence in this life-filled square (p86).

3 Live Jazz in Populart or Café Central
Listen to the greatest names in jazz (p206).

PASEO DEL PRADO & EL RETIRO

One of Europe's grandest boulevards, the Paseo del Prado is home to more museums and galleries than almost anywhere else on earth. Away to the east, the Botanical Gardens and Retiro Park are glorious oases of greenery in the city centre.

1 **Museo Thyssen-Bornemisza**
Explore centuries of the finest art in one extraordinary collection (p95).

2 **Plaza de la Cibeles**
Marvel at how a roundabout can be so beautiful in this iconic plaza (p97).

3 **Real Jardín Botánico**
Shelter from the noise of Madrid in the botanical gardens (p96).

4 **Iglesia de San Jerónimo El Real**
Sigh amid the extravagance of this former royal chapel (p94).

5 **Parque del Buen Retiro**
Take a break from city life in these glorious gardens (p98).

6 **Caixa Forum**
Enjoy the hanging garden and an innovative approach to architecture (p96).

7 **Museo del Prado**
Survey the work of Goya, Velázquez and other fine artists in this superior art gallery (p90).

SALAMANCA

Madrid's most exclusive barrio for more than a century, Salamanca is all about designer shopping, restaurants and refinement. That is, at least, until you arrive at the bullring where Madrid holds fast to that most controversial Spanish pastime.

❶ Salamanca Shopping

Get glamorous amid the surfeit of international brand names (see the boxed text, p138).

❷ Museo de la Escultura Abstracta

Stumble upon the open-air work of the country's big-name sculptors (p105).

❸ Museo Arqueológico Nacional

Step back into Spain's past at the archaeological museum (p104).

MALASAÑA & CHUECA

Two barrios that overflow with life, Malasaña and Chueca have two vastly different personalities – the former is grungy, eclectic and always fun, while the latter is gay, extravagant and sophisticated. Together they're two of the most diverse to explore.

❶ Sociedad General de Autores y Editores
Ask whether Gaudí has made a sudden appearance in Madrid (p108).

❷ Malasaña Nightlife
Indulge in the hard-living fun that's a Malasaña trademark (p192).

❸ Museo Municipal
Immerse yourself in the story of Madrid at the municipal museum (p108).

CHAMBERÍ & ARGÜELLES

Chamberí is the new Salamanca, a barrio where madrileños have perfected the art of living, while Argüelles extends on the theme. Out to the west, most of the neighbourhood's sights line up along the ridge looking out towards the setting sun.

❶ Templo de Debod
Relive ancient Egypt in the heart of Madrid (p115).

❷ Teleférico
Ride out across the city fringe on the slow-moving cable car (p119).

NORTHERN MADRID

The north of the capital is where Madrid works hard, celebrates the fact that it has the greatest football club of all time and generally goes out to eat when money is no object.

1 Estadio Santiago Bernabéu
Tour the temple of football or absorb the passion of Real Madrid match day (p122).

2 Santceloni
Dine alongside royalty in this gastronomic laboratory (p180).

BEYOND THE CENTRE

Beyond the confines of inner Madrid lie many of the mega-sites that need space to accommodate the crowds, from the massive stand of trees that is Casa de Campo to a range of sights for families.

1 Zoo Aquarium de Madrid
Talk to the animals at this fine city zoo (p128).

2 Ermita de San Antonio de la Florida
Catch your breath under the glorious frescoes of Goya (p124).

CONTENTS

Continued from previous page.

THE AUTHOR

Anthony Ham

After years of wandering the world Anthony has finally found his spiritual home. In 2001 he fell irretrievably in love with Madrid on his first visit to the city. Less than a year later he arrived here on a one-way ticket, with not a word of Spanish and not knowing a single person in the city. Now Anthony speaks Spanish with a Madrid accent, is married to Marina, a madrileña, and, together with their baby daughter, Carlota, they live overlooking their favourite plaza in the city. He adores just about everything about his adopted home (with the possible exception of *cocido a la madrileña* – a meat and chickpea stew that madrileños drool over – but he's working on it) and sometimes has to pinch himself to believe just how wonderfully life has turned out. When he's not writing for Lonely Planet, Anthony is the Madrid stringer for Melbourne's *Age* newspaper, and writes about and photographs Madrid, Africa and the Middle East for newspapers and magazines around the world.

ANTHONY'S TOP MADRID DAY

Madrid is not a city that gets up early and that suits me perfectly. I'd start with breakfast on Plaza de Olavide in Chamberí while I make my plans for the day. One of the things I love most about Madrid is that there's a different barrio to explore depending on my mood. My best possible day begins with browsing the shops in the lanes of Malasaña, then a quick metro trip to La Latina for tapas, especially those at Almendro 13, Taberna Txacoli, Corazon Loco or the *tortilla de patatas* (potato tortilla) at Juanalaloca. After resting in one of the glorious plazas in the city centre or a stroll around the Parque del Buen Retiro (best on a Sunday), I'd get my dose of high culture at the Paseo del Prado. Ignoring my body's demand for a siesta I'd head to Huertas for some live flamenco (Cardamomo is great), before cradling a *mojito* (rum with sugar and lashings of mint) in Café Belén in Chueca. I love the live music at Zanzibar, or any of the venues west of the Paseo de los Recoletos for that matter. After a late dinner along Calle de Manuela Malasaña, I'd be very happy to find myself nursing a *caipirinha* (Brazilian cocktail made with *cacheca*, sugar, lime and ice) in Conde Duque at Kabokla, before the city's all-night clubs erase all thoughts of tomorrow.

GETTING STARTED

A trip to Madrid doesn't require too much advance planning – it's the sort of city where you can just dive in and make it up as you go along. Apart from booking your flight (p259) and accommodation (p228), just about everything else can be sorted out upon your arrival. Then again, the planning stage of your trip to Madrid can be part of the pleasure and any preparation you do beforehand will surely only enhance your experience of this intoxicating city.

You want to see Real Madrid play live in front of 80,000 screaming fans or you really want to see a bullfight to see what all of the fuss is about? No problem. Turn to p220 for information on how to book ahead. You've heard that Madrid's live music and jazz scenes are the best in southern Europe? Easy, simply turn to p207 and p206 respectively. Not quite sure which barrio (neighbourhood) in Madrid best suits your personality and where you'd like to be based? We've reduced the barrios to their essence in the boxed text on p67. In short, everything you could possibly want in Madrid is covered in this book. For a quick overview of some of the advance planning you may want to do, see the boxed text on p21.

When it comes to planning your budget Madrid is a destination that's well suited to all pockets with hotels and hostels spanning the full spectrum of traveller means (from terrific backpackers' hang-outs to luxurious palaces) and restaurants ranging from quick meals on the run to all that's innovative (and expensive) about nouvelle Spanish cuisine.

WHEN TO GO

There's no bad time to visit Madrid. Given that there's always something going on, the weather can be an important factor when planning your visit. In winter Madrid most often enjoys cool but crystal-clear days, although cold winds blow in off the Sierra del Guadarrama and cold snaps can be bitterly cold (snowfalls are rare but do happen). In July and August expect unrelenting heat with occasional, apocalyptic storms. In August Madrid's frenetic energy takes a break and the city is uncharacteristically quiet. City streets empty, some restaurants close and offices run in neutral as locals head for the coast in search of a sea breeze or the hills in pursuit of high-altitude respite.

For more advice on Madrid's climate, turn to p268, while a full list of official public holidays in Madrid is covered in the Directory (p270).

If you have some flexibility about when you travel to Madrid, or you've a specialised interest, planning your trip around one of Madrid's many festivals (right) will be an important consideration.

If you're only here for a short stay, consider making it a weekend (ie Thursday to Sunday) when Madrid's nightclubs (p200) will have you dancing till dawn. If you're here for the major art galleries and museums, avoid Mondays when many are closed; the Centro de Arte Reina Sofía (p82) is a notable exception, clos-

ing on Tuesdays. If El Rastro (p136), Europe's largest flea market, is your thing, you'll need to be in Madrid on a Sunday morning.

FESTIVALS

Madrileños love to party. Most often that means an impromptu night out. However, there are times when there's method in the madness, whether it's Carnaval in the depths of February or the local fiestas in central Madrid's barrios in the stifling heat of August. What follows is a comprehensive guide to the major festivals, fairs and other important events in Madrid's calendar for which you may want to try to be in town. For a list of local fiestas in various Madrid barrios and surrounding towns, pick up a copy of the *Guía de Fiestas en la Comunidad de Madrid* (in Spanish) from the Comunidad de Madrid tourist office (p276).

January

AÑO NUEVO   1 Jan
Noche Vieja (New Year's Eve) is often celebrated at home with family, before people head out after midnight to paint the town red and all other sorts of colours. Many madrileños gather in Plaza de la Puerta del Sol to wait for the 12 *campanadas* (bell chimes) that signal Año Nuevo (New Year's Day), whereupon they try to stuff 12 grapes

(one for each chime) into their mouths and make a wish for the new year.

REYES
Epifanía (the Epiphany) is also known as the Día de los Reyes Magos (Three Kings' Day), or simply Reyes, perhaps the most important day on a madrileño kid's calendar. Although a December visit from Santa Claus has caught on, traditionally young Spaniards wait until Reyes. Three local politicians dress up as the three kings (three wise men) and lead a sweet-distributing frenzy of Cabalgata de Reyes, as horse-drawn carriages and floats make their way from the Parque del Buen Retiro to Plaza Mayor at 6pm on 5 January.

MADRID FUSION
www.madridfusion.net
All the Spanish chefs who have made it big on the national and international stage come to Madrid for this gastronomy summit. It's a cooking extravaganza where the masters of the Spanish kitchen show off their latest creations. Tickets can be difficult to come by, but your tastebuds will love you for it.

February
CARNAVAL
Carnaval spells several days of fancy-dress parades and merrymaking in many barrios across the Comunidad de Madrid, usually ending on the Tuesday, 47 days before Easter Sunday. Competitions for the best costume take place in the Círculo de Bellas Artes (p87). Carnaval in Madrid is not quite as big as in other parts of Spain, such as Cádiz, but it can still be a wild time. Depending on when Easter falls, Carnaval can spill over into March.

CAJA MADRID FLAMENCO FESTIVAL
A combination of big names and rising talents come together for five days of fine flamenco music in one of the city's theatres (often the Teatro Albéniz, but check). The dates are movable, but big names are guaranteed (in recent years including Enrique Morente and Pepe Habichuela).

PASARELA CIBELES
www.cibeles.ifema.es, in Spanish
The Pasarela Cibeles, staged in the Parque Ferial Juan Carlos I, is becoming an increasingly important stop on the European fashion circuit, especially for spring and autumn collections; the latter take to the catwalk in September.

ARCO
www.arco.ifema.es, in Spanish
One of Europe's biggest celebrations of contemporary art, the Feria Internacional de Arte Contemporánea draws gallery reps and exhibitors from all over the world. It's staged around mid-February in the Parque Ferial Juan Carlos I exhibition centre and lasts for five days.

March & April
JUEVES SANTO
Jueves Santo (Good Thursday) kicks off the official holiday period known in Spain as Semana Santa (Holy Week). Local *cofradías* (lay fraternities) organise colourful and often solemn religious processions where hooded men and barefoot women dragging chains around their ankles and bearing crosses are among the parading figures. The main procession concludes by crossing the Plaza Mayor to the Basílica de Nuestra Señora del Buen Consejo. For many madrileños it also marks the start of a much-needed *puente* (bridge, or long weekend) and they take the chance to escape the city.

VIERNES SANTO
Viernes Santo (Good Friday) and Easter in general are celebrated with greater enthusiasm in some of the surrounding towns. Chinchón, Ávila and Toledo in particular, are known for their lavish Easter processions.

ARTEMANÍA
The Feria de Arte y Antigüedades sees antique dealers from all over Spain converge on the Palacio de Congresos y Exposiciones on Paseo de la Castellana. You can admire anything from Picasso lithographs to ancient pottery. The fair usually lasts for a week and takes place towards the end of April.

JAZZ ES PRIMAVERA
www.sanjuanevangelista.org
Three weeks of jazz in the leading jazz venues across the city. Tickets can be bought online through www.elcorteingles.es.

May

SUMA FLAMENCA

www.sumaflamenca.com/eng/index.asp
Another soul-filled flamenco festival that draws some of the biggest names in the genre. Again the Teatro Albéniz provides one of the stages, but the big names also appear in some of the better-known *tablaos* (small stage theatres; p204) and other venues across the city.

FIESTA DE LA COMUNIDAD DE MADRID   2 May

On El Dos de Mayo (2 May) in 1808 Napoleon's troops put down an uprising in Madrid, and commemorating this day has become an opportunity for much festivity. The day is celebrated with particular energy in the bars of Malasaña, so much so that in recent years, this fiesta has seen pitched battles between police and rowdy revellers in Malasaña, so keep your wits about you.

FIESTAS DE SAN ISIDRO LABRADOR   15 May

The merry month of May is nowhere merrier than in Madrid. In the wake of the Dos de Mayo festivities comes the city's big holiday on 15 May, when it celebrates the feast day of its patron saint, San Isidro (the 'peasant'). On this day the townsfolk gather in central Madrid to watch the colourful procession, which kicks off a week of cultural events across the city. Locals also traipse across the Puente de San Isidro to the saint's chapel and spend the day there picnicking; many are in traditional dress, and sip holy water and munch on *barquillos* (sweet pastries). Goya depicted this feast day by the river at the tail end of the 18th century. In those days you looked across green fields back to Madrid – that view is now largely obstructed by high-rises! The country's most prestigious *feria* (bullfighting season) also commences and continues for a month at the bullring Plaza de Toros Monumental de Las Ventas.

FESTIMAD

www.festimad.es, in Spanish
This is the biggest of Spain's year-round circuit of major music festivals. Bands from all over the country and beyond converge on Móstoles or Leganés (on the MetroSur train network), just outside Madrid, for two days of indie music indulgence. Although usually held in May, Festimad sometimes spills over into (and even may begin in) June.

June

DÍA DE SAN JUAN   24 Jun

Celebrated in other parts of Spain with fireworks and considerable gusto, the eve of this holiday is a minor affair in Madrid. The action, such as it is, takes place in the Parque del Buen Retiro.

DÍA DEL ORGULLO DE GAYS, LESBIANAS Y TRANSEXUALES

www.orgullogay.org, in Spanish
The city's Gay and Lesbian Pride Festival and Parade take place on the last Saturday of the month. It's an international gig, with simultaneous parades taking place in cities across Europe, from Berlin to Paris. The inner-city barrio of Chueca is the place to be.

July

VERANOS DE LA VILLA

As if the traditional local fiestas weren't enough to amuse those madrileños forced to stay behind in the broiling city summer heat, the town authorities stage a series of cultural events, shows and exhibitions, known as 'Summers in the City'. Concerts, opera, dance and theatre are performed in the Centro Cultural de la Villa, in the Palacio del Conde Duque, the Jardines de Sabatini and outside the Templo de Debod, as well as other venues around town. The programme starts in July and runs to the end of August.

August

FIESTAS DE SAN LORENZO, SAN CAYETANO & LA VIRGEN DE LA PALOMA

These three local patron saints' festivities (which revolve around La Latina and Plaza de Lavapiés) keep the otherwise quiet central districts of Madrid busy during the first fortnight of August. An almighty din fills the hot night air as locals eat, drink, dance and generally let their hair down. Why not? It's too hot for sleep anyway.

LA ASUNCIÓN 15 Aug

Also known as the Fiesta de la Virgen de la Paloma, this is a solemn date in the city's religious calendar, celebrating the Assumption of the Virgin Mary.

September

LOCAL FIESTAS

Several local councils organise fiestas in the first and second weeks of September. They include Fuencarral-El Pardo, Vallecas, Arganzuela, Barajas, Moncloa-Aravaca and Usera. In the last week of the month you can check out the Fiesta de Otoño (Autumn Festival) in Chamartín. These are very local affairs and provide a rare insight into the barrio life of the average madrileño.

LA NOCHE EN BLANCO

'The White Night', first held in 2006 when it was a roaring success, is when Madrid (and many of its monuments, bars etc) stay open all night with a city-wide extravaganza of concerts and general revelry in 120 venues across the city. It's a participatory arts and culture festival and it rocks.

FIESTA DEL PCE

www.pce.es, in Spanish

In mid-September the Partido Comunista de España (PCE; Spanish Communist Party) holds its annual fundraiser in the Casa de Campo on the edge of the city. This mixed bag of regional-food pavilions, rock concerts and political soap-boxing lasts all weekend.

FIESTA DE OTOÑO

Since the early 1980s the city has thrown off the torpor of summer with the Autumn Festival, a busy calendar of musical and theatrical activity right up to the approach to Christmas. The nature and scope of the programme depends in no small measure on budget constraints.

November

DÍA DE LA VIRGEN DE LA ALMUDENA 9 Nov

Castizos (traditional madrileños) gather together in the Plaza Mayor to hear Mass on the feast day of the city's female patron saint.

top picks

UNUSUAL EVENTS

- **Fiesta de San Antón** The blessing of the pets takes place at the Iglesia de San Antón (Map pp110–11), home church of the patron saint of animals, on 17 January.
- **Jesús de Medinaceli** Up to 100,000 people crowd the Iglesia de Jesús de Medinaceli (Map pp84–5) on the first Friday of Lent to kiss the right foot of a wooden sculpture of Christ (*besapié,* kissing of the foot). Pilgrims make three wishes to Jesus, of which he is said to grant one.
- **Fiestas de San Isidro Labrador** (opposite) This is Madrid's biggest party, when *chulapos* (born-and-bred madrileños) dress in short jackets and berets, and *manolas* (the female version of a once-common Lavapiés first name) don their finest *mantón de Manila* (embroidered silk shawl). If you're lucky, they'll even dance the *choti* (a traditional working-class dance not unlike the polka).
- **Fiesta de San Antonio** Young women (traditionally seamstresses) flock to the Ermita de San Antonio de la Florida (p124) on 13 June to petition for a partner. Whether spiritually inclined or not, the attitude seems to be 'why chance it?'
- **Fiesta de Vallecas** The mischievous Brotherhood of Sailors in the working-class barrio of Vallecas stages a 'naval battle', in other words a massive water fight, in July to demand that the government provide Madrid with a seaport.

EMOCIONA JAZZ

Madrid loves its jazz too much to be confined to just one festival (Jazz es Primavera in spring is the other one). Groups from far and wide converge on the capital for a series of concerts in venues across town.

December

FESTIVAL DE GOSPEL & NEGRO SPIRITUALS

In the week running up to Christmas Madrid is treated to a feast of jazz, blues and gospel, usually in the Centro Cultural de la Villa.

NAVIDAD 25 Dec

Navidad (Christmas) is a fairly quiet family time, with the main meal being served on Nochebuena (Christmas Eve). Elaborate nativity scenes are set up in churches around the city and an exhibition of them is held in Plaza Mayor.

COSTS & MONEY

First, the bad news. Not so long ago, Madrid was the second-cheapest capital city in Europe. But soaring house prices and a significant rise in prices across the board since Spain adopted the euro in 2002 have made Madrid not only the most expensive city in Spain, but the 22nd most expensive city in the world in which to live.

Despite such a gloomy outlook Madrid remains generally cheaper for travellers than many major world capitals. If you're coming from Paris, London or New York, you may find most things cheaper than back home. Unlike elsewhere in cities of Madrid's stature, it's also still possible to find semi-luxurious boutique hotels for around €100 a double in the city centre. At the budget end of the market, dormitory beds shouldn't cost more than €20 and nice *hostales* (hostels) with private bathroom and TV rarely cost more than €60, sometimes even less. Eating out in a nice, midrange restaurant shouldn't cost much more than about €30 per person, although you can do it for a lot less, especially if you partake in the weekday lunchtime *menú del día* (see the boxed text, p159), a fixed-price, three-course set lunch that costs around €10. The *menú del día* is a great way to experience a more expensive restaurant without getting stung for à la carte prices. Transport (metro, city buses and even taxis) is still absurdly cheap and, if you time your visit well, it's possible to visit some mu-

seums at no cost (see boxed text on p104 for more information), including the must-see Museo del Prado and the Centro de Arte Reina Sofía.

INTERNET RESOURCES

A Tapear (www.atapear.com, in Spanish) Customer reviews and rankings of tapas bars in Madrid (370 at last count) and other Spanish cities under its 'Guía de Bares de Tapas'.

EsMadrid.com (www.esmadrid.com) The Ayuntamiento's recently revamped website is super-sexy, although it can be a little tough to navigate (scroll down and try the 'Site Map' if you're having trouble). Lots of info on upcoming events.

In Madrid (www.in-madrid.com) A direct line to Madrid's expat community with upcoming events, nightlife reviews, articles, a forum, classifieds and some useful practical information.

La Netro (http://madrid.lanetro.com, in Spanish) Allows you to search for bars, restaurants, nightclubs and just about any kind of Madrid business and most have customer reviews. Its TOP La Netro section lists top tens across a range of categories as voted by users.

Le Cool (www.lecool.com) Weekly updates on upcoming events in Madrid with an emphasis on the alternative, offbeat and avant-garde. The name is pretty accurate.

Mad About Madrid (www.madaboutmadrid.com) Reasonably comprehensive site with blogs, history and advice on exploring the city.

Multi Madrid (www.multimadrid.com) Traveller-driven website with chat forums, classifieds and loads of practical information.

Turismo Madrid (www.turismomadrid.es) Portal of the regional Comunidad de Madrid tourist office that's especially good for areas outside the city but still within the Comunidad de Madrid.

HOW MUCH?

El País newspaper €1

Souvenir T-shirt €10 to €25

Admission to the Prado €6

1L of mineral water in supermarket €0.50

10-trip metro ticket €6.70

Caña (small glass of beer) of Mahou €1.50 to €2.50

Tapa €2.50 to €4.50

Admission to dance clubs €10 to €20

Normal letter (up to 20g) within Europe €1.07

Cocktail €6.50 to €12

SUSTAINABLE MADRID

Travelling to Madrid by train allows you to see so much more as well as minimising your impact upon the environment. While it used to take days to get to Madrid by train, the expansion of Spain's high-speed train system has drastically reduced travelling time. For more information, see p264. If you're coming from the UK, another option is to travel by boat (see p262) from Plymouth to Santander or from Portsmouth to Bilbao; from both Bilbao and Santander there are regular train services to Madrid.

ADVANCE PLANNING

To find out what's going to be happening in Madrid while you're there, start perusing the local Spanish-language websites that give a rundown of upcoming concerts, exhibitions and other events. The better ones include Guía del Ocio (www.guiadelocio.com), La Netro (http://madrid.lanetro.com) and Salir Urban (www.salirsalir.com). If Spanish is a road too far, try the Madrid page of www.whatsonwhen.com, In Madrid (www.in-madrid.com) or the Madrid town hall's excellent multilingual website (www.esmadrid.com). If you find something you like, turn to the boxed text on p212 of this guide to see if you can book your concert or theatre performance online.

Although its unlikely you'll be able to book for the smaller venues, La Noche En Vivo (www.lanocheenvivo.com, in Spanish) and La Carega (www.lacarega.com, in Spanish) give a good rundown of where and when to turn up in time for live music.

For theatre performances, Real Madrid football games and bullfighting tickets, one recommended agency is Localidades Galicia (www.eol.es/lgalicia/). Tickets for football matches go on sale a week before the matches and we recommend trying to line up your tickets before arriving in town, especially if there's a big match on.

Most restaurants don't require bookings more than a day or two in advance during the week, but you should always book as early as possible for weekends – contact details for restaurants we recommend are found in the Eating chapter, which begins on p156. You should always book for the more expensive temples of gastronomy as soon as you know your travel dates. This is especially the case for Santceloni (p180), El Alboroque (p162), Sergi Arola Gastro (p178), Jockey (p178) and Zalacaín (p180).

It's supremely easy to keep your environmental credentials intact while travelling within Madrid, as much of the city is manageable on foot, and walking is a remarkably pleasant way to discover its unique barrios. Those areas not within walking distance are easily accessible on the city's excellent underground metro network (p263).

HISTORY

Founded as a Muslim garrison town in the 9th century and a squalid settlement for centuries thereafter, Madrid suddenly took centre stage in 1561 when it was unexpectedly chosen as Spain's capital. As the centre of a global empire on which the sun never set and as the seat of the Spanish royal court, Madrid was, at a stroke of the royal pen, transformed from a cultural backwater into the most important city in Spain. In the centuries that followed, the city grew into its role as capital, accumulating prestige, people from all across Spain and beyond, and the trappings of power and wealth. The end result is the most Spanish of all Spain's major cities.

ROMAN MADRID?

Amid the bustle of modern Madrid it can be difficult to imagine the scene that must have greeted the nomads who gathered along the banks of the Río Manzanares in Mesolithic and Neolithic times. If they came from the desolate plains that lie to the south or east, even Madrid's less-than-mighty river must have seemed like paradise. The rocky bluff where Madrid would later be founded, and where the Palacio Real (p67) now stands, must have offered welcome shelter amid a landscape of unrelenting monotony. If they came from the mountains in the north or west, this combination of river and rocky perch must have felt like the last place of safety before crossing the vast plateau, the *meseta* of central Iberia.

Thousands of years later the hagiographers of imperial Spain would, in an attempt to give Madrid an historical prestige it never truly had, argue that Madrid was later the site of a Roman city called Mantua Carpetana. Yes, the remains of Roman villas and inns have been found in the Madrid region, which fell under Roman control as they subdued the Celtiberian tribes between the 1st and 5th centuries AD. But the small Roman outpost known as Miacum, close to modern Madrid, was merely an obscure waystation on the important Roman road that criss-crossed the Iberian Peninsula.

MUSLIM MAYRIT

When the Muslim army of Tariq ibn Ziyad crossed the Straits of Gibraltar in the 8th century, it sparked an upheaval that would convulse the Iberian Peninsula for more than 700 years. In 756 the emirate of Córdoba was established in the south in what the Muslims called Al-Andalus. The soldiers and administrators of Córdoba, which became a beacon of religious tolerance and enlightened civilisation, would cover much of the peninsula until the beginning of the 9th century.

As Iberia's Christians began the Reconquista (Reconquest) – the centuries-long campaign by Christian forces to reclaim the peninsula – the Muslims of Al-Andalus constructed a chain of fortified positions through the heart of Iberia. One of these forts was built by Muhammad I, emir of Córdoba, in 854, on the site of what would become Madrid. They called the new

TIMELINE

1st–5th centuries AD	854	End 9th century
The Roman Empire subdues the Celtiberian tribes. The Roman road that connects Mérida with the Toledo (Toletum), Segovia, Alcalá de Henares and Zaragoza (Cesaraugusta) runs close to Madrid.	Muhammad I, emir of Córdoba, establishes the fortress of Mayrit (Magerit), one of many across the so-called Middle March, a frontier land connecting Al-Andalus with the small Christian kingdoms of the north.	Muhammad I orders the construction of a wall that ran along the ridgeline, enclosed the current Catedral de Nuestra Señora de la Almudena and what is now the Plaza de Oriente.

top picks

MADRID HISTORY BOOKS

- Madrid (Elizabeth Nash; 2001) An informative, entertaining and joyfully written account of various aspects of the city's past and present.
- A Traveller's Companion to Madrid (Hugh Thomas; 2005) A fascinating compendium of extracts about Madrid from the great and good.
- The New Spaniards (John Hooper; 2nd edition 2006) A highly readable account of the Franco years and the country's transition to democracy with Madrid taking centre stage.
- Hidden Madrid: A Walking Guide (Mark and Peter Besas; 2007) A quirky collection of anecdotes and curiosities about historical Madrid.
- Historia de la Villa de Madrid (José Antonio Vizcaíno; 2000) You'll need decent Spanish to enjoy this one, but there's no more comprehensive history of Spain's capital.
- Atlas Ilustrado de la Historia de Madrid (Pedro López Carcelén; 2004) Charts Madrid's growth into a modern metropolis using historical maps and clear, Spanish text.

settlement Mayrit (or Magerit), which comes from the Arabic word *majira*, meaning water channel. At first, Mayrit was merely one of a string of such forts across the so-called Middle March, a frontier land between Al-Andalus in the south and small Christian kingdoms of the north. As the Reconquista gathered strength, forts such as Mayrit grew in significance as part of a defensive line against Christian incursion.

With Christian forces massing to the north, Mayrit was small and vulnerable. Its hilltop location made it virtually impregnable from the north, west and south, but Mayrit lacked natural fortifications to the east. Recognising this, Muhammad I constructed a defensive wall within whose boundaries only Muslims could live; Mayrit's small Christian community lived outside, near what is now the Iglesia de San Andrés (p75). Wander down to the last remaining fragment of the Muralla Árabe (Arab Wall; p68), below the modern Catedral de Nuestra Señora de la Almudena (p68), and you can still get a sense of this isolated settlement surrounded by sweeping plains.

Above the more than 190 turrets, the imposing towers of the fort or *alcázar* (from the Arabic *al-qasr*) were visible where the Palacio Real now stands. Crouching beneath the walls was a tangle of lanes known as the *al-mudayna* (hence Almudena) in which soldiers lived with their families. It was a pattern that would be repeated over the centuries, with Madrid dominated by two mutually dependent communities who lived alongside but world's apart – the rulers in their castle and the ordinary people in small, squalid houses nearby.

Mayrit's strategic location in the centre of the peninsula drew an increasing number of soldiers and traders. To accommodate the many newcomers, Mayrit grew into a town. The main mosque was built on what is now the corner of Calle Mayor and Calle de Bailén, although only the smallest fragment remains (see p68). Muslim Mayrit survived through agriculture (irrigated by water) and produced its own pottery and ceramics.

For all its growth and attempts at fortifications, Mayrit was dispensable to its far-off Muslim rulers. When the emirate of Córdoba broke up into a series of smaller Muslim kingdoms called *taifas* in 1008, Mayrit was attached to Toledo. As the armies of Muslim and Christian Spain battled for supremacy elsewhere, Mayrit was not considered one of the great prizes and ultimately passed into Christian hands without a fight. In 1083 Toledo's ruler gave Mayrit to King Alfonso VI of Castile during a period of rare Muslim-Christian entente.

Around 1070	1083	1110
Madrid's patron saint, San Isidro Labrador, is born among the small community of Christians clustered around the Iglesia de San Andrés (where he was buried after his death in 1130) in Muslim Mayrit.	Mayrit passes into the hands of King Alfonso VI of Castile without a fight, ending Muslim rule over Mayrit, in return for the king's assistance in capturing Valencia.	Almoravid Muslims attack Madrid in an attempt to wrest the city back from Christian rule. They succeed in destroying Madrid's walls, but are unable to seize the Alcázar before being driven back.

BEAR NECESSITIES

Madrid's emblem – a bear nuzzling a *madroño,* or strawberry tree (so named because its fruit looks like strawberries), framed by seven five-point stars and topped by a crown – may be one of the most photographed corners of the Plaza de la Puerta del Sol (p68). But its origins remain something of a mystery, even to most madrileños.

When Alfonso VI accepted Mayrit from the Muslims in 1085, it was seen as an example of things to come for Christian forces hoping to sweep across Spain from the north. Taking the theme further, a group of seven stars that lies close to the North Star in the northern hemisphere forms a shape known as the Ursa Minor, or small she-bear. Thus the bear (once a common sight in the El Pardo area north of the city) and seven stars came to symbolise Madrid. The five points of the stars later came to represent the five provinces that surround Madrid (Segovia, Ávila, Toledo, Cuenca and Guadalajara).

The crown above the frame dates from the 16th century when Carlos I allowed Madrid to use the symbol of the imperial crown in its coat of arms after he cured a fever using *madroño* leaves (a popular medicinal herb).

This coat of arms appears on a deep-violet background to form the city's flag and adorns such important Madrid icons as the shirts of Atlético de Madrid football club (but not Real Madrid's).

A MEDIEVAL CHRISTIAN OUTPOST

Madrid never again passed into Muslim hands, although the city was often besieged by Muslim forces. As the frontline gradually pushed south, Christian veterans from the Reconquista and clerics and their orders flooded into Madrid and forever changed the city's character. A small Muslim community remained and south of what is now Calle de Segovia (then a stream), in the Vistillas area, emerged the busiest of the *arrabales* (suburbs beyond the city walls). To this day the warren of streets around Vistillas (p75) is known as the *morería* – the Moorish quarter. Nearby, the Plaza de la Paja was the site of the city's main market. By the end of the 13th century, a new city wall, bordered by what are now Calle Arenal, Cava de San Miguel, Calle de la Cava Baja, Plaza de la Puerta de Moros and Calle de Bailén, was built. To give you some idea of the scale of Madrid at this time, remember that where the Plaza Mayor (p61), Plaza de España (p70) and the Plaza de la Puerta del Sol (p68) all stand then lay beyond the walls.

Madrid may have been growing, but its power was negligible. Ruled by less-than-interested and usually distant rulers, the city existed in the shadow of the more established cities of Segovia and Toledo. Whereas other Castilian cities received generous *fueros* (self-rule ordinances), Madrid had to content itself with occasional, offhand royal decrees. Left largely to their own devices, a small number of local families set about governing themselves, forming Madrid's first town council, the Consejo de Madrid. The travelling Cortes (royal court and parliament) sat in Madrid for the first time in 1309. This first sign of royal favour was followed by others – Madrid (or rather the *alcázar*) was an increasingly popular residence with the Castilian monarchs, particularly Enrique IV. They found it a relaxing base from which to set off on hunting expeditions, especially for bears in the El Pardo district.

Whereas Madrid had once been susceptible to military conquest, it now succumbed to an altogether different threat, this time from poverty, isolation from power and terrible living conditions. In 1348 the horrors of the Black Death struck, devastating the population. In the same year the Castilian king began to tire of Madrid's growing independence and appointed *regidores* (governors) of Madrid and other cities in an attempt to tighten central control. Allying themselves with the royal family, a handful of families began to monopolise local power, ruling

1222	1309	1348
Madrid's emblem of seven stars and a bear nuzzling a *madroño* (strawberry tree) appears for the first time in historical records.	The Cortes (royal court and parliament) sits for the first time in Madrid. During the sitting, the royals declare war on Granada; the demands of the Reconquista mean that the royal court often travel throughout Spain.	The Black Death sweeps across Spain, killing King Alfonso XI and countless numbers of his compatriots. Estimates suggest that the plague kills anywhere between 20% and 50% of Madrid's population.

as petty oligarchs through a feudal system of government, the Comunidad de Villa y Tierra, in which the *villa* (town) lorded it over the peasants who worked the surrounding *tierra* (land).

Despite growing evidence of royal attention, medieval Madrid remained dirt-poor and small-scale. As one 15th-century writer observed, 'in Madrid there is nothing except what you bring with you'. It simply bore no comparison with other major Spanish, let alone European, cities.

Beyond the small-world confines of Madrid, however, Spain was being convulsed by great events that would ultimately transform Madrid's fortunes. The marriage of Isabel and Fernando united Christian Spain for the first time. Together they expelled the last of the Muslim rulers from Granada, financed Christopher Columbus' voyages of American discovery and ordered the expulsion of Jews who would not convert to Christianity from Spain – all in 1492.

Carlos I, the grandson of Isabel and Fernando, became the King of Spain in 1516. Three years later he succeeded to the Habsburg throne and so became Carlos V, Holy Roman Emperor. His territories stretched from Austria to the Netherlands and from Spain to the American colonies, but with such a vast territory to administer, he spent only 16 years of his 40-year reign in Spain. The Spanish nobility were not amused and rose up in what came to be known as the rising of the Comuneros. In March 1520 Toledo rebelled and Madrid quickly followed suit. Carlos and his forces prevailed, whereupon he retaliated by concentrating ever-more power in his own hands.

A TALE OF TWO CITIES

By the time that Carlos' son and successor, Felipe II, ascended the Spanish throne in 1556, Madrid was surrounded by walls that boasted 130 towers and six stone gates. Although it sounds impressive, these fortifications were largely built of mud and were designed more to impress than provide any meaningful defence of the city.

Such modest claims to significance notwithstanding, Madrid was chosen by Felipe II as the capital of Spain in 1561.

Suddenly thrust into the spotlight, Madrid took considerable time to grow into its new role. Felipe II was more concerned with the business of empire and building his monastic retreat at San Lorenzo de El Escorial (p252) than in developing Madrid. Despite a handful of elegant churches, the imposing *alcázar* and a smattering of noble residences, Madrid consisted, for the most part, of precarious, whitewashed houses that were little more than mud huts. They lined chaotic, ill-defined and largely unpaved lanes and alleys. The monumental Paseo del Prado, which now provides Madrid with so much of its grandeur, was nothing more than a small creek. Even so, Madrid went from having just 2000 homes in 1563 to more than 7000 just 40 years later as opportunists and impoverished rural migrants, would-be princes and fortune-seekers flocked to the city hoping for a share of the glamour and wealth that came from being close to royalty.

With more ostentatiousness than class, Madrid's indolent royal court retreated from reality and embarked on an era of decadence. Amid the squalor in which the bulk of Madrid's people toiled, royalty and the aristocracy gave themselves over to sickening displays of wealth and cavorted happily in their make-believe world of royal splendour. The sumptuous Palacio del Buen Retiro was completed in 1630 and replaced the *alcázar* as the prime royal residence (the former Museo del Ejército building and Casón del Buen Retiro (p99) are all that remain). Countless grand churches, convents and mansions were also built and, thanks to royal patronage,

1426	1479–81	1492
In the midst of a devastating drought, devout madrileños take the body of San Isidro, Madrid's patron saint, out onto the streets, whereupon it begins to rain.	Isabel, Queen of Castile, marries Fernando, King of Aragón; the two become the Catholic monarchs of Spain. An edict by Madrid's authorities turns Muslims into second-class citizens, forcing them to wear signs identifying their religion alongside other indignities.	The last Muslim rulers of Al-Andalus are defeated by Christian armies in Granada, uniting the peninsula for the first time in seven centuries.

A CAPITAL CHOICE

When Felipe II decided to make Madrid Spain's capital in 1561, you could almost hear the collective gasp of disbelief from Spain's great and good, few of whom lived in Madrid. Madrid was home to just 30,000 people, whereas Toledo and Seville each boasted more than 80,000. Even Valladolid, the capital of choice for Isabel and Fernando, had 50,000 inhabitants. What's more, in the 250 years since 1309, Madrid had hosted Spain's travelling road show of royalty just 10 times, far less than Spain's other large cities.

Madrid's apparent obscurity may, however, explain precisely why Felipe II chose it as the permanent seat of his court. Valladolid was considered to be of questionable loyalty. Toledo, which like Madrid stands close to the geographical heart of Spain, was known for its opinionated nobles and powerful clergy who had shown an annoying tendency to oppose the king's whims and wishes. In contrast, more than one king had described Madrid as 'very noble and very loyal'. By choosing Madrid Felipe II was choosing the path of least resistance. Felipe II also wanted the capital to be 'a city fulfilling the function of a heart located in the middle of the body'.

The decision saved Madrid from a life of provincial obscurity. This was most evident in 1601 when Felipe III, tired of Madrid, moved the court to Valladolid. Within five years, the population of Madrid halved. The move was so unpopular that the king, realising the error of his ways, returned to Madrid. *'Sólo Madrid es corte'* (roughly, 'Only Madrid can be home to the court') became the catchcry and thus it has been ever since.

this was the golden age of art in Spain (see p38). Velázquez, El Greco, José de Ribera, Zurbarán, Murillo and Coello were all active in Madrid in the 17th century. For the first time, Madrid began to take on the aspect of a city.

But for all its newfound wealth and status, Madrid suffered several handicaps compared with more illustrious capitals elsewhere in Europe: it was bereft of a navigable river, port, decent road links or the slightest hint of entrepreneurial spirit; agricultural land around the town was poor; and the immense wealth from the Americas was squandered on wars and on indulging the court. Madrid was, in fact, little more than a large grubby leech, bleeding the surrounding provinces and colonies dry.

By the middle of the 17th century Madrid had completely outgrown its capacity to cope: it was home to 175,000 people, making it the fifth-largest city in Europe. But if you took away the court, the city amounted to nothing and when Pedro Texeiro drew the first map of the city in 1656, the place was still largely a cesspit of narrow, squalid lanes.

THE BOURBONS LEAVE THEIR MARK

Such was the extent of Spain's colonial reach that events in Madrid could still alter the course of European history. After King Carlos II died in 1700 without leaving an heir, the 12-year War of the Spanish Succession convulsed Europe. While Europe squabbled over the Spanish colonial carcass, Felipe V (grandson of Louis XIV of France and Maria Teresa, a daughter of Felipe IV) ascended the throne. He may have founded the Bourbon dynasty, which remains at the head of the Spanish state today, but he also presided over the loss of most of Spain's European territories and was left with just Spain and a handful of colonial territories over which to rule.

Thankfully Felipe proved more adept at nation-building than military strategy. His centralisation of state control and attempts at land reform are viewed by some historians as the first steps in making Spain a modern European nation, and the former clearly cemented Madrid's claims

1520	1561	1601
Madrid joins Toledo in the rebellion of the Comuneros against Carlos I, a disastrous decision that prompts the victorious king to rein in Madrid's growing independence.	Against all the odds, Felipe II establishes his permanent court at Madrid which was, in Felipe II's words, 'a city fulfilling the function of a heart located in the middle of the body'.	Felipe III moves Spain's capital to Valladolid, but popular discontent convinces him of the error of his ways and the royal court returns to Madrid. It is the last serious challenge to Madrid's position as capital.

MADRID BEYOND THE ROYAL COURT

Travellers to Madrid in the 16th and 17th century found occasional beauty in the brick buildings with balconies of wrought iron, but the lasting impression was of streets 'which would be beautiful if it were not for the mud and filth'. The houses, such chroniclers wrote, were 'bad and ugly and almost all made of mud'. In the absence of a functioning government that took the needs of its citizens seriously, rubbish and human excrement were thrown from the balconies, 'a thing which afterwards creates an insupportable odour'. Undaunted by the squalor of the streets, madrileños had already begun a tradition that endures to this day, as one British traveller observed: 'In the evening, the people of Madrid go out to stroll and promenade and you see nothing more than a series of carriages.' Largely abandoned to their fate by their rulers, madrileños learned how to circumvent the often onerous decrees emanating from the royal court. When, in the 17th century, all home owners were ordered to reserve the second-storey of their homes for government bureaucrats and clergy newly arrived in the city, madrileños instead built homes with just a single-storey façade at street level, building additional storeys out the back, away from prying government eyes.

to being Spain's pre-eminent city. He preferred to live outside the noisy and filthy capital, but when in 1734 the *alcázar* was destroyed in a fire, the king laid down plans for a magnificent new Palacio Real (Royal Palace) to take its place.

His immediate successors, especially Carlos III (r 1759–88), also gave Madrid and Spain a period of comparatively common-sense governance. Carlos (with the big nose – his equestrian statue dominates the Puerta del Sol) came to be known as the best 'mayor' Madrid had ever had. By introducing Madrid's first programme of sanitation and public hygiene, he cleaned up a city that was, by all accounts, the filthiest in Europe. He was so successful that, near the end of Carlos III's reign, France's ambassador in Madrid described the city as one of the cleanest capitals in Europe. Mindful of his legacy, Carlos III also completed the Palacio Real (p67), inaugurated the Real Jardín Botánico (Royal Botanical Gardens; p96) and carried out numerous other public works. His stamp upon Madrid's essential character was also evident in his sponsorship of local and foreign artists, among them Goya and Tiepolo. Carlos III also embarked on a major road-building programme.

By the time Carlos III died in 1788, Madrid was in better shape than ever, even if Spain remained, despite all the improvements, an essentially poor country with a big-spending royal court.

NAPOLEON & EL DOS DE MAYO

Within a year of Carlos III's death Europe was again in uproar, this time as the French Revolution threatened to sweep away the old order of privileged royals and inherited nobility. Through the machinations of Carlos IV, the successor to Carlos III, and his self-seeking minister, Manuel Godoy, Spain incurred the wrath of both the French and the British. The consequences were devastating. First, Nelson crushed the Spanish fleet in the Battle of Trafalgar in 1805. Next, Napoleon convinced a gullible Godoy to let French troops enter Spain on the pretext of a joint attack on Portugal, whereby General Murat's French detachment took control of Madrid, easily defeating General Tomás de Morla's bands of hearty but unruly armed citizenry. By 1808 the French presence had become an occupation and Napoleon's brother, Joseph Bonaparte, was crowned king of Spain.

1622	Mid-17th century	1702
Seville-born Diego Rodríguez de Silva Velázquez moves to Madrid, takes up a position as a painter in the royal court and becomes synonymous with the golden age of Spanish art.	Madrid's population swells to 175,000 people, up from just 30,000 a century before. Only London, Paris, Constantinople and Naples can boast larger populations in Europe.	Felipe V is crowned king, beginning the Bourbon dynasty that still rules Spain and, save for four decades of the 20th century, has done so from Madrid.

Madrid did not take kindly to foreign rule and, on the morning of 2 May 1808 madrileños, showing more courage than their leaders, attacked French troops around the Palacio Real and what is now Plaza Dos de Mayo in Malasaña. Murat moved quickly and by the end of the day the rebels were defeated. Goya's masterpieces, *El Dos de Mayo* and *El Tres de Mayo,* on display in the Museo del Prado (p90), poignantly evoke the hope and anguish of the ill-fated rebellion.

Although reviled by much of Madrid's population, Joseph Bonaparte's contribution to Madrid in five short years should not be underestimated. Working hard to win popular support, Bonaparte staged numerous free *espectáculos* – bullfights, festivals of food and drink, and religious processions. He also transformed Madrid with a host of measures necessary in a city that had grown up without any discernible sense of town planning. These measures included the destruction of various churches and convents to create public squares (such as the Plaza de Oriente (p63), Plaza de Santa Ana (p86), Plaza de San Miguel, Plaza de Santa Bárbara, Plaza de Tirso de Molina and Plaza de Callao) and widening streets. He also conceived the viaduct that still spans Calle de Segovia (p75). Under Bonaparte sanitation was also improved and cemeteries were moved to the outskirts of the city.

But madrileños never forgave Bonaparte his foreign origins and the brutality with which he suppressed uprisings against his rule, mocking his yearning for legitimacy by calling him names that included the Cucumber King, Pepe Botella and King of the Small Squares. Perhaps their scepticism of foreign rule lay in the undeniable fact that life for madrileños was as difficult as ever.

The French were finally evicted from Spanish territory in 1813 as a result of the Guerra de la Independencia (War of Independence, or Peninsular War). But when the autocratic King Fernando VII returned in 1814, Spain was in disarray and, at one point, French troops even marched back into Spain to prop him up. Though Fernando was not given to frequent bouts of enlightenment, two of his projects would stand the test of time – he opened the renewed Parque del Buen Retiro (p98), which had been largely destroyed during the war, to the public and founded an art gallery in the Prado (p90). When he died in 1833 Fernando left Spain with little more than a three-year-old daughter to rule over them, a recipe for civil war, and an economy in tatters.

CAPITAL OF A COUNTRY DIVIDED

Isabel II, a toddler, was obviously not up to running the country, and power passed into the hands of her mother, María Cristina, who ruled as regent. Fernando's brother, Don Carlos, and his conservative supporters disputed Isabel's right to the throne, so María Cristina turned to the liberals for help, prompting what's known as the Carlist Wars. Throughout this period political upheaval remained part of Madrid's daily diet, characterised by alternating coups by conservative and liberal wings of the army. Madrileños must have rued the day their city became capital of this deeply fragmented country.

Apart from anything else, Madrid was incredibly backward. A discernible middle class only began to make a timid appearance from the 1830s. It was aided when the government ordered the *desamortización* (disentailment) of Church property in 1837. A speculative building boom ensued – if you've lived in Madrid since the late 1990s, you'll see that history has a habit of repeating itself – and its beneficiaries constituted the emerging entrepreneurial class. Indeed most historians agree that it was in the second half of the 19th century that Madrid's ordinary inhabitants finally began to emerge from the shadow of royalty and powerful clergy and play a defining role in the future of their city.

1734	1759–88	1808
The most enduring symbol of medieval Madrid, the *alcázar*, which had stood since the early days of the Muslim occupation, is destroyed by fire. Plans begin almost immediately to take its place.	Carlos III, King of Spain and patron of Madrid, cleans up the city, lays out the Parque del Buen Retiro and sponsors Goya, transforming Madrid from a squalid provincial city into a sophisticated European capital.	Napoleon's troops under General Murat march into Madrid and Joseph Bonaparte, Napoleon's brother, is crowned King of Spain, but only after Madrid's citizen-defenders bravely rose up in vain to protest against foreign rule.

Nonetheless, for 25 years after Isabel began to rule in her own right in 1843, Madrid was awash with coups, riots and general discontent. It is therefore remarkable that amid the chaos the city's rulers laid the foundations for modern Madrid's infrastructure. In 1851 the city's first railway line, operating between Madrid and Aranjuez, opened. Seven years later the Canal de Isabel II, which still supplies the city with water from the Sierra de Guadarrama, was inaugurated. Street paving, the sewage system and rubbish collection were improved, and gas lighting was introduced. More importantly, foreign (mostly French) capital was beginning to fill the investment vacuum.

Signs that Madrid was finally becoming a national capital worthy of the name also began to appear. In the years that followed, a national road network radiating from the capital was built and public works, ranging from the reorganisation of the Puerta del Sol to the building of the Teatro Real (p213), Biblioteca Nacional (p105) and Congreso de los Diputados (lower house of parliament), were carried out.

In the 1860s the first timid moves to create an Ensanche, or extension of the city, were undertaken. The initial spurt of building took place around Calle de Serrano, where the enterprising Marqués de Salamanca bought up land and built high-class housing. Poor old Salamanca – it was only after he died that Salamanca became one of Madrid's most exclusive barrios (neighbourhoods); see the boxed text, p105.

In 1873 Spain was declared a republic, but the army soon intervened to restore the Bourbon monarchy. Alfonso XII, Isabel's son, assumed power. In the period of relative tranquillity that ensued, the expansion of the Ensanche gathered momentum, the city's big train stations were constructed and the foundation stones of a cathedral were laid. Another kind of 'cathedral', the Banco de España, was completed and opened its doors in 1891. By 1898 the first city tramlines were electrified and in 1910 work began on the Gran Vía. Nine years later the first metro line started operation.

The 1920s were a period of frenzied activity, not just in urban construction but in intellectual life. As many as 20 newspapers circulated on the streets of Madrid and writers and artists (including Lorca, Dalí and Buñuel) converged on the capital, which hoped to the sounds of American jazz and whose grand cafés resounded with the clamour of *tertulias* (literary discussions). The '20s roared as much in Madrid as elsewhere in Europe.

However, dark clouds were gathering against this backdrop of a culturally burgeoning city.

IN THE EYE OF THE STORM

In 1923 the captain-general of Catalonia and soon-to-be dictator, General Miguel Primo de Rivera, seized power and held it until Alfonso XIII had him removed in 1930. Madrid erupted in joyful celebration, but it would prove to be a false dawn. By now, the Spanish capital, home to more than one million people, had become the seething centre of Spain's increasingly radical politics and the rise of the socialists in Madrid, and anarchists in Barcelona and Andalucía, sharpened tensions throughout the country.

Municipal elections in Madrid in April 1931 brought a coalition of republicans and socialists to power. Three days later a second republic was proclaimed and Alfonso XIII fled. The republican government opened up the Casa de Campo – until then a private royal playground – to the public and passed numerous reformist laws, but divisions within the government enabled a right-wing coalition to assume power in 1933. Again the pendulum swung and in

1812	1819	1833
Thirty thousand madrileños die from hunger caused by fighting against the French in the lead-up to the Guerra de la Independencia (War of Independence). The French were expelled from Spanish soil a year later.	Fernando VII opens the Museo del Prado with 311 Spanish paintings.	King Fernando VII dies, leaving three-year-old Isabel II as heir-apparent and Spain descends into the Carlist civil wars, devastating Madrid in the process.

February 1936 the left-wing Frente Popular (Popular Front) barely defeated the right's Frente Nacional (National Front) to power. General Francisco Franco was exiled, supposedly out of harm's way, to the Canary Islands, but with the army supporting the right-wing parties and the extreme left clamouring for revolution, the stage was set for a showdown. In July 1936 garrisons in North Africa revolted, quickly followed by others on the mainland. The Spanish Civil War had begun.

Having stopped Franco's nationalist troops advancing from the north, Madrid found itself in the sights of Franco's forces moving up from the south. Take Madrid, Franco reasoned, and Spain would be his. By early November 1936 Franco was in the Casa de Campo. The republican government escaped to Valencia, but the resolve of the city's defenders, a mix of hastily assembled and poorly trained recruits, sympathisers from the ranks of the army and air force, the International Brigades and Soviet advisers, held firm. Madrid became an international cause célèbre, drawing luminaries as diverse as Ernest Hemingway and Willy Brandt in defence of the city. For all the fame of the brigades, the fact remains, however, that of the 40,000 soldiers and irregulars defending Madrid, more than 90% were Spaniards.

Madrid's defenders held off a fierce nationalist assault in November 1936, with the fighting heaviest in the northwest of the city, around Argüelles and the Ciudad Universitaria. The Francoist general Emilio Mola assured a British journalist that he would soon take Madrid with his four columns of soldiers (20,000 in all) massed on the city's outskirts and with the help of his 'fifth column', a phrase that has since remained in the popular lexicon and referred to Franco's right-wing sympathisers in Madrid. But Mola's predictions came to nothing. Soldiers loyal to Franco inside Madrid were overpowered by local militias and 20,000 Franco supporters sought protection inside the walls of foreign embassies. Faced with republican intransigence – symbolised by the catchphrase 'No pasarán!' ('They shall not pass!') coined by the Communist leader Dolores Ibarruri – Franco besieged Madrid, bombarded the city from the air and waited for the capital to surrender. It didn't.

German bombers strafed Madrid, one of the first such campaigns of its kind in the history of warfare, although the Salamanca district was spared, allegedly because it was home to a high proportion of Franco supporters. The Museo del Prado was not so fortunate and most of its paintings were evacuated to Valencia. Hundreds of civilians were killed, although as many as 10,000 died in the Battle of Madrid, and Franco's approach was summed up by his promise that 'I will destroy Madrid rather than leave it to the Marxists'.

Encircled on all sides and with much of Spain falling to Franco's forces, madrileños lived a bizarre reality. People went about their daily business, caught the metro to work and got on with things as best they could. Like Londoners during the Blitz, madrileños who lived through the siege talk of the parallel realities of life in Madrid: the fear and the camaraderie of the bomb shelters, the mundane normalcy of daily life even as the bombs rained down. All the while, skirmishes continued around Argüelles and nationalist artillery intermittently shelled the city, particularly Gran Vía (nicknamed 'Howitzer Alley'), from the Casa de Campo. To maintain a minimum of functioning infrastructure, some of the city's vital industries were moved into disused metro tunnels.

By 1938 Madrid was in a state of near famine, with clothes and ammunition in equally short supply. As republican strongholds fell elsewhere across Spain, Madrid's republican defenders were divided over whether to continue the resistance. After a brief internal power struggle, those favouring negotiations won. On 28 March 1939 an exhausted Madrid finally surrendered.

1846	1860	1873
The French writer Alexandre Dumas visits Madrid, which he describes as 'a city of miracles. I have a terrible desire to become a naturalised Spaniard and live in Madrid'.	Even as Madrid's economy begins to shift away from the chasm that separated royalty and riff-raff, one-quarter of Madrid's working populace is still employed to serve in aristocratic households.	Spain's first, short-lived republic is declared, although the Bourbon monarchy soon returns to power in Madrid's Palacio Real with help from the army.

FRANCO'S MADRID

A deathly silence fell over the city as the new dictator made himself at home. Mindful that he was occupying a city that had hardly welcomed him with open arms, Franco considered shifting the capital south to the more amenable Seville. As if to punish Madrid for its resistance, he opted instead to remake Madrid in his own image and transform the city into a capital worthy of its new master. Franco and his right-wing Falangist Party maintained a heavy-handed repression, and Madrid in the early 1940s was impoverished and battle scarred, a 'city of a million cadavers', according to one observer.

In the Francoist propaganda of the day, the 1940s and 1950s were the years of *autarquía* (economic self-reliance, largely induced by Spain's international isolation after the end of WWII). For most Spaniards, however, these were the *años de hambre* (the years of hunger). Only in 1955 did the average wage again reach the levels of 1934. Throughout the 1940s, tens of thousands of suspected republican sympathisers were harassed, imprisoned, tortured and shot. Thousands of political prisoners were shipped off to Nazi concentration camps. Many who remained were put to work in deplorable conditions, most notably to construct the grandiose folly of Franco's Valle de los Caídos (p253) monument northwest of Madrid.

The dire state of the Spanish economy forced hundreds of thousands of starving *campesinos* (peasants) to flock to Madrid, increasing the already enormous pressure for housing. Most contented themselves with erecting *chabolas* (shanty towns) in the increasingly ugly satellite suburbs that began to ring the city.

By the early 1960s the so-called *años de desarollo* (years of development) industry was taking off in and around Madrid. Foreign investment poured in and the services and banking sector blossomed. Factories of the American Chrysler motor company were Madrid's single biggest employers in the 1960s. In 1960 fewer than 70,000 cars were on the road in Madrid. Ten years later more than half a million clogged the capital's streets.

For all the signs of development in Madrid, Franco was never popular in his own capital and an increased standard of living did little to diminish madrileños' disdain for a man who held the capital in an iron grip. From 1965 opposition to Franco's regime became steadily more vocal. The universities were repeatedly the scene of confrontation and clandestine trade unions, such as Comisiones Obreras (CCOO; Workers' Commissions) and the outlawed Union General de Trabajadores (UGT; General Workers' Union), also began to make themselves heard again.

The waves of protest were not restricted to Madrid. In the Basque Country the terrorist group Euskadi Ta Askatasuna (ETA; Basque Homeland and Freedom) began to fight for Basque independence. Their first important action outside the Basque Country was the assassination in Madrid in 1973 of Admiral Carrero Blanco, Franco's prime minister and designated successor.

Franco fell ill in 1974 and died on 20 November 1975.

THE TRANSITION TO DEMOCRACY

After the initial shock caused by the death of Franco, who had cast a shadow over Spain for almost four decades, Spaniards began to reclaim their country and Madrid took centre stage.

The Partido Socialista Obrero Español (PSOE; Spanish Socialist Workers' Party), Partido Comunista de España (PCE; Spanish Communist Party), trade unions and a wide range of opposition figures emerged from hiding and exile. Franco's trusted advisors remained in control

1881	1898	1919
The Partido Socialista Obrero Español (PSOE; Spanish Socialist Workers' Party) is founded in a back room of Casa Labra, still one of Madrid's most prestigious tapas bars.	Spain loses its remaining colonies of Cuba, Puerto Rico and the Philippines to the USA.	Madrid's first metro line starts running, crossing the city from north to south, with eight stations and a total length of 3.5km.

of both parliament and the armed forces but had neither the authority nor charisma necessary to hold back the tide of liberal optimism sweeping the country.

King Juan Carlos I, of the Bourbon family that had left the Spanish political stage with the flight of Alfonso XIII in 1931, had been groomed as head of state by Franco. But the king confounded the sceptics by entrusting Adolfo Suárez, a former moderate Francoist with whom he had long been in secret contact, with government in July 1976. With the king's approval Suárez quickly rammed a raft of changes through parliament while Franco loyalists and generals, suddenly rudderless without their leader, struggled to regroup.

Suárez and his centre-right coalition won elections in 1977 and set about writing a new constitution in collaboration with the now-legal opposition. It provided for a parliamentary monarchy with no state religion and guaranteed a large degree of devolution to the 17 regions (including the Comunidad de Madrid) into which the country was now divided.

Spaniards got the fright of their lives in February 1981 when a pistol-brandishing, low-ranking Guardia Civil (Civil Guard) officer, Antonio Tejero Molina, marched into the Cortes in Madrid with an armed detachment and held parliament captive for 24 hours. Throughout a day of high drama the country held its breath as Spaniards waited to see whether Spain would be thrust back into the dark days of dictatorship or whether the fledgling democracy would prevail. With the nation glued to their TV sets, King Juan Carlos I made a live broadcast denouncing Tejero and calling on the soldiers to return to their barracks. The coup fizzled out.

A year later Felipe González' PSOE won national elections. Spain's economic problems were legion – incomes were on a par with those of Iraq, ETA terrorism was claiming dozens of lives every year and unemployment was above 20%. But one thing that Spaniards had in abundance was optimism and when, in 1986, Spain joined the European Community (EC), as it was then called, the country had well and truly returned to the fold of modern European nations.

LA MOVIDA MADRILEÑA

Madrid's spirits could not be dampened and, with grand events taking place on the national stage, the city had become one of the most exciting places on earth. What London was to the swinging '60s and Paris to 1968, Madrid was to the 1980s. After the long, dark years of dictatorship and conservative Catholicism, Spaniards, especially madrileños, emerged onto the streets with all the zeal of ex-convent schoolgirls. Nothing was taboo in a phenomenon known as 'la movida madrileña' (the Madrid scene) as young madrileños discovered the '60s, '70s and early '80s all at once. Drinking, drugs and sex suddenly were OK. All night partying was the norm, drug taking in public was not a criminal offence (that changed in 1992) and the city howled. All across the city, summer terraces roared to the chattering, drinking, carousing crowds and young people from all over Europe flocked here to take part in the revelry.

What was remarkable about la movida is that it was presided over by Enrique Tierno Galván, an ageing former university professor who had been a leading opposition figure under Franco and was affectionately known throughout Spain as 'the old teacher'. A Socialist, he became mayor in 1979 and, for many, launched la movida by telling a public gathering 'a colocarse y ponerse al loro', which loosely translates as 'get stoned and do what's cool'. Unsurprisingly he was Madrid's most popular mayor ever and when he died in 1986 a million madrileños turned out for his funeral.

1920s	1931	1936–39
Madrid enjoys a cultural revival with Salvador Dalí, Federico García Lorca and Luis Buñuel bringing both high culture and mayhem to a city in love with jazz and *tertulias* (literary discussions).	After a period of right-wing dictatorship, Spain's Second Republic is proclaimed and King Alfonso XIII flees, leaving Spain in political turmoil and planting the seeds for civil war.	The Spanish Civil War breaks out. Nationalist forces bombard Madrid from the air and with artillery from the Casa de Campo and besiege the city for three years, before the exhausted city surrenders on 28 March 1939.

EYEWITNESS TO LA MOVIDA MADRILEÑA *Agatha Ruiz de la Prada, fashion designer*

Madrid during *la movida* was, for me, something marvellous because it coincided with my 20s and it was then that I started my first job. And so I arrived at work and thought, 'How much fun it is to work!' Imagine that you get to your first job and you are in the heart of *la movida*. At the time, I thought that was normal.

And the people who were very clever during *la movida* are still very clever, like Pedro Almodóvar and Alaska. Alaska was only 12 years old, but she was a spectacularly clever young woman. She was 12 years old but seemed like she was 40.

And then there was a time that was quite sad, at the end of *la movida*, when lots of people died from drugs. In the middle of the 1980s HIV was running wild and we were all very afraid. They were very black years, very sad, but I remember *la movida* as a wonderful thing, both for me and for Madrid. It was a moment during which there was so much freedom.

As told to Anthony Ham

But *la movida* was not just about rediscovering the Spanish art of *salir de copas* (going out for a drink). It was also accompanied by an explosion of creativity among the country's musicians, designers and film-makers keen to shake off the shackles of the repressive Franco years. The most famous of these was film director Pedro Almodóvar (see the boxed text, p42). Still one of Europe's most creative directors, his riotously colourful films captured the spirit of *la movida*, featuring larger-than-life characters who pushed the limits of sex and drugs. Although his later films became internationally renowned, his first film, *Pepi, Luci, Bom y Otras Chicas del Montón* (Pepi, Luci, Bom and the Other Girls), released in 1980, is where the spirit of the movement really comes alive. When he wasn't making films, Almodóvar immersed himself in the spirit of *la movida*, doing drag acts in smoky bars that people-in-the-know would frequent.

Among the other names from *la movida* that still resonate, the designer Agatha Ruiz de la Prada (see the boxed text, above) stands out. Also, start playing anything by Alaska, Los Rebeldes, Radio Futura or Nacha Pop and watch madrileños' eyes glaze over with nostalgia.

What happened to *la movida*? Many say that it died in 1991 with the election of the conservative Popular Party's José María Álvarez del Manzano as mayor. In the following years rolling spliffs in public became increasingly dangerous and creeping clamps (ie closing hours) were imposed on the almost lawless bars. Pedro Almodóvar was even heard to say that Madrid had become 'as boring as Oslo'. Things have indeed quietened down a little, but you'll only notice if you were here during the 1980s. If only all cities were this 'boring'.

MADRID SOBERS UP

Madrid is not a city that shifts its loyalties easily. After 12 years of Socialist rule, Madrid's political landscape fundamentally changed in 1991 with the election of its first democratically elected conservative mayor, José María Álvarez del Manzano of the Popular Party (PP), who earned the dubious distinction of bringing an end to the hedonistic Madrid of the 1980s. Álvarez del Manzano, who remained in power until 2003, became known as 'The Tunnelator' for beginning the ongoing mania of Madrid governments for semipermanent roadworks and large-scale infrastructure projects. His party remains in power to this day.

1960s	1973	1975–78
After two decades of extreme economic hardship, the decade became known as the *años de desarollo* (years of development) with investment and rural immigrants flooding into Madrid, even as opposition to Franco's rule begins to grow.	Admiral Carrero Blanco, Franco's prime minister and designated successor, is assassinated by ETA in a car bomb attack in Madrid's Salamanca district after the admiral left Mass at the Iglesia de San Francisco de Borga.	Franco dies in Madrid in his bed on 20 November 1975 after 39 years in power and following a year-long illness. Without an obvious successor to Franco, Spain returns to democratic rule three years later.

González and the PSOE remained in power at a national level until 1996 when the right-wing PP, which had been created by former Franco loyalists, picked up the baton under José María Aznar.

From 1996 until 2004, the three levels of government in Madrid (local, regional and national) remained the preserve of the PP, a dominance that prompted observers from other regions to claim that the PP overtly favoured development of the capital at the expense of Spain's other regions. Whatever the truth of such accusations, the city has moved ahead in leaps and bounds, and as the national economy took off in the late 1990s, Madrid reaped the benefits. Extraordinary expansion programmes for the metro, highways, airport, outer suburbs and for innercity renewal are unmistakable signs of confidence. By one reckoning, up to 75% of inward foreign investment into Spain is directed at the capital.

11-M

On 11 March 2004, just three days before the country was due to vote in national elections, Madrid was rocked by 10 bombs on four rush-hour commuter trains heading into the capital's Atocha station. When the dust cleared, 191 people had died and 1755 were wounded, many of them seriously. It was the biggest such terror attack in the nation's history. Madrid was in shock and, for 24 hours at least, this most clamorous of cities fell silent. Then, some 36 hours after the attacks, more than three million madrileños streamed onto the streets to protest against the bombings, making it the largest demonstration in Madrid's history. A further eight million marched in solidarity in cities across Spain. Although deeply traumatised, the mass act of defiance and pride began the process of healing.

Visit Madrid today and you'll find a city that has resolutely returned to normal. Bars and restaurants overflow with happy crowds and people throng the streets as they always have. Yes, security is a little tighter than before, but it's no more than in most other European cities. The only reminders of the bombings is the poignant Bosque de los Ausentes (Forest of the Absent; p98) in the Parque del Buen Retiro, which was planted as a memorial to the victims, and the 11 March 2004 Memorial (p86) at Atocha station.

Given the history of ETA violence, it came as no surprise that the ruling right-wing PP government insisted that ETA was responsible. But as evidence mounted that the attack might have come from a radical Islamic group in reprisal for the government's unswerving support for the deeply unpopular invasion of Iraq, angry Spaniards turned against the government. In a stunning reversal of prepoll predictions, the PP was defeated by the PSOE, whose leader, José Luis Rodríguez Zapatero, led the Socialists back to power after eight years in the wilderness.

In addition to withdrawing Spanish troops from Iraq, the new government introduced a raft of liberalising social reforms. Gay marriage was legalised, Spain's arcane divorce laws overhauled and, in 2005, almost a million illegal immigrants were granted residence. Although Spain's powerful Catholic Church has cried foul over many of the reforms, the changes played well with most Spaniards. As always, however, Madrid would become a battleground for the great issues of the day. It was here that the reforms were embraced with the greatest fervour, even as the streets filled with demonstrators (often bussed in from other Spanish regions).

In late 2007 21 people were convicted of involvement in the attacks, which were allegedly ordered by al-Qaeda.

1981	1980s	1991
Renegade Civil Guard officers march into the Spanish lower house of parliament (the Cortes) in Madrid in an attempted coup. After a day of high drama, the king orders a return to barracks and democracy survives.	La movida madrileña takes over the city, and becomes a byword for hedonism. The era produces such zany creative talents as Pedro Almodóvar, Agatha Ruiz de la Prada and Alaska.	Madrid elects a conservative mayor, José María Álvarez del Manzano of the Partido Popular (PP; Popular Party), for the first time, bringing an official end to la movida. A year later Madrid is designated a European Capital of Culture.

A CITY OF IMMIGRANTS

In a country where regional nationalisms abound – even Barcelona, that most European of cities, is fiercely and parochially Catalan – Madrid is notable for its absence of regional sentiment. If you quiz madrileños as to why this is so, they most often look mystified and reply, 'but we're *all* from somewhere else'.

It has always been thus in Madrid. In the century after the city became the national capital in 1561, the population swelled by more than 500%, from 30,000 to 175,000. Most were Spaniards (peasants and would-be nobles) who left behind the impoverished countryside and were drawn by the opportunities that existed on the periphery of the royal court.

During the first three decades of the 20th century Madrid's population doubled from half a million to almost one million; in 1930 a study found that less than 40% of the capital's population was from Madrid. The process continued in the aftermath of the civil war and in the 1950s alone more than 600,000 arrived from elsewhere in Spain.

In the late 20th century the process of immigration began to take on a new form, as Spain became the EU's largest annual recipient of immigrants. By early 2006 more than 16.5% of Madrid's population were foreigners, some 536,000 out of 3.29 million inhabitants and more than double the national average.

Unsurprisingly, true madrileños are something of a rare breed. Those who can claim four grandparents born in the city are dignified with the name *gatos* (cats). Although you could be forgiven for thinking that it reflects their tendency to crawl around the city until all hours; the term actually dates from when one of Alfonso VI's soldiers artfully scaled Muslim Mayrit's formidable walls in 1083. 'Look,' cried his comrades, 'he moves like a cat!'

MADRID TODAY

It comes as a surprise to many visitors that free-swinging Madrid is ruled by a conservative right-wing government. The PP's Alberto Ruiz-Gallardón, who was first elected mayor in 2003, increased the PP's stranglehold over the Ayuntamiento (town hall) with a landslide victory in 2007, winning 55% of the vote. His colleague, Esperanza Aguirre, became the country's first ever woman regional president in close-run elections for the Comunidad de Madrid in October 2003, but easily extended her majority in 2007. Madrid will, it seems, be ruled by conservatives for some time to come.

Despite belonging to the same party, the political marriage between Aguirre and Ruiz-Gallardón has not always been a happy one. Aguirre is a tough right-wing PP member who served as a senator and as national education and culture minister in José María Aznar's first PP government. Ruiz-Gallardón, on the other hand, comes unmistakeably from the liberal wing of the party. Aguirre makes little attempt to mask her dislike of Ruiz-Gallardón. Their simmering rivalry spilled over into open conflict on the national stage in early 2008, when the PP's leader of the national opposition, Mariano Rajoy, bowed to Aguirre's demand that Ruiz-Gallardón not be chosen as Rajoy's running mate in the national elections in March 2008, elections which the Socialists narrowly won.

Ruiz-Gallardón has been largely credited with feeding Madrid's burgeoning confidence, in part thanks to his aim of making Spain 'the city of reference in Southern Europe' by encouraging international organisations (such as the World Tourism Organisation) to set up their headquarters here. It seems to be working. In the first annual survey in June 2007 of 'The Good Life – Where to Live It', Madrid came in 10th, the highest ranking of any Spanish city. Madrid also came in a creditable seventh in a survey of the top ten European cities for business start-ups.

Yes, Ruiz-Gallardón saw his poll numbers briefly plummet in 2005 due to the disruption caused by a staggering 67 major infrastructure projects underway at the same time. But Madrid's impressive (albeit unsuccessful) bid for the 2012 Olympic Games reflected a mayor at the top of his game and a city that rightfully belongs in the company of Europe's great capitals.

11 March 2004	2005	2007
Terrorist bombings on four Madrid commuter trains kill 191 people and injure 1755. The next day three million madrileños take to the streets in protest, and the PSOE wins national elections on 14 March.	Madrid comes third in the competition to host the 2012 Summer Olympic Games, losing narrowly to Paris and London in the penultimate knock-out round of voting.	The PP's Alberto Ruiz-Gallardón, who first won election in 2003, wins an absolute majority in municipal elections, cementing the conservatives hold over Madrid's Ayuntamiento (town hall).

ARTS

Madrid is the cultural capital of the Spanish-speaking world. Yes, many quintessentially Spanish art forms may have had their origins elsewhere – flamenco, for example, has its roots in Andalucía. But it is to Madrid that Spain's major artists have always flocked in order to make their name, from the grand masters of Spanish painting down through the centuries – Velázquez and Goya are two shining examples – to Spain's famous film stars, acclaimed directors such as Pedro Almodóvar and flamenco greats like El Camarón de la Isla. As such, Madrid is easily Spain's premier cultural stage. Beyond the names that have received international recognition, many of Spain's greatest celebrities and finest performers may be unfamiliar to you, but that owes more to the Anglocentric international arts scene and its media than to the quality of their work. Madrid is a wonderful place to rectify such gaps in your knowledge, should they exist. Add to these elements an exciting contemporary arts scene where so much that is innovative in Spanish culture finds a stage in the capital – if it's happening in Spain, it will be happening here. Whether you're new to the arts of Spain or an old hand, you're in for a treat.

LITERATURE

From the Siglo de Oro to Pérez Galdós

Spanish literature began to come of age in the late 16th century as writers gravitated to the new capital, drawn by promises of royal patronage and endless material for stories as Madrid attracted a fascinating cast of characters eager for the glamour and opportunities that surrounded the royal court. The *Siglo de Oro* (Golden Age) of Spanish writing was very much Madrid's century and luminaries, such as Cervantes, Quevedo and Lope de Vega (p44), were all Madrid celebrities.

With the exception perhaps of the greatest of all Spanish poets, Seville-born Luis de Góngora (1561–1627), the greatest Spanish writers of the age were either born or spent much of their time in the young capital. Francisco de Quevedo (1580–1645), whose parents served in the royal court, went in search of grittier vignettes of local life and spent much of his time in Madrid taverns scribbling some of the most biting, nasty and entertaining prose to come out of 17th-century Spain. His *La Historia de la Vida del Buscón Llamado Don Pablos* (The Swindler; 1626), tracing the none-too-uplifting life of antihero El Buscón, is laced with venom and is his most enduring work.

Miguel de Cervantes Saavedra (1547–1616), regarded as the father of the novel, was born in Alcalá de Henares, lived in the Barrio de las Letras district in Huertas and ended his turbulent days in Madrid. He started writing *El Ingenioso Hidalgo Don Quijote de la Mancha* (Don Quijote) as a short story to earn a quick peseta. It turned instead into an epic tale in 1605 and is now widely considered the first and greatest novel of all time, charting the journey of the errant knight and his equally quixotic companion, Sancho Panza, through the foibles of his era.

Benito Pérez Galdós (1843–1920), alternately referred to as Spain's Balzac or the Iberian Tolstoy, spent virtually all his adult life in Madrid. His *Fortunata y Jacinta* recounts much more than a tormented love triangle, throwing light on the mores and social intrigues of late-19th-century Madrid.

FERIA DEL LIBRO

Bibliophiles will love being in Madrid around the last week of May and first two weeks of June for Madrid's Book Fair, the Feria del Libro de Madrid (www.ferialibromadrid.com), which has been running since 1933 and draws hundreds of booksellers from all over Spain, who set up stalls in the Parque del Buen Retiro. The Feria brings together some of the biggest names in Spanish literature for book signings and public events, although strolling amid the stalls in Madrid's most beautiful park on an early summer's day is reason enough to come. The books you'll come across are mostly in Spanish, but English-language titles are fairly widespread. For the duration of the Feria stalls open from 11am to 2pm and from 6pm to 9.30pm Monday to Friday, and from 10.30am to 2.30pm and from 5pm to 9.30pm Saturday and Sunday. Unless you like massive crowds, avoid Saturday and Sunday and come on a weekday.

top picks

GREAT MADRID READS

- Fortunata y Jacinta, Benito Pérez Galdós (1887)
- La Colmena (The Beehive), Camilo José Cela (1957)
- Capital de la Gloria, Juan Eduardo Zúñiga (2003)
- Un Corazon tan Blanco (A Heart So White), Javier Marías (2002)
- Historias del Kronen, José Ángel Mañas (1994)
- Winter in Madrid, CJ Sansom (2006)
- A Load of Bull: An Englishman's Adventures in Madrid, Tim Parfitt (2006)
- The Bad Girl, Mario Vargas Llosa (2007)

Contemporary Literature

The censors of Francoist Spain ensured that literary growth in the country was somewhat stunted; some outstanding writers emerged, but freedom of expression was limited and much of what was good in Spanish writing was penned by writers in exile. Since Spain's return to democracy in 1978 there has been a flowering of Spanish letters, and Madrid is at the heart of it.

Although not a madrileño by birth, Camilo José Cela (1916–2002) wrote one of the most talked about novels on the city in the 1950s, *La Colmena* (The Beehive). This classic takes the reader into the heart of Madrid, the beehive of the title, in what is like a photo album filled with portraits of every kind of Madrid punter in those grey days. For some readers Cela's reputation has been tarnished by rumours of his closeness to Franco's regime. Cela was nonetheless a writer of the highest quality and took the Nobel Prize in Literature in 1989 and the most important Spanish literature prize, the Premio Cervantes, six years later.

Francisco Umbral (b 1935), a prestigious journalist and winner in 2000 of the Premio Cervantes, is yet another chronicler of the city. *Trilogía de Madrid* (Madrid Trilogy; 1984), which explores a whole range of different circles of Madrid life in the Franco years, is just one of several Madrid-centric novels to his credit. Some have praised Umbral as the greatest prose writer in Spanish of the 20th century; Cela would no doubt snort in disagreement, as was his wont.

Spain and Madrid's experience of the civil war is better known through the works of foreigners like Orwell and Hemingway, but Madrid's own Juan Eduardo Zúñiga (b 1929) has written one of the most moving portrayals of Madrid life during the resistance. *Capital de la Gloria* consists of 10 stories set during the last, desperate months before Madrid finally capitulated.

Murcia's Arturo Pérez-Reverte (b 1951), long-time war correspondent and general man's man, has latterly become one of the most internationally read Spanish novelists. In *El Capitán Alatriste* (Captain Alatriste) we are taken into the decadent hurly-burly of 18th-century Madrid. The captain in question has become the protagonist of several novels and a blockbuster movie.

The author of *the* cult urban tribal novel in Madrid is without doubt José Ángel Mañas (b 1971). In *Historias del Kronen* (Stories from the Kronen; 1994) a band of young disaffected madrileños hangs out in the Kronen bar and throws itself into a whirlwind of sex, drugs, violence and rock 'n' roll.

Madrileño Javier Marías (b 1951; www.javiermarias.es) is a prolific and critically acclaimed novelist and essayist whose exceptional breadth and quality of work has led many to tip him as Spain's next Nobel Prize winner. His *Un Corazon tan Blanco* (A Heart So White; 2002), set in Madrid and centring on a tale of subtle family intrigue, shows a miniaturist's eye for detail throughout this outstanding work of digressive and intimate storytelling.

Another emerging talent is José Machado (b 1974), whose *Grillo* (2003) is a heavily autobiographical look at a young madrileño lad of good family determined to be a writer. It's a little like looking into a mirror that looks into a mirror. Other writers either born in Madrid or with strong connections to the city include: Almudena Grandes (b 1960), whose two novels *The Ages of Lulu* (2005) and *The Wind from the East* (2007) are both available in English; and Elvira Lindo (b 1962), who is a witty newspaper columnist for *El País* on matters of Madrid and national life as well as having written numerous books for children and adults.

PAINTING

The pantheon of master painters who called Madrid home for critical periods during their working lives runs from the old masters Velázquez, El Greco and Goya to doyens of contemporary art such as Picasso and Juan Gris. In centuries past Madrid's undeniable attraction was the patronage of

BACKGROUND ARTS

Spanish kings who lavished money on the great painters of the day. Spain's kings, who began the tradition in the 16th century, were a pretty vain and decadent lot and liked nothing better than to pose for portraits and to compete with other European royals for the fleeting prestige that came from association with the great artists of the day. Perhaps they also appreciated fine art. Whatever their motives, royal money and personal patronage transformed Madrid into one of the richest producers and storehouses of paintings anywhere in the world. From the early 20th century onwards, Madrid's role as the seat of Spain's finest artistic academies has drawn Spain's most creative talents.

The Early Days

The first Spaniard to find royal favour was Logroño-born Juan Navarrete (1526–79), also known as El Mudo (the Mute), one of Spain's first practitioners of tenebrism, a style that largely aped Caravaggio's chiaroscuro style. But Navarrete was an exception and Felipe II – the monarch who made Madrid the permanent seat of the royal court – preferred the work of Italian artists such as Titian ahead of home-grown talent. Even some foreign artists who would later become masters were given short shrift, suggesting that the king's eye for quality was far from perfect. One of these was the Cretan-born Domenikos Theotokopoulos (1541–1614), known as El Greco (the Greek; see the boxed text, p244), who was perhaps the most extraordinary and temperamental 'Spanish' artist of the 16th century, but whom Felipe II rejected as a court artist.

Velázquez & the Golden Age

As Spain's monarchs sought refuge from the creeping national malaise of the 17th century by promoting the arts, they fostered an artist who would rise above all others: Diego Rodríguez de Silva Velázquez (1599–1660). Born in Seville, Velázquez later moved to Madrid as court painter and stayed to make the city his own. He composed scenes (landscapes, royal portraits, religious subjects, snapshots of everyday life) that owe their vitality not only to his photographic eye for light and contrast but also to a compulsive interest in the humanity of his subjects so that they seem to breathe on the canvas. His masterpieces include *Las Meninas* (The Maids of Honour) and *La Rendición de Breda* (The Surrender of Breda), both on view in the Museo del Prado (p90).

Francisco de Zurbarán (1598–1664), a friend and contemporary of Velázquez, ended his life in poverty in Madrid and it was only after his death that he received the acclaim that his masterpieces deserved. He is best remembered for the startling clarity and light in his portraits of monks, a series of which hangs in the Real Academia de Bellas Artes de San Fernando (p71).

Other masters of the era whose works hang in the Prado, though their connection to Madrid was limited, include José (Jusepe) de Ribera (1591–1652), who was influenced by Caravaggio and produced fine chiaroscuro works, and Bartolomé Esteban Murillo (1618–82).

The Madrid School, Goya & Beyond

While the stars were at work, a second tier of busy baroque artists beavered away in the capital and collectively they came to be known as the Madrid School.

Fray Juan Rizi (1600–81) did most of his work for Benedictine monasteries across Castile; some hang in the Real Academia de Bellas Artes de San Fernando. Claudio Coello (1642–93) specialised in the big picture and some of his huge canvases adorn the complex at San Lorenzo de El Escorial (p252), including his magnum opus, *La Sagrada Forma* (The Holy Form).

But these were mere window dressing compared to Goya (see the boxed text, opposite), who cast such a long shadow that all other artists of the period have been largely obscured.

Although no-one of the stature of Goya followed in his wake, new trends were noticeable by the latter decades of the 19th century. Joaquín Sorolla (1863–1923) flew in the face of the French Impressionist style, preferring the blinding sunlight of the Valencian coast to the muted tones favoured in Paris. His work can be studied in Madrid's Museo Sorolla (p119).

Leading the way into the 20th century was Madrid-born José Gutiérrez Solana (1886–1945), whose disturbing, avant-garde approach to painting revels in low lighting, sombre colours and deathly pale figures. His work is emblematic of what historians now refer to as *España negra* (black Spain). A selection of his canvases is on display in the Centro de Arte Reina Sofía (p82).

GOYA – A CLASS OF HIS OWN

There was nothing in the provincial upbringing of Francisco José de Goya y Lucientes (1746–1828), who was born in the village of Fuendetodos in Aragón, to suggest that he would become one of the towering figures of European art.

Goya started his career as a cartoonist in the Real Fábrica de Tapices (Royal Tapestry Workshop) in Madrid. In 1776 Goya began designing for the tapestry factory, but illness in 1792 left him deaf; many critics speculate that his condition was largely responsible for his wild, often merciless style that would become increasingly unshackled from convention. By 1799 Goya was appointed Carlos IV's court painter.

Several distinct series and individual paintings mark his progress. In the last years of the 18th century he painted enigmatic masterpieces, such as *La Maja Vestida* (The Young Lady Dressed) and *La Maja Desnuda* (The Young Lady Undressed), identical portraits but for the lack of clothes in the latter. The rumour mill suggests the subject was none other than the Duchess of Alba, with whom he allegedly had an affair. Whatever the truth of Goya's sex life, the Inquisition was not amused by the artworks, which it covered up. Nowadays all is bared in the Prado.

At about the same time as his enigmatic *Majas*, the prolific Goya executed the playful frescoes in Madrid's Ermita de San Antonio de la Florida (p124), which have recently been restored to stunning effect. He also produced *Los Caprichos* (The Caprices), a biting series of 80 etchings lambasting the follies of court life and ignorant clergy.

The arrival of the French and war in 1808 had a profound impact on Goya. Unforgiving portrayals of the brutality of war are *El Dos de Mayo* (The Second of May) and, more dramatically, *El Tres de Mayo* (The Third of May). The latter depicts the execution of Madrid rebels by French troops.

After he retired to the Quinta del Sordo (Deaf Man's House) west of the Río Manzanares in Madrid, he created his nightmarish *Pinturas Negras* (Black Paintings). Executed on the walls of the house, they were later removed and now hang in the Prado. A scandal erupted recently when it was claimed that these chilling works were painted by the artist's son, Javier, and sold as genuine Goyas by his grandson. The Prado strenuously denies the claims.

Goya spent the last years of his life in voluntary exile in France, where he continued to paint until his death.

Picasso, Dalí & Juan Gris

The 17th century may have been Spain's golden age, but the 20th century was easily its rival.

The Málaga-born Pablo Ruiz Picasso (1881–1973) is one of the greatest and most original Spanish painters of all time. Although he spent much of his working life in Paris, he arrived in Madrid from Barcelona in 1897 at the behest of his father for a year's study at the Escuela de Bellas Artes de San Fernando. Never one to allow himself to be confined within formal structures, the precocious Picasso instead took himself to the Prado to learn from the masters, and to the streets to depict life as he saw it. Picasso went on to become the master of cubism, which was inspired by his fascination with primitivism, primarily African masks and early Iberian sculpture. This highly complex form reached its high point in *Guernica* (see the boxed text, p83), which hangs in the Centro de Arte Reina Sofía.

Picasso was not the only artist who found the Escuela de Bellas Artes de San Fernando too traditional for his liking. In 1922 Salvador Dalí (1904–89) arrived in Madrid from Catalonia, but he decided that the eminent professors of the renowned fine-arts school were not fit to judge him. He spent four years living in the 'Resi', the renowned students' residence (which still functions today) where he met poet Federico García Lorca and future film director Luis Buñuel. The three self-styled anarchists and bohemians romped through the cafés and music halls of 1920s Madrid, frequenting brothels, engaging in pranks, immersing themselves in jazz and taking part in endless *tertulias* (literary discussions). Dalí, a true original and master of the surrealist form, was finally expelled from art school and left Madrid, never to return. The only remaining link with Madrid is a handful of his hallucinatory works in the Centro de Arte Reina Sofía (p82).

In the same gallery is a fine selection of the cubist creations of Madrid's Juan Gris (1887–1927), who was turning out his best work in Paris while Dalí and his cohorts were up to no good in Madrid. Along with Picasso and Georges Braque, he was a principal exponent of the cubist style.

During the Franco years in Madrid, Antonio Saura (1930–98) was a shining light of surrealism and the dramatic brushstrokes of his portraits are sometimes seen as a reaction to the conventionality of public life under the dictator. In 1956 he publicly burned books of his paintings as a protest against Franco and the following year set up the El Paso group of artists whose aim was to provide a forum for contemporary art. Check out www.antoniosaura.org for more info.

Contemporary Art

The death of Franco in 1975 unleashed a frenzy of activity and artistic creativity was central to *la movida madrileña* (p32). The Galería Moriarty (p214) became a focal point of exuberantly artistic reference and is still going strong. A parade of artists marched through the gallery, including leading *movida* lights such as Ceesepe (b 1958), whose real name is Carlos Sánchez Pérez, and whose busy paintings full of people and activity (but recently veering towards surrealism), and eight short films capture the spirit of 1980s Madrid. Another Moriarty protégé was Ouka Lele (b 1957), a self-taught photographer whose sometimes weird works stand out for her tangy treatment of colour. Her photos can be seen at the Centro de Arte Reina Sofía, Museo Municipal (p108) and the Museo Municipal de Arte Contemporáneo (p108). Another *movida* photographer who still exhibits with Moriarty is Alberto García-Alix (b 1956).

The rebellious, effervescent activity in the 1980s tends to cloud the fact that the visual arts in the Franco years were far from dead, although many artists spent years in exile. The art of Eduardo Arroyo (b 1937) in particular is steeped in the radical spirit that kept him in exile for 15 years from 1962. His paintings tend in part towards pop art, brimming with ironic sociopolitical comment. Of the other exiles, one of Spain's greatest 20th-century sculptors, Toledo-born Alberto Sánchez (1895–1962), lived his last years in Moscow. He and Benjamín Palencia (1894–1980), an artist whose paintings occasionally show striking similarities with some of Sánchez' sculptures, were part of the so-called Escuela de Vallecas (Vallecas is now a working-class barrio in southern Madrid). The inheritors of their legacy, which is now more often called the Escuela de Madrid, include Francisco Arias, Gregorio del Olmo, Álvaro Delgado, Andrés Conejo and Agustín Redondela; all are on display at the Museo de Arte Contemporáneo. Carlos Franco (b 1951) painted the frescoes on the Real Casa de la Panadería on Playa Mayor (p61).

Antonio López García (b 1936) takes a photographer's eye to his hyperrealistic paintings. Settings as simple as *Lavabo y Espejo* (Wash Basin and Mirror, 1967) convert the most banal everyday objects into scenes of extraordinary depth and the same applies to his Madrid street scenes, which are equally loaded with detail, light play and subtle colour, especially *La Granvía* (1981) and *Vallecas* (1980). He won the coveted Premio Príncipe de Asturias for art in 1985. His contemporary, Alfredo Alcain (b 1936), whose textured paintings could at times be mistaken for aerial shots of patchwork fields, won the Premio Príncipe de Asturias in 2004.

Many of the most prominent new abstract painters have a relatively small body of work, but Alejandro Corujeira, Alberto Reguera, Xavier Grau and Amaya Bozal are all names to watch. In the figurative tradition, the same could be said of Juan Carlos Savater, Sigfrido Martín Begué, Abraham La Calle and Fernando Bellver. All can be seen at the Museo de Arte Contemporáneo.

The big event for contemporary art in Madrid is the annual midwinter Arco contemporary art fair (p16; www.arco.ifema.es), which goes from strength to strength as a showcase for both emerging and established Spanish talent, although as it gains in prestige, it's taking on a more international flavour.

MUSIC
Classical & Opera

Madrid has never been at the forefront of great classical music and opera, and the Spanish composers of note (Isaac Albéniz, Enrique Granados, Joaquín Rodrigo and Manuel de Falla) all came from elsewhere in Spain.

The single obvious exception to the general rule is Plácido Domingo (b 1934), the country's leading opera tenor and born *gato* (slang for madrileño, literally 'cat'). Early childhood was where the charming singer's relationship with Madrid more or less ended, as his parents, *zarzuela* (satirical dance and music) performers, moved to Mexico, where he made his singing debut years later. Along with the Catalan José Carreras, Spain contributed two of the Three Tenors.

Although not much of what you'll hear in Madrid originates here, you can still find a year-round programme of fine performances to choose from (see p212).

Contemporary Music

At the height of *la movida madrileña* in the 1980s Madrid's nights rocked to the sounds of more than 300 local rock bands. Most such groups fell by the wayside, but some have survived. Seguridad Social is a good old-fashioned hard-rock group that has remained a surprisingly constant force since it first started in 1982. Another legend is rock poet Rosendo Mercado, who started off with the group Leño in the late 1970s, later went solo and hasn't stopped since. Others that defined 1980s Madrid – Radio Futura, El Último de la Fila and Nacha Pop (and punkier ensembles such as Alaska and Kaka de Luxe) – came and went, but their music still holds a special place in the hearts of madrileños of a certain age.

One enduring group from *la movida*, Mecano, is now the subject of a blockbuster musical *Hoy No Me Puedo Levantar* (I Can't Get Out of Bed Today), named after its debut single; the musical ran in Madrid for three years from 2005 to sell-out crowds. The musical was written by Madrid-born Nacho Cano, former band member and now one of Madrid's most creative musical producers. At its peak Mecano sang many of the theme songs for the grittier side of *la movida*, dealing with teenage boredom, drugs and experimental love. Although the group went its separate ways in 1998, Mecano still provides the soundtrack for many a Madrid night.

top picks

MUSIC CDS

- Lo Mejor de Miguel Bosé (Miguel Bosé) Greatest hits of this veteran of the Madrid music scene.
- La Movida de los 80 All the biggies of *la movida*, including Alaska y Los Pegamoides, Radio Futura and Nacha Pop.
- Mecanografia (Mecano) All the hit singles from one of *la movida's* iconic bands.
- Canciones Hondas (Ketama) One of Ketama's best-ever CDs of rocky flamenco fusion; it's miles better than the Gypsy Kings!
- Pafuera Telearañas (Bebe) You can hear the smoky Madrid bar scene in every chord.
- Chicote Red Lounge – Cocktail (Sandro Bianchi) Downtempo rhythms mixed by DJs at Madrid's legendary Museo Chicote.
- Follow the City Lights (Dover) Catchy indie rock from Madrid's English-language sensations.
- El Mundo Se Equivoca (La Quinta Estación) Latin Grammy award-winning album in 2007.
- Con Otro Aire (Chambao) The latest flamenco fusion from Spain's hottest group of the moment.

Although born in Panama, Miguel Bosé was another *la movida* identity to make Madrid his own. Since the craziness of his early years, Bosé has mellowed into one of Spanish music's elder statesmen and most respected musicians with a base in pop but with inflections from myriad music genres.

Other echoes of *la movida* can be heard elsewhere. Three years after his band Nacha Pop split, Madrid-born Antonio Vega put out his first solo disc in 1991 and became one of the sensations of the mid-1990s with his soft pop-rock.

Madrid's rock scene is not what it once was but nonetheless continues to churn out class acts. Dover is one such group, a Madrid quartet that belts out energetic indie rock in English. Another pop-rock group to watch is La Quinta Estación, three Madrid-born musicians who left Spain to find success in Mexico before returning with a string of big hits.

Recently emerged from the rock bar scene in Malasaña is the pop quartet Balboa. Led by guitarist Carlos del Amo and his singer girlfriend, Lua Ríos, they've combined the energy of rock with a strong guitar lead and a soft-pop touch in Lua's voice and lyrics.

Another big star to recently emerge from the Madrid bar scene is Nieves Rebolledo, who goes by the stage name of Bebe. Her 2004 *Pafuera Telarañas* became one of the biggest albums of recent years and the signature track 'Malo' (Bad) managed that rare combination of becoming a dance-floor anthem while making serious social commentary (the song is an impassioned denunciation of domestic violence).

Other names enjoying huge popularity on the Spanish music scene include Estopa, La Oreja de Van Gogh, Amaral and the enduring Alejandro Sanz.

CINEMA & TELEVISION

The Spanish film industry, with Madrid as its uncontested capital, exists on two radically different levels. First there are the exceptional individual talents, such as Pedro Almodóvar (see the boxed text, p42), Penélope Cruz, Antonio Banderas and Javier Bardem, who have become international (and Hollywood) stars. At the same time the local film-making industry turns

PEDRO ALMODÓVAR'S MADRID

Plaza Mayor (p61) *La Flor de mi Secreto*
(The Flower of my Secret; 1995)

El Rastro (p74) *Laberinto de Pasiones* (Labyrinth of
Passion; 1982)

Villa Rosa (p204) *Tacones Lejanos* (High Heels; 1991)

Café del Círculo de Bellas Artes (p189) *Kika* (1993)

Acueducto de Segovia (p75) *Matador* (1986)

Museo del Jamón (p161) *Carne Trémula* (Live Flesh;
1997)

out work of real quality but struggles for both funding and international success, too often drowned out by the glamour and big budgets of that same Hollywood. Public funding for local film-making has consistently fallen over the past decade or so and, although audience numbers remain quite steady, less than 20% of Spanish box office takings are for Spanish films. These two strands come together for the annual Goya awards (Spain's Oscars), which are held in Madrid in February – it's the perfect stage for taking the pulse of the industry.

Pedro Almodóvar is not the only Spanish director to have earned critical international acclaim. The still-young Alejandro Amenábar (b 1973) is already one of Spain's most respected directors. He was born in Chile but his family moved to Madrid when he was a child. He announced his arrival with *Tesis* (1996), but it was with *Abre Los Ojos* (Open Your Eyes; 1997), which was later adapted for Hollywood as *Vanilla Sky*, that his name became known internationally. His first English-language film was *The Others* (2001), which received plaudits from critics, but nothing like the clamour that surrounded *Mar Adentro* (The Sea Inside; 2004), his stunning portrayal of a Galician fisherman's desire to die with dignity, which starred Javier Bardem. Not content with directing, Amenábar also writes his own films.

Madrid-born Fernando Trueba (b 1955) has created some fine Spanish films, the best of which was his 1992 release *Belle Epoque*. It portrays gentle romps and bed-hopping on a country estate in Spain in 1931 as four sisters pursue a slightly ingenuous young chap against a background of growing political turbulence. Behind the scenes on this and many Spanish movies is the publicity-shy, Madrid-based Rafael Azcona, surely one of the cinema's most prolific screenplay writers. *Belle Epoque* took an Oscar for Best Foreign Language Film in 1993. Truly versatile, Trueba is equally well known for his documentary *Calle 54* (2000), which did for Latin jazz

A DIRECTOR LIKE NO OTHER

When Pedro Almodóvar (b 1951) won an Oscar in 2000 for his 1999 hit, *Todo Sobre Mi Madre* (All About My Mother), the world suddenly discovered what Spaniards had known for decades – that Almodóvar was one of world cinema's most creative directors.

Born in a small, impoverished village in Castilla La Mancha, Almodóvar once remarked that in such conservative rural surrounds, 'I felt as if I'd fallen from another planet'. After he moved to Madrid in 1969 he found his spiritual home and began his career making underground Super-8 movies and making a living by selling second-hand goods at El Rastro flea market. He soon became a symbol of Madrid's counter-culture, but it was after Franco's death in 1975 that Almodóvar became a nationally renowned cult figure. His early films *Pepi, Luci, Bom y Otras Chicas del Montón* (Pepi, Luci, Bom and the Other Girls; 1980) and *Laberinto de Pasiones* (Labyrinth of Passion; 1982) – the film that brought a young Antonio Banderas to attention – announced him as the icon of *la movida madrileña* (p32), the explosion of hedonism and creativity in the early years of post-Franco Spain. Almodóvar had both in bucketloads; he peppered his films with candy-bright colours and characters leading lives where sex and drugs are the norm. By night Almodóvar performed in Madrid's most famous *movida* bars as part of a drag act called 'Almodóvar & McNamara'. He even appears in this latter role in *Laberinto de Pasiones*.

By the mid-1980s madrileños had adopted him as one of the city's most famous sons and he went on to broaden his fan base with such quirkily comic looks at modern Spain, generally set in the capital, as *Mujeres al Borde de un Ataque de Nervios* (Women on the Verge of a Nervous Breakdown; 1988) and *Átame* (Tie Me Up, Tie Me Down; 1990). *Todo Sobre Mi Madre* (All About My Mother; 1999) is also notable for the coming of age of the Madrid-born actress Penélope Cruz, who had starred in a number of Almodóvar films and was considered part of a select group of the director's leading ladies long before she became a Hollywood star. Other outstanding movies in a formidable portfolio include *Hable Con Ella* (Talk to Her; 2002), for which he won a Best Original Screenplay Oscar, *La Mala Educación* (Bad Education; 2004), a twisted story of a drag queen, his brother, an abusive priest and a school-friend-turned-filmmaker, and *Volver* (2006), which reunited Almodóvar with Penélope Cruz to popular and critical acclaim.

top picks

FILMS SET IN MADRID

Many famous movies have been filmed at least partly in Madrid, among them *Doctor Zhivago*, *El Cid* and *The Fall of the Roman Empire*. But the following are where Madrid really plays a starring role:

- *Pepi, Luci, Bom y Otras Chicas del Montón* (Pepi, Luci, Bom and the Other Girls; 1980) If you always wondered what Madrid was like during *la movida madrileña*, this early Almodóvar feature film takes you there in all its madness.

- *La Colmena* (The Beehive; 1982) Based on the classic novel by Camilo José Cela, this is a faithful rendition of Cela's portrait of Madrid during the grey years of the 1950s.

- *Historias del Kronen* (Stories from the Kronen; 1994) In Montxo Armendariz's film, a slightly depressing story of alienated urban youth emerges from the heart of Madrid.

- *Carne Trémula* (Live Flesh; 1997) This typically kaleidoscopic love thriller by Pedro Almodóvar contains the usual tortured themes of sex, violence and love, and stars Javier Bardem.

- *La Comunidad* (The Community; 2000) Directed by the generally wacky Alex de la Iglesia, this cheerfully off-the-wall tale of greed in a Madrid apartment block stars Carmen Maura.

- *Los Fantasmas de Goya* (Goya's Ghosts; 2006) Set in 1792 Madrid, this recent offering from Milos Forman tells the story of Goya, the Spanish Inquisition and the painter's many scandals; Javier Bardem and Natalie Portman play the lead roles.

- *Volver* (2006) This heartwarming Almodóvar film starring Penélope Cruz is set partly in the outer suburbs of Madrid.

what the *Buena Vista Social Club* (1999) did for ageing Cuban musicians. Trueba was a leading personality in the craziness that was *la movida madrileña* (see p32) in the 1980s.

Going back further, Luis Buñuel (1900–83) was another film identity obliquely associated with Madrid. He spent part of his formative professional years in Madrid, raising hell with his fellow surrealist Salvador Dalí, although he later spent much of his life in Paris and Mexico. Buñuel became something of a surrealist icon with his 1929 classic *Un Chien Andalou*, on which he collaborated with Dalí. His often-shocking films included *Los Olvidados* (The Forgotten Ones; 1950) and *Viridiana* (1961) – both won prizes at the Cannes Film Festival, although the latter was banned in Francoist Spain on the grounds of blasphemy.

Of Spain's best-loved actors, few are enjoying international popularity quite like the Oscar-winning heart-throb Javier Bardem, one of the best-known faces in Spanish cinema. Having made his name alongside Penélope Cruz in *Jamón Jamón* (1992), his best-loved roles include *Before Night Falls* (2000), *Mar Adentro* (The Sea Inside; 2004), *Love in the Time of Cholera* (2007) and *No Country for Old Men* (2007); remarkably his Oscar for Best Supporting Actor in 2008 was a first for Spanish actors. Like so many of Spain's best actors, Bardem has passed through the finishing school that are Pedro Almodóvar's movies, appearing in *Carne Trémula* (Live Flesh; 1997). Javier Bardem also comes from one of Spain's most distinguished film-making families and his uncle, Juan Antonio Bardem (1922–2002), is often considered Madrid's senior cinematic bard; Bardem Snr wrote the script for Luis García Berlanga's 1952 classic, *Bienvenido Mr Marshall* (Welcome Mr Marshall), and followed in 1955 with *Muerte de un Ciclista* (Death of a Cyclist). Although

from Spain's Canary Islands, the Bardems are Madrid identities and run a trendy tapas bar, La Bardemcilla (see p192), in the inner-city barrio of Chueca.

Penélope Cruz is another Hollywood actress with strong roots in Madrid (where she was born in 1974) and with an enduring love affair with Almodóvar. In the late 1990s Penélope Cruz took a leap of faith and headed for Hollywood where she had success in such films as *Captain Corelli's Mandolin* (2001) and *Vanilla Sky* (2001), but recognition of her acting abilities has come most powerfully for her roles in the Almodóvar classics, *Carne Trémula* (Live Flesh; 1997), *Todo Sobre Mi Madre* (All About My Mother; 1999) and *Volver* (2006); the latter was described by one critic as 'a raging love letter' to Cruz and earned her a Best Actress Oscar nomination, a remarkable achievement for a foreign-language film. Her conversion into one of Almodóvar's muses seems confirmed by news that she has agreed to appear in Almodóvar's next two movies.

Although not born in Madrid, Málaga-born Antonio Banderas moved to Madrid in 1981, at the age of 19, to launch his career and soon became caught up in the maelstrom of *la movida madrileña*, where he made the acquaintance of Almodóvar. After an early role in *Laberinto de*

Pasiones (Labyrinth of Passion; 1982), Banderas would return to the Almodóvar stable with *Mujeres al Borde de un Ataque de Nervios* (Women on the Verge of a Nervous Breakdown; 1988) as his glittering Hollywood career was taking off.

An eminent line-up of some of Spain's best actresses also come from Madrid, among them Victoria Abril (b 1959), Ana Belén (b 1950), Carmen Maura (b 1945), Belén Rueda (1965) and Maribel Verdú (b 1970).

Although existing in the shadow of Hollywood and its Spanish stars, *Alatriste* (2006) and *El Orfanato* (The Orphange; 2007) are among the Spanish movies to have made an international splash in recent years.

At first glance, Spanish TV may seem to be dominated by clones of international reality TV – especially *Gran Hermano* (Big Brother) and *Operación Triunfo* (which propels singing unknowns to stardom) – or endless gossip programmes (known by critics as *telebasura*, or TV rubbish) dissecting the lives of current celebrities.

That's true to a certain extent, but there are some excellent TV series to look out for. An outstanding series is *Cuéntame Cómo Pasó* (www.cuentamecomopaso.net), which is set in 1970s' Madrid. Telecinco's *Los Serrano* (www.losserrano.telecinco.es) is a mostly-comic, sometimes-serious family drama set in a Madrid chalet and featuring well-known movie actors. Anyone who has spent any time living in a Madrid apartment building will groan with recognition at *Aquí No Hay Quien Viva* (www.antena3.com/aquinohayquienviva/), a funny, fast-paced story of neighbours who know everyone else's business.

Most TVs receive six or seven channels – two from Spain's state-run Televisión Española (TVE1 and La 2), four independent (Antena 3, El Cuatro, Tele 5 and La Sexta) and the regional Telemadrid station – and a host of other local channels of varying quality.

News programmes are generally decent (especially on TVE1 at 3pm and 9pm) and you can often catch an interesting documentary (especially on La 2) or film. Some TVs allow you to switch from the dubbed version to the original on some channels. Otherwise the main fare is a rather nauseating diet of soaps (many from Latin America), endless talk shows and almost vaudevillian variety shows (with plenty of glitz and tits).

Many private homes and better hotels have satellite TV. Foreign channels include BBC World, CNN, Eurosport, Sky News and the German SAT 1, while places with digital decoders offer endless choices.

THEATRE

The literary *Siglo de Oro* (Golden Age) that characterised 17th-century Madrid also filled the sails of theatrical creation with the winds of genius. Some of the country's all-time greatest playwrights were at work in much the same period. One of Madrid's towering literary figures, Lope de Vega (1562–1635), also an exceptional lyric poet, was perhaps the most prolific: more than 300 of the 800 plays and poems attributed to him remain. He explored the falseness of court life and canvassed political subjects with his imaginary historical plays. You can still visit his house (p87) in the Barrio de las Letras. The work of Tirso de Molina (1581–1648) includes *El Burlador de Sevilla* (The Seducer of Seville), a play in which we encounter the immortal Don Juan, a likable seducer who meets an unhappy end.

A particularly Spanish genre that originated in Madrid is the *zarzuela*, light-hearted musical comedy in which the actors occasionally burst into song. Although it spread throughout the country in the 19th century it remains very much a Madrid phenomenon. The Teatro de la Zarzuela keeps busy with a year-round programme of these melodic social dramas. For more information on this uniquely Spanish drama form, see the boxed text on p215; for advice on where to see the best in Spanish theatre, turn to p215.

DANCE

Nacho Duato, head and principal dancer of the Madrid-based Compañía Nacional de Baile (http://cndanza.mcu.es/) since 1990, has transformed it from a low-profile classical company into one of the world's most dazzling and technically accomplished contemporary dance groups. Founded in 1978, the Ballet Nacional de España (http://balletnacional.mcu.es/) mixes classical ballet with Spanish dance. Both perform regularly in Madrid and around the country.

One performer that you absolutely must see if your visit coincides with her arrival in town is Sara Baras (www.sarabaras.com), a Cádiz-born performer whose flamenco ballet is unique and soul-stirring.

FLAMENCO

The musical and dance form most readily identified with Spain is rooted in the *cante jondo* (deep song) of the *gitanos* (Roma people) of Andalucía, and probably influenced by North African rhythms. The melancholy *cante jondo* is performed by a singer, who may be *cantaor* (male) or *cantaora* (female), to the accompaniment of a blood-rush of guitar from the *tocaor* (guitar player). The accompanying dance (not always present) is performed by one or more *bailaores* (flamenco dancers).

The genre flourished in the 1920s, but with the civil war things went downhill. Not until the 1950s did flamenco come to life again. In those dark years of austere dictatorship, even fun was considered suspect and so the hidden world of smoky cabarets and *tablaos* (small restaurants where flamenco is performed) was born.

Flamenco in Madrid

Although flamenco emerged in southern Spain, since the mid-19th century the best performers of flamenco have turned up at one time or another in Madrid. This statement distils in an essence the contribution Madrid has made to the development of flamenco: it has always been a stage, often a prestigious one, that has brought flamenco to a wider audience, but the roots of flamenco have always grown first elsewhere and the greatest proponents of the art have learned their craft in the south.

At first the *gitanos* and Andalucians were concentrated in the area around Calle de Toledo. The novelist Benito Pérez Galdós found no fewer than 88 Andalucian taverns along that street towards the end of the 19th century. The scene shifted in the early 20th century to the streets around Plaza de Santa Ana. Huertas is again the centre for some of the best flamenco venues and bars dedicated to all things flamenco, although *tablaos* are found across the capital.

As flamenco's appeal widened and became a tourist attraction, more *tablaos* sprang up throughout Madrid. For advice on Madrid's best flamenco venues, turn to p204, while a good website for all things flamenco is www.deflamenco.com. To learn more you could also pass by El Flamenco Vive (p132), Flamenco World (p136) or Espacio Flamenco (p135), all of which have a wide range of flamenco books and CDs. For flamenco courses see p269, while Madrid's excellent flamenco festivals are covered on p16.

Flamenco Stars

Two names loom large over the world of flamenco – Paco de Lucía and El Camarón de la Isla – who were responsible for flamenco's revival in the second half of the 20th century. Such is (or, in the case of El Camarón de la Isla, was) their dominance that theirs is the standard by which all other flamenco artists are measured.

Paco de Lucía (b 1947) is the doyen of flamenco guitarists with a virtuosity few can match. For many in the flamenco world, he is the personification of *duende,* that indefinable capacity to transmit the power and passion of flamenco. If he's playing in Madrid when you're there, don't miss it. Although existing somewhat in Paco de Lucía's shadow, other guitar maestros include members of the Montoya family (some of whom are better known by the sobriquet of Los Habichuela), especially Juan (b 1933) and Pepe (b 1944).

From 1964 Paco de Lucía teamed up with madrileño guitarist Ricardo Modrego, but began, in 1968, flamenco's most exciting partnership with his friend El Camarón de la Isla (1950–92); together they recorded nine classic albums. Until his premature death, El Camarón was the leading light of contemporary *cante jondo* and it's impossible to overstate his influence over the art; his introduction of electric bass into his songs, for example, paved the way for a generation of artists to take flamenco in hitherto unimagined directions. Although born in San Fernando in Andalucía's far south, El Camarón was the artist in residence at Madrid's Tablao Torres Bermejas for 12 years and it was during this period that his collaboration with Paco de Lucía was at its best. In his later years El Camarón teamed up with Tomatito, one of Paco de Lucía's protégés, and the results were similarly ground-breaking. The story of El Camarón's life (his real name was the far less evocative José Monje Cruz) has been made into an excellent movie (*Camarón*, 2005), directed by Jaime Chávarri. When El Camarón died in 1992 an estimated 100,000 people attended his funeral.

Another artist who has reached the level of cult figure is Enrique Morente (b 1942), referred to by one Madrid paper as 'the last bohemian'. While careful not to alienate flamenco purists, Morente, through his numerous collaborations across genres, helped lay the foundations for Nuevo Flamenco and Fusion. One of the most venerable *cantaoras* is Carmen Linares (b 1951), who has spent much of her working life in Madrid. Leading contemporary figures include the flighty, adventurous Joaquín Cortés (b 1969), and Antonio Canales (b 1962), who is more of a flamenco purist.

Nuevo Flamenco & Fusion

Possibly the most exciting recent developments in flamenco have occurred in its fusion with other musical forms. The purists loathe these changes – in the proud *gitano* world, innovation has often met with abrasive scorn – but a wider Spanish audience has enthusiastically embraced this innovative musical experimentation.

Two of the earliest groups to fuse flamenco with rock back in the 1980s were Ketama and Pata Negra, whose music is labelled by some as Gypsy rock. Ketama, in particular, have been wide-ranging in their search for complementary sounds and rhythms, and their collaborations with Malian kora (harp) player, Toumani Diabaté *(Songhai I and Songhai II)* are underrated works of rare beauty. In the early 1990s, Radio Tarifa emerged with a mesmerising mix of flamenco, North African and medieval sounds. A more traditional flamenco performer, Juan Peña Lebrijano, better known as El Lebrijano, has created some equally appealing combinations with classical Moroccan music. Diego Cigala, one of modern flamenco's finest voices, relaunched his career with an exceptional collaboration with Cuban virtuoso Bebo Valdés (*Lágrimas Negras,* 2004).

Chambao is the most popular of the *nuevo flamenco* bands doing the rounds at the moment. They first captured attention with their *Endorfinas a la Menta* (2003) and the excellent *Pokito a Poko* (2005). Also popular is Diego Amador (b 1973), a self-taught pianist. The piano is not a classic instrument of flamenco but Amador makes it work.

ARCHITECTURE

Madrid has long been defined by the grandeur of its public buildings. From the stately Palacio Real and *barroco madrileño* (Madrid baroque), the Spanish capital's muted contribution to world architectural textbooks, to the flights of fancy erected during the *belle époque* (beautiful time) period at the beginning of the 20th century, this is a city of exceptional beauty and variety. What has added depth to the visitor's architectural experience are two relatively recent phenomenon: innovative, eye-catching new structures (eg Caixa Forum Madrid and Terminal 4 at Barajas Airport) that were once the preserve of Barcelona, and iconic edifices (eg Museo del Prado, Centro de Arte Reina Sofía and the Antigua Estación de Atocha) transformed by extensions that take them to a whole new level. The overall effect is the unmistakable feel of a capital that other Spanish cities, however replete with history, could never exude.

MADRID TO THE 16TH CENTURY

Madrid's origins as a Muslim garrison town yielded few architectural treasures, or at least few that remain. The only reminder of the Muslim presence is a modest stretch of the town wall, known as the Muralla Árabe (Arab Wall; p68) below the Catedral de Nuestra Señora de la Almudena. Few examples of the rich *mudéjar* style (developed by the Moors who remained behind in reconquered Christian territory) that once adorned Madrid are the bell towers of the Iglesia de San Pedro El Viejo (p78) and Iglesia de San Nicolás de los Servitas (p63).

When Felipe II decided in 1561 to establish Madrid as the capital of Imperial Spain the city's architecture was unworthy of such grand aspirations with little more to distinguish

top picks

NOTABLE OLD BUILDINGS

- Palacio Real (p67)
- Plaza de la Villa (p62)
- Real Casa de la Panadería (p61)
- Palacio de Comunicaciones (p97)
- Sociedad General de Autores y Editores (p108)
- Plaza de Toros Monumental de Las Ventas (p101)
- Edificio Metrópolis (p70)

it than the odd grand church or palace; the elaborate edifices of Gothic architecture that prompted the erection of great soaring churches across medieval Europe largely passed Madrid by. After making Madrid his capital Felipe II became preoccupied with building his monumental mausoleum/palace/summer getaway at El Escorial and Madrid's architecture continued much as it had before. Unless you're content with the much interfered with, late-Gothic Casa de los Lujanes (p62) or the beautiful Capilla del Obispo (p75), you'll need to head for Toledo (p242), Segovia (p245) or Ávila (p249) for a greater appreciation of the genre.

MADRID BAROQUE & BEYOND

Juan de Herrera (1530–97) was perhaps the greatest figure of the Spanish Renaissance and his style, which was unlike anything else seen during the period, influenced a generation of Madrid architects and bequeathed to the city an architectural style all of its own. Herrera's austere masterpiece was the palace-monastery complex of San Lorenzo de El Escorial (p252), although the nine-arched Puente de Segovia (p75) is among the few buildings he left behind in Madrid.

But after his death Herrera's style would give Madrid some of its most distinguished buildings. The sternness of his Renaissance style fused with a timid approach to its successor, the more voluptuous, ornamental baroque, to create an architectural style known as *barroco madrileño* (Madrid baroque). The most successful proponent of this style was Juan Gómez de Mora (1586–1648), who was responsible for laying out the Plaza Mayor (p61), as well as the Ayuntamiento (p62), the Convento de la Encarnación (p70) and the Palacio de Santa Cruz (p62). Gómez de Mora's uncle, Francisco de Mora (1560–1610), added to an impressive family portfolio with the Palacio del Duque de Uceda (p62). Other exceptional examples of the style are the Real Casa de la Panadería (p61) and the main entrance of what is now the Museo Municipal (p108).

Ventura Rodríguez (1717–85) dominated the architectural scene in 18th-century Madrid much as Goya lorded it over the world of art. He redesigned the interior of the Convento de la Encarnación and conceived the Palacio de Liria (p109). He also sidelined in spectacular fountains, and it is Rodríguez whom we have to thank for the goddess Cybele in the Plaza de la Cibeles (p97) and the Fuente de las Conchas (p124) in the Campo del Moro.

Where Ventura Rodríguz leaned towards a neo-Classical style, Juan de Villanueva (1739–1811) embraced it wholeheartedly, most notably in the Palacio de Villanueva that would eventually house the Museo del Prado (p90). Villanueva also oversaw the rebuilding of the Plaza Mayor after it was destroyed by fire in 1790 and designed numerous outbuildings of the royal residences, such as San Lorenzo de El Escorial.

BELLE ÉPOQUE

As Madrid emerged from the chaos of the first half of the 19th century, a building boom began. The use of iron and glass, a revolution in building aesthetics that symbolised the embracing of modernity, became all the rage. The Palacio de Cristal (p98) in the Parque del Buen Retiro was built at this time.

By the dawn of the 20th century, known to many as the *belle époque*, Madrid was abuzz with construction. Headed by the prolific Antonio Palacios (1874–1945), architects from all over Spain began to transform Madrid into the airy city you see today. Many looked to the past for their inspiration. Neo-*mudéjar* was especially favoured for bullrings. The ring at Las Ventas (p101), finished in 1934, is a classic example. A more bombastic (and perhaps the most spectacular) interpretation of the Belle Époque style is Palacios' Palacio de Comunicaciones (p97) with its plethora of pinnacles and prancing ornaments, which was finished in 1917.

By the early 20th century architecture in Madrid had come to be known as the 'eclectic' style, a hybrid form of competing influences as architects mixed and matched. Among the joyous and eye-catching examples – Gran Vía (p70) is jammed with them – are the 1916 Edificio Grassy and the 1905 Edificio Metrópolis.

By the 1930s public architecture had taken on a more austere style with pretensions to grandeur. The signature building of this period was Nuevos Ministerios (1934–40; Map p123), whose architect, Segundino Zuazo, was said to have taken inspiration from San Lorenzo de El Escorial (p252), although the resemblance is more about scale than charm and which served as a precursor to the charmless style that would dominate the Franco years.

THE ARCHITECTURE OF DICTATORSHIP

After pounding Madrid into submission and seizing control of the country in 1939, General Francisco Franco was eager to leave behind an architectural legacy that would consist of enduring monuments to his rule. The results were either self-glorifying or grand structures of little discernible beauty.

Belonging to the former category were the Valle de los Caídos (p253) and the triumphal Arco de Victoria (Arch of Victory; Map pp116–17), which stands immediately northwest of the Plaza de la Moncloa. Now known more prosaically as the Puerta de Moncloa (Moncloa Gate), the arch was built in 1956 to commemorate his victorious troops' entry into Madrid and was adorned with references to his triumphs. After Spain's return to democracy all references to Franco were removed from the gate and only the *quadriga* (a chariot drawn by four horses) on the summit remains.

Skyscrapers were a Franco trademark. Given Franco's paranoia when it came to communism, the echoes in the Edificio España (1953) of a Soviet Monumentalist style are somewhat ironic. More in keeping with Franco's self-image was the Torre de Madrid (1957), which was for a time the tallest building in Europe. Both buildings overlook Plaza de España (p70). Far more striking and in keeping with the architecture of old Madrid was the Ministerio del Aire (Air Force Ministry; 1951) on the Plaza de la Moncloa.

Franco's impact on Madrid can also be seen along the grand, tree-lined Paseo de la Castellana, which took on much of its present aspect during Franco's rule. Sadly many fine old palaces that once lined the roadside were demolished in the process. These were replaced by such buildings as the none-too-elegant Torres de Colón, which was finished in 1976 after Franco's death.

CONTEMPORARY ARCHITECTURE

International experts are buzzing with the energy and creativity surrounding Spanish architecture. At one level Spanish architects such as Santiago Calatrava (who transformed Valencia and built the Olympic stadium in Athens among other signature projects) are taking the world by storm. At the same time architects from all over the world are clamouring for Spanish contracts, in part because the projects for urban renewal currently underway in Spain are some of the most innovative in Europe and municipal governments are funding this extraordinary explosion of architectural ambition.

Madrid has been slow in coming to the party, but things are changing rapidly, a fact that will become immediately obvious if you're arriving in town at Terminal Four (T4) of Madrid's Barajas International Airport. Designed by Richard Rogers, it's a stunning, curvaceous work of art, which deservedly won Rogers the prestigious Stirling Prize in October 2006; Spanish architect Carlos Lamela also worked with Rogers on the project.

Another significant transformation on a grand scale is to Madrid's once-low-rise skyline, with four skyscrapers rising up above the Paseo de la Castellana in northern Madrid. Of these, the Torre Caja Madrid (250m, designed

top picks

NOTABLE NEW OR FUSION BUILDINGS

- Centro de Arte Reina Sofía (p82)
- Caixa Forum (p96)
- Museo del Prado (p90)
- Antigua Estación de Atocha (p86)
- Teatro Valle-Inclán (p79)
- Terminal 4, Barajas International Airport (p260)

CONTEMPORARY ARCHITECTURE – FIND OUT MORE

Those keen to see beyond the major architectural landmarks of Madrid should pick up a copy of the *Plano de Arquitec-tura* (Architecture Map), which has photos of 258 distinguished Madrid buildings and a map of where to find them; it's usually available from the Centro de Turismo de Madrid (p276). Architecture buffs will also want to be in Madrid in late September or early October for the Semana de la Arquitectura (Architecture Week), with exhibitions, conferences and guided visits to signature architectural projects in Madrid; it's organised by the Fundación Arquitectura COAM (☎ 91 319 16 83; www.fucoam.es, in Spanish; Calle de Piamonte 23; Ⓜ Chueca or Colón). To find out more about Madrid's architectural direction, the June-July 2005, issue No 478, of *Techniques & Architecture* is entitled 'Madrid: A Challenge' and devoted solely to the Spanish capital. In early 2006 New York's Museum of Modern Art recognised the growing importance of Spanish architecture by launching an exhibition called 'On Site: New Architecture in Spain'. For these and other architectural publications, try Naos Libros (Map pp116–17; ☎ 91 547 39 16; www.naoslibros.es, in Spanish; Calle de Quintana 12).

by Sir Norman Foster) is Spain's tallest building, just surpassing its neighbour, the Torre de Cristal (249.5m, designed by César Pelli). The Torre de Espacio (236m, designed by Henry Cobb) has also won plaudits for its abundant use of glass.

Among the architectural innovations that travellers to Madrid are more likely to experience up close and at greater depth, the most exciting is perhaps the extension of the Museo del Prado, which opened in October 2007. The work of one of Spain's premier architects, the Madrid-based, Pritzker-prize-winning Rafael Moneo, the extension links the main gallery with what remains of the cloisters of the Iglesia de San Jerónimo el Real.

Tinkering with the 18th-century Palacio de Villanueva that houses the Prado was always going to be controversial and the appropriation of the cloisters to form part of the Prado's ever-growing empire was widely condemned when the plans were announced. The verdict, however, seems to be that Moneo has pulled it off with considerable aplomb. Much of the praise has centred around the use of traditional building materials like granite, red brick and oak, while the director of the Museo del Prado, Miguel Zugzaga, lauded the final effect as being 'like placing a still life by Juan Gris next to one by Zurbarán…discreet, elegant and profoundly modern'. Moneo is no stranger to urban challenges. One of his first major tasks was the construction of the Bankinter building in Madrid in 1976. After the mania of the 1960s for destroying 19th-century mansions and replacing them with bland blocks, Moneo demonstrated another way and thus may have saved old Madrid from disappearing under the crushing weight of a lack of imagination. Moneo met two other major Madrid challenges with his acclaimed remodelling of the Antigua Estación de Atocha and his conversion of the Palacio de Villahermosa into the Museo Thyssen-Bornemisza, both in the early 1990s.

Another landmark project in recent years has been the extension of the Centro de Arte de Reina Sofía by the French architect Jean Nouvel. It's a stunning red glass-and-steel complement to the old-world Antigua Estación de Atocha across the Plaza del Emperador Carlos V and the austerity of the remainder of the museum's 18th-century structure.

Between the Reina Sofía and the Prado and opposite the Real Jardín Botánico, the Caixa Forum Madrid (p96), completed in 2008, is one of Madrid's most striking buildings. Designed by the Swiss architects Jacques Herzog and Pierre de Meuron, its aesthetic seems to owe more to the world of sculpture than of architecture with its unusual iron-and-brick form. It's a worthy, surprising addition to the Paseo del Prado's grandeur.

One truly madrileño architectural team is the couple Ignacio García Pedrosa and Ángela García de Paredes, whose modern redesign of the Teatro Valle-Inclán (formerly the Teatro Olímpico) on the Plaza de Lavapiés has won much admiration. Emilio Tuñon and Luis Mansilla have joined forces to undertake the delicate work-in-progress of building the Museum of Royal Collections, close to the Palacio Real.

Other urban renewal projects are regenerating some of Madrid's satellite suburbs, such as Carabanchel to the south and Sanchinarro to the north, with innovative approaches to the city's urban sprawl.

And one final thing for those who love architecture: while in Madrid you really must stay at the Hotel Puerta América (p238), where each floor has been custom designed by a world-renowned architect.

ENVIRONMENT & PLANNING

Madrid is already feeling the effects of climate change, and although Spain and Madrid are not entirely to blame, the country's lamentable environmental record is nonetheless a major factor. At a city level some positive steps are being taken, but these pale in comparison to the problems the city itself seems to be creating, particularly when it come to pollution. On a planning front Madrid is, depending on your perspective, a massive building site or an exciting work-in-progress.

THE LAND

At 650m above sea level on a high continental plateau, Madrid is the highest capital city in Europe. The Comunidad de Madrid – in the centre of which lies Madrid in a rough triangle – covers 7995 sq km, less than 2% of Spain's territory.

Madrid's northwest boundary consists of a series of mountain ranges that run from the northeast to the southwest for 140km as part of the longer chain known as the Cordillera Central. Known by madrileños simply as the Sierra, they encompass the Somosierra, Sierra de Guadarrama and Sierra de Gredos. However, as the foothills of the Sierra lie a considerable distance from the city centre, little stands in the way of Madrid's relentless sprawl.

Within Madrid itself there are plenty of gentle rises and falls to test weary legs, the most significant surrounding the ridge along which the original Islamic fortress town (the *alcázar*) was raised. From the Palacio Real, the Catedral de Nuestra Señora de la Almudena and Vistillas, the land falls away into parks towards the Río Manzanares.

To the east, old Madrid rises almost imperceptibly, drops down again to the great north–south boulevard, the Paseo de la Castellana, before climbing again towards Salamanca and the Parque del Buen Retiro.

GREEN MADRID

Downtown Madrid has an abundance of parks and gardens. The most central and attractive is the Parque del Buen Retiro, an expansive manicured stretch of greenery that once constituted the eastern boundary of the city and was also the preserve of royalty and nobles. With its sculpted gardens, artificial lakes and roaming paths, it's a wonderful escape from the din of central Madrid. Just down the hill from the Retiro is the charming little Real Jardín Botánico, a botanical garden packed with all sorts of exotic species.

Equally green and enticing for a romantic stroll is the Campo del Moro, which slopes away west of the Palacio Real, while the nearby Parque del Oeste is similarly hilly and delightfully green. Altogether wilder is the Casa de Campo, west of the Manzanares and often called 'the lungs of Madrid'.

However, it must be acknowledged that this region's environmental problems are legion – the worst drought since records began, greenhouse gas emissions more than three times the level agreed to under the Kyoto Protocol – and the consequences for Madrid are potentially devastating. In the last 30 years Madrid has seen a rise of 2.2°C in its average temperature, a greater increase than for any other European capital. The Madrid authorities have begun campaigns to encourage sensible water use among the city's residents, but water restrictions are not yet in place and the government's strategy seems to rely more on hoping for rain than on serious water conservation. (In late 2005 the 5200 inhabitants of Miraflores de la Sierra, a village 50km north of the capital in the Sierra, woke up to find that the village had simply run out of water.) The rains may have stayed away, but there is also a man-made dimension to the problem – Madrid's 29 golf courses use as much water in a day as a city of 100,000 inhabitants and half remain under investigation for not using recycled water.

If Madrid never seems to have enough water, it has the reverse problem with pollution. Some four million car journeys are made in the capital every day, with one million vehicles entering and leaving the city. The resulting cloud of pollution that settles over Madrid on windless days – known locally as 'the grey beret' – means that breathing Madrid's air is equivalent to smoking 11 cigarettes a day. Spain's obsession with diesel-fuelled cars (which produce seven times more pollution than cars running on unleaded petrol) only exacerbates the problem.

Madrid's city authorities have considered introducing a London-style congestion charge in order to reduce pollution, but the plan remains nothing more than that. That's not to say that some concrete steps haven't been taken. One obvious measure has been the pedestrianisation of many inner-city streets, among them Calle de Arenal and some 40 hectares of streets in the barrio of Huertas, which have been closed to all but local traffic. The unsuccessful Socialist candidate for mayor in 2007 even proposed closing off Gran Vía to traffic.

The constant investment in Madrid's already impressive underground metro system – one of the 10 longest in the world and the third longest in Europe – ensures that Madrid's high pollution levels can in no way be blamed on inadequate public transport. Since 2000 more than 100km have been added to the network, drawing an ever-growing number of satellite towns into the system.

While rubbish is collected every night, recycling is optional and largely ignored. Noise pollution is another massive problem throughout the city. Residents in some Madrid barrios regularly suffer noise levels above 71 decibels; the World Health Organisation warns that anything above 65 decibels poses a health risk and a recent investigation found that a dozen sites consistently exceed such levels. Madrid's first noise survey found that the streets around Calle de O'Donnell, the Paseo de los Recoletos and Calle de Santa Engracia are among Madrid's noisiest. But at many points across the city, rowdy revellers, heavy traffic, late-night rubbish collection, all-night roadworks, the incessant sirens of emergency vehicles and horn-happy drivers all help to keep madrileños' nerves well jangled. Long live double glazing.

Beyond the city, the planned upgrading of the M-501 through the west of the Comunidad de Madrid has been hugely controversial. Environmentalists argue that the road expansion threatens 13 nesting pairs of the endangered Iberian Imperial Eagle, as well as destroying woodlands that shelter 10% of Spain's endangered species and possibly the world's most endangered cat species, the Iberian lynx. When environmentalists announced in 2007 that they had found droppings from a lynx, a species that was long thought to have died out in the Madrid region, the regional premier Esperanza Aguirre refused to conduct an investigation and accused them of faking the findings in order to halt the road's construction.

Madrid may also be endlessly expanding to swallow up previously nonurban areas, but some small steps are being taken in compensation. Among these are ambitious plans to reforest 15,000 hectares of land around the Comunidad de Madrid. Within metropolitan Madrid, 6km of the M-30 beltway has recently been driven underground, to be replaced by the Parque de Manzanares, 500,000 sq metres of landscaped greenery in southwestern Madrid that the mayor calls 'a giant green carpet'; local residents are still waiting to see whether the dust stirred up by three years of massive road works will prove to be worth it.

URBAN PLANNING & DEVELOPMENT

Madrid's mayors are nothing if not ambitious. Madrid's mayor from 1991 to 2003, José María Alvarez del Manzano, became known as 'The Tunnelator' because of his passion for building tunnels and rerouting the course of the city's traffic. But he was nothing compared to his successor, Alberto Ruiz-Gallardón, who has become known as 'The Pharaoh' (see the boxed text, p52) for the sheer scale of his infrastructure projects. Scarcely surprising, therefore, that Danny De Vito, when asked for his opinion of Madrid during a visit some years back, replied 'Tell the mayor to tell me when he's dug up the treasure'.

Madrid can seem to be perennially awash with *obras* (road or infrastructure works). At one level such major works are necessary in a city for whom urban planning was, for centuries, somewhat chaotic and rarely part of an overall plan to make the city more livable. As such some major infrastructure projects have been long overdue, from the extraordinary upgrading of the city's metro system (see opposite) to the proposed Parque de Manzanares (opposite). The shift towards massive skyscrapers in northern Madrid (see p48) has also been sold as a solution to Madrid's critical shortage of office and residential space. Although often heard complaining about the significant disruptions caused by the works, madrileños are generally quite proud that they live in a city that is constantly being improved.

But not all 'improvements' to the city have been welcomed. In 2006 the Baroness Carmen Thyssen-Bornemisza, who was responsible for convincing her husband to bequeath his unrivalled art collection to the Spanish capital (see p95), locked horns with Madrid's mayor Alberto

Ruiz-Gallardón. The reason? The mayor planned to divert traffic away from the Museo del Prado and create a pedestrian precinct outside the Prado. Although the idea sounds good in principle, the problem is that much of the traffic would move across the boulevard to run past the Museo Thyssen-Bornemisza. The proposed works would also have seen more than 700 trees removed, among them 95 trees that date back to the 18th century when Carlos III ruled Spain; Ruiz-Gallardón claimed that all would be replanted, the baroness threatened to chain herself to a tree. At the time of writing, the spat between two of Madrid's most powerful personalities was still to be resolved, although popular opinion seemed to be siding with the baroness.

For all the attempts to address the problems caused by a lack of historical planning, Madrid may already have reached the point of no return. Surrounded by ever-growing concentric ring roads, Madrid just can't stop growing. Whole new suburbs are under construction and will swallow up pretty much all that remains of the available land in the Madrid municipal area by around 2020. Such an approach (with its inevitably speculative side) is fairly typical of the PP, and opposition parties and environmentalists alike have slammed the programme. Whoever's to blame, it's already too late to stop Madrid's transformation from a compact, manageable and high-density city into one that sprawls endlessly to the horizon.

GOVERNMENT & POLITICS

Madrileños, like many Spaniards, have always had a fairly wary approach to the authorities who would try to rule over them. This is perhaps best summed up by the tale oft-told by straight-faced locals that every one of his compatriots carries a letter from the king that reads 'This Spaniard is entitled to do whatever he feels like doing'. Madrileños are nonetheless presided over by three layers of government.

At the national level, the Partido Socialista Obrero Español (PSOE; Spanish Socialist Workers' Party), of José Luis Rodríguez Zapatero, has held power since March 2004, winning re-election in 2008. The national Cortes (parliament) is divided into two houses, the Congreso de los Diputados (lower house) on Carrera de San Jerónimo, and the Senado (senate), off Plaza de España.

The Comunidad de Madrid, one of 17 Spanish autonomous regions, is led by Esperanza Aguirre of the conservative Partido Popular (PP; Popular Party), who is the country's first female president of a Spanish region. After a close-run election in 2003 Aguirre won an absolute majority of seats with 53.3% of the vote to the PSOE's 33.4% (the left-wing Izquierda Unida won 8.8%) in May 2007.

At a city level the government has been the preserve of the PP since 1991 and is led by the *alcalde* (mayor), currently Alberto Ruiz-Gallardón. Ruiz-Gallardón easily won the May 2007 election, winning 34 out of the 57 seats, and is one of Madrid's most popular politicians of recent times. Among his councillors (and a right-wing politician to watch) is Ana Botella, wife of José María

THE PHARAOH OF MADRID

Madrid's mayor, Alberto Ruiz-Gallardón, must be one of few mayors around the world to have been re-elected (in 2007) on a promise that he begin no new major infrastructure projects during his next term in office. It was a shrewd political move by a man dubbed by his subjects as 'The Pharaoh'.

Behind the nickname was a city thoroughly exhausted by the endless road works and infrastructure projects that had made Madrid Europe's largest building site. At the height of Ruiz-Gallardón's mania for tearing down, digging up and generally recasting the city in his own image, there were, in 2005, more than 900 holes officially open across Madrid, not to mention 75 large infrastructure projects underway. Within this context of perennial noise and stirred-up dust, it was more than a little galling for madrileños to find that they could be charged with a local law prohibiting 'the abusive use of the public street', when most such abuse was the work of lawmakers themselves.

Of equal concern to madrileños is the financial cost involved. The Parque de Manzanares project alone will end up costing local taxpayers almost €4 billion, while the city's annual budget has a gaping €5 billion hole in its centre.

Thus it is that when the dust settles and the city finally falls quiet, Madrid will be vastly improved, but very much in the red.

Aznar, the former PP Spanish president. The city council has operated for decades out of the Ayuntamiento on Plaza de la Villa in the heart of the old city, although many officials (including the mayor) have since moved to the Palacio de Comunicaciones on Plaza de la Cibeles.

The next city and regional elections are set for 2011, with national elections a year later. For more information on the machinations of political life Madrid style, see p35.

FASHION

In the 18th century madrileños rioted when told by the king that they could no longer wear the sweeping capes that so distinguished them. The days of Spanish capes may be long gone, but they still take their fashion seriously in Madrid.

The current buzz surrounding Spanish fashion began in the 1980s when Spain in general, and Madrid in particular, embraced all that was new and experimental after the fascist austerity of the Franco years; during *la movida madrileña* Madrid was said to be home to 1500 fashion designers. What has changed recently is that Madrid has come to surpass Barcelona as Spain's fashion capital; while Madrid may not yet rival Milan or Paris, Madrid's Pasarela Cibeles (p17) runway fashion shows have become increasingly important, especially for spring and autumn collections. As a result Madrid is considered by many in-the-know to rank among the five most important fashion cities in the world (along with New York and London).

One of the success stories of Spanish cultural life, the Spanish fashion industry now employs more than 500,000 people (more than three times the number employed by bullfighting and up from 180,000 in 1995). This is an industry that is aiming high and industry insiders admit that Spain's *fashionistas* won't be satisfied until Madrid has been elevated to the top tier of European fashion capitals. On current trends, they may not have that long to wait.

Colour is the key to Spanish fashion's individuality. The psychedelic colours of *la movida madrileña* (p32) in the 1980s have never really gone away and the candy-bright colours of Agatha Ruiz de la Prada (p137; Andy Warhol was a fan of this icon of modern Madrid) have now acquired something of a middle-class respectability; her work, widely available, encompasses everything from children's clothes to outrageous evening wear for adults. This stylish-but-anything-goes approach has morphed into a fashion scene dominated by bold colours equally well suited to the casual as to a more tailored look.

Classic and more conservative lines are the preserve of Loewe (see the boxed text, p139), Sybilla (see the boxed text, p140) and the madrileña Alma Aguilar (see the boxed text, p140). A more formal/casual mix is favoured by designers like Amaya Arzuaga (p137), Purificación García (see the boxed text, p139), Roberto Torretta (see the boxed text, p140) and Roberto Verino (see the boxed text, p139). Apart from the names already mentioned, others to watch out for on the catwalk include the madrileño Javier Larráinzar (one of the city's top haute couture icons), Pedro del Hierro, Kina Fernández, Nacho Ruiz and Montesinos Alama. More clean lined and casual is Armand Basi (p137), while the clothes of Davidelfín (p137) span the divide between edgy and exclusive.

Spain is also famous for the quality of its shoes and the designers once known only to Spaniards and madrileñas are fast becoming fixtures on the international scene. Manolo Blahnik (see the boxed text, p139) is perhaps the best known and beloved by red-carpet Hollywood stars. Many designers also do great lines in handbags and other accessories (they wouldn't maintain the loyalty of Madrileñas if they didn't) and there's no finer exponent of the art than the hand-painted sophisticated but fun masterpieces of Iñaki Sampedro (see the boxed text, p151).

The shopping explosion that began in the 1990s in Madrid shows no sign of abating and it's unlikely to end any time soon. It's not only upmarket designer wear that is dominating the madrileño wardrobe and capturing international headlines. A host of more affordable high-street fashions is also leading the way. Just about every Madrid barrio has at least one outlet for names like Zara (with 2244 shops in 56 countries), Adolfo Domínguez and Mango, which have in turn become some of Spain's leading exports. And where would you be without the cool and casual shoes of Camper (p137)? If these names have been your introduction to the world of Spanish fashion, you'll very much enjoy Madrid, but don't forget that these are merely an introduction to a far more sophisticated look.

Madrid has numerous places to shop. For Spanish designers, Salamanca in general is Madrid's and Spain's fashion capital, with exclusive Chueca outposts along Calle de Piamonte,

STORM IN A D-CUP

In recent years Madrid's annual Pasarela Cibeles international fashion week has been steadily growing in importance to the extent that it has surpassed Barcelona's fashion week and taken its place in the second tier of European fashion shows. In 2006, however, the Pasarela Cibeles shot to international attention when the Spanish Association of Fashion Designers announced that excessively thin models would be banned from the city's catwalk. The new policy, which fuelled an international debate on the image presented by catwalk models, was adopted after protests by doctors and women's rights groups who argued that the models at the previous year's fashion show were unhealthily thin and set a bad example for young girls and women. The organisers of the Pasarela Cibeles proved true to their word in February 2007 when five out of the 69 female models were disqualified for having a body mass-to-height ratio, or Body Mass Index (BMI), of less than 18, a benchmark set by UN health experts. One of the rejected models had a BMI of just 16 – the equivalent of being 175cm tall and weighing just 50kg. Apart from some fashion shows in New York, no other fashion show has yet followed Madrid's lead. The French Couture Federation dismissed the new rules, saying that 'everyone would laugh' if Paris were to adopt the change. Organisers of Milan fashion week, however, promised to release a new code of conduct and has begun to hold plus-size shows to show its support for Madrid's new policy.

Calle de Almirante and Calle del Conde Xiquena (Map pp110–11). Malasaña is the place for an altogether different fashion aesthetic with quirky, imaginative shops where the line between designer fashions and urban streetwear is decidedly blurred. Calle de Fuencarral (see the boxed text, p150) is Madrid's spiritual home for edgy urban fashion. For classy shoes and accessories at discounted prices, Chueca's Calle de Augusto Figueroa (Map pp110–11) is the stuff of shopping legend. For more details on shopping in Madrid, turn to p132.

NEIGHBOURHOODS

top picks

- **Museo del Prado** (p90)
  One of the great art galleries of the world with Goya and Velázquez the highlights.
- **Centro de Arte Reina Sofía** (p82)
  Stunning art gallery that's home to Picasso's *Guernica*.
- **Plaza Mayor** (p61)
  Glorious architecture in abundance.
- **Parque del Buen Retiro** (p98)
  Stately gardens where all the city comes to play.
- **Museo Thyssen-Bornemisza** (p95)
  Private art gallery with masters from every era.
- **Palacio Real** (p67)
  Madrid's lavish royal palace lords it over the elegant Plaza de Oriente.
- **El Rastro** (p74)
  Expansive Sunday flea market that tumbles down the hill and echoes out across the city.
- **Ermita de San Antonio de la Florida** (p124)
  Exquisite Goya frescoes in their original setting.

What's your recommendation? www.lonelyplanet.com/madrid

Madrid may be Europe's most dynamic city, but it doesn't have the immediate cachet of Rome, Paris or even that other city up the road, Barcelona. Its architecture is beautiful, but there's no Coliseum, no Eiffel Tower, no Gaudí-inspired zaniness to photograph and then tell your friends back home, 'this is Madrid'. As such, many first-time visitors wonder what there is to see in the Spanish capital. The answer is wonderful sights in abundance, so many in fact that few travellers leave disappointed with their menu of high culture and high-volume excitement.

For a start, Madrid has three of the finest art galleries in the world and if ever there was a golden mile of fine art, it has to be the combined charms of the Museo del Prado, Centro de Arte Reina Sofía and the Museo Thyssen-Bornemisza. There are so many works by the master painters in Madrid that masterpieces overflow from these three museums into dozens of museums and galleries across the city.

> 'Madrid has three of the finest art galleries in the world and if ever there was a golden mile of fine art, it has to be the combined charms of the Museo del Prado, Centro de Arte Reina Sofía and the Museo Thyssen-Bornemisza'

Exploring deeper into the city, the combination of stunning architecture and feel-good living has never been easier to access than in the beautiful plazas where *terrazas* (cafés with outdoor tables) provide a front-row seat for Madrid's fine cityscape and endlessly energetic street life. We challenge you to find a more spectacular and agreeable setting for your coffee than the Plaza Mayor, Plaza de Santa Ana or Plaza de Oriente. Throw in some outstanding city parks (the Parque del Buen Retiro in particular) and areas such as Chueca, Malasaña, Lavapiés and Salamanca, which each have their own alluring personalities, and you'll quickly end up wishing, like Hemingway, that you never had to leave.

Madrid is divided up into *distritos* (districts) and these are subdivided into *barrios* (neighbourhoods), the official names of which are largely ignored by madrileños. Indeed the word barrio has a very strong feel of local identity about it. Madrileños have their own city map in their heads and, since they know best, we follow them.

Los Austrias, Sol and Centro make up the bustling, compact and medieval heart of Madrid, where the village of Mayrit came to life. This area now yields an impossibly rich heritage of things to see, among them palaces, churches and grand squares. La Latina and Lavapiés, two of Madrid's oldest inner-city barrios, are immediately south and southeast of the centre, and have plenty to see and even more to experience. East of here takes in Huertas and Atocha, with the former the home to a labyrinth of more vibrant nightlife than seems possible, but also with its fair share of cultural sights that are well worth tracking down. Down the hill, Atocha is a gateway to the grand boulevard of the Paseo del Prado, a haven of culture boasting the city's finest museums. Part of the same barrio, the Parque del Buen Retiro is a refuge of green parkland and gardens, and serves as an entry point to the exclusive barrio of Salamanca. West of Salamanca, across the Paseo de los Recoletos, are two of modern Madrid's coolest barrios, Malasaña and Chueca, which have been transformed from gritty, working-class dives into cultural focal points. Neighbouring Chamberí and Argüelles have few sights to talk about, but offer an ambience that is rapidly making them the barrios of choice for discerning madrileños. The outer *distritos* of Madrid offer some parks and children's attractions, such as Warner Brothers Movie World.

See p259 for transport details of getting around Madrid.

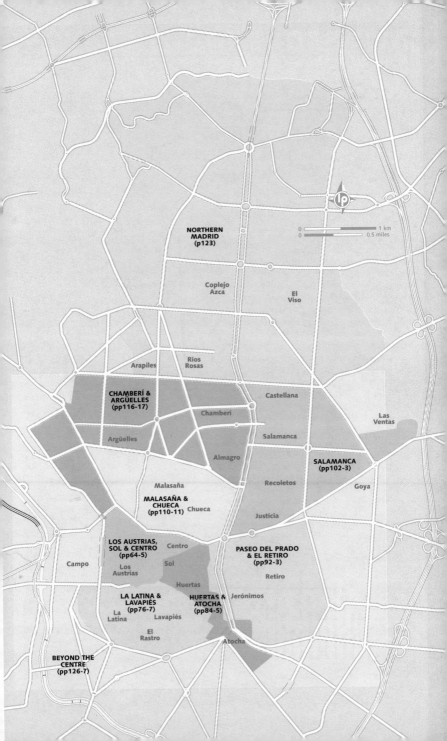

NORTHERN
MADRID
(p123)

0   1 km
0   0.5 miles

Coplejo
Azca

El
Viso

Arapiles

Ríos
Rosas

CHAMBERÍ &
ARGÜELLES
(pp116-17)

Castellana

Chamberí

Las
Ventas

Argüelles

Salamanca

Almagro

SALAMANCA
(pp102-3)

Malasaña

Recoletos

Goya

MALASAÑA &
CHUECA
(pp110-11) Chueca

Justicia

LOS AUSTRIAS,
SOL & CENTRO
(pp64-5)

Centro

PASEO DEL PRADO
& EL RETIRO
(pp92-3)

Campo

Los
Austrias

Sol

Retiro

Huertas

LA LATINA &
LAVAPIÉS
(pp76-7)

HUERTAS &
ATOCHA
(pp84-5)

Jerónimos

La
Latina

Lavapiés

El
Rastro

Atocha

BEYOND THE
CENTRE
(pp126-7)

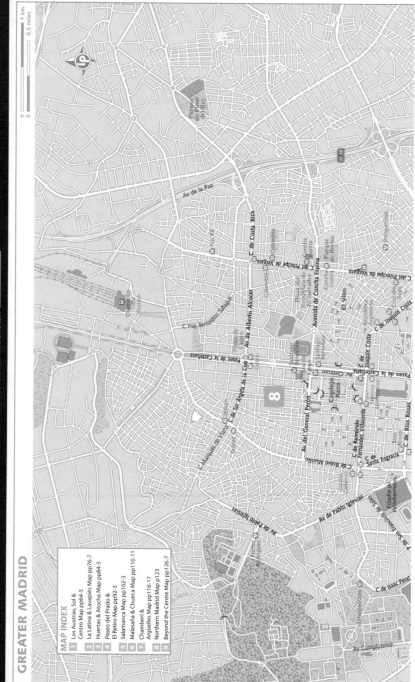

GREATER MADRID

ITINERARY BUILDER

The table below allows you to plan a day's worth of activities in any area of the city. Simply select which area you wish to explore, and then mix and match from the corresponding listings to build your day. The first item in each cell represents a well-known highlight of the area, while the other items are more off-the-beaten-track gems.

ACTIVITIES AREA	Sights	Eating	Shopping
Los Austrias, Sol & Centro	Plaza Mayor (opposite) Palacio Real (p67) Real Academia de Bellas Artes de San Fernando (opposite)	Restaurante Sobrino de Botín (p160) Casa Revuelta (p161) La Viuda Blanca (p160)	Antigua Casa Talavera (p133) El Arco Artesanía (p134) El Flamenco Vive (p134)
La Latina & Lavapiés	Basílica de San Francisco El Grande (p74) Iglesia de San Andrés (p75) Museo de San Isidro (p78)	Almendro 13 (p165) Taberna Txacoli (p165) Naïa Restaurante (p164)	El Rastro (p136) Del Hierro (p135) Helena Rohner (p136)
Huertas & Atocha	Centro de Arte Reina Sofía (p82) Plaza de Santa Ana (p86) Casa de Lope de Vega (p87)	Arola Madrid (p166) Casa Alberto (p166) Maceiras (p167)	México (p136) Gil (p137) Lomography (p137)
Paseo del Prado & Salamanca	Museo del Prado (p90) Museo Thyssen-Bornemisza (p95) Parque del Buen Retiro (p98)	Sula Madrid (p169) La Galette (p170) Biotza (p170)	Agatha Ruiz de la Prada Madrid (p138) Gallery (p139) Oriol Balaguer (p140)
Malasaña & Chueca	Sociedad General de Autores y Editores (p108) Museo Municipal (p108) Museo Municipal de Arte Contemporáneo (p108)	Nina (p171) La Musa (p172) Bazaar (p175)	Mercado de Fuencarral (p151) Isolée (p151) Gandolfi (p152)
Chamberí & Argüelles	Templo de Debod (p115) Museo de América (p118) Museo Sorolla (p119)	Las Tortillas de Gabino (p179) Sagarretxe (p179) Casa Ricardo (p178)	Antigüedades Hom (p153) Diedro (p153) DMR María Rivolta (p154)

LOS AUSTRIAS, SOL & CENTRO

Drinking p186; Eating p160; Nightlife p200; Shopping p132; Sleeping p229

Los Austrias, Sol and Centro is where the story of Madrid began and became the seat of royal power. This is where the splendour of Imperial Spain was at its most ostentatious and Spain's overarching Catholicism was at its most devout – think expansive palaces, elaborate private mansions, ancient churches and imposing convents amid the raucous clamour of modern Madrid.

From the tangle of streets tumbling down the hillside of Los Austrias and the busy shopping streets around the Plaza de la Puerta del Sol (the Gate of the Sun; more commonly known as Puerta del Sol) to the monumental Gran Vía, which marks the northern border of central Madrid, this is Madrid at its most clamorous and diverse. If other barrios all have their own distinctive character traits, then Los Austrias, Sol and Centro is the sum total of all Madrid's personalities. It's also where the madrileño world most often intersects with that of tourists and expats drawn to that feel-good Madrid vibe.

The area that slopes down the hill southwest of the Plaza Mayor is Madrid at its most medieval and has come to be known as Madrid de los Austrias, in reference to the Habsburg dynasty, which ruled Spain from 1517 to 1700. The busy and bustling streets between the Puerta del Sol and Gran Vía, form the heart and centre of Madrid, a designation that extends west to the Palacio Real, the royal jewel in Madrid's considerable crown. At the hub is the splendour of the glorious Plaza Mayor.

PLAZA MAYOR Map pp64–5

Ⓜ Sol

For centuries the centrepiece of Madrid life, the stately Plaza Mayor combines supremely elegant architecture with a history dominated by peculiarly Spanish dramas. Pull up a chair at the outdoor tables around the perimeter or laze upon the rough-hewn cobblestones as young madrileños have a habit of doing. All around you, the theatre that is Spanish street life buzzing through the plaza provides a crash course in why people fall in love with Madrid.

Ah, the history the plaza has seen! Designed in 1619 by Juan Gómez de Mora and built in typical Herrerian style, of which the slate spires are the most obvious expression, its first public ceremony was suitably auspicious – the beatification of San Isidro Labrador (St Isidro the Farm Labourer), Madrid's patron saint. Thereafter it was as if all that was controversial about Spain took place in this square. Bullfights, often in celebration of royal weddings or births, with royalty watching on from the balconies and up to 50,000 people crammed into the plaza were a recurring theme until 1878. Far more notorious were the *autos-da-fé* (the ritual condemnations of heretics) followed by executions – burnings at the stake and deaths by garrotte on the north side of the square, hangings to the south. These continued until 1790 when a fire largely destroyed the square, which was subsequently reproduced under the supervision of Juan de Villanueva who lent his name to the building that now houses the Museo del Prado.

Not all the plaza's activities were grand events and just as it is now surrounded by

ORIENTATION & TRANSPORT: LOS AUSTRIAS, SOL & CENTRO

With the Plaza de la Puerta del Sol (Spain's Kilometre Zero) at its heart, Los Austrias, Sol and Centro is bordered by Gran Vía to the north, Plaza de España and Calle de Bailén to the west, Calle de Segovia and Calle de la Concepción Jerónima to the south and Calle de Carretas and Calle de Alcalá to the east. Aside from Calle de Segovia, which cuts a swathe through Los Austrias, other atmospheric thoroughfares include Calle Mayor, the major shopping street of Calle de Preciados and the recently pedestrianised Calle del Arenal, which spills into Plaza de Isabel II, home of the Teatro Real, beyond which lies the Palacio Real. Landmark plazas include the cosy Plaza de la Villa and the majestic Plaza de Oriente.

Central Madrid is well-served by metro, although less so on its western perimeter and the southwestern corner. Along the northern rim handy metro stops include Gran Vía (lines 1 and 5), Callao (lines 3 and 5), Santo Domingo (line 2) and Plaza de España (lines 3 and 10). In the heart of the barrio getting out at either Sol (lines 1, 2 and 3) or Ópera (lines 2 and 5) puts you within walking distance of anywhere covered in this section.

shops, it was once filled with food vendors. In 1673, King Carlos II issued an edict allowing the vendors to raise tarpaulins above their stalls to protect their wares and themselves from the refuse and raw sewage that people habitually tossed out of the windows above! Well into the 20th century, trams ran through the Plaza Mayor.

The grandeur of the plaza is due in large part to the warm colours of the uniformly ochre apartments with 237 wrought-iron balconies offset by the exquisite frescoes of the 17th-century Real Casa de la Panadería (Royal Bakery). The present frescoes date to just 1992, the work of artist Carlos Franco who chose images from the signs of the zodiac and gods (eg Cybele) to provide a stunning backdrop. The frescoes were inaugurated to coincide with Madrid's 1992 spell as European Capital of Culture.

In the middle of the square stands an equestrian statue of the man who ordered its construction, Felipe III. Originally placed in the Casa de Campo, it was moved to the Plaza Mayor in 1848, whereafter it became a favoured meeting place for irreverent madrileños who arranged to catch up 'under the balls of the horse'.

To see the plaza's epic history told in pictures, check out the carvings on the circular seats beneath the lamp posts. On Sunday mornings, the plaza's arcaded perimeter is taken over by traders in old coins, banknotes and stamps, while December and early January sees the plaza occupied by a Christmas market selling kitsch, nativity scenes of real quality and drawing massive crowds.

PALACIO DE SANTA CRUZ Map pp64–5
Plaza de la Provincia; M Sol
Just off the southeast corner of Plaza Mayor and dominating Plaza de Santa Cruz is this baroque edifice, which houses the Ministerio de Asuntos Exteriores (Ministry of Foreign Affairs) and hence can only be admired from the outside. A landmark with its grey slate spires, it was built in 1643 and initially served as the court prison.

BASÍLICA DE SAN MIGUEL Map pp64–5
☎ 91 548 40 11; Calle de San Justo 4;
⏰ 9.45am-2pm & 5.30-9pm Mon-Fri mid-Sep–Jun, 9.45am-1pm & 5.30-9pm Mon-Fri Jul–mid-Sep;
M La Latina or Sol
Hidden away off Calle de Segovia, this basilica is something of a surprise. Its convex,

late-baroque façade sits in harmony with the surrounding buildings of old Madrid and among its fine features are statues representing the four virtues, and the reliefs of Justo and Pastor, the saints to whom the church was originally dedicated. The rococo and Italianate interior, completed by Italian architects in 1745, is another world altogether with gilded flourishes and dark, sombre domes.

CONVENTO DEL CORPUS CRISTI (LAS CARBONERAS) Map pp64–5
☎ 91 548 37 01; Plaza del Conde de Miranda; admission free; ⏰ 9.30am-1pm & 4-6.30pm; M Ópera
Architecturally nondescript but culturally curious, this church hides behind sober modern brickwork on the western end of a quiet square. A closed order of nuns occupies the convent building around it and, when Mass is held, the nuns gather in a separate area at the rear of the church. They maintain a centuries-old tradition of making sweet biscuits that can be purchased from the entrance just off the square on Calle del Codo (see p134).

PLAZA DE LA VILLA & AROUND Map pp64–5
☎ 010; ⏰ free guided tour of Ayuntamiento 5pm & 6pm Mon; M Ópera
There are grander plazas, but this intimate little square is one of Madrid's prettiest. Enclosed on three sides by pleasing and wonderfully preserved examples of 17th-century Madrid-style baroque architecture (barroco madrileño; see p47), it has been the permanent seat of Madrid's city government since the Middle Ages, although not for long…Madrid's city council has already begun the long process of relocating to the Palacio de Comunicaciones on Plaza de la Cibeles.

The 17th-century Ayuntamiento (town hall), on the western side of the square, is a typical Habsburg edifice with Herrerian slate-tiled spires. First planned as a prison in 1644 by Juan Gómez de Mora, who also designed the Convento de la Encarnación (p70), its granite and brick façade is a study in sobriety. The final touches to the Casa de la Villa (as the town hall was also known) were made in 1693, and Juan de Villanueva, of the Museo del Prado fame, made some alterations a century later.

The Ayuntamiento offers free tours (in Spanish) through various reception halls and into the Salón del Pleno (council chambers). The latter were restored in the 1890s and again in 1986; the decoration is sumptuous neo-Classical with late 17th-century ceiling frescoes. Look for the ceramic copy of Pedro Teixera's landmark 1656 map of Madrid just outside the chambers.

On the opposite side of the square the 15th-century Casa de los Lujanes is more Gothic in conception with a clear *mudéjar* influence. The brickwork tower is said to have been 'home' to the imprisoned French monarch François I and his sons after their capture during the Battle of Pavia (1525). As the star prisoner was paraded down Calle Mayor locals are said to have been more impressed by the splendidly attired Frenchman than they were by his more drab captor, the Spanish Habsburg emperor Carlos I.

The Casa de Cisneros, built in 1537 by the nephew of Cardinal Cisneros, a key adviser to Queen Isabel, is plateresque in inspiration, although it was much restored and altered at the beginning of the 20th century. The main door and window above it are what remains of the Renaissance-era building. It's now home to the Salón de Tapices (Tapestries Hall), adorned with exquisite 15th-century Flemish tapestries and is visited as part of the Ayuntamiento tour.

Other landmarks nearby include: the 19th-century Mercado de San Miguel (central produce market) in Plaza de San Miguel; the 18th-century baroque remake of the Iglesia del Sacramento, the central church of the Spanish army; and the Palacio del Duque de Uceda, which is now used as a military headquarters (the Capitanía General), but is a classic of the Madrid baroque architectural style and was designed by Juan Gómez de Mora in 1608. If you duck down behind this massive mansion, you'll end up in Calle de la Villa. At No 2 was once the Estudio Público de Humanidades. This was one of Madrid's more important schools in the 16th century and Cervantes studied here for a while.

The section of Calle Mayor that runs past the plaza witnessed one of the most dramatic moments in the history of early 20th-century Madrid. On 31 May 1906, on the wedding day of King Alfonso XIII and Britain's Victoria Eugenia, a Catalan anarchist Mateu Morral threw a bomb concealed in a bouquet of flowers at the royal couple. Several bystanders died, but the monarch and his new wife survived intact, save for her blood-spattered dress. During the Spanish Civil War, Madrid's republican government briefly renamed the street Calle Mateo Morral.

IGLESIA DE SAN NICOLÁS DE LOS SERVITAS Map pp64–5

☎ 91 548 83 14; Plaza de San Nicolás 6; admission free; ☺ 8am-1.30pm & 5.30-8.30pm Mon, 8-9.30am & 6.30-8.30pm Tue-Sat, 9.30am-2pm & 6.30-9pm Sun & holidays; M Ópera
Tucked away up the hill from Calle Mayor, this intimate little church is Madrid's oldest surviving building of worship. As such, it offers a rare glimpse of how medieval Madrid must have appeared before it took on the proportions of a city. It is believed to have been built on the site of Muslim Mayrit's second mosque. The most striking feature is the restored 12th-century *mudéjar* (decorative style of Islamic architecture as used on Christian buildings) bell tower, although much of the remainder dates in part from the 15th century. The vaulting is late Gothic while the fine timber ceiling, which survived a fire in 1936, dates from about the same period. Other elements inside this small house of worship include plateresque and baroque touches, although much of the interior is a study in simplicity. The architect Juan de Herrera (see p47), one of the great architects of Renaissance Spain, was buried in the crypt in 1597.

PLAZA DE RAMALES Map pp64–5

M Ópera
This pleasant little triangle of open space is not without historical intrigue. Joseph Bonaparte ordered the destruction of the Iglesia de San Juanito to open up a pocket of fresh air in the then-crowded streets. It is believed Velázquez was buried in the church; excavations in 2000 revealed the crypt of the former church and the remains of various people buried in it centuries ago, but Velázquez was nowhere to be found. On the west side of the plaza is the Escuela Superior de Música Reina Sofía (www.fundacion albeniz.com), a musical conservatory which hosts occasional concerts.

PLAZA DE ORIENTE Map pp64–5

M Ópera
A royal palace that once had aspirations to be the Spanish Versailles. Sophisticated

lonelyplanet.com

NEIGHBOURHOODS LOS AUSTRIAS, SOL & CENTRO

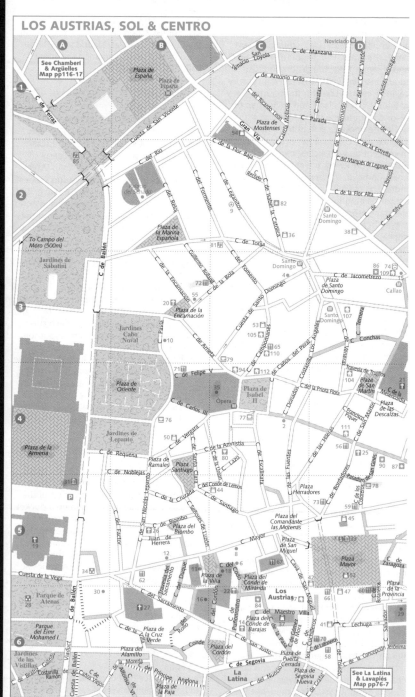

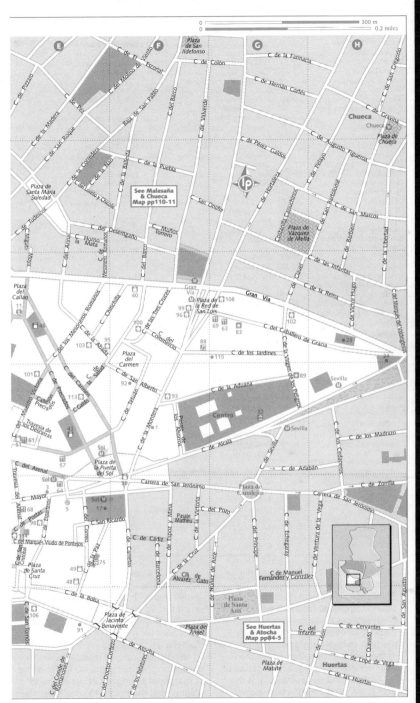

0   300 m
0   0.2 miles

Plaza de San Ildefonso

C de El Escorial
C del Molino de Viento
C de Colón
C de la Farmacia
C de Hernán Cortés
C de San Gregorio

C de Pizarro
C de Pez
C del Barco
C de Valverde
C de Pérez Galdós
C de Augusto Figueroa
C de Gravina

Chueca
Chueca
Plaza de Chueca

C de la Madera
Baja de San Pablo
C de Pelayo
C de San Bartolomé
C de San Marcos

C de San Roque
C de la Corredera
C de la Nau
C de la Ballesta
C de la Puebla
San Onofre

Plaza de Santa María Soledad
C del Loreto y Chicote
C del Desengaño
Muñoz Torrero
Costanilla Capuchinos
C de Hortaleza
C de Barbieri
C de la Libertad

C de Tudescos
Miguel Moya
C del Arnal
Horno Mata
Mesonero Romanos
C del Barco
Plaza de Vázquez de Mella
C de las Infantas
C del Marqués del Valdeiglesias

Plaza del Callao
11
46
C de los Mesoneros Romanos
Chinchilla
C de las Tres Cruces
40
Gran Vía
Gran Vía
108
C de la Reina
C de Victor Hugo
23

M Plaza de la Red de San Luis
99
96
69
63
83
102
C del Caballero de Gracia
24

103
C de la Abada
95
100
C del Comercio
88
115
C de los Jardines
89

101
C del Carmen
C de Salud
Plaza del Carmen
92
de San Alberto
C de la Virgen de los Peligros
Sevilla
M Sevilla

Teatro Victoria
Callejón Preciados
113
Caldo
93
C de la Aduana
Centro
32
C de los Madrazo

Travesía de los Descalzas
43
C de Tetuán
C de la Montera
Pasaje de los Austrias
C de Alcalá
Sevilla
C de Arlabán

5
61
1
C de Sevilla
C de Zorrilla

Sol
57
Plaza de la Puerta del Sol
Carrera de San Jerónimo
Plaza de Canalejas
Carrera de San Jerónimo

C del Arenal
Sol M
3
64
39
C de Ventura de la Vega

Travesía del Arenal
Mayor
5
C de Espartero
17
C del Pozo
C del Príncipe
C de Echegaray

68
C de Postas
San Ricardo
C de Espoz y Mina
Pasaje Matheu
C de la Victoria

98
114
C del Correo
C de Cádiz
C de la Cruz
C de Manuel Fernández y González
C de San Agustín

C del Marqués Viudo de Pontejos
C de Carretas
C de Barcelona
Cllj de Álvarez Gato
C de Núñez de Arce

Plaza de Santa Cruz
49
75
C de la Paz
Plaza de Santa Ana

48
C de la Bolsa
Plaza del Ángel
C del Infante
C de Cervantes
C de Quevedo

106
Plaza de Jacinto Benavente
91
C de Atocha
Plaza de Santa María
C de León
C de Lope de Vega

C de San Tomás
C del Conde de Romanones
C del Doctor Cortezo
C de los Relatores
Plaza de Matute
Huertas
C de las Huertas

See Malasaña & Chueca Map pp110-11

See Huertas & Atocha Map pp84-5

LOS AUSTRIAS, SOL & CENTRO

cafés watched over by apartments that cost the equivalent of a royal salary. Teatro Real, Madrid's Opera House and one of Spain's temples to high culture. Some of the finest sunset views in Madrid. Welcome to Plaza de Oriente, a living, breathing monument to imperial Madrid.

At the centre of the plaza, which the palace overlooks, is an equestrian statue of Felipe IV. Designed by Velázquez, it is the perfect place to take it all in with marvel-lous views wherever you look. If you're wondering how a heavy bronze statue of a rider and his horse rearing up can actually maintain that stance, the answer is simple – the hind legs are solid while the front ones are hollow. That idea was Galileo Galilei's.

Nearby are some 20 marble statues of mostly ancient monarchs. Local legend has it that these ageing royals get down off their pedestals at night to stretch their legs.

The adjacent Jardines Cabo Naval, a great place to watch the sun set, adds to the sense of a sophisticated oasis of green in the heart of Madrid.

PALACIO REAL Map pp64–5

☎ 91 542 69 47; www.patrimonionacional.es, in Spanish; Calle de Bailén; adult/student & EU senior €10/3.50, adult without guide €8, EU citizens free Wed, Armería Real €3.40/1.70; ☼ 9am-6pm Mon-Sat, 9am-3pm Sun & holidays Apr-Sep, 9.30am-5pm Mon-Sat, 9am-2pm Sun & holidays Oct-Mar; Ⓜ Ópera

In their modern manifestation, the Bourbons who rule Spain are one of Europe's more modest royal families, but their predecessors lived far more sumptuous lifestyles.

You can almost imagine how the eyes of Felipe V, the first of the Bourbon kings, lit up when the *alcázar* (Muslim-era fortress) burned down in 1734 on Madrid's most exclusive perch of real estate. His plan? Build a palace that would dwarf all its European counterparts. The Italian architect Filippo Juvara (1678–1736), who had made his name building the Basilica di Superga and the Palazzo di Stupinigi in Turin, was called in but, like Felipe, he died without bringing the project to fruition. On Juvara's death, another Italian, Giovanni Battista Sacchetti, took over, finishing the job in 1764.

The result was an Italianate baroque colossus with some 2800 rooms, of which around 50 are open to the public. It's occasionally closed for state ceremonies and official receptions, but the present king is rarely in residence, preferring to live somewhere more modest.

The Farmacia Real (Royal Pharmacy), the first set of rooms to the right at the southern end of the Plaza de la Armería (Plaza de Armas; Plaza of the Armoury) courtyard, contains a formidable collection of medicine jars and stills for mixing royal con-

top picks

SIGHTS IN LOS AUSTRIAS, SOL & CENTRO

- Plaza Mayor (p61)
- Palacio Real (left)
- Plaza de la Villa (p62)
- Plaza de Oriente (p63)
- Convento de las Descalzas Reales (p69)
- Real Academia de Bellas Artes de San Fernando (p71)

coctions, suggesting that the royals were either paranoid or decidedly sickly. West across the plaza is the Armería Real (Royal Armoury), a hoard of weapons and striking suits of armour, mostly dating from the 16th and 17th centuries.

From the northern end of the Plaza de la Armería, the main stairway, a grand statement of imperial power, leads to the royal apartments and eventually to the Salón del Trono (Throne Room). The latter is nauseatingly lavish with its crimson-velvet wall coverings complemented by a ceiling painted by the dramatic Venetian baroque master, Tiepolo, who was a favourite of Carlos III. Nearby, the Salón de Gasparini (Gasparini Room) has an exquisite stucco ceiling and walls resplendent with embroidered silks. The aesthetic may be different in the Sala de Porcelana (Porcelain Room), but the aura of extravagance continues with myriad pieces from the one-time Retiro porcelain factory screwed into the walls. In the midst of it all comes the spacious Comedor de Gala (Gala Dining Room). Only students with passes may enter the Biblioteca Real (Royal Library).

MADRID'S BARRIOS IN A NUTSHELL

Los Austrias, Sol & Centro Madrid's oldest quarter, home to some of Madrid's grandest monuments, and plenty of bars, restaurants and hotels.

La Latina & Lavapiés Narrow medieval streets, great bars for tapas, drinking and restaurants.

Huertas & Atocha Madrid's nightlife capital and home to the Centro de Arte Reina Sofía.

Paseo del Prado & El Retiro Grand boulevard with the great art galleries along its shores and the Parque del Buen Retiro.

Salamanca Upscale and upmarket, Madrid's home of designer shopping.

Malasaña & Chueca Inner-city barrios with eclectic nightlife, shopping and outstanding eating options.

Chamberí & Argüelles Residential barrios with a glimpse of Madrid away from the tourist crowds.

Northern Madrid High-class restaurants and the home of Real Madrid.

NEIGHBOURHOODS LOS AUSTRIAS, SOL & CENTRO

If you're lucky, you might just catch the colourful changing of the guard in full parade dress. This takes place at noon on the first Wednesday of every month (except July and August) between the palace and the Catedral de Nuestra Señora de la Almudena.

The French-inspired Jardines de Sabatini (9am-9pm May-Sep, 9am-8pm Oct-Apr) lie along the northern flank of the Palacio Real. They were laid out in the 1930s to replace the royal stables that once stood on the site.

Work is underway on the Museo de Colecciones Reales (Museum of Royal Collections; Map pp126–7) behind the Catedral de Nuestra Señora de la Almudena and adjacent to the Palacio Real, which is being built to house much of the Palace's collection.

CATEDRAL DE NUESTRA SEÑORA DE LA ALMUDENA Map pp64–5

☎ 91 542 22 00; Calle de Bailén; 9am-9pm; M Ópera

Paris has Notre Dame and Rome has St Peter's Basilica. In fact, almost every European city of stature has its signature cathedral, a stand-out monument to a glorious Christian past. Not Madrid. Although the exterior of the Catedral de Nuestra Señora de la Almudena sits in perfect harmony with the adjacent Palacio Real, Madrid's cathedral is cavernous and largely charmless within; its colourful, modern ceilings do little to make up for the lack of the old-world gravitas that so distinguishes great cathedrals.

Carlos I first proposed building a cathedral here back in 1518, but building didn't actually begin until the 1880s. Other priorities got in the way and it wasn't begun until 1879 and was finally finished in 1992. Unsurprisingly, the pristine, bright white neo-Gothic interior holds no pride of place in the affections of madrileños.

Just around the corner on Calle Mayor, the low-lying ruins of Santa María de la Almudena (Map pp64–5) are all that remain of Madrid's first church, which was built on the site of Mayrit's Great Mosque when the Christians arrived in the 11th century.

MURALLA ÁRABE Map pp64–5

Cuesta de la Vega; M Ópera

Behind the cathedral apse and down Cuesta de la Vega is a disappointingly short stretch of the original Arab Wall, the city wall built by Madrid's early-medieval Muslim rulers. Some of it dates as far back as the 9th century, when the initial Muslim fort was raised. Other sections date from the 12th and 13th centuries, by which time the city had been taken by the Christians. The earliest sections were ingeniously conceived – the outside of the wall was made to look dauntingly sturdy, while the inside was put together with cheap materials to save money. It must have worked, as the town was rarely ever taken by force. In summer the city council organises open-air theatre and music performances here.

TEATRO REAL Map pp64–5

☎ 91 516 06 96; www.teatro-real.com; Plaza de Oriente; admission by guided tour (in Spanish) adult/student up to 26yr & senior €4/2; 10.30am-1pm Mon & Wed-Fri, 11am-1.30pm Sat, Sun & holidays; M Ópera

Backing onto the Plaza de Oriente, Madrid's signature opera house does not have the most distinguished of histories. The first theatre was built in 1708 on the site of the public washhouses. Torn down in 1816, its successor was built in 1850 under the reign of Isabel II, whereafter it was burned down and later blown up in the civil war (when it was used as a powder store, resulting in the inevitable fireworks). It finally took its present neo-Classical form in 1997 and, viewed from Plaza de Isabel II, it's a fine addition to the central Madrid cityscape; in Plaza de Oriente, however, it's somewhat overshadowed by the splendour of its surrounds. The 1997 renovations combined the latest in theatre and acoustic technology with a remake of the most splendid of its 19th-century décor. The guided tours leave every half-hour and take about 50 minutes. See also p213.

PLAZA DE LA PUERTA DEL SOL Map pp64–5

M Sol

The official centrepoint of Spain is a gracious hemisphere of elegant façades and often overwhelming crowds. It is, above all, a crossroads with people forever passing through on their way elsewhere.

In Madrid's earliest days the Puerta del Sol (the Gate of the Sun) was the eastern gate of the city and from here passed a road through the peasant hovels of the outer 'suburbs' en route to Guadalajara, to the northeast. The name of the gate appears to

THINGS THEY SAID ABOUT...PUERTA DEL SOL

During the first days I could not tear myself away from the square of the Puerta del Sol. I stayed there by the hour, and amused myself so much that I should like to have passed the day there. It is a square worthy of its fame; not so much on account of its size and beauty as for the people, life and variety of spectacle which it presents at every hour of the day. It is not a square like the others; it is a mingling of salon, promenade, theatre, academy, garden, a square of arms, and a market. From daybreak until one o'clock at night, there is an immovable crowd, a crowd that comes and goes through the ten streets leading into it, and a passing and mingling of carriages which makes one giddy.

Edmondo De Amicis, Spain & the Spaniards (*1885*)

date from the 1520s, when Madrid joined the revolt of the Comuneros against Carlos I and erected a fortress in the east-facing arch in which the sun was depicted. The fort, which stood about where the metro station is today, was demolished around 1570.

The main building on the square houses the regional government of the Comunidad de Madrid. The Casa de Correos, as it is called, was built as the city's main post office in 1768. The clock was added in 1856 and on New Year's Eve people throng the square to wait impatiently for the clock to strike midnight, and at each gong swallow a grape – not as easy as it sounds! On the footpath outside the Casa de Correos is a plaque marking Spain's Kilometre Zero, the point from which Spain's network of roads is measured. The semicircular junction owes its present appearance in part to the Bourbon king Carlos III (r 1759–88), whose equestrian statue (the nose is unmistakable) stands in the middle.

Just to the north of Carlos, the statue of a bear nuzzling a *madroño* (strawberry tree) is the city's symbol; for more information, see the boxed text, p24.

CONVENTO DE LAS DESCALZAS REALES Map pp64–5

☎ 91 542 69 47; www.patrimonionacional.es, in Spanish; Plaza de las Descalzas 3; adult/student & EU senior €5/2.50, EU citizens free Wed, combined ticket with Convento de la Encarnación €6/3.40; ☽ 10.30am-12.45pm & 4-5.45pm Tue-Thu & Sat, 10.30am-12.45pm Fri, 11am-1.45pm Sun & holidays; Ⓜ Callao

The grim, prisonlike walls of this one-time palace keep modern Madrid at bay and offer no hint that behind the sober platesque façade lies a sumptuous stronghold of the faith.

The compulsory guided tour (in Spanish) leads you up a gaudily frescoed Renais-

sance stairway to the upper level of the cloister. The vault was painted by Claudio Coello, one of the most important artists of the Madrid School (p38) of the 17th century and whose works adorn San Lorenzo de El Escorial.

You then pass several of the convent's 33 chapels – a maximum of 33 Franciscan nuns is allowed to live here (perhaps because Christ is said to have been 33 when he died) as part of a closed order. These nuns follow in the tradition of the Descalzas Reales (Barefooted Royals), a group of illustrious women who cloistered themselves when the convent was founded in the 16th century. The first of these chapels contains a remarkable carved figure of a dead, reclining Christ, which is paraded in a moving Good Friday procession each year. At the end of the passage is the antechoir, then the choir stalls themselves, where Doña Juana – the daughter of Carlos I and who in a typical piece of 16th-century collusion between royalty and the Catholic Church, commandeered the palace and had it converted into a convent – is buried. A *Virgen la Dolorosa* by Pedro de la Mena is seated in one of the 33 oak stalls.

In the former sleeping quarters of the nuns are some of the most extraordinary tapestries you're ever likely to see. Woven in the 17th century in Brussels, they include four based on drawings by Rubens. To produce works of this quality, four or five artisans could take up to a year to weave just 1 sq m of tapestry.

IGLESIA DE SAN GINÉS Map pp64–5

☎ 91 366 48 75; Calle del Arenal 13; admission free; ☽ for services only; Ⓜ Sol or Ópera

Due north of Plaza Mayor, San Ginés is one of Madrid's oldest churches: it has been here in one form or another since at least the 14th century. It is speculated that, prior to the arrival of the Christians in 1085, a Mozarabic community (Christians in Muslim territory) lived around the stream that later became Calle del Arenal and that their parish church stood on this site. What you see today was built in 1645 but largely reconstructed after a fire in 1824. The church houses some fine paintings, including El Greco's *Expulsion of the Moneychangers from the Temple* (1614), which is beautifully displayed; the glass is just 6mm from the canvas to avoid reflections. The church has stood at the centre of Madrid life for centuries; Spain's premier playwright Lope de Vega was married here and novelist Francisco de Quevedo was baptised in its font. Sadly, the church opens to the public only once a week (at the time of research, that day was Saturday but was expected to change).

CONVENTO DE LA ENCARNACIÓN
Map pp64–5

☎ 91 542 69 47; www.patrimonionacional.es, in Spanish; Plaza de la Encarnación 1; adult/student & EU senior €3.60/2, EU citizens free Wed, combined ticket with Convento de las Descalzas Reales €6/3.40; ⏱ 10.30am-12.45pm & 4-5.45pm Tue-Thu & Sat, 10.30am-12.45pm Fri, 11am-1.45pm Sun & holidays; Ⓜ Ópera

Founded by Empress Margarita de Austria, this 17th-century mansion built in the Madrid baroque style (a pleasing amalgam of brick, exposed stone and wrought iron) is still inhabited by nuns of the Augustine order. The large art collection dates mostly from the 17th century and among the many gold and silver reliquaries is one that contains the blood of San Pantaleón, which purportedly liquefies each year on 27 July. The convent also sits on a pretty plaza with lovely views down towards the Palacio Real.

PLAZA DE ESPAÑA Map pp64–5
Ⓜ Plaza de España

It's hard to know what to make of this curiously unprepossessing square. The 1953 Edificio de España (Spain Building; Map pp110–11) on the east side clearly sprang from the totalitarian recesses of Franco's imagination such is its resemblance to austere Soviet monumentalism, but there's also something strangely grand and pleasing about it. To the north stands the rather ugly and considerably taller 35-storey Torre de Madrid (Madrid Tower; Map pp116–17). Taking centre

stage in the square is a statue of Cervantes. At the writer's feet is a bronze of his immortal characters, Don Quijote and Sancho Panza. The monument was erected in 1927. But Plaza de España is at its best down in its lower (western) reaches where abundant trees are remarkably successful in keeping Madrid's noise at bay. It's probably best avoided after dark.

GRAN VÍA Map pp64–5
Ⓜ Gran Vía or Callao

It's difficult to imagine Madrid without Gran Vía, the grand boulevard that climbs through the centre of Madrid from Plaza de España down to Calle de Alcalá, but it has only existed since 1911 when it was bulldozed through what was then a labyrinth of old streets. It may have destroyed whole barrios, but it is still considered one of the most successful examples of urban planning in central Madrid since the late 19th century. It wasn't always thus: plans for the boulevard were first announced in 1862 and so interminable were the delays that a famous *zarzuela* (satirical musical comedy), La Gran Vía, first performed in 1886, was penned to mock the city authorities and remains popular to this day.

Its short history has been eventful and its very existence was controversial from the start, sweeping away a lively inner-city community, including the house where Goya had once lived, to be replaced by the towering Belle Époque façades that lord it over the street below. In all, 14 streets disappeared off the map, as did 311 houses.

One eye-catching building, the Carrión (Map pp64–5), on the corner of Gran Vía and Calle de Jacometrezo, was Madrid's first tower-block apartment hotel and caused quite a stir when it was put up during the pre-WWI years; it's once again a hotel. Also dominating the skyline about one-third of the way along Gran Vía stands the 1920s-era Telefónica building (Map pp110–11), which was for years the highest building in the city. During the civil war, when Madrid was besieged by Franco's forces and the boulevard became known as 'Howitzer Alley' due to the artillery shells that rained down upon it, the Telefónica building was a favoured target.

Among the more interesting buildings is the stunning, French-designed Edificio Metrópolis (Map pp64–5; 1905), which marks the southern end of Gran Vía. The winged victory statue atop its dome was added in 1975 and is best seen from Calle de Alcalá or Plaza de Cibeles. A little up the boulevard is the Edificio Grassy (with the Piaget sign; Map pp64–5), built in 1916. With its circular 'temple' as a crown, and profusion of arcs and slender columns, it's one of the most elegant buildings on the Gran Vía.

Otherwise, Gran Vía proliferates with luxury hotels and cheap *hostales* (hostels), pinball parlours and dark old cinemas, as well as everything from jewellery shops, banks and high fashion to fast food and sex shops. It's home to twice as many businesses (1051 at last count) as homes (592), over 13,000 people work along the street and up to 50,000 vehicles pass through every day (including almost 200 buses an hour during peak periods). In 2007 the failed Socialist mayoral candidate for Madrid proposed closing Gran Vía to traffic. In short, Gran Vía is central Madrid in microcosm: clamorous, hard-working and always with a controversial story behind it.

REAL ACADEMIA DE BELLAS ARTES DE SAN FERNANDO Map pp64–5

☎ 91 524 08 64; http://rabasf.insde.es, in Spanish; Calle de Alcalá 13; adult/student/child under 18yr & senior €3/1.50/free; 9am-7pm Tue-Fri, 9am-2.30pm & 4-7pm Sat, 9am-2.30pm Sun & Mon Sep-Jun, varied hours in Jul & Aug; M Sevilla

In any other city, this gallery would be a stand-out attraction, but in Madrid it often gets forgotten in the rush to the Prado, Thyssen or Reina Sofía. A visit here is a fascinating journey into another age of art; when we tell you that Picasso and Dalí studied at this academy (long the academic centre of learning for up-and-coming artists), but found it far too stuffy for their liking, you'll get an idea of what to expect. A centre of excellence since Fernando VI founded the academy in the 18th century, it remains a stunning repository of works by some of the best-loved old Spanish masters.

The 1st floor, mainly devoted to 16th- to 19th-century paintings, is the most noteworthy of those in the academic gallery. Among relative unknowns you come across a hall of works by Zurbarán – especially arresting is the series of full-length portraits of white-cloaked friars – and a *San Jerónimo* by El Greco.

At a 'fork' in the exhibition a sign points right to Rooms 11 to 16, the main one

showcasing Alonso Cano (1601–67) and José de Ribera (1591–1652). In the others a couple of minor portraits by Velázquez hang alongside the occasional Rubens, Tintoretto and Bellini, which have somehow been smuggled in. Rooms 17 to 22 offer a roomful of Bravo Murillo and last, but most captivating, more than a dozen pieces by Goya, including self-portraits, portraits of King Fernando VII and the infamous minister Manuel Godoy, along with one on bullfighting.

The 19th and 20th centuries are the themes upstairs. It's not the most extensive or engaging modern collection, but you'll find drawings by Picasso as well as works by Joaquín Sorolla, Juan Gris, Eduardo Chillida and Ignacio Zuloaga, in most cases with only one or two items each.

OLD MADRID
Walking Tour

1 Plaza de Oriente (p63) Begin in this splendid arc of greenery and graceful architecture, which could be Madrid's most agreeable plaza. You'll find yourself surrounded by gardens, the Palacio Real and the Teatro Real, and peopled by an ever-changing cast of madrileños at play. Spend as long as you can here before setting out.

2 Palacio Real (p67) Spain's seat of royal power for centuries, the Royal Palace imposes itself upon the Plaza de Oriente and stands as one of the capital's most emblematic sights when seen from the west. Its interior is lavish, crammed with the accumulated extravagance of royal excess.

3 Catedral de Nuestra Señora de la Almudena (p68) Madrid's modern cathedral may lack the old-world gravitas of other Spanish cathedrals, but it's a beautiful part of the skyline when combined with the adjacent Palacio Real. Take a quick look within, if only to see a rare example of pop art in a house of worship.

4 Plaza de la Villa (p62) From the cathedral, climb gently up Calle Mayor, pausing to admire the last remaining ruins of Madrid's first cathedral, Santa María de la Almudena, then on to Plaza de la Villa, a cosy square surrounded on three sides by some of the best examples of Madrid baroque architecture.

5 Plaza Mayor (p61) Up the hill to the east, the Plaza Mayor is one of Spain's grandest and most beautiful plazas and is always filled with life. The frescoes on the north side perfectly complement the slate spires and ochre tones that surround a square that has witnessed many of the grand events of the city's history.

6 Casa Revuelta (p161) Just southwest of the plaza, Casa Revuelta is a terrific place to recharge the batteries and to pause long enough to sample the tapas of *bacalao* (cod) in Madrid. It's an old place, with an old owner and a loyal clientele and, when they're on song, the banter is pure theatre.

7 Plaza de la Puerta del Sol (p68) Return to the Plaza Mayor and leave it via the northeast corner, down to Calle de Postas to the Puerta del Sol. This is Madrid's heartbeat, a clamorous wedge of activity and pretty architecture dead in the centre of Madrid.

8 Iglesia de San Ginés (p69) The pedestrianised Calle del Arenal, which leads northwest from the plaza, takes you past the pleasing brick-and-stone Iglesia de San Ginés, one of the longest-standing relics of Christian Madrid. If you're able to peek inside, make straight for the El Greco masterpiece.

WALK FACTS

Start Plaza de Oriente
End Plaza de España
Distance 3km
Time Two to three hours

OLD MADRID

9 Chocolatería de San Ginés (p186) Tucked away in the lane behind the church, this bar-café is justifiably famous for its *churros y chocolate* (Spanish donuts with chocolate), the ideal Madrid hangover cure or a delicious indulgence at any hour of the day.

10 Convento de las Descalzas Reales (p69) Across the other side of Calle del Arenal, in the Plaza de San Martín, this austere convent has an extraordinarily rich interior behind the high brick walls, loaded with tapestries, master paintings and a jaw-dropping Renaissance stairway.

11 Gran Vía (p70) Up the hill to the northeast lies Gran Vía, the grand boulevard that consists of an endless tide of human and vehicular traffic. Along its shores are formidable examples of early 20th-century architecture. Along its footpaths passes Madrid in all its madness.

12 Plaza de España (p70) Down the bottom of Gran Vía to the northwest, Plaza de España is a rare stand of greenery in downtown Madrid. Watched over by architectural monuments to a dictator's folly, the plaza has a far more cultured statue of Cervantes and his two most famous literary creations in the centre.

LA LATINA & LAVAPIÉS

Drinking p187; Eating p162; Nightlife p200; Shopping p135; Sleeping p232

La Latina combines many of the best things about Madrid: arguably the Spanish capital's best selection of tapas bars and a medieval streetscape studded with elegant churches. The barrio's heartland is centred on the area between (and very much including) Calle de la Cava Baja and the beautiful Plaza de la Paja. It's always lively here, but while the rest of the city sleeps off its hangover from the night before, La Latina throngs with crowds on Sunday on their way home from the unrivalled El Rastro flea market. The web of lanes around Calle de Segovia and Calle de Bailén once constituted the *morería*, the Moorish quarter of Mayrit, while the medieval city walls once loosely followed Calles de la Cava Baja and de la Cava Alta. The barrio still represents something of a meeting point between the old-world elegance of Madrid de los Austrias and working-class Lavapiés.

Lavapiés, on the other hand, is a world away from the sophistication of modern Madrid. This is one of the city's oldest and most traditional barrios. It's at once deeply traditional – when madrileños dress up for the Fiestas de San Isidro Labrador (p18), they don the outfits of working-class *chulapas* and *manolos* who frequented Lavapiés in centuries past – and home to more immigrants than any other central Madrid barrio. Black Africans, Moroccans, South Americans and Chinese live cheek by jowl with locals whose grandparents also lived here and who wouldn't live anywhere else; according to one count, over 50 nationalities are represented in an area made up of a couple of dozen streets. It's quirky, alternative and a melting pot all in one, a long-standing community and one constantly in the making. It's not without its problems and the barrio has a reputation for either antiglamour cool or as a no-go zone.

EL RASTRO Map pp76–7
Ribera de Curtidores; ⏱ **8am-3pm Sun & holidays;**
Ⓜ **La Latina**

The crowded Sunday flea market was, back in the 17th and 18th centuries, largely dedicated to a meat market (the word *rastro*, which means 'stain', referred to the trail of blood left behind by animals dragged down the hill). The road leading to the market, Ribera de Curtidores, translates as Tanners' Alley and further evokes this sense of a slaughterhouse past. On Sunday mornings this is *the* place to be, with all of Madrid in all its diversity here in search of a bargain (see p136).

BASÍLICA DE SAN FRANCISCO EL GRANDE Map pp76–7
☎ 91 365 38 00; Plaza de San Francisco; admission €3; ⏱ 8-11am Mon, 8am-1pm & 4-6.30pm Tue-Fri, 4-8.45pm Sat; Ⓜ La Latina or Puerta de Toledo

Lording it over the southwestern corner of La Latina, this imposing and recently restored baroque basilica is one of Madrid's grandest old churches – although it's a little off the normal tourist trail, it feels more like a local church than a tourist attraction. Beneath the frescoed cupolas (restored in 2000–01) and the appealing chapel ceilings by Francisco Bayeu, old women seem lost amid the empty pews as priests try to ignore the fact that church attendance in Spain is at an all-time low.

Legend has it that St Francis of Assisi built a chapel on this site in 1217. The current version – one of the city's largest – was designed by Francesco Sabatini, who also designed the Puerta de Alcalá and finished off the Palacio Real. He designed the church with a highly unusual floor plan: when you enter, the building arcs off

ORIENTATION & TRANSPORT: LA LATINA & LAVAPIÉS

La Latina forms a rough triangle bordered by Calle de Segovia, Calle de Bailén (which becomes the Gran Vía de San Francisco) and the Calle de Toledo, which separates it from Lavapiés. There aren't many metro stops within La Latina, although La Latina station (line 5) is the most convenient. The Puerta de Toledo stop is handy only if your business is a long way down the hill.

From Plaza de Tirso de Molina and Calle de Atocha, a series of long narrow lanes drops downhill into Lavapiés. The barrio's most obvious nerve centre is the small triangular Plaza de Lavapiés. Lavapiés is cordoned off to the south by Ronda de Toledo and Ronda de Atocha, noisy avenues that head east to Atocha station. Lavapiés metro stop (line 3) drops you in the heart of the barrio, although if you prefer a downhill walk, Tirso de Molina (line 1) and Antón Martín (line 1) are better. For El Rastro, the best stops are La Latina (line 5) or Tirso de Molina.

THINGS THEY SAID ABOUT... EL RASTRO

The Rastro was itself a curious place then, almost medieval. There was sold almost everything imaginable: used clothes, pictures, false teeth, books, medicines, chestnuts, coach wheels, trusses, shoes. There one met all types: Moors, Jews, blacks, travelling charlatans, rat-catchers and sellers of caged birds.

Pío Baroja, Desde la Última Vuelta del Camino (1948)

to the left and right in a flurry of columns. Off this circular nave lie several chapels, while a series of corridors behind the high altar is lined with works of art from the 17th to 19th centuries. A guide usually directs you to the sacristy, which features fine Renaissance *sillería* – the sculpted walnut seats where the church's superiors would meet.

A 19th-century plan to create a grand linking square supported by a viaduct between this church and the Palacio Real never left the drawing board, but you can see a model in the Museo Municipal.

LAS VISTILLAS, VIADUCT & CALLE DE SEGOVIA Map pp76–7
Ⓜ Ópera

Jardines de las Vistillas, the leafy area around and beneath the southern end of the viaduct that crosses Calle de Segovia, is an ideal spot to pause and ponder the curious history of one of Madrid's oldest barrios.

Probably the best place to do this is just across Calle de Bailén where the *terrazas* (oper-air cafés) of Las Vistillas offer one of the best vantage points in Madrid for a drink, with views towards the Sierra de Guadarrama. During the civil war, Las Vistillas was heavily bombarded by Nationalist troops from the Casa de Campo, and they in turn were shelled from a republican bunker here.

The adjacent viaduct, which was built in the 19th century and replaced by a newer version in 1942, would also become a place associated with death, albeit of a different kind. It was the suicide launch pad of choice until plastic barriers were erected in the late 1990s. They obscure the views, but one assumes the local death rate has dropped, too.

Before the viaduct was built, anyone wanting to cross over was obliged to make their way down to Calle de Segovia and back up the other side. If you feel like re-enacting the journey, head down to Calle de Segovia and cross to the southern side. Just east of the viaduct, on a characterless apartment block (No 21) wall, is one of the city's oldest coats of arms. The site once belonged to Madrid's Ayuntamiento. A punt would ferry people across what was then a trickling tributary of the Río Manzanares.

Climbing back up the southern side from Calle de Segovia you reach Calle de la Morería. The area south to the Basílica de San Francisco El Grande and southeast to the Iglesia de San Andrés was the heart of the *morería* (Moorish quarter). The Muslim population of Mayrit was concentrated here following the 11th-century Christian take over. Strain the imagination a little and the maze of winding and hilly lanes even now retains a whiff of a North African medina; for more information on the history of the period, turn to p24.

Another option is to follow Calle de Segovia west, down to the banks of the Manzanares and a nine-arched bridge, the Puente de Segovia (Map pp126–7), which Juan de Herrera built in 1584. The walk is more pleasant than the river, a view shared by the writer Lope de Vega who thought the bridge a little too grand for the 'apprentice river'. He suggested the city buy a bigger river or sell the bridge!

IGLESIA DE SAN ANDRÉS Map pp76–7
☎ 91 365 48 71; Plaza de San Andrés; ⏰ 8am-1pm & 6-8pm; Ⓜ La Latina

This proud church is more imposing than beautiful and what you see today is the result of restoration work completed after the church was gutted during the civil war.

The interior is not without its appeal, most notably its extraordinary baroque altar. Stern, dark columns with gold-leaf capitals against the rear wall lead your

top picks

SIGHTS IN LA LATINA & LAVAPIÉS

- El Rastro (opposite)
- Basílica de San Francisco El Grande (opposite)
- Iglesia de San Andrés (above)
- Museo de San Isidro (p78)

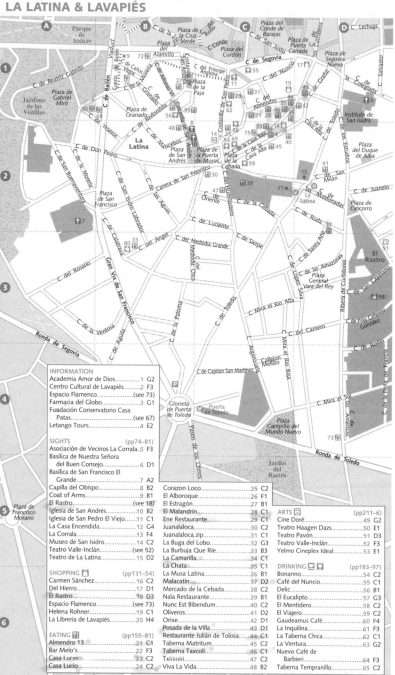

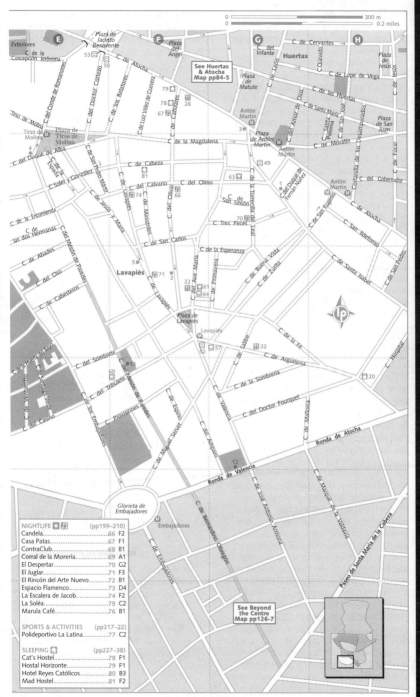

Exteriores

C de la Concepción Jerónima

Plaza de Jacinto Benavente

Plaza del Ángel

Plaza del Infante

C de Cervantes

Huertas

C de Lope de Vega

Plaza de Jesús

See Huertas & Atocha Map pp84-5

Plaza de Matute

Antón Martín

C de las Huertas

C de Atocha

C de Luis Vélez de Guevara

C de Cañizares

Plaza de Tirso de Molina

Tirso de Molina

C de la Magdalena

Plaza de Antón Martín

Antón Martín

C del Duque de Fernán Núñez

C del Duque de Alba

C de Cabeza

C del Calvario

C del Olmo

C de San Simón

C de la Torrecilla del Leal

Anton Martín

C del Gobernador

C de Atocha

C de la Encomienda

C de las dos Hermanas

C del Mesón de Paredes

C de Jesús y María

C de Ministriles

C del Olivar

Tres Peces

C de San Carlos

C de la Esperanza

Lavapiés

C de Ave María

C de Primavera

C de Buena Vista

C de Zurita

C de Santa Isabel

C de la Fe

Lavapiés

C de Argumosa

C de Sumbre

C de la Sombrería

C del Doctor Fourquet

C de Valencia

C de Mallorca

Ronda de Atocha

Ronda de Valencia

Glorieta de Embajadores

Embajadores

See Beyond the Centre Map pp126-7

Paseo de Santa María de la Cabeza

eyes up into the dome, all rose, yellow and green, and rich with sculpted floral fantasies and cherubs poking out of every nook and cranny.

Around the back, on the delightful Plaza de la Paja (Straw Square), is the Capilla del Obispo, a hugely important site on the historical map of Madrid. It was here that San Isidro Labrador, patron saint of Madrid, was first buried. When the saint's body was discovered there in the late 13th century, two centuries after his death, decomposition had not yet set in. Thus it was that King Alfonso XI ordered the construction in San Andrés of an ark to hold his remains and a chapel in which to venerate his memory. In 1669 (47 years after the saint was canonised) the last of many chapels was built on the site and that's what you see today.

Restoration of the chapel was nearing completion at the time of writing and when it reopens to the public, note the Gothic vaulting in the ceilings and the fine Renaissance reredos (screens), a combination that's quite rare in Madrid. But don't go looking for the saint's remains because San Isidro made his last move to the Basílica de Nuestra Señora del Buen Consejo in the 18th century.

MUSEO DE SAN ISIDRO Map pp76–7
☎ 91 366 74 15; www.munimadrid.es/museo sanisidro; Plaza de San Andrés 2; admission free; ☾ 9.30am-8pm Tue-Fri, 10am-2pm Sat & Sun; Ⓜ La Latina

Next door to the Iglesia de San Andrés is this engaging museum on the spot where San Isidro Labrador is said to have ended his days around 1172. For an overview of Madrid's history this place is hard to beat with archaeological finds from the Roman period (including a 4th-century mosaic found on the site of a Roman villa in the barrio of Carabanchel); maps, scale models, paintings and photos of Madrid down through the ages; and detailed sections on the Alcázar and the Parque del Buen Retiro when it was exclusively a royal playground. A particular highlight is the large model based on Pedro Teixeira's famous 1656 map of Madrid. Of great historical interest (though not much to look at) is the 'miraculous well' where the saint called forth water to slake his master's thirst. In another miracle, the son of the saint's master fell into a well, whereupon Isidro prayed and prayed until the water rose and lifted his son to

safety. The museum is housed in a largely new building with a 16th-century Renaissance courtyard and a 17th-century chapel.

IGLESIA DE SAN PEDRO EL VIEJO Map pp76–7
☎ 91 365 12 84; Costanilla de San Pedro; Ⓜ La Latina

This fine old church is one of the few remaining windows on post-Muslim Madrid, most notably its clearly *mudéjar* brick bell tower, which dates from the 14th century. The church is generally closed to the public, but it's arguably more impressive from the outside (you'll probably have to take our word for it); the Renaissance doorway has stood since 1525. If you can peek inside, the nave dates from the 15th century, although the interior largely owes its appearance to 17th-century renovations. Along with the Iglesia de San Nicolás de los Servitas (p63), the Iglesia de San Pedro El Viejo is one of very few sites where traces of *mudéjar* Madrid remain *in situ*. Otherwise, you need to visit Toledo (p242), 70km south of Madrid, to visualise what Madrid once was like.

BASÍLICA DE NUESTRA SEÑORA DEL BUEN CONSEJO Map pp76–7
☎ 91 369 20 37; Calle de Toledo 37; ☾ 8am-1pm & 6-9pm; Ⓜ Tirso de Molina or La Latina

Towering above the northern end of bustling Calle de Toledo, and visible through the arches from the Plaza Mayor, this imposing church long served as the city's de facto cathedral until Nuestra Señora de la Almudena was completed in 1992.

Still known to locals as the Catedral de San Isidro, the austere baroque basilica was

---

THINGS THEY SAID ABOUT... LAVAPIÉS

Old Madrid, the Madrid of my childhood, is a great surge of clouds or of waves, I do not know which. But beyond all those whites and blues, beyond all the songs and sounds and vibrations, there is one permanent strain: El Avapiés. At that time it was the frontier of Madrid. It was the end of Madrid, and the end of the world...It was another world indeed. So far civilisation and the city reached, and there they ended.

Arturo Barea, The Forging of a Rebel

founded in the 17th century as the head-quarters for the Jesuits and today is home to the remains of the city's main patron saint, San Isidro (in the third chapel on your left after you walk in). His body, apparently remarkably well preserved, is only removed from here on rare occasions, such as in 1896 and 1947 when he was paraded about town in the hope he would bring rain (he did, at least in 1947).

Next door, the Instituto de San Isidro once went by the name of Colegio Imperial and, from the 16th century on, was where many of the country's leading figures were schooled by the Jesuits. You can wander in and look at the elegant courtyard.

PLAZA DE LA CEBADA Map pp76–7
Ⓜ La Latina

Just west of La Latina metro station, the busy and bar-strewn corner of Madrid marked by the ill-defined 'Barley Square' is important to understanding what medieval Madrid was like, although it requires a little imagination.

In the wake of the Christian conquest the square was, for a time, the site of a Muslim cemetery, and the nearby Plaza de la Puerta de Moros (Moors' Gate) underscores that this area was long home to the city's Muslim population. The square later became a popular spot for public executions – until well into the 19th century, the condemned would be paraded along Calle de Toledo, before turning into the square and mounting the gallows.

The Teatro de la Latina, at the Calle de Toledo end of the elongated square, stands where one of Queen Isabel's closest advisers, Beatriz Galindo, built a hospital in the 15th century. A noted humanist, Galindo was known as 'La Latina' for her prodigious knowledge of Latin (which she taught Queen Isabel) and general erudition. Only Galindo's nickname reminds us of what once stood here.

Not far from the theatre, the narrow streets of Calle de la Cava Alta and Calle de la Cava Baja delineate where the second line of medieval Christian city walls ran (see p24 for more information). They continued up along what is now Calle de los Cuchilleros (Knife-makers St) and along the Cava de San Miguel, and were superseded by the third circuit of walls, which was raised in the 15th century. The cavas were initially ditches dug in front of the walls, later used as refuse dumps and

WHAT'S IN A NAME?
The name Lavapiés comes from aba-puest (place of the Jews) because the bulk of the city's Jewish population once lived in the eastern half of Lavapiés (the existence, centuries ago, of at least one synagogue in the area is documented) in what was then known as the judería (Jewish quarter). The bulk of them left after the Catholic Monarchs ordered the expulsion of Jews and Muslims from Spain in 1492. Those who remained behind became conversos (converts to Christianity).

finally given over to housing when the walls no longer served any defensive purpose.

PLAZA DE LAVAPIÉS & AROUND Map pp76–7
Ⓜ Lavapiés

The triangular Plaza de Lavapiés is one of the few open spaces in the barrio and it's a magnet for all that's good (a thriving cultural life) and bad (drugs and a high police presence) about the barrio. The Teatro Valle-Inclán (p216), on the southern edge of the plaza, is a stunning contemporary addition to the eclectic Lavapiés streetscape. To find out what makes this barrio tick, consider dropping in to the Asociación de Vecinos La Corrala (☎ 91 467 05 09; www.avvlacorrala.org, in Spanish; Calle de Lavapiés 38; Ⓜ Lavapiés), just up the hill from the plaza, where staff are happy to highlight all that's good about Lavapiés without dismissing its problems.

In the surrounding streets, one building that catches the community spirit of this lively barrio is La Corrala (Map pp76–7; cnr Calle del Mesón de Paredes & Calle del Tribulete; Ⓜ Lavapiés), an example of an intriguing traditional (if much tidied up) tenement block, with long communal balconies built around a central courtyard; working-class Madrid was once strewn with buildings like this and very few survive. Almost opposite are the ruins (Map pp76–7; cnr Calle del Sombrete & Calle del Mesón de Paredes; Ⓜ Lavapiés) of an old church, now converted into a library and the stunning Gaudeamus Café (p188), with its views over the rooftops of the barrio.

LA CASA ENCENDIDA Map pp76–7
☎ 902 430 322; www.lacasaencendida.com; Ronda de Valencia 2; 10am-10pm; Ⓜ Embajadores
This cultural centre is utterly unpredictable, if only because of the quantity and scope

of its activities – everything from exhibitions, cinema sessions, workshops and more. The focus is often on international artists or environmental themes, and if it has an overarching theme, it's the alternative slant it takes on the world.

TAPAS IN MEDIEVAL MADRID
Walking Tour

1 Basílica de Nuestra Señora del Buen Consejo (p78) If it's not Sunday and time for El Rastro (p74), begin at what once served as Madrid's interim cathedral and last resting place of the city's patron saint. At once austere and gilded in gold leaf, this imposing basilica has much greater resonance for most madrileños than the cathedral that replaced it.

WALK FACTS

Start Basílica de Nuestra Señora del Buen Consejo
End Almendro 13
Distance 2.5km
Time Two to three hours

---

2 Calle de la Cava Baja Head across the Plaza de Segovia Nueva and turn left in Calle de la Cava Baja, a winding medieval street along the site of Madrid's old city walls. This is Madrid's tapas central, with wonderful bars like Taberna Txacoli (p165), Casa Lucas (p164) and the extravagantly tiled La Chata (p163).

3 Juanalaloca (p163) You haven't come very far, but walking La Latina means regular tapas pit stops. Purple-clad Juanalaloca, just off the southwestern end of Calle de la Cava Baja, is the place for what's possibly Madrid's best *tortilla de patatas* (potato *tortilla*) and fine wines. Try other things if you wish, but *don't* pass on the *tortilla*.

4 Basílica de San Francisco El Grande (p74) All the way down the bottom of Carrera de San Francisco, this formidable basilica looms over southwestern Madrid. Inside, note the unusual floor plan and marvel at the walls strewn with masterpieces and consider how far this patch of land has come since St Francis of Assisi passed through in the 13th century.

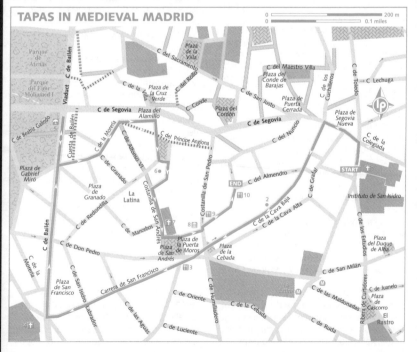

TAPAS IN MEDIEVAL MADRID

5 Las Vistillas (p75) Calle de Bailén runs north to Las Vistillas, with it's sweeping views out over Madrid's sprawl, and the viaduct from where there are even better views back towards the spires and terracotta roofs of Los Austrias. You're now looking at the *morería* (Moorish Quarter) from medieval times and it's here that you're headed.

6 Plaza de la Paja (p75) Take Calle de la Morería as far as Calle de Segovia, then climb back up to Plaza de la Paja, which is unlike any other Madrid square. Feeling for all the world like you've stumbled upon a *plaza del pueblo* (village square) in the heart of the city, Plaza de la Paja is possibly our favourite little corner of medieval Madrid.

7 Iglesia de San Andrés (p75) Overlooking the plaza (although entry is from the southern side), this imposing church is glorious when floodlit at night and filled with baroque flourishes within, especially the altar and the sculpted columns. If it has reopened, don't miss the Capilla del Obispo.

8 Museo de San Isidro (p78) Time for a history lesson. Along the Plaza de San Andrés, this fine museum takes you on a journey through Madrid's history through maps, old photos and memorabilia from San Isidro – this was where he performed his first miracle.

9 Corazon Loco (p165) One of the best tapas bars in the barrio, if not all of Madrid, Corazon Loco is the sort of place where you could easily spend an entire afternoon. The reason not to is that there's one more tapas stop before you finish the walking tour.

10 Almendro 13 (p165) Rest your weary legs perched atop one of Almendro 13's wooden stools and cast a lingering look over the extensive menu. And hold on to your seat – this is among the most celebrated tapas bars in Madrid and tables are at a premium.

HUERTAS & ATOCHA

Drinking p189; Eating p165; Nightlife p200; Shopping p136; Sleeping p232

The noise of Huertas' nights rolls out across the city like the clamour of a not-so-distant war. If Huertas is known for anything, it's for nightlife that never seems to abate once the sun goes down. Such fame is well deserved, but there's so much more to Huertas than immediately meets the eye.

By day it's a place to enjoy the height of sophisticated European café culture in the superb Plaza de Santa Ana. Down the hill, in the impossibly narrow and largely traffic-free lanes, you'll find restaurants, bars of every description, some of the city's best live music venues, quirky shops and signposts to the days when Madrid's writers made this their home – the other name for this area is the Barrio de las Letras (Barrio of Letters). Keep going down the slope and Huertas becomes less clamorous by degrees, shifting from Madrid's culture of excess to the paragons of high culture that line up along the Paseo del Prado. Down the bottom of Calle de Atocha, in particular, the Centro de Arte Reina Sofía is one of the finest contemporary art galleries in Europe, home to works by Dalí and Miró as well as Picasso's *Guernica*, and just across from the Antigua Estación de Atocha – a landmark for architects as for train travellers alike.

Unsurprisingly, Huertas and Atocha draw a diverse crowd that ranges from those hellbent on having a good time to aesthetes who love the intimacy and choice that the barrio has to offer. It's at once cultural, casual and, dare we say it, downright intoxicating. If you love narrow Spanish streets that seem to close off the horizon and run at all angles, if you like a barrio with multiple personalities, you'll love Huertas.

CENTRO DE ARTE REINA SOFÍA Map pp84–5

☎ 91 774 10 00; www.reinasofia.es; Calle de Santa Isabel 52; adult/student/child under 12yr & senior over 65yr €6/4/free, free to all Sat 2.30-9pm & Sun, handset guide €3; ⏰ 10am-9pm Mon & Wed-Sat, 10am-2.30pm Sun; Ⓜ Atocha

Adapted from the shell of an 18th-century hospital, the Centro de Arte Reina Sofía houses the best Madrid has to offer in modern Spanish art, principally spanning the 20th century up to the 1980s (for more recent works, visit the Museo Municipal de Arte Contemporáneo; p108). The occasional non-Spaniard artist makes an appearance, but most of the collection is strictly peninsular.

While the stately grandeur of the 18th-century palace that houses the Museo del Prado is an essential part of the Prado's charm, the state-of-the-art Reina Sofía is a perfect showpiece for converting old-world architecture to meet the needs of a dynamic modern collection. This is especially the case in the stunning extension that spreads along the western tip of the Plaza del Emperador Carlos V, and which hosts temporary exhibitions, auditoriums, the bookshop, a café and the museum's library.

The main gallery's permanent display ranges over the 2nd (Rooms 1 to 12) and 4th floors (Rooms 13 to 39). Note that the room numbers have recently been changed to accommodate temporary exhibitions and may change again, so pick up a floor plan from the information desk just inside the museum's entrance. As you skip from room to room and from floor to floor,

---

ORIENTATION & TRANSPORT: HUERTAS & ATOCHA

The Huertas area owes its name to the mostly traffic-free Calle de las Huertas, which starts just southwest of the Plaza de Santa Ana and runs through the heart of the barrio and all the way down the hill to the Paseo del Prado. The Calle del Prado also cuts a swathe through the neighbourhood. Otherwise, Huertas is bounded to the south by Calle de Atocha, which ends at the thundering roundabout of Plaza del Emperador Carlos V, which marks the beginning of Atocha, while Calle de Alcalá (north), Paseo del Prado (east) and Calle de Carretas (west) mark the Huertas perimeter.

The major metro stations for Huertas and Atocha all lie around the outside of the barrio, with Sol (lines 1, 2 and 3), Sevilla (line 2) and Antón Martín (line 1). Atocha station (line 1) and, to a lesser extent, Banco de España (line 2) are useful if your business lies down the hill and closer to Atocha or the Paseo del Prado.

GUERNICA

Guernica is one of the most famous paintings in the world, a signature work of cubism whose disfiguration of the human form would become an eloquent symbol of a world's outrage at the horrors wrought upon the innocent by modern warfare.

After the civil war broke out in 1936 Picasso was commissioned by the Republican government of Madrid to do the painting for the Paris Exposition Universelle in 1937. As news filtered out about the bombing of Gernika (Guernica) in the Basque Country by Hitler's Legión Condor, at the request of Franco, on 26 April 1937 (almost 2000 people died in the attack and much of the town was destroyed), Picasso committed his anger to canvas. To understand the painting's earth-shattering impact at the time, it must be remembered that the attack on Guernica represented the first use of airborne military hardware to devastating effect.

Guernica has always been a controversial work and was initially derided by many as being more propaganda than art. The 3.5m by 7.8m painting subsequently migrated to the USA and only returned to Spain in 1981, in keeping with Picasso's wish that the painting return to Spanish shores (first to the Museo del Prado, then to its current home) once democracy had been restored. The Basques believe that its true home is in the Basque Country and calls to have it moved there continue unabated, although such a move is unlikely to happen anytime soon with the Reina Sofía arguing that the painting is too fragile to be moved again.

the peaceful courtyard offers a peaceful respite from the clamour of Madrid, while the views over the city from the external glass lift, especially on the top floor, are outstanding.

The big attraction for most visitors is Picasso's *Guernica* (see the boxed text, above), in Room 6 on the 2nd floor, which is worth the entrance price even if you see nothing else. Alongside this masterwork is a plethora of the artist's preparatory sketches, offering an intriguing insight into the development of this seminal work.

Rush straight for it if you must, but don't make the mistake of neglecting the other outstanding works on show here.

Primary among the other stars in residence is the work of Joan Miró (1893–1983), which adorns Room 12, a long gallery adjacent to the Picasso collection. Amid his often delightfully bright primary-colour efforts are some of his equally odd sculptures. Since his paintings became a symbol of the Barcelona Olympics in 1992, his work has begun to receive the international acclaim it so richly deserves and this is the best place to get a representative sample of his innovative work.

You'll also want to rush to Room 10 to view the 20 or so canvases by Salvador Dalí (1904–89), especially the surrealist extravaganza *El Gran Masturbador* (1929). Amid this collection is a strange bust of a certain *Joelle* done by Dalí and his friend Man Ray (1890–1976). Other surrealists, including Max Ernst (1891–1976), appear in Room 11.

If you can tear yourself away from the big names, the Reina Sofía proffers a terrific opportunity to learn more about lesser-known 20th-century Spanish art, examples of which are littered throughout the gallery. Room 12, for example, concentrates on madrileño artist José Gutiérrez Solana (1886–1945). He depicts himself in gloomy fashion in *La Tertulia del Café de Pombo* (The Circle of the Café Pombo; 1920). Room 3 hosts works by the better-known Juan Gris, and these spill over into Room 4. Among the bronzes of Pablo Gargallo (1881–1934) in Room 5 is a head of Picasso. Also on the 2nd floor, in Room 1, you'll find the excellent works of the important Basque painter Ignazio Zuloaga (1870–1945).

Room 12 has a display dedicated to Luis Buñuel, including a portrait of the filmmaker by Dalí and sketches by the poet Federico García Lorca. Room 13 hosts a long list of artists active in the turbulent decades of the 1920s and 1930s, including Benjamín Palencia. Luis Fernández (1900–73) dominates Room 14.

The collection on the 4th floor takes up the baton and continues from the 1940s until the 1980s. A new approach to landscapes evolved in the wake of the civil war, perhaps best exemplified by the work of Juan Manuel Díaz Caneja (1905–88) in Room 18. In the following room you can study works by two important groups to emerge after WWII, Pórtico and Dau al Set. Among artists of the latter was Barcelona's Antoni Tàpies (b 1923), some of whose later pieces also appear in Rooms 34 and 35.

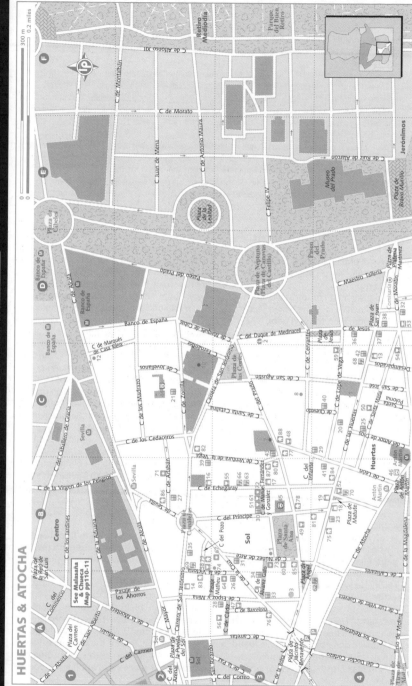

HUERTAS & ATOCHA

See Paseo del Prado & El Retiro Map pp92-3

Real Jardín Botánico

C de Alfonso XII

Paseo del Prado

Plaza del Emperador Carlos V

Atocha

C de Claudio Moyano

Paseo de la Infanta Isabel

Paseo de las Delicias

C de Méndez Álvaro

C de Tortosa

Ronda de Atocha

C del Doctor Drumen

C de Cenicero

C de la Almudena

C del Gobernador

C de San Pedro

C del Hospital

C de Santa Isabel

C de Atocha

C de Fúcar

C de Verónica

Costanilla de los...

Antón Martín

C de San Ildefonso

C de Sánchez Bustillo

Atocha Train Station

See La Latina & Lavapiés Map pp76-7

INFORMATION	
Babylon Idiomas	1 B3
Comunidad de Madrid Tourist Office	2 D3
La Bolsa de Minutos	3 A3
Tourist Information Point	4 D7

SIGHTS	(pp82–9)
11 March 2004 Memorial	5 F8
Antigua Estación de Atocha	6 E7
Ateneo Científico, Literario y Artístico de Madrid	7 C3
Casa de Lope de Vega	8 C3
Centro de Arte Reina Sofía	9 D7
Congreso de los Diputados	10 C2
Convento de las Trinitarias	11 C4
Círculo de Bellas Artes	12 C1
Teatro Español	(see 45)

SHOPPING	(pp131–54)
Flamenco World	13 C4
Gil	14 A2
La Central–Librería de Centro de Arte Reina Sofía	15 D7
Lomography	16 B2
María Cabello	17 B3
México	18 B4
México II	19 B4

EATING	(pp155–81)
A Tasca do Bacalhau Português	20 C4
Al Natural	21 C2
Arola Madrid	22 D7
Casa Alberto	23 B4
El Brillante	24 E6
La Biotika	25 C4
La Casa del Abuelo	26 A3
La Finca de Susana	27 B2
La Negra Tomasa	28 A3
La Piola	29 C4
La Trucha	30 B3
La Trucha	31 B3
La Vaca Verónica	32 D4
Las Bravas	33 A3
Las Bravas	34 A3
Lhardy	35 B2
Los Gatos	36 D4
Maceiras	37 D4
Maceiras	38 D4
Restaurante Integral Artemisa	39 B2
Sidrería Vasca Zerain	40 C4
Vinos González	41 B4
Viva La Vida	42 C4
Ølsen	43 C3

ARTS	(pp211–6)
Teatro de la Zarzuela	44 C2
Teatro Español	45 B3
Teatro Monumental	46 B4

DRINKING	(pp183–97)
Café del Círculo de Bellas Artes	(see 12)
Café del Soul	47 A3
Casa Alberto	(see 23)
Casa Pueblo	48 C3
Cervecería Alemana	49 B3
Dos Gardenias	50 C4
El Callejón	51 B3
El Imperfecto	52 B4
El Oasis	53 D4
La Venencia	54 C4
Malaspina	55 B3
Melounge	56 A3
Ølsen	57 D5
Taberna Alhambra	58 B2
Taberna de Dolores	59 C4
The Penthouse	60 B3
Viva Madrid	61 B3

NIGHTLIFE	(pp199–210)
Café Central	62 A4
Cardamomo	63 B3
El Son	64 A3
Kapital	65 E6
La Boca del Lobo	66 B3
La Cartuja	67 B3
La Fidula	68 C4
La Fontana de Oro	69 B2
Populart	70 B4
Room at Stella	71 B2
Sol y Sombra	72 B3
Villa Rosa	73 B3

SPORTS & ACTIVITIES	(pp217–22)
La Central Bullfight Ticket Office	74 B3

SLEEPING	(pp227–38)
Chic & Basic	75 B4
Hostal Adria Santa Ana	(see 76)
Hostal Adriano	76 A3
Hostal Sardinero	77 C3
Hotel Alicia	78 B3
Hotel El Pasaje	79 B2
Hotel El Prado	80 B3
Hotel Miau	81 B4
Hotel Urban	82 C2
Hotel Victoria 4	83 A2
International Youth Hostel – La Posada de Huertas	84 B4
Me by Meliá	85 B3
Quo	86 B2
Suite Prado Hotel	87 B3
Vincci Soho	88 C3

Rooms 20 to 23 offer a representative look at abstract painting in Spain. Among the more significant contributors are Eusebio Sempere (1923–85) and members of the Equipo 57 group (founded in 1957 by a group of Spanish artists in exile in Paris), such as Pablo Palazuelo. Rooms 24 to 35 leads you through Spanish art of the 1960s and 1970s. Some external reference points, such as works by Francis Bacon (1909–92) and Henry Moore (1831–95), both in Room 24, are thrown in to broaden the context.

Closer to the present day, Room 38 is given over to work by Eduardo Arroyo, while beautiful works of the Basque sculptor Eduardo Chillida (1924–2002) fill Rooms 42 and 43.

ANTIGUA ESTACIÓN DE ATOCHA Map pp84–5
Plaza del Emperador Carlos V; M Atocha Renfe
Large areas of central Madrid may have been blighted by ill-conceived and downright ugly apartment blocks in the 1970s, but by the 1990s the city's developers had learned to make use of the elegant architecture of yesteryear. Nowhere is this more evident than at the Antigua Estación de Atocha (Atocha train station) where the grand iron-and-glass relic from the 19th century was preserved and artfully converted in 1992 into a surprising tropical garden with more than 500 plant species. Amid the greenery are various shops, cafés and restaurants, and it also houses the Renfe train information offices. The project was the work of architect Rafael Moneo, the man behind the still-more-ambitious Museo del Prado extension that was completed in 2007. The tropical garden certainly makes a pleasant, although slightly humid, departure or arrival point in Madrid and the cavernous ceiling resonates with the grand old European train stations of another age.

11 MARCH 2004 MEMORIAL Map pp84–5
1st fl, Estación de Atocha; Admission free; 10am-8pm; M Atocha Renfe
This moving monument to the victims of the worst terrorist attack on European soil at Atocha station is partially visible from the street, but the memorial is best viewed from below. A glass panel shows the names of those killed, while the airy glass-and-Perspex dome is inscribed with the messages of condolence and solidarity left by well-wishers in a number of languages in the immediate aftermath of the attack. The 12m-high dome is designed so that the sun highlights different messages at different times of the day, while the effect at night is akin to flickering candles. It's a simple but powerful memorial to an unsettling event.

PLAZA DE SANTA ANA Map pp84–5
M Sevilla, Sol or Antón Martín
The Plaza de Santa Ana is a delightful confluence of elegant architecture and irresistible energy. Situated in the heart of Huertas, it was laid out in 1810 during the controversial reign of Joseph Bonaparte (p27), giving breathing space to what had hitherto been one of Madrid's most claustrophobic barrios. It quickly became a focal point for the intellectual life of the day, and the cafés surrounding the plaza thronged with writers, poets and artists engaging in endless *tertulias* or literary and philosophical discussions; the Teatro Español (previously the Teatro del Príncipe) at the plaza's eastern end was a centre for performances long before the plaza was laid out. The statue of Federíco García Lorca was added in 1998, on the 100th anniversary of his birth. These days the plaza has become the vibrant hub of Huertas, a base from which to explore the bars, restaurants and live music venues in the surrounding streets. Sure, it was discovered long ago by residents and visiting *guiris* (foreigners). And true, some *gatos* (madrileños) haughtily avoid it for that very reason. But many an authentic *gato* still winds up here for an afternoon coffee or a long, long evening.

top picks
SIGHTS IN HUERTAS & ATOCHA
- Centro de Arte Reina Sofía (p82)
- Plaza de Santa Ana (right)
- Antigua Estación de Atocha (above)
- Casa de Lope de Vega (opposite)

CERVANTES IN THE BARRIO DE LAS LETRAS

Miguel de Cervantes Saavedra, the author of *Don Quijote*, spent much of his adult life living in Madrid and, unsurprisingly, he chose the Barrio de las Letras for his home. A plaque (dating from 1834) above the door of Calle de Cervantes 2 announces that Spain's most famous writer lived and later died at this address in 1616. Sadly, the house was torn down in the early 19th century. When Cervantes died his body was interred around the corner at the Convento de San Ildefonso de las Trinitarias (Calle de Lope de Vega 16), which is marked by another plaque. Still home to cloistered nuns, the convent is closed to the public, which saves the authorities' embarrassment at the fact that no-one really knows where in the convent the bones of Cervantes lie.

CASA DE LOPE DE VEGA Map pp84–5

☎ 91 429 92 16; Calle de Cervantes 11; adult/ student & senior €2/1, free Sat; ☼ 9.30am-2pm Tue-Fri, 10am-2pm Sat; Ⓜ Antón Martín

Lope de Vega (see p44) may be little known outside the Spanish-speaking world, but he was one of the greatest playwrights ever to write in Spanish, not to mention one of Madrid's favourite and most colourful literary sons. What Real Madrid's footballers now are to Madrid's celebrity rumour mill, Lope de Vega was to scandalised Madrid society in the 17th century; he shared the house, where he lived and wrote for 25 years until his death in 1635, with a mistress and four children by three different women. Today the house, which was restored in the 1950s, is filled with memorabilia related to his life and times. Lope de Vega's house was a typical *casa de malicia* (roughly translated, 'house of ill-repute'). Out the back is a tranquil garden, a rare haven of birdsong in this somewhat claustrophobic district.

ATENEO CIENTÍFICO, LITERARIO Y ARTÍSTICO DE MADRID Map pp84–5

☎ 91 429 17 50; www.ateneodemadrid.com, in Spanish; Calle del Prado 21; Ⓜ Sevilla

Nestled away in the heart of the Barrio de las Letras, this venerable club of learned types was founded in 1821, although the building took on its present form in 1884. Its library and meetings of the great minds prompted Benito Pérez Galdós to describe it as the most important 'intellectual temple' in Madrid and a reference point for the thriving cultural life of the Barrio de las Letras. It's not really open to the public, but no-one seems to mind if you wander into the foyer, which is lined with portraits of terribly serious-looking fellows. They may even let you amble upstairs to the library, a jewel of another age, with dark timber stacks, weighty tomes and

creakily quiet reading rooms dimly lit with desk lamps.

CONGRESO DE LOS DIPUTADOS Map pp84–5

☎ 91 390 65 25; www.congreso.es; Plaza de las Cortes; admission free; ☼ guided tours 10.30am-12.30pm Sat; Ⓜ Sevilla

Spain's lower house of parliament was originally a Renaissance building, but it was completely revamped in 1850 and given a façade with a neo-Classical portal. The imposing lions watching over the entrance were smelted from cannons used in Spain's African wars during the mid-19th century. Before becoming the official seat of Spain's parliament, the building was home to a church, the Iglesia de Espíritu Santo. The modern extension tacked onto it seems a rather odd afterthought. It was here, on 11 February 1981, that renegade members of Spain's Guardia Civil launched a failed coup attempt (see p31). Be sure to bring your passport if you want to visit.

CÍRCULO DE BELLAS ARTES Map pp84–5

☎ 91 360 54 00; www.circulobellasartes.com; Calle de Alcalá 42; Ⓜ Banco de España

The 'Fine Arts Circle' has just about every kind of artistic expression on show, including exhibitions, concerts, short films and book readings. It's an elegant space with a programme that's anything but staid, allowing it to remain at the forefront of Madrid's cultural life.

KILLING THE NIGHT
Walking Tour

1 Plaza de Santa Ana (opposite) There are more beautiful squares in Madrid, but none more filled with life, making it the perfect place to begin your walking tour. To gather your energy, take up residence in a *terraza*

and watch the passing parade, all the while nursing a glass of La Rioja.

2 Casa Alberto (p166) Just off the southeast corner of the plaza, along the iconic nightlife street of Calle de las Huertas, Casa Alberto is a classic Madrid tapas bar, laden with history and a menu even more laden with tempting choices. Bull's tail would be a fine way to start the evening.

3 Maceiras (p167) Now that you're getting the hang of Huertas nights, amble all the way down Calle de las Huertas to Maceiras, a casual, often rowdy Galician bar-restaurant with the fresh tastes of Spain's northern Atlantic coast. Order what you will, but we'd be going for the *pulpo a la gallega* (octopus cooked in the Galician style, boiled

and served with paprika, potatoes and rock salt).

4 Taberna La Dolores (p189) With your stomach suitably fortified, head just around the corner to the Plaza de Jesús. There, Taberna La Dolores draws a quintessentially Madrid crowd of celebrities and casual locals drawn by cheap, fine wines. If you've still got the munchies, order a *tapa* of *anchóas* (anchovies), ideal for building up a thirst.

5 La Venencia (p190) Climb up the hill along Calle de Cervantes, which runs through the heart of the Barrio de las Letras, then wind your way to Calle de Echegaray, home to La Venencia. This is Madrid's most authentic bar for *fino* (sherry) straight from the barrel and it's a quiet place offering respite from Huertas' clamour.

6 Sol y Sombra (p203) Back down Calle de Echegaray and you find yourself at sleek Sol y Sombra, where you'll be glad you remembered to dress well. Great music, slick décor and a sophisticated crowd are what this place is all about.

WALK FACTS

Start **Plaza de Santa Ana**
End **Villa Rosa**
Distance **1.5km**
Time **All night**

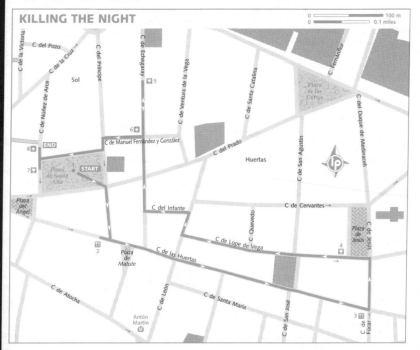

KILLING THE NIGHT

NEIGHBOURHOODS HUERTAS & ATOCHA

7 The Penthouse (p190) Make sure you leave early enough (around 2.30am) to get to The Penthouse before closing time (4am). Looking down over Plaza de Santa Ana, and frequented by a groovy, upmarket crowd, this place oozes style, quite apart from letting you look out over Madrid from a whole new perspective.

8 Villa Rosa (p204) The night is nearly at an end and, if you're like us, you just want something you can dance to without being too heavy on the ear at a place that's not too strict at the door. Villa Rosa is just such a place with tunes you can sing along to with like-minded and similarly worse-for-wear patrons.

PASEO DEL PRADO & EL RETIRO

Eating p168; Shopping p137; Sleeping p235

If you've just come down the hill from Huertas, you'll feel like you've left behind a mad house for an oasis of greenery, fresh air and culture. The Museo del Prado and the Museo Thyssen-Bornemisza are among the richest galleries of fine art in the world and plenty of other museums lurk in the quietly elegant streets close to the Prado. Rising up the hill to the east are the stately gardens of the marvellous Parque del Buen Retiro.

The Paseo del Prado – which becomes the Paseo de los Recoletos and then the Paseo de la Castellana further north – cuts through the heart of modern Madrid. Once, it was a stream that marked the city's eastern extremity. The *prado* (field) was the preserve of gardens and palaces that were green playgrounds for Madrid's swollen nobility.

MUSEO DEL PRADO Map pp92–3

☎ 91 330 28 00; http://museoprado.mcu.es; Paseo del Prado; adult/student/child under 18yr & senior over 65yr €6/4/free, free to all Sun, headset guide €3.50; ⏱ 9am-8pm Tue-Sun; Ⓜ Banco de España

Welcome to one of the best and most important art galleries anywhere in the world. The more than 7000 paintings held in the Museo del Prado's collection (although just over half are currently on display) are like a window on the historical vagaries of the Spanish soul, at once grand and imperious in the royal paintings of Velázquez, darkly tumultuous in *Las Pinturas Negras* (Black Paintings) of Goya and outward-looking with sophisticated works of art from all across Europe. Spend as long as you can at the Prado or, better still, plan to make a couple of visits because it can be a little overwhelming if you try to absorb it all at once. Either way, it's an artistic feast that is many visitors' main reason for visiting Madrid.

Part of the Prado's appeal is the fact that the building in which it is housed is itself a masterpiece, although its early days were less than momentous. Completed in 1785, the neo-Classical Palacio de Villanueva was conceived as a house of science but served, somewhat ignominiously, as a cavalry barracks for Napoleon's troops during their occupation of Madrid between 1808 and 1813. In 1814 King Fernando VII decided to use the palace as a museum, although his purpose was more about finding a way of storing the hundreds of royal paintings gathering dust than any high-minded civic ideals – this was an era where art was a royal preserve. Five years later the Museo del Prado opened with 311 Spanish paintings on display. The Prado has never looked back.

In late 2007 the long-awaited extension of the Prado opened to the public to critical acclaim; for more information on the extension, see p48. For more information on many of the artists covered in the Prado, turn to p37.

Entrance to the Prado is via the western Puerta de Velázquez (in the old part of the Prado) or the eastern Puerta de los Jerónimos (the extension), but first, tickets must be purchased from the ticket office at the northern end of the building, opposite the Hotel Ritz. Groups sometimes also enter via the southern Puerta de Murillo. Our own preference, but only just, is to start from the Puerta de Velázquez, because it takes you into the heart of the permanent collection in the original Edificio Villanueva (Villanueva Building).

If you've entered this way, turn right into Room 75, home to works by Tintoretto and Titian, but your primary aim should be Rooms 66 and 67, where the darkest and most disturbing works of Francisco José de

ORIENTATION & TRANSPORT: PASEO DEL PRADO & EL RETIRO

The Paseo del Prado runs north–south from the Plaza de la Cibeles to the Plaza del Emperador Carlos V. Huertas rises up to the west, while atop the hill to the east is the Parque del Buen Retiro, which can be reached by any of the streets running east from the Paseo.

The only metro stations are those at either end of the Paseo del Prado – Banco de España (line 2) on Plaza de la Cibeles to the north, and Atocha (line 1) to the south. For the Parque del Buen Retiro, the best station is Retiro (line 2), but Príncipe de Vergara (lines 2 and 9) and Ibiza (line 9) also leave you on the eastern perimeter of the park.

top picks

PAINTINGS IN THE MUSEO DEL PRADO

- Las Meninas (Velázquez; Room 12)
- Las Hilanderas (Velázquez; Room 15A)
- La Maja Desnuda & La Maja Vestida (Goya; Room 39)
- El Tres de Mayo (Goya; Room 39)
- Las Pinturas Negras (Black Paintings, Goya; Rooms 66 & 67)
- The Garden of Earthly Delights (El Jardín de las Delicias, Hieronymus Bosch; Room 56A)
- Adam & Eve (Adán y Eva, Dürer; Room 55B)
- El Lavatorio (Tintoretto; Room 75)
- La Trinidad (El Greco; Room 9A)
- David Vencedor de Goliath (Caravaggio; Room 5)
- El Sueño de Jacob (Ribera; Room 26)
- The Three Graces (Las Tres Gracias, Rubens; Room 9)
- Artemisa (Rembrandt; Room 7)

Goya y Lucientes (Goya; see the boxed text, p39) reside. Las Pinturas Negras are so-called because of the dark browns and black that dominate, but more for the distorted animalesque appearance of their characters. The Saturno Devorando a Su Hijo (Saturn Devouring His Son) captures the essence of Goya's genius and La Romería de San Isidro and El Akelarre (El gran cabrón) are profoundly unsettling. The former evokes a writhing mass of tortured humanity, while the latter is dominated by the compelling individual faces of the condemned souls of Goya's creation.

After such a disconcerting introduction to the museum, it's time for a dramatic change of pace. There is no more weird-and-wonderful painting in the Prado than The Garden of Earthly Delights by Hieronymus Bosch (c1450–1516) in Room 56A. No-one has yet been able to provide a definitive explanation for this hallucinatory work, although many have tried. While it is, without doubt, the star attraction of this fantastical painter's collection, all his work rewards inspection. The closer you look, the harder it is to escape the feeling that he must have been doing some extraordinary drugs.

Before heading upstairs, don't miss the paintings by German artist Albrecht Dürer (1471–1528) in Room 55B, or Italy's Rafael (1483–1520) in Room 49.

The 1st floor is where the Prado really struts its stuff. Room 39 has two of the Prado's greatest masterpieces, Goya's El Dos de Mayo and El Tres de Mayo. Two of Madrid's most emblematic paintings, they bring to life the 1808 anti-French revolt and subsequent execution of insurgents in Madrid. They were under restoration at the time of research and be warned that they may be moved upon their return. In the same room are two more of Goya's best-known and most intriguing oils, La Maja Vestida and La Maja Desnuda. These portraits of an unknown woman commonly believed to be the Duquesa de Alba (who may have been Goya's lover) are identical save for the lack of clothing in the latter. You can enjoy the rest of Goya's works in Rooms 32, 29 and 16B.

From the latter room, it's a short stroll to Room 12 where you'll encounter the extraordinarily life-filled paintings of one of the greatest figures of Spanish art. Of the many paintings by Diego Rodríguez de Silva y Velázquez (p38) that so distinguish the Prado by their presence, Las Meninas is what most people come to see. Completed in 1656, it is more properly known as La Família de Felipe IV (The Family of Felipe IV). It depicts Velázquez himself on the left and, in the centre, the infant Margarita. There's more to it than that: the artist in fact portrays himself painting the king and queen, whose images appear, according to some experts, in mirrors behind Velázquez. His mastery of light and colour is never more apparent than here. An interesting detail of the painting, aside from the extraordinary cheek of painting himself in royal company, is the presence of the cross of the Order of Santiago on his vest. The artist was apparently obsessed with being given a noble title. He got it shortly before his death, but in this oil painting he has awarded himself the order years before it would in fact be his!

There are more fine works by Velázquez in Rooms 14, 15, 16 and 18. Watch out in particular for his stunning paintings of various members of royalty who seem to spring off the canvas – Felipe II, Felipe IV, Margarita de Austria (a younger version of whom features in Las Meninas), El Príncipe Baltasar Carlos and Isabel de Francia – on horseback; but you could pick any work of Velázquez and not be disappointed.

Having captured the essence of the Prado, you're now free to select from the diverse works that remain. If Spanish

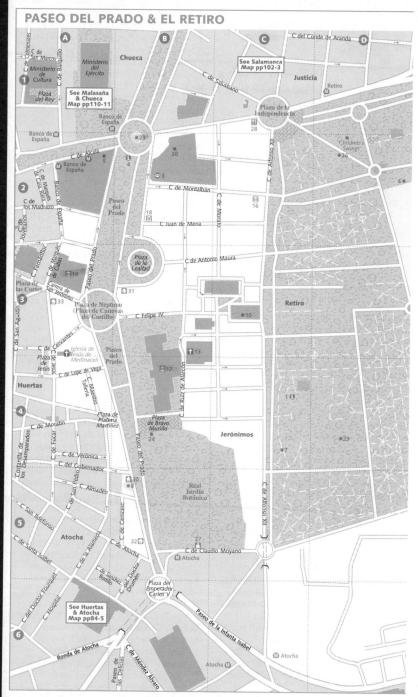

PASEO DEL PRADO & EL RETIRO

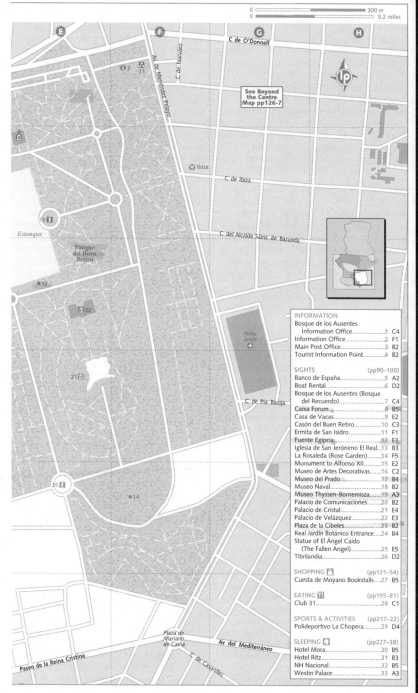

0   300 m
0   0.2 miles

C de O'Donnell

Av de Menéndez Pelayo

C de Narváez

See Beyond
the Centre
Map pp126–7

Ⓜ Ibiza

C de Ibiza

C del Alcalde Sainz de Baranda

Estanque

Parque
del Buen
Retiro

Niño
Jesús

C de Pío Baroja

Plaza de
Mariano
de Cavia

Av del Mediterráneo

Paseo de la Reina Cristina

C de Cavanilles

INFORMATION
Bosque de los Ausentes
  Information Office...................1 C4
Information Office........................2 F1
Main Post Office..........................3 B2
Tourist Information Point.............4 B2

SIGHTS   (pp90–100)
Banco de España...........................5 A2
Boat Rental..................................6 D2
Bosque de los Ausentes (Bosque
  del Recuerdo)...........................7 C4
Caixa Forum.................................8 B5
Casa de Vacas..............................9 E2
Casón del Buen Retiro.................10 C3
Ermita de San Isidro....................11 F1
Fuente Egipcia............................12 E3
Iglesia de San Jerónimo El Real...13 B3
La Rosaleda (Rose Garden).........14 F5
Monument to Alfonso XII............15 E2
Museo de Artes Decorativas........16 C2
Museo del Prado.........................17 B4
Museo Naval...............................18 B2
Museo Thyssen-Bornemisza........19 A3
Palacio de Comunicaciones.........20 B2
Palacio de Cristal.........................21 E4
Palacio de Velázquez...................22 E3
Plaza de la Cibeles......................23 B2
Real Jardín Botánico Entrance.....24 B4
Statue of El Ángel Caído
  (The Fallen Angel)...................25 E5
Titirilandia.................................26 D2

SHOPPING 🛍   (pp131–54)
Cuesta de Moyano Bookstalls....27 B5

EATING 🍽   (pp155–81)
Club 31.......................................28 C1

SPORTS & ACTIVITIES (pp217–22)
Polideportivo La Chopera............29 D4

SLEEPING 🏠   (pp227–38)
Hotel Mora.................................30 B5
Hotel Ritz...................................31 B3
NH Nacional...............................32 B5
Westin Palace.............................33 A3

ONLY IN MADRID

Spaniards love to take to the streets, whether it be to demonstrate against the war in Iraq, protest against social reforms by the government of the day, or to march in solidarity with the victims of terrorism. But Madrid must be the only city in the world where a near riot was caused by an art exhibition.

John Hooper in his fine book *The New Spaniards* tells the story of how in 1990 the Prado brought an unprecedented number of works by Velázquez out of storage and opened its doors to the public. The exhibition was so popular that more than half a million visitors came to see the rare showing. Just before the exhibition was scheduled to end, the Prado announced that they would keep the doors open for as long as there were people wanting to enter. When the doors finally shut at 9pm, several hundred people were still outside waiting in the rain. They chanted, they shouted and they banged on the doors of this august institution with their umbrellas. The gallery was reopened, but queues kept forming and when the doors shut on the exhibition for good at 10.30pm, furious art lovers clashed with police. At midnight, there were still almost 50 people outside chanting 'We want to come in'.

painters have piqued your curiosity, the stark figures of Francisco de Zurbarán dominate Rooms 18 and 18A, while Bartolomé Esteban Murillo (Room 28) and José de Ribera (Rooms 25 and 26) should also be on your itinerary. The vivid, almost surreal works by the 16th-century master El Greco (see the boxed text, p244), whose figures are characteristically slender and tortured, are to be found in Rooms 10 and 10A.

Another alternative is the Prado's outstanding collection of Flemish art. The fulsome figures and bulbous cherubs of Peter Paul Rubens (1577–1640) provide a playful antidote to the darkness of many of the other Flemish artists and can be enjoyed in Rooms 8 to 11. His signature *Las Tres Gracias* (The Three Graces) is in Room 9, while the stand-out *Adoración de los Reyes Magos* is in Room 9B. Other fine works in the vicinity include those by Anton Van Dyck (Rooms 9B, 10A and 10B) and on no account miss Rembrandt in Room 7.

From the 1st floor of the Edificio Villanueva, passageways lead to the Edificio Jerónimos (Jerónimos Building), the Prado's stunning modern extension. The main hall (where you enter if coming through the Puerta de los Jerónimos) contains information counters, the Prado's excellent new bookshop and its café. Continue across the hall where Rooms A and B (and Room C on the 1st floor) host temporary exhibitions, often including many Prado masterpieces that were held in storage for decades for lack of wall space. If you continue up to the 2nd floor, you'll reach the cloisters, the undoubted architectural highlight of the extension. Built in 1672 of local granite, they were until recently attached to the adjacent Iglesia de San Jerónimo El Real

(right), but were in a parlous state. As part of their incorporation into the Prado, they were painstakingly dismantled, restored and reassembled. They're a stunning way to end (or begin) your Prado visit – look in particular for the royal coats of arms on the four compass points, while the Italianate bronze and marble sculptures date back to the 16th century.

IGLESIA DE SAN JERÓNIMO EL REAL Map pp92–3

☎ 91 420 35 78; Calle de Ruiz de Alarcón; admission free; ☽ 10am-1pm & 5-8pm Mon-Sat; Ⓜ Atocha or Banco de España

Tucked away behind the Museo del Prado, this lavish chapel was traditionally favoured by the Spanish royal family. Here, amid the mock-Isabelline splendour, King Juan Carlos I was crowned in 1975 upon the death of Franco. The interior is actually a 19th-century reconstruction that took its cues from the Iglesia de San Juan de los Reyes in Toledo; the original was largely destroyed during the Peninsular War. Being a chapel of royal choice did little to protect it from the Museo del Prado's inexorable expansion – what remained of the cloisters next door was appropriated by the Museo del Prado (see p90).

PLAZA DE NEPTUNO Map pp92–3

Ⓜ Banco de España

Officially known as Plaza de Cánovas del Castillo, the next roundabout south of Cibeles is something of a crossroads of Spanish nobility. The Ritz and the Palace, two of Madrid's longest-standing and most exclusive hotels, glower at each other across the plaza with self-righteous grandeur, while the Museo Thyssen-Bornemisza and the Prado do likewise in competition for the title of Madrid's best loved repository of fine art. The centrepiece is an ornate fountain and 18th-century sculpture of Neptune, the sea god, by Juan Pascual de Mena. But madrileños, never the most reverent lot, know it better as the celebration venue of choice for fans of Atlético de Madrid who lose all sense of decorum when their team wins a major trophy. The last time this happened, in 1996, the hundreds of thousands of success-starved Atlético fans celebrated in anything but noble style and Neptune was relieved of a few fingers. Charges are still pending.

MUSEO THYSSEN-BORNEMISZA
Map pp92–3

☎ 91 369 01 51; www.museothyssen.org; Paseo del Prado 8; adult/student & senior €6/4, temporary exhibitions adult/student & senior/child under 12yr €6/4/free, headset guide €3; ⏱ 10am-7pm Tue-Sun; Ⓜ Banco de España

The Museo Thyssen-Bornemisza is the favourite art gallery of many visitors to Madrid, home as it is to the most wide-ranging private collection of predominantly European art in the world. If you want to study the body of work of a particular artist in depth, head to the Museo del Prado or Centro de Arte Reina Sofía. But the Thyssen has something for everyone, with a breathtaking breadth of artistic styles from the masters of medieval art down to the zany world of contemporary painting. All the big names are here, sometimes with just a single painting, but the Thyssens' gift to Madrid and the art-loving public is to have them all under one roof. Its simple-to-follow floor plan also makes it one of the most easily navigable galleries in Madrid and means that you can be selective about your viewing by heading straight to the paintings where your interest lies.

The collection is spread out over three floors, with the oldest works on the top floor down to the contemporary scene on the ground floor.

The 2nd floor, which is home to medieval art, includes some real gems hidden among the mostly 13th- and 14th-century and predominantly Italian, German and Flemish religious paintings and triptychs. Unless you've a specialist's eye, pause in Room 5 where you'll find one work by Italy's Piero della Francesca (1410–92) and the instantly recognisable *Henry VIII* by Holbein the Younger (1497–1543), before continuing on to Room 10 for the Brueghel-like and evocative 1586 *Massacre of the Innocents* by Lucas Van Valckenberch. Room 11 is dedicated to El Greco (with three pieces) and his Venetian contemporaries Tintoretto and Titian, while Caravaggio and the Spaniard José de Ribera dominate Room 12. A single painting each by Murillo and Zurbarán add further Spanish flavour in the two rooms that follow, while the exceptionally rendered views of Venice by Canaletto (1697–1768) should on no account be missed.

But best of all on this floor is the extension (Rooms A to H) built to house the burgeoning collection with more Canalettos hanging alongside Monet, Sisley, Renoir, Pissarro, Degas, Constable and Van Gogh.

Before heading downstairs, a detour to Rooms 19 through to 21 will satisfy those devoted to 17th-century Dutch and Flemish masters, Anton van Dyck, Jan Brueghel the Elder and Rembrandt (one painting).

THE THYSSEN-BORNEMISZA LEGEND

The collection held in the Museo Thyssen-Bornemisza is a very Spanish story that has a celebrity love affair at its heart. The paintings held in the museum are the legacy of Baron Thyssen-Bornemisza, a German-Hungarian magnate. Spain managed to acquire the prestigious collection when the baron married Carmen Tita Cervera, a former Miss España and ex-wife of Lex Barker (of *Tarzan* fame). The deal was sealed when the Spanish government offered to overhaul the neo-Classical Palacio de Villahermosa specifically to house the collection. Although the baron died in 2002, his glamorous wife has shown that she has learned much from the collecting nous of her late husband. In early 2000 the museum acquired two adjoining buildings, which have been joined to the museum to house approximately half of the collection of Carmen Thyssen-Bornemisza.

When Madrid City Council announced plans in April 2006 to reroute the traffic lanes in front of the Museo del Prado on the eastern side of the Paseo del Prado so that they ran past the Thyssen, the baroness threatened to publicly chain herself to a tree if the plan went ahead. The prospect of taking on one of Madrid's favourite daughters proved too much for the council who quietly shelved the plans, although for how long no-one knows – recent reports suggest the council hasn't yet given up on the idea.

DISCOUNTS & CLOSING TIMES

The Paseo del Arte ticket covers the big three galleries (Museo del Prado, Museo Thyssen-Bornemisza and Centro de Arte Reina Sofía) for €14.40 and is valid for up to 12 months (one visit to each). Never has €14.40 been better spent. For unlimited visits to either the Prado or the Reina Sofía, a year's ticket costs €36. A yearly ticket to both these galleries and eight other museums throughout the country is also available (€36.06); you'll need to present two passport photographs and a photocopy of your passport.

A more extensive system of discounts is available if you buy the Madrid Card; see p269 for details.

Most, but not all, museums and monuments close on Monday (the Reina Sofía is an exception and closes on Tuesday). Some also shut on Sunday afternoons, although the Prado and the Thyssen are notable exceptions. In July and August some close parts of their displays for want of staff, most of whom take annual leave around this time. A few minor museums close entirely throughout August.

If all that sounds impressive, the 1st floor is where the Thyssen really shines. English visitors may want to pause in Room 28 where you'll find a Gainsborough, but if you've been skimming the surface of this at times overwhelming collection, Room 32 is the place to linger over each and every painting. The astonishing texture of Van Gogh's *Les Vessenots* is a masterpiece, but the same could be said for *Woman in Riding Habit* by Manet, *The Thaw at Véthueil* by Monet and Pissarro's quintessentially Parisian *Rue Saint-Honoré in the Afternoon*.

Rooms 33 to 35 play host to Modigliani, Picasso, Cezanne, Matisse and Egon Schiele, while the baroness' eye for quality is nowhere more evident than in the extension (Rooms I to P). Juan Gris, Matisse, Picasso, Kandinsky, Georges Braque, Toulouse-Lautrec, Degas, Sorolla, Sisley and Edward Hopper are all present, but our favourites include the rich colours of Gauguin's *Mata Mua*, Monet's dreamlike *Charing Cross Bridge* and the rare appearance of Edvard Munch with *Geese in an Orchard*. Quite simply, it's an outrageously rich collection.

On the ground floor, the foray into the 20th century that you began in the 1st-floor extension takes over with a fine spread of paintings from cubism through to pop art. Like much modern art, some of it may be an acquired taste, but bypassing most of it would be a grievous error.

In Room 41 you'll see a nice mix of the big three of cubism, Picasso, Georges Braque and Madrid's own Juan Gris, along with several other contemporaries. Picasso pops up again in Room 45, another one of the gallery's stand-out rooms. Its treasures include works by Marc Chagall, Kandinsky, Paul Klee and Joan Miró.

Room 46 is similarly rich, with the splattered craziness of Jackson Pollock's *Brown and Silver I* and the deceptively simple but strangely pleasing *Green on Maroon* by Mark Rothko taking centre stage. In Rooms 47 and 48 the Thyssen builds to a stirring climax, with Salvador Dalí, Francis Bacon, Roy Lichtenstein, Edward Hopper and Lucian Freud, Sigmund's Berlin-born grandson, all represented. The latter's distinguished *Portrait of Baron HH Thyssen-Bornemisza*, the man who made it all possible, is a nice way to finish.

CAIXA FORUM Map pp92–3

☎ 91 330 73 00; www.fundacio.lacaixa.es, in Spanish; Paseo del Prado 36; admission free; ⏲ 10am-10pm; Ⓜ Atocha

This extraordinary edifice, which opened in early 2008 down towards the southern end of the Paseo del Prado, is one of the most exciting architectural innovations to emerge in Madrid in recent years. Seeming to hover above the ground, this brick edifice is topped by an intriguing summit of what looks like rusted iron. On an adjacent wall is the *jardín colgante* (hanging garden), a lush vertical wall of greenery almost four storeys high. Inside there are four floors of exhibition and performance space awash in stainless steel and with soaring ceilings. What's on show comes from the extensive archives and treasures held by the Catalan building society, La Caixa. They're impressive, but the building is the star attraction.

REAL JARDÍN BOTÁNICO Map pp92–3

☎ 91 420 30 17; Plaza de Bravo Murillo 2; adult/student/children under 11yr & EU senior €2/1/free; ⏲ 10am-9pm May-Aug, 10am-8pm Apr & Sep, 10am-7pm Oct & Mar, 10am-6pm Nov-Feb; Ⓜ Atocha

Although not as expansive or as popular as the Parque del Buen Retiro, Madrid's botan-

top picks

SIGHTS IN PASEO DEL PRADO & EL RETIRO

- Museo del Prado (p90)
- Museo Thyssen-Bornemisza (p95)
- Parque del Buen Retiro (p98)
- Plaza de la Cibeles (right)
- Caixa Forum (opposite)

ical gardens are another leafy oasis in the centre of town. With some 30,000 species crammed into a relatively small 8-hectare area, it's more a place to wander at leisure than laze under a tree, although there are benches dotted throughout the gardens where you can sit.

In the centre stands a statue of Carlos III, who in 1781 moved the gardens here from their original location at El Huerto de Migas Calientes, on the banks of the Río Manzanares. In the Pabellón Villanueva, on the northern flank of the gardens, art exhibitions are frequently staged – the opening hours are the same as for the park and the exhibitions are usually free.

MUSEO NAVAL Map pp92–3

☎ 91 523 87 89; www.museonavalmadrid.com, in Spanish; Paseo del Prado 5; admission free; ☾ 10am-2pm Tue-Sun; Ⓜ Banco de España
A block south of Plaza de la Cibeles, this museum will appeal to those who love their ships or who have always wondered what the Spanish armada really looked like. On display are quite extraordinary models of ships from the earliest days of Spain's maritime history to the 20th century. Lovers of antique maps will also find plenty of interest, especially Juan de la Cosa's parchment map of the known world, put together in 1500. The accuracy of Europe is astounding, and it's supposedly the first map to show the Americas (albeit with considerably greater fantasy than fact). Littered throughout this pleasant, though rarely cluttered, exhibition space are dozens of uniforms, arms, flags (including a Nazi flag from the German warship *Deutschland*, which was bombed by Republican planes off Ibiza in 1937) and other naval paraphernalia.

MUSEO DE ARTES DECORATIVAS Map pp92–3

☎ 91 532 64 99; http://mnartesdecorativas.mcu .es; Calle de Montalbán 12; child, student or senior/adult €1.20/2.40, free Sun; ☾ 9.30am-3pm Tue-Sat, 10am-3pm Sun & holidays; Ⓜ Retiro
This niche museum won't appeal to everyone, but those who love sumptuous period furniture, ceramics, carpets, tapestries and the like will find themselves passing a worthwhile hour or two here. The exhibits span the 15th- to the late-19th-centuries and are spread over five floors.

There's plenty to catch your eye and the ceramics from around Spain are a definite feature, while the re-creations of kitchens from several regions are curiosities. Reconstructions of regal bedrooms, women's drawing rooms and 19th-century salons also help shed light on how the privileged classes of Spain have lived through the centuries.

PLAZA DE LA CIBELES Map pp92–3

Ⓜ Banco de España
Of all the grand roundabouts that punctuate the elegant boulevard of Paseo del Prado, Plaza de la Cibeles most evokes the splendour of imperial Madrid.

The jewel in the crown is the astonishing Palacio de Comunicaciones. Built between 1904 and 1917 by Antonio Palacios, Madrid's most prolific architect of the *belle époque*, it combines elements of the North American monumental style of the period with Gothic and Renaissance touches. Newcomers find it hard to accept that this is merely the central post office. Clearly the city council thought the same and are in the process of taking most of it over as the Ayuntamiento, although the post office will remain accessible from a side entrance. Other landmark buildings around the perimeter include the Palacio de Linares and Casa de América (p104), the Palacio Buenavista (1769; p109) and the national Banco de España (1891). The views east towards the Puerta de Alcalá or west towards the Edificio Metrópolis are some of Madrid's finest.

The spectacular fountain of the goddess Cybele at the centre of the plaza is also one of Madrid's most beautiful. Ever since it was erected in 1780 by Ventura Rodríguez, it has been a Madrid favourite. Carlos III liked it so much that he tried to have it moved to the gardens of the Granja de San Ildefonso, on the road to Segovia, but the madrileños kicked up such a fuss that he let it be.

For all its popularity, symbolism of ancient mythology and role as exemplar of centuries-old public art, Cibeles endures madrileños' affection as hard love. For over a century, the Cibeles fountain has been the venue for joyous and often destructive celebrations by players and supporters of Real Madrid whenever the side has won anything of note. In recent years the frenzy of clambering all over the fountain and chipping bits off as souvenirs has seen the city council board up the statue and surround it with police on the eve of important matches.

PARQUE DEL BUEN RETIRO Map pp92–3

admission free; ⊙ 6am-midnight May-Sep, 6am-11pm Oct-Apr; Ⓜ Retiro, Príncipe de Vergara, Ibiza or Atocha

The glorious gardens of El Retiro are as beautiful as any you'll find in a European city. Littered with marble monuments, landscaped lawns, the occasional elegant building and abundant greenery, it's quiet and contemplative during the week, but comes to life on weekends.

Laid out in the 17th century by Felipe IV as the preserve of kings, queens and their intimates, the park was opened to the public in 1868 and ever since, whenever the weather's fine and on Sundays in particular, madrileños from all across the city gather here to stroll, read the Sunday papers in the shade, take a boat ride (€4 for 45 minutes) or take a cool drink at the numerous outdoor *terrazas*. Weekend buskers, Chinese masseurs and tarot readers ply their trades, while art and photo exhibitions are sometimes held at the various sites around the park. Puppet shows for the kids are another summertime feature (look for Titirilandia, or Puppet Land; check out www.titirilandia.com for show times).

Most of the activity takes place around the artificial lake *(estanque)*, but the park is large enough to allow you to escape the crowds (apart from the lovers under trees locked in seemingly eternal embraces).

The lake is watched over by the massive ornamental structure of the Monument to Alfonso XII on the east side of the lake, complete with marble lions. If you want to catch the essence of Madrid's endless energy, come here as sunset approaches on a summer Sunday afternoon – as the crowd

top picks

FOR CHILDREN

- Warner Brothers Movie World (p128)
- Teleférico (p119)
- Faunia (p129)
- Estadio Santiago Bernabéu (p122)
- Parque del Buen Retiro (left)
- Museo de Cera (Wax Museum; p112)
- Museo del Ferrocarril (p129)
- Parque de Atracciones (p128)
- Zoo Aquarium de Madrid (p128)
- Madrid Snow Zone (p219)
- Parque Secreto (p267)

grows, bongos sound out across the park and people start to dance.

On the southern end of the lake, the odd structure decorated with sphinxes is the Fuente Egipcia (Egyptian Fountain) and legend has it that an enormous fortune buried in the park by Felipe IV in the mid-18th century rests here. Park authorities assured us that we could put away our spade and that the legend is rot.

Hidden among the trees south of the lake, the Palacio de Cristal (☎ 91 574 66 14; ⊙ 11am-8pm Mon-Sat, 11am-6pm Sun & holidays May-Sep, 10am-6pm Mon-Sat, 10am-4pm Sun & holidays Oct-Apr), a charming metal and glass structure, was built in 1887 as a winter garden for exotic flowers; it's now used for temporary exhibitions organised by the Centro de Arte Reina Sofía. Just north of here, the Palacio de Velázquez was built in 1883 for a mining exposition. Now it is generally used for temporary exhibitions, although it was closed for renovations at the time of writing. Another building occasionally used for temporary exhibitions is the Casa de Vacas (☎ 91 409 58 19; ⊙ 11am-10pm).

At the southern end of the park, near La Rosaleda (Rose Garden), on a roundabout, is a statue of El Ángel Caído (the Fallen Angel, aka Lucifer), one of the few statues to the devil anywhere in the world.

In the southwest corner of the park is the moving Bosque de los Ausentes (Forest of the Absent), also known as the Bosque del Recuerdo (Memorial Forest), an understated memorial to the 191 victims of the 11 March 2004 train bombings. For each victim stands an olive or cypress tree. About 200m north of the monument is the Bosque de los Ausentes information office (🕙 10am-2pm & 4-7pm Sat, Sun & holidays).

In the northeastern corner of the park, there's another information office (🕙 10am-2pm & 4-7pm Sat, Sun & holidays) in the cute Casita del Pescador. Inquire here for the guided tours (☎ 662 149 054; inforetiuro@yahoo.es; admission free; 🕙 11am Sat) of the Parque del Buen Retiro; reservations are essential.

A stone's throw from this information office are the pleasing ruins of the Ermita de San Isidro (Cnr Calle de O'Donnell & Avenida de Menéndez Pelayo; Ⓜ Príncipe de Vergara), a small country chapel noteworthy as one of the few, albeit modest, examples of extant Romanesque architecture in Madrid. Parts of the wall, a side entrance and part of the apse were restored in 1999 and are all that remain of the 13th-century building. When it was built Madrid was a little village more than 2km away.

CASÓN DEL BUEN RETIRO Map pp92–3
Calle de Alfonso XII 28; Ⓜ Retiro
One of the few vestiges of the 17th-century Palacio del Buen Retiro, this somewhat austere building overlooking the Parque del Buen Retiro is administered by the Museo del Prado for its students and is, sadly, otherwise closed to the public other than for occasional temporary exhibitions. If you're lucky enough to see inside, make straight for the Hall of the Ambassadors where the expansive 1697 ceiling fresco *The Apotheosis of the Spanish Monarchy* by Luca Gordano is astonishing. The rest of the building has been renovated in a modern style.

PASEO DEL ARTE
Walking Tour
1 Parque del Buen Retiro (opposite) Wandering through El Retiro is one of Madrid's greatest pleasures, its combination of expansive greenery and marble or glass monuments littered among the trees. Start at the lake *(Estanque)* and consider taking a leisurely detour via the Monument to Alfonso XII, the statue of El Ángel Caído and completing a circuit via the Ermita de San Isidro before making your way west.

2 Casón del Buen Retiro (above) Just outside one of the western gates of the park, the Casón

del Buen Retiro, which in the 17th century formed part of the royal residence, was recently renovated, although unless there's a temporary exhibition in the building, you'll probably only be able to admire it from the outside. With El Retiro on your doorstep, you can't help but feel it must have been a lovely place to live.

3 Plaza de la Cibeles (p97) Head north along Calle de Alfonso XII, admire the Puerta de Alcalá, then turn left down the hill to Plaza de la Cibeles, one of the world's most beautiful roundabouts. Surrounded as it is by soaring architectural triumphs, you'll nonetheless be unable to tear your eyes away from the Palacio de Comunicaciones, a glorious remnant of the Belle Époque architectural period.

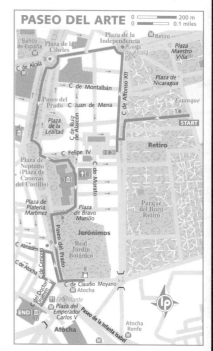

WALK FACTS
Start **Parque del Buen Retiro**
End **Centro de Arte Reina Sofía**
Distance **4km**
Time **Two hours, plus gallery time**
Fuel Stop **El Brillante** (p168)

4 Museo Thyssen-Bornemisza (p95) Walk south along the Paseo del Prado (in the tree-lined centre of the boulevard, not the side footpaths) until you reach the Museo Thyssen-Bornemisza (closed Monday) on your right. This marvellous museum gives you a taste of the major epochs of European art before you narrow in on the more specialist collections elsewhere.

5 Museo del Prado (p90) Diagonally across the other side of the Plaza de Neptuno awaits the Prado, one of the greatest galleries in the world of fine art. If time is short, restrict yourself to the works of Velázquez and Goya, the two towering masters of Spanish painting.

6 Iglesia de San Jerónimo El Real (p94) The Museo del Prado extension has recently swallowed up the cloisters of the Iglesia de San Jerónimo El Real, but the church itself has all the unmuted extravagance as befits the royal chapel of choice for the royal family.

7 Real Jardín Botánico (p96) Skirting around the back of the Museo del Prado, you'll soon come to Madrid's Botanical Gardens. There's no more shady spot in central Madrid, a green oasis while the modern, mechanised world rushes past just outside. Budding botanists will love the variety of trees, but we love it more for its respite from the outside world.

8 Cuesta de Moyano Bookstalls (p137) Outside the southern end of the Botanical Gardens, these second-hand bookstalls climb up towards the backside of El Retiro. They're something of a Madrid landmark and are well worth casting an eye over, especially the significant collection of fine arts books.

9 Caixa Forum (p96) Across the other side of the Paseo del Prado, Caixa Forum is Madrid's most stunning architectural innovation. Its hanging garden alongside the earth-toned façade only serves to accentuate the sense that the building is floating above the ground.

10 Centro de Arte Reina Sofía (p82) Even if you've had enough of galleries for one day, don't forsake the Reina Sofía. Head straight for Picasso's *Guernica*, a breathtaking masterpiece, seek out the Miró and Salvador Dalí, then take in the stunning new extension around the corner.

SALAMANCA

The barrio of Salamanca is Madrid's most exclusive quarter, a barrio defined by grand and restrained elegance. This is a place to put on your finest clothes and be seen (especially along Calle de Serrano or Calle de José Ortega y Gasset), to stroll into shops with an affected air and resist asking the prices, or to promenade en route between the fine museums and parks that make you wonder whether you've arrived at the height of civilisation. Everything about the barrio – its fine restaurants, its upmarket wine bars, its niche museums – are merely variations on this exclusive theme but, above all else, Salamanca lives and breathes shopping, from chic boutiques by leading Spanish designers to the emporiums of the great names in world fashion. As such, Salamanca is the antithesis of Lavapiés, its quiet streets suggesting an enclave of long-standing prosperity, of old money. For more earthy delights, the Plaza de Toros and Museo Taurino to the east of the barrio is the spiritual home of Spanish bullfighting; it's technically part of Salamanca even if the señoras of the barrio would love to disown it, even as their husbands sneak out for an occasional *corrida* (bullfight).

PLAZA DE TOROS & MUSEO TAURINO Map pp102–3

☎ 91 556 92 37; www.las-ventas.com, in Spanish; Calle de Alcalá 237; ⏰ museum 9.30am-2.30pm Tue-Fri & 10am-1pm Sun Jun-Sep; Ⓜ Las Ventas

The Plaza de Toros Monumental de Las Ventas (often known simply as Las Ventas) is not the most beautiful bullring in the world – that honour probably goes to Ronda in Andalucía – but it is the most important.

A classic example of the neo-*mudéjar* style, it was opened in 1931 and hosted its first *corrida* (bullfight) three years later. Like all bullrings, the circle of sand enclosed by four storeys, which can seat up to 25,000 spectators, evokes more a sense of a theatre than a sports stadium; it also hosts concerts; see p210. To be carried high on the shoulders of aficionados out through the grand and decidedly Moorish Puerta de Madrid is the ultimate dream of any torero (bullfighter) – if you've made it at Las Ventas, you've reached the pinnacle of the bullfighting world. The gate is known more colloquially as the gate of glory.

THINGS THEY SAID ABOUT…THE PLAZA DE TOROS

'The next afternoon all the world crowds to the Plaza de Toros. You need not ask the way; just launch into the tide, which in these Spanish affairs will assuredly carry you away. Nothing can exceed the gaiety and sparkle of a Spanish public going, eager and full-dressed, to the fight.'

Richard Ford, Gatherings from Spain (1861)

If your curiosity is piqued, wander into the Museo Taurino, and check out the collection of paraphernalia, costumes, photos and other bullfighting memorabilia up on the top floor above one of the two courtyards by the ring. There are guided tours of the museum from 10am to 2pm from Tuesday to Friday.

The area where the Plaza de Toros is located is known as Las Ventas because, in times gone by, several wayside taverns *(ventas)*, along with houses of ill repute, were to be found here.

ORIENTATION & TRANSPORT: SALAMANCA

Paseo de los Recoletos and its continuation, Paseo de la Castellana, delineate the western end of Salamanca's neat grid of streets tacked on to the northern sides of the Parque del Buen Retiro. Calle de María de Molina, Calle de Francisco Silvela and Calle de Alcalá rule Salamanca off neatly to the north, east and southeast. The posher parts of Salamanca centre around Calle de Serrano, Calle del Príncipe de Vergara and Calle de Goya.

The most useful metro stations that encircle the barrio's perimeter include Colón (line 4), Banco de España (line 2), Retiro (line 2), Príncipe de Vergara (lines 2 and 9), Goya (lines 2 and 4), Manuel Becerra (lines 2 and 6) and Gregorio Marañón (lines 7 and 10). Those that deposit you in the heart of the barrio include Serrano (line 4), Velázquez (line 4) and Nuñez de Balboa (lines 5 and 9).

lonelyplanet.com

SALAMANCA

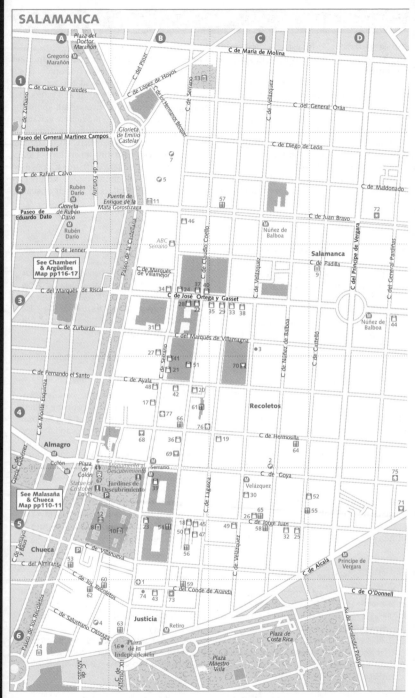

NEIGHBOURHOODS SALAMANCA

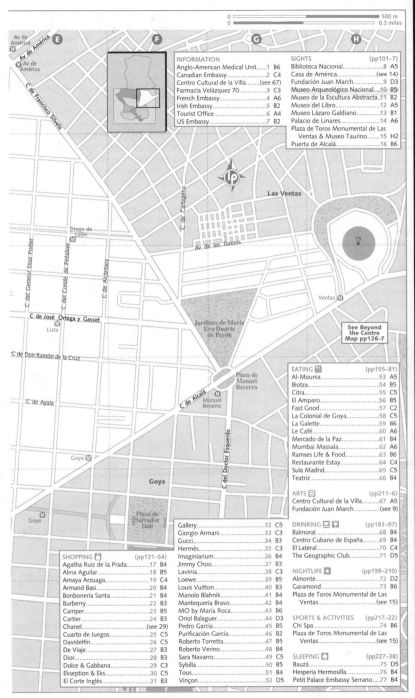

500 m
0.3 miles

Av de América

Av de América

C de Francisco Silvela

INFORMATION
Anglo-American Medical Unit......1 B6
Canadian Embassy.........................2 C4
Centro Cultural de la Villa........(see 67)
Farmacia Velázquez 70.............3 C3
French Embassy..........................4 A6
Irish Embassy..............................5 B2
Tourist Office..............................6 A4
US Embassy.................................7 B2

SIGHTS (pp101–7)
Biblioteca Nacional......................8 A5
Casa de América...................(see 14)
Fundación Juan March...............9 D3
Museo Arqueológico Nacional...10 B5
Museo de la Escultura Abstracta.11 B2
Museo del Libro..........................12 A5
Museo Lázaro Galdiano.............13 B1
Palacio de Linares.......................14 A6
Plaza de Toros Monumental de Las
   Ventas & Museo Taurino......15 H2
Puerta de Alcalá........................16 B6

C de Cartagena

Las Ventas

Diego de León

C del General Díaz Porlier

C del Conde de Peñalver

C de Alcántara

Av de los Toreros

15

C de José Ortega y Gasset

Lista

C de Don Ramón de la Cruz

Jardines de María Eva Duarte de Perón

Ventas

See Beyond the Centre Map pp126–7

C de Ayala

Plaza de Manuel Becerra

C de Alcalá

Manuel Becerra

Goya

C del Doctor Esquerdo

Goya

Goya

Plaza de Salvador Dalí

EATING (pp155–81)
Al-Mounia..................................53 A5
Biotza..54 B5
Citra..55 C5
El Amparo..................................56 B5
Fast Good..................................57 C2
La Colonial de Goya...................58 C5
La Galette...................................59 B6
Le Café......................................60 A6
Mercado de la Paz.....................61 B4
Mumbai Massala........................62 A6
Ramses Life & Food....................63 B6
Restaurante Estay.......................64 C4
Sula Madrid................................65 C5
Teatriz..66 B4

ARTS (pp211–6)
Centro Cultural de la Villa..........67 A5
Fundación Juan March...........(see 9)

DRINKING (pp183–97)
Balmoral....................................68 B4
Centro Cubano de España.........69 B4
El Lateral....................................70 C4
The Geographic Club.................71 D5

NIGHTLIFE (pp199–210)
Almonte....................................72 D2
Garamond..................................73 B6
Plaza de Toros Monumental de Las
   Ventas...............................(see 15)

SPORTS & ACTIVITIES (pp217–22)
Chi Spa......................................74 B6
Plaza de Toros Monumental de Las
   Ventas...............................(see 15)

SLEEPING (pp227–38)
Bauzá..75 D5
Hesperia Hermosilla...................76 B4
Petit Palace Embassy Serrano....77 B4

SHOPPING (pp131–54)
Agatha Ruiz de la Prada...........17 B4
Alma Aguilar..............................18 B5
Amaya Arzuaga........................19 C4
Armand Basi..............................20 B4
Bonbonería Santa......................21 B4
Burberry....................................22 B3
Camper......................................23 B5
Cartier.......................................24 B3
Chanel.................................(see 29)
Cuarto de Juegos......................25 C5
Davidelfin..................................26 C5
De Viaje....................................27 B3
Dior...28 B3
Dolce & Gabbana.....................29 C3
Ekseption & Eks.........................30 C5
El Corte Inglés...........................31 B3

Gallery.......................................32 C5
Giorgio Armani..........................33 C3
Gucci...34 B3
Hermés......................................35 C3
Imaginarium..............................36 B4
Jimmy Choo...............................37 B3
Lavinia......................................38 C3
Loewe.......................................39 B5
Louis Vuitton..............................40 B3
Manolo Blahnik.........................41 B4
Mantequería Bravo....................42 B4
MO by María Roca....................43 B6
Oriol Balaguer...........................44 D3
Pedro García.............................45 B5
Purificación García....................46 B2
Roberto Torretta........................47 B5
Roberto Verino..........................48 B4
Sara Navarro.............................49 C5
Sybilla.......................................50 B5
Tous..51 B4
Vinçon.......................................52 D5

103

PUERTA DE ALCALÁ Map pp102–3

Plaza de la Independéncia; Ⓜ **Retiro**

This stunning triumphal gate was once the main entrance to the city (its name derives from the fact that the road that passed under it led to Alcalá de Henares) and was surrounded by the city's walls. It was here that the city authorities controlled access to the capital and levied customs duties.

The first gate to bear this name was built in 1599, but Carlos III was singularly unimpressed and had it demolished in 1764 to be replaced by another, the one you see today. It's best viewed from Plaza de la Cibeles to the west from where it complements the grandeur of the Palacio de Comunicaciones as part of one of Madrid's most attractive vistas. From the east, the views through the arch down towards central Madrid are similarly special. Our only complaint? It could do with a clean. Twice a year, in autumn and spring, cars abandon the roundabout and are replaced by flocks of sheep being transferred in an age-old ritual from their summer to winter pastures (and vice versa). And the Puerta de Alcalá was immortalised in the cultural lexicon in 1986 when Ana Belén and Victor Manuel's mediocre but strangely catchy song 'La Puerta de Alcalá' became an unlikely smash hit.

PALACIO DE LINARES & CASA DE AMÉRICA Map pp102–3

☎ 91 595 48 00; www.casamerica.es, in Spanish; Plaza de la Cibeles 2; adult/student or senior/child €7/4/free; Ⓨ guided tours half-hourly 10am-2pm Sat & Sun; Ⓜ Banco de España

So extraordinary is the Palacio de Comunicaciones on Plaza de la Cibeles that many visitors fail to notice this fine 19th-century pleasure dome that stands watch over the northeastern corner of the plaza. Built in 1873, the Palacio de Linares is a worthy member of the line-up of grand façades on the plaza, while its interior is notable for the copious use of Carrara marble. Tours can take an hour and can be reserved on ☎ 902 400 222. In the palace's grounds is the Casa de América, a modern exhibition centre which, also hosts all sorts of events and concerts.

MUSEO ARQUEOLÓGICO NACIONAL Map pp102–3

☎ 91 577 79 12; http://man.mcu.es/, in Spanish; Calle de Serrano 13; admission free until renova-

tions complete, then admission €3, free after 2.30pm Sat & all day Sun; Ⓨ 9.30am-8pm Tue-Sat, 9.30am-3pm Sun & holidays; Ⓜ Serrano

On the east side of the building housing the Biblioteca Nacional, the National Archaeology Museum hides behind a towering façade. Within, with typical Spanish flair for presentation – lighting is perfect and the large collection of artefacts is never cluttered – this delightful collection spans everything from prehistory to the Iberian tribes, Imperial Rome, Visigothic Spain, the Muslim conquest, and specimens of Romanesque, Gothic and *mudéjar* handiwork.

The ground floor is the most interesting. Highlights include the stunning mosaics taken from Roman villas across Spain (the 4th-century *Mosaico de las Musas* from Navarra and the incomplete *Triumph of Bacchus* will particularly catch the eye); the stunning gilded *mudéjar*-domed ceiling and the arches taken from Zaragoza's Aljafería; and the more sombre Christian Romanesque and later-Gothic paraphernalia. Elsewhere, sculpted figures, such as the historically significant *Dama de Ibiza* and *Dama de Elche*, reveal a flourishing artistic tradition among the Iberian tribes – no doubt influenced by contact with Greek, Phoenician and Carthaginian civilisation. The latter bust continues to attract controversy over its authenticity, a century after it was found near the Valencian town.

top picks

IT'S FREE

- Museo del Prado (admission free 6-8pm Tue-Sat, 5-8pm Sun; p90)
- Centro de Arte Reina Sofía (admission free 2.30-9pm Sat, 10am-2.30pm Sun; p82)
- Museo Municipal de Arte Contemporáneo (admission free Tue-Sun; p108)
- Museo Arqueológico Nacional (admission free 2.30-8.30pm Sat & all day Sun; left)
- Ermita de San Antonio de la Florida (admission free Tue-Sun; p124)
- Templo de Debod (admission free Tue-Sun; p115)
- Museo de América (admission free Sun; p118)
- Museo de la Escultura Abstracta (admission free daily; opposite)
- Museo de la Ciudad (admission free Tue-Sun; p122)

The basement contains displays on prehistoric man and spans the Neolithic period to the Iron Age – it's probably more of interest to dedicated archaeological buffs. Modest collections from ancient Egypt, Etruscan civilisation in Italy, classical Greece and southern Italy under Imperial Rome take their place alongside the ancient civilisations in the Balearic and Canary Islands. The 1st floor contains all sorts of items pertaining to Spanish royalty and court life from the 16th to the 19th centuries. Outside, stairs lead down to a partial copy of the prehistoric cave paintings of Altamira (Cantabria).

The museum was undergoing a major renovation at the time of writing, so the location of some of the exhibits may have changed by the time you read this.

BIBLIOTECA NACIONAL & MUSEO DEL LIBRO Map pp102–3
☎ 91 580 78 05, 91 580 77 59; www.bne.es, in Spanish; Paseo de los Recoletos 20; admission free; 🕑 10am-9pm Tue-Sat, 10am-2pm Sun; Ⓜ Colón
One of the most outstanding of the many grand edifices erected in the 19th century along the Paseo de los Recoletos, the 1892 Biblioteca Nacional (National Library) dominates the southern end of Plaza de Colón. The reading rooms are more for use by serious students. Downstairs, and entered via a separate entrance, the fascinating and recently overhauled Museo del Libro (otherwise known as the Museo de la Biblioteca Nacional) is a must for bibliophiles with interactive displays on printing presses and other materials, illuminated manuscripts, the history of the library and literary cafés, although our favourite is Sala 3 (Sala de las Musas), with priceless original works such as a 1626 map

top picks

SIGHTS IN SALAMANCA

- Plaza de Toros & Museo Taurino (p101)
- Museo Arqueológico Nacional (opposite)
- Museo de la Escultura Abstracta (below)

of Spain, Picasso's *Mademoiselle Léonie en un Sillón* and other gorgeous artefacts.

MUSEO DE LA ESCULTURA ABSTRACTA Map pp102–3
www.munimadrid.es/museoairelibre/; Paseo de la Castellana; Ⓜ Rubén Darío
This fascinating open-air collection of 17 abstracts includes works by the renowned Basque artist Eduardo Chillida, the Catalan master Joan Miró as well as Eusebio Sempere and Alberto Sánchez, one of Spain's foremost sculptors of the 20th century. The sculptures are beneath the overpass where Paseo de Eduardo Dato crosses Paseo de la Castellana. All but one are on the eastern side of Paseo de la Castellana.

MUSEO LÁZARO GALDIANO Map p102–3
☎ 91 561 60 84; www.flg.es, in Spanish; Calle de Serrano 122; adult/student €4/3, free Sun; 🕑 10am-4.30pm Wed-Mon; Ⓜ Gregorio Marañón
This is just the sort of place you expect to find along Calle de Serrano, with an imposing early 20th-century Italianate stone mansion set discreetly back from the street. And Don José Lázaro Galdiano (1862–1947), a successful and cultivated businessman, was just the sort of man you'd expect to find in Salamanca. A patron of the arts, he built

SALAMANCA'S DIFFICULT BIRTH

Salamanca, with its expensive boutiques, high-class restaurants and luxury apartments, was born with a silver spoon in its mouth. When Madrid's authorities were looking to expand beyond the newly inadequate confines of the medieval capital, the Marqués de Salamanca, a 19th-century aristocrat and general with enormous political clout, heard the call. He threw everything he had into the promotion of his barrio in the 1870s, buying up land cheaply, which he later hoped to sell for a profit. He was ahead of his time – the houses he built contained Madrid's first water closets, the latest in domestic plumbing and water heating for bathrooms and kitchens, while he also inaugurated horse-drawn tramways. In the year of his death, 1883, the streets got electric lighting. Hard as it is now to imagine, there was little enthusiasm for the project and the marques quickly went bankrupt. Towards the end of his life, he wrote: 'I have managed to create the most comfortable barrio in Madrid and find myself the owner of 50 houses, 13 hotels and 18 million feet of land. And I owe more than 36 million reales on all of this. The task is completed but I am ruined.' It was only later that madrileños saw the error of their ways.

up an astonishing private collection that he bequeathed to the city upon his death. It was no mean inheritance with some 13,000 works of art and *objets d'art*, a quarter of which are on show at any time. The highlights are the works by Van Eyck, Bosch, Zurbarán, Ribera, Goya, Claudio Coello, El Greco, Gainsborough and Constable.

The ground floor is largely given over to a display setting the social context in which Galdiano lived, with hundreds of curios on show. The 1st floor is dominated by Spanish artworks up until Goya, the 2nd floor continues with Goya and paintings from the rest of Europe. The top floor is jammed with all sorts of ephemera (such as Mrs Galdiano's fan collection). A lawyer and journalist, Galdiano also collected a library of some 20,000 volumes.

The ceilings of each room are painted in different styles, the most beautiful of which is Room 14, featuring a collage from some of Goya's more famous works, in honour of the genius.

FUNDACIÓN JUAN MARCH Map pp102–3
☎ 91 435 42 40; www.march.es; Calle de Castelló 77; admission free; ⏰ 11am-8pm Mon-Sat, 10am-2pm Sun & holidays; Ⓜ Núñez de Balboa
This foundation organises some of the better temporary exhibitions in Madrid each year and it's always worth checking its website, the listings pages of local papers or *EsMadrid Magazine* (from the tourist office) to see what exhibitions are happening. The foundation also stages concerts and other events throughout the year (see p213 for more info).

DESIGNER BARRIO
Walking Tour
1 Plaza de la Independencia (Map pp102–3)
From this roundabout crowned with the monumental Puerta de Alcalá you've many of Madrid's highlights on your doorstep. Southeast is the Parque del Buen Retiro, down the hill to the west is the glorious Plaza de la Cibeles and, beyond, the city centre. But you're headed north, into the distinguished Salamanca barrio.

2 Calle de Serrano (see the boxed text, p139)
Sweeping away to the north is Calle de Serrano, which is to Madrid what Boulevard Haussmann is to Paris. This street is glamour central, the

most prestigious shopping street in Spain and just about every Spanish designer of international repute has a boutique lining its shores.

3 Museo Arqueológico Nacional (p104)
Just before you reach Plaza de Colón (it's the one with the largest Spanish flag you'll ever see) is the grand Archaeological Museum. If the renovations have finished, take the time

---

WALK FACTS
Start **Plaza de la Independencia**
End **Museo de la Escultura Abstracta**
Distance **4km**
Time **Two hours, plus shopping time**
Fuel Stop **Biotza** (p170)

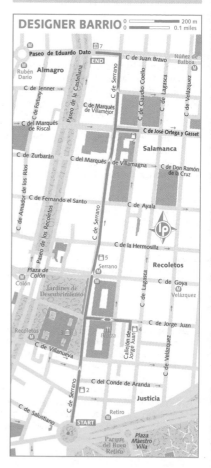

DESIGNER BARRIO

to wander through this fascinating journey spanning Spanish prehistory through to the glories of Muslim Spain. Be sure to check out the stunning Roman mosaics.

4 Callejón de Jorge Juan (see the boxed text, p140) A brief detour from Calle de Serrano along Calle de Jorge Juan brings you to its smaller cousin Callejón de Jorge Juan. It's only short, but this little pedestrian street is lined with designer boutiques of Spanish haute couture. This is where discerning Salamanca shoppers with fat wallets love to browse, especially in Alma Aguilar, Sybilla and Roberto Torretta.

5 Calle de Serrano Part Two (see the boxed text, p139) Back on Calle de Serrano, stop in at Loewe. Thus initiated into the world of classy Spanish fashion, continue north to the cheerful, bright colours of Agatha Ruiz de la Prada before toning things down a little in the boutique of Roberto Verino.

6 Calle de José Ortega y Gasset (see the boxed text, p138) Shopping in Salamanca can give you a newly acquired Spanish look, but Calle de José Ortega y Gasset is all about international glamour with just about every mainstream luxury clothes designer having a shopfront here. To treat yourself head east as far as Oriol Balaguer (p140), where chocolate becomes art.

7 Museo de la Escultura Abstracta (p105) Retrace your steps to Calle de Serrano, turn right, then left on Calle de Juan Bravo. Beneath the bridge where the street starts to cross the Paseo de la Castellana, the open-air Museum of Abstract Art is about Spanish design of a more enduring kind, with the works of big-name Spanish sculptors on permanent display.

MALASAÑA & CHUECA

Drinking p192; Eating p170; Nightlife p200; Shopping p149; Sleeping p236

The two inner-city barrios of Malasaña and Chueca are where Madrid gets up close and personal. Yes, there are rewarding museums and examples of landmark architecture sprinkled throughout. But these two barrios are more about doing than seeing, more an experience of life as it's lived by madrileños than the traditional traveller experience of ticking off from a list of wonderful, if more static, attractions that may have made the city famous but which only tell half the story. These are barrios with attitude and personality, barrios where Madrid's famed nightlife, shopping and eating choices live and breathe and take you under the skin of the city.

Malasaña lives in the past. The barrio where, in 1808, locals rose up in rebellion against the French occupiers (p27) has never quite lost its rebellious spirit. It was here, two centuries later in the 1980s, that *la movida madrileña* (p32) found its most authentic expression, rebelling against Spain's Franco past and pushing hedonism to new limits. Most of the city may have moved on, but Malasaña remains a barrio of narrow streets where the shopfronts announce names like 'True Love Tattoo', 'Blue Rabbit Sex Shop' and 'Retro City', and where graffiti and posters to heavy-rocking bands have become an integral part of its gritty urban charm. From the Plaza Dos de Mayo in the heart of the barrio, the clamour of Malasaña rolls out across the city, reminding madrileños where they came from.

If Malasaña holds fast to its roots, Chueca has become a symbol for all the extravagance, tolerance and sometime sophistication of the new Madrid. Chueca wears its heart on its sleeve, a barrio that gay and lesbians have transformed from a down-at-heel symbol of urban decay into one of the coolest places in Spain. Sometimes it's in-your-face, more often it's what locals like to call not gay-friendly, but hetero-friendly. As such, you don't have to be gay to enjoy Chueca. The diversity of the gay and lesbian communities who have made Chueca their own is reflected in its polyglot character: it's a place of rainbow flags and open-fronted gay bookshops, of bars for bears and boutiques for an exclusive clientele. Above all, it's a feel-good barrio whose moment is very much now.

The major sights in Malasaña and Chueca are covered in the pages that follow, but for the small, boutique galleries of contemporary art that abound throughout Chueca, turn to p214.

SOCIEDAD GENERAL DE AUTORES Y EDITORES Map pp110–11

☎ 91 349 95 50; ww.sgae.es, in Spanish; Calle de Fernando VI 4; Ⓜ Alonso Martínez

This swirling, melting wedding cake of a building is as close as Madrid comes to the work of Antoni Gaudí, which so illuminates Barcelona. It's a joyously self-indulgent ode to modernismo and virtually one of a kind in Madrid. Casual visitors are actively discouraged, although what you see from the street is impressive enough. The only exceptions are on the first Monday of October, International Architecture Day, and during the Noche en Blanco festivities (see p19). We've had a peek inside and it's interior staircase alone is worth coming here for if you're here on one of these two days.

MUSEO MUNICIPAL Map pp110–11

☎ 91 588 86 72; www.munimadrid.es/museomunicipal; Calle de Fuencarral 78; admission free; ⏰ 9.30am-8pm Tue-Fri, 10am-2pm Sat & Sun Sep-Jun, 9.30am-2.30pm Tue-Fri, 10am-2pm Sat & Sun Jul & Aug, closed holidays; Ⓜ Tribunal

The entrance of this fine museum is extraordinary – an elaborate and restored baroque entrance, a flight of churrigueresque fancy raised in 1721 by Pedro de Ribera. The interior is dominated by paintings and other memorabilia charting the historical evolution of Madrid.

On the ground floor Madrid de los Austrias (Habsburg Madrid) is brought to life with paintings and by an absorbing and expansive model of 1830s Madrid. Note especially the long-disappeared bullring next to the Puerta de Alcalá and the absence of the Gran Vía through the centre of Madrid. On the 1st floor the various rooms take you from Bourbon Madrid through to the final years of the 19th century.

Sadly, the museum was due to close for extensive renovations in October 2008 and may not reopen until 2010.

MUSEO MUNICIPAL DE ARTE CONTEMPORÁNEO Map pp110–11

☎ 91 588 59 28; www.munimadrid.es/museoartecontemporaneo, in Spanish; Calle del

ORIENTATION & TRANSPORT: MALASAÑA & CHUECA

Malasaña is enclosed by Gran Vía (south), Calle de la Princesa (west), Calle de Alberto Aguilera (north) and Calle de Fuencarral (east). The heart of Chueca starts not far east of the latter street and extends down as far as the Paseo de los Recoletos, with Gran Vía and Calle de Génova enclosing Chueca to the south and north, respectively. The major, roughly north–south thoroughfares through the area are Calle de San Bernardo, Calle de Fuencarral and Calle de Hortaleza.

Six out of the 10 main metro lines pass through one of these two barrios or deposit you conveniently around the perimeter. For Malasaña, Bilbao (lines 1 and 4) and San Bernardo (lines 2 and 4) sit on the barrio's northern rim and allow a downhill walk into the barrio, while Noviciado (lines 2 and 10) lies where Malasaña segues into Conde Duque. Alonso Martínez (lines 4, 5 and 10) allows a downward stroll into Chueca, while Colón (line 4) and Banco de España (line 2) also surround the barrio. Gran Vía (lines 1 and 5), at the southern end, and Tribunal (lines 1 and 10) are handy for both barrios. Chueca (line 5) sits in the heart of the barrio of the same name. Plaza de España (lines 3 and 10) is helpful for the lower corner of Malasaña and Conde Duque.

Conde Duque 9-11; admission free; ☉ 10am-2pm & 5.30-9pm Tue-Sat, 10.30am-2.30pm Sun & holidays; Ⓜ Noviciado or San Bernardo

Spread over two floors, this is a rich collection of modern Spanish art, mostly paintings and graphic art with a smattering of photography, sculpture and drawings. Running throughout much of the gallery are works showcasing creative interpretations of Madrid's cityscape – avant-garde splodges and almost old-fashioned visions of modern Madrid side by side – and, for many lay visitors, therein lies the museum's greatest appeal. Some examples include Juan Moreno Aquado's (b 1954) *Chamartín* (2000), Luis Mayo's *Cibeles* (1997) and a typically fantastical representation of the Cibeles fountain by one-time icon of *la movida madrileña*, Ouka Lele. The 1st floor is a mix of works acquired between 1999 and 2001, while the 2nd floor contains a chronological display (starting with the 1920s). The many talented artists represented here include Eduardo Arroyo and Basque sculptor Jorde Oteiza.

ANTIGUO CUARTEL DEL CONDE DUQUE Map pp110–11

☎ 91 588 57 71; Calle del Conde Duque 9-11; Ⓜ Noviciado or San Bernardo

This grand former barracks dominates Conde Duque on the western fringe of Malasaña with its imposing façade stretching 228m down the hill. Built in 1717 under the auspices of architect Pedro de Ribera, its highlight is the extravagant 18th-century doorway, which is a masterpiece of the baroque churrigueresque style. Now it's home by day to a cultural centre, which hosts government archives, libraries, the Hemeroteca Municipal (the biggest collection of newspapers and magazines in Spain), temporary exhibitions and the Museo Municipal de Arte Contemporáneo (opposite). By night, in summer, one of the two large patios becomes an atmospheric venue for concerts; programmes for exhibitions and concerts are posted outside. In the gardens to the northeast of the building, most mornings you'll find old men playing *petanca (pétanque)* under the trees like a scene from Madrid's village past.

PALACIO DE LIRIA Map pp110–11

☎ 91 547 53 02; Calle de la Princesa 20; admission on guided visit by prior arrangement only; ☉ 11am & noon Fri; Ⓜ Ventura Rodríguez

This 18th-century mansion, rebuilt after a fire in 1936, nestles amid the modern architecture just north of Plaza de España as a reminder of the days when the streets were lined with mansions like these. It holds an impressive collection of art, period furniture and *objets d'art*. To join a guided visit you need to send a formal request with your personal details to the palace, which is home to the Duke and Duchess of Alba, one of the grandest names in Spanish nobility. The waiting list is long and most mere mortals content themselves with staring through the gates into the grounds.

PALACIO BUENAVISTA & CASA DE LAS SIETE CHIMENEAS Map pp110–11

Plaza de la Cibeles; Ⓜ Banco de España

Set back amid gardens on the northwest edge of Plaza de la Cibeles stands the Palacio Buenavista, now occupied by the army. It once belonged to the Alba family, and the young Duchess of Alba, Cayetana, who was widely rumoured to have had an affair with the artist Goya, lived here for a time.

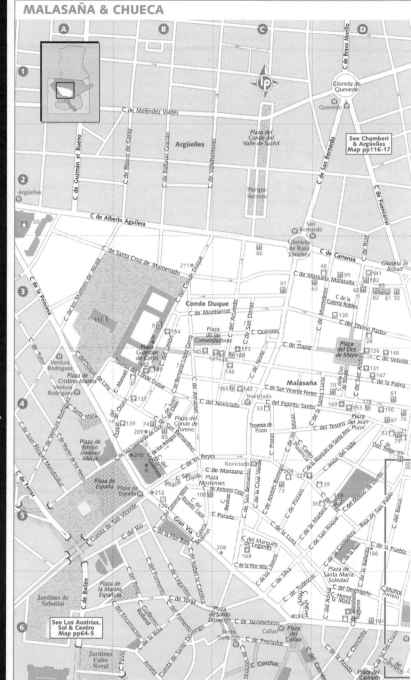

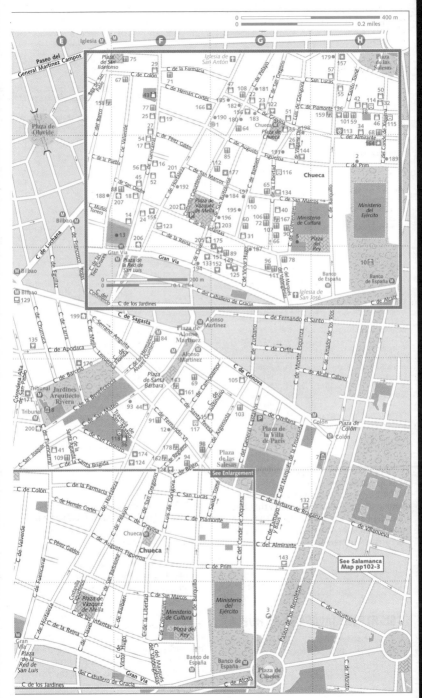

A block behind it to the west, on the tiny Plaza del Rey, is the Casa de las Siete Chimeneas, a 16th-century mansion that takes its name from the seven chimneys it still boasts and which gives a tantalising glimpse of the sort of residences that once lined the Paseo de la Castellana. They say that the ghost of one of Felipe II's lovers still runs about here in distress on certain

top picks

SIGHTS IN MALASAÑA & CHUECA

- Museo Municipal (p108)
- Museo Municipal de Arte Contemporáneo (p108)
- Sociedad General de Autores y Editores (p108)

evenings. Nowadays, it's home to the Ministry of Education, Culture and Sport.

MUSEO DE CERA Map pp110–11
☎ 91 319 26 49; www.museoceramadrid.com; Paseo de los Recoletos 41; adult/child under 10yr €15/9; ⏰ 10am-2.30pm & 4.30-8.30pm Mon-Fri, 10am-8.30pm Sat-Sun & holidays; Ⓜ Colón
If wax museums are your thing, this one with more than 450 characters is a fairly standard version of the genre. With models ranging from the Beatles to Bart Simpson, from Raúl to Cervantes, Dalí and Picasso, it's a typically broadranging collection of international and Spanish figures down through the centuries. If you're drawn to the darker side of life, there's everything from the Inquisition to Freddy Krueger, while the Tren del Terror is not for the faint-hearted. Other attractions include the

MALASAÑA & CHUECA

Simulador, which shakes you up a bit, as though you were inside a washing machine, and the Multivisión journey through Spanish history. It claims to be Madrid's seventh most-visited museum, although it's hard to see why, unless you've got kids.

OFF THE TOURIST TRAIL
Walking Tour

1 Plaza de Chueca (Map pp110–11) Welcome to the heart of gay Madrid, a barrio of over-the-top sexuality and devil-may-care hedonism. If you like what you see and plan to return after dark, take note of Antigua Casa Ángel Sierra (p196), right on the plaza, and Café Acuarela (p225) to return later to catch the buzz.

2 Sociedad General de Autores y Editores (p108) Take Calle de Luis de Góngora

heading north to Calle de Belén, mark the location of Café Belén (p194) for a later *mojito*, then make for Calle de Fernando VI, where the General Society of Authors and Editors is housed in a Modernista masterpiece that would have made Gaudí proud.

3 Museo Municipal (p108) Continue northwest along Calle de Mejía Lequerica, then left on Calle de la Beneficencia. At the end of this street on the right is the Municipal Museum, an intriguing repository of historical Madrid artworks and a wonderful scale map. If the renovations haven't finished, you can at least admire its astonishing baroque doorway.

4 Café Comercial (p193) Calle de Fuencarral heads north to the Glorieta de Bilbao and it's here you'll find the old-world literary Café

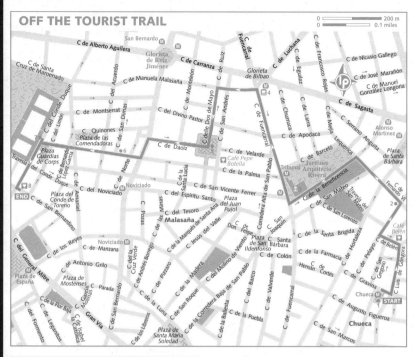

OFF THE TOURIST TRAIL

WALK FACTS

Start Plaza de Chueca
End El Jardín Secreto
Distance 5km
Time Three hours
Fuel Stop Café Pepe Botella (p194)

Comercial. One of the most famous old cafés in Madrid, a coffee here is a journey back to the thriving intellectual life of Madrid in the 1950s.

5 Plaza del Dos de Mayo (Map pp110–11) Crossing into Malasaña, stroll west along Calle de Manuela Malasaña, a name you'll want to remember for its fine range of restaurants (see the boxed text, p171). We especially like La Isla del Tesoro, Nina and La Musa, but they're all good. Down the hill to the south is Plaza Dos de Mayo, the beating heart of Malasaña.

6 Conde Duque (Map pp110–11) Any of the streets leading west out of Malasaña lead down to Calle de San Bernardo, across which lies the barrio of Conde Duque. Its impossibly narrow streets shelter a number of excellent live music venues, among them Kabokla (p209) and Café La Palma (p207).

7 Antiguo Cuartel del Conde Duque (p109) Make your way down to the Plaza Guardias de Corps, a pleasing little square overshadowed by the Antiguo Cuartel del Conde Duque. This immense cultural space is architecturally distinguished, but its treasures lie within, most notably in the Museo Municipal de Arte Contemporáneo (p108).

8 El Jardín Secreto (p194) You've covered a lot of ground. Now your reward lies in El Jardín Secreto. There's no more romantic café in Madrid than this cosy, candlelit bar with its exotic décor and wide range of drinks.

CHAMBERÍ & ARGÜELLES

Drinking p196; Eating p178; Nightlife p200; Shopping p178; Sleeping p178

Chamberí, north of the city centre, is one of the most *castizo* (typically madrileño) barrios in Madrid. At once traditional and sophisticated, this leafy barrio has in recent years become the most sought-after address in Madrid for madrileños and prices have even begun to surpass those of Salamanca. In the early 19th century the barrio was an insignificant village beyond the then city boundaries – Napoleon himself is believed to have spent the night here in December 1808, in the early months of his occupation of Spain.

Argüelles is similar, a predominantly residential barrio whose streets are lined with elegant early 20th-century apartment buildings, although it's far from uniform; the barrio was the scene of heavy fighting during the Spanish Civil War, acting as the buffer between Franco's forces in the Ciudad Universitaria area and downtown Madrid. Argüelles, like Chamberí, is home to a smattering of small shops and restaurants that are very much a part of barrio life.

You don't come to Chamberí or Argüelles for the sights, although there are some fine museums, as well as outstanding places to eat, drink and watch live music. More than that, Chamberí and, to a lesser extent, Argüelles may be fairly well off today, but they lack the snootiness of Salamanca. As such, it's here perhaps more than anywhere else in Madrid that you get a sense of Madrid as the madrileños experience it away from the tourist crowds.

TEMPLO DE DEBOD Map pp116–17

☎ 91 366 74 15; www.munimadrid.es/ templodebod/, in Spanish; Paseo del Pintor Rosales; admission free; ☷ 10am-2pm & 6-8pm Tue-Fri, 10am-2pm Sat & Sun Apr-Sep, 9.45am-1.45pm & 4.15-6.15pm Tue-Fri, 10am-2pm Sat & Sun Oct-Mar; Ⓜ Ventura Rodríguez

Yes, this is an Egyptian temple in downtown Madrid. No matter which way you look at it, there's something incongruous about finding the Templo de Debod in the Parque de la Montaña northwest of Plaza de España. How did it end up in Madrid? The temple was saved from the rising waters of Lake Nasser in southern Egypt as Egyptian president Gamal Abdel Nasser built the Aswan High Dam. After 1968 it was sent block by block to Spain as a gesture of thanks to Spanish archaeologists in the Unesco team that worked to save the extraordinary monuments that would otherwise have disappeared forever.

Begun in 2200 BC and completed over many centuries, the temple was dedicated to the god Amon of Thebes, about 20km south of Philae in the Nubian desert of southern Egypt. According to some authors of myth and legend, the goddess Isis gave birth to Horus in this very temple, although obviously not in Madrid.

The views from the surrounding gardens towards the Palacio Real are something special.

MUSEO DE CERRALBO Map pp116–17

☎ 91 547 36 46; http://museocerralbo.mcu .es; Calle de Ventura Rodríguez 17; ☷ closed for renovations; Ⓜ Ventura Rodríguez

Huddled beneath the modern apartment buildings northwest of Plaza de España, this noble old mansion is like an apparition of how wealthy madrileños once lived. The former home of the 17th Marqués de Cerralbo (1845–1922) – politician, poet and

ORIENTATION & TRANSPORT: CHAMBERÍ & ARGÜELLES

For the purposes of this book, Chamberí and Argüelles stretch westward from Paseo de la Castellana, across Calle de la Princesa and then doglegs south; Chamberí occupies the east, Argüelles the west. Sloping parkland along Paseo del Pintor Rosales closes off the area to the west. Calle de Cea Bermúdez and Calle de José Abascal seal the area off to the north, while Calle de Génova, Calle de Sagasta, Calle de Carranza and Calle de Alberto Aguilera demarcate the south from Chueca and Malasaña. The Parque del Oeste also drops away from Argüelles, while the Teleférico cable car sets off from a nearby perch for its little jaunt across to the Casa de Campo. Nearby, across the Avenida del Arco de la Victoria, are the Museo de América and the Faro, an observation tower open to the public.

Numerous metro stations circle the area. The most useful are: Colón (line 4), Gregorio Marañón (lines 7 and 10), Islas Filipinas (line 7), Moncloa (lines 3 and 6), Argüelles (lines 3, 4 and 6), San Bernardo (lines 2 and 4), Bilbao (lines 1 and 4) and Alonso Martínez (lines 4, 5 and 10). In the heart of Chamberí you'll find Quevedo (line 2) and Iglesia (line 1).

CHAMBERÍ & ARGÜELLES

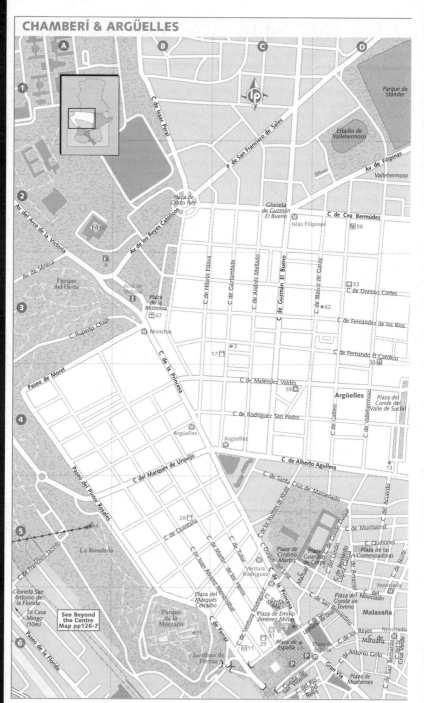

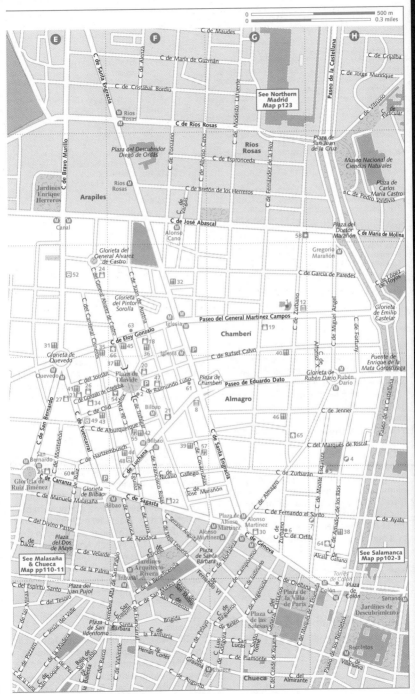

0   500 m
0   0.3 miles

C de Maudes

Paseo de la Castellana

C de Grijalba

C de María de Guzmán

C de Jorge Manrique

C de Santa Engracia

C de Atenza

C de Cristóbal Bordiú

C de Modesto Lafuente

C de Vitruvio

C de Particular

Ríos Rosas

C de Ríos Rosas

Plaza del Descubridor Diego de Ordás

C de Fonzano

C de Alonso Cano

C de Espronceda

C de Fernández de la Hoz

Plaza de San Juan de la Cruz

Ríos Rosas

C de Bravo Murillo

Ríos Rosas

C de Bretón de los Herreros

Museo Nacional de Ciencias Naturales

Plaza de Carlos María Castro

C de Pedro Valdivia

Jardines Enrique Herreros

Arapiles

C de Vargas

C de José Abascal

Canal

Alonso Cano

Plaza del Doctor Marañón

C de María de Molina

58

Glorieta del General Álvarez de Castro

Gregorio Marañón

C de García de Paredes

C de López de Hoyos

52

24

C de Juan de Austria

32

Glorieta del Pintor Sorolla

Glorieta de Emilio Castelar

C del General Álvarez de Castro

C de Zurbano

12

Paseo del General Martínez Campos

1

C de Miguel Ángel

C de Fortuny

Iglesia

63

C de Eloy Gonzalo

Chamberí

19

Puente de Enrique de la Mata Gorostizaga

31

Glorieta de Quevedo

35

C del Cardenal Cisneros

45

18

37

66

C de Rafael Calvo

40

Glorieta de Rubén Darío

Rubén Darío

Iglesia

36

Quevedo

C del Jordán

20

Plaza de Olavide

Plaza de Chamberí

Paseo de Eduardo Dato

41

26

23

C de Gonzalo de Córdoba

47

C de Raimundo Lulio

61

Almagro

27

34

54

C de Olid

C de Trafalgar

C de Pastor

Bilbao

8

C de Jenner

C de San Bernardo

49

43

C de Alburquerque

21

46

65

C del Marqués de Riscal

44

55

42

C de Fuencarral

C de Hartzembusch

Bilbao

C de Santa Engracia

4

San Bernardo

48

39

57

C de Monteleón

C de Luchana

C de Covarrubias

C de Zurbarán

C de Monte Esquinza

C de Amador de los Ríos

Glorieta de Ruiz Jiménez

25

60

C de Carranza

C de Ríos

C de Francisco de Rojas

Gallego

C de José Marañón

C de Almagro

C de Fernando el Santo

C de Ayala

C de Manuela Malasaña

Glorieta de Bilbao

Bilbao

C de Sagasta

22

C de Nicasio Gallego

Plaza de Alonso Martínez

Alonso Martínez

6

7

C del Divino Pastor

C de Manuel Silvela

C de Orfila

38

64

Plaza del Dos de Mayo

Plaza del Juan Pujol

C de Apodaca

Alonso Martínez

C de Génova

Alcalá Galiano

See Salamanca Map pp102-3

See Malasaña & Chueca Map pp110-11

C de Velarde

30

C de Zurbano

Torres de Colón

C de Daoíz

C de la Palma

C de Barceló

Plaza de Santa Bárbara

C de Campoamor

C de Orellana

Colón

Plaza de Colón

C del Espíritu Santo

Plaza del Dos de Mayo

Jardines Arquitecto Rivera

Fernando VI

C de Luminio

Plaza de la Villa de París

Serrano

Jardines de Descubrimiento

C de las Minas

Tribunal

C de San Mateo

C de Hortaleza

C de Argensola

C del Marqués de la Ensenada

C de Jesús del Valle

Plaza de San Ildefonso

C de San Vicente Alta

C de la Beneficencia

Fernando VI

C de Regueros

Plaza de las Salesas

Paseo de los Recoletos

Recoletos

C de la Madera

Plaza de Santa Bárbara

Santa Bárbara

C de la Farmacia

Brígida

C de Belén

C de Piamonte

C del Conde de Xiquena

C de Villanueva

C del Pez

C de San Joaquín

Plaza de San Ildefonso

C de Fuencarral

C de Pelayo

C de Góngora

San Lucas

C de San Lorenzo

C de Santo Tomé

C de la Luna

C de San Roque de Pe...

Bala de San...

C de Valverde

Hernán Cortés

C de Gravina

C del Barco

C de la Ballesta

C de Augusto

Chueca

Chueca

C del Almirante

117

CHAMBERÍ & ARGÜELLES

INFORMATION
British Council....1 G3
Escuela Popular de Musica y Danza....2 F4
European Vibe....3 C3
German Embassy....4 H4
Goethe Institut....5 H5
International House....6 G5
UK Embassy....7 H5

SIGHTS (pp115–21)
Estación de Chamberí....8 F4
Faro de Madrid....9 A3
Museo de América....10 A2
Museo de Cerralbo....11 C6
Museo Sorolla....12 G3
Parque Secreto....13 D4
Teleférico....14 A5
Templo de Debod....15 B6
Torre de Madrid....16 C6

SHOPPING (pp131–54)
Altaïr....17 C3
Antigüedades Hom....18 F3
Booksellers....19 G3
Booksellers....20 F4
Casa Carril....21 F4
Diedro....22 F5
DMR María Rivolta....23 E4
Harley Davidson Madrid....24 E3
Imaginarium....25 E5
Los Bebés de Chamberí....26 E4
Massimo Dutti....27 E4
Naos Libros....28 B5
Ocho y Medio....29 C6
Pasajes Librería Internacional....30 G5

EATING (pp155–81)
Bajo Cero....31 E3
Bodega de la Ardosa....32 F3
Cachabacha....(see 26)
Casa Ricardo....33 D3
Cavatappi....34 E4
El Brillante....35 E3
El Pedrusco....36 F3
Il Casone....37 F4
Jockey....38 H5
La Favorita....39 F4
Las Tortillas de Gabino....40 G3
Locandita....41 E4
Moma 56....(see 58)
Nagoya....42 F4
Restaurante Collage....43 E4
Restaurante La Giralda....44 F4
Sagarretxe....45 F3
Sergi Arola Gastro....46 G4
Things You Miss....47 F4

ARTS (pp211–16)
Cine Palafox....48 F4
Cinesa Proyecciones....49 E4
Princesa....50 C6
Renoir Plaza de España....51 C6
Verdi....52 E3

DRINKING (pp183–97)
Djénné....53 D3
Krypton....54 F4

NIGHTLIFE (pp199–210)
Clamores....55 F4
Galileo Galilei....56 D2
Honky Tonk....57 F4
Moma 56....58 G2
Supersonic....59 C4

SPORTS & ACTIVITIES (pp217–22)
City Pilates....60 E5
Gimnasio Chamberí....61 F4
Zensei....62 D3

GAY & LESBIAN (pp223–6)
Fundación Triángulo....63 F3

SLEEPING (pp227–38)
Amador de los Ríos Espahotel....64 H5
Hotel AC Santo Mauro....65 G4
Hotel Trafalgar....66 F3

TRANSPORT (pp259–65)
Herranz....(see 67)
Intercambiador de Autobuses de Moncloa....67 B3
Pepecar....68 C6

archaeologist – is a study in 19th-century opulence. The museum was closed for renovations at the time of writing, so for now you'll have to admire it from the outside.

When it reopens, the upper floor boasts a gala dining hall and a grand ballroom. The mansion is jammed with the fruits of the collector's eclectic meanderings – from Oriental pieces to religious paintings and clocks.

On the main floor are spread suits of armour from around the world, while the Oriental room is full of carpets, Moroccan kilims, tapestries, musical instruments and 18th-century Japanese suits of armour, much of it obtained at auction in Paris in the 1870s. The music room is dominated by a gondola of Murano glass and pieces of Bohemian crystal. The house is also replete with porcelain, including Sèvres, Wedgwood, Meissen and local ceramics. Clearly the marqués was a man of diverse tastes and it can all be a little overwhelming, especially once you factor in artworks by Zurbarán, Ribera, van Dyck and El Greco.

top picks

SIGHTS IN CHAMBERÍ & ARGÜELLES

- Templo de Debod (p115)
- Museo de América (right)
- Museo Soralla (opposite)
- Estación de Chamberí (opposite)

MUSEO DE AMÉRICA Map pp116–17

☎ 91 549 26 41; http://museodeamerica.mcu.es, in Spanish; Avenida de los Reyes Católicos 6; adult/student €3.01/1.50, free to all Sun; 9.30am-3pm Tue-Sat, 10am-3pm Sun & holidays; M Moncloa

Empire may have become a dirty word but it defined how Spain saw itself for centuries. Spanish vessels crossed the Atlantic to the Spanish colonies in Latin America carrying adventurers one way and gold and other looted artefacts from indigenous cultures on the return journey. These latter pieces – at once the heritage of another continent and a fascinating insight into Imperial Spain – are the subject of this excellent museum.

The two levels of the museum show off a representative display of ceramics, statuary, jewellery and instruments of hunting, fishing and war, along with some of the paraphernalia of the colonisers. The display is divided into five thematic zones: El Conocimiento de América (which traces the discovery and exploration of the Americas), La Realidad de América (a big-screen summary of how South America wound up as it has today), and others on society, religion and language, which each explore tribal issues, the clash with the Spanish newcomers and its results. The Colombian gold collection, dating as far back as the 2nd century AD, and a couple of shrunken heads are particularly eye-catching.

Temporary exhibitions with various Latin American themes are regularly held here.

FARO DE MADRID Map pp116–17
☎ 91 544 81 04; Avenida de los Reyes Católicos; lift €1.20; 🕑 closed for renovations; Ⓜ Moncloa
The odd tower (lighthouse) just in front of the Museo de América is the place to go for panoramic views of Madrid if they ever reopen after slow-moving renovations. It was built in 1992 to commemorate the 500th anniversary of the discovery of America and to celebrate Madrid's role that year as the European Cultural Capital.

TELEFÉRICO Map pp116–17
☎ 91 541 74 50; www.teleferico.com, in Spanish; adult one way/return €3.50/5, child 3-7yr one way/ return €3.40/4; 🕑 hours vary; Ⓜ Argüelles
One of the world's most horizontal cable cars (it never hangs more than 40m above the ground), the Teleférico putters out from the slopes of La Rosaleda (the rose garden of Parque del Oeste). The 2.5km journey takes you into the depths of the Casa de Campo, Madrid's enormous green (in summer more a dry olive hue) open space to the west of the city centre. It's relaxing, a very local thing to do and offers some good views of Madrid's skyline. Try to time it so you can settle in for a cool lunch or evening tipple on one of the *terrazas* along Paseo del Pintor Rosales.

PARQUE DEL OESTE Map pp116–17
Avenida del Arco de la Victoria; Ⓜ Moncloa
Sloping down the hill behind the Moncloa metro station, Parque del Oeste (Park of the West) is quite beautiful, with plenty of shady corners where you can recline under a tree in the heat of the day and fine views out to the west towards Casa de Campo. It has been a madrileño favourite ever since its creation in 1906, and one of the country's greatest-ever writers Benito Pérez Galdós

(p36) took his last ride in Madrid here in August 1919. He soon fell ill and died in his house in Salamanca in January 1920.

In recent years the park has become the unofficial base of some new madrileños, the large Latin American community who gather here on weekend afternoons in large numbers to pass the time with barbecues and impromptu football games.

Until a few years ago, the Paseo de Camoens, a main thoroughfare running through the park, was lined with prostitutes by night. To deprive the prostitutes of clients, the city authorities now close the park to wheeled traffic from 11pm on Friday until 6am on Monday.

ESTACIÓN DE CHAMBERÍ Map pp116–17
Cnr Calle de Santa Engracia & Calle de Luchana; admission free; 🕑 11am-7pm Tue-Fri, 10am-2pm Sat & Sun; Ⓜ Iglesia
For years, madrileños wandered what happened to the metro station called Chamberí – they knew it existed yet it appeared on no maps and no trains ever stopped there. Over four decades later, the mystery has been solved. The answer was that Chamberí station lay along Line 1, between the stops of Bilbao and Iglesia, until 1966 when Madrid's trains (and, where possible, platforms) were lengthened. Logistical difficulties meant that Chamberí could not be extended and the station was abandoned. In early 2008 the Estación de Chamberí finally reopened to the public, if not for trains, serving as a museum piece that re-creates the era of the station's inauguration in 1919 with advertisements from the time (including with Madrid's then-four-digit phone numbers), ticket offices and other memorabilia almost a century old. It's an engaging journey down memory lane. While admission was free at the time of research, there are plans to charge a small fee in the future.

MUSEO SOROLLA Map pp116–17
☎ 91 310 15 84; http://museosorolla.mcu.es, in Spanish; Paseo del General Martínez Campos 37; adult/student/child under 18yr & senior €2.40/1.20/ free; 🕑 9.30am-3pm Tue & Thu-Sat, 9.30am-6pm Wed, 10am-3pm Sun & holidays; Ⓜ Iglesia or Gregorio Marañón
The Valencian artist Joaquín Sorolla immortalised the clear Mediterranean light of the Valencian coast. His Madrid house, a quiet mansion surrounded by lush gardens that

he designed himself, was inspired by what he had seen in Andalucía and now contains the most complete collection of the artist's works.

On the ground floor you enter a cool *patio cordobés*, an Andalucian courtyard off which is a room containing collections of Sorolla's drawings. The 1st floor, with the main salon and dining areas, was mostly decorated by the artist himself. On the same floor are three separate rooms that Sorolla used as studios. In the second one is a collection of his Valencian beach scenes. The third was where he usually worked. Upstairs, works spanning Sorolla's career are organised across four adjoining rooms.

FROM TRADITIONAL BARRIO LIFE TO EGYPT

Walking Tour

1 Plaza de Olavide (Map pp116–17) This lovely circular plaza is a main reason why madrileños love to live in Chamberí. It's a real slice of barrio life with bars around the perimeter, children's playgrounds and a fountain as its centrepiece. It's a wonderful place to begin your walking tour, even if it will make you wish that you, too, could call it home.

2 Calle de Fuencarral (Map pp116–17) Take Calle de Gonzalo de Córdoba, which runs southwest from the plaza into Calle de Fuencarral. Another barrio favourite, this wide street has more pedestrians than cars and is lined with shops and cinemas. On Sunday mornings, it's closed to traffic and the kids come out to play.

3 Faro de Madrid (p119) You've a long walk ahead of you, down through the east–west running streets of residential Argüelles. You'll eventually reach the Plaza de la Moncloa, watched over by the eye-catching Air Force Ministry. Just beyond here is the rather ugly Faro de Madrid. Fortunately, the view from the summit is excellent.

WALK FACTS

Start **Plaza de Olavide**
End **Templo de Debod**
Distance **4km**
Time **Three hours**

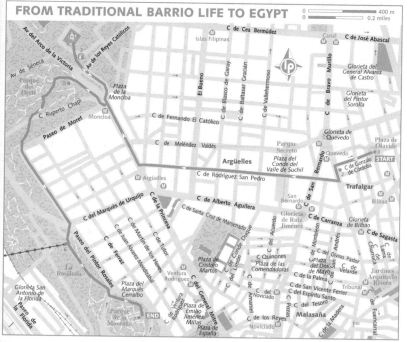

FROM TRADITIONAL BARRIO LIFE TO EGYPT

4 Museo de América (p118) Almost next door, the Museo de América promises a close-up look at the treasures looted from Spain's Latin American colonies. It's one of the more interesting museums in Madrid and promises many insights into how Spaniards see their own history.

5 Parque del Oeste (p119) Across the busy road to the south, the sloping lawns and shady nooks of the Parque del Oeste are a pleasure to wander through. They may lack the grandeur of the Parque del Buen Retiro, but they're a delightful place to stroll as you make your way roughly south–southeast.

6 Teleférico (p119) Emerging from the park along the Paseo del Pintor Rosales, you'll see the station for the Teleférico on your right. If you've the time, take a return trip out to the Casa de Campo, enjoying particularly the views of central Madrid on the return journey.

7 Templo de Debod (p115) With your feet back on the ground, the Paseo del Pinto Rosales leads to the Templo de Debod, a 4200-year-old Egyptian temple transplanted into the heart of Madrid. It's an intriguing apparition and don't neglect to wander in the gardens behind the temple for fine views (especially at sunset) towards the Palacio Real.

NORTHERN MADRID

Drinking p197; Eating p180; Nightlife p200; Shopping p154; Sleeping p238

Madrileños like to keep business and play separate and, except for one of the world's most famous football stadiums, northern Madrid concerns itself more with business than play. Most of the gracious old palaces and mansions that once lined the Paseo de la Castellana were long ago replaced by office buildings and apartments, many of which have appeared since the 1940s. Northern Madrid does have some good bars and a handful of some of the city's most celebrated restaurants.

ORIENTATION & TRANSPORT: NORTHERN MADRID

Just about everything you're likely to need in northern Madrid is on, or just off, Paseo de la Castellana, which runs through the striking Torres Puerta de Europa on Plaza de Castilla close to its northern end. These remarkable leaning towers are 115m high and with a 15° tilt, and have become a symbol of modern Madrid. Just northeast of the towers is the Chamartín train station.

The main metro stations you're likely to need are Gregorio Marañón (lines 7 and 10), Nuevos Ministerios (lines 6, 8 and 10), Santiago Bernabéu (line 10; for Real Madrid) and Chamartín (lines 1 and 10).

ESTADIO SANTIAGO BERNABÉU Map p123
☎ 91 398 43 00, 902 291 709; www.realmadrid .com; Avenida de Concha Espina 1; tour adult/child under 14yr €10/8; ☻ 10am-7pm Mon-Sat, 10.30am-6.30pm Sun, closed game day; Ⓜ Santiago Bernabéu
Football fans and budding Madridistas (Real Madrid supporters) will want to make a pilgrimage to this temple to all that's extravagant and successful in football. For a tour of the stadium, buy your ticket at ticket window 10 (next to gate 7), then self-guided tours take you through the extraordinary

Exposición de Trofeos (trophy exhibit), presidential box, press room, dressing rooms, players' tunnel and even onto the pitch itself. For details on getting tickets to a Real Madrid game, turn to p220, while the club's astonishing history is covered on p220. Details of Real Madrid's club shop are found on p154.

MUSEO DE LA CIUDAD Map p123
☎ 91 588 65 99; www.munimadrid.es/museo delaciudad/; Calle del Príncipe de Vergara 140; admission free; ☻ 9.30am-8pm Tue-Fri, 10am-2pm Sat & Sun Sep-Jun; Ⓜ Cruz del Rayo
The highlights of this museum are the scale models of various Madrid landmarks, among them the Plaza de Toros and equestrian statues of Felipe IV and Carlos III. Other models cover whole barrios or features, such as Plaza de la Villa and Paseo de la Castellana. The exhibits take you from Madrid and its beginnings to the Enlightenment, through the 19th century and to the present. The displays on the airport and how the gas, electricity and telephone systems work, however, are as dry as dust and may offer just a bit too much discovery for some tastes.

2012 OLYMPICS – SO NEAR…

Few people outside Madrid gave Madrid a chance in challenging heavyweights Paris and London for the right to host the 2012 Olympic Games. And so it proved: Madrid came in a respectable third, dropping out in the penultimate round of voting. But few people realise just how close Madrid came to hosting the games. According to senior members of the International Olympic Committee (IOC), the vote cast for Paris by the Greek member of the IOC was actually intended for Madrid. Indeed, the announcement of the results of the third-round vote was delayed as the IOC member in question complained that his vote has been miscast.

If the vote had gone to Madrid, Paris and the Spanish capital would have tied on 32 votes. In a head-to-head vote, many IOC members believe, the votes of delegates supporting London would have gone to Madrid. With Paris eliminated, so the theory goes, most of the Paris-supporting delegates would have thrown their weight behind London in order to deny the British capital its prize. 'That's now what we think happened,' Alex Gilady, a senior IOC member who now serves on the IOC's London 2012 team, told the BBC. 'This is what you call good fortune and good luck.' At least for London.

Whatever the truth of the story, London will host the 2012 Games and Madrid will be trying to learn the lessons to help its 2016 bid. But still it hurts. 'We were very close to winning,' said Feliciano Maroyal, CEO of the Madrid bid. 'We can never know if the Greek vote would have been decisive, but it is lamentable for one human error to have ruined all our hard work.'

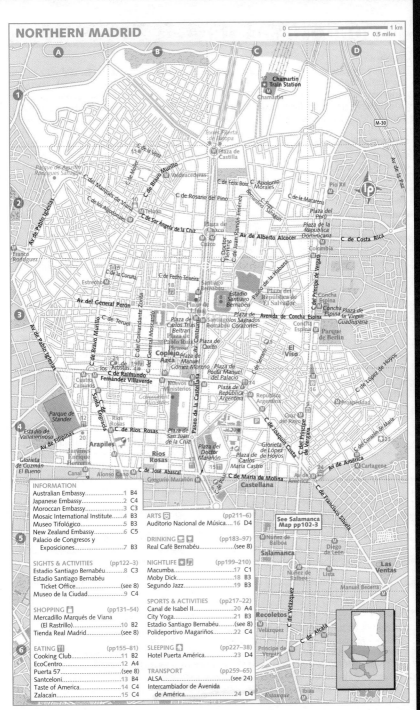

lonelyplanet.com

NEIGHBOURHOODS NORTHERN MADRID

0			1 km
0			0.5 miles

INFORMATION
Australian Embassy.....................1 B4
Japanese Embassy......................2 C4
Moroccan Embassy......................3 C3
Mosaic International Institute......4 B3
Museo Tifológico.......................5 B3
New Zealand Embassy.................6 C5
Palacio de Congresos y
　Exposiciones..........................7 B3

SIGHTS & ACTIVITIES (pp122–3)
Estadio Santiago Bernabéu..........8 C3
Estadio Santiago Bernabéu
　Ticket Office.......................(see 8)
Museo de la Ciudad....................9 C4

SHOPPING (pp131–54)
Mercadillo Marqués de Viana
　(El Rastrillo)........................10 B2
Tienda Real Madrid...............(see 8)

EATING (pp155–81)
Cooking Club............................11 B2
EcoCentro.................................12 A4
Puerta 57.............................(see 8)
Santceloni................................13 B4
Taste of America.......................14 C4
Zalacaín..................................15 C4

ARTS (pp211–6)
Auditorio Nacional de Música....16 D4

DRINKING (pp183–97)
Real Café Bernabéu...............(see 8)

NIGHTLIFE (pp199–210)
Macumba.................................17 C1
Moby Dick................................18 B3
Segundo Jazz............................19 B3

SPORTS & ACTIVITIES (pp217–22)
Canal de Isabel II.......................20 A4
City Yoga..................................21 B3
Estadio Santiago Bernabéu.....(see 8)
Polideportivo Magariños............22 C4

SLEEPING (pp227–38)
Hotel Puerta América................23 D4

TRANSPORT (pp259–65)
ALSA................................(see 24)
Intercambiador de Avenida
　de América............................24 D4

See Salamanca
Map pp102–3

123

BEYOND THE CENTRE

Nightlife p200

In general the attractions beyond Madrid's central barrios are spread pretty far and wide, and in most cases, there's little reason to do anything other than see the sight and come back. There are, however, exceptions. The Ermita de San Antonio de la Florida, which on no account should be missed, lies just beyond the Argüelles district and is easily reached by public transport. The Real Fábrica de Tapices and Casa de la Moneda are similarly close, away to the east and southeast.

ERMITA DE SAN ANTONIO DE LA FLORIDA Map pp126–7

☎ 91 542 07 22; Glorieta de San Antonio de la Florida 5; admission free; ⏱ 9.30am-8pm Tue-Fri, 10am-2pm Sat & Sun (varied hours Jul-Aug); Ⓜ Príncipe Pío

Simply extraordinary: the frescoed ceilings of this humble hermitage are among Madrid's most surprising secrets. Recently restored – and also known as the Panteón de Goya – the southern of the two chapels is one of the few places to see Goya masterworks in their original setting, as painted by the master in 1798 on the request of Carlos IV.

Figures on the dome depict the miracle of St Anthony. The saint, who lived in Padua in Italy, heard word from his native Lisbon that his father had been unjustly accused of murder. The saint was whisked miraculously to his hometown from northern Italy, where he tried in vain to convince the judges of his father's innocence. He then demanded that the corpse of the murder victim be placed before the judges. Goya's painting depicts the moment in which St Anthony calls on the corpse (a young man) to rise up and absolve his father. Around them swarms a typical Madrid crowd. It was customary in such works that angels and cherubs appear in the cupola, above all the terrestrial activity, but Goya, never one to let himself be confined within the mores of the day, places the human above the divine.

The painter is buried in front of the altar. His remains were transferred in 1919 from Bordeaux (France), where he had died in self-imposed exile in 1828. Oddly, the skeleton that was exhumed in Bordeaux was missing one important item – the head.

On 13 June every year, it is a Madrid tradition for seamstresses to come here to pray for a partner, although the tradition now extends to many young women from all walks of life.

CEMENTERIO DE LA FLORIDA Map pp126–7

Calle de Francisco Jacinto y Alcantara; Ⓜ Príncipe Pío

Across the train tracks from the Ermita de San Antonio de la Florida is the cemetery where 43 rebels executed by Napoleon's troops lie buried. They were killed on the nearby Montaña del Príncipe Pío in the predawn of 3 May 1808, after the Dos de Mayo uprising. The event was immortalised by Goya and a plaque placed here in 1981. The forlorn cemetery, established in 1796, is usually closed.

CAMPO DEL MORO Map pp126–7

☎ 91 454 88 00; Paseo de la Virgen del Puerto; ⏱ 10am-8pm Mon-Sat, 9am-8pm Sun & holidays Apr-Sep, 10am-6pm Mon-Sat, 9am-6pm Sun & holidays Oct-Mar; Ⓜ Príncipe Pío

From this park you can gain an appreciation of Madrid in its earliest days – it was from here, in what would become known as Campo del Moro (Moor's Field), that an Almoravid army laid siege to the city in 1110. The troops occupied all but the fortress (where the Palacio Real now stands), but the Christian garrison held on until the Al-

ORIENTATION & TRANSPORT: BEYOND THE CENTRE

You'll find the Casa de Campo west of the city centre; it's also home to the Zoo Aquarium de Madrid and Parque de Atracciones. The Museo del Ferrocarril is about 1km south of Atocha station in the former Las Delicias train station. South of Madrid near the town of San Martín de la Vega is Madrid's answer to Disney World: Warner Brothers Movie World. Faunia is southeast of the city centre.

The most efficient way to get to the sights in this section (with the exception of Warner Brothers Movie World, which requires a regional train) is by metro. In some cases you have a short walk afterwards, but overall it's quicker than taking the bus or even driving. The appropriate metro stations are indicated in each entry.

moravid fury abated and their forces retired south. The 20 hectares of gardens that now adorn the site were first laid in the 18th century, with major overhauls in 1844 and 1890. The gardens combine quiet corners that feel like an expansive private garden with the monumental grandeur designed to mimic the gardens surrounding the palace at Versailles; nowhere is the latter more in evidence than along the east–west Pradera, a lush lawn with the Palacio Real as its backdrop. The gardens' centrepiece, which stands halfway along the Pradera, is the elegant Fuente de las Conchas (Fountain of the Shells) designed by Ventura Rodríguez, the Goya of Madrid's 18th-century architecture scene. The only entrance is from Paseo de la Virgen del Puerto.

CASA DE CAMPO Map pp126–7
🚇 Batán

Sometimes called the 'lungs of Madrid', this 17 sq km semiwilderness stretches west of the Río Manzanares. There are prettier and more central parks in Madrid but such is its scope that there are plenty of reasons to visit. And visit the madrileños do, nearly half a million of them every weekend, celebrating the fact that the short-lived republican government of the 1930s opened the park to the public (it was previously the exclusive domain of royalty).

For city-bound madrileños with neither the time nor the inclination to go further afield, it has become the closest they get to nature, despite the fact that cyclists, walkers and picnickers overwhelm the byways and trails that crisscross the park. There are tennis courts and a swimming pool, as well as a zoo (Zoo Aquarium de Madrid; p128) and an amusement park (Parque de Atracciones; p128). At Casa de Campo's southern end, restaurants specialise in wedding receptions, ensuring plenty of bridal parties roam the grounds in search of an unoccupied patch of greenery where they can take photos. Also in the park, the Andalucian-style ranch known as Batán is used to house the bulls destined to do bloody battle in the Fiestas de San Isidro Labrador.

Although it's largely for the better, something has definitely been lost from the days before 2003 when unspoken intrigues surrounded the small artificial lake (🚇 Lago), where several lakeside terrazas and eateries were frequented by an odd combination

of day-trippers, working girls and clients. By night, prostitutes jockeyed for position while punters kept their places around the lakeside chiringuitos (open-air bars or kiosks) as though nothing out of the ordinary was happening. The traffic in the middle of the night here was akin to rush hour in the city centre. The police shut this scene down and, thankfully, there are no more louche traffic jams, at least on weekends.

REAL FÁBRICA DE TAPICES Map pp126–7
🕿 91 434 05 50; www.realfabricadetapices.com, in Spanish; Calle de Fuenterrabía 2; admission €2.50; ⏰ 10am-2pm Mon-Fri Sep-Jul; 🚇 Atocha or Menéndez Pelayo

If a wealthy Madrid nobleman wanted to impress, he came here to the Royal Tapestry Workshop where royalty commissioned the pieces that adorned their palaces and private residences. The Spanish government, Spanish royalty and the Vatican were the biggest patrons of the tapestry business: Spain alone is said to have collected four million tapestries. With such an exclusive clientele, it was a lucrative business and remains so, 300 years after the factory was founded. Its connections to the Madrid of the 18th century become even more important when it is remembered that Goya began his career here, first as a cartoonist and later as a tapestry designer. Given such an illustrious history, it is, therefore, somewhat surprising that coming here today feels like visiting a carpet shop with small showrooms strewn with fine tapestries and carpets. If you know your stuff, however, you'll soon see that what's on display is of the highest quality (with prices to match). If you're lucky, you'll get to see how they're made.

CASA DE LA MONEDA Map pp126–7
🕿 91 566 65 44; www.fnmt.es; Calle del Doctor Esquerdo 36; admission free; ⏰ 10am-5.30pm Tue-Fri, 10am-2pm Sat & Sun & holidays; 🚇 O'Donnell

The national mint (literally the 'house of coin') is a collectors' treasure-trove of coins from Ancient Greece and Roman Spain and proceeds through the Byzantine, Visigothic and Islamic periods. The latter period is particularly well represented. Coins from the days of the Catholic Monarchs abound, and the collection continues through to the establishment of the peseta as the Spanish currency – only consigned to history by the introduction of the euro in 2002. Paper

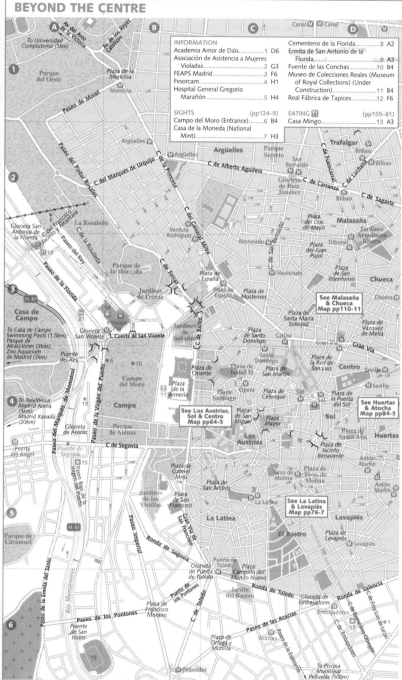

INFORMATION

Academia Amor de Diós............1	D6
Asociación de Asistencia a Mujeres Violadas.....................2	G3
FEAPS Madrid.........................3	F6
Fesorcam................................4	H1
Hospital General Gregorio Marañón............................5	H4

SIGHTS (pp124–9)

Campo del Moro (Entrance)......6	B4
Casa de la Moneda (National Mint)...............................7	H3
Cementerio de la Florida............8	A2
Ermita de San Antonio de la Florida...............................9	A3
Fuente de las Conchas..............10	B4
Museo de Colecciones Reales (Museum of Royal Collections) (Under Construction).....................11	B4
Real Fábrica de Tapices............12	F6

EATING (pp155–81)

Casa Mingo.............................13	A3

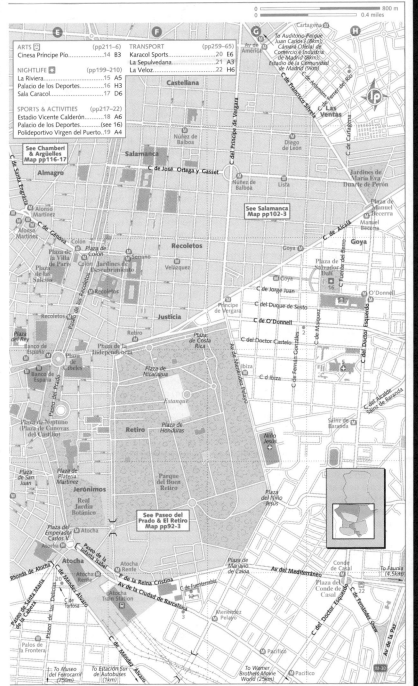

See Chamberí & Argüelles Map pp116–17

See Salamanca Map pp102–3

See Paseo del Prado & El Retiro Map pp92–3

To Auditorio Parque Juan Carlos I (8km);
Cámara Oficial de Comercio e Industria de Madrid (8km);
Estadio de la Comunidad de Madrid (9km)

To Museo del Ferrocarril (750m)

To Estación Sur de Autobuses (1km)

To Warner Brothers Movie World (25km)

To Faunia (4.5km)

top picks

SIGHTS BEYOND THE CENTRE

- Ermita de San Antonio de la Florida (p124)
- Warner Brothers Movie World right
- Casa de Campo (p125)
- Faunia (opposite)
- Zoo Aquarium de Madrid (below)

money ranges from a 14th-century Chinese note to revolutionary Russian cash. Also on display is an extensive collection of prints and *grabados* (etchings), lottery tickets since 1942 and stamps. You can also follow the processes involved in coining money and even strike your own medal. If you're an old-money buff, a visit to the Plaza Mayor (p61) on Sunday morning, when the porticoes are crowded with dealers selling coins, stamps and banknotes, will nicely complement your visit to the mint.

ZOO AQUARIUM DE MADRID

☎ 91 512 37 70; www.zoomadrid.com; Casa de Campo; adult/child 3-7yr & senior €16.90/13.70; ☼ hours vary; Ⓜ Batán

Madrid's zoo, in the Casa de Campo, is a fairly standard European city zoo and home to about 3000 animals. Exhibits range from Emperor scorpions to scary green mambas, as well as zebras, giraffes, rhinoceroses, leopards, flamingos, grey kangaroos, rattlesnakes, wolves and some recently arrived celebrity pandas. There's also a fine aquarium and you can watch dolphins and sea lions get up to their tricks in the Delfinario. Shows are held at least a couple of times a day. The 3000 sq metre Aviario (aviary) contains some 60 species of eagle, condor and vulture.

PARQUE DE ATRACCIONES

☎ 91 463 29 00; www.parquedeatracciones .es in Spanish; Casa de Campo; admission €9.30, admission & unlimited rides adult/child under 7yr €27.50/18; ☼ hours vary; Ⓜ Batán

There's not much that's especially Spanish about this amusement park, located about 300 m from the Parque de Atracciones, but it's got the usual collection of high-adrenaline rides, shows for the kids and kitsch at every turn. In the Zona de Máquinas (the rather omi-

nous sounding Machines Zone) are most of the bigger rides, such as the Siete Picos (Seven Peaks, a classic roller coaster), the Lanzadera (which takes you up 63m and then drops you in a simulated bungee jump), La Máquina (a giant wheel that spins on its axis) and the favourite of all, the Tornado, a kind of upside-down roller coaster that zips along at up to 80km per hour. Strictly for those with cast-iron stomachs.

After all that gut-churning stuff, you'll be grateful for the Zona de Tranquilidad, where you can climb aboard a gentle Ferris wheel, take a theme ride through the jungle or just sit back for a snack. Of course, tranquillity is relative – El Viejo Caserón (haunted house) is not for the nervous among you (in our experience, it's the adults who get spooked). La Zona de la Naturaleza (Nature Zone) offers, among other things, Dodgems and various water rides.

Finally, in the Zona Infantil, younger kids can get their own thrills on less hair-raising rides, such as a Ford-T, the Barón Rojo (Red Baron) and Caballos del Oeste (Horses of the Wild West).

The park, in the Casa de Campo, has all sorts of timetable variations, so it is always a good idea to check before committing yourself.

WARNER BROTHERS MOVIE WORLD

☎ 902 024 100; www.parquewarner.com; San Martín de la Vega; 11-59yr €33, 5-10yr €25; ☼ from 10am, closing hours vary; cercanías train (line C3 for Pinto) from Atocha stops in park near San Martín de la Vega

Disney World it ain't but this movie theme-park, 25km south of central Madrid, has much to catch the attention. Kids will love the chance to hang out with Tom and Jerry, while the young-at-heart film buffs among you will be similarly taken with the Wild West or remakes of the studio sets for such Hollywood 'greats' as *Police Academy*. Entrance to the park is via Hollywood Boulevard, not unlike LA's Sunset Boulevard, whereafter you can choose between Cartoon World, the Old West, Hollywood Boulevard, Super Heroes (featuring Superman, Batman and the finks of Gotham City) and finally Warner Brothers Movie World Studios. It's all about the stars of the silver screen coming to life as life-sized cartoon characters roam the grounds, and rides and high-speed roller coasters (up to 90km per hour!) distract you if attention starts to wane. There are also restaurants and shops.

To get here by car, take the N-IV (the Carretera de Andalucía) south out of Madrid and turn off at Km22 for San Martín de la Vega, about 15km east of the exit. Follow the signs to the car park, where parking is available for €5.

Opening times are complex and do change – check before heading out.

MUSEO DEL FERROCARRIL
☎ 902 228 822; Paseo de las Delicias 61; adult/student & senior €4/2.50; ⏰ 10am-3pm Tue-Sun Sep-Jul; Ⓜ Delicias

You don't have to be a trainspotter to enjoy this railway museum – you'll see as many kids as anoraks – but it helps. Housed in the disused 1880s Estación de Delicias south of Lavapiés, this museum has about 30 pieces of rolling stock lined up along the platforms, ranging from the earliest steam locomotives to a sleeping car from the late 1920s and the *Talgo II*, which ran on the country's long-distance routes until 1971. Several rooms off the platforms are set aside for dioramas of train stations, memorabilia, station clocks and the like. There are plenty of model trains and tracks at the shop on the way out.

FAUNIA
☎ 91 301 62 35; www.faunia.es, in Spanish; Avenida de las Comunidades 28; adult/child under 12yr & senior €23/17; ⏰ hours vary; Ⓜ Valdebernardo

This modern animal theme park takes you through a range of thematic areas, including an aviary, an insectarium, a parade of more than 70 penguins in the snow, an Amazon jungle scene (complete with simulated tropical storm), and performing dolphins and sea lions. Faunia is located east of the M-40, about 7km from the city centre.

SHOPPING

top picks

- **El Rastro** (p136)
  A bargain-hunter's Sunday paradise.
- **Mercado de Fuencarral** (p151)
  Down-and-dirty streetwear with dozens of shops.
- **Antigua Casa Talavera** (p133)
  Traditional ceramics like they used to be made.
- **El Arco Artesanía** (p134)
  Creative modern souvenirs just off the Plaza Mayor.
- **Helena Rohner** (p136)
  Designer jewellery from the catwalks.
- **Agatha Ruiz de la Prada** (p138)
  Spain's premier and most colourful designer.
- **Gallery** (p139)
  Salamanca fashions for the male sophisticate.
- **Diedro** (p153)
  Brand-name clothes and designer homewares.
- **Tienda Real Madrid** (p154)
  Memorabilia from the world's greatest football club.

What's your recommendation? www.lonelyplanet.com/madrid

SHOPPING

Eager to change your look to blend in with the casual-but-sophisticated Spanish crowd? Tired of bull postcards and tacky flamenco posters? Convinced that your discerning friends back home have taste that extends beyond a polka-dot flamenco dress? In Madrid you'll find it all, as well as English-language bookshops, stores selling Spanish food delicacies and cutting-edge homewares. This is a fantastic city in which to shop and madrileños are some of the finest exponents of the art.

The key to shopping Madrid style is knowing where to look. Salamanca is the home of upmarket fashions, with chic boutiques lining up to showcase the best that Spanish and international designers have to offer. Some of it spills over into Chueca, but Malasaña is Salamanca's true alter ego, home to fashion that's as funky as it is offbeat and ideal for that studied underground look that will fit right in with Madrid's hedonistic after-dark crowd. Central Madrid – whether it's Sol, Huertas or La Latina – offers plenty of individual surprises, although there's little uniformity in what you'll find. That sense is multiplied a hundred-fold in El Rastro market, where madrileños converge in epic numbers on Sunday to pick through the junk in search of treasure.

LOS AUSTRIAS, SOL & CENTRO

The maze of streets around the Plaza Mayor and extending up towards Gran Vía have something for everyone. These are fine streets in which to window-shop unless you're after something specific.

CASA DEL LIBRO Map pp64–5   Bookshop
☎ 91 524 19 00; www.casadellibro.com, in Spanish; Gran Vía 29; ☯ 9.30am-9.30pm Mon-Sat, 11am-9pm Sun; Ⓜ Gran Vía
Spain's answer to Borders, this sprawling megabookshop has titles on just about any topic you can think of. There's a large English- and foreign-language literature section on the ground floor at the back, and nonfiction books in English are elsewhere mixed alongside Spanish titles.

FNAC Map pp64–5   Bookshop
☎ 91 595 61 00; www.fnac.es, in Spanish; Calle de Preciados 28; ☯ 10am-9.30pm Mon-Sat, noon-9.30pm Sun; Ⓜ Callao

This four-storey megastore has a terrific range of CDs, DVDs, electronics and books; English-language books are on the 3rd floor. There's also a news kiosk on the 1st floor with a good range of magazines.

LA BUENA VIDA Map pp64–5   Bookshop
☎ 91 542 91 42; labuenavida@cafedellibro.es; Calle de Vergara 10; ☯ noon-midnight; Ⓜ Ópera
If your idea of browsing in bookshops involves perusing a range of choices over a coffee, you don't have many options in Madrid – most Spanish bookshops are a commercial transaction of buying, then leaving. Thankfully, this new bookshop allows you to do both; we could spend hours in here. It has plans to stock a small selection of books in English and French alongside the mostly Spanish titles.

PETRA'S INTERNATIONAL BOOKSHOP Map pp64–5   Bookshop
☎ 91 541 72 91; Calle de Campomanes 13; ☯ 11am-9pm Mon-Sat; Ⓜ Ópera or Santo Domingo
A wonderful little bookshop (with mostly second-hand stock), Petra's has a great

SALES & OPENING HOURS

The peak shopping season is during *las rebajas,* the annual winter and summer sales, when prices are slashed on just about everything. The winter sales begin around 7 January, just after Three Kings' Day, and last well into February. Summer sales begin in early July and last into August.

The shopping day starts at about 10am and is often broken up by a long lunch from 2pm to 5pm, except in larger stores. Shops reopen after lunch and stay busy until 8pm or even later. Shops selling music and books, as well as some convenience stores, are the only outlets allowed to open every Sunday, although all shops may (and most usually do) open on the first Sunday of every month and throughout December. There are plans to allow more shops to open on Sunday.

top picks

FOR CASUAL FASHION

- Adolfo Domínguez (see the boxed text, p150)
- Mango (see the boxed text, p150)
- Massimo Dutti (Map pp116–17; ☎ 91 593 82 68; www.massimodutti.com; Calle de Fuencarral 139; Ⓜ Quevedo) From the Zara stable; a step up in elegance.
- Zara (Map pp110–11; ☎ 91 521 12 83; www.zara.es; Gran Vía 34; Ⓜ Gran Vía) Popular men's, women's and kids' wear with a sideline in homewares.

selection in all major languages and across most major genres; it's also something of a meeting place for the lively expat community. The friendly owners can point you in the direction of activities in English and other languages. We also like a bookshop with a cat – Safi is its name.

ANTIGUA CASA TALAVERA
Map pp64–5   Ceramics
☎ 91 547 34 17; Calle de Isabel la Católica 2; ⏰ 10am-1.30pm & 5-8pm Mon-Fri, 10am-1.30pm Sat; Ⓜ Santo Domingo
The extraordinary tiled façade of this wonderful old shop conceals an Aladdin's cave of ceramics from all over Spain. This is not the mass-produced stuff aimed at a tourist market, but comes from the small family potters of Andalucía and Toledo, ranging from the decorative (tiles) to the useful (plates, jugs and other kitchen items). The old couple who run the place are delightful.

ASÍ Map pp64–5   Children's
☎ 91 548 28 28; Gran Vía 47; ⏰ 10am-8.30pm Mon-Sat; Ⓜ Callao or Santo Domingo
Exquisite handmade children's dolls, all beautifully attired and overflowing from the shop window, are proffered here. Inside it also sells children's clothes and intricate dolls' houses that are works of art; for the latter, every single item (furniture, saucepans etc) can be purchased individually. None of it's cheap, but they're once-in-a-lifetime purchases.

FLIP Map pp64–5   Clothes & Accessories
☎ 91 366 44 72; www.flipmadrid.com, in Spanish; Calle Mayor 19; ⏰ 10.30am-9pm Mon-Sat; Ⓜ Sol

Too cool for its own good, Flip is funky and edgy with its designer T-shirts, G-Star jeans and brand names like Franklin Marshall, Carhartt, Guess and Diesel, as well as a groovy and often offbeat collection of belts, caps and bags. Staff are as hip as the clothing and always ready with advice. The changing rooms, however, require a contortionist's flexibility.

SALVADOR BACHILLER
Map pp64–5   Clothes & Accessories
☎ 91 559 83 21; www.salvadorbachiller.com; Gran Vía 65; ⏰ 10am-9pm Mon-Thu, to 9.30pm Fri & Sat; Ⓜ Plaza de España or Santo Domingo
The stylish and high-quality leather bags, wallets, suitcases and other accessories of Salvador Bachiller are a staple of Spanish shopping aficionados. This is leather with a typically Spanish twist – the colours are dazzling in bright pinks, yellows and greens. Sound garish? You'll change your mind once you step inside. It also has an outlet in Chueca (Map pp110–11; ☎ 91 523 30 37; Calle de Gravina 11; ⏰ 10.30am-9.30pm Mon-Thu, to 10pm Fri & Sat; Ⓜ Chueca) for superseded stock.

EL CORTE INGLÉS Map pp64–5 Department Store
☎ 91 418 88 00; www.elcorteingles.es, in Spanish; Calle de Preciados 3; ⏰ 10am-10pm Mon-Sat; Ⓜ Sol
In the great tradition of department stores the world over, there's everything you need here from food and furniture to clothes, appliances, toiletries, electronics, books and music. Although you'll pay extra for the convenience of one-stop shopping, the after-sales service is better than most. Branches are scattered throughout the city, including one in Malasaña (Map pp110–11; ☎ 91 454 60 00; Calle de Princesa 56; ⏰ 10am-10pm Mon-Sat;

top picks

FOR ENGLISH-LANGUAGE BOOKS

- Pasajes Librería Internacional (p153)
- Petra's International Bookshop (opposite)
- Booksellers (p153)
- J&J Books & Coffee (p149)
- Altaïr (p153)
- De Viaje (p138)
- Fnac (opposite)
- Casa del Libro (opposite)

top picks

SHOPPING STREETS

- Calle de Serrano (see the boxed text, p139) – for Spanish designers.
- Calle de José Ortega y Gasset (see the boxed text, p138) – for international glamour.
- Calle de Fuencarral (see the boxed text, p150) – for quirky and alternative cool.
- Callejón de Jorge Juan (see the boxed text, p140) – for Spanish designer shoes.
- Calle de Piamonte (see the boxed text, p151) – for exclusive accessories.

(M) Argüelles) and one in Salamanca (Map pp102–3; ☎ 91 432 54 90; Calle de Serrano 47; 🕐 10am-10pm Mon-Sat; (M) Serrano).

CONVENTO DEL CORPUS CRISTI (LAS CARBONERAS) Map pp64–5   Food & Drink
☎ 91 548 37 01; Plaza del Conde de Miranda; 🕐 9.30am-1pm & 4-6.30pm; (M) Ópera
The cloistered nuns at this convent also happen to be fine pastry chefs. You make your request through a door, then grille on Calle del Codo and the products are delivered through a little revolving door that allows the nuns to remain unseen by the outside world.

EL FLAMENCO VIVE Map pp64–5   Music
☎ 91 547 39 17; www.elflamencovive.es; Calle Conde de Lemos 7; 🕐 10am-2pm & 5-9pm Mon-Sat; (M) Ópera
This temple to flamenco has it all, from guitars and songbooks to well-priced CDs, polka-dotted dancing costumes, shoes, colourful plastic jewellery and literature about flamenco. It's the sort of place that will appeal as much to curious first-timers as to serious students of the art. It also organises classes in flamenco guitar (see p269).

EL ARCO ARTESANÍA Map pp64–5   Souvenirs
☎ 91 365 26 80; www.elarcoartesania.com, in Spanish; Plaza Mayor 9; 🕐 11am-9pm; (M) Sol or La Latina
This original shop in the southwestern corner of Plaza Mayor sells an outstanding array of homemade designer souvenirs, from stone and glasswork to jewellery and home fittings. The papier mâché figures are

gorgeous, but there's so much else here to turn your head.

FORTUNATA – LA TIENDA DE MADRID Map pp64–5   Souvenirs
☎ 91 364 16 82; www.latiendademadrid.com; Calle de Toledo 3; 🕐 11am-2.30pm & 5-8.30pm Tue-Sat, 11am-2pm Sun; (M) Sol
For quality Spanish souvenirs and books about Madrid (mostly in Spanish), Fortunata is a cut above most souvenir shops in the city centre. There's very little of the mass-produced tourist kitsch here.

CASA DE DIEGO Map pp64–5   Specialist
☎ 91 522 66 43; www.casadediego.com; Plaza de la Puerta del Sol 12; 🕐 9.30am-8pm Mon-Sat; ☎ Sol
This classic shop has been around since 1858, selling and repairing Spanish fans, shawls, umbrellas and canes. Service is old style and occasionally grumpy, but the fans are works of antique art.

CASA HERNANZ Map pp64–5   Specialist
☎ 91 366 54 50; Calle de Toledo 18; 🕐 9am-1.30pm & 4.30-8pm Mon-Fri, 10am-2pm Sat; ☎ La Latina or Sol
Comfy, rope-soled alpargatas (espadrilles), Spain's traditional summer footwear, are worn by everyone from the King of Spain to the Pope, and you can buy your own pair at this humble workshop, which has been hand-making the shoes for five generations; you can even get them made to order. Queues form whenever the weather starts to warm up.

JOSÉ RAMÍREZ Map pp64–5   Specialist
☎ 91 531 42 29; www.guitarrasramirez.com; Calle de la Paz 8; 🕐 10am-2pm & 4.30-8pm; (M) Sol
José Ramírez is one of Spain's best guitar makers and his guitars have been strummed by a host of flamenco greats and international musicians (even the Beatles). Using Honduran cedar, Cameroonian ebony and Indian rosewood among other materials, and based on traditions dating back over generations, this is craftsmanship of the highest order. Out the back there's a little museum with guitars dating back to 1830.

JUSTO ALGABA Map pp64–5   Specialist
☎ 91 523 35 95; www.justoalgaba.com, in Spanish; Calle de la Paz 4; 🕐 10am-2pm & 5-8pm Mon-Fri, 10am-2pm Sat; (M) Sol

TAXES & REFUNDS

Value-added tax (VAT) is known as *impuesto sobre el valor añadido* (IVA; EE-ba). On accommodation and restaurant prices, IVA is 7% and is usually – but not always – included in quoted prices. On retail goods IVA is 16%.

Visitors are entitled to a refund of the 16% IVA on purchases costing more than €90.16, from any shop, if the goods are taken out of the European Union (EU) within three months. Ask the shop for a cashback refund form showing the price and IVA paid for each item, and identifying the vendor and purchaser; then present the form at the customs booth for IVA refunds when you depart from Spain (or elsewhere from the EU). At this point, you'll need your passport and a boarding card that shows you're leaving the EU. The officer will stamp the invoice and you hand it in at a bank at the departure point for the reimbursement. There are refund offices in terminals T1, T2 and T4 at Barajas airport as you're departing from Madrid.

Always wanted to be a torero but didn't have a thing to wear? This is where Spain's toreros come to have their *traje de luces* (suit of lights, the traditional glittering bullfighting suit) made in all its intricate excess. A custom-made suit starts at €2500, a *muleta* (cape) goes for €155, while the sexy pink tights are a steal at €50.

MATY Map pp64–5   Specialist

☎ 91 531 32 91; www.maty.es, in Spanish; Calle del Maestro Victoria 2; ☀ 10am-1.45pm & 4.30-8pm Mon-Fri, 10am-2pm & 4.30-8pm Sat; Ⓜ Sol
Wandering around central Madrid, it's easy to imagine that flamenco outfits have been reduced to imitation dresses sold as souvenirs to tourists. That's why places like Maty matter. Here you'll find dresses, shoes and all the accessories that go with the genre, with sizes for children and adults. It also does quality disguises for Carnaval. These are the real deal, with prices to match, but they make brilliant gifts.

LA LATINA & LAVAPIÉS

La Latina is very much an after-dark or weekend barrio. That said, this is one of the most popular barrios for a hip, well-to-do urban crowd and the small boutiques dotted around the narrow streets reflect this clientele, especially when it comes to designer jewellery. But it's also the barrio that throngs with Sunday bargain hunters drawn here by El Rastro and you'll also come across curio shops so specialised that you wonder how they ever keep going. Down into Lavapiés, the barrio's large immigrant population has fostered a fascinating mix of ethnic shops (Asian food markets, Muslim halal butchers and stores selling gifts imported from China).

LA LIBRERÍA DE LAVAPIÉS

Map pp76–7   Bookshop

☎ 91 527 89 92; www.libreriadelavapies.com, in Spanish; Calle de Argumosa 39; ☀ 10am-10pm Mon-Sat, 11am-9pm Sun; Ⓜ Lavapiés or Atocha
If you value personal service, a community feel and the sort of cosy charm that lends itself to browsing, this alternative bookshop is perfect. There's a carefully chosen English section, as well as contemporary literature, the arts, and books for families and children.

DEL HIERRO Map pp76–7   Clothes & Accessories

☎ 91 364 58 91; Calle de la Cava Baja 6; ☀ 11.30am-2.30pm & 5-9pm Mon-Sat, noon-3pm Sun; Ⓜ La Latina or Tirso de Molina
If you're looking for a handbag that captures the essence of chic, modern Spain, then this small boutique has an exceptional selection from designers such as Iñaki Sampedro, Quique Mestre and Carlos de Caz. The look is sophisticated but colourful.

ESPACIO FLAMENCO Map pp76–7   Flamenco

☎ 91 298 70 45; www.deflamenco.com/tiendas/espacioflamenco/indexi.jsp; Calle de la Ribera de Curtidores 26; ☀ 11am-2pm & 5.30-8.30pm Mon-Fri, 11am-2.30pm Sat & Sun; Ⓜ Puerta de Toledo
This small temple to all things flamenco has just about any flamenco CD you could want, from classic Camarón to nuevo flamenco, as well as castanets, flamenco dresses and shoes, and DVDs.

CARMEN SÁNCHEZ Map pp76–7   Jewellery

☎ 91 366 74 01; carmensanchezjoyas@hotmail.com; Calle de la Cava Baja 25; ☀ noon-3pm & 7-9pm Tue-Sat, noon-5pm Sun; Ⓜ La Latina
This charming little boutique serves up sophisticated, individually crafted jewellery with the occasional quirky twist. Silver, enamel and beautiful colour combinations

EL RASTRO & THE FLEA MARKETS OF MADRID

Flea markets, fresh markets, crafts markets…bargain hunters will have a field day in Madrid. The city's biggest and best-known market is El Rastro, by some accounts the largest flea market in Europe and a thriving mass of vendors, buyers, pickpockets and the generally curious. This classic flea market, open on Sunday morning only, has been an open-air market for half a millennium.

The madness begins at the Plaza de Cascorro, near La Latina metro stop, and worms its way downhill along the Calle de la Ribera de Curtidores and the streets off it. The shopping starts at about 8am and lasts until 2pm or 3pm, but for many madrileños the best of El Rastro comes after the stalls have shut and everyone crowds into the nearby bars of La Latina for an *aperitivo* (appetizer) of vermouth and tapas.

Apart from El Rastro, other curious local markets include the following:

Art Market (Map pp64–5; Plaza del Conde de Barajas; ☽ 10am-2pm Sun; Ⓜ Sol) Local art and prints of the greats.

Cuesta de Moyano Bookstalls (opposite)

Mercadillo Marqués de Viana (El Rastrillo; Map p123; Calle del Marqués de Viana; ☽ 9am-2pm Sun; Ⓜ Tetuán) A calmer version of El Rastro in northern Madrid.

Mercado de Monedas y Sellos (Map pp64–5; Plaza Mayor; ☽ 9am-2pm Sun; Ⓜ Sol) Old coins and stamps.

---

are the hallmark. If you're on your way back from El Rastro, this is a good way to add a touch of class to your treasure hunting.

HELENA ROHNER Map pp76–7 Jewellery
☎ 91 365 79 06; www.helenarohner.com; Calle del Almendro 4; ☽ 9am-8.30pm Mon-Fri, noon-2.30pm & 3.30-8pm Sat, noon-3pm Sun; Ⓜ La Latina or Tirso de Molina
One of Europe's most creative jewellery designers, Helena Rohner has a spacious, chic boutique in La Latina. Working with silver, stone, porcelain, wood and Murano glass, she makes inventive pieces and her work is a regular feature of Paris fashion shows. In her own words, she seeks to re-create 'the magic of Florence, the vitality of London and the luminosity of Madrid'. She has also recently branched out into homewares.

EL RASTRO Map pp76–7 Market
Calle de la Ribera de Curtidores; ☽ 8am-3pm Sun; Ⓜ La Latina, Puerta de Toledo or Tirso de Molina
A Sunday morning at El Rastro is a Madrid institution. You could easily spend an entire morning inching your way down the Calle de la Ribera de Curtidores and through the maze of streets that hosts El Rastro flea market every Sunday morning. Cheap clothes, luggage, old flamenco records, even older photos of Madrid, faux designer purses, grungy T-shirts, household goods and electronics are the main fare, but for every 10 pieces of junk, there's a real gem (a lost masterpiece, an Underwood typewriter) waiting to be found. Antiques

are also a major drawcard for traders and treasure hunters alike.

A word of warning: pickpockets love El Rastro as much as everyone else, so keep a tight hold on your belongings and don't keep valuables in easy-to-reach pockets.

For information on the history of El Rastro, see p74.

HUERTAS & ATOCHA

Although you'll stumble across some quirky little boutiques tucked away in the lanes of the Barrio de las Letras, you wouldn't come to Huertas just for the shopping. Most of the shops of interest are in the streets close to the Plaza de la Puerta del Sol.

MÉXICO Map pp84–5 Antiques
☎ 91 429 94 76; Calle de las Huertas 20; ☽ 9am-2pm & 5-8pm Mon-Fri, 9am-2pm Sat; Ⓜ Antón Martín
A treasure chest of original old maps, this is a great place to find a unique souvenir of Spain. Some 160 folders hold antique, original maps of Madrid, Spain and the rest of the world. These are all originals or antique copies, not modern reprints, so prices range from a few hundred to thousands of euros. Just down the road, México II (☎ 91 429 58 12; Calle de las Huertas 17) sells cheaper reprints.

LA CENTRAL – LIBRERÍA DE CENTRO DE ARTE REINA SOFÍA Map pp84–5 Bookshop
☎ 91 787 87 82; www.lacentral.com, in Spanish; Ronda de Atocha 2; ☽ 10am-9pm Mon-Sat, to 2.30pm Sun; Ⓜ Atocha

Part of the stunning extension to the Centro de Arte Reina Sofía, this outstanding shop is Madrid's best gallery bookshop, with a range of posters and postcards as well as extensive sections on contemporary art, design, architecture and photography.

GIL Map pp84–5 — Clothes & Accessories

☎ 91 521 25 49; Carrera de San Jerónimo 2; ⏰ 9.30am-1.30pm & 4.30-8pm Mon-Fri, 9.30am-1.30pm Sat; Ⓜ Sol

You don't see them much these days, but the exquisite fringed and embroidered *mantones* and *mantoncillos* (traditional Spanish shawls worn by women on grand occasions) and delicate *mantillas* (Spanish veils) are stunning and uniquely Spanish gifts. Gil also sells *abanicos* (Spanish fans). Inside this dark shop, dating back to 1880, the sales clerks still wait behind a long counter to attend to you; the service hasn't changed in years and that's no bad thing. Our only complaint? Kitsch tourist souvenirs (T-shirts and the like) have made an appearance here.

FLAMENCO WORLD Map pp84–5 — Flamenco

☎ 91 360 08 65; www.flamenco-world.com; Calle de las Huertas 62; ⏰ 11am-2.30pm & 4.30-8pm Mon-Fri; Ⓜ Antón Martín

For a terrific range of flamenco CDs and other flamenco-related items, this is one of the better shops in Madrid. The CDs range from the big names to harder-to-find disks, and it sells a small range of other flamenco items.

MARÍA CABELLO Map pp84–5 — Food & Drink

☎ 91 429 60 88; Calle de Echegaray 19; ⏰ 9.30am-3pm & 5.30-9pm Mon-Fri, 9.30am-3pm & 6-9.30pm Sat; Ⓜ Sevilla or Antón Martín

top picks

FOR QUALITY GIFTS

- Antigua Casa Talavera (p133)
- Antigüedades Hom (p153)
- El Arco Artesanía (p134)
- Gil (above)
- México (opposite)
- Casa de Diego (p134)
- Fortunata – La Tienda de Madrid (p134)

You just don't find wine stores like this any more – family run, friendly, with knowledgeable staff, and still decorated in the original 1913 style with wooden shelves and even a ceiling fresco. There are fine wines in abundance (mostly Spanish, and a few foreign bottles) with some 500 labels on show or tucked away out the back.

LOMOGRAPHY Map pp84–5 — Specialist

☎ 91 369 17 99; www.lomospain.com, in Spanish; Calle de Echegaray 5; ⏰ 11am-8.30pm Mon-Fri, to 2pm Sat; Ⓜ Sevilla or Sol

This just proves you can find anything in Madrid. Dedicated to a Russian Kompakt camera that has acquired cult status for its zany colours, fish-eye lenses and anti-cool clunkiness, this eclectic shop sells the cameras (an original will set you back €295), as well as offbeat design items from bags and mugs to kitsch-cool memorabilia loved by adherents of 'lomography'. You can even develop your photos here. And no, there's not a *lomo* (of the cured Spanish meat variety) in sight.

PASEO DEL PRADO & EL RETIRO

The Paseo del Prado is more about grand art galleries and afternoon promenades, but there is one Madrid shopping tradition that you really must seek out.

CUESTA DE MOYANO BOOKSTALLS

Map pp92–3 — Bookshop

Calle de Claudio Moyano; ⏰ 9am-dusk Mon-Sat, to 2pm Sun; Ⓜ Atocha

Madrid's answer to the booksellers that line the Seine in Paris, these second-hand bookstalls are an enduring Madrid landmark. Most titles are in Spanish, but there's a handful of offerings in other languages.

SALAMANCA

Salamanca is Madrid's designer central, home to the richest concentration of exclusive boutiques anywhere in Spain. Shopping here is a social event where people put on their finest and service is often impeccable, if a little stuffy. Fashions range from classically elegant to cool and cutting edge, from leading and upcoming Spanish designers to the big names in international fashion. But above all, this is the

CLOTHING SIZES

Women's clothing

Aus/UK	8	10	12	14	16	18
Europe	36	38	40	42	44	46
Japan	5	7	9	11	13	15
USA	6	8	10	12	14	16

Women's shoes

Aus/USA	5	6	7	8	9	10
Europe	35	36	37	38	39	40
France only	35	36	38	39	40	42
Japan	22	23	24	25	26	27
UK	3½	4½	5½	6½	7½	8½

Men's clothing

Aus	92	96	100	104	108	112
Europe	46	48	50	52	54	56
Japan	S		M	M		L
UK/USA	35	36	37	38	39	40

Men's shirts (collar sizes)

Aus/Japan	38	39	40	41	42	43
Europe	38	39	40	41	42	43
UK/USA	15	15½	16	16½	17	17½

Men's shoes

Aus/UK	7	8	9	10	11	12
Europe	41	42	43	44½	46	47
Japan	26	27	27½	28	29	30
USA	7½	8½	9½	10½	11½	12½

Measurements approximate only, try before you buy

barrio to take the pulse of the Spanish fashion scene and you'll likely find it in rude health. (For the lowdown on Spain's fashion industry, turn to p53). Throw in a sprinkling of gourmet food shops and designer homewares and you could easily spend days doing little else but shop.

DE VIAJE Map pp102–3   Bookshop

☎ 91 577 98 99; www.deviaje.com, in Spanish; Calle de Serrano 41; ☒ 10am-8.30pm Mon-Fri, 10.30am-2.30pm & 5-8pm Sat; Ⓜ Serrano
Whether you're after a guidebook, a coffee-table tome or travel literature, De Viaje probably has it. Covering every region of the world, it has mostly Spanish titles, but plenty in English as well. Staff are incredibly helpful and very knowledgeable. There's also a travel agency, with a travel gear section and regular exhibitions of travel photos.

IMAGINARIUM Map pp102–3   Children's

☎ 91 781 33 37; www.imaginarium.es, in Spanish; Calle de Claudio Coello 45; ☒ 10am-8.30pm Mon-Sat; Ⓜ Serrano
This wonderfully personal toy shop sells creative toys, books and games; it treats kids respectfully here, with separate entrances for kids and adults. There are other branches all across town, including one in Argüelles (Map pp116–17; ☎ 91 444 56 09; Calle de Carranza 20; ☒ 10am-8.30pm Mon-Sat; Ⓜ San Bernardo).

AGATHA RUIZ DE LA PRADA

Map pp102–3   Clothes & Accessories
☎ 91 319 05 01; www.agatharuizdelaprada.com; Calle de Serrano 27; ☒ 10am-8.30pm Mon-Sat; Ⓜ Serrano
This boutique has to be seen to be believed, with pinks, yellows and oranges everywhere you turn. It's fun and exuberant, but not just for kids. It also has serious and highly original fashion; Agatha Ruiz de la Prada is one of the enduring icons of Madrid's 1980s outpouring of creativ-

SHOPPING STREET – CALLE DE JOSÉ ORTEGA Y GASSET

The world's most exclusive international designers occupy what is known as la milla del oro (the golden mile) along Calle de José Ortega y Gasset (Map pp102–3; Ⓜ Nuñez de Balboa), close to the corner with Calle de Serrano. All of the following shops are open from 10am to 8.30pm Monday to Saturday unless otherwise stated.

On the south side of the street, there's Giorgio Armani (☎ 91 577 58 07; www.armani.com; Calle de José Ortega y Gasset 16), Dolce & Gabbana (☎ 91 781 09 10; www.dolcegabbana.es; Calle de José Ortega y Gasset 14), Chanel (☎ 91 431 30 36; www.chanel.com; Calle de José Ortega y Gasset 14), Hermès (☎ 91 577 76 09; www.hermes.com; Calle de José Ortega y Gasset 12), Burberry (☎ 91 575 82 99; www.burberry.com; Calle de José Ortega y Gasset 8) and Dior (☎ 91 781 08 10; www.dior.com; Calle de José Ortega y Gasset 6). Just across the road is Louis Vuitton (☎ 91 575 13 08; www.louisvuitton.com; Calle de José Ortega y Gasset 17), Jimmy Choo (☎ 91 781 86 08; www.jimmychoo.com; Calle de José Ortega y Gasset 15) and Cartier (☎ 91 576 22 81; www.cartier.com; cnr Calles de José Ortega y Gasset & de Serrano). Also in the vicinity is Gucci (☎ 91 431 17 17; www.gucci.com; cnr Calles de José Ortega y Gasset & de Serrano). What more could you want?

SHOPPING STREET – CALLE DE SERRANO

Sometimes likened to Paris' Champs Élysées, glamorous Calle de Serrano (Map pp102–3; M Serrano) is lined with big-name Spanish designers – opening a boutique along this street is an announcement of arrival as a national fashion icon. The colours of Agatha Ruiz de la Prada (p137) find their classy (and expensive) counterpoint in Loewe (☎ 91 426 35 88; Calle de Serrano 34; ☼ 9.30am-8.30pm Mon-Sat; M Serrano), whose clothes and accessories are regulars on the Paris catwalk. Purificación García (☎ 91 576 72 76; Calle de Serrano 92; ☼ 10am-8.30pm Mon-Sat; M Nuñez de Balboa) is one of the most successful Spanish designers, offering elegant, mature designs for men and women that are as at home in the workplace as at a wedding. Roberto Verino (☎ 91 426 04 75; Calle de Serrano 33; ☼ 10am-9pm Mon-Sat; M Serrano) is the purveyor of simple, classy designs for men and women. Manolo Blahnik (☎ 91 575 96 48; Calle de Serrano 58; ☼ 10am-2pm & 4.30-8.30pm Mon-Sat; M Serrano) is one of Spain's women's shoe designers *par excellence*; the shoes are displayed in the shop like works of art and have appeared more times at the Oscars than Javier Bardem.

ity known as *la movida madrileña* (see the boxed text, p33).

AMAYA ARZUAGA
Map pp102–3   Clothes & Accessories
☎ 91 426 28 15; www.amayaarzuaga.com; Calle de Lagasca 50; ☼ 10.30am-8.30pm Mon-Wed, to 9pm Thu-Sat; M Velázquez

Amaya Arzuaga has sexy, bold options. She loves mixing black with bright colours (one season it's 1980s fuchsia and turquoise, the next it's orange or red) and has earned a reputation as one of the most creative designers in Spain today.

ARMAND BASI Map pp102–3 Clothes & Accessories
☎ 91 577 79 93; www.armandbasi.com; Calle de Claudio Coello 52; ☼ 10am-2pm & 5-9pm Mon-Sat; M Serrano

With hip, urban designs for men and women, this is the place to go when you want to look fashionable but carelessly casual; the look is perfectly suited to a night out in the city's bars, especially Chueca.

CAMPER Map pp102–3   Clothes & Accessories
☎ 91 578 25 60; www.camper.es; Calle de Serrano 24; ☼ 10am-8.30pm Mon-Sat; M Serrano

Spanish fashion is not all *haute couture*, and this world-famous cool and quirky shoe brand from Mallorca offers bowling-shoe chic with colourful, fun designs that are all about comfort. There are other outlets throughout the city.

DAVIDELFÍN Map pp102–3   Clothes & Accessories
☎ 91 700 04 53; www.davidelfin.com; Calle de Jorge Juan 31; ☼ 10.30am-2.30pm & 4.30-8.30pm Mon-Sat; M Velázquez

This young Spanish designer combines catwalk fashions with a rebellious spirit. The look is young, sometimes edgy and an enthusiastic nod to the avant-garde.

EKSEPTION & EKS
Map pp102–3   Clothes & Accessories
☎ 91 577 43 53; Calle de Velázquez 28; ☼ 10.30am-2.30pm & 5-9pm Mon-Sat; M Velázquez

The catwalk-like entrance is the perfect introduction to brand names dedicated to urban chic, with Balenciaga, Kokosalaki and Dries van Noten displayed like a gallery showroom in one shop and younger, more casual lines next door.

GALLERY Map pp102–3   Clothes & Accessories
☎ 91 576 79 31; www.gallerymadrid.com; Calle de Jorge Juan 38; ☼ 10.30am-8.30pm Mon-Sat; M Príncipe de Vergara or Velázquez

This stunning showpiece of men's fashions and accessories (shoes, bags, belts and the like) is the new Madrid in a nutshell – stylish, brand conscious and all about having the right look. With an interior designed by Tomas Alia, it's one of the city's coolest shops for men.

MO BY MARÍA ROCA
Map pp102–3   Clothes & Accessories
☎ 91 577 88 04; www.mobymariaroca.com, in Spanish; Calle del Conde de Aranda 10; ☼ 10.30am-8pm Mon-Sat; M Retiro

Tucked away in a quiet corner of Salamanca, this wonderful boutique sells handbags, jewellery and other accessories. The look ranges from classical to quirky and colourful – only a shop with a loyal following such as this one dares to make leopard skin fashionable again.

SHOPPING STREET – CALLEJÓN DE JORGE JUAN

The small pedestrianised street of Callejón de Jorge Juan (Map pp102–3; M Serrano) is a sanctuary of civility, lined with *haute couture* boutiques whose designers are regulars on the catwalk of Madrid's Pasarela Cibeles. Alma Aguilar (☎ 91 577 66 96; www.almaaguilar.com; Callejón de Jorge Juan 12; ☾ 10am-2pm & 5-8pm Mon-Sat) is a classy Madrid designer known for her stylish formal wear for women. Roberto Torretta (☎ 91 435 79 89; www.robertotorretta.com, in Spanish; Callejón de Jorge Juan 14; ☾ 10.30am-2pm & 5-8.30pm Mon-Fri, 11am-2pm & 5-8.30pm Sat) specialises in romantic, yet practical design, combining casual and formal wardrobes. Sybilla (☎ 91 578 13 22; Callejón de Jorge Juan 12; ☾ 10.30am-8.30pm Mon-Sat) is one of the more original Spanish designers, who combines local and international styles with strong, Spanish colours and deceptively simple pieces with stylish cuts that stand out in the crowd. The trademark of Pedro García (☎ 91 575 34 41; www.pedrogarcia.com; Callejón de Jorge Juan 14; ☾ 10.30am-8.30pm Mon-Fri, 10.30am-2pm & 5-8.30pm Sat) is elegant shoes for women.

SARA NAVARRO
Map pp102–3　　　　　　Clothes & Accessories
☎ 91 576 23 24; www.saranavarro.com; Calle de Jorge Juan 22; ☾ 10.30am-8.30pm Mon-Sat; M Velázquez

Spanish women love their shoes and, perhaps above all, they love Sara Navarro. This designer seems to understand that you may only rarely buy expensive shoes like these – so why not make each into a perfect work of art? The shop is a temple to good taste, with fine bags, belts and other accessories. It also does a line in matching mother-daughter sets.

BOMBONERÍA SANTA
Map pp102–3　　　　　　　　　　Food & Wine
☎ 91 576 86 46; Calle de Serrano 56; ☾ 10am-3pm & 3.30-8.30pm Mon-Sat; M Serrano

If your style is as refined as your palate, the exquisite chocolates in this tiny shop will satisfy. The packaging is every bit as pretty as the *bonbones* within, but they're not cheap – a large box will cost around €120!

LAVINIA　Map pp102–3　　　　　Food & Wine
☎ 91 426 06 04; Calle de José Ortega y Gasset 16; ☾ 10am-9pm Mon-Sat; M Núñez de Balboa

Although we love the intimacy of old-style Spanish wine shops, they can't match the selection of Spanish and international wines available at Lavinia, which has more than 4500 bottles to choose from. It also organises wine courses (see p185), wine tastings and excursions to nearby *bodegas* (wineries).

MANTEQUERÍA BRAVO
Map pp102–3　　　　　　　　　　Food & Wine
☎ 91 576 02 93; Calle de Ayala 24; ☾ 9.30am-2.30pm & 5.30-8.30pm Mon-Fri, 9.30am-2.30pm Sat; M Serrano

Behind the attractive old façade lies a connoisseur's paradise, filled with local cheeses, sausages, wines and coffees. The products here are great for a gift, but everything's so good that you won't want to share. Mantequería Bravo won the prize for Madrid's best gourmet food shop or delicatessen – it's as simple as that.

ORIOL BALAGUER　Map pp102–3　　Food & Wine
☎ 91 401 64 63; www.oriolbalaguer.com; Calle de José Ortega y Gasset 44; ☾ 10am-2.30pm & 5-8.30pm Mon-Sat; M Núñez de Balboa

Catalan pastry chef Oriol Balaguer has a formidable CV – he worked in the kitchens of Ferran Adrià in Catalonia and won the prize for the World's Best Dessert (the 'Seven Textures of Chocolate') in 2001. His hugely anticipated chocolate boutique opened with much fanfare in Madrid in March 2008 and it's a combination of a small art gallery and a fashion boutique, except that it's dedicated to exquisite finely crafted chocolate collections and cakes. You'll never be able to buy ordinary chocolate again after a visit here. For an interview with Oriol Balaguer, see p143.

VINÇON　Map pp102–3　　　　　　Homewares
☎ 91 578 05 20; www.vincon.com, in Spanish; Calle de Castelló 18; ☾ 10am-8.30pm Mon-Sat; M Príncipe de Vergara

Conceived in Barcelona when the city was Europe's centre of cool, Vinçon's popularity here recognises the fact that cutting-edge Catalan *disseny* (design) is fast taking hold in the Spanish capital. Sleek and often fun homewares and all sorts of gadgets that you never knew you needed – but suddenly feel you must have – are what it's all about.

(Continued on page 149)

SHOPPING SALAMANCA

LOCAL VOICES

Madrileños are a gregarious lot and boy do they love to talk, often at full volume, often all at once. Walk into any crowded Spanish bar and you'll be assailed by a chattering din to the extent that you'll struggle to make yourself heard by the bar staff, let alone the person next to you. It's not because they love the sound of their own voices. Rather, life Madrid-style is a social event and the art of good conversation is alive and well in the Spanish capital.

The young, laid-back and sassy Madrid of the 21st century is a radically different world to that of the parents and grandparents of today's younger generation. Old Madrid was a world of strictures and strong social codes, of dour Francoist limits on freedom, and conservative Catholic mores. These madrileños developed a reputation for reserve and conservatism, forced to focus inwards due to bleak Castilian winters and by living in close proximity to the powers that be.

Younger madrileños couldn't be more different. Liberated from the shackles that bound their parents, those who grew up in the post-Franco years did so believing that theirs was a world without limits. They're not entirely sure about the changing face of their city as a result of immigration – one-in-five Madrid residents has relocated here from elsewhere – but by and large newcomers are made to feel welcome. Through it all madrileños manage that rare city combination – leading generally frenetic lives but giving the impression of being quite relaxed about it all. What follows are conversations with seven locals, adopted or otherwise, as diverse as the city itself.

'Killing the night', à la Hemingway, in one of Madrid's many bars

Name Agatha Ruiz de la Prada
Occupation Fashion designer
Interviewed in Salamanca

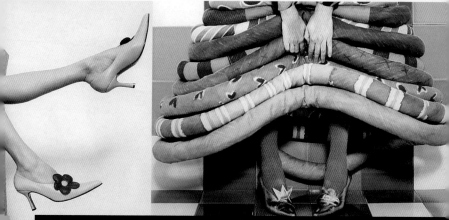

Kick up your heels and celebrate the vibrant, oh-so-madrileño edge of the city's doyenne of cool, Agatha Ruiz de la Prada (below), at her Salamanca store (p138)

What is it about Madrid? Madrid has very good vibrations. It's a very happy city. From the outset, people in Madrid are very open and you can make friends easily.

What do you miss when you're not in Madrid? The climate. It can make you feel quite euphoric and gives you lots of energy. And the light in Madrid is very beautiful.

What's special about people in Madrid? Madrid is a city where we don't have anything. We don't have the sea etc. So we have to go in search of life.

What's the biggest change you've seen in Spain in your lifetime? When I was a child Spain was really poor, so poor that we used to go to France to buy butter. Now we're a rich country. We were the worst country in the world and now, all of a sudden, we're the best brand name in the world.

Would you like to be mayor of Madrid one day? I would love to. I would stop all my designing just to be mayor of Madrid. It would be so much fun, organising parties, organising parties…

Name Oriol Balaguer
Occupation Chocolate revolutionary, pastry chef and proprietor of Oriol Balaguer Chocolate Boutique, Salamanca
Interviewed in Sol

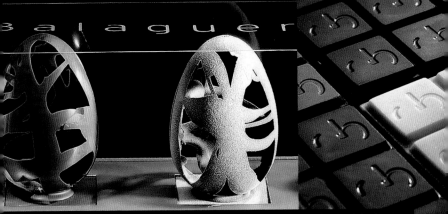

Death by chocolate courtesy of the delicacies on offer at Oriol Balaguer's chocolate laboratory (p140), including his prize-winning Seven Textures of Chocolate (bottom); talking sweet treats with fellow gastronomer Tetsuya Wakuda (middle)

Your father was also a pastry chef. I was born wrapped in the smell of chocolate. I became impregnated by it.

You worked with master chef Ferran Adrià. What did you learn? A way of cooking and thinking that I had never seen before and to always believe that you can go one step further.

In 2001 you won the prize for the 'Best Dessert in the World'. What was it? The Seven Textures of Chocolate where I amalgamated seven different textures of chocolate. It's a dessert for lovers and for those obsessed with chocolate.

What's your philosophy of desserts? A dessert must create happiness, excitement.

What role does tradition have in your cooking? I have a series of recipes based around memories of my childhood, which I have updated for the 21st century. But I am much more motivated if I start with something unknown.

Why is Spanish food all the rage? We have great designers, sculptors, creators, painters and architects and this creative atmosphere has spilled over into the world of gastronomy.

If your work were to have a parallel in music, what would it be? There are moments when it could be jazz, others classical music and, occasionally, Bruce Springsteen.

Name Carlos Baute
Occupation Latin American music star and Madrid resident
Interviewed in Salamanca

The life, the music, the marcha: *Madrid's many action-filled plazas bring out the locals to enjoy the night*

What do you like most about Madrid? How open the people are, the great weather, the *marcha* (action or nightlife).

Where do you go for a late-night *copa* (drink)? Café Olivier and The Penthouse at Me by Meliá.

A favourite nightclub? Pachá.

Best barrios for shopping? Salamanca and Calle de Fuencarral.

Favourite Spanish designers? For men Davidelfín, for women Alma Aguilar.

Have you seen many changes in Madrid? Since I arrived seven years ago, Madrid has become a modern city, opening so many new places, following all the latest trends and even setting a few of its own.

Madrid or Barcelona? They're very different. Madrid is much more traditional, classic, but I love that because it never goes out of fashion. I love the modern and avant-garde of Barcelona, but I'll stick with classic Madrid.

Name Fernando
Occupation Waiter at Café Comercial
Interviewed in Malasaña

Serving the perfect cup of coffee is serious business at Café Comercial (p193), traditional coffee house and scene of many an intellectual tertulia *(literary discussion) in the '50s and '60s*

This café's been around for a while. It was opened in 1860 by a priest and it's been in my family for four generations.

How long have you been a waiter here? I grew up in here, but 20 years as a waiter and behind the bar.

Has the café changed over the years? Not a bit. The last renovations were in 1958.

No changes at all? Ten or 12 years ago we put an internet café upstairs. Downstairs is now nonsmoking. And, as of three years ago, we finally have female waiters!

Are they good? They work better than the men.

Has the clientele changed? We've always had customers from children to old people, which is very typical of Madrid. Many famous people as well.

And what they order? People are more health-conscious now – even though later they go out and smoke.

You must have seen some changes. Look at this café and you see Madrid. If the economy's going well, we're going well.

And now? Things are going well, but people have started to order just a coffee instead of coffee and a pastry. So maybe things are starting to change.

Name Manolo Osuna
Occupation President of La Corrala Lavapiés
Neighbours' Association (Asociación de Vecinos La Corrala)
Interviewed in Lavapiés

Explore Lavapiés and discover tranquil streets (bottom) and its lively multicultural spirit in the streetside entertainment (above) around El Rastro market (p74)

Lavapiés is pretty multicultural. There are people living here from every country of the world and from every corner of Spain.

That's quite a mix. Madrid has always grown thanks to the arrival of immigrants from the rest of Spain, then later from the rest of the world. In Lavapiés we've had more practice than anywhere else, but everyone in Madrid is from somewhere else.

What's Lavapiés' secret? This is a very traditional Madrid barrio, but people who live in Lavapiés are neighbours, not immigrants, regardless of the colour of their skin.

And it works? Here you won't find the problems of France for example, or even those in other parts of Madrid. We're like a laboratory for Spain because we started receiving immigrants from the beginning. There are some 'immigrants' here who've been in the barrio longer than I have.

The best thing about living here is…that it's like living in a village where everyone knows and greets each other and it doesn't matter where they're from.

It's not a ghetto? Some Chinese community leaders came to us recently and asked if we wanted to turn Lavapiés into Madrid's Chinatown. We said yes, but we'd also like to turn it into a Moroccantown, a Senegalesetown…

Name James Nicol
Occupation Long-time British resident of Madrid and head of IT in film distribution
Interviewed in Los Austrias/La Latina

Live music is thriving in Madrid and the energy of the city's nightlife is captured perfectly at many venues around town, including Café Central (p206)

How long have you lived here? Seven years working and living in Madrid: classy Chamberí, multicultural Tetuán (Northern Madrid) and now Los Austrias right in the centre.

What was the most difficult thing to get used to here? The relentless pace of the city. It can be exhausting due to the sensation of never getting out of fifth gear. Now it fills me with energy when I'm short of it and I live, breathe and sleep Spanish.

Where will we find you on Friday or Saturday night? I love the jazz or blues sessions at El Junco or Café Central on Fridays and a more energetic Saturday night dancing to the early hours in any of the bars and discotheques in Huertas.

The secret to living like a local? Make Spanish friends, enrol in a Spanish course and take part in the *intercambios* (cultural language exchanges) that are advertised around town. And be adventurous with the cuisine.

What's the best thing about living here? The energy, vitality, *joie de vivre*, variety and, of course, my great friends. Culture, climate and sheer fun all rolled into one.

Would you ever move back to the UK? Not a chance.

Wandering Madrid's sunny and life-filled streets, you'll never be far from mouth-watering tapas and other delights

It must be tough surviving Madrid nights with so little sleep. It's easy when you're having so much fun and every place is busy. People go out till all hours, even when they have to work the next day!

A favourite barrio? I love Malasaña.

Any good recent discoveries? I just discovered an amazing place, Viva la Vida in Costanilla de San Andrés in La Latina. It's an organic market and vegetarian buffet. Once you finish you can go next door to Café Bar Delic and have a digestive cocktail, such as a *mojito* or *caipirinha*, and cake. And Baco y Beto in Chueca has some of the best tapas in Madrid.

The best thing about living in Madrid? Living right in the city centre. You can enjoy Madrid just going for a walk. If you want peace and solitude, you can find it too – just get lost along its narrow streets and in its cosy squares.

Madrid's best-kept secret? Its never-ending activity. The city never sleeps, always spying, mixing and changing…A refreshing spirit!

The best thing about being a woman in Madrid? When you go out, the sun shines on your face and you feel so warm and beautiful that you want to merge into the city.

Madrid is…whatever you want it to be.

(Continued from page 140)

TOUS Map pp102–3 Jewellery

☎ 91 575 51 71; www.tous.com; Calle de Claudio Coello 65; ⏰ 10am-2pm & 5-8.30pm Mon-Sat; Ⓜ Serrano

No self-respecting Spanish *pija* (yuppie) could do without the trendy jewellery by Rosa Tous. Some of it's teddy bear–cutesy striving for serious elegance that may seem like an odd combination, but not to Spanish shoppers.

CUARTO DE JUEGOS Map pp102–3 Specialist

☎ 91 435 00 99; Calle de Jorge Juan 42; ⏰ 10am-2pm & 5-8pm Mon-Fri, 5-8pm Sat; Ⓜ Velázquez or Príncipe de Vergara

We're not sure if it's an official rule, but batteries seem to be outlawed at this traditional toy shop, where the kinds of games, puzzles and toys mum and dad used to play with are still sold. They're not just for kids.

MALASAÑA & CHUECA

Malasaña is one of Madrid's quirkiest barrios in which to shop, home to edgy clothing stores, shops where mainstream designers show off their street cred and highly original jewellery boutiques. Shop staff here won't look down their noses at you no matter what you wear – they've seen it all before. Chueca, on the other hand, can be zany or elegant and caters as much for explicit gay clubbers as for a refined gay sensibility. Where Chueca eases gently down the hill towards the Paseo de los Recoletos and beyond to Salamanca, niche designers take over with exclusive boutiques and the latest individual fashions. In short, it's Madrid in microcosm and ideal for those style-conscious shoppers who value an alternative look at life.

J&J BOOKS & COFFEE Map pp110–11 Bookshop

☎ 91 521 85 76; www.jandjbooksandcoffee .com; Calle del Espíritu Santo 47; ⏰ 11am-midnight Mon-Thu, 11am-2am Fri & Sat, 2-10pm Sun; Ⓜ Noviciado

Downstairs from this bar that serves as a meeting place for Madrid's expats, this place claims to have more than 150,000 books for sale. A fair proportion of these are in English and the bar is the perfect place to flick through those you're considering buying.

BIBLIOKETA Map pp110–11 Children's

☎ 91 391 00 99; www.biblioketa.com, in Spanish; Calle de Justiniano 4; ⏰ 10.30am-8pm Mon-Sat; Ⓜ Alonso Martínez

Biblioketa is perhaps the best multilingual children's bookshop in Madrid with a range of quality titles in English, Spanish and French. Check out the basement 'cave', where it runs a range of activities offering an 'apprenticeship' in reading with an emphasis on fun.

EL TEMPLO DE SUSU
Map pp110–11 Clothes & Accessories

☎ 91 523 31 22; Calle del Espíritu Santo 1; ⏰ 11am-2.30pm & 5.30-9pm Mon-Sat; Ⓜ Tribunal

It won't appeal to everyone, but El Templo de Susu's second-hand clothes from the 1960s and 1970s have clearly found a market among Malasaña's too-cool-for-the-latest-fashions types. It's kind of like charity shop meets unreconstructed hippie, which is either truly awful or retro cool, depending on your perspective.

EL TINTERO Map pp110–11 Clothes & Accessories

☎ 91 308 14 18; www.eltintero.es, in Spanish; Calle de Gravina 5; ⏰ 10.30am-2pm & 5-9pm Mon-Fri, 11am-2.30pm & 5-9pm Sat; Ⓜ Chueca

Terrific T-shirts are all that El Tintero sells, so if you're looking for a colourful *camiseta* with Spanish-language slogans that translate as 'I'm tired of being good' and 'Looking for a habitable planet', this is your place. A few doors down, El Tintero Niños (☎ 91 310 44 02; Calle de Gravina 9; ⏰ 10.30am-2pm & 5-9pm Mon-Fri, 11am-2.30pm & 5-9pm Sat) takes the

top picks

SPANISH FASHION ICONS

- Agatha Ruiz de la Prada (p138)
- Amaya Arzuaga (p139)
- Camper (p139)
- Custo Barcelona (see the boxed text, p150)
- Davidelfín (p139)
- Divina Providencia (see the boxed text, p150)
- Iñaki Sampedro (see the boxed text, p151)
- Loewe (see the boxed text, p139)
- Manolo Blahnik (see the boxed text, p139)
- Purificación García (see the boxed text, p139)
- Sybilla (see the boxed text, p140)

SHOPPING STREET – CALLE DE FUENCARRAL

As the sign outside the iconic Mercado de Fuencarral (p149) says, 'They say that fashion comes from the street, but which street?' The answer to that question is that much of Madrid's fashion comes from the Calle de Fuencarral (Map pp110–11; M Gran Via). All of the following shops are open 10am to 9pm Monday to Saturday.

For landmark Spanish fashion, there's the colourful and consciously cool Adolfo Domínguez (☎ 91 523 39 38; www.adolfodominguez.com; Calle de Fuencarral 5; M Gran Via), Mango (☎ 91 523 04 12; www.mango.es; Calle de Fuencarral 70; M Tribunal), often-outlandish Custo Barcelona (☎ 91 360 46 36; www.custo-barcelona.com; Calle de Fuencarral 29; M Gran Vía), Spain's casual shoe king Camper (☎ 91 522 67 35; www.camper.com; Calle de Fuencarral 22; M Gran Vía or Tribunal) and Divina Providencia (☎ 91 522 02 65; www.divinaprovidencia .com; Calle de Fuencarral 42; M Tribunal), whose offbeat retro and Asian influences have made the transition to mainstream stylish.

International names with an outlet along the street include Geox (☎ 91 531 64 62; Calle de Fuencarral 53; ☻ 10am-8.30pm Mon-Sat; M Tribunal), Fun & Basics (☎ 91 523 36 91; Calle de Fuencarral 43; M Tribunal), Salsa (☎ 91 523 19 45; Calle de Fuencarral 42; M Tribunal), G-Star Raw (☎ 91 523 80 48; Calle de Fuencarral 39; M Gran Vía or Tribunal), Thomas Burberry (☎ 91 523 38 14; Calle de Fuencarral 33; M Gran Vía or Tribunal), Pepe Jeans (☎ 91 701 06 42; Calle de Fuencarral 23; M Gran Vía or Tribunal), Skunkfunk (☎ 91 391 12 68; Calle de Fuencarral 20; M Gran Vía or Tribunal), Diesel (☎ 91 522 69 24; Calle de Fuencarral 19; M Gran Vía) and Friday's Project (☎ 91 522 93 00; Calle de Fuencarral 6; M Gran Vía).

same approach but with kids' wear, from newborns to those aged 10 years.

HOLALÁ Map pp110–11   Clothes & Accessories
☎ 91 521 96 78; www.zombiestudio.es, in Spanish; Calle del Pez 7; ☻ 11am-3pm & 5-10pm Mon-Sat; M Noviciado
If you're into tattoos, Black Sabbath and can relate to T-shirts that announce 'My Space is the Devil', Holalá is your spiritual home. Zombie Clothing is the name that drives everything you'll find here, from cool-again fur coats to retro sportswear that wouldn't look out of place on a Malasaña night out.

LA TIPO CAMISETAS
Map pp110–11   Clothes & Accessories
☎ 91 547 78 39; www.latipo.es, in Spanish; Calle del Conde Duque 7; ☻ 11am-2.30pm & 5-9pm Mon-Sat; M Plaza de España or Ventura Rodríguez
T-shirts in bright colours, T-shirts you'd have to be feeling pretty preppy to wear and T-shirts with witty (Spanish-language) slogans that rarely stray into the questionable taste that can be Malasaña's forte are what this shop is all about. It's all good, clean fun that would be out of place in the heart of hard-rocking Malasaña, but they've found a good home here in Conde Duque.

L'HABILLEUR Map pp110–11 Clothes & Accessories
☎ 91 531 32 22; Plaza de Chueca 8; ☻ 11am-2pm & 5-9pm Mon-Sat; M Chueca

This popular Paris boutique now has a branch on Plaza de Chueca and the deal is the same: designer names at discounted prices, especially downstairs. For women, top names include Forte-Forte, Dr Fango, Marlota and Sofie Doore, while men are served by Hartford, Ganesh and Vintage.

MADERFAKER INDUSTRY
Map pp110–11   Clothes & Accessories
☎ 91 523 80 36; www.maderfaker.com, in Spanish; Calle del Pez 14; ☻ 11am-2.30pm & 5-9pm Mon-Sat; M Noviciado
Malasaña's love affair with all things retro takes a funky twist here with a line in clothing, accessories, DVDs and posters that pays homage to black music and cinema from the 1970s. The shop is understated classy, having shed the barrio's often grungy look without losing any of its look-back-in-anger spirit.

MALA MUJER Map pp110–11 Clothes & Accessories
☎ 91 523 29 26; www.malamujer.net, in Spanish; Calle de la Libertad 12; ☻ 11am-3pm & 5-8pm Mon-Fri, 11am-9pm Sat; M Chueca
Clothing and accessories for women with attitude is the name of the game here at 'The Bad Woman'. The look is playful yet provocative and everything for sale is designed to make a statement. It's kind of like Germaine Greer meets Agatha Ruiz de la Prada.

MERCADO DE FUENCARRAL

Map pp110–11   Clothes & Accessories

☎ 91 521 41 52; Calle de Fuencarral 45; ⏰ 11am-9pm Mon-Sat; Ⓜ Tribunal

Madrid's home of alternative club-cool is still going strong, revelling in its reverse snobbery. With shops like Fuck, Ugly Shop and Black Kiss, it's funky, grungy and filled to the rafters with torn T-shirts and more black leather and silver studs than you'll ever need.

POPLAND Map pp110–11   Clothes & Accessories

☎ 91 591 21 20; www.popland.es, in Spanish; Calle de Manuela Malasaña 24; ⏰ 11am-8.30pm Mon-Sat; Ⓜ San Bernardo

'Curiosity and Retro' are the buzzwords here and Popland has both by the vinyl-suitcase load. 'Go Eighties' T-shirts, Pink Panther dolls, Elvis card games, candy handcuffs, mirrored disco balls, space invaders handbags… If you can't find it here, it simply didn't exist in the world of street pop art.

SNAPO Map pp110–11   Clothes & Accessories

☎ 91 532 12 23; www.fuckingbastardz.com; Calle del Espíritu Santo 5; ⏰ 11am-2pm & 5-8.30pm Mon-Sat; Ⓜ Tribunal

Snapo is rebellious Malasaña to its core, thumbing its nose at the niceties of fashion respectability – hardly surprising given that its line of clothing is called Fucking Bastardz Inc. It does jeans, caps and jackets, but its T-shirts are the Snapo trademark. Expect a mocked-up cover of 'National Pornographic' or Pope John Paul II with fist raised and 'Vatican 666' emblazoned across the front. Need we say more?

UNDERNATION Map pp110–11 Clothes & Accessories

☎ 902 445 575; www.undernation.es, in Spanish; Calle de Barquillo 38; ⏰ 10am-8pm Mon-Sat; Ⓜ Chueca

Undernation would look right at home in Malasaña with hard-core clothing and accessories with black and underground slogans the recurring themes. But, perhaps in a nod to its Chueca locale, Undernation stocks brands like Franklin & Marshall and the shop has none of the grungy atmosphere that usually accompanies the look.

VESTIUM Map pp110–11   Clothes & Accessories

☎ 91 702 40 72; Calle de Barquillo 41; ⏰ 11am-2pm & 5-9pm Mon-Sat; Ⓜ Chueca

Vestium made its name in Ibiza and brought with it to Madrid clothes by Diesel, Dolce & Gabbana, Jordi Cuesta and Emporio Armani. The selection is small, but with designers like this on the shelves, what's there is always worth a look.

CACAO SAMPAKA Map pp110–11 Food & Wine

☎ 91 521 56 55; Calle de Orellana 4; ⏰ 10am-9.30pm; Ⓜ Alonso Martínez

If you thought chocolate was about fruit 'n' nut, think again. This gourmet chocolate shop is a chocoholic's dream come true, with more combinations to go with humble cocoa than you ever imagined possible.

ISOLÉE Map pp110–11   Food & Wine

☎ 91 522 81 38; www.isolee.com; Calle de las Infantas 19; ⏰ 10am-10pm Mon-Wed, to 12.30am Thu-Sun; Ⓜ Gran Vía or Chueca

Multipurpose lifestyle stores are all the rage in Madrid, and there's none more stylish than Isolée. It sells a select range of everything

SHOPPING STREET – CALLE DE PIAMONTE & AROUND

Three streets – Calle de Piamonte, Calle del Conde de Xiquena and Calle del Almirante (Map pp110–11; Ⓜ Chueca or Colón) – have the Chueca market cornered when it comes to exclusive, personalised boutiques for designer accessories. What follows are just a few of our favourites among many. Start at Piamonte (☎ 91 522 45 80; Calle de Piamonte 16; ⏰ 10.30am-8.30pm Mon-Sat), a favourite haunt of madrileñas looking for special shoes or handbags. The shoes at the cave-like Las Bailarinas (☎ 91 319 90 69; Calle de Piamonte 19; ⏰ 11am-2pm & 5-8pm Mon-Sat) are popular with Spanish celebrities. French Connection and other stylishly casual lines are found at Martel Kee (☎ 91 319 86 11; Calle de Piamonte 15; ⏰ 11am-2pm & 5-8.30pm Mon-Sat). Stunning hand-painted handbags and other accessories are available just around the corner at Iñaki Sampedro (☎ 91 319 45 65; Calle del Conde de Xiquena 13; ⏰ 10.30am-2pm & 5-8.30pm Mon-Sat), one of Spain's most innovative accessories designers. For glamorous evening wear for ladies (not 'women', we were informed by the shop assistant), it's difficult to go past the Spanish designer Jesús del Pozo (☎ 91 531 36 46; www.jesusdelpozo.com; Calle del Almirante 9; ⏰ 11am-2pm & 5-8.30pm Mon-Fri, 11am-2pm Sat).

SHOPPING MALASAÑA & CHUECA

from clothes (Levi's to Davidelfín) and shoes to CDs and food. It also has a trendy café.

MAISON BLANCHE Map pp110–11 Food & Wine
☎ 91 522 82 17; Calle de Piamonte 10; ☺ 10am-midnight Mon-Sat, noon-6pm Sun; Ⓜ Chueca
A small but extremely tasteful selection of cookbooks, homemade pastas, wines and other delicacies are beautifully displayed here.

PATRIMONIO COMUNAL OLIVARERO
Map pp110–11   Food & Wine
☎ 91 308 05 05; www.pco.es, in Spanish; Calle de Mejía Lequerica 1; ☺ 10am-2pm & 5-8pm Mon-Fri, 10am-1.30pm Sat; Ⓜ Alonso Martínez
You could buy your Spanish olive oil at El Corte Inglés, but to catch the real essence of the country's olive-oil varieties (Spain is the world's largest producer), Patrimonio Comunal Olivarero is perfect. With examples of the extra-virgin variety (and nothing else) from all over Spain, you could spend ages agonising over the choices. The staff know their oil and are happy to help out.

PLAISIR GOURMET Map pp110–11 Food & Wine
☎ 91 702 55 01; www.plaisirgourmet.com, in Spanish; Calle de Gravina 1; ☺ 10.30am-10pm Mon-Sat; Ⓜ Chueca
This is not your ordinary delicatessen. With products from every corner of the globe, you'll find all manner of things that you didn't know existed (who knew that essence of cotton from Mali could be used in cooking?) or can't find anywhere else in Madrid. At noon on Saturday, it has tastings of wine and cheese, a nod to the shop's French owners. In 2008 this stylish place won second prize for Madrid's best deli; Mantequería Bravo (p140) came first.

RESERVA & CATA Map pp110–11 Food & Wine
☎ 91 319 04 01; www.reservaycata.com, in Spanish; Calle del Conde de Xiquena 13; ☺ 11am-2.30pm & 5-9pm Mon-Fri, 11am-2.30pm Sat; Ⓜ Colón or Chueca
This old-style shop stocks an excellent range of local wines, and the knowledgeable staff can help you pick out a great one for your next dinner party or a gift for a friend back home. It specialises in quality Spanish wines that you just don't find in El Corte Inglés and there's often a bottle open so that you can try before you buy.

FUTURAMIC Map pp110–11 Homewares
☎ 91 531 63 57; www.futuramics.com, in Spanish; Calle de Válgame Dios 5; ☺ variable hours; Ⓜ Chueca
Looking for that 1960s jukebox? Or a real-life parking meter? Just about anything you can imagine in memorabilia (either original or in replica) from the 1930s to the 1980s is available here. Not everything is for sale (the life-size London phone booth, for example), as many of the items are in demand for movie sets, but much of it is. Ring before you head here as it's often out on location.

GANDOLFI Map pp110–11 Jewellery
☎ 91 591 93 77; www.gandolfi.es; Calle de San Andrés 28; ☺ 11am-9.30pm Mon-Sat; Ⓜ Bilbao
A jewellery store with attitude, Gandolfi blends Malasaña edge with the sophistication of the new Madrid. The rings and other accessories are pretty outlandish, but you'll figure that out as soon as you walk in and find yourself confronted with a full-size Texaco petrol tank and larger-than-life human statues as props, which are works of art in themselves.

UNO DE 50 Map pp110–11 Jewellery
☎ 91 523 99 75; Calle de Fuencarral 25; ☺ 10am-8.30pm Mon-Sat; Ⓜ Gran Vía or Tribunal
Close to where in-your-face Malasaña intersects with could-go-either-way Chueca, Uno de 50 offers up silver jewellery that wouldn't look out of place in either barrio. It's chunky and loud and not very subtle, but there are some great pieces here.

RADIO CITY DISCOS Map pp110–11 Music
☎ 91 547 77 67; www.radiocitydiscos.com, in Spanish; Plaza Guardias de Corps 2; ☺ 11am-2pm & 5-9pm Mon-Sat; Ⓜ Plaza de España or Ventura Rodríguez
In these days of music megastores and internet downloads, it's nice to find small, specialist music shops still going strong. True to Malasaña's roots, Radio City's small collection of CDs and vinyl spans the 1970s, roots, funk, rock and occasional pop, with a small section devoted to Brazil's Tropicalismo.

LA JUGUETERÍA Map pp110–11 Sex Shop
☎ 91 308 72 69; Travesía del San Mateo 12; ☺ 11am-3pm & 5-9pm Mon-Sat; Ⓜ Alonso Martínez

We don't normally include sex shops in our guides but this softly lit one tickled our fancy (so to speak). Home to sultry staff and carefully chosen feathers and erotic toys, there's nothing brown paper bag and men in anoraks about this place; you won't feel guilty entering. It's very Chueca.

CHAMBERÍ & ARGÜELLES

One of Madrid's trendiest barrios, Chamberí is dotted with great shops, although for designer gear it's not a patch on Salamanca and it doesn't have the quirks of Malasaña and Chueca. Some of it spills over into Argüelles, although the latter is primarily residential and not generally known for its shopping.

ANTIGÜEDADES HOM Map pp116–17 Antiques

☎ 91 594 20 17; Calle de Juan de Austria 31; 5-8pm Mon-Wed, noon-2pm & 5-8pm Thu & Fri; M Iglesia

Specialising in antique Spanish fans, this tiny shop is a wonderful place to browse or to find a special gift, especially delicately painted fans and fans made with bone. It's open most afternoons only because the owner spends the morning restoring the fans you see for sale. It's also a purveyor of other treasures/bric-a-brac.

ALTAÏR Map pp116–17 Bookshop

☎ 91 543 53 00; www.altair.es; Calle de Gaztambide 31; 10am-2pm & 4.30-8.30pm Mon-Fri, 10.30am-2.30pm; M Argüelles

One of the best travel bookshops in Madrid, Altaïr has an exceptional range of books, maps and magazines covering Spain and every region of the world. Most are in Spanish, but there are loads of English-language titles scattered throughout, as well as calendars and world-music CDs. Altaïr is the Spanish distributor for Moleskine notebooks, once beloved of Hemingway and Chatwin, and now enjoying a revival.

BOOKSELLERS Map pp116–17 Bookshop

☎ 91 442 79 59; Calle de Fernández de la Hoz 40; 9.30am-2pm & 5-8pm Mon-Fri, 10am-2pm Sat; M Iglesia

This suburban bookshop has close to the largest selection of English-language titles in town, covering novels, history, travel literature and Spanish themes. There's another Booksellers (☎ 91 702 79 44; Plaza de Olavide 10; 9.30am-2pm & 5-8pm Mon-Fri, 10am-2pm Sat; M Bilbao, Iglesia or Quevedo) that specialises in multilingual children's books.

PASAJES LIBRERÍA INTERNACIONAL
Map pp116–17 Bookshop

☎ 91 310 12 45; www.pasajeslibros.com; Calle de Génova 3; 10am-8pm Mon-Fri, to 2pm Sat; M Alonso Martínez

Definitely one of the best English-language bookshops in Madrid, Pasajes has an extensive English section (downstairs at the back), which includes high-quality fiction (if it's a new release, it'll be the first bookshop in town to have it), history, Spanish subject matter and travel, as well as a few literary magazines. There are also French, German, Italian and Portuguese books, and a useful noticeboard.

LOS BEBÉS DE CHAMBERÍ
Map pp116–17 Children's

☎ 91 444 05 96; www.losbebesdechamberi.com, in Spanish; Calle de Gonzalo de Córdoba 7; 11am-2.30pm & 5.30-8.30pm Mon-Fri, 11am-2.30pm Sat; M Quevedo

This small shop showcases the wonderful individuality of Spanish children's clothes; you'll leave laden with bags for your own kids and for friends back home. Bright colours are a recurring theme, the stuffed toys are always more original than you'll find elsewhere and the wares cater to all ages from newborns to six-year-olds.

DIEDRO Map pp116–17 Clothes & Accessories

☎ 91 444 59 59; www.diedro.com; Calle de Sagasta 17; 10am-10pm Mon-Sat, noon-10pm Sun; M Bilbao or Alonso Martínez

top picks

CHILDREN'S SHOPS

- Así (p133)
- Imaginarium (p138)
- Los Bebés de Chamberí (above)
- Biblioketa (p149)
- El Tintero Niños (p149)
- Cuarto de Juegos (p149)
- Agatha Ruiz de la Prada (p138)

One of the most innovative gift shops in Madrid, Diedro has designer jewellery, clothes, stationery and homewares. It's a wonderful space spread over three floors that span just about every taste, as long as it's design conscious. Leading brand names include Calvin Klein, Guess, Bodum and Alessi.

DMR MARÍA RIVOLTA Map pp116–17 Jewellery
☎ 91 448 02 57; www.mariarivolta.com, in Spanish; Calle de Fuencarral 146; ☺ 10am-8.30pm Mon-Fri, 10am-2pm & 5-8.30pm Sat; Ⓜ Quevedo
It's practically impossible to walk out of this tiny jewellery boutique without buying something. The speciality of this Argentine designer is colourful glass and enamel rings, necklaces and bracelets, and each piece is a reasonably priced work of art.

CASA CARRIL Map pp116–17 Specialist
☎ 91 447 05 12; www.casacarril.com, in Spanish; Calle de Luchana 27; ☺ 9am-8pm Mon-Fri; Ⓜ Bilbao
You could go to any photography shop in Madrid for your camera needs, but why not go where the professionals go? This place has knowledgeable staff who are as savvy with older cameras as with digital ones. It also develops photos and sells a range of other accessories, including camera bags.

HARLEY DAVIDSON MADRID
Map pp116–17 Specialist
☎ 91 591 32 50; www.hdofmadrid.com; Calle del General Álvarez de Castro 26; ☺ 10am-2pm & 5-8pm Mon-Fri, 10am-2pm Sat; Ⓜ Canal

For the Harley Davidson fans who long to connect with like-minded motorcyclists in Madrid, this is the place to go. You can ooh and ah over the bikes on show, and you'll also find Harley jackets, T-shirts, pins and all sorts of must-have motorbike paraphernalia.

OCHO Y MEDIO Map pp116–17 Specialist
☎ 91 559 06 28; Calle de Martín de los Heros 11; ☺ 10am-2pm & 5-8.30pm Mon-Sat; Ⓜ Plaza de España
Close to a number of the best foreign-language cinemas in Madrid, this is a terrific resource for film buffs, with a huge range of books, posters, magazines and other memorabilia. Much of the stock is in Spanish, but there's a smattering of English-language titles and the friendly staff knows its films.

NORTHERN MADRID
TIENDA REAL MADRID Map p123 Specialist
☎ 91 458 74 22; Estadio Santiago Bernabéu, Avenida de Concha Espina 1; ☺ 10am-9pm Mon-Thu, to 8pm Fri & Sat, 11am-8pm Sun; Ⓜ Santiago Bernabéu
The club shop of Real Madrid sells replica shirts, posters, caps and just about everything under the sun to which it could attach a club logo. From the shop window, you can see down onto the stadium itself. For information on stadium tours, turn to p122.

top picks

- **Restaurante Sobrino de Botín** (p160)
  The world's oldest restaurant – simple as that.
- **Casa Revuelta** (p161)
  Outstanding tapas of cod in a very Madrid atmosphere.
- **Santceloni** (p180)
  Michelin-starred dining for a special occasion.
- **Almendro 13** (p165)
  Perhaps our favourite Madrid tapas bar.
- **Corazon Loco** (p165)
  Creative tapas in the heart of La Latina.
- **Bazaar** (p175)
  Clean lines and celebrity diners in Chueca's hottest restaurant.
- **Sula Madrid** (p169)
  Designer food in designer surrounds.
- **La Musa** (p172)
  Malasaña cool with surprising food combinations.
- **Nina** (p171)
  Sophisticated Malasaña restaurant with a touch of class.

What's your recommendation? www.lonelyplanet.com/madrid

After holding fast to its rather unexciting local cuisine for centuries (aided, it must be said, by loyal locals who never saw the need for anything else), Madrid has finally become one of Europe's culinary capitals.

There's everything to be found here, not least the rich variety of regional Spanish specialities from across the country. This is a city that grew and became great because of the immigrants from all over Spain who made Madrid their home. On their journey to the capital, these immigrants carried with them recipes and ingredients from their villages, thereby bequeathing to the city an astonishing variety of regional flavours that you just don't find anywhere else. Travel from one Spanish village to the next and you'll quickly learn that each has its own speciality. Travel to Madrid and you'll find them all. Throw in some outstanding restaurants serving international cuisine and the choice of where to eat well is almost endless.

There's not a barrio where you can't find a great meal. Restaurants in Malasaña, Chueca and Huertas range from glorious old *tabernas* (taverns) to boutique eateries across all price ranges. For more classically elegant surrounds, Paseo del Prado, El Retiro, Salamanca and Northern Madrid are generally pricey but of the highest standard and ideal for a special occasion or for spotting royalty and celebrities. In the central barrios of Los Austrias, Sol and Centro, as is their wont, there's a little bit of everything. Splendid tapas bars abound everywhere, but La Latina is the undoubted king.

Almost more than the myriad tastes on offer, however, is the buzz that accompanies eating that defines the city as a gastronomic experience. In Madrid eating is not a functional pastime to be squeezed in between other more important tasks; instead it is one of life's great pleasures, a social event always taken seriously enough to allocate hours for the purpose and to be savoured like all good things in life.

In January Spain's most prestigious chefs arrive in town to showcase the latest innovations in Spain's world-famous cuisine at the Madrid Fusion (www.madridfusion.net) gastronomy summit.

HISTORY

Medieval Madrid was a simple place. On the bleak *meseta* (plateau) of inland Spain, food was a necessity, good food a luxury, and the dishes that developed were functional and well suited to a climate dominated by interminable, bitterly cold winters. Most madrileños scraped by on a limited diet, the staple of which was cereals (often barley). Bread was a rarity, as was meat. Fruit and vegetables, typically grown along the Manzanares, were by no means available to all. Olive oil was an expensive luxury.

With little to contribute of its own, Madrid became dependent on emerging cuisines from elsewhere in Spain and from its colonies in Latin America. Slowly but surely, dishes from across Spain – paella from Valencia, *marisco* (seafood) and *pescado* (fish) from Galicia and Andalucía, the many and varied uses of *bacalao* (cod), *solomillo* (steak) and *pimientos* (peppers) to name a few – made their way to the capital. As Madrid grew in wealth, meat was added to the diet, especially *cordero asado* (roast lamb), *cochinillo* (suckling pig), *jamón* (ham), chorizo (seasoned pork sausage), *lomo* (loin, usually pork) and *salchichón* (salami-like sausage).

WOULD YOU LIKE SMOKE WITH THAT, SIR?

If you're from a country where smoking is banned in restaurants, you're in for a rude shock in Madrid.

Since 1 January 2006 all Spanish bars, restaurants, offices and other enclosed public places have, in theory, become subject to strict antismoking legislation. Smoking is now banned in all workplaces, schools (like they had to ban this?), sports and cultural centres, and on public transport. The law also extends to bars and restaurants, although these have an opt-out clause, and therein lies the key. Those establishments over 100 sq metres must have designated smoking areas, while smaller bars must make a choice – ban smoking or make the bar off-limits to children. In practice, and despite polls showing that a majority of Spaniards supports the law, many restaurants and most bars remain dominated by *zonas de fumadores* (smoking sections).

THE ORIGIN OF TAPAS

Medieval Spain was a land of isolated settlements and people on the move – traders, pilgrims, emigrants and journeymen – who had to cross the lonely high plateau of Spain en route elsewhere. All along the route, travellers holed up in isolated inns where innkeepers, concerned about drunken men on horseback setting out from their village, developed a tradition of putting a *tapa* (lid) of food atop a glass of wine or beer. Their purpose was partly to keep the bugs out, but primarily to encourage people not to drink on an empty stomach.

In this sense, little has changed and the *tapa* continues to serve the dual purposes of lid and sustenance to enable you to develop new levels of stamina during long Spanish nights.

Over time Madrid has become one of the biggest fish- and seafood-consuming cities in the world; it's often said that Madrid is the best 'port' in Spain. In the early days this meant *bacalao* was carried by horse-drawn cart from the coast. Nowadays, tonnes of fish and seafood are trucked in daily from Mediterranean and Atlantic ports to satisfy the madrileño taste for the sea.

ETIQUETTE

Spanish waiters – love them or hate them, they're unlikely to leave you indifferent. In smarter establishments waiters are often young, attentive and switched on to the needs of patrons. In more traditional places waiting is a career, often a poorly paid one, which is the preserve of old men (sometimes one old man, sometimes one grumpy old man) in white jackets and bow ties and for whom service with a smile is not part of the job description. In such places, they shuffle amid the tables, the weight of the world upon their shoulders, struggling with what seems a Sisyphean task. Getting their attention can be a challenge. On the other hand, they know their food and, if you speak Spanish, can help tailor your order in the best possible way.

If you're just eating tapas, in many bars you can either take a small plate and help yourself or point to the morsel you want. If you do this, it's customary to keep track of what you eat (by holding on to the toothpicks for example) and then tell the barman when it comes time to pay. Otherwise you can order a *media ración* (half ration) or a full *ración* from the menu. In some bars you'll also get a small (free) *tapa* when you buy a drink.

In simpler restaurants you may keep the same knife and fork throughout the meal. As each course is finished you set the cutlery aside and the waiter whisks away the plates.

Don't jump out of your seats if people passing your table address you with a hearty '*buen provecho!*' They're just saying 'Enjoy your meal!'

And if you're in a bar, don't be surprised to see people throwing their serviettes and olive stones on the floor – you might as well join them because a waiter will come around from time to time to sweep them all up.

SPECIALITIES

Madrileños love their food. When the weather turns chilly, that means *legumbres* (legumes), such as *garbanzos* (chickpeas), *judias* (beans) and *lentejas* (lentils). Hearty stews are the order of the day and there are none more hearty than *cocido a la madrileña*; it's a kind of hotpot or stew that starts with a noodle broth and is followed by, or combined with – there are as many ways of eating *cocido* as there are madrileños – carrots, chickpeas, chicken, *morcilla* (blood sausage) beef, lard and possibly other sausage meats, too. *Repollo* (cabbage) sometimes makes an appearance. Madrileños love *cocido*. They dream of it while they're away from home and they wonder why it hasn't caught on elsewhere. There was even a hit song written about it in the 1950s. However, we'll put this as gently as we can: you

top picks

MADRID SPECIALITIES & WHERE TO FIND THEM

- *Cocido a la madrileña* (Madrid stew) – Taberna La Bola (p160), Malacatín (p164), Lhardy (p166) or La Tasca Suprema (p175)
- *Callos a la madrileña* (tripe casserole with chorizo and chillies) – Oliveros (p164) or Casa Revuelta (p161)
- *Sopa de ajo or sopa castellana* (garlic broth with floating egg and bread) – Posada de la Villa (see the boxed text, p163)
- *Chocolate con churros* (deep-fried doughnut strips dipped in hot chocolate) – El Brillante (p168) or Chocolatería de San Ginés (p186)
- *Bocadillo de calamares* (a roll stuffed with calamari) – Cervecería Compano (p162)

have to be a madrileño to understand what all the fuss is about because it may be filling but it's not Spain's most exciting dish.

Other popular staples in Madrid include *cordero asado* (roast lamb), *patatas con huevos fritos* (baked potatoes with eggs), *tortilla de patatas* (a thick potato omelette) and endless variations on *bacalao*.

VEGETARIANS & VEGANS

Pure vegetarianism remains something of an alien concept in most Spanish kitchens; cooked vegetable dishes, for example, often contain ham. That said, Madrid has a growing cast of vegetarian restaurants. Even in those restaurants that serve meat or fish dishes, salads are a Spanish staple and, in some places, can be a meal in themselves. You'll also come across the odd vegetarian paella, as well as dishes such as *verduras a la plancha* (grilled vegetables), *garbanzos con espinacas* (chickpeas and spinach) and numerous potato dishes, such as *patatas bravas* (potato chunks bathed in spicy tomato sauce) and the *tortilla de patatas* (potato and onion omelette). The prevalence of legumes ensures that *lentejas* and *judías* are also easy to track down, while *pan* (bread), *quesos* (cheeses), *alcachofas* (artichokes) and *aceitunas* (olives) are always easy to find. If vegetarianism is rare among Spaniards, vegans will feel as if they've come from another planet. However, some of the established vegetarian restaurants may have certain vegan dishes; otherwise, an option is self-catering (see opposite).

COOKING COURSES

There are plenty of places to learn Spanish cooking. In most cases, you'll need at least passable Spanish, but some run special classes for English speakers.

top picks

FOR VEGETARIANS & VEGANS

- La Isla del Tesoro (p171)
- El Estragón (p164)
- La Galette (p170)
- Restaurante Integral Artemisa (p167)
- Viva La Vida (p165)
- La Biotika (p168)

OPENING HOURS

In this chapter, 'lunch' means a venue is open 1pm to 4pm, and 'dinner' means 8.30pm to midnight; exceptions are noted in reviews.

Alambique (Map pp64–5; ☎ 91 547 42 20; www .alambique.com; Plaza de la Encarnación 2; Ⓜ Ópera or Santo Domingo) Cooking classes start at around €50, with English-speaking courses from €70.

Cooking Club (Map p123; ☎ 91 323 29 58; www .club-cooking.com, in Spanish; Calle de Veza 33; Ⓜ Valdeacederas) The regular, respected programme of classes encompasses a range of cooking styles.

La Maison (Map pp110–11; ☎ cooking 620 566 676, wine 649 803 283; www.lamaison.es, in Spanish; 3rd fl, Calle de San Mateo 26; Ⓧ by appointment; Ⓜ Alonso Martínez or Tribunal) Try creative cooking and wine classes (around €25 per class) as part of this fascinating designer/ decoration/artist space.

Gaudeamus Café (p188) International and occasionally local cooking courses.

PRACTICALITIES

Most visitors complain not about the quality of Spanish food but about its timing. *Comida/almuerzo* (lunch) rarely begins before 2pm (restaurant kitchens usually open from 1pm until 4pm), and for *cena* (dinner) few madrileños would dream of turning up before 9.30pm, although restaurants open 8.30pm to midnight, later on weekends. On weekends some restaurants take reservations for two sittings, one starting at 9pm, the other at 11pm! Stay in Madrid long enough and you'll soon get used to it.

In the intervening hours, many bars serve tapas and *raciones* throughout the day. *Bocadillos* (filled rolls, usually without butter) are another option. Cafés tend to open from 8am or 9am through to at least 9pm, and often to midnight or beyond if they double as bars. Most restaurants are shut on Christmas Eve and many on New Year's Eve (or Christmas Day and New Year's Day), while some have a night off on Sunday and many don't open at all on Monday. Some close over Easter and a good many shut for at least part of August as well.

Desayuno (breakfast) is generally a no-nonsense affair taken at a bar on the way to work. A *café con leche* (half coffee and half warm milk) with a *bollo* (pastry) is the

MENÚ DEL DÍA

One great way to cap prices at lunchtime Monday to Friday is to order the *menú del día*, a full set meal (usually with several options), water, bread and wine. These meals start from around €8.50, although €10 and up is increasingly the norm. You'll be given a menu with five or six entrées, the same number of mains and a handful of desserts – choose one from each category and don't even think of mixing and matching.

The philosophy behind the *menú del día* is that, during the working week, few madrileños have time to go home to have their lunch. Taking a packed lunch is just not the done thing, so the majority of people end up eating in restaurants, and all-inclusive three-course meals are as close as they can get to eating home-style food without breaking the bank.

typical breakfast. Croissants or a cream-filled pastry are also common. Some people prefer a savoury start – try a *sandwich mixto*, a toasted ham and cheese; a Spanish *tostada* is simply buttered toast. Others, especially party animals heading home at dawn after a night out, go for an all-Spanish favourite, *chocolate con churros*, a deep-fried stick of plain pastry immersed in thick hot chocolate.

A full meal generally comprises an *entrante* (entrée), *plato principal* (main course) and *postre* (dessert). Bread is routinely served with meals, but you pay extra for it (usually around €1.20). If you can't face a full menu, a simpler option is the *plato combinado*, basically a meat-and-three-veg dish that will hardly excite taste buds but will have little fiscal impact.

In the following pages a 'meal' is understood to mean an entrée, main course and dessert, including a little modestly priced wine. Prices have risen pretty steadily in Madrid over the past few years, but eating out here is still cheaper than in most other major European cities.

At many of the midrange restaurants and simpler taverns with *comedores* (dining rooms) you can generally turn up and find a spot without booking ahead. You should reserve a table at sit-down restaurants, especially on Friday or Saturday night.

PRICE GUIDE

Throughout this chapter, restaurants are listed according to the barrio (area of Madrid), then by price range from most expensive to least expensive, then in alphabetical order. Each place is accompanied by one of the following symbols:

€€€	more than €50 a meal per person
€€	€20-50 a meal per person
€	less than €20 a meal per person

Tipping

A service charge is generally calculated into most bills in Madrid, so any further tipping is a matter of personal choice. Spaniards themselves are pretty stingy when it comes to tipping and often leave no more than €1 per person or nothing more than small change. If you're particularly happy, 5% on top would be fine.

Self-Catering

Some of the better food markets in town:

Mercado de la Cebada (Map pp76–7; Plaza de la Cebada; 9am-2pm & 5-8pm Mon-Fri, 9am-2.30pm Sat; M La Latina) Slated for major renovations.

Mercado de la Paz (Map pp102–3; off Calle de Alcalá; 9am-8pm Mon-Sat; M Serrano)

Mercado de San Miguel (Map pp64–5; Plaza de San Miguel; 9am-2.30pm & 5.15-8.15pm Mon-Fri, 9am-2.30pm Sat; M Sol) Currently under renovation.

Other specialist food stores include Maison Blanche (p152) and Mantequería Bravo (p140). For Spanish and other European cheeses, Poncelet (Map pp110–11; ☎ 91 308 02 21; www.poncelet.es, in Spanish; Calle de Argensola 27; 10.30am-8.30pm Mon-Sat; M Alonso Martínez) should be your first stop.

For more international flavours, try:

Cavatappi (Map pp116–17; ☎ 91 446 98 85; Calle de Gonzalo de Córdoba 6; 11am-3pm & 5-9pm Mon-Fri, 11am-3pm Sat; M Quevedo) Freshly made pasta and other Italian delicacies.

Plaisir Gourmet (p152) Products from all over the world.

Taste of America (Map p123; ☎ 91 562 16 32; Calle de Serrano 149; 9am-9pm Mon-Fri, 10am-9pm Sat; M República Argentina)

Things You Miss (Map pp116–17; ☎ 91 447 07 85; www.thethingsyoumiss.com; Calle de Juan de Austria 11; 9.30am-2.30pm & 5-8.30pm Mon-Fri, 10am-2.30pm Sat Sep-Jul; M Iglesia or Bilbao) For all things British.

LOS AUSTRIAS, SOL & CENTRO

From the world's oldest restaurant to down-tempo fusion places, from regional tapas to Asian flavours, from old Spanish bars where the ambience owes everything to impromptu theatre to brightly painted vegetarian restaurants, downtown Madrid has a little bit of everything. This is the part of the capital where you're most likely to find English menus (which we welcome), as well as loads of places with brightly photographed paellas out the front (of which we're always suspicious). Around here, you'll also find waiters roaming outside spruiking for business – we haven't listed such places here because if they're good, they'll be filled with locals anyway.

TABERNA DEL ALABARDERO

Map pp64–5   Tapas €€

☎ 91 547 25 77; Calle de Felipe V 6; meals €40-45; Ⓜ Ópera

This fine old Madrid *taberna* is famous for its *montaditos de jamón* or *bonito* (small rolls of cured ham or tuna) in the bar, while out the back the more classic cuisine includes fine *croquetas* (croquettes), *morcilla* (blood sausage) and *rabo de toro* (bull's tail, usually in a stew). Prices aren't cheap, but Madrid's notoriously fussy diners generally accept that it's worth it.

RESTAURANTE SOBRINO DE BOTÍN

Map pp64–5   Spanish €€

☎ 91 366 42 17; www.botin.es; Calle de los Cuchilleros 17; set menu €37, meals €35-45; Ⓜ La Latina or Sol

It's not every day that you can eat in the oldest restaurant in the world (the *Guinness Book of Records* has recognised it as the oldest – established in 1725) that has also appeared in many novels about Madrid,

most notably Hemingway's *The Sun Also Rises*. The secret of its staying power is fine *cochinillo* (€21.10) and *cordero asado* (€21.10) cooked in wood-fired ovens. Eating in the vaulted cellar is a treat. Yes, it's filled with tourists. And yes, staff are keen to keep things ticking over and there's little chance to linger. But the novelty value is high and the food excellent.

LA VIUDA BLANCA   Map pp64–5   Fusion €€

☎ 91 548 75 29; www.laviudablanca.com; Calle de Campomanes 6; menú del día €13.50, meals €35-40; Ⓥ lunch & dinner Tue-Sat, lunch Mon; Ⓜ Ópera

Calle de Campomanes is fast becoming one of central Madrid's coolest streets, and La Viuda Blanca is an essential part of its charm. The dining room is flooded with sunshine through the glass roof by day, the crowd is young and trendy, and the cooking of madrileño chef César Augusto is filled with flavour; try, for example, the rice with mushrooms from Madrid's Sierra de Guadarrama and tiger prawns or duck with caramelised apple and raspberries in pastry.

TABERNA LA BOLA   Map pp64–5   Madrileño €€

☎ 91 547 69 30; www.labola.es; Calle de la Bola 5; meals €30-35; Ⓥ lunch & dinner Mon-Sat, lunch Sun; Ⓜ Santo Domingo

In any poll of food-loving locals seeking the best and most traditional Madrid cuisine, Taberna La Bola (going strong since 1880) always features near the top. We're inclined to agree and if you're going to try *cocido a la madrileña* (€20) at some stage while you're in Madrid, this is a good place to do so (although we'd only recommend it in winter). It's busy and noisy and very Madrid. It serves other Madrid specialities, such as *callos* (tripe, but which the website translates as callouses…) and *sopa de ajo*.

LA GLORIA DE MONTERA

Map pp64–5   Spanish €€

☎ 91 523 44 07; Calle del Caballero de Gracia 10; meals €20-25; Ⓥ lunch & dinner daily; Ⓜ Gran Vía

La Gloria de Montera combines classy décor with eminently reasonable prices. It's not that the food is especially creative, but rather the tastes are fresh and the surroundings sophisticated, and you'll get a good initiation into Spanish cooking without paying over the odds. It doesn't take reservations, so turn up early or be prepared to wait.

top picks

EAT STREETS

- Calle de la Cava Baja (see the boxed text, p163)
- Calle de Manuela Malasaña (see the boxed text, p171)
- Calle de la Libertad (see the boxed text, p177)

PINK SUSHIMAN Map pp64–5   Japanese €€

☎ 91 360 56 08; www.pinksushiman.com; Calle de Caballero de Gracia 8; meals €15-25; ☯ 1.30pm-midnight daily; Ⓜ Gran Vía

The revolving sushi bar has finally arrived in Madrid. Other Japanese restaurants may have this, but they're restaurants first and foremost, whereas Pink Sushiman is more like a fast and cheerful tapas bar with modern décor. Colour-coded sushi plates cost €1.50 to €4.50, although the weekday lunchtime choice of any five for €9.90 is a steal. It also cooks noodle dishes to order.

YERBABUENA Map pp64–5   Vegetarian €€

☎ 91 548 08 11; www.yerbabuena.ws, in Spanish; Calle de Bordadores 3; set menu €12, meals €15-25; ☯ lunch & dinner daily; Ⓜ Sol or Ópera

Cheerful bright colours, a full range of vegetarian staples (vegetable sausages, soya-bean hamburgers, biological rice and home-made yogurt) and plenty of creatively conceived salads add up to one of central Madrid's best restaurants for vegetarians. The *alubias de Tolosa* (white Navarran beans) cooked Mexican style is a good choice.

BANGKOK CAFÉ Map pp64–5   Thai €

☎ 91 559 16 96; 1st fl, Calle de Bordadores 15; meals €15-20; ☯ lunch & dinner daily; Ⓜ Sol or Ópera

Great Thai food, reasonable prices, good service and a Thai-style dining area make for a terrific meal in the heart of town. If you're lucky, you'll get one of the tables overlooking the busy pedestrian thoroughfare of Calle del Arenal. Unusually for Madrid, it's a wholly nonsmoking restaurant.

CASA LABRA Map pp64–5   Tapas €

☎ 91 531 00 81; www.casalabra.es; Calle de Tetuán 11; meals €15-20; ☯ 11am-3.30pm & 6-11pm; Ⓜ Sol

Casa Labra has been going strong since 1860, an era that the décor strongly evokes. Locals love their *bacalao* and ordering it here (either as deep-fried tapas or croquetas) is a Madrid rite of initiation. This is also a bar with history – it was here that the Partido Socialista Obrero Español (PSOE; Spanish Socialist Party) was formed on 2 May 1879. It was a favourite of Lorca, the poet, as well as appearing in Pío Baroja's novel *La Busca*. It's the sort of place that fathers bring their sons as their fathers did before them in what has become a rite of madrileño passage.

CASA REVUELTA Map pp64–5   Tapas €

☎ 91 366 33 32; Calle de Latoneros 3; meals €15-20; ☯ lunch & dinner Tue-Sat, lunch Sun; Ⓜ Sol or La Latina

Casa Revuelta puts out Madrid's finest tapas of *bacalao* bar none. While aficionados of Casa Labra may disagree, the fact that the octogenarian owner, Señor Revuelta, painstakingly extracts every fish bone in the morning and serves as a waiter in the afternoon wins the argument for us. Early on a Sunday afternoon, as the Rastro crowd gathers here, it's filled to the rafters, although old locals who've been coming here for decades always manage to find room. It's also famous for its *callos*, *torreznos* (bacon bits) and *albóndigas* (meatballs).

MUSEO DEL JAMÓN Map pp64–5   Spanish €

☎ 91 531 45 50; www.museodeljamon.com, in Spanish; Calle Mayor 7; meals €10-20; ☯ 8am-midnight; Ⓜ Sol

Famous for having appeared in Pedro Almodóvar's 1997 film *Carne Trémula* (Live Flesh), and equally beloved by first-time visitors to Spain for the sight of hundreds of hams hanging from the ceiling, Museo del Jamón is definitely a local landmark. Prices range from €2.50 up to €15.50, depending on the quality, for a plate of *jamón*.

FAST GOOD Map pp64–5   Healthy Fast Food €

www.fast-good.com, in Spanish; Calle de Tetuán 2; meals €10; ☯ 8am-midnight Mon-Fri, noon-midnight Sat & Sun; Ⓜ Sol

When Ferran Adrià, the star Catalan chef, became concerned about Spaniards' growing obsession with fast food, he decided to do something about it. Fast Good is a wonderfully simple concept (food that's fast but healthy) and it's a terrific place to get a freshly prepared hamburger using Spanish ground beef with olive tapenade, roast chicken, sandwiches with Spanish ham, paninis, or French fries cooked in fresh olive oil. We also love the curvy white and lime-green décor. There's another Fast Good pp102–3; Calle de Juan Bravo 3; ☯ noon-5pm & 8pm-midnight Mon-Fri, 12.30-5.30pm & 8pm-midnight Sat & Sun; Ⓜ Núñez de Balboa) in Salamanca.

CERVECERÍA 100 MONTADITOS
Map pp64–5   Bocadillos €

☎ 902 197 494; www.cerveceria100montaditos .com; Calle Mayor 22; meals €5-10; Ⓜ Sol

CULINARY TOURS OF MADRID

If you'd like an insider's take on Madrid's (often lesser-known) tapas restaurants, Adventurous Appetites (☎ 639 331 073; www.adventurousappetites.com; 4hr tour incl 1st drink €50, food extra; ☺ 8pm-midnight Mon-Sat) runs English-language tours through central Madrid from the bear statue in Puerta del Sol.

Another good choice is Letango Tours (Map pp76–7; ☎ 91 369 47 52; www.letango.com; 3hr tour incl light tapas Mon-Fri €95, Sat & Sun €135).

This bar with outlets all across the city serves up no fewer than 100 different varieties of mini-*bocadillos* (filled rolls, without butter) that span the full range of Spanish staples, such as chorizo, *jamón*, *tortilla*, a variety of cheeses and seafood, in more combinations than you could imagine; there are even four possibilities with chocolate. Each one costs a princely €1.20 and four will satisfy most stomachs. You fill out your order, take it up to the counter and your name is called in no time. Menus in English are available.

CERVECERÍA COMPANO
Map pp64–5   Bocadillos €
Calle de Botaneros; bocadillos €2.30; ☺ **lunch & dinner until late;** Ⓜ **Sol**
Spanish bars don't come any more basic than this, but it's the purveyor of an enduring and wildly popular Madrid tradition – a *bocadillo de calamares* at any hour of the day or night. If it's closed, which is rare, Bar La Ideal next door is the same deal.

LA LATINA & LAVAPIÉS

Although facing stiff competition elsewhere, La Latina is simply the best barrio in Madrid for tapas. If you're only planning one tapas crawl while in town, do it here. It also ranks with Malasaña and Chueca for stylish dining and innovative cooking; take your pick of any of the restaurants around Calle de la Cava Baja and you won't leave disappointed.

Lavapiés is more eclectic and multicultural and, generally speaking, the further down the hill you go, the better it gets, especially along Calle de Argumosa.

EL ALBOROQUE Map pp76–7 Spanish Fusion €€€
☎ 91 389 65 70 or 902 203 025; www.alboroque .es in Spanish; Calle de Atocha 34; meals €55-80;

☺ lunch & dinner Tue-Sat; Ⓜ Antón Martín or Tirso de Molina
The new home kitchen of Madrid's hottest home-grown chef, Andrés Madrigal, is all that you'd expect from a temple of gastronomy, with experiments in flavours and textures that never miss a beat. Dishes like cherry gazpacho, smoked crayfish with cardamom and pear, and rocket and parmesan ice cream are the star turns, but everything's a revelation. The evening set menu for €55 gives you a range of the chef's latest experiments. Fine wines and a refined setting in a mid-19th-century palace make it one of Madrid's best new restaurants.

CASA LUCIO Map pp76–7 Spanish €€
☎ 91 365 32 52; www.casalucio.es, in Spanish; Calle de la Cava Baja 35; meals €40-50; ☺ lunch & dinner Sun-Fri, dinner Sat Sep-Jul; Ⓜ La Latina
Lucio has been wowing madrileños with his light touch, quality ingredients and home-style local cooking for ages – think seafood, roasted meats and, a Lucio speciality, eggs in abundance. There's also *rabo de toro* during the Fiestas de San Isidro Labrador and plenty of rioja to wash away the mere thought of it. Casa Lucio draws an august, always well-dressed crowd, which has included the King of Spain, former US president Bill Clinton and Penélope Cruz.

ENE RESTAURANTE
Map pp76–7   Tapas & Fusion €€
☎ 91 366 25 91; www.enerestaurante.com; Calle del Nuncio 19; meals €30-35, brunch €20; Ⓜ La Latina
Just across from Iglesia de San Pedro El Viejo, one of Madrid's oldest churches, Ene

top picks

TAPAS

- Sagarretxe (p179)
- Biotza (p170)
- Taberna Txacoli (p165)
- Almendro 13 (p165)
- Taberna Matritum (p164)
- Juanalaloca (opposite)
- Txirimiri (p164)
- Casa Lucas (p164)
- Baco y Beto (p176)
- Bocaito (p176)

EAT STREETS – CALLE DE LA CAVA BAJA

Calle de la Cava Baja (Map pp76–7; M La Latina) is jam-packed with great tapas bars and sit-down restaurants. For tapas, there is none finer than Taberna Txacoli (p165), La Chata (below) and Casa Lucas (p164). Other outstanding choices include La Camarilla (☎ 91 354 02 07; www.lacamarillarestaurante.com, in Spanish; Calle de la Cava Baja 21; meals €25-30, tapas tasting menu €17.90; ☺ lunch & dinner Mon, Tue & Thu-Sat, lunch Sun; M La Latina) and the Galician cuisine of Orixe (☎ 91 354 04 11; www.orixerestaurante.com, in Spanish; Calle de la Cava Baja 17; meals €25-30; ☺ dinner Mon-Fri, lunch & dinner Sat, lunch Sun; M La Latina).

For a sit-down meal, it's difficult to beat Casa Lucio (opposite), but other bastions of tradition worth splashing out for include the Madrid-through-and-through Posada de la Villa (☎ 91 366 18 60; Calle de la Cava Baja 9; meals €35-40; ☺ lunch & dinner Mon-Sat, lunch Sun Sep-Jul; M La Latina), in a restored 17th-century inn, and the refined Navarran cooking of Restaurante Julián de Tolosa (☎ 91 365 82 10; Calle de la Cava Baja 8; meals €45-50; ☺ lunch & dinner Mon-Sat, lunch Sun; M La Latina). For something a little more varied, try just around the corner at El Malandrín (☎ 91 354 00 82; Calle de Almendro 9; meals €25-30; ☺ lunch & dinner Tue-Sat, lunch Mon & Sun; M La Latina), which cooks Indian-Spanish food, has saints' effigies of Raquel Welch and Steve McQueen, and does a Sunday Menú del Rastro (€12).

is anything but old world. The design is cutting edge and awash with reds and purples, while the young and friendly waiters circulate to the tune of lounge music. The food is Spanish-Asian fusion and there are also plenty of *pintxos* (Basque tapas) to choose from. The chill-out beds downstairs are great for an after-dinner cocktail or even a meal, although they're always reserved well in advance. The brunch (12.30pm to 4.30pm Saturday and Sunday) includes fine pastries and a Bloody Mary.

JUANALALOCA Map pp76–7 Tapas €€
☎ 91 364 05 25; Plaza de la Puerta de Moros 4; meals €30-35; ☺ lunch & dinner Tue-Sun, dinner Mon; M La Latina

You can't miss 'Juana the Crazy One' with its bright purple façade and nor would you want to. We're still convinced that the wife of one Lonely Planet author cooks the best *tortilla de patatas* in Madrid, but we have to confess that Juanalaloca gives her a run for her money – it's a far cry from your average bar tortilla and the secret lies in the caramelised onions. With more than 70, mostly Basque-influenced tapas to choose from, there are so many possibilities and fine wines, but quality here doesn't come cheap. There's another branch, Juanalaloca.zip (Calle del Nuncio 17; ☺ dinner Tue-Fri, 1pm-1am Sat & Sun), just down the hill.

NUNC EST BIBENDUM Map pp76–7 Spanish €€
☎ 91 366 52 10; Calle de la Cava Alta 13; meals €30-35; ☺ lunch & dinner Mon-Sat, lunch Sun; M La Latina

Calle de la Cava Alta doesn't have the sex appeal (or the crowds) of its neighbour, Calle de la Cava Baja, but it has some wonderful little bar-restaurants. Nunc est Bibendum combines a classy, clean-lined look with a varied menu that defies categorisation – sometimes it's a Basque base; other flavours come from the south or from France – but it's always good, with plenty of meat and fish dishes, and crêpes, foie gras and rice dishes built in. The wine list is also thoughtfully chosen, with some lesser-known Spanish wines.

LA BUGA DEL LOBO Map pp76–7 Spanish €€
☎ 91 467 61 51; www.labocadellobo.com; Calle de Argumosa 11; meals €25-30, menú del día €10-11; ☺ 11am-2am Wed-Mon; M Lavapiés

La Buga del Lobo has been one of the 'in' places in cool and gritty Lavapiés for years now and it's still hard to get a table. The atmosphere is bohemian and inclusive with funky, swirling murals, contemporary art exhibitions and jazz or lounge music. The food's good and traditional with meat and fish dishes for mains and *croquetas*, cheeses or salads for entrées, but it's best known for its groovy vibe at any time of day or night.

LA CHATA Map pp76–7 Tapas €€
☎ 91 366 14 58; Calle de la Cava Baja 24; meals €25-30; ☺ lunch & dinner Thu-Mon, dinner Wed; M La Latina

Behind the lavishly tiled façade, La Chata looks for all the world like a neglected outpost of the past. The décor may be rundown and the bullfighting memorabilia not to everyone's taste, but this is an essential stop on a tapas tour of La Latina. The dishes are mainstays of the local diet (tripe and plenty of seafood), but don't come here without ordering a *cazuela* (stew cooked and served in a ceramic pot).

LA MUSA LATINA Map pp76–7 Fusion €€
☎ 91 354 02 55; www.lamusalatina.com; Costanilla de San Andrés 1; meals €25-30, menú del día €11; ☺ lunch & dinner daily; Ⓜ La Latina
La Musa Latina is back and better than ever with an ever-popular dining area and food that's designed to bring a smile to your face. It's the same deal as at its other restaurant in Malasaña (p172) and the downstairs bar in the former wine cellar is ideal for an after-dinner drink.

MALACATÍN Map pp76–7 Madrileño €€
☎ 91 365 52 41; www.malacatin.com, in Spanish; Calle de Ruda 5; meals €25-30; ☺ lunch & dinner Mon-Fri, lunch Sat; Ⓜ La Latina
If you want to see madrileños enjoying their favourite local food, this is arguably the best place to do so. The clamour of conversation – an essential part of the local eating experience – bounces off the tiled walls of the cramped dining area adorned with bullfighting memorabilia. The speciality is as much *cocido* (stew) as you can eat (€18). The *degustación de cocido* (taste of *cocido*; €5) at the bar is a great way to try Madrid's favourite dish without going all the way, although locals would argue that doing that is like smoking without inhaling.

NAÏA RESTAURANTE Map pp76–7 Fusion €€
☎ 91 366 27 83; www.naiarestaurante.com, in Spanish; Plaza de la Paja 3; meals €25-30; ☺ lunch & dinner Mon-Sat; Ⓜ La Latina
On the lovely Plaza de la Paja, Naïa has a real buzz about it, with a cooking laboratory overseen by Carlos López Reyes, delightful modern Spanish cuisine and a chill-out lounge downstairs. The emphasis throughout is on natural ingredients, healthy food and exciting tastes. The Iberian meats cooked with vanilla and smoked potato mash is intense and surprising, while the fish dishes are equally fresh.

OLIVEROS Map pp76–7 Madrileño €€
☎ 91 354 62 52; Calle de San Milán 4; meals €25-30; ☺ lunch & dinner Tue-Sat, noon-6pm Sun mid-Sep–mid-Aug; Ⓜ La Latina

This famous old *taberna* has been in the Oliveros family since 1921 and nothing seems to have changed much since it opened. It's a tiny, warm, bottle-lined den that doesn't disappoint with its local dishes of *cocido a la madrileña* or *callos de la Abuela* (grandma's tripe).

TXIRIMIRI Map pp76–7 Tapas €€
☎ 91 364 11 96; Calle del Humilladero 6; meals €25-30; ☺ noon-midnight Tue-Sun; Ⓜ La Latina
This Basque *pintxo* bar is a great little discovery just down from the main La Latina tapas circuit. Wonderful wines, gorgeous *pintxos* (tapas; the *tortilla de patatas* is superb) and more substantial dishes with a nod to Italian influences, such as duck lasagne and fine risottos, add up to a pretty special combination. It's always full and the atmosphere is sophisticated and casual.

TABERNA MATRITUM Map pp76–7 Tapas €€
☎ 91 365 82 37; Calle de la Cava Alta 17; meals €20-30; ☺ lunch Mon-Fri, lunch & dinner Sat & Sun; Ⓜ La Latina
This little gem is reason enough to detour from the more popular Calle de la Cava Baja next door. Terrific *tostas* (toasts, especially those with foie gras, caramelised onion and baked apple) and tapas, such as Spanish ham with cream of truffle, are complemented by a good wine list and a cosy ambience. An outstanding choice.

CASA LUCAS Map pp76–7 Tapas €€
☎ 91 365 08 04; Calle de la Cava Baja 30; meals €20-25; ☺ lunch & dinner Thu-Tue, dinner Wed; Ⓜ La Latina
It's always a close-run thing between Casa Lucas and Almendro 13 (opposite) for the best tapas bar in La Latina, if not all Madrid. It's a small place where there's hardly room to bend your elbow, but persist you should because this bar has been doing creative tapas long before they became fashionable. The grilled chicken with sesame, soy sauce and corn mousse is typical. We only ever hear praise about this place.

EL ESTRAGÓN Map pp76–7 Vegetarian €€
☎ 91 365 89 82; Plaza de la Paja 10; meals €20-25, menú del día €9.99; ☺ lunch & dinner daily; Ⓜ La Latina
A delightful spot for crepes, veggie burgers and other vegetarian specialities, El Estragón is undoubtedly one of Madrid's best vegetar-

ian restaurants, although attentive vegans won't appreciate the use of butter. Apart from that, we're yet to hear a bad word about El Estragón. It's also on one of old Madrid's quieter and more delightful squares.

LA BURBUJA QUE RÍE Map pp76–7 Asturian €€
☎ 91 366 51 67; Calle del Ángel 16; meals €20; ⌚ lunch & dinner daily; Ⓜ La Latina
'The Laughing Bubble' is an excellent Asturian tavern that serves up nourishing and hearty dishes with cider; the *patatas con cabrales* (potato with blue cheese) is a fine order. It's all very noisy and casual, like a genuine Asturian *taberna*, and you'd hard-pressed to find a more popular restaurant dedicated to this fine regional cuisine.

ALMENDRO 13 Map pp76–7 Tapas €€
☎ 91 365 42 52; Calle del Almendro 13; meals €15-25; ⌚ lunch & dinner daily; Ⓜ La Latina
Regularly voted among the top 10 tapas bars in Madrid, Almendro 13 is a charming, wildly popular *taberna* where you come for traditional Spanish tapas with an emphasis on quality rather than frilly elaborations. Cured meats, cheeses, tortillas, *huevos rotos* (literally, 'broken eggs') and many variations on the themes dominate the menu; it serves both *raciones* and half-sized plates. The only problem is that the wait for a table (low, with wooden stools) requires the patience of a saint, so order a fine wine or manzanilla (dry sherry) and soak up the buzz. Unusually, it opens at 7.30pm (8pm on weekends), when your chances of finding a perch are higher.

CORAZON LOCO Map pp76–7 Tapas €€
☎ 91 366 57 83; Calle del Almendro 22; meals €15-25; ⌚ lunch & dinner Tue-Sun; Ⓜ La Latina
In a barrio replete with tapas options, it takes something pretty special to catch our eye. Corazon Loco is just such a place, a splendid little tapas bar blending subtle tastes (the canapés, for €3.90, include *solomillo* with brie or salmon with Roquefort). It also has a special dish each day, which can range from couscous to *cocido*. Wine by the glass never costs more than €2.50 and the service is friendly. Every time we pass by here it's full and deservedly so.

TYAKo LiNA

TABERNA TXACOLI Map pp76–7 Tapas €
☎ 91 366 48 77; Calle de la Cava Baja 26; meals €15-20; ⌚ Tue & Thu-Sat lunch & dinner, lunch Sun, dinner Wed; Ⓜ La Latina

Taberna Txacoli calls its *pintxos* 'high cuisine in miniature' – the first part is true, but these are some of the biggest *pintxos* (€2.80 to €5) you'll find and some are a meal in themselves. If ordering tapas makes you nervous because you don't speak Spanish or you're not quite sure how it works, it couldn't be easier here – they're lined up on the bar, Basque style, in all their glory and you can simply point. Whatever you order, wash it down with a *txacoli*, a sharp Basque white.

VIVA LA VIDA Map pp76–7 Tapas €
☎ 91 366 33 49; www.vivalavida.vg; Costanilla de San Andrés 16; veg buffet per 100g €1.80; ⌚ 11am-midnight; Ⓜ La Latina
This organic food shop has as its centrepiece an enticing vegetarian buffet with hot and cold food that's always filled with flavour. With a laid-back vibe and being on the cusp of Plaza de la Paja, it's a great place at any time of the day, especially outside normal Spanish eating hours when your stomach's rumbling. It has another branch (Map pp84–5; ☎ 91 369 72 54; Calle de las Huertas 57; Ⓜ Antón Martín) in Huertas, although it's more takeaway with only a handful of stools.

BAR MELO'S Map pp76–7 Tapas & Bocadillos €
☎ 91 527 50 54; Calle del Ave María; meals €10-15; ⌚ 9pm-2am Tue-Sat; Ⓜ Lavapiés
One of those Spanish bars that you'd normally walk past without a second glance, Bar Melo's is famous across the city for its *zapatillas* (great, spanking *bocadillos* of *lacón* – cured shoulder of pork – and cheese). They're big, they're greasy and they're damn good; the place is packed on a Friday or Saturday night when a *zapatilla* is the perfect accompaniment to a night of drinking. The *croquetas* are also famously good.

HUERTAS & ATOCHA
The noise surrounding Huertas nightlife can obscure the fact that the barrio is a terrific place to eat out. Its culinary appeal lies in a hotchpotch of styles rather than any overarching personality. It's a state of affairs perhaps best summed up by the presence of restaurants Arola Madrid, one of the home kitchens of master chef Sergi Arola, and down-and-dirty tapas bars selling *oreja* (pig's ear). In between,

there's Basque, Galician, Andalucian, Scandinavian and Italian from which to choose.

LHARDY Map pp84–5   Madrileño €€€

☎ 91 522 22 07; www.lhardy.com; Carrera de San Jerónimo 8; meals €50-60; ⊗ lunch & dinner Mon-Sat, lunch Sun; Ⓜ Sol or Sevilla

This Madrid landmark (since 1839) is an elegant treasure-trove of takeaway gourmet tapas. Upstairs is the upscale preserve of house specialities, such as *callos, cocido*, pheasant in grape juice and lemon soufflé. It's expensive, but the quality and service are unimpeachable, and the great and good of Madrid have all eaten here at some stage.

AROLA MADRID Map pp84–5 Nouvelle Cuisine €€

☎ 91 467 02 02; www.arola-madrid.com, in Spanish; Calle de Argumosa 43; meals €50; ⊗ 10am-9pm Mon & Wed-Sat, to 5pm Sun; Ⓜ Atocha

What do you get if you cross one of Spain's most celebrated young chefs and a designer, blood-red space in one of Europe's most innovative galleries? A terrific place to eat, drink or simply hang out and feel stylish in one of the great art cities of the world. The food is nouvelle cuisine with an emphasis on presentation and variations on a traditional Spanish base.

A TASCA DO BACALHAU
PORTUGUÊS Map pp84–5   Portuguese €€

☎ 91 429 56 75; Calle de Lope de Vega 14; meals €30-40, menú del día €21.50; ⊗ lunch & dinner Tue-Sat, lunch Mon; Ⓜ Antón Martín

One of the few authentically Portuguese restaurants in Madrid, A Tasca do Bacalhau doesn't have a particularly extensive menu, but it's dominated by excellent *bacalhau* (cod) and rice dishes. It's pricey, but if you're not familiar with Portuguese cooking, this is a good place to have your first taste.

ØLSEN Map pp84–5   Scandinavian €€

☎ 91 429 36 59; www.olsenmadrid.com; Calle del Prado 15; meals €30-40, menú del día €10-15; ⊗ lunch & dinner daily; Ⓜ Antón Martín

With everything you'd expect from a Scandinavian restaurant – minimalist décor, an extensive vodka menu and creatively conceived tastes from the north – Ølsen confirms that Huertas has more than its share of classy establishments. The service is casual but attentive, the food (eg reindeer) delicious and the crowd young and well heeled. Service can, however, be a little slow.

SIDRERÍA VASCA ZERAIN
Map pp84–5   Basque €€

☎ 91 429 79 09; Calle de Quevedo 3; meals €30-40; ⊗ Mon-Sat; Ⓜ Antón Martín

In the heart of the Barrio de las Letras, this sophisticated Basque restaurant is one of the best places in town to sample Basque cuisine. The essential staples include cider, *bacalao* and wonderful steaks, while there are also a few splashes of creativity thrown in (the secret's in the sauce).

LA VACA VERÓNICA
Map pp84–5   Italian/Argentine €€

☎ 91 429 78 27; www.lavacaveronica.es, in Spanish; Calle de Moratín 38; meals €25-30, menú del día €15; ⊗ lunch & dinner Mon-Sat, dinner Sun; Ⓜ Antón Martín

Plenty of red meat, pastas and salads are the staples of this long-standing local favourite in the Paseo del Prado hinterland. There's an agreeable buzz about this place most nights and the service is excellent. If there's two of you, try the *bandeja de la vaca* (€35), a meat platter that groans under the weight of steak, chorizo, *morcilla, mollejas* (sweetbreads), potatoes… It's proud of its smokers-allowed policy, boasting that Humphrey Bogart would feel comfortable here.

AL NATURAL Map pp84–5   Vegetarian €€

☎ 91 369 47 09; www.alnatural.biz; Calle de Zorrilla 11; meals €20-30; ⊗ lunch & dinner Mon-Sat, lunch Sun; Ⓜ Sevilla or Banco de España

Tucked behind the Spanish parliament, Al Natural has an intimate ambience and terrific vegetarian food. There are the usual suspects, such as salads and pastas, but some welcome creative touches, including grilled provolone cheeses, make this a good choice.

CASA ALBERTO Map pp84–5 Traditional Spanish €€

☎ 91 429 93 56; www.casaalberto.es, in Spanish; Calle de las Huertas 18; meals €20-25; ⊗ noon-1.30am Tue-Sat, to 4pm Sun; Ⓜ Antón Martín

One of the most atmospheric old *tabernas* of Madrid, Casa Alberto has been around since 1827. The secret to its staying power is vermouth on tap (see p191), excellent tapas and fine sit-down meals; *rabo de toro* is a good order. As the antique wood-pannelled decoration will suggest straight away, the *raciones* have none of the frilly innovations that have come to characterise Spanish tapas, and *jamón*, Manchego cheese and anchovies are recurring themes.

LA FINCA DE SUSANA

Map pp84–5   Mediterranean €€

☎ 91 369 35 57; www.lafinca-restaurant.com;
Calle de Arlabán 4; meals €20-25; ☷ lunch &
dinner daily; Ⓜ Sevilla

Just because you're paying relatively low
prices for your meal doesn't mean you have
to dine in *cutre* (rough-and-ready) surrounds. The softly lit dining area is bathed
in greenery and the sometimes innovative,
sometimes traditional food draws a hip
young crowd. The *ensalada de aguacate con
cinturón de bacalao* (avocado salad with a
cod 'belt') is a fine choice. It doesn't take
reservations.

LA TRUCHA Map pp84–5   Tapas €€

☎ 91 532 08 82; Calle de Núñez de Arce 6; meals
€20-25; ☷ lunch & dinner Tue-Sat; Ⓜ Sol

'The Trout' is an outpost of Andalucía
in central Madrid and is one of Madrid's
longest-standing and most popular tapas
bars. The counter is loaded with enticing
choices, but seafood is why most people
come here and the bar staff will have their
own idea about what's good to try. The
menu lists a staggering 95 possibilities. If
it's too crowded, try the other branch (Map
pp84–5; ☎ 91 429 58 33; Calle de Manuel Fernández y
González 3) nearby.

LOS GATOS Map pp84–5   Tapas €€

☎ 91 429 30 67; Calle de Jesús 2; meals €20-25;
☷ noon-1am Sun-Thu, to 2am Fri & Sat;
Ⓜ Antón Martín

Tapas you can point to without deciphering the menu and eclectic old-world décor
(from bullfighting memorabilia to a fresco
of skeletons at the bar) make this a popular
choice down the bottom end of Huertas.
The most popular order is the *tostas* (tapas
on toast), which, we have to say, is rather
delicious.

MACEIRAS Map pp84–5   Galician €€

☎ 91 429 15 84; Calle de las Huertas 66; ☷ lunch
& dinner daily; meals €20-25; Ⓜ Antón Martín

Galician tapas (think octopus, green peppers etc) never tasted so good as in this
agreeably rustic bar down the bottom of
the Huertas hill, especially when washed
down with a crisp white Ribeiro. The
simple wooden tables, loyal customers
and handy location make this a fine place
to rest after (or en route to) the museums
along the Paseo del Prado. Galician music

also plays in the background. There's
another branch (Map pp84–5; Calle de Jesús 7;
☷ lunch & dinner Tue-Sun, dinner Mon) around
the corner.

VINOS GONZÁLEZ Map pp84–5   Deli Café €€

☎ 91 429 56 18; Calle de León 12; meals €20-25;
☷ 9am-midnight Tue-Thu, to 1am Fri & Sat;
Ⓜ Antón Martín

Ever dreamed of a deli where you could
choose a tasty morsel and sit down and eat
it right there? Well, here you can. On offer
is a tempting array of cheeses, cured meats
and other typically Spanish delicacies. The
tables are informal, café style and it also
does takeaway, but we recommend eating
here if you can find a table.

LA CASA DEL ABUELO Map pp84–5   Tapas €€

☎ 91 521 23 19; Calle de la Victoria 12; meals €15-
25; ☷ 11.30am-3.30pm & 6.30-11.30pm; Ⓜ Sol

The 'House of the Grandfather' is an age-
less, popular place where the traditional
order is a *chato* (small glass) of the heavy,
sweet El Abuelo red wine (made in Toledo
province) and the heavenly *gambas a la
plancha* (grilled prawns) or *gambas al ajillo*
(prawns sizzling in garlic on little ceramic
plates).

RESTAURANTE INTEGRAL ARTEMISA

Map pp84–5   Vegetarian €€

☎ 91 429 50 92; Calle de Ventura de la Vega 4;
meals €15-25; ☷ lunch & dinner daily; Ⓜ Sevilla

With a couple of options for meat eaters,
this mostly vegetarian restaurant does a
brisk trade with its salads, moussaka and
rice dishes. The décor is simple, the service
is no-nonsense and there are more than
50 dishes to choose from. The salads are
what marks this place out as worthy of a
visit.

LA NEGRA TOMASA Map pp84–5   Cuban €

☎ 91 523 58 30; Calle de Cádiz 9; meals €15-20;
☷ noon-3.30am Sun & Mon, to 5.30am Tue-Sat;
Ⓜ Sol

Bar, restaurant and magnet for all things
Cuban, La Negra Tomasa is a boisterous
meeting place for the Havana set with
waitresses dressed in traditional Cuban
outfits (definitely pre-Castro), decent
food such as *cojimar* (shrimps in a tomato
sauce with rice and slices of banana frit-
ter) and typical drinks of the Caribbean.

LATE BITES & DAWN DINING

Way past midnight and your stomach's growling? If you know where to look, meals are available in Madrid up to 2am, and sometimes later. In Huertas try La Negra Tomasa (p167) or Malaspina (p191). Around Plaza Mayor Cervecería Compano (p162) serves *bocadillos de calamares* (rolls stuffed with calamari) until the wee hours, while the kitchen might still be open at Delic (p188) down on Plaza de la Paja. In Lavapiés the *bocadillos* of Bar Melo's (p165) are a Madrid institution, while La Buga del Lobo (p163) is another possibility. In Malasaña Casa Do Compañeiro (p172) stays open till 2am, as does Giangrossi (p174) on Friday and Saturday for ice creams. For a *chocolate con churros* (Spanish donuts with chocolate) at any time of night, Chocolatería de San Ginés (see the boxed text, p173) rarely closes. Chinese vendors often set up snack stalls at all hours along Gran Vía on weekends.

There's often live Cuban music in the evening.

LA PIOLA Map pp84–5 Italian Café €
Calle de León 9; meals €15-20; ☺ 10am-2am Mon-Sat; Ⓜ Antón Martín
This charming Italian place is part café and part bar. The small range of pasta on offer is well priced and filled with subtle flavours. In addition to the simple tables and bar stools, there's a sofa that has to be the best seat in the house. You're likely to find it full most nights of the week, which has as much to do with the atmosphere as the food.

LAS BRAVAS Map pp84–5 Tapas €
☎ 91 532 26 20; Callejón de Álvarez Gato 3; meals €15; ☺ 10am-11.30pm; Ⓜ Sol
Las Bravas has long been the place for a *caña* (small glass of beer) and the best *patatas bravas* (fried potatoes with a spicy tomato sauce) in town; other good orders include *pulpo a la gallega,* (octopus Galician style), *calamares* (calamari) and *oreja a la plancha* (grilled pig's ear). The antics of the bar staff are enough to merit a stop, and the distorting mirrors are a minor Madrid landmark. Elbow your way to the bar and be snappy about your orders. There are three other branches dotted around Huertas, including one on the corner of Calle de Espoz y Mina and Callejón Álvarez Gato (Map pp84–5).

LA BIOTIKA Map pp84–5 Vegetarian €
☎ 91 429 07 80; Calle del Amor de Dios 3; meals €10-15; ☺ lunch & dinner daily; Ⓜ Antón Martín
The macrobiotic, café-style La Biotika, out the back of a health-food shop, takes its vegetarianism seriously with an emphasis on simplicity and healthy eating with not too many creative twists: *seitan* (wheat meat), tofu-based dishes and generous salads. If you're a vegetarian, you'll love it. If you're not, you might want to go elsewhere as the variety is limited.

PASEO DEL PRADO & EL RETIRO

In the discreet residential enclave between the Parque del Buen Retiro and the Paseo del Prado you'll find a handful of exclusive restaurants where eating is taken seriously, elegant, classic charm is the pervasive atmosphere, and limousines wait outside to ferry the well-heeled back home.

CLUB 31 Map pp92–3 Spanish €€€
☎ 91 532 00 92; Calle de Alcalá 58; meals €50-60; ☺ lunch & dinner daily Sep-Jul; Ⓜ Retiro
An old Madrid classic, Club 31 has a vaguely contemporary design with long black seats, leaning wall mirrors and bright white designer lamps hanging from the ceiling, but the cuisine is classic. The accent is on fish and game, with the occasional modern touch. You could set your watch by the old-style, professional service. Last time we were here, royalty were at the next table.

EL BRILLANTE Map pp92–3 Bocadillos €
☎ 91 528 69 66; Calle del Doctor Drumén 7; bocadillos €4-6; ☺ 6.30am-12.30am; Ⓜ Atocha
Just by the Centro de Arte Reina Sofía, this breezy, no-frills bar-eatery is a Madrid institution for its *bocadillos* (the *bocadillo de calamares* is an old favourite) and other snacks (*raciones* cost €7.50 to €12). It's also famous for *chocolate con churros* or *porras* (deep-fried doughnut strips) in the wee hours after a hard night on the tiles. There's another branch (Map pp116–17; ☎ 91 448 19 88; Calle de Eloy Gonzalo 14; Ⓜ Quevedo) in Chamberí.

SALAMANCA

Eating out in Salamanca is traditionally as exclusive as the shops that fill the barrio, the sorts of places where the keys to Jags and BMWs are left for valet parking, only the impeccably dressed are allowed through the doors, and prices and quality are high. But Salamanca is also home to some of Madrid's best-kept eating secrets, from *pintxos* (Basque tapas) to fusion restaurants and intimate dens of creative home cooking – all very handy options for refuelling after a big day shopping in the barrio.

EL AMPARO Map pp102–3 Basque & Creative €€€

☎ 91 431 64 56; Calle de Puigcerdà 8; meals €80-100; ❤ lunch & dinner Mon-Fri, dinner Sat; Ⓜ Serrano

Hidden away down a charming alley in the heart of Salamanca, El Amparo is one of the more exclusive restaurants in town. The cuisine has been variously described as Basque and *nueva cocina madrileña* (nouvelle Madrid cuisine); try the *cigala salteadas con raviolis de queso, miel y romero* (sautéed crayfish with cheese, honey and rosemary ravioli). The service is impeccable, the wine list admirable and the food is generally excellent. Some of the home-made desserts are simply divine.

SULA MADRID Map pp102–3 Fusion €€€

☎ 91 781 61 97; www.sula.es; Calle de Jorge Juan 33; meals €70-80; ❤ lunch & dinner Mon-Sat; Ⓜ Velázquez

If you want to catch Salamanca's happening vibe, head for Sula, a gourmet food store, super-stylish tapas bar and clean-lined restaurant where gastronomic wunderkind Quique Dacosta (voted Spain's best chef in 2005) serves up a range of Mediterranean dishes that you won't find anywhere else. Design touches added by Amaya Arzuaga help to make this one of Madrid's coolest, black-clad spaces. Rumour has it that David Beckham had one of his farewell parties here.

RAMSES LIFE & FOOD
Map pp102–3 Fusion & Spanish €€

☎ 91 435 16 66; www.ramseslife.com; Plaza de la Independencia 4; meals €35-60; ❤ noon-11.30pm; Ⓜ Retiro

Opened in December 2007 and designed by Philippe Starck, Ramses Life & Food is all the rage among Madrid's trendy, well-to-do set. The decoration is baroque and upmarket kitsch (the reproduction of an El Greco on the ceiling sets the standard), while there are two spaces, the more informal El Petit and the seriously formal bistro. The food gets mixed reviews (far more than it should for these prices), but the aubergine croquettes and curry mussels are well worth trying. You won't get past the doorman unless you're well dressed (the first thing he does is look at your shoes), but it's worth experiencing this place at least once. It also does brunch and is a great choice for a late-night *copa* after the kitchen closes.

CITRA Map pp102–3 Mediterranean €€

☎ 91 575 28 66; Calle de Castelló 18; meals €35-40; ❤ lunch & dinner Mon-Sat; Ⓜ Príncipe de Vergara or Velázquez

When the *New York Times* declared Citra the best new restaurant in Madrid a couple of years ago, it must have been thinking of the cod taco or any other of the unusual Mediterranean dishes on offer. The dining area is cosy, colourful and consciously cool, and you can order tapas if you just want to catch the vibe.

TEATRIZ Map pp102–3 Fusion €€

☎ 91 577 53 79; Calle de Hermosilla 15; meals €35-40; ❤ 11.30am-12.30pm; Ⓜ Serrano

Also designed by Philippe Starck, the former Teatro Beatriz has an eerily lit bar right on the stage and it's the kind of place where you'll need to look like George Clooney to feel like you fit in. The food follows the fashion, ranging from 'Made in Spain' to 'Fusion'. While you're there, check out the loos, where you leave luminous footprints!

MUMBAI MASSALA Map pp102–3 Indian €€

☎ 91 435 71 94; www.mumbaimassala.com; Calle de los Recoletos 14; meals €35; ❤ lunch & dinner daily; Ⓜ Retiro

Enter through the heavy red curtain and into a brightly coloured Indian world where the food and service are good and the ambience is very laid-back. Servings aren't enormous, but they're superbly done with dishes spanning the subcontinent from southern India (think hot and spicy) to Pakistan. If you can't decide, it has a range of set menus (€14 to €30) to choose from.

AL-MOUNIA Map pp102–3 Moroccan €€

☎ 91 435 08 28; www.almounia.es, in Spanish; Calle de los Recoletos 5; meals €30-35; ⏲ lunch & dinner Mon-Sat Sep-Jul; Ⓜ Recoletos

One of the longest-standing Moroccan restaurants in town, Al-Mounia has a loyal following. The best couscous in Madrid (it bears little relation to the couscous you buy in a packet) is a menu highlight, as are the subtly spiced lamb tagines (stew cooked in a ceramic pot) and the *asado berebere* (Berber roast; €24.50). The hand-crafted traditional décor is breathtaking and greatly complements the cuisine.

LA GALETTE

Map pp102–3 Vegetarian & European €€

☎ 91 576 06 41; Calle del Conde de Aranda 11; meals €30-35; ⏲ lunch & dinner Mon-Sat, lunch Sun; Ⓜ Retiro

This lovely little restaurant combines an intimate dining area with checked table-cloths and cuisine that the owner describes as 'baroque vegetarian'. The food is a revelation, blending creative flavours with a strong base in traditional home cooking. The *croquetas de manzana* (apple croquettes) are a house speciality, but the truth is everything on the extensive menu is good. The only problem is that the tables are so close together you get the feeling that diners need to breathe in at the same time for everyone to fit.

LE CAFÉ Map pp102–3 Spanish €€

☎ 91 781 15 86; Calle de los Recoletos 13; meals €25-30; ⏲ lunch & dinner Mon-Sat, lunch Sun; Ⓜ Retiro

It can be almost impossible to get a table here at lunchtime on a weekday when locals stream in from surrounding offices for the buzzy atmosphere and orange décor. The food is largely traditional Spanish fare (rice dishes are a recurring theme) and they're done well, but dishes such as smoked reindeer carpaccio with mushrooms and a lime vinaigrette (€14.50) show more than a touch of flair.

BIOTZA Map pp102–3 Basque Tapas €€

☎ 91 781 03 13; Calle de Claudio Coello 27; meals €25; ⏲ 9am-midnight Mon-Thu, to 1am Fri & Sat; Ⓜ Serrano

This breezy Basque tapas bar is one of the best places in Madrid to sample the creativity of bite-sized *pintxos* as only the Basques can make them. It's the perfect combina-

tion of San Sebastián bars laden with food and Madrid style in the pale-green, red-black decoration and unusual angular benches. The *pintxos* cost from €2.40 to €3.70 apiece, but we suggest one of the *degustación de pintxos* (tasting menus; €17 to €21) where you get a selection. The prices quickly add up, but it's highly recommended nonetheless.

RESTAURANTE ESTAY Map pp102–3 Tapas €€

☎ 91 578 04 70; www.estayrestaurante.com; Calle de Hermosilla 46; meals €20-30; ⏲ 8am-12.30am Mon-Sat; Ⓜ Velázquez

Restaurante Estay is partly a standard Spanish bar where besuited waiters serve *café con leche* (it does breakfasts) and partly a cool tapas bar known for its range of *pintxos* (mostly €2 to €4), international wines and contemporary art on the walls. It may seem rather an odd mix, but somehow it works.

LA COLONIAL DE GOYA Map pp102–3 Tapas €€

☎ 91 575 63 06; Calle de Jorge Juan 34; meals €20; ⏲ 8am-midnight Mon-Fri, to 1am Sat; Ⓜ Velázquez

This engaging little tapas bar all dressed in white serves 68 varieties of *pinchos* (€2.40 to €4.30), as well as more hearty *raciones*, internationally flavoured salads and carefully chosen wines. We especially liked the prawns with guacamole and the goats-cheese croquettes with quince jam and pine nuts. The chill-out music on the sound system and the dull roar of popularity only add to the charm.

MALASAÑA & CHUECA

Cool barrios. Cool places to eat. Chueca and Malasaña may be radically different, one newly modern, the other rooted firmly in the past, but their restaurants are remarkably similar. Blending old *tabernas* with laid-back temples to nouvelle Spanish cuisine, eating here revolves around an agreeable buzz, innovative cooking and casual but stylish surrounds. Some streets stand out, especially Calle de Manuela Malasaña (see the boxed text, opposite) in Malasaña and Calle de la Libertad (see the boxed text, p177) in Chueca. For cheap but decent international cuisine (eg Asian, Indian, Thai, Persian), head down to Calle de San Bernardino (Map pp110–11) at the lower end of Calle del Conde Duque.

MALASAÑA

LA ISLA DEL TESORO

Map pp110–11   Vegetarian €€

☎ 91 593 14 40; Calle de Manuela Malasaña 3; meals €30-35, menú del día €10; ⏰ lunch & dinner daily; Ⓜ Bilbao

Unlike some vegetarian restaurants that seem to work on the philosophy that a basic décor signifies healthy food, La Isla del Tesoro is loaded with quirky charm; the dining area is like someone's fantasy of a secret garden come to life. The cooking here is assured and wide ranging in its influences; the jungle burger is typical in a menu that's full of surprises. The weekday, lunchtime *menú del día* is more varied than most in Madrid, with Indonesian, Lebanese, Moroccan, French and Mexican among others all getting a run. Our only complaint? The otherwise friendly waiters are often too keen to free up your table for the next punters on weekends.

LAYDOWN REST CLUB Map pp110–11 Fusion €€

☎ 91 548 79 37; www.laydown.es, in Spanish; Plaza Mostenses 9; meals €30-35, menú del día €11; ⏰ 2-4pm & 9.30pm-2.30am Tue-Fri, 9.30pm-2.30am Sat & Sun, 2-4pm Mon; Ⓜ Plaza de España or Noviciado

The name says it all. Part of the ongoing craze in concept dining, Laydown Rest Club is whiter than white and completely devoid of tables – you eat Roman style while reclining on beds where you're served by toga-clad waiters with huge feather fans. Incredible. The menu changes daily, but it never strays too far from its variations on

top picks

INTERNATIONAL CUISINE

- Al-Mounia (opposite) Moroccan
- Arabia (p177) Middle Eastern
- Nagoya (p179) Japanese
- Mumbai Massala (p169) Indian
- Kim Bu Mbu (p176) African
- Ølsen (p166) Scandinavian
- A Tasca do Bacalhau Português (p166) Portuguese
- La Negra Tomasa (p167) Cuban
- Bangkok Café (p161) Thai
- La Mordida (p176) Mexican
- Il Casone (p179) Italian

a Mediterranean theme. It can be difficult to find – from Plaza Mostenses, head east along Calle del General Mitre then take the first lane on the right.

NINA Map pp110–11 Mediterranean Fusion €€

☎ 91 591 00 46; Calle de Manuela Malasaña 10; meals €30-35, menú del día €12.20; ⏰ lunch & dinner daily; Ⓜ Bilbao

Sophisticated, intimate and wildly popular, Nina has an extensive menu (available in English) of nouvelle Mediterranean cuisine that doesn't miss a trick; the deboned pig's trotters filled with boletus, foie gras and truffles with fried prawns is as weird and wonderful as it sounds. We like the décor, all exposed brick and subtle lighting, we love just about everything on the menu, but

EAT STREETS – CALLE DE MANUELA MALASAÑA

Calle de Manuela Malasaña (Map pp110–11; Ⓜ Bilbao) has long been one of Madrid's best streets for eating out, its appeal founded on creative approaches to Mediterranean cuisine and designer décor. While the buzz has revolved around three flagship restaurants – Nina (above), La Musa (p172) and La Isla del Tesoro (above) – others have been drawn here to transform the street into one of Madrid's most varied eating experiences.

Starting from the east, El Sitio de Malasaña (☎ 91 446 68 76; Calle de Manuela Malasaña 7; meals €20-25, menú del día €10.50; ⏰ lunch & dinner Tue-Sat, lunch Sun; Ⓜ Bilbao) has a cosy, modern charm and innovative dishes, such as turkey and truffle ravioli in a mushroom sauce (€10). Almost next door, Este o Este (☎ 91 445 33 57; Calle de Manuela Malasaña 9; meals €15-25, menú del día €9.50; ⏰ lunch & dinner Tue-Sat, lunch Sun & Mon; Ⓜ Bilbao) balances a largely Spanish menu with Moroccan touches, such as the Sunday couscous special (€15). Alongside is El Txoko (☎ 620 639 142; Calle de Manuela Malasaña 9; meals €30-35; ⏰ lunch & dinner Fri & Sat, lunch Mon-Thu; Ⓜ Bilbao), which does classic Basque staples such as bacalao (cod) and solomillo (steaks). Albur (☎ 91 594 27 33; Calle de Manuela Malasaña 15; meals €20-30, menú del día €11; Ⓜ Bilbao), is known for terrific rice dishes and tapas, and has a well-chosen wine list. Further west, Allora Qui (☎ 91 593 93 86; www.alloraqui.com, in Spanish; Calle de Manuela Malasaña 33; meals €20-25, menú del día €9.50; Ⓜ San Bernardo) is a swish trattoria with a lounge-club ambience and good Italian food.

we adore the *foie fresco a la plancha* (grilled foie gras). What we're not so keen on is the policy of two sittings (at 9.15pm and 11.30pm), which inevitably means that staff can start to hover when your time's nearly up. The weekend brunch (€19.90, noon to 6pm Saturday and Sunday) is wide ranging but, in our view, a touch overpriced.

LA MUSA Map pp110–11 Fusion €€
☎ 91 448 75 58; www.lamusa.com.es; Calle de Manuela Malasaña 18; meals €25-30, menú del día €11; ⏰ lunch & dinner daily; Ⓜ Bilbao or San Bernardo

Snug yet loud, a favourite of Madrid's hip young crowd yet utterly unpretentious, La Musa is all about designer décor, lounge music on the sound system and food that will live long in the memory. The fried green tomatoes with strawberry jam and great meat dishes are fun and filled with flavour. It doesn't take reservations, so sidle up to the bar, add your name to the waiting list and soak up the ambient buzz of Malasaña at its best. If you don't fancy waiting, try the sister restaurant nearby, Ojalá Awareness Club (p195).

CON DOS FOGONES
Map pp110–11 Spanish & International €€
☎ 91 559 63 26; www.condosfogones.com; Calle de San Bernardino 9; meals €25-30, day/night menú €9.50/16.90; ⏰ lunch & dinner daily; Ⓜ Plaza de España

A welcome addition to the Madrid culinary scene, Con Dos Fogones is cool and classy with bright colours softly lit by designer lamps. The food is everything from salads and quality hamburgers to great slabs of fine Argentine beef with plenty of unexpected twists like brie tempura or cod paté.

A DOS VELAS
Map pp110–11 Spanish & International €€
☎ 91 446 18 63; www.adosvelas.net, in Spanish; Calle de San Vicente Ferrer 16; meals €20-25, menú del día €9.50; ⏰ lunch & dinner Mon-Sat; Ⓜ Tribunal

We're fans of this place and Madrid's discerning restaurant public clearly agrees. The food is always creative with Mediterranean cooking fused with occasional Indian or even Argentine flavours, a lovely dining area with soft lighting and exposed brick, and service that's attentive without being intrusive. The lime-marinated swordfish with avocado salad is among our many favourites.

CASA DO COMPAÑEIRO
Map pp110–11 Galician Tapas €€
☎ 91 521 57 02; Calle de San Vicente Ferrer 44; meals €20-25, menú del día €9; ⏰ 1.30pm-2am; Ⓜ Tribunal

Tucked away in the streets just up from Plaza del Dos de Mayo, this atmospheric old Madrid *taberna* is like Spanish bars used to be made, with a wonderful tiled and wood façade, basic wooden stools and marble-topped tables. It's renowned for its *pulpo a la gallega* (Galician-style octopus), *pimientos de padrón* (grilled little green peppers) and *lacón* (cured shoulder of pork).

EL PLACER DEL ESPÍRITU SANTO
Map pp110–11 Spanish & International €€
☎ 91 360 45 16; www.elplacerdelespiritusanto .com in Spanish; Calle del Espíritu Santo 3; meals €20-25; ⏰ lunch & dinner Wed-Sat, lunch Tue & Sun; Ⓜ Tribunal

Surrounded by retro clothing shops, El Placer del Espíritu Santo is a sanctuary in the heart of hard-living Malasaña with food 'for body and soul' and a clean-lined dining area in which to enjoy it. The rice dishes stand out, as does the *carpaccio de pulpo* (octopus carpaccio; €10.50).

RIBEIRA DO MIÑO Map pp110–11 Seafood €€
☎ 91 521 98 54; Calle de la Santa Brigida 1; meals €20-25; ⏰ lunch & dinner Tue-Sat; Ⓜ Tribunal

This riotously popular seafood bar and restaurant is where madrileños with a love for seafood indulge their fantasy. The *mariscada de la casa* (€30 for two) is a platter of seafood so large that even the hungriest of visitors will be satisfied. Leave your name with the waiter and be prepared to wait up to an hour for a table.

COMOMELOCOMO
Map pp110–11 Spanish & International €
☎ 91 523 13 23; www.comomelocomo.com, in Spanish; Calle de Andrés Borrego 16; meals €15-25, menú del día €9.50; ⏰ lunch & dinner Mon-Sat; Ⓜ Noviciado

Traditional Spanish dishes given the odd international twist to suit 21st-century palates and excellent value for money are the hallmarks of this trendy place down Malasaña's lower end. Elsewhere, beautifully presented meals and agreeable surrounds too often mean meagre portions, but not here. The friendly service is another winner, as is the three-course evening menu for €16.90.

MADRID FOR THE SWEET TOOTH

Tapas may be a Spanish institution, but what madrileños really love are their pastries, especially at breakfast, although any excuse will do. These are our favourite classic Madrid pastry shops, which we were forced to visit (purely for research purposes, you understand).

Chocolatería de San Ginés (p186) Perhaps the best known of Madrid's *chocolate con churros* vendors. Its main market is clubbers with the munchies, pouring out of the city's nearby dance palaces.

Horno de San Onofre (Map pp110–11; ☎ 91 532 90 60; Calle de San Onofre 3; 8am-9pm; Gran Vía) and **Horno de Santiguesa** (Map pp64–5; ☎ 91 559 62 14; Calle Mayor 73; 8am-9pm; Ópera) These are owned by the same family and everything's a speciality, from cakes and pastries to bite-sized sweets and Christmas *turrón* (a nougat-like sweet).

La Duquesita (Map pp110–11; ☎ 91 308 02 31; Calle de Fernando VI 2; 9.30am-2.30pm & 5-9pm Tue-Sun; Alonso Martínez) Another lavish step back in time with wonderful traditional pastries.

La Mallorquina (Map pp64–5; ☎ 91 521 12 01; Plaza de la Puerta del Sol 8; 9am-9.15pm; Sol) A classic pastry shop that's packed to the rafters by madrileños who just couldn't pass by without stopping. Treat yourself to a takeaway *ensaimada* (a light pastry dusted with icing sugar) from Mallorca.

Niza (Map pp110–11; ☎ 91 308 13 21; Calle de Argensola 24; 10am-2.30pm & 5.30-8.30pm Mon-Sat, 10am-2.30pm Sun Sep-Jul; Alonso Martínez) Astonishing, old-Madrid interior decoration; it's worth a visit here just to admire the stunning ceiling and other fittings. But buy you should, especially the *rusos* (cream-filled pastries) and delicious *tarta de milhojas* (layered cake with custard cream).

CONACHE Map pp110–11 Spanish €
☎ 91 522 95 00; Plaza de San Ildefonso; meals €15-25, menú del día €9; 9.30am-1.30am Mon-Thu, to 2.30am Fri & Sat; Tribunal

With Asian and African decoration, creative Mediterranean cooking and a noisy Spanish clientele, Conache is a hub of barrio life and is as good for breakfast as for dinner. The food is outstanding; the *salmorejo* (cold tomato soup made with bread, oil, garlic and vinegar) is among the best we've tasted this far from Córdoba. Follow it up with the tuna fillet with ginger marmalade.

EL LATERAL Map pp110–11 Tapas €
☎ 91 531; www.cadenalateral.es; Calle de Fuencarral 43; meals €15-25; 1pm-1am; Tribunal

Although it has an excellent à la carte menu (salads, *raciones*), we love El Lateral for its pinchos, which make a perfect accompaniment to the fine wines on offer. At €3 per pincho, you could easily pass an evening here savouring every bite. Personally, we'd consider starting with stuffed pepper or chickpeas with *chistorra* (similar to chorizo, but cooked in a ceramic pot), but if you can't decide, try the *degustación de pinchos* (€14). Service is restaurant standard, rather than your average tapas bar brusqueness.

CRÊPERIE MA BRETAGNE Map pp110–11 Crêpes €
☎ 91 531 77 74; Calle de San Vicente Ferrer; meals €20; dinner Thu-Sun; Tribunal

What a wonderful little place this is – dark, candlelit and all about delicious crêpes. After eating a main meal of crêpes from the rustic wooden tables, there are more crêpes, this time sweet, for dessert. You'll never want to see a crêpe again after over-indulging here, but it's a great way to go out.

BODEGA DE LA ARDOSA Map pp110–11 Tapas €
☎ 91 521 49 79; Calle de Colón 13; meals €15-20; 8am-1.30am Sun-Thu, to 2.30am Fri & Sat; Tribunal

Going strong since 1892, the charming, wood-panelled bar of Bodega de la Ardosa could equally be recommended as a favourite Malasaña drinking hole. Then again, to come here and not try the *salmorejo*, *croquetas*, *patatas bravas* or *tortilla de patatas* would be a crime. On weekend nights there's scarcely room to move.

EL REY DE TALLARINES Map pp110–11 Asian €
☎ 91 542 68 97; Calle de San Bernardino 5; meals €15-20, menú del día €8.90-11.50; lunch & dinner daily; Plaza de España

This is one of Madrid's longest-standing and best-loved Asian restaurants; it's been here so long its décor has come to resemble a generic Spanish bar. The secret of its longevity is its dedication to the dying art of La Mian (pulled noodles), which it makes here on the spot. Add Chinese and Thai sauces and reasonable prices and we expect it'll be around for a while yet.

HOME BURGER BAR

Map pp110–11   Hamburgers €

☎ 91 522 97 28; www.homeburgerbar.com; Calle del Espíritu Santo 12; meals €15-20; ⏱ lunch & dinner Tue-Sun; Ⓜ Tribunal

There are times when you just need a burger. Home Burger Bar is terrific, with an interesting mix of vegetarian, gourmet and classic hamburgers served by friendly waiters in an American diner–style setting. The meat is 'ecologically sound' and, in the Spanish style, medium-rare (the chef will cook it more if you ask).

LA TABERNA DE SAN BERNARDO

Map pp110–11   Tapas €

☎ 91 445 41 70; Calle de San Bernardo 85; meals €15-20; ⏱ 2.30-4.30pm & 8.30pm-2.30am; Ⓜ San Bernardo

Stick your head in the door and there's not a lot to catch your attention in this agreeable brick-lined bar, but pause long enough to read the menu and you'll be hooked. The *raciones* (€6.50 to €9) include plenty of Spanish staples (eg *chistorra, bacalao, pisto* etc) with a few surprising twists – the *berenjenas con miel de caña* (deep-fried aubergine with honey) is brilliant.

GIANGROSSI

Map pp110–11   Ice Cream €

☎ 900 555 009; www.giangrossi.es, in Spanish; Calle de Alberto Aguilera 1; meals €10; ⏱ 9am-1am Mon-Thu, to 2am Fri & Sat, noon-1am Sun; Ⓜ San Bernardo

Designer chill-out lounge meets ice-cream parlour at Giangrossi and it's a fine combination. It serves natural flavours blended in creative ways, great coffee, delicious cakes and a range of other tasty sweets, as well as a small range in breakfasts and sandwiches, all against a backdrop of high ceilings and laid-back music. Sink into the super-comfy chairs and you may never want to leave.

LA VITA É BELLA

Map pp110–11   Italian Takeaway €

☎ 91 521 41 08; Plaza de San Ildefonso 5; meals €5-10; ⏱ 2pm-1am; Ⓜ Tribunal

With tasty, authentic Italian dishes that would put many sit-down restaurants to shame, the Italian-run La Vita é Bella does a roaring trade in pizza, pasta, calzone, salad and tiramisú. Take the plate of your choice down to Plaza del Dos de Mayo (Map pp110–11) and watch the barrio life.

CHUECA

SUA

Map pp110–11   Nouvelle Spanish Cuisine €€

☎ 91 523 20 04; www.sua.es, in Spanish; Calle del Marqués de Valdeiglesias 3; meals €40-45; ⏱ lunch & dinner daily; Ⓜ Banco de España

Sua is the height of softly lit sophistication and cooking that provides a new slant on nouvelle cuisine. Dishes are organised around four temperatures – 25°C, 50°C, 75°C and -2°C (desserts) – and it draws its inspiration from the Basque Country, Spain's hothouse for culinary innovation. The service is faultless and adept at helping you negotiate your way through the menu, but we suggest the €36 *menú de degustación* (tasting menu), which gradually increases the temperature.

BOGA BAR

Map pp110–11   Seafood €€

☎ 91 532 18 50; Calle del Almirante 11; meals €35-40; ⏱ lunch & dinner Mon-Sat, lunch Sun; Ⓜ

Boga Bar identifies its target market as 'lovers of lobster' and there's plenty of that in this fine restaurant that's right at home in this exclusive corner of Madrid. The round arches, fire-red walls and deep-green fronds make for one of the barrio's most agreeable dining atmospheres, and the seafood is high quality.

CASA HORTENSIA

Map pp110–11   Asturian €€

☎ 91 539 00 90; 2nd fl, Calle de la Farmacia 2; meals €30-40; ⏱ lunch & dinner Tue & Thu-Sat, lunch Sun & Wed; Ⓜ Tribunal or Gran Vía

With all the innovations happening elsewhere in Madrid, it's good to know that some things don't change. Casa Hortensia doesn't bother much with decoration, allowing you to concentrate on the Asturian specialities, such as *fabada asturiana* (white-bean stew with pork and blood sausage; €12.50). *Sidra* (cider) is, of course, obligatory.

EL ORIGINAL

Map pp110–11   Traditional Spanish €€

☎ 91 522 90 69; www.eloriginal.es, in Spanish; Calle de las Infantas 44; meals €25-30; ⏱ lunch & dinner Mon-Sat; Ⓜ Chueca or Banco de España

With the best products and signature dishes from each of the regions of Spain, you might expect El Original to be a bastion of traditionalism. Indeed, it describes its cooking as classic Spanish. Then you step into the dining area and find trees growing in the sleek dining room. Prices are reasonable, another reason why this relatively new place seems to be lasting the distance.

JANATOMO Map pp110–11 Japanese €€
☎ 91 521 55 66; Calle de la Reina 27; meals €25-30; 🕑 lunch & dinner Tue-Sun; Ⓜ Gran Vía
Restaurateur Eiko Ikenaga arrived in Spain in the 1950s and has watched Spaniards slowly become accustomed to foreign cuisines. Her patience has paid off and now her restaurant, Janatomo, has undergone a style overhaul, adding a Zen ambience to its splendid Japanese cooking. The sight of tour groups from the home country piling in is all the confirmation we need.

LA PAELLA DE LA REINA Map pp110–11 Paella €€
☎ 91 531 18 85; www.lapaelladelareina.com; Calle de la Reina 39; meals €25-30; 🕑 lunch & dinner daily; Ⓜ Banco de España
Madrid is not renowned for its paella (Valencia is king in that regard), but Valencianos who can't make it home are known to frequent La Paella de la Reina. Like any decent paella restaurant, you need two people to make an order but, that requirement satisfied, you've plenty of choice. The typical Valencia paella is cooked with beans and chicken, but there are also plenty of seafood varieties on offer, including *arroz negro* (black rice whose colour derives from squid ink).

LA TASCA SUPREMA
Map pp110–11 Traditional Madrileño €€
☎ 91 308 03 47; Calle de Argensola 7; meals €20-25; 🕑 lunch Mon-Sat; Ⓜ Alonso Martínez or Chueca
Going strong since the 19th century, La Tasca Suprema is one of the most traditional restaurants north of Gran Vía. It's famous for its *cocido a la madrileña* (see p157); if you're wondering why it only opens for lunch, the answer is that no self-respecting madrileño would eat a heavy *cocido* in the evening. It also does *callos*, *fabada* (white-bean stew), *chipirones* (baby squid) and home-made desserts.

SALVADOR Map pp110–11 Spanish €€
☎ 91 521 45 24; Calle de Barbieri 12; meals €25-30; 🕑 lunch & dinner Mon-Sat, lunch Sun, closed Aug; Ⓜ Chueca
This old Hemingway favourite is typical of many Madrid classics – walking past, you

top picks

ICE CREAM

- Giangrossi (opposite)
- Bajo Cero (p180)
- Palazzo (Map pp110–11; ☎ 91 532 26 42; Gran Vía 32; 🕑 11am-10pm; Ⓜ Gran Vía) The best vanilla ice cream with a hint of lemon.
- Los Caprichos de Martina (Map pp64–5; ☎ 91 365 04 19; Calle de Toledo 4; 🕑 11am-2am; Ⓜ Sol) Just down the steps from Plaza Mayor and good for home-made ice cream.

wouldn't give it a second look. Since 1941, locals have been coming to the 'Saviour' for lashings of hearty Madrid cooking, and among them are plenty of bullfighting aficionados and *toreros* (bullfighters, or matadors), especially during the Fiestas de San Isidro Labrador. Ordering a plate of *rabo de toro* is a way to win friends, while the remainder is simple, no-nonsense fare.

TEPIC Map pp110–11 Mexican €€
☎ 91 522 08 50; www.tepic.es, in Spanish; Calle de Pelayo 4; meals €25-30; 🕑 lunch & dinner daily; Ⓜ Chueca
Chueca's young professional crowd loves these sorts of places – chic dining rooms, gay-friendly service and international flavours that come with a label, in this case 'Urban Mexican Food'. Tepic's signature dish is the Acapulco Tropical, a cheese taco with meat and pineapple, but it's all good and leaves you with none of that heavy after-dinner feel that spoils the aftermath of so many Mexican meals.

BAZAAR Map pp110–11 Nouvelle Spanish Cuisine €€
☎ 91 523 39 05; www.restaurantbazaar.com; Calle de la Libertad 21; meals €25; 🕑 lunch & dinner daily; Ⓜ Chueca
Bazaar's popularity among the well-heeled and often famous shows no sign of abating. Its pristine white interior design with theatre lighting may draw a crowd that looks like it stepped out of the pages of *Hola!* magazine, but the food is extremely well priced and innovative. The *carpaccio de gambas con vinagreta de setas* (prawn carpaccio with mushroom vinaigrette; €6.98) is typical of the dishes that caught our eye.

EATING CHUECA

With the energy of Chueca swirling outside the wall-length windows, Bazaar has none of the stuffiness that you might expect to find. It doesn't take reservations, so get here early or be prepared to wait, regardless of whether you're famous or not.

BACO Y BETO Map pp110–11 Tapas €€
☎ 91 522 84 81; www.bacoybeto.com, in Spanish; Calle de Pelayo 24; meals €20-25; ⏰ lunch & dinner Sat, dinner Mon-Fri; Ⓜ Chueca
Friends of ours in Madrid begged us not to include this place in the guide and we must admit that we were tempted to keep this secret all to ourselves. Some of the tastiest tapas in Madrid are what you find here, either ordered as a *tapa* (eg quail's eggs with *salmorejo*) or *raciones* (eg aubergine with parmesan). The clientele is predominantly gay, but they, like our friends, can't have it all to themselves.

BOCAITO Map pp110–11 Tapas €€
☎ 91 532 12 19; Calle de la Libertad 4-6; meals €20-25; ⏰ lunch & dinner Mon-Fri, dinner Sat; Ⓜ Chueca or Banco de España
Film-maker Pedro Almodóvar finds this bar and restaurant in the traditional Madrid style 'the best antidepressant'. Forget about the sit-down restaurant and jam into the bar shoulder to shoulder with the casual crowd, order a few Andalucian *raciones* off the menu, slosh them down with some gritty red or a *caña* and enjoy the theatre in which these busy barmen excel. Specialities include the smoked fish salad, scrambled eggs with garlic and *jamón*.

KIM BU MBU Map pp110–11 African €€
☎ 91 521 26 81; www.kimbumbu.com, in Spanish; Calle de Colmenares 7; meals €20-25; ⏰ lunch & dinner daily; Ⓜ Chueca or Banco de España
Stepping inside this fine African restaurant, with stunning African décor and a tranquil air, is like entering another world. The *menú de degustación* (€21) is a good way to get acquainted with Senegalese and other predominantly West African tastes. Then again, the *gambas con mango y batata dulce* (prawns with mango and sweet potato) are pretty self-explanatory and very tasty.

LA MORDIDA Map pp110–11 Mexican €€
☎ 91 308 20 89; www.lamordida.com, in Spanish; Calle de Belén 13; meals €20-25; ⏰ lunch & dinner Sun-Fri, 1.30pm-1am Sat; Ⓜ Chueca

If your idea of Mexican food was born in Taco Bell, La Mordida will show you a whole new world. This is home-style Mexican cooking, the sort of place where most of the names on the menu will need explanation from the waiters. With Mexican cantina-style décor, Coronitas for just €3.15 and hearty servings, this could just be our favourite Mexican restaurant in a city overflowing with them.

RESTAURANTE VEGA VIANA
Map pp110–11 Vegetarian €€
☎ 91 308 03 81; www.accua.com/vegaviana, in Spanish; Calle de Pelayo 35; meals €20-25; ⏰ lunch & dinner Mon-Sat; Ⓜ Chueca
Chueca is surprisingly lacking in vegetarian restaurants and even this one does a small sideline in chicken dishes (albeit of the free-range variety); not surprisingly, vegans need not apply. Dishes like zucchini burritos with Manchego cheese and carrot croquettes with sultanas and yoghurt cream should nonetheless keep most vegetarians happy. It has an English-language menu. Smoking is not permitted.

MAISON BLANCHE Map pp110–11 Gourmet Café €€
☎ 91 522 82 17; Calle de Piamonte 10; meals €20; ⏰ 10am-midnight Mon-Sat, noon-6pm Sun; Ⓜ Chueca
If you've got a friend from Barcelona who's too cool for Madrid, bring them here and they might just change their mind. A gourmet-food store and designer café, this has become one of the most fashionable places in town for A-list celebrities; one newspaper called it 'paradise for sybarites'. The food ranges far and wide, but quiche Lorraine and duck are among the most popular choices. It also serves up live jazz (€5) from 2.30pm to 4.30pm on Sunday. This is the new Madrid and it's very cool.

RESTAURANTE MOMO Map pp110–11 Spanish €€
☎ 91 532 73 48; Calle de la Libertad 8; meals €20; ⏰ lunch & dinner Mon-Sat; Ⓜ Chueca
Momo is a Chueca beacon of reasonably priced home cooking for a casual crowd. It has an artsy vibe and is ideal for those who want a hearty meal without too much elaboration; the trout with soy and lemon sauce is recommended. The three-course dinner *menú* (€12.80) is one of Madrid's best bargains and the famous chocolate

EAT STREETS – CALLE DE LA LIBERTAD & AROUND

You can eat well in most corners of Chueca, but one street and its immediate vicinity stand out for variety and value for money. Central to Calle de la Libertad's appeal are Bazaar (p175), Bocaito (opposite) and Restaurante Momo (opposite), and one of Chueca's most popular cafés, Diurno (p193).

Circus (Map pp110–11; ☎ 91 522 52 15; Calle de la Libertad 13; Ⓜ Chueca or Plaza de España) serves fast and abundant Asian noodle dishes with plenty of coconut milk and lime juice; its motto is 'Very Fashion Fast Food'. Restaurante Extremadura (Map pp110–11; ☎ 91 531 88 82; Calle de la Libertad 13; meals €35-40; Ⓜ Chueca) is a complete change of pace, with hearty, meat-dominated cooking from the Spanish interior; *jamón* is a key fixture (some of the best *jamón* comes from Extremadura). Just down the road, El Original (p174) lives up to its name, while 4 de Tapas (below) is one of the barrio's best tapas bars.

moco (chocolate 'snot', but really homemade chocolate pudding) is the tastiest of dessert dishes despite the worrying name. It's a mostly gay crowd, but everyone's welcome.

ARABIA Map pp110–11   Middle Eastern €€

☎ 91 532 53 21; Calle de Piamonte 12; meals €20; Ⓨ lunch & dinner Sat & Sun, dinner Mon-Fri; Ⓜ Chueca

Fine Middle Eastern cuisine, reasonable prices and the aesthetics of an Arab diwan with cushions strewn around some of the softly lit, low-lying tables make for a fine change to your Spanish diet. We especially enjoyed the *cordero con miel y piñones* (lamb with honey and pine nuts; €9.40) and the *cuscus de pollo con pasas y cebolla* (couscous with raisins and onion; €8.80).

4 DE TAPAS Map pp110–11   Tapas €€

☎ 91 532 94 64; Calle de Barbieri 4; meals €20; Ⓨ 9am-5pm & 8pm-2.30am Mon-Sat; Ⓜ Chueca or Gran Vía

Tapas is not just about Andalucian-themed, tiled bars and shouting waiters. 4 de Tapas has a lounge-bar atmosphere and young and friendly waiters, quite apart from terrific tapas. The specialities are *tostas* (around €3 to €4) and *cazuelas* (from €7). For the former, brie with raspberry jam just has to be ordered, while the *cazuelas* range from Roquefort croquettes to the more traditional scrambled eggs with ham. The kitchen closes around midnight, an hour later on weekends.

GASTROMAQUIA Map pp110–11   Tapas €

☎ 91 522 64 13; Calle de Pelayo 8; meals €15; Ⓨ dinner Mon-Sat; Ⓜ Chueca

The exciting reimagining of tapas that would have Hemingway turning in his grave long ago swept through Madrid, but few places have recognised the possibilities of bringing world cuisines (eg couscous) into the mix. The philosophy behind Gastromaquia (the brainchild of renowned chef Ivan Sánchez) is to encourage Spaniards to relearn the art of eating tapas, taking them on a journey into what he calls 'universal tapas'. To do so, Gastromaquia maintains a base in Spanish cooking (helped by its location in an old Chueca *taberna*), but the tastes are always fresh and surprising, not to mention very good. There are plans to open for lunch, and the menu changes as often as new ideas emerge from the kitchen.

CACAO SAMPAKA

Map pp110–11   Snacks & Light Meals €

☎ 91 521 56 55; www.cacaosampaka.com; Calle de Orellana 4; meals €15; Ⓨ 10am-9pm; Ⓜ Alonso Martínez

Although better known as a gourmet chocolate shop (p151), Cacao Sampaka also has a lovely little café where it serves snacks and light meals (sandwiches, pastries, cakes and the like). It's a good choice if you haven't become accustomed to the Spanish habit of full meals at lunchtime.

FRESC CO Map pp110–11   Buffet €

☎ 91 521 60 52; Calle de Sagasta 30; meals €8.50-9.95; Ⓨ 12.30pm-1am; Ⓜ Alonso Martínez

If you just can't face deciphering another Spanish menu or are in dire need of a do-it-yourself salad, Fresc Co is a fresh, well-priced and all-you-can-eat antidote. OK, so the atmosphere is cafeteria and none too exciting, but the extensive choice of self-service salads, soups, pasta and pizza more than make up for it; the price includes a drink. Queues often go out the door at lunchtime.

CHAMBERÍ & ARGÜELLES

At first glance Chamberí and Argüelles seem more residential than great places to go out. With so many young and upwardly mobile madrileños clamouring to live here, however, there are some fine choices if you know where to look. Another advantage is that there's rarely another tourist in sight and you'll feel much more a part of the barrio than in the town centre.

SERGI AROLA GASTRO

Map pp116–17   Nouvelle Cuisine €€€

☎ 91 308 72 40; www.sergiarola.es; Calle de Zurbano 31; meals €100-200; Ⓜ Alonso Martínez

Sergi Arola, a young Catalan acolyte of the world-renowned chef Ferran Adrià, has abandoned La Broche and opened his second, personalised temple to all that's innovative in Spanish gastronomy. You pay for the privilege of eating here – the standard Menú Gastro costs €140 without wine and taxes – and you may leave hungry as this is the sort of place where presentation and taste are elevated above the need to fill hungry stomachs. But oh, what tastes…

JOCKEY Map pp116–17   Spanish €€€

☎ 91 319 24 35; www.restaurantejockey.es, in Spanish; Calle de Amador de los Ríos 6; meals €70-100; Ⓨ lunch & dinner Mon-Sat Sep-Jul; Ⓜ Colón

Fine Spanish cooking, with the occasional nod to international sophistication, and celebrities and royalty dotted around the dining room (Prince Felipe, heir to the Spanish throne, and Letizia Ortiz chose the Jockey chefs for their wedding banquet in May 2004) make for a top-quality dining experience. The menu is more traditionally European than most in this price range, although there are some innovative flourishes. Otherwise, it's along the lines of Persian caviar, snails and soufflés. If we could choose one dish, it would probably be lobster ragout with truffles and fresh pasta. Men must wear a tie and a jacket.

LA FAVORITA Map pp116–17   Navarran €€

☎ 91 448 38 10; www.restaurante-lafavorita .com in Spanish; Calle de Covarrubias 25; menú del día €15, meals €40-50; Ⓨ lunch & dinner Mon-Fri, dinner Sat; Ⓜ Alonso Martínez

top picks

REGIONAL SPANISH SPECIALITIES

- Casa Hortensia (p174) Asturias
- La Burbuja Que Ríe (p165) Asturias
- Restaurante Julián de Tolosa (see the boxed text, p163) Navarra
- Sidrería Vasca Zerain (p166) Basque Country
- Sagarretxe (opposite) Basque Country
- Restaurante Extremadura (see the boxed text, p177) Extremadura
- Maceiras (p167) Galicia
- Restaurante La Giralda (opposite) Andalucía
- La Trucha (p167) Andalucía
- La Paella de la Reina (p175) Valencia

Set in a delightful old mansion and famous for its opera arias throughout the night sung by professional opera singers, La Favorita has an ambience all of its own. The outdoor garden courtyard is delightful on a summer's evening, while the music and food are top drawer. Our only complaint is that the tables are too close together.

MOMA 56 Map pp116–17   Fusion €€

☎ 91 399 09 00; www.moma56.com, in Spanish; Calle de José Abascal 56; meals €30-50; Ⓨ 8am-1am Mon-Wed, to 2am Thu & Fri, 10am-2am Sat, noon-2am Sun; Ⓜ Gregorio Marañón

Still one of the places to be seen, Moma 56 is two diverging options in one. Momabar is to the left, where you can perch on slippery metallic bar stools or take a table for Basque pintxos. To the right is the minimalist white Moma Gold (open for lunch and dinner Monday to Friday, dinner on Saturday), where Mediterranean flavours predominate. The buzz about Moma is considerable and it's always packed, although food critics with whom we spoke felt that it's not quite worth the rave. It also has a popular nightclub (p202).

CASA RICARDO Map pp116–17   Spanish €€

☎ 91 447 61 19; www.casaricardo.net; Calle de Fernando el Católico 31; meals €30-40; Ⓨ lunch & dinner Mon-Sat, lunch Sun; Ⓜ Argüelles or Quevedo

This brilliant little 1930s-era taberna is tucked away in residential Argüelles, but it's well worth venturing out for. The specialities are *callos* (€13.35) and *rabo de toro* (€16.25), but there's plenty more to choose from, including the outstanding *calamares en su propia tinta* (calamari in its own ink). Like any old Spanish bar worth its salt, it's cramped, tiled, adorned with bullfighting photos and aimed at aficionados rather than tourists.

EL PEDRUSCO Map pp116–17 · Spanish €€
☎ 91 446 88 33; www.elpedruscodealdealcorvo.com, in Spanish; Calle de Juan de Austria 27; meals €30-35; ☼ lunch Mon-Thu, lunch & dinner Fri & Sat; Ⓜ Iglesia
If you haven't time to visit one of the *asadores* (restaurants specialising in roasted food, particularly meat) of Segovia (p248), head to this fine restaurant where the roasted meats are as good as any in Madrid. The *cochinillo asado* (€60 for two or three people) and ¼ *lechazo* (quarter roast lamb; €38 for two) are succulent. It's the sort of place where a salad is a must and you'll be delighted to see a vegetable.

LAS TORTILLAS DE GABINO
Map pp116–17 · Spanish €€
☎ 91 319 75 05; www.lastortillasdegabino.com, in Spanish; Calle de Rafael Calvo 20; meals €30-35; ☼ lunch & dinner Mon-Fri, dinner Sat; Ⓜ Iglesia
It's a brave Spanish chef that fiddles with the iconic *tortilla de patatas,* but the results here are delicious – tortilla with cockles, with octopus, with all manner of surprising combinations. This place also gets rave reviews for its *croquetas*. The service is excellent and the bright yet classy dining area adds to the sense of a most agreeable eating experience. Reservations are highly recommended.

RESTAURANTE COLLAGE
Map pp116–17 · Swedish €€
☎ 91 448 45 62; www.restaurantecollage.com, in Spanish; Calle de Olíd 6; menú del día €8.90, meals €25-35; ☼ lunch & dinner Tue-Fri, lunch Mon, dinner only Sat; Ⓜ Quevedo or Bilbao
One of our favourite restaurants in the barrio, Restaurante Collage serves wonderful food; the *rollitos de alce* (elk spring rolls; €9.25) are a spectacular entrée and the *solomillo de reno* (reindeer sirloin; €22.45) is tender and utterly delicious. The *menú de noche* (evening set menu; €21.95) is excellent and Swedish in orientation, while the daytime *menú del día* is supercheap

by barrio standards, more basic and caters to hungry local workers in search of home cooking. The whole atmosphere is casual but sleek in a Swedish kind of way.

NAGOYA Map pp116–17 · Japanese €€
☎ 91 448 69 07; www.nagoya.es, in Spanish; Calle de Trafalgar 7; menú del día from €8.55, meals €25-30; ☼ lunch & dinner daily; Ⓜ Bilbao
Madrid has its fair share of Japanese restaurants, but you won't find any better than this one. The service is friendly and fast, and the food is outstanding – from the tempura and sushi to the *kami yaki soba* (duck with noodles and teriyaki sauce). Ask for your *maki* with *sesamo por fuera* (sesame on the outside) and you'll be in heaven.

IL CASONE Map pp116–17 · Italian €€
☎ 91 591 62 66; Calle de Trafalgar 25; meals €20-25; ☼ lunch & dinner daily; Ⓜ Quevedo, Iglesia or Bilbao
With its outdoor tables on the lovely Plaza de Olavide in summer, reasonable prices, and fresh and inventive Italian cooking, Il Casone is excellent. We always order the *tagliatelle scampi* (€8.95), which is perfect, but there are flashes of creativity, such as fagottini with black truffles and cream of foie gras and mushroom. The carpaccios or grilled provolone are great entrées.

RESTAURANTE LA GIRALDA
Map pp116–17 · Andalucian €€
☎ 91 445 17 43; www.restauranteslagiralda.com, in Spanish; Calle de Hartzembusch 12 & 15; meals €20-25; ☼ lunch & dinner Mon-Sat, lunch Sun; Ⓜ Bilbao
For just about every kind of fried or fresh Mediterranean seafood you can imagine (and many you can't), Restaurante La Giralda feels like you've landed in Sevilla or Cádiz. The quality is high so it's hugely popular, but the downstairs dining area is surprisingly large.

SAGARRETXE Map pp116–17 · Basque Tapas €€
☎ 91 446 25 88; Calle de Eloy Gonzalo 26; meals €15-25; ☼ noon-5pm & 7pm-1am; Ⓜ Iglesia
One of the best Basque *pintxos* bars in Madrid, Sagarretxe takes the stress out of eating tapas. Simply point and any of the wonderful selection will be plated up for you. Better still, order the *surtido de 8/12 pintxos* (your own selection of 8/12 tapas)

for €15/24. There's a more expensive but equally good restaurant downstairs.

LOCANDITA Map pp116–17   Tapas €€
☎ 91 444 11 97; Calle de Fuencarral 148; menú del día €10.50, meals €15-25; ⏰ 7am-10.30pm Mon-Thu, 9am-10.30pm Fri & Sat; Ⓜ Quevedo

Good for a breakfast pastry, lunch or a drink at any hour of the day, this friendly little brasserie is a bright place to rest during your Chamberí explorations. We especially like the thought that goes into the *menú del día*, where the kitchen accompanies your main choices to make sure you get a healthy balance of all the food groups.

CASA MINGO Map pp126–7   Asturian €
☎ 91 547 79 18; Paseo de la Florida 34; meals €15-20; ⏰ 11am-midnight; Ⓜ Príncipe Pío

Built in 1916 to feed workers building the Príncipe Pío train station, Casa Mingo is a large Asturian cider house known by just about every madrileño. It's kept simple here, focusing primarily on the signature dish of *pollo asado* (roast chicken) accompanied by a bottle of cider. There are also a few Asturian specialities, such as *chorizo a la sidra* (chorizo in cider) and *queso de cabrales* (aged blue cheese).

BODEGA DE LA ARDOSA
Map pp116–17   Tapas €
☎ 91 446 58 94; Calle de Santa Engracia 70; meals €10-15; ⏰ 9am-3pm & 6-11.30pm Thu-Tue; Ⓜ Iglesia

Tucked away in a fairly upscale and modern corner of Chamberí, this fine old relic has an extravagantly tiled façade. Locals have been coming here for their morning tipple for decades and for some of the best traditional Spanish *patatas bravas* (fried potatoes with a spicy tomato sauce) in town. It also has vermouth on tap.

CACHABACHA Map pp116–17   Bocadillos €
☎ 690 265 556; Calle de Gonzalo de Córdoba; meals €5-10; ⏰ 9am-11pm Mon-Fri, 1-4pm & 8-11pm Sat; Ⓜ Quevedo

Wandering around Chamberí and you can't face a three-course Spanish meal? Cachabacha has a bar ambience with brick arches, and an excellent meal of soup, *bocadillo* and drink for €8.90. The service is relaxed and friendly, and the value is excellent.

BAJO CERO Map pp116–17   Ice Cream €
☎ 902 113 377; www.bajocero.es, in Spanish; Glorieta de Quevedo 6; snacks €5-10; ⏰ 8am-midnight Mon-Thu, to 1am Fri, 9am-1am Sat, 9am-midnight Sun; Ⓜ Quevedo

You can tell that a barrio is going upmarket when even its ice creameries have a super-cool style. Curvaceous chairs, bright colours, friendly service and a sophisticated vibe (not to mention brilliant ice creams, milkshakes and cakes) are what it's all about.

NORTHERN MADRID

The business and well-to-do clientele who eat in the restaurants of northern Madrid know their food and they're happy to pay for it. Often it's a fair metro or taxi ride north of the centre, but well worth it for a touch of class.

SANTCELONI Map p123   Catalan €€€
☎ 91 210 88 40; www.restaurantesantceloni.com; Paseo de la Castellana 57; set menus €125-155, meals from €100; Ⓜ Gregorio Marañón

The Michelin-starred Santceloni is one of Madrid's best restaurants, with luxury décor that's the work of star interior designer Pascual Ortega, and nouvelle cuisine from the kitchen of master Catalan chef Santi Santamaría. Each dish is an exquisite work of art – try for example the lobster with vegetables and an oil-mint emulsion. But we'd recommend one of the set menus to really sample the breadth of exquisite tastes on offer.

ZALACAÍN Map p123   Basque & Navarran €€€
☎ 91 561 48 40; www.restaurantezalacain.com; Calle de Álvarez de Baena 4; meals €90-100; ⏰ lunch & dinner Mon-Fri, dinner Sat Sep-Jul; Ⓜ Gregorio Marañón

Where most other fine-dining experiences centre on innovation, Zalacaín is a bastion of tradition with a refined air and a loyal following among Spain's great and good. Everyone who's anyone in Madrid, from the king down, has eaten here since the doors opened in 1973. The pig's trotters filled with mushrooms and lamb is a house speciality, as is the lobster salad. The wine list is purported to be one of the best in the city (it stocks an estimated 35,000 bottles). You should certainly dress to impress (men will need a tie and a jacket).

top picks

FINE DINING

- Santceloni (opposite)
- Sergi Arola Gastro (p178)
- Arola Madrid (p166)
- El Amparo (p169)
- Sula Madrid (p169)
- Sua (p174)
- Jockey (p178)
- Zalacaín (opposite)
- El Alboroque (p162)

PUERTA 57 Map p123 Spanish €€€

☎ 91 457 33 61; www.puerta57.com, in Spanish; gate 57, Estadio Santiago Bernabéu, Calle de Padre Damián; meals €75-80; ☯ lunch & dinner Mon-Sat, lunch Sun; Ⓜ Santiago Bernabéu

There are many reasons to recommend this place, but the greatest novelty lies in its location – inside the home stadium of Real Madrid; its Salón Madrid (one of a number of dining rooms) looks out over the playing field. Needless to say, you'll need to book a long time in advance for a meal during a game. The cuisine is traditional Spanish with an emphasis on seafood and it gets rave reviews.

ECOCENTRO Map p123 Vegetarian €€

☎ 91 553 55 02; www.ecocentro.es, in Spanish; Calle de Esquilache 2-12; menú del día €10.50, meals €25-35; ☯ lunch & dinner daily; Ⓜ Canal or Ríos Rosas

Ecocentro is a vegetarian's paradise. Depending on which door you enter, there's an extensive organic food shop, a cheap cafeteria-style eatery or a basement restaurant that serves wonderful veggie food. The *menú del día* changes daily and has plenty of choice.

DRINKING

top picks

- **Chocolatería San Ginés** (p186)
  Chocolate con churros became an institution here.
- **The Penthouse** (p190)
  Rooftop terrace that's the height of refinement.
- **Taberna Tempranillo** (p188)
  Busy bar that showcases all that's good about La Latina.
- **Taberna Alhambra** (p190)
  One of the most agreeable bars in central Madrid.
- **Taberna de Dolores** (p189)
  Great wines and a who's who of Madrid society.
- **Café Comercial** (p193)
  One of Madrid's oldest and most famous literary cafés.
- **Café Belén** (p194)
  Fine *mojitos* and a chilled vibe.
- **Museo Chicote** (p195)
  Legendary cocktail bar that draws the celebrities.
- **Ojalá Awareness Club** (p195)
  Fun and funky Malasaña watering hole.

What's your recommendation? www.lonelyplanet.com/madrid

DRINKING

Madrid has more bars than any city in the world, six, in fact, for every 100 inhabitants – wherever you are in town, there'll be a bar close by. That's because your average Spanish bar is not just a place to drink. Instead they form the centre of community life, usually filled with a cast of old-time regulars alongside people of all ages. Madrileños drink often and seem up for a drink almost any time of the day or night, but they rarely do so to excess; drinking is almost never an end in itself, but rather an accompaniment to good conversation, food or music. Perhaps they've learned that pacing themselves is the key to lasting until dawn – it's a key strategy to learn if you want to make the most of your Madrid night.

In addition to local corner bars, Madrid is replete with late-night temples to good taste that have something special about them – these are the places we've concentrated on here. Places to drink listed throughout this chapter are divided into cafés and bars, although the dividing line between the two is often blurred – just as you can order a coffee in many bars, they won't look strangely at you if you order something stronger in a café.

BEER

If madrileños mostly drink wine with their meals, they drink lager-style beer for much of the rest of the time. In the majority of bars you won't have much choice, but thankfully Madrid's flagship beer, Mahou, goes down well. Mahou was first produced in Madrid by a French entrepreneur in 1890 and comes as both draught and bottled. Cruzcampo is a lighter beer. Otherwise, two Catalan companies, Damm and San Miguel, each produce about 15% of all Spain's beer. Foreign beers are becoming more widely available, but you'll have to ask for them and don't expect too much choice other than in Irish bars. The Mexican Coronita is also widely on sale.

WINE

Although beer drinking now outstrips wine, Spaniards love their wine, not least because they produce some of the best wines in Europe. They even have a saying to convince the sceptics: *comer sin vino, comer mosquino* (a meal without wine is a stingy one).

Unlike France and many other wine-producing countries, Spanish wine is labelled primarily according to region and quality, rather than the type of grape. Most of the best Spanish wine, whether *blanco* (white), *tinto* (red) or *rosado* (rosé), is produced in northern Spain. The most famous wine region is La Rioja, whose wines (mostly reds) are generally of the highest order. Not far behind are the regions of Ribera del Duero (along the Duero River in Castilla y León) and Navarra, while Valdepeñas in Castilla-La Mancha has less variety but is generally well priced. For white wines the Ribeiro wines of Galicia are well regarded, and have traditionally been popular, while the Penedès area in Catalonia produces whites and sparkling wine, such as *cava*, the champagne-like toasting drink of choice for Spaniards at Christmas. Jeréz sherry is the most famous alcoholic drink to emerge from Andalucía. All are widely available in Madrid.

THE SECRET LANGUAGE OF BEER

To slake your thirst at the bar you could just ask for a *cerveza* (beer), but why not give the bartender an idea of exactly what you're after?

The most common order is a *caña*, a small glass of *cerveza de barril* (draught beer). In the heat of the summer, this is the best way to make sure they keep coming cold. A larger beer (about 300ml), more common in the hipper bars and clubs, usually comes in a *tubo* (a long, straight glass). The equivalent of a pint is a *pinta*, while a *jarra* refers to a jug of beer. A *clara* is a shandy, a beer cut with *gaseosa* (lemonade or soda water) or *limón* (lemon).

A small bottle of beer is called a *botellín* or *quinto* because it contains a fifth of a litre. A larger one (330ml) is often referred to as a *tercio* (ie a third of a litre).

Some bars also provide extremely large plastic beakers of beer (usually for the younger crowd); with no little irony, these huge containers are called *minis*. The beer's not always great (and often watered down).

MADRID WINES

The Comunidad de Madrid is not renowned for the quality of its wines and locals are more likely to order a bottle from La Rioja or Ribera del Duero than one from their own backyard. That said, *vinos de Madrid* have *Denominación de Origen* (DO) standing and their reputation is growing among wine experts. When Madrid first received DO status two decades ago, wine production was restricted to just five *bodegas* (wineries). Now there are 39 wineries with 80 sq km of grape-growing areas (mostly around Aranjuez, Navalcarnero and San Martín de Valdeiglesias) producing four million bottles a year. Grapes range from the indigenous malvar to grenache, syrah and cabernet sauvignon. Perhaps the most important mark of the region's growing wine success is that Madrid waiters will no longer look down their noses at you if you order a *vino de Madrid*, especially one under the labels of Divo, Tapón de Oro, Montazo and Qubél.

For information on wines from Madrid, see the boxed text, above.

Spanish wine is subject to a complicated system of wine classification, ranging from the straightforward *vino de mesa* (table wine) to *vino de la tierra*, which is a wine from an officially recognised wine-making area. If they meet certain strict standards for a given period, they receive *Denominación de Origen* (DO) status. An outstanding wine region gets the *Denominación de Origen Calificada* (DOC) while *reserva* and *gran reserva* are other indications of quality. The only DOC wines come from the Rioja region in northern Spain, which was demarcated in 1926, and the small Priorat area in Catalonia.

Wine Appreciation Courses & Tours

A number of wine shops and other organisations run wine tours and courses in wine appreciation if you'd like to understand more about Spanish wines.

Lavinia (p140) Wine courses (in Spanish) and tours to nearby *bodegas* (wineries).

Planeta Vino (☎ 91 310 28 55; www.planetavino.net) Tastings in an English-language wine school from €25.

Poncelet (see the boxed text, p159) Monthly primers on cheese and wine appreciation for around €50.

The Wellington Society (☎ 609 143 203; www.wellsoc.org; tours €85) Quirky and informative tours of the wines of La Rioja and Ribera del Duero in Madrid wine bars.

OTHER DRINKS

Sangria is a red wine–and–fruit punch (usually with lemon, orange and cinnamon), sometimes laced with brandy or whisky. It's refreshing going down but too many on a summer's afternoon will soon catch up with you. A variation on the theme is *tinto de ve-rano*, a mix of wine and Casera, a brand of *gaseosa* (lemonade or soda water).

Although it's becoming less common, you will on occasion be asked if you'd like a *chupito* to round off a meal (usually it's on the house). This is a little shot of liqueur or liquor and the idea is to help digestion. Popular and refreshing Spanish ones are *licor de manzana verde* (green apple liqueur), *licor de melocotón* (peach) or *pacharán* (made from the sloe berry).

Once the pleasurable business of eating is over, Spaniards invariably turn to *copas* (literally 'cups', but used to describe spirits), with *whisky, ron* (rum) and *gin-tonic* (gin and tonic) the most popular orders. You'll be expected to watch while the bartender pours your whisky…and sometimes continues pouring until you tell them to stop. You pay no extra regardless of the amount! Foreign whiskies are widely available, but Dyc (known locally as El Segoviano) is cheaper and fine if you're mixing it with coke. Rum with coke is known as a *cubata*, while for G&T lovers, Larios is a common brand of gin, although it gets mixed reviews from resident Brits. There's also no shortage of imported and Spanish-produced top-shelf stuff – *coñac* (brandy) is popular.

Other popular drinks include *sidra* (cider, usually poured from the barrel), an Asturian staple that has caught on elsewhere, vodka mixed with just about anything or a Brazilian *caipirinha* (made with *cacheca*, a spirit similar to rum). But madrileños have, above all, fallen in love with the *mojito* (rum with sugar and lashings of mint). Our pick of Madrid's *mojitos* are found in the boxed text on p196.

Further drinks produced locally include *licor de madroño* (strawberry-tree liqueur), a light-brown, high-octane drop extracted from the fruit of Madrid's symbolic strawberry tree, and *anisado de Chinchón*, a very popular *anis* (aniseed-based drink) produced in the town of the same name south of Madrid.

HOT DRINKS – A PRIMER

Café con leche About half coffee and half hot or *templada* (tepid) milk. Ask for *grande* or *doble* if you want a large cup, *en vaso* if you want a smaller shot in a glass, or a *sombra* if you want lots of milk.

Café solo (un solo) A short black.

Café cortado A short black with a little milk (*macchiato* in Italy).

Café con hielo A glass of ice and a hot cup of black coffee, to be poured over the ice; it's as close as Spaniards come to iced coffee.

Té and infusions Teas and herbal teas. Locals tend to drink tea black, so if you want milk (*leche*), ask for it to come separately (*a parte*).

Chocolate caliente Hot chocolate – it's dark and sweet and so thick you could stand your spoon up in it. If you want something less thick, ask for a *colacao* or *nesquik*.

PRACTICALITIES

As Spanish bars double as breakfast and, later, tapas bars, they tend to open all day, sometimes from around 8am until 1am, until 3am or later on weekends; this is especially true of cafés. Newer bars that don't serve breakfast or food usually open late afternoon or early evening.

Although prices can be much higher, expect to pay around €2.50 and up for a *caña* (small glass of beer), *copas* (spirits) hover around €5, while cocktails start from around €6.50. Wine is incredibly cheap in supermarkets; in restaurants, apart from *vino de la casa* (house wine), which you usually order by the glass, prices start from around €15 for a reasonable bottle and considerably more for something classy.

Spaniards don't usually tip in bars.

LOS AUSTRIAS, SOL & CENTRO

Downtown Madrid has a number of splendid cafés that span a range of tastes, but we're none too excited about the bars in the city centre (apart from the two listed). Tapas bars where you can also enjoy a drink include Casa Revuelta (p161) and Casa Labra (p161). Otherwise you've far more choice in neighbouring La Latina (opposite) or Huertas (p189).

CAFÉ DE ORIENTE Map pp64–5   Café
☎ 91 541 39 74; Plaza de Oriente 2; 🕙 9am-midnight Sun-Thu, 9am-2am Fri & Sat; Ⓜ Ópera
On a pretty square in what was once part of a long-gone, 17th-century convent, this place feels like a set out of Mitteleuropa. It's the perfect spot for a coffee (surprisingly, only €2.50), especially on the *terraza* (open-air bar) when the weather's fine. There's also a pricy restaurant attached.

CAFÉ DEL REAL Map pp64–5   Café
☎ 91 547 21 24; Plaza de Isabel II 2; 🕙 9am-1am Sun-Thu, 10am-2am Fri & Sat; Ⓜ Ópera
One of the nicest cafés in central Madrid, this place serves a rich variety of creative coffees and a few cocktails to the soundtrack of chill-out music. The best seats are upstairs, where the low ceilings, wooden beams and leather chairs are a great place to pass an afternoon with friends.

EL CAFÉ DE LA ÓPERA Map pp64–5   Café
☎ 91 542 63 82; www.elcafedelaopera.com; Calle de Arrieta 6; 🕙 8am-midnight; Ⓜ Ópera
Opposite the Teatro Real, this classic before-performance café has one unusual requirement for would-be waiters – they have to be able to sing opera. If you pass by here at most hours, it's a quite, classic café and your attention will be caught by the décor (floral wallpaper and stainless-steel tables) as it's rare that the waiters break into song until dinner time – then you'll pay around €55 for a meal, which is not bad value if you don't have tickets for the show across the road.

CHOCOLATERÍA SAN GINÉS
Map pp64–5   Chocolate Con Churros Café
☎ 91 365 65 46; Pasadizo de San Ginés 5; 🕙 9am-7am Wed-Sun, 6pm-7am Mon & Tue; Ⓜ Sol
Perhaps the best known of Madrid's *chocolate con churros* (Spanish donuts with chocolate) vendors, this Madrid institution is at its most popular from 3am to 6am as clubbers make a last stop for sustenance on their way home. Only in Madrid.

GAIA COCKTAIL LOUNGE
Map pp64–5   Cocktail Bar
☎ 610 737 639; www.gaiacocktail.com, in Spanish; Calle de la Amnistía 5; 🕙 10pm-3am Tue-Thu, 8.30pm-3.30am Fri & Sat; Ⓜ Ópera

Heartbreakingly sleek and oh-so-cool, Gaia is one of the best bars in the city centre, serving up delicious cocktails to a DJ-soundtrack of jazz, funk, lounge and occasional house music. It's not like you'd stumble onto Gaia on your way elsewhere, so the crowd tends to be a pretty discerning, sophisticated lot.

LA VIUDA NEGRA Map pp64–5   Cocktail Bar

☎ 91 548 75 29; Calle de Campomanes 6; ☺ 5-9pm Sun & Mon, 9pm-2am Tue & Wed, 9pm-3am Thu-Sat; Ⓜ Ópera

The 'Black Widow' is an all-dressed-in-orange, lounge-like cocktail bar that's minimalist enough for Manhattan and genuinely cool enough to satisfy the sophisticated new-Madrid crowd. If you're the sort that likes to settle in for the night, you can eat first at the sister restaurant La Viuda Blanca (The White Widow; p160) next door, then ease over to the bar for funky house music until late. Sunday afternoons are jazzy and very mellow.

LA LATINA & LAVAPIÉS

Two different barrios, two very different vibes.

Most nights (and Sunday afternoons), crowds of happy madrileños hop from bar to bar across La Latina. This is a barrio beloved by a discerning crowd of 20- and 30-something urban sophisticates who ensure there's little room to move in the good places and the bad ones don't survive long; the scene is a little more diverse on Sundays as crowds fan out from El Rastro. Most of the action takes place along Calle de la Cava Baja, the western end of Calle del Almendro and Plaza de la Paja. La Latina is not really a late-night barrio (by Madrid's standards), so if you're keen to keep going after 3am, you'll probably need to move elsewhere. And drinking in La Latina is usually combined with the tapas for

which the barrio is famed – many great tapas bars listed on p162 are also terrific places in which to drink.

Lavapiés is a completely different kettle of fish altogether – working class and multicultural, with an alternative, often bohemian crowd and quirky bars brimful of personality. Not everyone loves Lavapiés, but we do.

CAFÉ DEL NUNCIO Map pp76–7   Bar

☎ 91 366 08 53; Calle de Segovia 9; ☺ 12.30pm-2.30am Sun-Thu, 12.30pm-3.30am Fri & Sat; Ⓜ La Latina

Café del Nuncio straggles down a stairway passage to Calle de Segovia. You can drink on one of several cosy levels inside or, better still in summer, enjoy the outdoor seating. On summer weekends this place hums with the sort of clamour that newcomers to Madrid find irresistible.

EL MENTIDERO Map pp76–7   Bar

☎ 91 354 64 92; Calle del Almendro 22; ☺ 7pm-2am Mon-Fri, 1pm-2.30am Sat & Sun; Ⓜ La Latina

Get the night started at this fun flamenco bar that's also popular for its wines. Downstairs is somewhat more low-key, a place where groups of friends huddle around tall barrels that serve as tables.

EL VIAJERO Map pp76–7   Bar

☎ 91 366 90 64; Plaza de la Cebada 11; ☺ 2pm-2am Tue-Thu & Sun, 2pm-3am Fri & Sat; Ⓜ La Latina

This landmark of La Latina nights may have lost a little of its glamour, but it's nonetheless essential for a drink in the barrio. Its undoubted highlight is the open-air, rooftop *terraza*, which boasts fine views down onto the thronging streets, although when the weather's warm, it's nigh-on impossible to get a table. Our secret? It often closes the *terraza* around 8pm to spruce it up a little and you should be ready to pounce when it reopens and thereafter guard your table with your life.

LA INQUILINA Map pp76–7   Bar

☎ 627 511 804; Calle del Ave María 39; ☺ 7pm-2am Tue-Thu, 1-4pm & 8pm-3am Fri-Sun; Ⓜ Lavapiés

This could just be our favourite bar in Lavapiés. It's partly about the cool-and-casual vibe, partly because it's a bar run by women and partly because of its community spirit with deep roots in the Lavapiés soil. Contemporary artworks by budding local artists adorn the walls and you can either gather around the bar or take a table out the back.

LA TABERNA CHICA Map pp76–7 Bar
☎ 91 364 53 48; Costanilla de San Pedro 7;
🕑 8pm-1.30am Mon-Thu, 1.30pm-2am Fri-Sun;
Ⓜ La Latina
Most of those who come to this narrow little bar are after one thing, the famous Santa Teresa rum that comes served in an extra-large mug. The music is chill-out with a nod to lounge, which makes it an ideal pit-stop if you're hoping for conversation.

LA VENTURA Map pp76–7 Bar
☎ 91 521 48 54; Calle del Olmo 21; 🕑 10.30pm-2.30am Wed-Sat, 8pm-2am Sun; Ⓜ Antón Martín
One of many Lavapiés secrets hidden behind nondescript doors, La Ventura is a smoky, underground, alternative-cool bar with a cut-off-from-the-outside-world feel. It's always filled with locals and don't believe everything you read – we've been there long after closing time, but we didn't tell you that.

GAUDEAMUS CAFÉ Map pp76–7 Café
☎ 91 528 25 94; www.gaudeamuscafe.com, in Spanish; 4th fl, Calle de Tribulete 14; 🕑 3.30pm-midnight Mon-Fri, 8pm-midnight Sat; Ⓜ Lavapiés
What a place! Decoration that's light and airy with pop-art posters of Audrey Hepburn and James Bond. A large terrace with views over the Lavapiés rooftops. A stunning backdrop of a ruined church atop which the café sits. With so much else going for it, it almost seems incidental that it also serves great teas, coffees and snacks. The only criticism we can think of is that it doesn't stay open later. It's definitely a candidate for Madrid's best-kept secret.

top picks

ROOFTOP TERRAZAS (OPEN-AIR BARS)

- The Penthouse (p190)
- Gaudeamus Café (above)
- Bonanno (right)
- Hotel de las Letras (p229)

NUEVO CAFÉ DE BARBIERI Map pp76–7 Café
☎ 91 527 36 58; Calle del Ave María 45; 🕑 3pm-12.30am Mon-Wed, 3pm-2am Thu, 3pm-2.30am Fri & Sat, 1pm-12.30am Sun; Ⓜ Lavapiés
This barrio classic is Lavapiés' grandest old café, the sort of place for quiet conversation amid the columns and marble-topped tables right on the Plaza de Lavapiés. It does everything from coffees to cocktails and it's always been an intellectual hub of barrio life. If it all sounds a bit staid, it gets busy with a young crowd on weekend nights.

EL EUCALIPTO Map pp76–7 Cocktail Bar
Calle de Argumosa 4; 🕑 5pm-2am Mon-Sat, 4pm-1am Sun; Ⓜ Lavapiés
You'd be mad not to at least pass by this fine little bar with its love of all things Cuban: from the music to the clientele and the Caribbean cocktails (including non-alcoholic), it's a sexy, laid-back place. Not surprisingly, the mojitos are a cut above the average.

DELIC Map pp76–7 Mojito Bar-Café
☎ 91 364 54 50; Costanilla de San Andrés 14; 🕑 11am-2am Tue-Sun, 8pm-2am Mon; Ⓜ La Latina
We could go on for hours about this long-standing café-bar, but we'll reduce it to its most basic elements: nursing an exceptionally good mojito or three on a warm summer's evening at Delic's outdoor tables on one of Madrid's prettiest plazas is one of life's great pleasures. Bliss.

TABERNA TEMPRANILLO
Map pp76–7 Wine Bar
☎ 91 364 15 32; Calle de la Cava Baja 38; 🕑 1-4pm & 8pm-midnight; Ⓜ La Latina
You could come here for the tapas, but we recommend Taberna Tempranillo primarily for its wines, of which it has a selection that puts most Spanish bars to shame. It's not a late-night place, but it's always packed with an early evening crowd and on Sundays after El Rastro.

BONANNO Map pp76–7 Wine & Cocktail Bar
☎ 91 366 68 86; Calle del Humilladero 4; 🕑 noon-2am Sun-Thu, noon-2.30am Fri & Sat; Ⓜ La Latina
If much of Madrid's nightlife starts too late for your liking, Bonanno could be for you. It made its name as a cocktail bar, but many people come here for the great wines and

LA HORA DEL VERMUT

Sunday. One o'clock in the afternoon. A dark bar off Calle de la Cava Baja would be shut tight, but in Madrid the place is packed because it's *la hora del vermut* (vermouth hour), when friends and families head out for a quick apéritif before Sunday lunch. Sometimes referred to as *ir de Rastro* (going to the Rastro) because so many of the traditional vermouth bars are in and around El Rastro market, this Sunday tradition is deeply engrained in madrileño culture. Some of the best bars for vermouth are along Calle de la Cava Baja (Map pp76–7), while Casa Alberto (p191) is another legendary part of this fine tradition.

it's usually full with young professional madrileños from early evening onwards. In fact, it's still so full on Sunday lunchtime that we wonder why it bothers closing at all. Be prepared to snuggle up close to those around you if you want a spot at the bar.

HUERTAS & ATOCHA

Huertas comes into its own after dark and stays that way until close to sunrise. Bars are everywhere, from Sol down to the Paseo del Prado hinterland, but it's in Plaza de Santa Ana and along Calle de las Huertas that most of the action is concentrated. Huertas draws a mixed local and international crowd and your standard Huertas bar has touts outside offering a cheap first drink; we haven't bothered to list these as they'll find you before you find them. But Huertas is big enough for everyone and, for the most part, we've concentrated instead on places with what Spaniards call *encanto* (charm) that will appeal to the more discerning among you. Down the hill, Atocha is not really known for its interesting bars, although like many Madrid barrios, you'll find standard Spanish bars on most streets.

TABERNA DE DOLORES Map pp84–5   Bar
☎ 91 429 22 43; Plaza de Jesús 4; ☼ 11am-1am Sun-Thu, 11am-2am Fri & Sat; Ⓜ Antón Martín
Old bottles and beer mugs line the shelves behind the bar at this Madrid institution, known for its blue-and-white tiled exterior and for a 30-something crowd that often includes the odd *famoso* (celebrity) or two. It claims to be 'the most famous bar in Madrid' – that's pushing it but it's

invariably full most nights of the week, so who are we to argue? You get good house wine, great anchovies and some of Madrid's best beer for prices that haven't been seen elsewhere in Madrid since the euro sent prices soaring.

VIVA MADRID Map pp84–5   Bar
☎ 91 429 36 40; www.barvivamadrid.com; Calle de Manuel Fernández y González 7; ☼ 1pm-2am Sun-Thu, 1pm-3am Fri & Sat; Ⓜ Antón Martín or Sol
The tiled façade of Viva Madrid is one of Madrid's most recognisable and it's an essential landmark on the Huertas nightlife scene. It's packed to the rafters on weekends and you come here in part for some of the best *mojitos* in town and also for the casual, friendly atmosphere.

CAFÉ DEL CÍRCULO DE BELLAS ARTES Map pp84–5   Café
☎ 91 521 69 42; Calle de Alcalá 42; ☼ 9am-1am Sun-Thu, 9am-3am Fri & Sat; Ⓜ Sevilla
This wonderful Belle Époque café was designed by Antonio Palacios in 1919 and boasts chandeliers and the charm of a bygone era. You have to buy a token temporary club membership (€1) to drink here, but it's worth every cent, even if the waiters are not averse to looking aggrieved if you put them out.

EL OASIS Map pp84–5   Café
☎ 91 429 93 56; www.el-oasis-madrid.es, in Spanish; Calle de Moratín 36; ☼ 4pm-2am Sun & Tue-Thu, 4pm-2.30am Fri & Sat; Ⓜ Antón Martín
When Spain does teahouses, they're often awash in faux-*mudéjar* interiors, but this lovely little café down the Huertas hill breaks the mould with clean-lined modern décor. Exotic teas and coffees and free wi-fi make this a fine spot to kick back in the late afternoon, while cocktails and *copas* mean that you could move on to the harder stuff without leaving your chair.

EL IMPERFECTO Map pp84–5   Café-Bar
Plaza de Matute 2; ☼ 3pm-2am Sun-Thu, 3pm-3am Fri & Sat; Ⓜ Antón Martín
Its name notwithstanding, the 'Imperfect One' is our ideal Huertas bar, with live jazz on Tuesdays (and sometimes other nights) and a drinks menu as long as a saxophone, ranging from cocktails (€6.50) and spirits to milkshakes, teas and creative coffees.

CAFÉ DEL SOUL Map pp84–5 Chill-Out Bar

☎ 91 523 16 06; www.cafedelsoul.es, in Spanish;
Calle de Espoz y Mina 14; ⏲ 4pm-2am Mon-Thu,
4pm-3am Fri, 2pm-3am Sat, 2pm-2am Sun; Ⓜ Sol
Cocktails (with or without alcohol) for €6.50
are a big selling point these days in Madrid.
If you add chill-out music (that turns to
chill-house later in the night) and curious
décor that incorporates Moroccan lamps,
Café del Soul is more mellow than many.

MELOUNGE Map pp84–5 Chill-Out Bar

☎ 91 369 26 41; www.espaciomelounge.com;
Calle de San Pedro 22; ⏲ 7pm-3am Thu-Sat;
Ⓜ Antón Martín
On a quiet backstreet just in from the Paseo
del Prado, Melounge is a colourful, but cosy
split-level little bar with an artsy vibe and
where *mojitos*, daiquiris and piña coladas
cost an eminently reasonable €5.50. From
time to time it has small shows or exhibitions and it's always worth stopping by to
see what's happening.

DOS GARDENIAS Map pp84–5 Cocktail Bar

☎ 91 429 29 69; Calle de Santa María 13;
⏲ 6pm-2am Mon-Thu, 6pm-3am Fri & Sat,
5pm-1am Sun; Ⓜ Antón Martín
When Huertas starts to overwhelm, this
soothing little bar is the perfect antidote.
The flamenco and chill-out music ensure a
relaxed vibe, while sofas, softly lit colours
and some of the best *mojitos* (and exotic
teas) in the barrio make this place perfect
to ease yourself into or out of the night.

THE PENTHOUSE Map pp84–5 Cocktail Bar

☎ 91 701 60 20; Plaza de Santa Ana 14;
⏲ 9pm-4am Wed-Sat, 5pm-midnight Sun;
Ⓜ Antón Martín or Sol
High above the clamour of Huertas, this
exclusive cocktail bar has a delightful terrace overlooking Plaza de Santa Ana and
the rooftops of downtown Madrid from the
7th floor. It's a place for sophisticates with
chill-out areas strewn with cushions, funky
DJs and a dress policy designed to sort out
the classy from the wannabes. If you suffer
from vertigo, consider the equally sybaritic
Midnight Rose on the ground floor.

EL CALLEJÓN Map pp84–5 Flamenco Bar

☎ 91 429 83 97; Calle de Manuel Fernández y
González 5; ⏲ 7.30pm-2.30am Sun-Thu, 7.30pm-
3.30am Fri & Sat; Ⓜ Sevilla or Antón Martín

Tiny El Callejón lives and breathes flamenco
from the music coming from the sound
system to the stars of *cante jondo* (deep
flamenco song) who adorn the walls. The
clientele includes flamenco stars who
recognise authentic flamenco when they
hear it.

TABERNA ALHAMBRA Map pp84–5 Flamenco Bar

☎ 91 521 07 08; Calle de la Victoria 9; ⏲ 10am-
2am; Ⓜ Sol
There can be a certain sameness about
the bars between Sol and Huertas, which
is why this fine old *taberna* (tavern) stands
out. The striking façade and exquisite
tilework of the interior are quite beautiful;
however, this place is anything but stuffy
and the vibe is cool, casual and busy. Later
at night there are some fine flamenco
tunes.

CASA PUEBLO Map pp84–5 Jazz Bar

☎ 91 420 20 38; Calle de León 3; ⏲ 8.30pm-
2.30am Tue-Sun; Ⓜ Antón Martín
Jazz may be all the rage in Madrid, but
Casa Pueblo was onto it long before the
fad started and will remain so long after it
passes. As such, it has a whiff of authenticity about it. Tango is also a staple of the bar
and there are occasional live acts and great
drinks to be had.

JAZZ BAR Map pp84–5 Jazz Bar

☎ 91 429 70 31; www.jazzbar.es, in Spanish;
Calle de Moratín 35; ⏲ 3pm-2.30am Sun-Thu,
3pm-3.30am Fri & Sat; Ⓜ Antón Martín
Jazz aficionados will love this place for its
endless jazz soundtrack and private booths
(at last, a bar that has gone for privacy
instead of trying to cram too many people
in) and there's plenty of greenery to keep
you cheerful. If you want live jazz, head
elsewhere (p206), but this place is unbeatable for its cruisy jazz vibe.

LA VENENCIA Map pp84–5 Sherry Bar

☎ 91 429 73 13; Calle de Echegaray 7;
⏲ 1-3.30pm & 7.30pm-1.30am Sun-Thu, 1-3.30pm
& 7.30pm-2.30am Fri & Sat; Ⓜ Sol
This is how sherry bars should be – old-
world, drinks poured straight from the
dusty wooden barrels and none of the frenetic activity for which Huertas is famous.
La Venencia is a barrio classic, with fine
sherry from Sanlúcar and manzanilla from

Jeréz. There's no music, no flashy decorations; it's all about you, your *fino* (sherry) and your friends.

MALASPINA Map pp84–5   Tapas Bar

☎ 91 523 40 24; Calle de Cádiz 9; ☽ 11am-2am Sun-Thu, 11am-2.30am Fri & Sat; Ⓜ Sol

Although it serves inviting tapas, we like this cosy place with its wooden tables and semirustic décor as a mellow place for a quiet drink before you head home for an early night. Many of the bars in this area lack character or have sold their soul to the god of tourism. This place is different.

CASA ALBERTO Map pp84–5   Tapas Tavern

☎ 91 429 93 56; www.casaalberto.es, in Spanish; Calle de las Huertas 18; ☽ noon-1.30am Tue-Sat, noon-4pm Sun; Ⓜ Antón Martín

Since 1827 madrileños have been getting their vermouth from this elegant bar, where the hard stuff is served on tap. It's also famous as a restaurant (p166), but come here on Sunday at 1pm and you're halfway towards being considered an honorary madrileño. Cervantes lived in this building before it became a bar.

CERVECERÍA ALEMANA

Map pp84–5   Tapas Tavern

☎ 91 429 70 33; Plaza de Santa Ana 6; ☽ 10.30am-12.30am Sun-Thu, 10.30am-2am Fri & Sat, closed August; Ⓜ Antón Martín or Sol

If you've only got time to stop at one bar on Plaza Santa Ana, let it be this classic *cervecería* (beer bar), renowned for its cold, frothy beers. It's fine inside, but snaffle a table outside in the plaza on a summer's evening and you won't be giving it up without a fight. This was one of Hemingway's haunts, and neither the wood-lined bar nor the bow-tied waiters have changed much since his day.

ØLSEN Map pp84–5   Vodka Bar

☎ 91 429 36 59; www.olsenmadrid.com; Calle del Prado 15; ☽ 1-4pm & 8pm-2am Tue-Sun; Ⓜ Antón Martín

This classy and clean-lined bar is a temple to Nordic minimalism and comes into its own after the Scandinavian restaurant out the back closes. We think the more than 80 varieties of vodka are enough to satisfy most tastes. You'll hate vodka the next day, but Madrid is all about living for the night.

SALAMANCA

Salamanca is the land of the beautiful people and it's all about gloss and glamour: heels for her and hair gel for him. As you glide through the *pijos* (beautiful people or yuppies), keep your eyes peeled for Real Madrid players, celebrities and designer clothes. If nothing else, you'll see how the other half lives.

THE GEOGRAPHIC CLUB Map pp102–3   Bar

☎ 91 578 08 62; Calle de Alcalá 141; ☽ 1pm-1.30am Sun-Thu, 1pm-3.30am Fri & Sat; Ⓜ Goya

With its elaborate stained-glass windows, ethno-chic from all over the world and laid-back atmosphere, the Geographic Club is an excellent choice in Salamanca for an early evening drink. We like the table built around an old hot-air balloon basket almost as much as the cavernlike pub downstairs.

BALMORAL Map pp102–3   Cocktail Bar

☎ 91 431 41 33; Calle de Hermosilla 10; ☽ 12.30-3pm & 7pm-2am Mon-Sat; Ⓜ Serrano

Very Salamanca. This cocktail bar is something of a barrio antique, open since 1955 and with a dignified, moneyed British atmosphere. The cocktails are exceptional and original – we couldn't quite bring ourselves to try the 'bull shot', which consists of vodka and beef consommé...

CENTRO CUBANO DE ESPAÑA

Map pp102–3   Cuban Bar

☎ 91 575 82 79; www.elcentrocubano.com; 1st fl, Calle de Claudio Coello 41; ☽ 2pm-2am Sun-Wed, 2pm-2.30am Thu-Sat; Ⓜ Serrano

top picks

MADRID TERRAZAS (OPEN-AIR BARS)

- Plaza de Santa Ana (Map pp84–5)
- Paseo de la Castellana and Paseo de los Recoletos (Map pp102–3)
- Plaza de Olavide (Map pp116–17)
- Plaza de Oriente (Map pp64–5)
- Plaza de Chueca (Map pp110–11)
- Plaza de la Paja (Map pp76–7)
- Plaza Mayor (Map pp64–5)

Always dreamed of Havana, Cuba? Come here and you'll be a whole lot closer. This is where Cubans from all over Madrid come to be reminded of their homeland via the flavours (in the restaurant) and fine rum-based drinks such as *mojitos* (in the bar).

EL LATERAL Map pp102–3 — Wine Bar
☎ 91 435 06 04; Calle de Velázquez 57; Ⓒ 1pm-1am; Ⓜ Velázquez or Núñez de Balboa
It doesn't get much more *pijo* than this chic wine bar, where hair gel seems to be required for entry. Don't bother coming here after work unless you're in an Armani suit; at other times, the excellent wines and other drinks loosen up the crowd (if not the ties) more than you'd think.

MALASAÑA & CHUECA

Drinking in Malasaña and Chueca is like a journey through Madrid's multifaceted past. Around the Glorieta de Bilbao and along the Paseo de los Recoletos you encounter the stately old literary cafés that revel in their grandeur and late-19th-century ambience. Throughout Malasaña, *rockeros* nostalgic for the hedonistic Madrid of the 1970s and 1980s will find ample bars in which to indulge their memories. At the same time all across the barrios, especially in gay Chueca and away to the west in Conde Duque, modern Madrid is very much on show with chill-out spaces and swanky, sophisticated bars. And Madrid's best cocktail bars are to be found in Chueca between Calle de la Reina and Gran Vía. Going out to drink in Malasaña and Chueca is the stuff of Madrid legend, whatever your era, whatever your drink, whatever your sexual preference, whatever your look.

BAR EL 2D Map pp110–11 — Bar
☎ 91 445 88 39; Calle de Velarde 24; Ⓒ 1pm-2am Sun-Wed, 1pm-3am Thu-Sat; Ⓜ Tribunal
One of the enduring symbols of *la movida*, El 2D's fluted columns, 1970s-brown walls and 1980s music (with a nod to America's Deep South) suggest that it hasn't quite arrived in the 21st century yet. No-one seems to care, mind you. It also serves its spirits in big glasses, *movida*-style, which may explain it.

EL CLANDESTINO Map pp110–11 — Bar
☎ 91 521 55 63; Calle de Barquillo 34; Ⓒ 8pm-3am; Ⓜ Chueca

We've been wandering around the barrios of Madrid for years and this is one bar we always find full. What it's doing right is a low-key atmosphere, excellent (and occasionally live indie rock) music and good *mojitos*.

LA BARDEMCILLA Map pp110–11 — Bar
☎ 91 521 42 56; Calle de Augusto Figueroa 47; Ⓒ noon-2am Mon-Fri, 6pm-2am Sat; Ⓜ Chueca
Run by the family of film heart-throb Javier Bardem, this bar has an agreeable buzz most nights of the week. A comfortable space to relax, a slightly bohemian air and a loyal following add up to a great package.

LA PALMERA Map pp110–11 — Bar
Calle de la Palma 67; Ⓒ 7.30pm-1am Mon-Thu, 7.30pm-2.30am Fri & Sat; Ⓜ Noviciado
Tucked away in the quiet-by-day laneways of Conde Duque, this tiny place is a gem. Covered in blue and yellow tiles and with an antique bar that looks like an animal eating trough, La Palmera draws an artsy crowd who come to sit at the small wooden tables and nurse a drink or two. The atmosphere is very low-key. In summer the outdoor tables are the place to be.

LA VÍA LÁCTEA Map pp110–11 — Bar
☎ 91 446 75 81; Calle de Velarde 18; Ⓒ 7.30pm-3am; Ⓜ Tribunal
Another living, breathing and somewhat grungy relic of *la movida*, La Vía Láctea remains a Malasaña favourite for a mixed, informal crowd who seems to live for the 1980s – eyeshadow for boys and girls is a recurring theme. There are plenty of drinks to choose from and by late Saturday night anything goes. Expect long queues to get in on weekends.

EL BANDIDO DOBLEMENTE ARMADO Map pp110–11 — Bar & Bookshop
☎ 91 522 10 51; Calle de Apodaca 3; Ⓒ 5pm-1am Mon-Wed, 5pm-2am Thu-Sat; Ⓜ Bilbao or Tribunal
Part cool cocktail bar and part bookshop, the 'Double-armed Bandit' is run by the writer Soledad Puértolas and is popular with an artsy crowd keen to keep abreast of the literary scene (it's the focus for numerous literary events). They're also drawn by the smoky, funky music (think Tom Waits and beyond).

CONDE DUQUE NIGHTLIFE – DIY

Conde Duque (Map pp110–11) is one of Madrid's best-kept secrets when it comes to nightlife. There are some long-standing favourites here, among them the café and live music venue Café La Palma (p207), the cosy La Palmera (opposite), the wildly popular nightclub Siroco (p203) and the home all things Brazilian Kabokla (p209).

Calle de la Palma is the centre of most of the action and the following four places, in addition to those mentioned above, cover a range of tastes: old-world El Maño (No 64); the dark and crowded 4 de Latas (No 66); quirky La Caracola (No 70); and dance-crazy Estocolmo (No 72). Just down the road, little El Naranja (Calle de San Vicente Ferrer 53; ⏰ 7pm-midnight Tue-Thu & Sun, 8pm-2.30am Fri & Sat; Ⓜ Noviciado) is packed to its orange rafters from Thursday to Saturday.

J&J BOOKS & COFFEE
Map pp110–11   Bar & Bookshop
☎ 91 521 85 76; www.jandjbooksandcoffee .com; Calle del Espíritu Santo 47; ⏰ 11am-midnight Mon-Thu, 11am-2am Fri & Sat, 2-10pm Sun; Ⓜ Noviciado

If you're new in town and keen to meet other members of Madrid's (mostly English-speaking) expat community, J&J Books is a fun place to do so. In this agreeable bar atmosphere, it has international exchange nights from 8pm on Wednesday and Thursday and happy hour from 4pm to 7pm Monday to Friday, as well as plenty of books for sale (see p149) downstairs.

CAFÉ COMERCIAL Map pp110–11   Café
☎ 91 521 56 55; Glorieta de Bilbao 7; ⏰ 7.30am-midnight Mon, 7.30am-1am Tue-Thu, 7.30am-2am Fri, 8.30am-2am Sat, 9am-midnight Sun; Ⓜ Bilbao

This glorious old Madrid café proudly fights a rearguard action against progress with heavy leather seats, abundant marble and old-style waiters. As close as Madrid came to the intellectual cafés of Paris' Left Bank, the cafés of the Glorieta de Bilbao were in the 1950s and 1960s a centre of coffee-house intellectualism with their *tertulias* (literary discussions) and intrigues. Café Comercial is the largest to remain and has changed little

top picks

GRAND OLD CAFÉS

- Café Comercial (above)
- Café del Círculo de Bellas Artes (p189)
- Café de Oriente (p186)
- El Parnasillo (right)
- Café-Restaurante El Espejo (right)
- Gran Café de Gijón (p194)

since those days, although the clientele has broadened to include just about anyone.

CAFÉ ISADORA Map pp110–11   Café
☎ 91 445 71 54; Calle del Divino Pastor 14; ⏰ 4pm-2am Tue-Thu, 4pm-3am Fri & Sat, 4pm-1am Sun; Ⓜ Bilbao or San Bernardo

Echoing the distinguished cafés that once dominated northern Malasaña, Café Isadora has the old-world signposts of another age with the memorabilia of high culture adorning its walls and mid-20th-century décor. But this being Malasaña, it's as good for a mellow evening coffee or a somewhat more raucous middle-of-the-night *copa*.

CAFÉ-RESTAURANTE EL ESPEJO
Map pp110–11   Café
☎ 91 308 23 47; Paseo de los Recoletos 31; ⏰ 10.30am-1am Sun-Thu, 10.30am-2am Fri & Sat; Ⓜ Colón

Once a haunt of writers and intellectuals, this *modernista* gem could well overwhelm you with all the mirrors, chandeliers and bow-tied service of another era; it's quiet and refined, although the outdoor tables are hugely popular in summer.

DIURNO Map pp110–11   Café
☎ 91 522 00 09; www.diurno.com, in Spanish; Calle de San Marcos 37; ⏰ 10am-midnight Mon-Thu, 10am-1am Fri, 11am-1am Sat, 11am-midnight Sun; Ⓜ Chueca

It's not often that we recommend DVD stores in our guidebooks, but the attached café is always full with a fun Chueca crowd relaxing amid the greenery. We recommend that you join them because this has become one of the most laid-back centres of barrio life.

EL PARNASILLO Map pp110–11   Café
☎ 91 447 00 79; Calle de San Andrés 33; ⏰ 2.30pm-3am Sun-Thu, 2.30pm-3.30am Fri & Sat; Ⓜ Bilbao

Another of the grand old literary cafés to have survived close to the Glorieta de Bilbao, El Parnasillo has seigneurial décor with muted Art Nouveau frescoes and stained glass adorning the walls, but it's a favourite drinking hole for the diverse crowd drawn to the Malasaña night for reasons other than the heavy rock scene.

GRAN CAFÉ DE GIJÓN Map pp110–11   Café
☎ 91 521 54 25; Paseo de los Recoletos 21; ⏲ 8am-2am; Ⓜ Chueca or Banco de España
This graceful old café has been serving coffee and meals since 1888 and has long been a favourite with Madrid's literati for a drink or a meal. You'll find yourself among intellectuals, conservative Franco diehards and young madrileños looking for a quiet drink. Come here for the history, but you do pay above the odds for the experience.

ANTIK CAFÉ Map pp110–11   Café-Bar
☎ 620 427 168; Calle de Hortaleza 4 & 6; ⏲ 5pm-2am Sun-Thu, 5pm-3am Fri & Sat; Ⓜ Gran Vía
The dimly lit interior of Antik Café whispers intimacy and discretion with deep purple walls, antique candlesticks and chandeliers, while downstairs it's dungeon-dark with quiet corners in which to enjoy a private conversation. It draws a pretty sophisticated crowd and the menu includes coffee laced with something a little stronger from the extensive range of spirits.

CAFÉ PEPE BOTELLA Map pp110–11 Café-Bar
☎ 91 522 43 09; Calle de San Andrés 12; ⏲ 10am-2am Sun-Thu, 10am-3am Fri & Sat; Ⓜ Bilbao or Tribunal
Pepe Botella has hit on a fine formula for success. As good in the wee small hours as it is in the afternoon when its wi-fi access draws the laptop-toting crowd, it's a classy bar with green-velvet benches, marble-topped tables, and old photos and mirrors covering the walls. The faded elegance gives the place the charm that's made it one of the most enduringly popular drinking holes in the barrio.

CAFEINA Map pp110–11   Café-Bar
Calle del Pez 18; ⏲ 3pm-3am Mon-Sat; Ⓜ Noviciado
Although it lies just before Malasaña disappears into the seedy hinterland of Gran Vía, Calle del Pez is becoming an increasingly hip place and Cafeina is one of the landmarks of the street's regeneration. It's a lovely downtempo bar with soft lighting, cool music and a mellow crowd. On weekends DJs spice things up a bit upstairs, but it's laid-back and classy most other times.

AREIA Map pp110–11   Chill-Out Bar
☎ 91 310 03 07; www.areiachillout.com; Calle de Hortaleza 92; ⏲ 12.30pm-3am Mon-Thu, 12.30pm-3.30am Fri-Sun; Ⓜ Chueca or Alonso Martínez
The ultimate lounge bar by day (cushions, chill-out music and dark, secluded corners where you can hear yourself talk, or even snog quietly), this place is equally enjoyable by night. That's when groovy DJs take over (from 11pm Sunday to Wednesday, and from 9pm the rest of the week) with deep and chill house, nu jazz, bossa and electronica. It's cool, funky and low-key all at once, although the cocktails can be pricey.

CAFÉ BELÉN Map pp110–11   Chill-Out Bar
☎ 91 308 24 47; Calle de Belén 5; ⏲ 3.30pm-3am; Ⓜ Chueca
Café Belén is cool in all the right places – lounge and chill-out music, dim lighting, a great range of drinks (the *mojitos* are as good as you'll find in Madrid and that's saying something) and a low-key crowd that's the height of casual sophistication.

EL JARDÍN SECRETO
Map pp110–11   Chill-Out Bar
☎ 91 541 80 23; Calle del Conde Duque 2; ⏲ 5.30pm-12.30am Sun-Thu, 6.30pm-2.30am Fri & Sat; Ⓜ Plaza de España
'The Secret Garden' oozes intimacy and romance in a barrio that's one of Madrid's best-kept secrets. Lit by Spanish designer candles, draped in organza from India and serving up chocolates from the Caribbean, El Jardín Secreto is one of our favourite drinking corners. It's at its best on a summer's evening, but the atmosphere never misses a beat with a loyal and young professional crowd.

LOLA BAR Map pp110–11   Chill-Out Bar
☎ 91 522 34 83; www.lola-bar.com; Calle de la Reina 25; ⏲ 6pm-3am Wed-Sun; Ⓜ Gran Vía
If you like your music chilled, Lola Bar is a great place to start your night. On weekends, the DJ ups the tempo a little, but it's more lounge than house and you may find yourself staying longer than you planned.

OJALÁ AWARENESS CLUB
Map pp110–11   Chill-Out Bar
☎ 91 523 27 47; Calle de San Andrés 1;
⌚ 8.30am-1am Sun-Wed, 8.30am-2am Thu-Sat;
Ⓜ Tribunal

From the people who brought you La Musa
(p172), Ojalá is every bit as funky and has a
lot more space to enjoy it. Yes, you eat well
here, but we love it first and foremost for a
drink (especially a daiquiri) at any time of
the day. Its lime-green colour scheme, zany
lighting and a hip, café-style ambience all
make it an extremely cool place to hang out,
but the sandy floor and cushions downstairs
take chilled to a whole new level.

SANDSET CHILL-OUT LOUNGE
Map pp110–11   Chill-Out Bar
☎ 91 542 00 00; Calle del Conde Duque 30;
⌚ 10am-1pm & 5pm-midnight Sun-Thu, 10am-
1pm & 5pm-3am Fri & Sat; Ⓜ San Bernardo or
Ventura Rodríguez

Whether for your morning coffee or a
weekend *copa* after midnight, Sandset is a
welcome recent addition to Conde Duque's
emerging cachet. Upstairs is a lazy café
with a sense of light and space (it serves
great cakes and breakfasts to accompany
your coffee), but it's downstairs that wins
prizes for imagination with tinkling water,
sand on the floor, cushions, wicker beach
furniture and sheeshas (€4) to smoke. It's
an eclectic mix, but it works.

BAR COCK Map pp110–11   Cocktail Bar
☎ 91 532 28 26; Calle de la Reina 16; ⌚ 7pm-3am
Mon-Thu, 7pm-3.30am Fri & Sat; Ⓜ Gran Vía

With a name like this, Bar Cock could go
either way, but it's definitely cock as in
'rooster' so the atmosphere is elegant and
classic rather than risqué. The décor resem-
bles an old gentleman's club, but it's beloved by A-list celebrities, those who'd like
to be and a refined 30-something crowd
who come here for a lively atmosphere and
great cocktails. On weekends all the tables
seem to be reserved, so be prepared to
hover on the fringes of fame.

DEL DIEGO Map pp110–11   Cocktail Bar
☎ 91 523 31 06; Calle de la Reina 12; ⌚ 7pm-3am
Mon-Thu, 7pm-3.30am Fri & Sat; Ⓜ Gran Vía

Calle de la Reina is much loved by *famosos*,
especially models, actors and designers,
as a place for terrific cocktails in stately
surrounds. Del Diego fits this bill perfectly

with a vaguely old-world café-style ambience where you can hear yourself talk. The
cocktails (mostly around €9) are among the
best in the barrio.

MERCADO DE LA REINA GIN CLUB
Map pp110–11   Cocktail Bar
☎ 91 521 31 98; Calle de la Reina 16;
⌚ 4pm-2am; Ⓜ Gran Vía

In this area of Madrid known for its classy
cocktails, this gin club fits right in. But
unlike other choices nearby (eg Bar Cock,
Del Diego and Museo Chicote), this place
has no pretensions to former grandeur;
the décor is super-modern and, like the
clientele, all dressed in black. With 20 types
of gin (€7 to €12) and DJs at night from
Thursday to Saturday, it's a happening
place.

MUSEO CHICOTE Map pp110–11   Cocktail Bar
☎ 91 532 67 37; www.museo-chicote.com;
Gran Vía 12; ⌚ 8am-4am Mon-Sat; Ⓜ Gran Vía

The founder of this Madrid landmark is
said to have invented more than a hundred
cocktails, which the likes of Hemingway,
Ava Gardner, Sophia Loren and Frank Si-
natra all enjoyed at one time or another. It's
still frequented by film stars and top social-
ites, and it's at its best after midnight when
a lounge atmosphere takes over, couples
cuddle on the curved benches and some
of the city's best DJs do their stuff (CDs
are available). The 1930s-era interior only
adds to the cachet of this place. We don't
say this often, but if you haven't been here,
you haven't really been to Madrid – it's that
much of an icon.

EL MOJITO Map pp110–11   Mojito Bar
Calle del Duque de Osuna 6; ⌚ 10pm-4am;
Ⓜ Plaza de España

El Mojito is a modern temple to one of
the favourite drinks of madrileños. In fact,
it doesn't really serve much else, but the
price is right (€6) and the crowd is oh-so-
cool and all dressed in black; the music
(often live on Thursdays) is as Cuban as the
mojitos. Space is always at a premium (the
wall-to-ceiling mirrors make it look larger
than it is).

MADERFAKER FUNK CLUB
Map pp110–11   Music Bar
Calle de San Vicente Ferrer 17; ⌚ 10pm-3am Thu,
10pm-3.30am Fri & Sat; Ⓜ Tribunal

Dedicated to the black arts of funk, soul and blues, this narrow bar is laid-back cool. It rarely draws the crowds it deserves, but that makes it all the more mellow.

EL REFUGIO DE MADRID Map pp110–11 Rock Bar
Calle del Conde Duque 14; 🕙 **9pm-6am Mon-Sat;** Ⓜ **Plaza de España**
Styling itself as a bastion of classic rock, this brick-lined bar keeps it simple with beer on tap, posters on the walls of its heroes (among them Jimi Hendrix and ZZ Top) and video clips running around the clock in the background. Unlike some Malasaña rock bars you won't find too many heavy rockers here; it's more filled with young, professional punters who love their rock.

LA VACA AUSTERA Map pp110–11 Rock Bar
☎ **91 523 14 87; Calle de la Palma 20;** 🕙 **10pm-late Mon-Sat;** Ⓜ **Tribunal**
Old habits die hard at this veteran bar, which became famous during the heady days of *la movida* in the 1980s and is still going strong. Its warehouse feel and pool table won't be to everyone's taste, but it's a local icon and a totally unpretentious place to hear alternative rock music and just about anything from the '60s and '70s.

ANTIGUA CASA ÁNGEL SIERRA
Map pp110–11 Tapas Tavern
☎ **91 531 01 26; Calle de Gravina 11;** 🕙 **noon-1am;** Ⓜ **Chueca**
This historic old *taberna* is the antithesis of modern Chueca chic – it has hardly changed since it opened in 1917. As Spaniards like to say, the beer on tap is very

'well pulled' here and it also has vermouth on tap. Fronting onto the vibrant Plaza de Chueca, it can get pretty lively of a weekend evening when it spills over onto the plaza. Just don't expect service with a smile.

STOP MADRID Map pp110–11 Tapas Tavern
☎ **91 521 88 87; Calle de Hortaleza 11;** 🕙 **12.30-4pm & 6.30pm-2am;** Ⓜ **Gran Vía**
The name may not be Madrid's most evocative but this terrific old *taberna* is friendly, invariably packed with people and wins the vote of at least one Lonely Planet author for the best sangria in Madrid. The tapas are also outstanding and there's always a buzz here in the evenings.

VINOTECA BARBECHERA
Map pp110–11 Wine Bar
☎ **91 523 98 16; Calle de Gravina 6;** 🕙 **1pm-midnight Sun-Wed, 1pm-1am Thu-Sat;** Ⓜ **Chueca**
Amid the frenetic and often suggestive nightlife that rolls across Chueca, this wine bar adds a touch of refinement and caters to Chueca's professional gay and straight crowd. The wine list is more like a menu, and although you'll find occasional drops from elsewhere, Spanish wines across all price ranges are what you come here for.

CHAMBERÍ & ARGÜELLES

Like any barrios in the capital, Chamberí and Argüelles have bars on practically every street corner, but for us there are really only a couple that stand out.

DJÉNNÉ Map pp116–17 Bar
☎ **91 448 84 18; Calle de Galileo 74;** 🕙 **8pm-3am Mon-Sat;** Ⓜ **Islas Filipinas**
Styling itself as a bar with a passion for travel, this bar *could* be a real find. The wall-sized mural of Mali's Djenné market and photos from around the world give it something special, but the music is of a fairly standard, late-night bar variety – if only they'd play a few world music tunes, the cocktails would go down a treat. We wouldn't travel all across town to get here, but if you're on your way to or from Galileo Galilei (p208), it's worth a stop.

top picks

MADRID'S BEST MOJITOS
- Café Belén (p194)
- El Eucalipto (p188)
- Dos Gardenias (p190)
- Delic (p188)
- Museo Chicote (p195)
- El Mojito (p195)
- Viva Madrid (p189)
- Centro Cubano de España (p191)

KRYPTON Map pp116–17   Cocktail Bar

☎ 91 591 54 32; www.kryptonbar.com, in Spanish; Calle de Gonzalo de Córdoba 20; 🕐 6pm-2.30am Thu-Sat, 6-11pm Sun; Ⓜ Bilbao or Quevedo

In the heart of Chamberí, Krypton is a dimly lit, smoky bar with quirky decoration dedicated to the edgy art of Japanese comics, music that could be jazz, electronica or hip-hop, and good cocktails (including *mojitos*). We love it, but it won't be to everyone's taste.

NORTHERN MADRID

REAL CAFÉ BERNABÉU Map p123   Bar

☎ 91 458 36 67; www.realcafebernabeu.es; Gate 30, Estadio Santiago Bernabéu, Avenida de Conche Espina; 🕐 10am-2am; Ⓜ Santiago Bernabéu

Overlooking one of the most famous football fields on earth, this place will appeal to those who live and breathe football. Views are exceptional, although it closes two hours before a game and doesn't open until an hour after. There's also a good restaurant.

NIGHTLIFE

top picks

- **Cool** (p201)
  Super-sleek nightclub with an upmarket crowd.
- **Room at Stella** (p203)
  Great DJs and a crowd that never pauses for breath.
- **Costello Café & Niteclub** (p201)
  A slice of New York in downtown Madrid.
- **Cardamomo** (p205)
  Authentic live flamenco that never disappoints.
- **Las Tablasp206**
  The best flamenco floor show in Madrid.
- **Café Central** (p206)
  Distinguished live jazz café that draws the big names.
- **Café La Palma** (p207)
  Eclectic but always buzzing live music venue.
- **Clamores p208**
  Top-notch live music across all genres.
- **Kaboklap209**
  Madrid's home of all things Brazilian.

What's your recommendation? www.lonelyplanet.com/madrid

Madrid's nightlife rocks. Brilliant clubs that stay open until dawn and cater to just about every dance-floor taste have earned the city a well-deserved reputation for being one of Europe's nightlife capitals and what Hemingway wrote of the place in the 1930s remains true to this day: 'Nobody goes to bed in Madrid until they have killed the night.' But Madrid nights are about far more than dancing the night away. Excellent flamenco venues, funky jazz clubs and an outstanding live music scene are all part of an intoxicating mix.

Although every barrio in the city (with the exception of Paseo del Prado and El Retiro) makes its contribution to the pulsating after-dark *marcha* (action), some barrios definitely offer more *marcha* than others. Los Austrias, Sol and Centro have the widest selection of venues across a range of genres, while Huertas attracts a local and international crowd most nights of the week. Chueca is exuberantly and extravagantly gay (see p224), although everyone's welcome. Neighbouring Malasaña, the spiritual home of *la movida madrileña* (see p32), has never really grown up and is the barrio of choice for grunge rockers, sideburns and an eclectic crowd; it's the antithesis of Salamanca, where it's all about hair gel and designer clothing. Lavapiés and, to a lesser extent, La Latina are gritty, groovy and cool all at once, and definitely among night-time Madrid's best-kept secrets, while Chamberí and Argüelles don't have many venues, but they're worth checking out.

For the best places to find out what's on and where, turn to p212, while a list of places to buy tickets appears in the boxed text, p212.

CLUBBING

People here live fully for the moment. Today's encounter can be tomorrow's distant memory, but you need to know how things work. Don't even think of starting your night until after midnight (most madrileños will be too busy eating up to that point anyway), hence our suggestion of a late-afternoon siesta. Don't expect the dance clubs or *discotecas* (nightclubs) to really get going until after 1am, and some won't even bat an eyelid until 3am, when the bars elsewhere have closed.

Club prices vary widely, depending on the time of night you enter, the way you're dressed and the number of people inside. The standard entry fee is €10, which usually includes the first drink, although megaclubs and swankier

places charge a few euros more (listed below). Even those that let you in for free will play catch-up with hefty prices for drinks, so don't plan your night around looking for the cheapest ticket.

No barrio in Madrid is without a decent club or disco, but the most popular dance spots are in the city centre. For intimate dancing or quirky décor, head to Chueca or Malasaña.

AKBAR Map pp110–11

☎ 91 532 34 09; Calle de Barquillo 44; admission Mon-Thu free, Fri & Sat €8; ☼ 7pm-5am Mon-Fri, 11pm-6am Sat; Ⓜ Chueca or Alonso Martínez
All decked out in red and drawing a multicultural crowd, Akbar is slightly more nuanced than your average Madrid nightclub. It plays chill-out early in the evening, before upping the tempo to funk, R&B and soul, but it's not averse to a little rap or hip-hop if the mood takes it. There are cushions on the floor and occasional live bands (Wednesday at 8.30pm).

ALMONTE Map pp102–3

☎ 91 563 25 04; Calle de Juan Bravo 35; ☼ 9pm-5am Sun-Thu, to 6am Fri & Sat; Ⓜ Nuñez de Balboa or Diego de León
If flamenco has captured your soul, but you're keen to do more than watch, head to Almonte where the whitewashed façade

top picks

CLUBS

tells you that this is all about Andalucía, the home of flamenco. The young and the beautiful who come here have *sevillanas* (a flamenco dance style) in their soul and in their feet, so head downstairs to see the best dancing. Dance if you dare.

CAPOTE Map pp110–11

☎ 91 319 01 38; Calle de Santa Teresa 3; admission free; 🕑 7pm-3am Tue-Thu, to 3.30am Fri, 8.30pm-3.30am Sat; Ⓜ Alonso Martínez
Most of the nightlife around Alonso Martínez can be pretty juvenile, but Capote gets an older, more sophisticated crowd. House music with jazz inflections from DJs Kalero and Mikeel Molina gets things going, but it's pretty laid-back and you can hear yourself speak, at least early in the evening.

COOL Map pp64–5

☎ 902 499 994; Calle de Isabel la Católica 6; admission €12; 🕑 11pm-6am Thu-Sat; Ⓜ Santo Domingo
Cool by name, cool by nature. One of the hottest clubs in the city, the curvy white lines, discreet lounge chairs in dark corners and pulsating dance floor are decked by gorgeous people, gorgeous clothes and a strict entry policy; if a famous DJ is on the bill, expect to pay at least €30. The sexy, well-heeled crowd includes a lot of sleek-looking gay men and model-like women. Things don't really get going until 3am, and the music's a mix of electronica and house with themed gay and rock nights.

COSTELLO CAFÉ & NITECLUB Map pp64–5

www.costelloclub.com; Calle del Caballero de Gracia 10; admission free; 🕑 6pm-3am; Ⓜ Gran Vía
Costello Café & Niteclub is smooth-as-silk ambience wedded with an innovative mix of pop, rock and fusion in Warholesque surrounds. It may close earlier than we'd like, but we still think this is one of the coolest places in town.

EL SON Map pp84–5

☎ 91 532 32 83; Calle de la Victoria 6; 🕑 8pm-5am; Ⓜ Sol
If you're looking for salsa, merengue or some sexy tangos, look no further than El Son. This is one of the top places in town for Latin music, and it's very popular with Madrid's South and Central American population.

EÓ Map pp110–11

☎ 91 521 73 79; Calle de Almirante 12; 🕑 10pm-3am Tue-Sat; Ⓜ Chueca
If you bottle the energy of Chueca and add the sophistication of Salamanca, you end up with EÓ. The cocktails are first rate, there seems to be a door policy of only admitting the beautiful people of Madrid and, though the clientele is mainly Spanish, there are enough gorgeous foreigners to lend the place an international feel. *Famosos* (celebrities) love this place.

GARAMOND Map pp102–3

☎ 91 578 19 74; www.garamond.es, in Spanish; Calle de Claudio Coello 10; admission €20; 🕑 10pm-6.30am; Ⓜ Retiro
Better look snazzy, 'cause this place has what's known as a *puerta rigurosa*, which translates roughly as 'we won't let you in unless you look like you belong in Salamanca'. Although it's aimed at a 30-plus crowd, the atmosphere can get pretty charged and there seems to be enough hormones here to fill a school disco. The decoration is mock-medieval and the music Spanish pop-rock.

KAPITAL Map pp84–5

☎ 91 420 29 06; www.grupo-kapital.com, in Spanish; Calle de Atocha 125; admission €20; 🕑 6-10pm & midnight-6am Thu-Sun; Ⓜ Atocha
One of the most famous megaclubs in Madrid, this massive seven-storey nightclub has something for everyone: from cocktail bars and dance music to karaoke, salsa, hip-hop and more chilled spaces for R&B and soul. The crowd is sexy, well heeled and up for a good time. On Sunday, 'Sundance' (otherwise known as 'Kapital Love') is definitely for those who have no intention of appearing at work on Monday, while other nights belong more to the Real Madrid set. We reckon €2 to use the cloak room cheapens an otherwise great package.

LA CARTUJA Map pp84–5

☎ 91 521 55 89; Calle de la Cruz 10; 🕑 11pm-5.30am; Ⓜ Sol or Sevilla
A real mixed bag of styles, La Cartuja is many people's favourite late-night Huertas club. The decoration is from Andalucía and the music's a mix of Spanish and Latin American tunes with salsa on Wednesday night.

LA LUPE Map pp110–11

Calle de Hortaleza 51; ⏰ 6pm-3am; Ⓜ Chueca
This fun dance spot at the top end of
Chueca is always packed to the rafters
on weekends. Its success is based on a
none-too-challenging playlist of mainstream tunes you can dance to. It doesn't
try to be anything else, and although few
people would identify it as their favourite
nightspot in Madrid, it's where many of
them end up when in search of a catchy
tune that's not house. The crowd is mixed
straight-gay.

MACUMBA Map p123

Plaza Estación de Chamartín; ⏰ 11pm-7am Thu &
Fri, 5.30-10.30pm & midnight-7am Sat, 10am-mid-
night Sun; Ⓜ Chamartín
Macumba, in the Chamartín train station,
hardly bothers closing from Thursday night
through to Sunday night, with a range of
sessions for all ages and styles. Sunday
(Space of Sound) is for those who can't
bear their Saturday night to end. You could,
of course, time your departure to coincide
with your train, but you'd be feeling pretty
rough.

MOMA 56 Map pp116–17

☎ 91 395 20 59; Calle de José Abascal 56;
admission €15; ⏰ midnight-6am Wed-Sat;
Ⓜ Gregorio Marañón
Two words: beautiful people. Get your
Prada gear on and that studied look of
sophistication, and join the small-time
celebrities and owners of the flashy sports
cars parked out the front. The décor (red
padded walls, red lighting) is as sleek as the
too-cool crowd who shake off their pretensions once the live percussion fuses into
DJ house. There's nowhere quite like it in
Madrid.

MOROCCO Map pp110–11

☎ 91 531 51 67; Calle del Marqués de Leganés
7; ⏰ midnight-3am Thu, to 5.30am Fri & Sat;
Ⓜ Santo Domingo
Owned by the zany Alaska, the standout
musical personality of *la movida*, Morocco
has décor that's so kitsch it's cool, and a
mix of musical styles that never strays too
far from 1980s Spanish and international
tunes. The bouncers have been known
to show a bit of attitude, but then that's
almost come to be expected these days,
hasn't it?

NASTI CLUB Map pp110–11

☎ 91 521 76 05; www.nasti.es, in Spanish; Calle de
San Vicente Ferrer 33; ⏰ 1-5.30am Thu, 1-6am Fri
& Sat; Ⓜ Tribunal
It's hard to think of a more off-putting
entrance with Nasti Club's graffiti and
abandoned-building look. You also won't
find the name outside – if you want to
come here you're supposed to know where
to find it. Its staple, appropriately, is a faith-
fully grungy approach to the 1970s (pop,
rock and punk), both in terms of music and
décor. But it's not as nasty as it sounds and
the crowd can span the full range of 1970s
throwbacks from a Who's Who of Madrid's
underground to some surprisingly respectable types. Very Malasaña.

OBA OBA Map pp64–5

Calle de Jacometrezo 4; ⏰ 11pm-5.30am Sun-Thu,
6am Fri & Sat; Ⓜ Callao
This nightclub is Brazilian down to its
G-strings with live music some nights and
dancing till dawn every night of the week.
You'll find plenty of Brazilians in residence,
which is the best recommendation we can
give for the music and the authenticity of
its caipirinhas.

PACHÁ Map pp110–11

☎ 91 447 01 28; www.pacha.com; Calle de
Barceló 11; admission €10; ⏰ 12.30-5am Thu-Sat;
Ⓜ Tribunal
This megaclub is one of the international
chain of clubs that earned its fame in Ibiza
and became a major Madrid club during *la
movida*. As serious clubbers have moved
on, the oh-my-gosh, barely out of school
set turns up in droves for the fun mixture of
house, Latin and Spanish music, and mixes
it with 30-somethings who never grew up.
The name still has a certain cachet on the
Madrid nightlife scene, so the odd celebrity
turns up here.

PALACIO GAVIRIA Map pp64–5

☎ 91 526 60 69; Calle del Arenal 9; ⏰ 11pm-4am
Sun-Wed, 10pm-6am Thu, 11pm-7am Fri & Sat;
Ⓜ Sol
An elegant palace converted into one of
the most popular dance clubs in Madrid,
this is the kind of place where you're guaranteed to meet the locals and probably
even a few compatriots as it's beloved of
a newly arrived international crowd. The
scene can be pretty young and boisterous,

the queues are long, and Thursday is international student and house-music night – international relations have never been such fun. Other themed nights include samba on Monday and Reggaeton Tuesday, but we love Sunday with Latin Lover and Bacchanal House Party.

PENTA BAR Map pp110–11

☎ 91 447 84 60; Calle de la Palma 4; ⏲ 9pm-3am; Ⓜ Tribunal

A night out here and you could be forgiven for believing that *la movida* never died down. It's an informal place where you can groove to the '80s music you love to hate; don't even think of turning up before midnight.

ROOM AT STELLA Map pp84–5

☎ 91 531 63 78; www.theroomclub.com; Calle de Arlabán 7; admission €14; ⏲ 1-6am Thu-Sat; Ⓜ Sevilla

If you arrive here after 3am, there simply won't be room and those inside have no intention of leaving until dawn. The DJs here are some of Madrid's best, and the great visuals will leave you cross-eyed if you weren't already from the house, electronica, new wave or funk in this vibrant, heady place.

SALA FLAMINGO Map pp110–11

Calle de Mesonero Romanos 13; ⏲ 11pm-6am Thu & Sat, 1-7am Fri, 10pm-3am Sun; Ⓜ Callao or Gran Vía

One of the most 'in' places in Madrid, Sala Flamingo opens four nights for four very different sessions. Thursday night is 'Frenela Dance Hall', where the '70s is about as modern as it gets. Friday night is 'Ocho y Media', which does modern pop-rock and what is called *rockotrónica* – this is the night when local celebrities flood through the doors. 'Darkhole' on Saturday is all black and Gothic, while Sunday is the '60s with a more chilled atmosphere and occasional live acts.

SIROCO Map pp110–11

☎ 91 593 30 70; www.siroco.es, in Spanish; Calle de San Dimas 3; ⏲ 10pm-6am Thu-Sat; Ⓜ Noviciado

One of the most popular and eclectic nightclubs in Madrid, Siroco does everything from reggae to acid jazz, from '70s to funk, house and hip-hop. As such it gets a diverse crowd and queues can be long. The one unifying theme is the commitment to Spanish music (sometimes live) and it's a good place to hear local music before it becomes too mainstream.

SOL Y SOMBRA Map pp84–5

☎ 91 542 81 93; www.solysombra.name; Calle de Echegaray 18; admission free; ⏲ 10pm-3.30am Tue-Sat; Ⓜ Sevilla

Not so long ago, this was one of the coolest live jazz venues in Madrid, with a real buzz attached to it, and it was pretty fussy about who it let in. But the last time we were here, staff were out on the street spruiking for punters on a mild Thursday night. A dispute with the local council has left live music off the menu and with it has gone much of the place's magic and sophistication. It's still a temple to good taste when it comes to the décor (the work of master designer Tomas Alia) and there are plans to restart the live gigs, which is why we include it here.

STROMBOLI CAFÉ Map pp110–11

☎ 91 319 46 28; Calle de Hortaleza 96; admission free; ⏲ 4pm-3am Thu & Fri, to 3.30am Sat; Ⓜ Chueca or Tribunal

One of Chueca's best smaller clubs, Stromboli somehow manages to stay hip and happening with its lounge, nu jazz and deep house beats from some of the best local DJs who love the cosy lounge feel almost as much as the punters do.

SUITE CAFÉ CLUB Map pp64–5

☎ 91 521 40 31; www.suitecafeclub.com, in Spanish; Calle de la Virgen de los Peligros 4; admission free; ⏲ 9pm-3am Tue-Sat; Ⓜ Sevilla

A café-restaurant downstairs, a sleek dance floor up stairs, Suite Café Club is one of the trendiest little clubs in the area (as a glance at the slickly dressed and mainly gay crowd will show), with DJs cooking up some seriously funky sounds.

SUPERSONIC Map pp116–17

Calle de Meléndez Valdés 25; ⏲ 9.30pm-3.30am Thu-Sat; Ⓜ Argüelles

Madrid has nightclubs in the most unlikely places… On a quiet residential Argüelles street, this great little *discoteca* is one of the best venues for indie music, with a mix of '70s diehard to everything that we loved to hate about Britpop (The Smiths, Oasis etc).

SUSAN CLUB Map pp110–11

www.susanclub.com, in Spanish; Calle de la Reina 23; ⏰ 8pm-3.30am Mon-Sat; Ⓜ Gran Vía

It's hard to know what sort of music you'll find at the cosy little Susan Club because the bar staff readily admit that they play whatever takes their fancy given the mood of the evening. As a general rule, it's quite funky and downtempo early in the night, with more frenetic and popular tunes, and occasional hip-hop, as the crowd starts to sweat. With smooth cocktails, comfy sofas and the promise of a good time for those who turn up alone, we think it's a good choice.

TEATRO JOY ESLAVA Map pp64–5

Joy Madrid; ☎ 91 366 54 39; www.joy-eslava.com, in Spanish; Calle del Arenal 11; admission €12-15; ⏰ 11.30pm-6am; Ⓜ Sol

The only things guaranteed at this grand old Madrid dance club (housed in a 19th-century theatre) are a crowd and the fact that it'll be open (it claims to have operated every single day for the past 27 years). The music and the crowd are a mixed bag, but queues are long and invariably include locals and tourists, and even the occasional *famoso*.

TUPPERWARE Map pp110–11

☎ 91 446 42 04; Corredera Alta de San Pablo 26; ⏰ 8pm-3.30am Sun-Wed, 9pm-3.30am Thu-Sat; Ⓜ Tribunal

A Malasaña stalwart, Tupperware draws a 30-something crowd, spins indie rock with a bit of soul and classics from the '60s and '70s, and generally revels in its kitsch (eyeballs stuck to the ceiling, and plastic TVs with action-figure dioramas lined up behind the bar). It can get pretty packed on a weekend after 1am. By the way, locals pronounce it 'Tupper-warry'.

VILLA ROSA Map pp84–5

☎ 91 521 36 89; Plaza de Santa Ana 15; ⏰ 11pm-6am Mon-Sat; Ⓜ Sol

The extraordinary tiled façade of this long-standing nightclub is a tourist attraction in itself; the club even appeared in the Pedro Almodóvar film *Tacones Lejanos* (High Heels; 1991). The music is what is known as '*comercial*', which basically means the latest dance hits with nothing too challenging. As such, it's more about Madrid's energy than its latest trends.

WHY NOT? Map pp110–11

Calle de San Bartolomé 7; ⏰ 10.30pm-6am; admission €10; Ⓜ Chueca

Narrow and packed with bodies, gay-friendly Why Not? is the sort of place where nothing's left to the imagination (the gay and straight crowd who come here are pretty amorous) and it's full nearly every night of the week. Pop and top-40 music are the standard here, and the dancing crowd is mixed and as serious about having a good time as they are about heavy petting. We're not huge fans of the bouncers here, but once you get past it's all about having fun.

FLAMENCO

First, a few home truths about Madrid's flamenco scene. Seeing flamenco in Madrid is, with some worthy exceptions (listed here), expensive – at the *tablaos* (restaurants where flamenco is performed) expect to pay €30 to €35 just to see the show. The admission price usually includes your first drink, but you pay extra for meals (up to €50 per person) that, put simply, are rarely worth the money. For that reason, we suggest you eat elsewhere and simply pay for the show (after having bought tickets in advance), albeit on the understanding that you won't have a front-row seat. The other important thing to remember is that most of these shows are geared towards tourists. That's not to say that the quality isn't often top-notch – often it's magnificent, spine-tingling stuff. It's just that they sometimes lack the genuine, raw emotion of real flamenco and the atmosphere is not as spontaneous as being surrounded by a knowledgeable crowd who can lift a performer to new heights.

There are alternatives, some of which are listed here, although the dark, smoky bars of flamenco's origins are now pretty thin on the ground. One bar that's always brimful of flamenco atmosphere is El Callejón (p190), while for those of you keen to dance your own version of the *sevillana* (flamenco dance style), Al Monte (p200) is a good choice.

If you don't fancy paying the steep prices of the *tablaos*, other live music venues also have live flamenco, usually one night a week. Such places include Bar&Co (p207), Clamores (p208), ContraClub (p208), El Juglar (p208) and Galileo Galilei (p208).

Festivals are another place to find flamenco; February's Festival Flamenco (p17) and Suma

top picks

FLAMENCO VENUES

- Cardamomo (below)
- Las Tablas (p206)
- Las Carboneras (p206)
- Corral de la Morería (right)
- Café de Chinitas (below)

Flamenca (p18) in May are the city's biggest flamenco events and attract the biggest names in the genre.

For more information about flamenco as art form, turn to p45.

CAFÉ DE CHINITAS Map pp64–5

☎ 91 559 51 35; www.chinitas.com; Calle de Torija 7; admission €32; ☼ 9pm-2.30am Mon-Sat, shows 10.30pm; ☎ Santo Domingo

For a high-end flamenco show in an elegant setting, this traditional *tablao* is the perfect choice. It attracts top performers and big crowds, so book in advance. There's a minimum meal charge of €18 in addition to the admission charge. It may attract loads of tourists, but flamenco aficionados also give it top marks.

CANDELA Map pp76–7

☎ 91 467 33 82; Calle del Olmo 3; ☼ 10.30pm-late; ☎ Antón Martín

Although not quite what it was, Candela draws a foreign crowd upstairs for fairly formal flamenco, while many of Madrid's young performers hang out downstairs in an informal bar where spontaneous music often breaks out late in the evening. To see Candela at its best, come after 1am and respect the atmosphere.

CARDAMOMO Map pp84–5

☎ 91 369 07 57; www.cardamomo.es, in Spanish; Calle de Echegaray 15; admission €10; ☼ 9pm-3.30am, live shows 10.30pm Tue & Wed; ☎ Sevilla

If you believe flamenco is best enjoyed in a dark, smoky bar where the crowd is predominantly local and where you can dance, clap and even sing along, Cardamomo is ideal. Flamenco and flamenco-fusion tunes are played until late with live shows Tuesday and Wednesday night.

CASA PATAS Map pp76–7

☎ 91 369 04 96; www.casapatas.com, in Spanish; Calle de Cañizares 10; admission €31; ☼ shows 10.30pm Mon-Thu, 9pm & midnight Fri & Sat; ☎ Antón Martín or Tirso de Molina

One of the top flamenco stages in Madrid, this *tablao* always offers unimpeachable quality that serves as a good introduction to the art. It's not the friendliest place in town, especially if you're only here for the show, and you're likely to be crammed in a little, but no-one complains about the standard of the performances.

CORRAL DE LA MORERÍA Map pp76–7

☎ 91 365 84 46; www.corraldelamoreria.com; Calle de la Morería 17; admission €32-35; ☼ 8.30pm-2.30am, shows 10pm; ☎ Ópera

This is one of the most prestigious flamenco stages in Madrid, with 50 years as a leading flamenco venue and top performers most nights. The stage area has a rustic feel, and tables are pushed up close. We'd steer clear of the restaurant, which is overpriced, but the performances have a far higher price-quality ratio. This is where international celebrities (eg Marlene Dietrich, Marlon Brando, Muhammad Ali, Omar Sharif) have always gone for their flamenco fix when in town.

ESPACIO FLAMENCO Map pp76–7

☎ 91 298 19 55; http://espacio.deflamenco.com; Calle de la Ribera de Curtidores 26; admission €30; ☼ 10pm-1am Thu-Sat; ☎ Puerta de Toledo

Way down the bottom of the El Rastro hill, this little-known but nonetheless excellent *tablao* draws occasional big names, but most often showcases young performers before they make the big stage. There's also a commitment here to authentic flamenco and its director, Mari Paz Lucena, is a leading flamenco *bailaora*, who often takes the stage.

LA SOLÉA Map pp76–7

☎ 91 366 05 34; Calle de la Cava Baja 34; admission free; ☼ 10pm-5am Mon-Thu, to 6am Fri & Sat; ☎ La Latina

This long-standing flamenco bar has live flamenco of a much more improvised kind and which bears little resemblance to the *tablao* floor shows. Usually from around midnight, a knowledgeable crowd of flamenco insiders provides the closest flamenco comes to a jam session. Like any such session, sometimes it works and sometimes it doesn't, but when it does it has a soulful authenticity that more formal *tablaos* can't quite match.

LAS CARBONERAS Map pp64–5

☎ 91 542 86 77; www.tablaolascarboneras.com, in Spanish; Plaza del Conde de Miranda 1; admission from €33; ⏰ shows 9pm & 11.30pm Mon-Thu, 8.30pm & 11pm Fri & Sat; Ⓜ Ópera, Sol or La Latina
Like most of the *tablaos* around town, this place sees far more tourists than locals, but the quality is top-notch. It's not the place for gritty, soul-moving spontaneity, but it's still an excellent introduction and one of the few places that flamenco aficionados seem to have no complaints about.

LAS TABLAS Map pp64–5

☎ 91 542 05 20; www.lastablasmadrid.com, in Spanish; Plaza de España 9; admission €10-30; ⏰ 7pm-1am, shows 10.30pm; Ⓜ Plaza de España
One of the relatively recent newcomers to Madrid's flamenco scene, Las Tablas has quickly earned a reputation for quality flamenco and it could just be the best choice in town. Most nights you'll see a classic flamenco show, with plenty of throaty singing and soul-baring dancing. Antonia Moya and Marisol Navarro are leading lights in the flamenco world and often take the stage.

JAZZ CLUBS

Madrid was one of Europe's jazz capitals in the 1920s. It's taken a while, but it's once again among Europe's elite for live jazz. You'll pay about €10 to get into most places, but special concerts can run up to €20 or more.

In addition to the places listed here, other places where you'll often hear jazz include Bar&Co (opposite), Zanzibar (p210) and Clamores (p208).

BOGUI JAZZ Map pp110–11

☎ 91 521 15 68; www.boguijazz.com in, Spanish; Calle de Barquillo 29; admission €5-10; ⏰ 10pm-5.30am Mon-Sat; Ⓜ Alonso Martínez
It's always worth checking out what's happening at Bogui Jazz, where it likes a big-band sound as much as it does intimate ensembles, whether big international names or well-established local groups. If you can't decide between the many groups on offer, the Tuesday-night jam sessions (11pm to 3am) are a good way to get a feel for this terrific venue.

top picks

JAZZ VENUES

- Café Central (below)
- Populart (opposite)
- El Berlín Jazz Café (below)
- El Junco Jazz Club (opposite)

CAFÉ CENTRAL Map pp84–5

☎ 91 369 41 43; www.cafecentralmadrid.com, in Spanish; Plaza del Ángel 10; admission €9-15; ⏰ 1pm-2.30am Sun-Thu, to 4am Fri & Sat; Ⓜ Antón Martín or Sol
This Art Deco bar has consistently been voted one of the best jazz venues in the world by leading jazz magazines, and with more than 8000 gigs under its belt, it rarely misses a beat. Big international names like Chano Domínguez, Tal Farlow and Wynton Marsalis have all played here, and there's everything from Latin jazz and fusion to tango and classic jazz. Performers usually play here for a week and then move on, so getting tickets shouldn't be a problem, except on weekends; shows start at 10pm and tickets go on sale an hour before the set starts.

EL BERLÍN JAZZ CAFÉ Map pp64–5

☎ 91 521 57 52; www.cafeberlin.es, in Spanish; Calle de Jacometrezo 4; admission €6-12; ⏰ 7pm-2.30am Tue-Sun; Ⓜ Callao or Santo Domingo
El Berlín is something of a Madrid jazz stalwart and the kind of place that some serious jazz fans rave about as the most authentic in town. The atmosphere is vaguely cabaret and the headline acts a Who's Who of world jazz; in the past Al Foster (Miles Davis' drummer), Santiago de Muela and the Calento Jazz Orchestra have all taken to the stage.

EL DESPERTAR Map pp76–7

☎ 91 530 80 95; www.cafeeldespertar.com, in Spanish; Calle de la Torrecilla del Leal 18; admission €6; ⏰ 7.30pm-late Wed-Mon; Ⓜ Antón Martín
El Despertar is all about jazz down to its roots. Everything about this place harks back to the 1920s, with a commitment to old-style jazz and décor to match from its days as a meeting point for the barrio's intelligentsia. There are live performances

every Friday and Saturday, as well as most Thursdays and Sundays. Concerts start at 10.30pm.

EL JUNCO JAZZ CLUB Map pp110–11
☎ 91 319 20 81; Plaza de Santa Bárbara 10; admission free; ⏰ 11pm-6am; Ⓜ Alonso Martínez
El Junco has quickly established itself on the Madrid nightlife scene, appealing as much to jazz aficionados as to clubbers. Its secret is high-quality live jazz gigs from Spain and around the world at 11.30pm every night, followed by DJs spinning funk, soul, nu jazz and innovative groove beats. There are also jam sessions in jazz (Tuesday) and blues (Sunday). The emphasis is on black music (music from the American south) and the crowd is classy and casual.

LA FIDULA Map pp84–5
☎ 91 429 29 47; www.cafeconciertolafidula.com; Calle de las Huertas 57; admission free-€6; ⏰ 8pm-3am Mon-Wed, to 3.30am Thu-Sun; Ⓜ Antón Martín
Less sophisticated than the other live jazz venues in the barrio, La Fidula is nonetheless a longstanding favourite for people who know their jazz and like it spontaneous. Drinks are reasonably priced and there are Sunday jazz jam sessions (9pm to midnight). Blues performers occasionally take to the stage here as well.

POPULART Map pp84–5
☎ 91 429 84 07; www.populart.es, in Spanish; Calle de las Huertas 22; admission free; ⏰ 6pm-2.30am Mon-Fri, to 3am Fri & Sat; Ⓜ Antón Martín or Sol
One of Madrid's classic jazz clubs, this place offers a low-key atmosphere and top-quality music, which is mostly jazz with occasional blues, swing and even flamenco thrown into the mix. Think Compay Segundo, Sonny Fortune and the Canal Street Jazz Band and you'll get an idea of the quality on offer here. The shows start at 11pm, but if you want a seat get here early.

SEGUNDO JAZZ Map p123
☎ 91 554 94 37; Calle del Comandante Zorita 8; admission €5-10; ⏰ 7pm-4am; Ⓜ Nuevos Ministerios or Cuatro Caminos
This well-regarded jazz venue focuses on up-and-coming local talents as well as a few international acts. It's an agreeable, unpretentious place where the quality is always high and the atmosphere nice and

laid-back. Tuesday is given over to jam sessions from 11pm, while other concerts start anywhere from 9pm to midnight.

LIVE MUSIC

Madrid is Spain's undisputed king of live music and it just keeps getting better. It wasn't always thus. Madrid made its name as a live music city back in the 1980s when drugs and rock music fuelled the decade-long fiesta known as *la movida madrileña* (see p32), but it was all pretty one-dimensional. And so it stayed until the late 1990s when big international names began once again including the Spanish capital on their European tours and, perhaps more importantly, live music venues catering to all tastes began populating just about every barrio of the city. While rock remains a Madrid mainstay and the doors of a handful of classic venues (Clamores, Honky Tonk and Moby Dick) remain open, the live music scene is in rude health covering every genre – world music, soul, blues, singer-songwriter, acoustic – on just about every night of the week. Many of these concert venues double as clubs where DJs follow the live acts, making it possible to start off the night with a great concert and stay on to party until late.

In addition to checking the websites of each individual club, a good website to find out what's happening is La Noche En Vivo (www.lanocheenvivo.com in Spanish); click on 'Actuaciones' for upcoming concerts and on 'Sala' for a list of venues. Another good source is La Carega (www.lacarega.com in Spanish).

BAR&CO Map pp110–11
☎ 91 521 24 47; www.barcobar.com, in Spanish; Calle del Barco 34; admission free-€6; ⏰ 8pm-5.30am Sun-Thu, 10.30pm-6am Fri & Sat; Ⓜ Tribunal
Just before Malasaña spills over into the seedy backside of Gran Vía, Bar&Co is an outstanding live venue with jazz, flamenco, Latin music, funk, rock or blues. There's room to dance if the mood takes you and the crowd is almost exclusively local. There's a jazz jam session at 12.15am on Sunday, and flamenco star Enrique Morente is known to turn up here as well.

CAFÉ LA PALMA Map pp110–11
☎ 91 522 50 31; www.cafelapalma.com, in Spanish; Calle de la Palma 62; admission free-€6; ⏰ 4pm-2am Sun-Thu, to 3.30am Fri & Sat; Ⓜ Noviciado

top picks

LIVE MUSIC VENUES

- Café La Palma (p207)
- Clamores belowGalileo Galilei right
- Honky Tonk (opposite)
- Kabokla (opposite)
- La Escalera de Jacobopposite
- Zanzibar p210

It's amazing how much variety Café la Palma has packed into its labyrinth of rooms. Live shows featuring hot local bands are held at the back, while DJs mix up the front. Some rooms have a café style, while others evoke an Arab tearoom, pillows on the floor and all. You might find live music other nights, but there are always two shows at 10pm and midnight from Thursday to Saturday. Every night is a little different.

CLAMORES Map pp116–17

☎ 91 445 79 38; www.clamores.es, in Spanish; Calle de Alburquerque 14; admission €5-20; ⏱ 6pm-3am Sun-Thu, to 4am Fri & Sat; Ⓜ Bilbao
Clamores is a one-time classic jazz café that has morphed into one of the most diverse live music stages in Madrid. Jazz is still a staple, but world music, flamenco, soul fusion, singer-songwriter, pop and rock all make regular appearances. Live shows can begin as early as 9pm but sometimes really get going after 1am on weekends.

CONTRACLUB Map pp76–7

☎ 91 523 15 11; www.contraclub.es, in Spanish; Calle de Bailén 16; admission €6-10; ⏱ 10pm-5.30am Wed & Thu, to 6am Fri & Sat, 7pm-3am Sun; Ⓜ La Latina
ContraClub is a crossover live music venue and nightclub, with live flamenco on Wednesday and an eclectic mix of other live music (jazz, blues, world music and rock) from Thursday to Sunday; after the live acts (which start at 10.30pm), the resident DJs serve up equally eclectic beats to make sure you don't move elsewhere. To get a feel for their concerts, check out www.contraclub.tv. You'll see plenty of well-known Spanish actors here as one of the owners is Antonio Molero,

who plays Fiti in the Telecinco TV series *Los Serrano*.

COSTELLO CAFÉ & NITECLUB Map pp64–5

www.costelloclub.com; Calle del Caballero de Gracia 10; admission free-€7; ⏱ 6pm-3am; Ⓜ Gran Vía
This funky little nightclub has live pop, rock and occasional electronica from 9pm Thursday to Saturday and sometimes on other nights. Even if there's nothing live on stage, it's still a great place to be (see p201).

EL BUHO REAL Map pp110–11

☎ 91 319 10 88; www.buhoreal.com, in Spanish; Calle de Regueros 5; admission €4-6; ⏱ 8pm-3am Sun-Thu, to 3.30am Fri & Sat; Ⓜ Alonso Martínez or Chueca
It looks like your average Madrid *bar de copas*, but El Buho Real (The Royal Owl) is all about acoustic music. It interprets the term pretty widely to include flamenco and singer-songwriter solo acts, and it's been around long enough to have drawn a loyal following. Concerts start at 9.30pm.

EL JUGLAR Map pp76–7

☎ 91 528 43 81; www.salajuglar.com; Calle de Lavapiés 37; admission €5-20; ⏱ 9pm-3am Sun-Wed, to 3.30am Thu-Sat; Ⓜ Lavapiés
One of the hottest spots in Lavapiés, this great venue is for a largely bohemian crowd with a rock-dominated programme leavened with flamenco on Sunday and occasional rumba, jazz and soul beats. Concerts begin around 9.30pm and then it's DJ-spun Latin tunes after midnight.

EL RINCÓN DEL ARTE NUEVO Map pp76–7

☎ 91 365 50 45; www.rincondelartenuevo.com, in Spanish; Calle de Segovia 17; admission €7-10; ⏱ 9.30pm-4.30am Sun-Thu, to 6am Fri & Sat; Ⓜ La Latina
With 29 years in the business, this small venue knows what its punters like and it serves up a nightly feast of singer-songwriters for an appreciative crowd. The acts are as diverse as the genre itself, with Melendi, Fran Postigo and Diego El Negro among the recent performers. Concerts start at 10pm.

GALILEO GALILEI Map pp116–17

☎ 91 534 75 57; www.salagalileogalilei.com, in Spanish; Calle de Galileo 100; admission free-€16; ⏱ 6pm-4.30am; Ⓜ Islas Filipinas

There's no telling what will be staged here next, but it's sure to be good as the list of past performers attests: Jackson Browne, El Cigala, Kiko Veneno, Niña Pastori and Brazilian songstress Cibelle among others. The programme changes nightly, with singer-songwriters, jazz, flamenco, folk, fusion, indie, world music and even comedians. Most performances start at 10.30pm.

HONKY TONK Map pp116–17

☎ 91 445 61 91; www.clubhonky.com, in Spanish; Calle de Covarrubias 24; admission free; ⏰ 9pm–5am; Ⓜ Alonso Martínez

Despite the name, this is a great place to see local rock 'n' roll, though many acts have a little country or some blues thrown into the mix, too. It's a fun vibe in a small-ish club that's been around since the heady 1980s. Arrive early as it fills up fast.

KABOKLA Map pp110–11

☎ 91 532 59 66; www.kabokla.es, in Spanish; Calle de San Vicente Ferrer 55; admission free; ⏰ 9pm–3am Tue-Thu, to 5am Fri & Sat, 2.30pm–midnight Sun; Ⓜ Noviciado

Run by Brazilians and dedicated to all things Brazilian, Kabokla is terrific. Live Brazilian groups play most nights from around 10pm (from percussion to samba and cover bands playing Chico Buarque). When there's no live music, the DJ gets the crowd dancing. It also serves Madrid's smoothest caipirinhas and runs samba and capoeira classes outside opening hours (see p269).

LA BOCA DEL LOBO Map pp84–5

☎ 91 429 70 13; www.labocadellobo.com, in Spanish; Calle de Echegaray 11; admission free-€10; ⏰ 9.30pm–3am Tue-Thu & Sun, to 3.30am Fri & Sat; Ⓜ Sol or Sevilla

Known for offering mostly rock and alternative concerts, La Boca del Lobo (The Wolf's Mouth) is as dark as its name suggests and has broadened its horizons, adding country and jazz to the line-up, with weekly roots and groove jam sessions on Wednesday. Concerts start at 10.30pm most nights and DJs take over once the live acts leave the stage.

LA ESCALERA DE JACOB Map pp76–7

☎ 64 942 32 54; www.laescaleradejacob.es, in Spanish; Calle de Lavapiés 11; admission €5-10; ⏰ 8pm–3am Wed-Sat; Ⓜ Antón Martín or Tirso de Molina

'Jacob's Ladder' is a perfect fit for Lavapiés, with world music (especially African) on Saturday and sometimes other nights, as well as indie, jazz, soul, funk, folk, fusion, and even theatre and short films. Behind this intimate venue is a philosophy of crossing boundaries and refusing to be contained within specific genres and this alternative slant on life makes for some terrific live performances and a crowd of like-minded patrons.

LA FONTANA DE ORO Map pp84–5

☎ 91 531 04 20; www.lafontanadeoro.net, in Spanish; Calle de la Victoria 1; admission free; ⏰ 1pm–6am; Ⓜ Sol

This Irish bar lays claim to being the oldest bar in Madrid, dating back to 1789. Mentioned in La Fontana de Oro, the novel by Benito Pérez Galdós (see p36), the upstairs bar is dedicated in part to the author and it's here that nightly Celtic or rock groups take to the stage at 10pm. Wander downstairs to see the original decoration with stained-glass windows.

LIBERTAD 8 Map pp110–11

☎ 91 532 11 50; Calle de la Libertad 8; admission free-€6; ⏰ 5pm–2.30am Mon-Fri, 6pm–3am Sat, 4pm–1am Sun; Ⓜ Chueca

At 9pm every night a storyteller does their stuff, often role-playing and drawing the audience into the performance. Half an hour later, a local or international singer-songwriter takes to the stage. We like the mix, and it's intimate venues like these that add depth to the Madrid night.

MARULA CAFÉ Map pp76–7

☎ 91 366 15 96; Calle de Caños Viejos 3; admission free-€10; ⏰ 10.30pm–5.30am Sun-Thu, to 6am Fri & Sat; Ⓜ La Latina

An Afro haircut would be the perfect look here, where the music (concerts at 11.30pm, DJs until sunrise) is all about funk, soul, jazz, music from the American South, Afrobeat and even a little hip-hop. It's a club with attitude and always has a great rhythm.

MOBY DICK Map p123

☎ 91 555 76 71; www.mobydickclub.com, in Spanish; Avenida del Brasil 5; admission free-€18; ⏰ 9.30pm–5am Mon-Sat; Ⓜ Santiago Bernabéu

In a corner of Madrid that works hard by day and parties even harder on weekends,

Moby Dick is a stalwart of the live music scene. It's mostly well-known rock bands who can't quite fill the 25,000-seater venues, and there are plenty of dance bars alongside if the music's not to your liking. The house band plays at 11.30pm on Monday, with the programme chosen by the punters.

SALA CARACOL Map pp126–7

☎ 91 527 35 94; www.salacaracol.com, in Spanish; Calle de Bernardino Obregón 18; admission €6-25; ☽ 8pm-2am Thu-Sun; Ⓜ Embajadores

The 'Snail Room' is a long-standing, small live venue with industrial décor and it plays host to everything from jazzy flamenco to heavy metal. Unlike other places, it only opens when it has concerts, so check the programme and never just turn up.

SALA EL SOL Map pp64–5

☎ 91 532 64 90; www.elsolmad.com, in Spanish; Calle de los Jardines 3; admission €9; ☽ midnight-5.30am Tue-Sat; Ⓜ Gran Vía

Sala El Sol opened in 1979, just in time for *la movida*, and quickly established itself as a leading stage for all the icons of the era, such as Nacha Pop and Alaska y los Pegamoides. *La movida* may have faded into history, but it lives on at El Sol, where the music rocks and rolls and always resurrects the '70s and '80s.

TABOÓ Map pp110–11

☎ 91 524 11 89; www.taboo-madrid.com, in Spanish; Calle de San Vicente Ferrer 23; admission €10; ☽ 10.30pm-6am Thu-Sat; Ⓜ Tribunal

With everything from pop to hard-core punk and a whole lot of house music in between, Taboó likes to keep its options open. Check out the website to see which way it's leaning, and spend as little time as

possible talking to the bouncers while you wait in the queue.

ZANZIBAR Map pp110–11

☎ 91 319 90 64; www.zanzibarmadrid.com, in Spanish; Calle de Regueros 9; admission €4; ☽ 8pm-3am Sun-Thu, to 3.30am Fri & Sat; Ⓜ Alonso Martínez or Chueca

What a fantastic little venue this is. Styled with African décor, it does indeed have world music (and sometimes a jam session) most Tuesdays, but its repertoire extends to jazz, singer-songwriter, soul-rap and even storytelling. Concerts start at 9.30pm or 11.30pm, and there's a lovely café-style intimacy about the place. Many of its concerts are replayed on www.zanzibarmadrid.tv.

MEGA-VENUES

Madrid is a major stop on the European tour circuit. Summer is undoubtedly the best time to see the big names, but headline acts arrive in town throughout the year and play at the following venues:

Auditorio Parque Juan Carlos I (☎ 91 721 00 79; www.parquejuancarlos.net/parquejuancarlosi/auditorio.htm; Avenida de Logroño; Ⓜ Campo de las Naciones)

Estadio de la Comunidad de Madrid (☎ 91 720 24 00; Avenida de Arcentales; Ⓜ Las Musas) Also known as 'La Peineta'.

Palacio de los Deportes (Map pp126–7; ☎ 91 258 60 16; www.palaciodedeportes.com; Calle de Jorge Juan 99; Ⓜ Goya or O'Donnell)

Plaza de Toros Monumental de Las Ventas (Map pp102–3; ☎ 91 356 22 00; www.las-ventas.com, in Spanish; Calle de Alcalá 237; Ⓜ Ventas)

La Riviera (Map pp126–7; ☎ 91 365 24 15; Paseo Bajo de la Virgen del Puerto; ☽ midnight-6am Tue-Sun; Ⓜ Puerta de Ángel)

THE ARTS

top picks

- **Teatro Real** (p213)
  Madrid's opera house and premier classical music venue.
- **Cine Doré** (p214)
  Wonderful old cinema showing Spanish-language films.
- **Yelmo Cineplex Ideal** (p214)
  One of the best cinemas for films in their original version
  with Spanish subtitles.
- **Galería Moriarty** (p214)
  Near-mythical private Madrid gallery.
- **Teatro de la Zarzuela** (p215)
  Home to Madrid's musical *zarzuela* extravaganzas.

You've killed the night by staying out till dawn and you've raced around to the major monuments and art galleries for which Madrid is famous. Time for a change of pace. Madrid's contribution to high artistic culture extends beyond the Museo del Prado and the city is an excellent place to take in a classical music, opera or dance performance, visit the engaging little private galleries scattered across the city or watch a blockbuster musical in one of the city's many theatres. Such performances are attended more often by locals than tourists, which may be an attraction in itself, but these genres take you deeper into the world of the Spanish-language arts that receive little coverage beyond the Spanish-speaking world. Indeed this is the best place in the world to see Spanish drama (both classical and modern) and *zarzuela* (a Madrid cross between opera and dance). Then again, you could always just join the throngs of Madrid's cinema-goers, either in English or in Spanish.

Although Spaniards consider those quintessentially Spanish pursuits of flamenco and bullfighting to be artistic endeavours, an overall look at flamenco appears on p45, flamenco venues are covered on p204 and bullfighting can be found on p221.

WHAT'S ON

All of the following publications and websites provide comprehensive, updated listings of showings at Madrid's theatres, cinemas and concert halls:

EsMadrid Magazine (www.esmadrid.com) Monthly tourist office listings for concerts and other performances; available at tourist offices, some hotels and online.

Guía del Ocio (www.guiadelocio.com, in Spanish) A Spanish-only weekly magazine available for €1 at news kiosks.

In Madrid (www.in-madrid.com) The monthly English-language expat publication is given out free at some hotels, original-version cinemas, Irish pubs and English bookshops, and has lots of information about what to see and do in town.

La Netro (http://madrid.lanetro.com) Comprehensive online guide to everything that's happening in Madrid.

Metropolis (www.elmundo.es/metropolis) *El Mundo*'s Friday supplement magazine has information on the week's offerings.

On Madrid (www.elpais.com) *El País* also has a Friday supplement with listings for the week.

Salir Urban (www.salirsalir.com) The magazine (€2.50) is mostly for bars, restaurants and live music, but its online version has a section on theatres.

What's on When (www.whatsonwhen.com) The Madrid page covers the highlights of sports and cultural activities, with some information on getting tickets.

CLASSICAL MUSIC & OPERA

Yes, Madrid loves to party, but scratch beneath the surface and you'll find a thriving city of high culture, with venues dedicated to year-round opera and classical music. Orchestras from all over Europe perform regularly here, but Madrid's own Orquesta Sinfónica (www.osm.es, in Spanish) is a splendid orchestra that normally performs (or accompanies) in the Teatro Real or Audi-

---

BOOKING CONCERT & THEATRE TICKETS

Outlets selling tickets online for concerts, theatre and other live performances include the following:

Caixa Catalunya's Tel-Entrada (☎ 902 101 212; www.telentrada.com)

El Corte Inglés (☎ 902 400 222; www.elcorteingles.es, in Spanish) Click on 'Entradas' on its website.

Entradas.com (☎ 902 221 622; www.entradas.com, in Spanish)

Fnac (☎ 91 595 62 00; www.fnac.es) Click on 'Venta de Entradas', though it's mostly modern, big-name music groups.

Localidades Galicia (Map pp64–5; ☎ 91 531 27 32, 91 531 91 31; www.eol.es/lgalicia/, in Spanish; Plaza del Carmen 1; 🕒 9.30am-1pm & 4.30-7pm Tue-Sat; Ⓜ Sol)

Servicaixa (www.servicaixa.com) You can also get tickets in Servicaixa ATMs.

Tick Tack Ticket (☎ 902 150 025; www.ticktackticket.com)

torio Nacional de Música. The Banda Sinfónica Municipal de Madrid (www.munimadrid.es/bandasinfonica, in Spanish) plays at the Teatro Monumental.

AUDITORIO NACIONAL DE MÚSICA
Map p123

☎ 91 337 01 40; www.auditorionacional.mcu.es; Calle del Príncipe de Vergara 146; Ⓜ Cruz del Rayo
When it's not playing the Teatro Real, Madrid's Orquesta Sinfonía plays at this modern venue, which also attracts conductors from all over the world. It's usually fairly easy to get your hands on tickets at the box office.

FUNDACIÓN JUAN MARCH Map pp102–3
☎ 91 435 42 40; www.march.es; Calle de Castelló 77; Ⓜ Núñez de Balboa
A foundation dedicated to promoting music and culture (as well as exhibitions; see p106), the Juan March Foundation stages free concerts throughout the year. Performances range from solo recitals to themed concerts dedicated to a single style or composer.

TEATRO MONUMENTAL Map pp84–5
☎ 91 429 12 81, 91 429 81 19; Calle de Atocha 65; Ⓜ Antón Martín
The main concert season runs from October to March, when concerts include those of Madrid's municipal orchestra, the Orquesta Sinfónica de RTVE, and occasional operas or zarzuelas show off this modern theatre's fabulous acoustics. Tickets are a bargain €3 to €10.

TEATRO REAL Map pp64–5
☎ 902 244 848, 91 516 06 60; www.teatro-real .com; Plaza de Oriente; Ⓜ Ópera
After spending €100 million-plus on a long rebuilding project, the Teatro Real is as technologically advanced as any venue in Europe, and is the city's grandest stage for elaborate operas, ballets and classical music. You'll pay as little as €15 for a spot so far away you will need a telescope, although the sound quality is consistent throughout. For the best seats, don't expect change from €100.

DANCE

Spain's lively Compañía Nacional de Danza (☎ 91 354 50 53; http://cndanza.mcu.es/), under director Nacho Duato, performs worldwide and has won ac-

colades for its marvellous technicality and original choreography. The company, made up mostly of international dancers, performs contemporary pieces and is considered a main player on the international contemporary dance scene. When in town, which is not often, it performs at various venues, including the Teatro de la Zarzuela (p215).

Madrid is also home to the Ballet Nacional de España (☎ 91 517 99 99; http://balletnacional.mcu.es/), a classical company known for its unique mix of ballet and traditional Spanish styles, such as flamenco and zarzuela. When in Madrid, it's usually on stage at the Teatro Real (left) or the Teatro de la Zarzuela (p215).

FILM

Madrileños are among Europe's most devoted movie-goers and on Sunday evenings just about every sala (venue) in town is packed and queues stretch down the street. Most people buy tickets at the door, but turning up a couple of hours early or ringing the cinema to make a booking can be a good idea. Regular tickets cost about €6, rising to €7 on weekends, though there's a discount on Wednesdays, the día de espectador (spectator's day). There are further discounts one day a week (also usually Wednesday) for seniors.

ORIGINAL-VERSION CINEMAS

Plenty of cinemas offer versión original (VO; original version) films, which are shown in the original language with Spanish subtitles; otherwise foreign-language films are dubbed in mainstream cinemas. The epicentre of original-version cinemas is around Plaza de Emilio Jiménez Millas (known locally as Plaza de los Cubos), just north of Plaza de España. The major Spanish newspapers have full film listings. The following are the best original-version cinemas:

Princesa (Map pp116–17; ☎ 91 541 41 00; Calle de Princesa 3; Ⓜ Plaza de España) One of the larger original-version cinemas.

Renoir Plaza de España (Map pp116–17; ☎ 91 541 41 00; Calle de Martín de los Heros 12; Ⓜ Plaza de España) Plenty of latest-release films but some interesting documentaries and Asian flicks as well.

Verdi (Map pp116–17; ☎ 91 447 39 30; www.cines-verdi .com, in Spanish; Calle de Bravo Murillo 28; Ⓜ Canal or Quevedo) Neighbourhood cinema that cherry-picks the best, big-budget art-house movies.

Yelmo Cineplex Ideal (Map pp76–7; ☎ 902 220 922; Calle del Doctor Cortezo 6; M Sol or Tirso de Molina) Close to Plaza Mayor, with a wide selection of films.

SPANISH-LANGUAGE CINEMAS

The highest concentration of Spanish-language cinemas is on Gran Vía and Calle Fuencarral. Watch in particular for the massive painted billboards outside, although this traditional form of advertising is a dying art. Those looking for cult movies in Spanish also have a couple of options.

Cine Doré (Map pp76–7; ☎ 91 369 11 25; Calle de Santa Isabel 3; Tue-Sun; M Antón Martín) A wonderful old cinema that's home to the Filmoteca Nacional (national film library) and an excellent Spanish-language cinema bookshop. Best of all, it shows classics past and present for just €2 (a 10-session ticket costs €15). Four movies are shown nightly, the first at 5.30pm and the last around 10pm.

Cine Palafox (Map pp116–17; ☎ 91 446 18 87; Calle de Luchana 15; M Bilbao)

Cinesa Capitol (Map pp64–5; ☎ 902 333 231; Gran Vía 41; M Callao)

Cinesa Príncipe Pío (Map pp126–7; ☎ 902 333 231; Estación de Príncipe Pío, Paseo de la Florida; M Príncipe Pío)

Cinesa Proyecciones (Map pp116–17; ☎ 902 333 231; Calle de Fuencarral 136; M Bilbao or Quevedo) Wonderful Art Deco exterior, wonderful modern cinema within.

La Enana Marrón (Map pp110–11; ☎ 91 308 14 97; www.laenanamarron.org; Travesía de San Mateo 8; admission €4; M Alonso Martínez) Artsy, alternative and independent (mostly Spanish) films that don't get a run elsewhere, from documentaries to animated films, international flicks and oldies. A great little cinema.

GALLERIES

For those with an interest in contemporary art that extends beyond what you'll find at the Centro de Arte Reina Sofía (p82) or the Museo Municipal de Arte Contemporáneo (p108), central Madrid is studded with small galleries showcasing up-and-coming and longer established painters, sculptors and photographers. For a near-complete list check out Arte Madrid (www.artemadrid.com); its brochure of the same name, available from most galleries, contains a map and programme of upcoming exhibitions. Many of these galleries are regulars at Madrid's Arco fair (p17).

ANNTA GALLERY Map pp110–11
☎ 91 521 23 53; www.anntagallery.com, in Spanish; Calle del Almirante 1; 10.30am-2pm Mon, 10.30am-2pm & 5.30-8.30pm Tue-Sat; M Chueca
Spread over two levels, this gallery has painting, sculpture and photography exhibitions, although recent offerings have tended towards the latter.

CRISTÓBAL BENITEZ ARTE AFRICANO Map pp110–11
☎ 91 521 53 54; www.angelmartin.es, in Spanish; Calle de Piamonte 21; 11am-2.30pm & 5-8.30pm Mon-Sat; M Chueca
For something a little different and anything but contemporary, this gallery of antique African art is quite extraordinary and a must for anyone with a love of Africa.

GALERÍA ANTONIO MACHÓN Map pp110–11
☎ 91 532 40 93; www.antoniomachon.com, in Spanish; Calle del Conde de Xiquena 8; 11am-2pm & 5-9pm Tue-Fri, 11am-2pm Sat; M Chueca or Colón
A delightful gallery dedicated primarily to painters with the occasional sculpture, the Galería Antonio Machón has hosted names as varied as Chema Chobo, Laura Lio and Gerardo Delgado.

GALERÍA MORIARTY Map pp110–11
☎ 91 531 43 65; www.galeriamoriarty.com; Calle de la Libertad 22; 11am-2pm & 5-8.30pm Tue-Sat; M Chueca
During *la movida madrileña* in the 1980s, Galería Moriarty (then in Calle del Almirante) was one of Madrid's most important meeting places of culture and counter-culture, drawing the iconic Agatha Ruiz de la Prada, film-maker Pedro Almodóvar and the photographer García Alix among others to attend its exhibitions and parties. It may have moved, but it remains one of the most important small galleries in Madrid.

GALERÍA MULTIPLE Map pp110–11
☎ 91 319 98 69; www.galeriamultiple.com, in Spanish; Calle de Santa Teresa 10; 10.30am-2pm & 4.30-8.30pm Tue-Fri, 10.30am-2pm Sat; M Alonso Martínez
Showcasing painters and photographers of the highest standing (Pablo Palazuelo, Eduardo Arroyo and Eduardo Chillida have

LA ZARZUELA

What began in the late 17th century as a way to amuse King Felipe IV and his court has become Spain's own unique theatre style. With a light-hearted combination of music and dance, and a focus on everyday people's problems, *zarzuelas* quickly became popular in Madrid, which remains the genre's undoubted capital. Although you're likely to have trouble following the storyline (*zarzuelas* are notoriously full of local references and jokes), seeing a *zarzuela* gives an entertaining look into local culture. The best place to catch a show is the Teatro de la Zarzuela (below), while for a history of *zarzuela* in English, translations of *zarzuela* songs and storylines, CD and DVD reviews, and a critical look at current *zarzuela* shows, check out the terrific website zarzuela.net (www.zarzuela.net).

recently held exhibitions here and their work is available for viewing upon request), Galería Multiple is one of our favourite contemporary Madrid galleries.

THEATRE

Madrid's theatre scene is a year-round affair, but it really gets going in autumn. Most shows are in Spanish, but those who don't speak the language may still enjoy musicals or *zarzuela*, Spain's own singing-and-dancing version of musical theatre. Tickets start at around €10 and run up to €50. Mostly you can buy tickets at the box office on the day of the performance, but for new, popular or weekend shows you should book ahead. Note that box offices are usually closed on Mondays and sometimes Tuesdays, when there are no shows. On other days they're generally open from about 10am until 1pm and again from 5pm until the start of the evening's show.

CENTRO CULTURAL DE LA VILLA Map pp102–3
☎ 91 480 03 00; www.esmadrid.com/ccvilla/; Plaza de Colón; Ⓜ Colón or Serrano
Located under the waterfall at Plaza de Colón, the Centro Cultural has exhibition and performance spaces where it stages everything from classical concerts to comic theatre, opera and flamenco.

TEATRO ALBÉNIZ Map pp64–5
☎ 91 531 83 11, 902 488 488; Calle de la Paz 11; Ⓜ Sol
One of the premier venues for popular Spanish dramas with well-known casts, the Albéniz also hosts the Caja Madrid flamenco festival (see p16) in late winter and concerts during the Festival de Otoño.

TEATRO ALFIL Map pp110–11
☎ 91 521 45 41; www.teatroalfil.com, in Spanish; Calle del Pez 10; Ⓜ Noviciado

Staging a broad range of alternative and experimental Spanish-language theatre, Teatro Alfil is a good place to catch up-and-coming Spanish actors and comedians, and mingle with an eclectic crowd.

TEATRO COLISEUM Map pp110–11
☎ 91 547 66 12; Gran Vía 78; Ⓜ Plaza de España
One of the larger theatres in the city, here you can expect to see major musicals, often Broadway or West End hits, but usually with an all-Spanish cast and in Spanish, such as *La Bella y La Bestia* (Beauty and the Beast).

TEATRO DE LA ZARZUELA Map pp84–5
☎ 91 524 54 00; http://teatrodelazarzuela.mcu .es/; Calle de Jovellanos 4; Ⓜ Banco de España
This theatre, built in 1856, is the premier place to see *zarzuela* (see the boxed text, above). It also hosts a smattering of classical music and opera, as well as the cutting edge Compañía Nacional de Danza.

TEATRO ESPAÑOL Map pp84–5
☎ 91 360 14 84; www.esmadrid.com/teatro espanol; Calle del Príncipe 25; Ⓜ Sevilla, Sol or Antón Martín
This theatre has been here since the 16th century and is still one of the best places to catch mainstream Spanish drama from the works of Lope de Vega to more recent playwrights.

TEATRO HAAGEN DAZS Map pp76–7
☎ 91 420 37 97; www.teatrohaagen-dazs.es, in Spanish; Calle de Atocha 18; Ⓜ Tirso de Molina
Big budget musicals take the stage in this grand old theatre (formerly Teatro Calderón) and stay for months. Recent shows include *Queen* and *Fame*.

TEATRO PAVÓN Map pp76–7
☎ 91 528 28 19; teatroclasico.mcu.es/; Calle de los Embajadores 9; Ⓜ La Latina or Tirso de Molina

The home of the National Classical Theatre Company, this theatre has a regular calendar of classical shows by Spanish and European playwrights.

TEATRO VALLE-INCLÁN Map pp76–7

☎ 91 505 88 00; http://cdn.mcu.es; tickets €15-18; Plaza de Lavapiés; Ⓜ Lavapiés

The stunning refurbishment of this theatre has brought new life (and quality plays) to this once run-down corner of Lavapiés. Located on the southern end of the Plaza de Lavapiés, it is now the headquarters for the Centro Dramático Nacional (National Drama Centre) and puts on landmark plays by (mostly) Spanish playwrights.

SPORTS & ACTIVITIES

top picks

- **Hammam Medina Mayrit** (p218)
  Wonderful day spa with Arab-style ambience.
- **City Yoga** (p218)
  The best place in town for yoga.
- **Estadio Santiago Bernabéu** (p221)
  Home of Real Madrid where you can take a tour or watch a game.
- **Plaza de Toros Monumental de Las Ventas** (p222)
  The most prestigious bullring in Spain.

SPORTS & ACTIVITIES

It doesn't come much more Spanish than Real Madrid or bullfighting. Watching a live game involving Real Madrid is an unforgettable experience. Attending a *corrida* (bullfight) at the Plaza de Toros Monumental de Las Ventas is a very local thing to do – love it or loathe it, you won't leave indifferent. Basketball is another spectator sport option.

For those who prefer getting all sweaty and making their own sport, there are gyms, health centres, swimming pools and tennis courts scattered throughout the city. Excellent spas and massage centres represent the height of pampering for those keen not to get too active.

HEALTH & FITNESS
HEALTH & DAY SPAS

CHI SPA Map pp102–3
☎ 91 578 13 40; www.thechispa.com; Calle del Conde de Aranda 6; �] 10am-9pm Mon-Fri, to 6pm Sat; Ⓜ Retiro

Wrap up in a robe and slippers and prepare to be pampered in one of Spain's best day spas. There are separate areas for men and women, and services include massage (from €65 per hour), facials (€65 to €125), manicures (€25) and pedicures (€35). Now, what was it you were stressed about?

HAMMAM MEDINA MAYRIT Map pp64–5
☎ 902 333 334; www.medinamayrit.com; Calle de Atocha 14; �] 10am-midnight; Ⓜ Sol

Medina Mayrit is both an architectural jewel and a sensory indulgence that takes your senses back in time. Housed in the excavated cellars of old Madrid, this imitation traditional Arab bath offers massages and aromatherapy beneath graceful arches and accompanied by the sound of tinkling water. Prices are at their cheapest from 10am to 4pm Monday to Friday (from €24); otherwise, you'll pay from €36. Reservations are required. There's also a Moroccan-style tearoom and restaurant upstairs.

SPA RELAJARSE Map pp110–11
☎ 91 308 61 48; www.sparelajarse.com, in Spanish; Calle de Barquillo 43; �] 11am-11pm Mon-Sat, 1-9pm Sun; Ⓜ Chueca

Step inside this intimate little spa and you can't help but felt relaxed. With a range of options (the Especial Spa includes a hydro-massage pool with strawberries and Möet Chandon for €140, while the Especial Spa with a 'romantic dinner' costs €220), this may be one for a special occasion. Discre-

tion and privacy are its trademarks, with most sessions popular with couples.

ZENSEI Map pp116–17
☎ 91 549 60 49; www.zensei.net, in Spanish; Calle de Blasco de Garay 64; �] 10am-10pm Mon-Sat; Ⓜ Moncloa or Quevedo

Hidden away on a suburban Argüelles street, this Japanese relaxation centre is an oasis of civility and promises the ultimate in Zen massage, acupuncture, reiki, shiatsu and yoga, not to mention origami or Japanese tea-ceremony classes. The two-hour relaxation or beauty programmes are also highly recommended. Prices start at €30 for a massage, and you'll come out floating on air.

YOGA & PILATES

In addition to the places listed here, many private gyms, such as Gimnasio Chamberí (opposite), also offer yoga and Pilates.

CITY PILATES Map pp116–17
☎ 91 445 13 03; www.city-pilates.com, in Spanish; Calle de Ruiz 27; classes from €15; �] 10am-10pm Mon-Fri, to 2pm Sat; Ⓜ San Bernardo or Bilbao

Opened in January 2008, this state-of-the-art Pilates centre has classes across all styles of the genre and, like its sister centre City Yoga (see below), it offers programmes for soon-to-be and recovering mums.

CITY YOGA Map p123
☎ 91 553 47 51; www.city-yoga.com, in Spanish; Calle de los Artistas 43; classes from €15; �] 10am-10pm Mon-Fri; Ⓜ Cuatro Caminos or Nuevos Ministerios

Don't be put off by the somewhat gritty barrio because this yoga and Pilates centre is one of the most popular in the city, with classes suiting all styles and ability levels. It also offers massages, Pilates and pre- and post-natal activities. There's a one-off joining fee of €30.

GYMS

Public gyms and indoor pools (normally for lap swimming only) are scattered throughout Madrid. They generally charge a modest €3.50 to €7 for one-day admission and can get pretty crowded at weekends and after work hours. More expensive (€10 to €15 per one-day admission), privately owned health centres usually have less crowded workout rooms.

GIMNASIO CHAMBERÍ Map pp116–17
☎ 91 448 0460; Calle de Raimundo Lulio 18; admission around €10; ☽ 7.45am-11pm Mon-Fri, 9am-3pm Sat & Sun; Ⓜ Iglesia
This privately run suburban gym doesn't have a pool, but it does offer yoga, Pilates, aerobics of most descriptions and a well-equipped workout room. Monthly memberships start from around €40.

POLIDEPORTIVO LA CHOPERA Map pp92–3
☎ 91 420 11 54; Parque del Buen Retiro; admission €5; ☽ 9am-8pm Mon-Fri; Ⓜ Atocha
With a fine workout centre, several football fields and a few tennis courts, this *polideportivo* (sports centre and gym) in the southwestern corner of El Retiro is one of Madrid's most attractive and central.

POLIDEPORTIVO LA LATINA Map pp76–7
☎ 91 365 80 31; Plaza de la Cebada; pool adult/child €4/2.35; ☽ 8.15am-7pm Mon-Thu, to 6pm Fri, 10am-8.30pm Sat & Sun; Ⓜ La Latina
This centrally located municipal gym (and one of few that has a pool) is busy day and night. While not all that new or clean, it offers decent weight and workout rooms. This whole complex is slated for renovation.

ACTIVITIES
SWIMMING
If you'd rather splash around than labour over laps, the following public pools are worth trying, although they can be completely overwhelmed in summer.

CANAL DE ISABEL II Map p123
☎ 91 533 17 91; Avenida de Filipinas 54; admission €4; ☽ 11am-8pm Jun-early Sep; Ⓜ Ríos Rosas or Canal

Open only in summer, this large outdoor pool is easily accessible by metro from the city centre. It also has a football field, a basketball court and a weights room, and across the road there's a running track and a golf driving range.

CASA DEL CAMPO
☎ 91 463 00 50; Avenida Ángel; pool €4.50; ☽ 11.30am-9pm summer, 9am-noon, 3-7pm & 9-10pm winter; Ⓜ Lago
The outdoor pools at this sprawling park are overrun in summer. The rest of the year (October to April) swimming is indoors.

PISCINA MUNICIPAL PEÑUELAS
off Map pp126–7
☎ 91 474 28 08; Calle de Arganda; admission €4; ☽ 11am-9pm Jun-Aug; Ⓜ Acacias, Pirámides or Embajadores
With two gloriously cool pools and another smaller one for infants, this outdoor complex south of the city centre is a popular place for a summer dip, but like any place where there's water in Madrid, it gets excessively crowded on summer weekends.

TENNIS
If you fancy a game of tennis surrounded by the greenery of the Parque del Buen Retiro, consider the Polideportivo La Chopera (left).

POLIDEPORTIVO VIRGEN DEL PUERTO Map pp126–7
☎ 91 366 28 40; Paseo de la Virgen del Puerto; court hire from €6.50; ☽ 8.30am-8.30pm; Ⓜ Príncipe Pío
Run by the municipal government, this modern sports centre near the Puente de Segovia has eight regulation-size tennis courts, eight paddle-ball courts and 12 table-tennis tables.

SKIING
MADRID XANADÚ Map pp126–7
☎ 902 361309; www.madridsnowzone.com; Calle Puerto de Navacerrada, Arroyomolinos; 1hr adult/child €19/16; ☽ 10am-10pm Sun-Thu, to midnight Fri & Sat
Far out to the east of Madrid, in the massive Xanadú shopping centre, you'll find the largest covered ski centre in Europe. Open 365 days a year, it's kept at a decidedly cool -2°C, so rug up before hitting

the surprisingly good slopes. To get here, take bus 529, 531 or 536 from the Méndez Álvaro transportation hub.

SPECTATOR SPORT

Watching Real Madrid play at its glorious Estadio de Santiago Bernabéu or taking in a bullfight at the Plaza de Toros Monumental de Las Ventas are high on the list of must-sees for a number of visitors to Madrid. There's also high-quality basketball if that's your thing.

SEASONS

The Spanish football season runs from September (or the last weekend in August) until May, with a two-week break just before Christmas until early in the New Year. Spain's top toreros (bullfighters) do their thing at Las Ventas bullring from early to mid-May to coincide with the Fiestas de San Isidro Labrador (see p16), continuing daily for a month, with further weekend fights until October. The basketball season shadows the football season, from September through to the second half of May.

Sports-only dailies such as *Marca* (www .marca.com, in Spanish) and *AS* (www.as.com, in Spanish) are wildly popular and will give you the inside scoop on upcoming matches and events, provided you read basic Spanish. They're available from any newspaper kiosk.

PRICES & RESERVATIONS
Football

Tickets for football matches in Madrid start at around €15 and run up to the rafters for major matches; you pay in inverse proportion to your distance from the pitch. For bigger games, such as Real Madrid against Barcelona or Atlético de Madrid, or a Champions League game, *entradas* (tickets) are nigh-on impossible to find unless you're willing to take the risk with scalpers. For less important matches, you shouldn't have too many problems.

Unless you book your Real Madrid ticket through a ticket agency, turn up at the Estadio Santiago Bernabéu ticket office (Map p123) at Gate 42 on Calle de Conche de Espina early in the week before a scheduled game (eg a Tuesday morning for a Sunday game). The all-important telephone number for booking tickets (which you later pick up at Gate 42) is ☎ 902 324 324, which only works if you're calling from within Spain. To see an Atlético de Madrid game, try

calling ☎ 91 366 47 07, but you're most likely to manage a ticket if you turn up at the ground a few days before the match.

If you're booking from abroad, try Localidades Galicia (Map pp64–5; ☎ 91 531 27 32, 91 531 91 31; www .eol.es/lgalicia/; Plaza del Carmen 1; ⏰ 9.30am-1pm & 4.30-7pm Tue-Sat; Ⓜ Sol). Numerous websites also sell tickets to Real Madrid games, including www .madrid-tickets.net, www.madrid-tickets.com and www.ticket-finders.com.

Bullfighting

Tickets for *corridas* (bullfights) are divided into *sol* (sun) and *sombra* (shade) seating, the former cheaper than the latter. Ticket sales begin a few days before the fight, at Plaza de Toros Monumental de Las Ventas ticket office (Map pp102–3; ☎ 91 356 22 00; www .las-ventas.com, in Spanish; Calle de Alcalá 237; ⏰ 10am-2pm & 5-8pm; Ⓜ Ventas). A few agencies sell before then, adding an extra 20% for their trouble; one of the best is Localidades Galicia (Map pp64–5; ☎ 91 531 27 32, 91 531 91 31; www.eol.es/lgalicia/; Plaza del Carmen 1; ⏰ 9.30am-1pm & 4.30-7pm Tue-Sat; Ⓜ Sol). You can also get tickets at La Central Bullfight Ticket Office (Map pp84–5; Calle de la Victoria). Mostly, you'll have no problem getting a ticket at the gate, but during the Fiestas de San Isidro, or when a popular torero comes to town, book ahead.

The cheapest tickets (around €5) are for standing-room *sol*, though on a hot summer day you might want to pay the extra €4 for *sombra* tickets. The premium seats – on the front row in the shade – are the preserve of celebrities and cost more than €100.

For information on who'll be in the ring, check out the colourful posters tacked around town or the daily newspapers.

Basketball

Tickets range from about €15 to €50 for regular season games. You can buy MMT Estudiantes tickets through El Corte Inglés (☎ 902 400 222; www.elcorteingles.es, in Spanish) or at the Polideportivo Magariños (Map p123; ☎ 91 562 40 22; Calle de Serrano 127; ⏰ 10am-2pm & 4-8pm). Real Madrid tickets go on sale two hours before the game, and you can buy them directly at the stadium box office.

FOOTBALL

Depending on your perspective, Real Madrid (www.realmadrid.com) is either the best football club in the world (in 1998, FIFA declared it the greatest club of all time) or the symbol of a game gone mad with money.

RIGHT ROYAL FOOTBALLERS

Few football teams arouse such contradictory passions as Real Madrid – *los blancos* (whites), *merengues* (meringues), *los galacticos* or simply *El Madrid*, as the team is variously known – and a quick look at its history shows why.

In 1920, King Alfonso XIII bestowed the *real* (royal) title upon the club. Fans of arch rival FC Barcelona will tell you that in the years of Primo de Rivera's dictatorship (1920s), and later under Franco, their team was frequently the victim of dodgy decisions. It's certainly true that Real Madrid dominated Spanish and European football throughout the Franco period and the little dictator frequently basked in Real Madrid's successes as if they were his own. Most famously, Barcelona won the first leg of its 1943 Spanish Cup semi-final against Real Madrid 3-0. Legend has it that before the return leg in Madrid, Franco's Director of State Security visited the Barcelona changing room and issued thinly veiled threats and berated the Catalans for their lack of patriotism. Madrid defeated a clearly frightened Barcelona 11-1 in the second leg.

When it comes to history, no-one can match Real Madrid's record at home or abroad: 31 Spanish *liga* (league) titles, the last in 2008; 17 Copas del Rey; nine European Cups (now known as the Champions League), including 1998, 2000 and 2002; two Uefa Cups; and the Spanish Supercopa a mere seven times.

Even against such a backdrop, however, the recent headlines surrounding the club have been extraordinary. After construction magnate Florentino Perez became club president in 2000, the club spent hundreds of millions of euros buying the best players in the world, in the process building a team known as *los galacticos*. There was just one problem: while these superstars of the world game shone as individuals, they never really gelled as a team. In the three seasons following its Spanish league title in 2003, Real Madrid won nothing (the longest drought in the club's history) as the team went through four coaches and reports began to emerge of a changing room divided into camps of overswelled egos. In March 2006, Florentino Perez resigned, blaming the prima donnas whom he himself had brought to the club. Against all the odds and after a stuttering season, Real Madrid won the 2007 *la liga* title, and followed it up with another in 2008, although success still eludes them on the European stage, and the club's embarrassed administration have pronounced an end to the *galactico* era.

Even amid all the tarnished glamour, El Estadio Santiago Bernabéu is one of the world's great football arenas; watching a game here is akin to a pilgrimage for sports fans and doing so alongside 80,000 passionate Madridistas (Real Madrid supporters) in attendance will send chills down your spine. If you're lucky enough to be in town when Real Madrid wins a major trophy, head to Plaza de la Cibeles and wait for the all-night party to begin.

It surprises many visitors that a significant proportion of the population can't stand Real Madrid and actually support the capital's other team, Atlético de Madrid (www.clubatleticodemadrid.com). Though existing in the shadow of its more illustrious city rivals, Atlético have won nine *liga* titles (a feat bettered only by Real Madrid and FC Barcelona), the latest in 1996, and nine Copas del Rey. Atlético, which has a cult following, attracts passionate support and fans of the *rojiblancos* (red-and-whites) declare theirs to be the *real* Madrid team, unlike the reviled and aristocratic 'Madridistas' up the road.

For details on how to see a Real Madrid or Atlético game, turn to opposite.

ESTADIO SANTIAGO BERNABÉU Map p123
☎ 91 398 43 00, 902 324 324; www.realmadrid .com; Calle de Concha Espina 1; ☒ 10.30am-6.30pm except day of or after game; Ⓜ Santiago Bernabéu

Holding 80,000 delirious fans, the Santiago Bernabéu (named after the long-time club president) is a mecca for Real Madrid football fans worldwide. Those who can't come to a game can at least stop by for a tour (p122), a peek at the trophies or to buy Real Madrid memorabilia in the club shop.

ESTADIO VICENTE CALDERÓN Map pp126–7
☎ 91 366 47 07; www.clubatleticodemadrid.com; Calle de la Virgen del Puerto; Ⓜ Pirámides

The home of Atlético de Madrid isn't as large as Real Madrid's (the Vicente Calderón seats fewer than 60,000), but what it lacks in size it makes up for in raw energy. A game at the Estadio Vicente Calderón has a passionate, more carnivalesque feel to it than most Real Madrid games.

BULLFIGHTING
An epic drama of blood and sand or a cruel blood 'sport' that has no place in modern Europe? This most enduring and controversial

of Spanish traditions is all this and more, at once picturesque, compelling theatre and an ancient ritual that sees 40,000 bulls killed in around 17,000 bullfights every year in Spain. Perhaps it was best summed up by Ernest Hemingway – a bullfighting aficionado – who described it as 'a wonderful nightmare'.

Whatever your viewpoint, an afternoon of *la corrida* is an essential part of Madrid life, particularly during the month-long season beginning with the Fiestas de San Isidro Labrador. This is Spain's premier bullfighting season and its most prestigious venue – when toreros put in a starring performance at Las Ventas, their career is made.

On an afternoon ticket there are generally six bulls and three star toreros dressed in the dazzling *traje de luces* (suit of lights). The torero leads a *cuadrilla* (team) of fighters who make up the rest of the colourful band in the ring. It's a complex business, but in essence the toreros aim to impress the crowd and jury with daring and graceful moves as close to an aggressive bull as possible. It's a one-sided event – the death of the bull is close to inevitable – but it's still a dangerous business. Despite the spectre of death that pervades *la corrida*, a day out at the bullring is a festive occasion for aficionados, dressed to the nines and wine flowing freely.

Still, there are signs that bullfighting's popularity may be waning, especially among younger Spaniards. A recent poll found that just 17% of Spaniards under 25 had any interest in bullfighting, compared with 41% of those aged over 64. Similar polls show that three-quarters of Spaniards have no interest in the sport.

While few modern fighters match the courage and skill of former greats, such as Juan Belmonte (1892–1962), Manuel 'Manolete' Rodríguez Sánchez (1917–47), Antonio Ordoñez (1932–98) and Luis Miguel Dominguín (1926–96), there are some names to look out for. Juan Antonio Ruiz (Espartaco) was unbeatable in the early 1990s, while current toreros include Jesulín de Ulbrique, Julián 'El Juli' López, José Miguel Arroyo (Joselito), Enrique Ponce and Manuel Díaz (El Cordobés).

For advice on how to see a bullfight in Madrid, see p220.

PLAZA DE TOROS MONUMENTAL DE LAS VENTAS Map pp102–3

☎ 91 356 22 00; www.las-ventas.com, in Spanish; Calle de Alcalá 237; Ⓜ Ventas
One of the largest rings in the bullfighting world, Las Ventas has a grand *mudéjar* (a Moorish architectural style) exterior and a

suitably coliseum-like arena surrounding the broad sandy ring. For more information, see p101.

BASKETBALL

Although they don't get the same publicity, Real Madrid's basketball players are as much champions as their footballing counterparts and their rivalry with Barcelona is equally fierce. The team has won 30 Spanish league titles, 22 Copas del Rey and eight European championships. Also popular is the less successful MMT Estudiantes side. Real Madrid plays at the recently rebuilt and state-of-the-art Palacio de los Deportes, while MMT Estudiantes plays at the Telefónica Madrid Arena in Casa del Campo.

For match information, see p220.

MMT ESTUDIANTES

☎ 902 400 002; www.clubestudiantes.com, in Spanish; Telefónica Madrid Arena, Calle de las Aves; Ⓜ Lago or Alto de Extremadura
MMT Estudiantes are the Atlético de Madrid of the city's basketball scene and Madrid's most popular team. Games in the excellent Telefónica Madrid Arena are usually played in front of a packed house.

REAL MADRID

☎ 91 258 60 16, 91 523 09 51; www.realmadrid .com; Palacio de los Deportes, Calle de Jorge Juan 99; Ⓜ Goya or O'Donnell
The Real Madrid basketball team, Madrid's most glamorous, is a great team to watch live. See a game at the state-of-the-art Palacio de los Deportes (Map pp126–7).

MARATHONS

In late April, the Maratón de Madrid (www .maratonmadrid.org) cuts a swathe through the city and attracts athletes from all over the world.

Less serious athletes may find the wonderfully festive San Silvestre Vallecana (www .sansilvestrevallecana.com) more to their liking. Staged on 31 December at 6pm, the 10km course leads from Plaza de Castilla all the way down Paseo de la Castellana to Vallecas, to the south. Although the professional section of the race attracts leading runners, the amateur section is one of the more unusual races in Europe. Many athletes wear fancy dress; musicians line the route and runners, who must pass through streets warming up for New Year's Eve, are pelted with eggs and tomatoes.

GAY & LESBIAN MADRID

top picks

- **Mamá Inés** (p225)
  Café that serves as the unofficial gay meeting point in Chueca.
- **Wagaboo** (p224)
  Fun restaurant with an unmistakeably gay ambience.
- **B Aires Café** (p225)
  Chueca bar-café where so many nights start.
- **Local Café Bar Lounge** (p225)
  Intimate lounge-bar where you can't help but dance.
- **La Fulanita de Tal** (p225)
  Outrageously lesbian club.
- **Sunrise** (p225)
  Extravagantly gay nightclub that parties until dawn.
- **Hostal La Zona** (p226)
  Great little *hostal* on the fringe of Chueca.
- **Chueca Pensión** (p226)
  Lovely *pensión* in the heart of Chueca.

What's your recommendation? www.lonelyplanet.com/madrid

GAY & LESBIAN MADRID

Madrid has always been one of Europe's most gay-friendly cities. The city's gay community is credited with reinvigorating the once down-at-heel inner-city barrio of Chueca, where Madrid didn't just come out of the closet, it ripped the doors off in the process. Today the barrio is one of Madrid's most vibrant and it's very much the heart and soul of gay Madrid. Restaurants, cafés and bars clearly oriented to a gay clientele abound, and new book, video and adult-toy shops aimed at gay people continue to spring up in and around Chueca, as well as gay-friendly hostels. But there's nothing ghetto-like about Chueca. Its extravagantly gay and lesbian personality is anything but exclusive and the crowd is almost always mixed gay-straight. As gay and lesbian residents like to say, Chueca isn't gay-friendly, it's hetero-friendly.

It's a great time to be gay in Madrid. Under laws passed by the Spanish Congress in June 2005, same-sex marriages now enjoy the same legal protection as those between heterosexual partners. At the time there was a conservative backlash, but opinion polls showed that the reforms were supported by more than two-thirds of Spaniards. The best time of all to be in town if you're gay or lesbian is around the last Saturday in June for Madrid's gay and lesbian pride march (p18).

The places listed throughout this chapter are overwhelmingly aimed at a gay and/or lesbian clientele. Loads of other places in town are gay-friendly; some of these are cross-referenced below.

SHOPPING

LIBRERÍA BERKANA Map pp110–11   Bookshop
☎ 91 522 55 99; www.libreriaberkana.com, in Spanish; Calle de Hortaleza 64; ☾ 10.30am-9pm Mon-Fri, 11.30am-9pm Sat, noon-2pm & 5-9pm Sun; Ⓜ Chueca
One of the most important gay and lesbian bookshops in Madrid, Librería Berkana stocks gay books, movies, magazines, music, clothing, and a host of free magazines for nightlife and other gay-focused activities in Madrid and around Spain; this is the place to pick up your copy of *Shanguide*, *Shangay Express* and *MENsual* (see p226).

A DIFFERENT LIFE Map pp110–11   Sex Shop
☎ 91 532 96 52; www.lifegay.com, in Spanish; Calle de Pelayo 30; ☾ 10.30am-9.30pm Mon-Thu, to 10pm Fri & Sat, 12.30-9.30pm Sun; Ⓜ Chueca
Yes, A Different Life has the usual sex-shop products – DVDs, magazines and 'erotic gifts' – but it also does a line in gay novels and DVDs focusing on gay themes or with predominantly gay characters. As such, it's somewhat less in-your-face than other shops.

AMANTIS.NET Map pp110–11   Sex Shop
☎ 91 702 05 10; www.amantis.net, in Spanish; Calle de Pelayo 46; ☾ 10am-10pm Mon-Sat, 4.30pm-9pm Sun; Ⓜ Chueca

A fairly standard gay sex shop, Amantis.Net is open to the street; by entering, there's no sense that you're doing anything illicit, as can be the case with other sex shops.

EATING

If they're in Chueca, restaurants simply wouldn't survive if they weren't gay-friendly, so turn to p174 for a more extensive list. Among these, some stand out, such as Restaurante Momo (p176), Baco y Beto (p176), Tepic (p175) and Restaurante Vega Viana (p176). See p158 for a guide to price symbols.

TXUECA Map pp110–11   Basque €€
☎ 91 522 16 91; Plaza de Vázquez de Mella 10; meals €20-25; ☾ 1pm-1am Sun-Thu, to 2am Fri & Sat; Ⓜ Gran Vía
Txueca has clean lines, tasty Basque cuisine and friendly waiters. The crepes start at around €8, but there are a host of cold *pintxos* (tapas; around €3) after the restaurant empties. Basque cooking and Chueca innovation combine for some pretty creative choices, and if you can't choose, there's always the plate of six *pintxos* (€13).

WAGABOO Map pp110–11   Fusion €
☎ 91 531 65 67; www.wagaboo.com; Calle de Gravina 18; meals €15-25; Ⓜ Chueca
Serving an almost exclusively gay clientele, Wagaboo offers cheap and cheerful pasta

and noodle dishes (the tagliatelle Stolichnaya is an acquired taste, though) and an unmistakeable *frisson* ripples across the room whenever the door opens. There's another Wagaboo (Calle de San Marcos 28) not far away.

DRINKING

Apart from the Chueca landmarks that follow, other good watering holes with a partly gay or lesbian vibe include Antik Café (p194), Antigua Casa Ángel Sierra (p196) and Diurno (p193).

B AIRES CAFÉ Map pp110–11   Café-Bar
☎ 91 532 98 79; Calle de Gravina 4; ☽ 3pm-1am Sun-Wed, to 2am Thu & Fri, to 2.30am Sat; Ⓜ Chueca
This oasis of sophistication in anything-goes Chueca is perfect for a quiet conversation, and most gays and lesbians passing through Chueca spend some time here, either resting from nights of partying, taking some down time in preparation for the night ahead or simply as an end in itself.

CAFÉ ACUARELA Map pp110–11   Café-Bar
☎ 91 522 21 43; Calle de Gravina 10; ☽ 2pm-3am; Ⓜ Chueca
Right on Plaza de Chueca and long a centrepiece of gay Madrid – a huge statue of a nude male angel guards the doorway – this is an agreeable, dimly lit salon decorated with, among other things, religious icons! It's ideal for quiet conversation and catching the weekend buzz as people plan their forays into the more clamorous clubs in the vicinity.

MAMÁ INÉS Map pp110–11   Café-Bar
☎ 91 523 23 33; Calle de Hortaleza 22; ☽ 10am-2am Sun-Thu, to 3.30am Fri & Sat; Ⓜ Gran Vía or Chueca
A gay meeting place with its low lights and low music, this café-bar is never sleazy and has a laid-back ambience by day and a romantic air by night. You can get breakfast, yummy pastries and all the gossip on where that night's hot spot will be.

LOCAL CAFÉ BAR LOUNGE
Map pp110–11   Café-Bar
☎ 91 532 76 10; Calle de la Libertad 28; ☽ 5pm-3am; Ⓜ Chueca
With its swirling colour scheme and funky soul, hip-hop, disco and deep house beats,

Local has drawn a loyal following. The crowd can be mixed gay-hetero, but don't hold that against them as no-one else in Chueca will.

NIGHTLIFE

The proportion of gay and lesbian revellers in many nightclubs is high, among them Cool (p201), Suite Café Club (p203), Susan Club (p204) and La Lupe (p202). The nightclubs listed are overwhelmingly gay.

LA FULANITA DE TAL Map pp110–11
☎ 91 360 47 02; www.fulanitadetal.com, in Spanish; Calle del Conde de Xiquena 2; ☽ 10pm-3am Sun-Wed, to 4am Thu-Sat; Ⓜ Chueca
Run by women, this outrageously uninhibited nightclub draws a predominantly lesbian crowd, but the club's refusal to stay within boundaries means gay men, hetero couples and just about anyone can turn up here. The music's mostly pop dance tunes, with a bit of funk and R&B.

OHM Map pp110–11
Sala Bash; ☎ 91 531 01 32; Plaza del Callao 4; ☽ midnight-6am Fri & Sat; Ⓜ Callao
The DJs who get you waving your hands in the air like you just don't care have made this club one of the most popular nightspots for Madrid's gay community, although, typically, everyone's welcome. The music never strays far from techno-house.

SUNRISE Map pp110–11
www.sunrisechueca.com, in Spanish; Calle de Barbieri 7; ☽ midnight-6am Thu-Sat; Ⓜ Chueca
Sunrise could just be Chueca's most popular gay nightclub and it's definitely the barrio at its most outrageous, with a mostly gay crowd on the prowl and often playing dress ups. There's occasional live cabaret. This place goes wild during the Orgullo Gay festivities (see p18).

SLEEPING

Most Madrid hotels won't bat an eyelid if you're a same-sex couple asking for a double bed. One place that goes out of its way to make gay couples welcome is Hotel Óscar (p237), which also applies to other Room Mate hotels; see the boxed text, p236. For a guide to price symbols, see p229.

HOSTAL LA ZONA Map pp110–11 Hostel €

☎ 91 521 99 04; www.hostallazona.com; 1st fl, Calle de Valverde 7; s/d/tr from €50/60/85; Ⓜ Gran Vía
Catering primarily to a gay clientele, the stylish Hostal La Zona has exposed brickwork, subtle colour shades and wooden pillars. We like a place where a sleep-in is encouraged – breakfast is served from 9am to noon, which is exactly the understanding Madrid's nightlife merits. There's free internet and wi-fi, Arnaldo and Vincent are friendly hosts, and every room has air-conditioning/heating.

CHUECA PENSIÓN Map pp110–11 Hostel €

☎ 91 523 14 73; www.chuecapension.com; 2nd fl, Calle de Gravina 4; s/d/tr €40/60/85; Ⓜ Gran Vía
There are few better Chueca bases than this lovely pensión. Features include hardwood floors, free wi-fi and large rooms, while the bright bedspreads add a splash of colour lacking in many hostales in this price range. Best of all, Beni Uria, the owner, is a welcoming host. There's no lift.

CASA CHUECA Map pp110–11 Hostel €

☎ 91 523 81 27; www.casachueca.com; 2nd fl, Calle de San Bartolomé 4; s/d/tr from €40/50/70; Ⓜ Gran Vía
If you don't mind lugging your suitcase up to the 2nd floor, Casa Chueca is outstanding. The rooms are modern, colourful and a cut above your average hostal; in keeping with the barrio that it calls home, Casa Chueca places a premium on style. Add casual, friendly service and you'd be hard pressed to find a better price-to-quality ratio anywhere in central Madrid.

FURTHER RESOURCES
MAGAZINES

A few informative free magazines are in circulation in gay bookshops (especially Librería Berkana (p224) and gay-friendly bars. One is the biweekly *Shanguide*, which is jammed with listings (including saunas and hard-core clubs) and contact ads. Its companion publication *Shangay Express* is better for articles with a handful of listings and ads. The *Mapa Gaya de Madrid* lists gay bars, discos and saunas. Also useful is the *Punto Guía de España para Gays y Lesbianas*, a countrywide guide for gay and gay-friendly bars, restaurants, hotels and shops around the country. The monthly *MENsual* costs €2.20 at newsstands; there's a web version at www.mensual.com.

WEBSITES

You can also check out the following sites on the web:

Chueca.com (www.chueca.com, in Spanish) Its Guía de Locales (for bars and clubs) is only available to subscribers to Chueca XL (the members-only section of the website; €20 per year).

Guía Gay (www.guiagay.com, in Spanish) Forums, news and public events.

Nación Gay (www.naciongay.com) News on the gay community across Spain.

Orgullo Gay (www.orgullogay.org, in Spanish) Website for the gay and lesbian pride march and links to gay organisations across the country.

ORGANISATIONS

The Colectivo de Gais y Lesbianas de Madrid (Cogam; Map pp110–11; ☎ 91 522 45 17; www.cogam.es; Calle de la Puebla 9; Ⓜ Callao or Gran Vía) offers activities, has an info office and social centre, and runs an information line (☎ 91 523 00 70; ☽ 5-9pm Mon-Fri).

The Comunidad de Madrid's Programa de Información y Atención a Homosexuales y Transexuales (Map pp110–11; 4th fl, Gran Vía 16; ☽ 10am-2pm & 5-9pm Mon-Fri Sep-May, 8am-3pm Mon-Fri Jun-Aug; Ⓜ Gran Vía) also has a toll-free information line (☎ 900 720 569).

The Federación Estatal de Lesbianas, Gays, Transexuales & Bisexuales (Felgt; Map pp110–11; ☎ 91 360 46 05; www.felgt.org; 1st fl, Calle de las Infantas 40; Ⓜ Chueca) is a national advocacy group that played a leading role in lobbying for the legalisation of gay marriages.

Fundación Triángulo (Map pp126–7; ☎ 91 593 05 40; www.fundaciontriangulo.es; 1st fl, Calle de Eloy Gonzalo 25; Ⓜ Iglesia) is another source of information on gay issues; it has a separate information line, Información LesGai (☎ 91 44 66 394).

SLEEPING

top picks

- **Albergue Juvenil** (p237)
  Super-new everything at this terrific youth hostel.
- **Cat's Hostel** (p232)
  Backpackers hostel with a stunning courtyard.
- **Los Amigos Backpackers Hostel** (p231)
  Lively traveller meeting place in the centre of town.
- **Hotel Meninas** (p229)
  Designer rooms on one of our favourite streets.
- **Hotel Óscar** (p237)
  Outrageously stylish rooms in a wonderful location.
- **Quo** (p233)
  One of the city's longest-standing boutique hotels.
- **Hotel Abalú** (p236)
  High-quality boutique hotel tucked away in Malasaña.
- **Hotel Puerta América** (p238)
  Madrid's style temple with rooms by world-famous architects.
- **Hotel Urban** (p232)
  Oh-so-sleek with antiques strewn amid a super-modern tower of glass.

SLEEPING

Madrid once trailed far behind Barcelona when it came to cool accommodation, but not any more. Having undergone something of a hotel revolution, the city now has high-quality accommodation across all price ranges and catering to every taste.

Each barrio has its own distinctive identity and where you decide to stay will play an important role in your experience of Madrid, although all are just a few metro stops from each other. Los Austrias, Sol and Centro put you in the heart of the busy downtown area, while La Latina (the best barrio for tapas) and Lavapiés, and Huertas (nightlife) and Atocha, are good for those who love Madrid nights but don't want to stagger too far to get back to their hotel in the wee small hours. Staying along the Paseo del Prado is ideal for those here to spend most of their time in galleries, while Salamanca is quiet, upmarket and perfect for serial shoppers. You don't have to be gay to stay in Chueca, but you'll love it if you are, while Malasaña is another inner-city barrio with great restaurants and bars. Chamberí removes you from the tourist scrum and lets you experience Madrid as the locals do.

Accommodation that caters primarily (but by no means exclusively) to a gay clientele is found on p225.

ACCOMMODATION STYLES

At the budget end of the market, there are plenty of buzzing backpacker places and cheap hostels for those who value a private room. You'll rarely pay more than €60 for a double room with private bathroom, TV and towels, which can't be said about many major European cities.

Midrange is where there's the widest variety of choice, with charming traditional architecture converted into chic designer hotels offering rooms for a fraction of the price you'd pay in most other European capitals. These *hoteles con encanto* (hotels with charm) share the market with stylish, modern monuments to 21st-century fashions. Entirely devoid of stuffiness, hotels and *hostales* (hostels) in this category enable you to feel pampered without the price tag.

At the top end of the market, the sky's the limit when it comes to luxury and price, with refined hotels valuing old-world elegance as well as innovative temples to modern design.

Three final things: in Spain a *habitación doble* (double room) usually indicates a room with two single beds. Cuddly couples should request a *cama de matrimonio* (literally, a marriage bed). All but the most basic *hostales* have free internet access. And check-out in almost all places is noon.

ROOM RATES

Some top-end places have separate price structures for *temporada alta* (high season), *temporada media* (midseason) or *temporada baja* (low season), all usually displayed on a notice in reception. But there's little agreement among hoteliers about when the seasons actually begin and end, and prices can vary on a daily basis according to occupancy, trade fairs and other major events in Madrid. Many of the top, business-oriented hotels cut good deals for weekend stays. Given this occasionally fluid price structure, accommodation prices in this book are a guide only and you should always check room charges before putting down your bags; and remember that prices can and do change with time. Booking ahead is always a good idea.

Virtually all accommodation prices are subject to 7% IVA (the Spanish version of value-added tax). This is often included in the quoted price at cheaper places, but less often at more expensive ones. To check, ask: '*¿Está incluido el IVA?*' ('Is IVA included?'). In some cases you will be charged the IVA only if you ask for a receipt.

LOS AUSTRIAS, SOL & CENTRO

With a wealth of historical sites, accommodation across a range of budgets, and traditional taverns, restaurants and shops within a stone's throw, this area is probably where you'll spend the most time while in town, making it a good place to be based. It's also where all the world congregates and where old Madrid meets the new; as such, it can be at once exhilarating and slightly seedy (especially along Calle de la Montera). For more information on the barrio, see p61.

CASA DE MADRID Map pp64–5   Hotel €€€

☎ 91 559 57 91; www.casademadrid.com; 2nd fl, Calle de Arrieta 2; s €220, d €240-390; Ⓜ Gran Vía

Refined, extravagantly decorated rooms make Casa de Madrid a luxurious choice overlooking the Teatro Real. The rooms are decorated in old-world style, with each built around a theme (eg the Spanish Room, the Indian Room, the Damascus Suite) and it's difficult not to feel like royalty here. It's a little like staying at the Ritz but without the price tag.

HOTEL DE LAS LETRAS
Map pp64–5   Boutique Hotel €€€

☎ 91 523 79 80; www.hoteldelasletras.com; Gran Vía 11; d from €165; Ⓜ Gran Vía

If you want to cause a stir in Madrid with a new hotel, make sure it has a rooftop bar overlooking the city. They're all the rage, but Hotel de las Letras started the craze. The bar's wonderful, but the whole hotel is excellent, with individually styled rooms, each with literary quotes from famous writers written on the walls. We don't always get the colour scheme, but it may just come down to personal taste. The build-

APARTMENTS

If you'll be in Madrid for more than a few days and you'd like the comfort and space of your own apartment, consider Apartasol (☎ 91 512 81 16; www .apartasol.com; apt per night per person for 1/5 persons €69/27). This traveller-friendly agency has well-equipped modern apartments scattered around the vicinity of the Puerta del Sol and Gran Vía. Prices are first-rate and there are discounts available for longer stays.

PRICE GUIDE

Throughout this chapter, accommodation is listed according to barrio, then by price range (starting with the most expensive). Each place is accompanied by one of the following symbols:

€€€	more than €150 a night per double
€€	€71-150 a night per double
€	up to €70 a night per double

ing dates from 1917 and the public areas retain original features, including mosaic tiles.

HOTEL SENATOR Map pp64–5   Hotel €€€

☎ 91 531 41 51; www.playasenator.com; Gran Vía 21; s/d from €145/160; Ⓜ Gran Vía

One of central Madrid's prettiest façades conceals some of the most attractive accommodation in the city centre. Unusually, only one room on each floor doesn't face onto the street and the views down Gran Vía from the corner rooms are brilliant. Rooms are sophisticated and come with armchairs and, wait for it, reclinable beds.

HOTEL MENINAS Map pp64–5   Boutique Hotel €€

☎ 91 541 28 05; www.hotelmeninas.com; Calle de Campomanes; s/d from €109/129; Ⓜ Ópera

This is a classy, cool choice. Opened in 2005, it's the sort of place where an interior designer licked their lips and created a master work of understated, minimalist luxury. The colour scheme is blacks, whites and greys, with dark-wood floors and splashes of fuchsia and lime-green. Flat-screen TVs in every room, modern bathroom fittings, internet access points, and even a laptop in some rooms, round out the clean lines and latest innovations. We love the location as well.

HOTEL VINCCI CAPITOL Map pp64–5 Hotel €€

☎ 91 521 83 91; www.vinccihoteles.com; Gran Vía 41; d €125-180; Ⓜ Gran Vía

Opened in 2007 in the landmark Carrión building, this modern hotel has large rooms with muted tones, and some even have the novelty of circular beds. But what makes it stand out are the views – straight down Gran Vía with its life and grandeur. Not all rooms have views, but there's a 9th-floor viewing area for guests. One local newspaper gave the hotel a '9' for architecture, a '4' for decoration and a '6' for the comfort of the rooms; they're being a little harsh, but we know what they mean.

HOTEL PRECIADOS Map pp64–5   Hotel €€
☎ 91 454 44 00; www.preciadoshotel.com, in Spanish; Calle de Preciados 37; s/d from €122/125; Ⓜ Santo Domingo or Callao
With a classier feel than many of the other business options around town, the Preciados gets rave reviews for its service. Soft lighting, light shades and plentiful glass personalise the rooms and provide an intimate feel.

PETIT PALACE POSADA DEL PEINE
Map pp64–5   Boutique Hotel €€
☎ 91 523 81 51; www.hthoteles.com; Calle de Postas 17; d €115-150; Ⓜ Sol
This outstanding hotel combines a splendid historic building (dating to 1610), brilliant location (just 50m from the Plaza Mayor) and modern hi-tech rooms. The bathrooms sparkle with stunning fittings and hydromassage showers, and the rooms are beautifully appointed; many historical architectural features remain *in situ* in the public areas. It's just a pity some of the rooms aren't larger.

HOTEL II CASTILLAS Map pp64–5   Hotel €€
☎ 91 524 97 50; www.hoteldoscastillas.com; Calle de la Abada 7; s/d around €95/110; Ⓜ Sol
A little bit of inside knowledge makes all the difference here. Ask for a corner room and you'll be rewarded with a light-filled space with hardwood floors and three windows – good value for the price in the city centre. We also love the heated towel rails. The location, just away from busier streets but within easy walking distance of most of them, is excellent.

ATENEO HOTEL Map pp64–5   Hotel €€
☎ 91 521 20 12; www.hotel-ateneo.com; Calle de la Montera 22; s/d from €75/107; Ⓜ Sol
Rooms here are quiet and come with attractive parquet floors as well as private balcony; there's ample floor space and the bathrooms have designer fittings. The only drawback is that Calle de la Montera can be pretty seedy. You're probably close enough to Sol for it not to be too much of an issue.

PETIT PALACE LONDRES Map pp64–5 Hotel €€
☎ 915 31 41 05; www.hthoteles.com; Calle Galdo 2; d from €105; Ⓜ Sol

This former palace is the ideal Madrid address – situated right in the city centre, but surrounded by traffic-free shopping streets with few bars to keep you awake at night. Rooms vary, but there are a few mainstays – modern black-and-white photos adorning the walls, light colour schemes, parquet floors, and hi-tech bathrooms with hydromassage showers and modern fittings.

HOTEL CARLOS V Map pp64–5   Hotel €€
☎ 91 531 41 00; www.hotelcarlosv.com; Calle del Maestro Victoria 5; s/d from €81/101; Ⓜ Callao
A loyal following is drawn to this family-run hotel with an old-fashioned style, right down to the suit of armour in the lobby. The rooms are fine, though more functional than filled with charm; those on the top floors have large balconies. An added bonus is that as you're on a pedestrianised street and there are not too many bars in the immediate vicinity, noise shouldn't be an issue.

MARIO ROOM MATE
Map pp64–5   Boutique Hotel €€
☎ 91 548 85 48; www.room-matehoteles.com; Calle de Campomanes 4; s €90-120, d €100-140; Ⓜ Ópera
Entering this swanky boutique hotel is like crossing the threshold of Madrid's latest nightclub – staff dressed all in black, black walls and swirls of red lighting in the lobby. Rooms are spacious, with high ceilings and simple furniture, light tones contrasting smoothly with muted colours and dark surfaces; some rooms are pristine white, others have splashes of colour with zany murals. The first of the Room Mate chain of hotels to open, Mario prides itself on being 'intimate, elegant and serene', and we have to agree with it.

HOTEL ANACO Map pp64–5   Hotel €€
☎ 91 522 46 04; www.anacohotel.com; Calle de las Tres Cruces 3; s/d from €80/95; Ⓜ Gran Vía
Don't be put off by the grim exterior, or even the lobby – the rooms here are great. Indeed, we like a place that spends its renovation euros on the rooms rather than the lobby – the latter is of a tired, 1970s vintage, but the rooms are decorated in neutral tones with touches of red, and include modern fixtures such as stainless-steel basins.

HOTEL LAURA Map pp64–5   Boutique Hotel €€

☎ 91 701 16 70; www.room-matehoteles.com; Travesía de Trujillos 3; d €90-200, ste €150-280; Ⓜ Sol or Ópera

Another fine offering from the Room Mate chain, Hotel Laura combines location with interiors that are the work of the famous interior designer Tomas Alia. It's all very slick, contemporary and colourful behind the somewhat staid façade.

HOTEL PLAZA MAYOR Map pp64–5   Hotel €€

☎ 91 360 06 06; www.h-plazamayor.com; Calle de Atocha 2; s/d from €65/85; Ⓜ Sol or Tirso de Molina

We love this place. Sitting just across from the Plaza Mayor, here you'll find stylish décor, charming original elements of this 150-year-old building and extremely helpful staff. The rooms are attractive, some with a light colour scheme and wrought-iron furniture. The attic rooms boast dark wood and designer lamps, and have lovely little terraces with wonderful rooftop views of central Madrid.

HOSTAL MADRID Map pp64–5   Apartments €€

☎ 91 522 00 60; www.hostal-madrid.info; 2nd fl, Calle de Esparteros 6; s/d from €57/78, apt per night/month from €100/1300; Ⓜ Sol

The excellent apartments here range in size from 33 sq metres to 130 sq metres and each has a fully-equipped kitchen, its own sitting area, bathroom and, in the case of the larger ones (room 51 on the 5th floor is one of the best), an expansive terrace with glorious views over central Madrid. Tastefully modern wrought-iron furniture and attractive colour schemes combine with period pieces throughout. The double rooms are fairly standard Madrid fare.

HOSTAL MACARENA Map pp64–5   Hostel €€

☎ 91 365 92 21; www.silserranos.com, in Spanish; Cava de San Miguel 8; s/d/tr €59.80/73.83/93.50; Ⓜ Sol

On one of the lovely old cobblestone streets that run past the Plaza Mayor, this charming hostal is at once homey and loaded with impeccable, old-style charm. The rooms are nicely spacious and decorated in warm colours, with the occasional antique writing desk. The centralised location is ideal and with not too much of the traffic noise you find elsewhere downtown.

HOSTAL ACAPULCO Map pp64–5   Hostel €

☎ 91 531 19 45; www.hostalacapulco.com; 4th fl, Calle de la Salud 13; s/d/tr €52/62/79; Ⓜ Gran Vía

A cut above many other hostels in Madrid, this immaculate little hostal has marble floors, recently renovated bathrooms (with bathtubs!), double-glazed windows and comfortable beds. Street-facing rooms have balconies overlooking a sunny plaza and are flooded with natural light. The staff are also friendly and always more than happy to help you plan your day in Madrid.

HOSTAL LUIS XV Map pp64–5   Hostel €

☎ 91 522 13 50; www.hrluisxv.net, in Spanish; 8th fl, Calle de la Montera 47; s/d/tr €45/59/75; Ⓜ Gran Vía

Everything here – especially the spacious rooms and the attention to detail – makes this family-run place feel pricier than it is. You'll find it hard to tear yourself away from the balconies outside every exterior room, from where the views are superb (especially from the triple in room 820) and you're so high up that noise is rarely a problem. If you come out the door, head left onto Gran Vía, rather than seedy Calle de la Montera.

HOSTEL METROPOL Map pp64–5   Hostel €

☎ 93 231 20 45; www.metropolhostel.com; 1st fl, Calle de la Montera 47; dm/s/d €17/45/60; Ⓜ Gran Vía

It's not that the rooms are great; in fact, they're simple and don't have a whole lot of character. But young travellers congregate here for that special something that few hostels have – an attitude, a young vibe. You'll also find art exhibitions, plenty of tourist information, young staff that merge seamlessly with the travellers, a few comfy chairs, picnic lunches, a laundry and a hint of alternative, street-wise advice. The street is not Madrid's finest, but if you turn left onto Gran Vía, you may not even notice.

LOS AMIGOS BACKPACKERS HOSTEL
Map pp64–5   Hostel €

☎ 915 47 17 07; www.losamigoshostel.com; 4th fl, Calle de Campomanes 6; dm €17-19, d €50; Ⓜ Ópera

If you arrive in Madrid keen for company, this could be the place for you – lots of students stay here, the staff are savvy (and speak English) and there are bright dorm-style rooms (with free lockers) that sleep from four to 12 people. A steady stream of repeat visitors is the best recommendation we can give. Los Amigos also has another hostel a couple of blocks away, the equally excellent Los Amigos Sol Backpackers Hostel (Map pp64–5; ☎ 91 559 24 72; 4th fl, Calle de Arenal 26; dm €17-20, d €50; Ⓜ Ópera).

LA LATINA & LAVAPIÉS

Places to stay are pretty thin on the ground in these two barrios, but what's here is just back from the clamorous streets of downtown and yet still close enough to get around the centre on foot. For more information on the barrio, see p74.

HOTEL REYES CATÓLICOS

Map pp76–7   Hotel €€

☎ 91 365 86 00; www.hotelreyescatolicos .com; Calle del Ángel 18; s €99-119, d €109-129; Ⓜ Puerta de Toledo or La Latina
If you like to be removed from the bustle of downtown Madrid but on the cusp of fascinating La Latina, this place is a good choice. While the rooms are simple and eccentric (what's with the stripy wallpaper?), they do have bright décor and lots of natural light. They also look onto a quiet street or the Basilica de San Francisco, and the double-glazed windows should be a lesson to other Madrid hotels.

HOSTAL HORIZONTE Map pp76–7   Hostel €

☎ 91 369 09 96; www.hostalhorizonte.com; 2nd fl, Calle de Atocha 28; s €29, with private bathroom €40, d €44, with private bathroom €55; Ⓜ Antón Martín
Billing itself as a hostel run by travellers for travellers, Hostal Horizonte is a well-run place. The rooms have far more character than your average hostel, with high ceil-

ings, deliberately old-world furnishings and modern bathrooms. The King Alfonso XII room (€72) is especially well presented. All in all it's a good package.

CAT'S HOSTEL Map pp76–7   Hostel €

☎ 91 369 28 07; www.catshostel.com; Calle de Cañizares 6; dm €19, d from €24; Ⓜ Antón Martín
Now here's something special. Forming part of a 17th-century palace, the internal courtyard is Madrid's finest – lavish Andalucian tilework, a fountain, a spectacular glass ceiling and stunning Islamic decoration, surrounded on four sides by an open balcony. There's a super-cool basement bar with free internet connections and fiestas, often with live music. One small complaint: Cat's standards of maintenance haven't quite kept pace with its popularity.

MAD HOSTEL Map pp76–7   Hostel €

☎ 915 06 48 40; www.madhostel.com; Calle de Cabeza 24; dm €20; Ⓜ Antón Martín
From the people who brought you Cat's Hostel, Mad Hostel is similarly filled with a buzzing vibe. The 1st-floor courtyard – with retractable roof – re-creates an old Madrid corrala and is a wonderful place to chill, while the four- to eight-bed rooms are smallish but new and clean. There's a small, rooftop gym equipped with state-of-the-art equipment. Great choice.

HUERTAS & ATOCHA

If you're opening a swish new designer hotel in Madrid, Huertas seems to be the place to do it. Some of the most exciting new upmarket hotels are to be found near in a barrio that seems hellbent on reinventing itself as the Spanish capital's home of accommodation chic. Huertas nights will, however, quickly bring you back down to earth, filled as they are with the roar of Madrid at play; going to sleep in Huertas can seem like something of a lost cause on weekends, although, thankfully, most of the newer places have double glazing. For more information on the sights of the barrio, see p82.

HOTEL URBAN Map pp84–5   Hotel €€€

☎ 91 787 77 70; www.derbyhotels.com; Carrera de San Jerónimo 34; d €200-350; Ⓜ Sevilla
The towering glass edifice of Hotel Urban is the epitome of art-inspired designer cool. With its clean lines and original artworks

top picks

FOR BACKPACKERS

- Albergue Juvenil (p237)
- Cat's Hostel (right)
- Mad Hostel (right)
- Los Amigos Backpackers Hostel (p231)
- International Youth Hostel – La Posada de Huertas (p235)

from Africa and Asia (there's a small museum to Egyptian art in the basement), it's a wonderful antidote to the more classic charm of Madrid's five-star hotels of longer standing. Dark-wood floors and dark walls are offset by plenty of light, while the dazzling bathrooms have wonderful designer fittings – the washbasins are sublime. The rooftop swimming pool is one of Madrid's best and the gorgeous terrace is heaven on a candle-lit summer's evening. If money were no object, we would need a good reason to stay anywhere else.

ME BY MELIÁ Map pp84–5 Hotel €€€
☎ 91 701 60 00; www.mebymelia.com; Plaza de Santa Ana 14; d without/with plaza view from €200/250; Ⓜ Sol or Antón Martín
Once the landmark Gran Victoria Hotel, the Madrid home of many a famous bullfighter, this audacious new hotel is fast becoming a landmark of a different kind. Overlooking the western end of Plaza de Santa Ana, this luxury hotel is decked out in minimalist white with curves and comfort in all the right places; this is one place where it's definitely worth paying extra for the view. Its two bars – The Penthouse and Midnight Rose (see p190) – are as lavish as the hotel.

HOTEL EL PRADO Map pp84–5 Hotel €€
☎ 91 369 02 34; www.pradohotel.com; Calle del Prado 11; s €80-120, d €125-195, ste €165-225; Ⓜ Antón Martín or Sevilla
This is one of Madrid's most welcoming three-star hotels, offering style and service beyond its modest rating. There's a wine theme running throughout the spacious rooms, which have parquet floors, light tones, and places to sit and write. The double-glazed windows are also important, especially if you're here on a weekend, when prices are at their cheapest.

VINCCI SOHO Map pp84–5 Hotel €€
☎ 91 141 41 00; www.vinccihoteles.com; Calle del Prado 18; d €90-470; Ⓜ Sevilla or Antón Martín
A refined sense of style permeates everything about this hotel from the subtly lit public areas to the rooms that combine vaguely Zen aesthetics with blood-red bathrooms. As ideal a base for the museums along the Paseo del Prado as for the clamour of central Madrid, it gets just about everything right. So why wouldn't you stay here? Well, on the rare occasions

when a standard double room goes for €470 it's just being silly. A more normal price hovers around €125, which is worth every euro.

QUO Map pp84–5 Boutique Hotel €€
☎ 91 532 90 49; www.hotelesquo.com; Calle de Sevilla 4; s €90-160, d €90-195; Ⓜ Sevilla
Quo is one of Madrid's homes of chic with black-clad staff, minimalist designer furniture, tall ceilings and huge windows that let light flood in. The colour scheme is black and red, with light surfaces providing perfect contrast and a resolutely contemporary look. We're also big fans of the bathrooms, with glass doors, glass benches and stainless-steel basins. All rooms have flat-screen TVs, black-and-white photos of Madrid, dark-wood floors and comfy armchairs; rooms on the 7th floor have Jacuzzis and private terraces with terrific views over the rooftops.

HOTEL ALICIA Map pp84–5 Boutique Hotel €€
☎ 91 389 60 95; www.room-matehoteles.com; Calle del Prado 2; d €90-200, ste €150-280; Ⓜ Sol, Sevilla or Antón Martín
One of the landmark properties of the designer Room Mate chain of hotels, Hotel Alicia overlooks Plaza de Santa Ana with beautiful, spacious rooms. The style (the work of Pascua Ortega) is a touch more muted than in other Room Mate hotels, but the supermodern look remains intact, the downstairs bar is oh-so-cool, and the service is young and switched on. Two of the duplex suites have their own terrace with a little private pool.

SUITE PRADO HOTEL Map pp84–5 Suites €€
☎ 91 420 23 18; www.suiteprado.com; Calle de Manuel Fernández y González 10; ste €90-160; Ⓜ Sevilla

The spacious modern suites at this centrally located hotel have plenty of space and are semiluxurious, although they don't have a whole lot of character; some are cavernous, as if the decorators didn't quite know what to do with so much space. All have sitting rooms, good bathrooms and kitchenettes, and the price is fine for the location.

HOTEL EL PASAJE Map pp84–5   Hotel €€
☎ 91 521 29 95; www.elpasajehs.com; Calle del Pozo 4; d incl breakfast Sun-Thu €90, Fri & Sat €110; Ⓜ Sol
If you were to choose your ideal location in Huertas, Hotel El Pasaje would be hard to beat. Set on a quiet lane largely devoid of bars, yet just around the corner from the Plaza de la Puerta del Sol, it combines a central location with a quiet night's sleep, at least by the standards of Huertas. The feel is intimate and modern (except for the tired-coloured bedspreads – what was it thinking?), with good bathrooms, minibars and enough space to leave your suitcase without tripping over it. The twins have balconies; the doubles are on the inside of the building.

HOTEL MIAU Map pp84–5   Hotel €€
☎ 91 369 71 20; www.hotelmiau.com; Calle del Príncipe 26; s/d incl breakfast €85/95; Ⓜ Sol or Antón Martín
If you want to be close to the nightlife of Huertas or can't tear yourself away from the beautiful Plaza de Santa Ana, then Hotel Miau is your place. Light tones, splashes of colour and modern art adorn the walls of the rooms, which are large and well equipped. It can be noisy, but you chose Huertas…

CHIC & BASIC Map pp84–5   Hostel €€
☎ 91 429 69 35; www.7colorsrooms.com; 2nd fl, Calle de las Huertas 14; s/d incl breakfast from €57/77; Ⓜ Antón Martín
It's all about colours here at this fine little hotel/hostel. The rooms are white in a minimalist style with free internet, flat-screen TVs, dark hardwood floors with a bright colour scheme superimposed on top with every room a different shade. It's all very comfortable, contemporary and casual. Only three of the rooms look out onto the street, but those on the inside of the building don't feel quite as claustrophobic as in some places. Prices increase by €10 per room on Friday and Saturday.

HOTEL VICTORIA 4 Map pp84–5   Hotel €€
☎ 91 523 84 30; www.hotelvictoria4.com; Calle de Victoria 4; d incl breakfast €75-143; Ⓜ Sol
We like a place where you can feel like you're in an oasis of calm even as carousing crowds pass by your front door. A great location, handy for some of Madrid's best nightlife, and attractive, well-equipped rooms add up to a package that represents outstanding value for the centre of a major European capital.

HOSTAL SARDINERO Map pp84–5   Hostel €
☎ 91 429 57 56; fax 91 429 41 12; 3rd fl, Calle del Prado 16; s/d from €47/67; Ⓜ Sol or Antón Martín
More than the cheerful rooms (which have high ceilings, air-conditioning, a safe, hairdryers and renovated bathrooms), it's the friendly old couple who run this place that gives it its charm. They love it if you take the time to sit down for a chat – preferably in Spanish or French, as the owners speak both.

HOSTAL ADRIANO Map pp84–5   Hostel €
☎ 91 521 13 39; www.hostaladriano.com; 4th fl, Calle de la Cruz 26; s/d/tr €49/63/83; Ⓜ Sol
They don't come any better than this bright and cheerful hostel wedged in the streets that mark the boundary between Sol and Huertas. Most rooms are well sized and each has its own colour scheme. Indeed, more thought has gone into the decoration than in your average hostel, from the bed covers to the pictures on the walls. On the same floor, the owners run the Hostal Adria Santa Ana (Map pp84–5; www.hostaladriasantaana.com; d/tr €70/90), which is a step up in price, style and luxury.

INTERNATIONAL YOUTH HOSTEL – LA POSADA DE HUERTAS
Map pp84–5   Hostel €

☎ 91 429 55 26; www.posadadehuertas.com; Calle de las Huertas 21; dm €17-21, s/d €40/50; Ⓜ Antón Martín

There's no better place to base yourself if you've come to Madrid to party and prefer to spend your money on your drinks rather than your bed. Rooms are simple, modern bog-standard dorms, and include free internet, breakfast, locker, and your own key that lets you come and go as you please. Staff are young and live Madrid's nightlife when they're not working; they're happy to advise on the latest in places.

PASEO DEL PRADO & EL RETIRO

The artistic splendour of the art galleries along the magnificent Paseo del Prado is a fine reason for choosing to stay in this former barrio of choice for Madrid's royalty; the sophisticated Parque del Buen Retiro is another of the joys of staying in this green and relatively tranquil barrio. For more information on the barrio, see p90.

HOTEL RITZ Map pp92–3   Hotel €€€

☎ 91 701 67 67; www.ritzmadrid.com; Plaza de la Lealtad 5; d €562-675, ste €1124-5136; Ⓜ Banco de España

The grand old lady of Madrid, the Hotel Ritz is the height of exclusivity. One of the most lavish buildings in the city, it has classic style and impeccable service that is second to none. Unsurprisingly it's the favoured hotel of presidents, kings and celebrities. The public areas are palatial and awash with antiques, while the rooms are extravagantly large, opulent and supremely comfortable. In the Royal Suite, the walls are covered with raw silk and there's a personal butler to wait upon you. We challenge you to find a more indulgent hotel experience anywhere in Spain.

WESTIN PALACE Map pp92–3   Hotel €€€

☎ 91 360 80 00; www.westinpalacemadrid.com; Plaza de las Cortes 7; d €369-470, ste €659-1265; Ⓜ Banco de España or Antón Martín

An old Madrid classic, this former palace of the Duque de Lerma opened as a hotel in 1911 and was Spain's second luxury hotel.

Ever since, it has looked out across Plaza de Neptuno at its rival, the Ritz, like a lover unjustly scorned. Its name may not have the world-famous cachet of the Ritz, but it's not called the Palace for nothing and is extravagant in all the right places. After the snooty Ritz banned actors and other public performers in the early 20th century, the Palace became the hotel of choice for celebrities – Mata Hari lived here during WWI and her ghost reportedly occupies the corridors, while Hemingway, Dalí and Lorca were all regulars in the cocktail bar. The 1999 renovations cost €144,000 per room…

HOTEL MORA Map pp92–3   Hotel €€

☎ 91 420 15 69; www.hotelmora.com; Paseo del Prado 32; s/d €60/78; Ⓜ Atocha

Near the main museums and a short walk from the city centre, this simple, friendly hotel is a fine choice. You have to feel for the owners, who endured years of massive building works right behind the hotel. Their (and your) reward is the architecturally stunning Caixa Forum, which is already one of the great landmarks along a boulevard of many. Rooms are a bit sparse, and their furnishings a little tired, but they're spacious and clean, and some look out across the Paseo del Prado.

NH NACIONAL Map pp92–3   Hotel €€

☎ 91 429 66 29; www.nh-hotels.com; Paseo del Prado 48; d Fri-Sun €147-185, Mon-Thu €169; Ⓜ Atocha

The excellent NH chain of hotels doesn't get any better than this place, where the stylish rooms are beautifully decorated in warm colours, and combine luxury comfort with all the necessary technology. It's also close to both Atocha train station and Madrid's big three art galleries.

top picks

LAP OF LUXURY

- Hotel Ritz (left)
- Westin Palace (left)
- Hotel Puerta América (p238)
- Hotel Urban (p232)
- Hotel AC Santo Mauro (p238)

SALAMANCA

Salamanca is Madrid's most exclusive address, home to suitably grand sights and the best shopping that the city has to offer. It's generally a quieter choice than anywhere else in the capital and good restaurants abound. For more information on the barrio, see p101.

BAUZÁ Map pp102–3 Boutique Hotel €€€
☎ 91 435 75 45; www.hotelbauza.com; Calle de Goya 79; s/d/ste from €150/200/340; Ⓜ Goya
Minimalist and modern, the Bauzá would be right at home in SoHo, New York. The generous rooms boast dark-wood floors, soothing greys and blues, and flashes of originality like Indian textile prints. Computers, sound systems, designer lamps and even plants add appeal without crowding the rooms.

PETIT PALACE EMBASSY SERRANO
Map pp102–3 Hotel €€€
☎ 91 431 30 60; www.hthoteles.com; Calle de Serrano 46; d from €165; Ⓜ Serrano
Part of the High Tech chain of hotels, this is the premier address for those who'll be spending their time shopping in Salamanca. On the boutique-rich Calle de Serrano, the Petit Palace has rooms classy and large enough to accommodate all your shopping bags and so much more – many have their own computer and exercise bike.

HESPERIA HERMOSILLA Map pp102–3 Hotel €€
☎ 91 246 88 00; www.hesperia.com; Calle de Hermosilla; s/d from €125/135; Ⓜ Serrano
If you're here on a mission to shop or you otherwise value quiet, exclusive streets away from the noise of central Madrid, this modern and subtly stylish hotel is a terrific choice. The furnishings are vaguely minimalist, especially in the public areas, and LCD flat-screen TVs and other creature comforts are rare luxuries in this price range.

MALASAÑA & CHUECA

Staying in Malasaña or Chueca keeps you within walking distance of (or a short metro ride from) most of Madrid's major sights but immerses you in the sometimes gritty, usually cool personalities of these two inner-city barrios. There's not a lot to see here – a few museums is about it – but both barrios are wonderful places to eat out or drink the night

top picks

HOTEL CHAINS

- Room Mate (www.room-matehoteles.com)
- Hi Tech (www.hthoteles.com)
- Vincci (www.vinccihoteles.com)
- NH (www.nh-hotels.com)
- AC (www.ac-hoteles.com)

away. It's a generally young vibe, and Chueca can be extravagantly gay, but it's almost always inclusive regardless of your age or sexual orientation.

PETIT PALACE HOTEL DUCAL
Map pp110–11 Hotel €€
☎ 91 521 10 43; www.hthoteles.com; Calle de Hortaleza 3; d from €115; Ⓜ Gran Vía
Fusing elegant old buildings with state-of-the-art rooms and hi-tech facilities is the hallmark here. The rooms boast strong, contrasting colours, polished floorboards, clean lines, comfy beds and armchairs, and plenty of light and mirrors. Each room also has its own computer with free internet connection. The hi-tech theme continues in the bathrooms, where hydromassage showers are standard.

SIETE ISLAS HOTEL Map pp110–11 Hotel €€
☎ 91 523 46 88; www.hotelsieteislas.com; Calle de Valverde 14-16; s/d from €103/114; Ⓜ Gran Vía
Rooms here are comfortable and stylish, with generous, marble-lined bathrooms and cool beige-and-navy-blue tones throughout. The owners hail from the Canary Islands and each room is themed to a different village from the islands. There's also a nautical flourish in some of the public areas.

HOTEL ABALÚ Map pp110–11 Boutique Hotel €€
☎ 91 531 47 44; www.hotelabalu.com; Calle del Pez 19; s/d from €74/105, ste €140-200; Ⓜ Noviciado
You may love the mean streets of Malasaña, but that doesn't mean you want to sleep rough. At last, Malasaña has its own boutique hotel, an oasis of style amid the barrio's timeworn feel. Each room has its own design drawn from the imagination of Luis Delgado, from retro chintz to Zen, Baroque and pure white and most aesthet-

ics in between. Some of the suites have Jacuzzis and large-screen home cinemas. You're close to Gran Vía, but away from the tourist scrum.

HOTEL ÓSCAR Map pp110–11 Boutique Hotel €€
☎ 91 701 11 73; www.room-matehoteles.com; Plaza Vázquez de Mella 12; d €90-200, ste €150-280; Ⓜ Gran Vía
Outstanding. Hotel Óscar belongs to the highly original Room Mate chain of hotels and the designer rooms ooze style and sophistication. Some have floor-to-ceiling murals, the lighting is always funky, and the colour scheme is splashed with pinks, lime greens, oranges or a more minimalist black and white. Like all Room Mate hotels, this one's themed around an individual personality, in this case Oscar, who describes himself as 'nocturnal, cosmopolitan and ready for anything'.

APARTHOTEL TRIBUNAL
Map pp110–11 Aparthotel €€
☎ 91 522 14 55; www.aparthotel-tribunal.com, in Spanish; Calle de San Vicente Ferrer 1; s apt €60-100, d apt €70-120; Ⓜ Tribunal
If you're looking for apartments for short stays (there are no cheaper weekly rates), Aparthotel Tribunal is a good choice. All the rooms come with kitchenette and satellite TV, and sizes range from 25 sq metres to 50 sq metres; they're more like studios than apartments. They're well maintained, although some are starting to show their age.

HOSTAL SAN LORENZO Map pp110–11 Hostel €
☎ 91 521 30 57; www.hotel-sanlorenzo.com; Calle de Clavel 8; s €45-75, d €59-98; Ⓜ Gran Vía
Hostal San Lorenzo is generally an excellent deal: original stone walls and some dark-wood beams from the 19th century in the public areas, and modern, comfortable and bright rooms (some with splashes of old-world charm) that you'll be more than happy to return to at the end of the day. Some of the rooms could be larger and, depending on who you encounter, the service can be a little off-hand.

HOSTAL AMÉRICA Map pp110–11 Hostel €
☎ 91 522 64 48; www.hostalamerica.net; 5th fl, Calle de Hortaleza 19; s/d €40/55; Ⓜ Gran Vía
Run by a lovely mother-son-dog team (the dog's called Ronnie and has quite a following among guests), the América has superclean, spacious and IKEA-dominated rooms. As most rooms face onto the usual interior 'patio' of the building, you should get a good night's sleep despite the busy area. For the rest of the time, there's an expansive terrace – quite a luxury for a hostel in downtown Madrid – with tables, chairs and a coffee machine. There's free wi-fi, but if you're too far down the hall, the connection can be a little tenuous.

HOSTAL DON JUAN Map pp110–11 Hostel €
☎ 91 522 31 01; 2nd fl, Plaza de Vázquez de Mella 1; s/d/tr €38/53/71; Ⓜ Gran Vía
Paying cheap rates for your room doesn't mean you can't be treated like a king. This elegant two-storey *hostal* is filled with original artworks and antique furniture that could grace a royal palace, although mostly it's restricted to the public areas. Rooms are large and simple but luminous; most have a street-facing balcony. The location is good, close to where Chueca meets Gran Vía.

ALBERGUE JUVENIL Map pp110–11 Hostel €
☎ 91 593 96 88; www.ajmadrid.es; Calle de Mejía Lequerica 21; dm €18-24; Ⓜ Bilbao or Alonso Martínez
If you're looking for dormitory-style accommodation, you'd need a good reason to stay anywhere other than here while you're in Madrid. Opened in 2007, the Albergue has spotless rooms, no dorm houses more than six beds (each has its own bathroom), and facilities include a pool table, a gymnasium, wheelchair access, free internet, laundry and a TV/DVD room with a choice of movies. All the facilities are supermodern, and breakfast is included in the price. Yes, there are places with more character or a more central location, but we'd still rate this as one of Madrid's best hostels for backpackers.

CHAMBERÍ & ARGÜELLES
Chamberí has bars, shops, cinemas and restaurants in just the right measure, and you'll quickly feel less like a tourist and more like a local by staying here. There aren't many places to stay, but those that are here are excellent, and you're only a short metro ride from the main sites of interest. For more information on the barrio, see p115.

HOTEL AC SANTO MAURO

Map pp116–17   Hotel €€€

☎ 91 319 69 00; www.ac-hoteles.com;
Calle de Zurbano 36; d €279-355, ste €425-1070;
Ⓜ Alonso Martínez

Everything about this recently renovated place oozes exclusivity and class, from the address – one of the elite patches of Madrid real estate – to the 19th-century mansion that's the finest in a barrio of many. It's a place of discreet elegance and warm service, and rooms are suitably lavish, with Persian carpets on the floor and the latest technology at your disposal; the Arabian-styled indoor pool isn't bad either. David Beckham may well be derided for many things, but the fact that he chose to make this his home for six months certainly suggests he has a higher degree of taste than people usually give him credit for. Madonna and Richard Gere have been other notable guests.

AMADOR DE LOS RÍOS ESPAHOTEL

Map pp116–17   Boutique Hotel €€

☎ 91 310 75 00; www.espahotel.es; Calle de Amador de los Ríos 3; s/d €120/150; Ⓜ Colón

Tucked away in an exclusive corner of Chamberí and just set back in behind the Paseo de la Castellana, Amador de los Ríos is a terrific hotel where all the rooms are apartments or suites. The interior design by Pascual Ortega blends the classic with the contemporary and the rooftop swimming pool is pure luxury. The rooms themselves are bathed in warm colours with soft lighting.

HOTEL TRAFALGAR   Map pp116–17   Hotel €€

☎ 91 445 62 00; www.hotel-trafalgar.com; Calle de Trafalgar 35; s/d from €93/132; Ⓜ Quevedo

If you asked madrileños where they would most like to live, the chances are it would be within a 1km radius of this hotel. The hotel itself is modern and comfortable, with good-sized rooms and all the mod-cons (in-room movies, internet and good bathrooms). There's not a lot of character, but you'll love strolling down to the Plaza de Olavide for breakfast.

NORTHERN MADRID

HOTEL PUERTA AMÉRICA

Map p123   Hotel €€€

☎ 917 44 54 00; www.hotelpuertamerica.com; Avenida de América 41; d from €239; Ⓜ Cartagena

When the owners of this hotel saw their location – halfway between the city and the airport – they knew they had to do something special, to build a self-contained world so innovative and luxurious that you'll never want to leave. Their idea? Give 22 of world architecture's most creative names (eg Zaha Hadid, Sir Norman Foster, Ron Arad, David Chipperfield, Jean Nouvel) a floor each to design. The result? An extravagant pastiche of styles, from zany montages of 1980s chic to bright-red bathrooms that feel like a movie star's dressing room. Even the bar ('a temple to the liturgy of pleasure'), restaurant, façade, gardens, public lighting and car park had their own architects. It's an extraordinary, astonishing place.

DAY TRIPS

DAY TRIPS

Located as it is in the geographical heart of Spain, Madrid is an ideal base for exploring the country. While well-developed road and rail networks connect the city to just about anywhere in Spain, there are a host of beautiful historical towns and other extraordinary sights, all of which can easily be visited as a day trip from the capital.

If you're a city person, Toledo, Segovia and Ávila can all be reached in an hour by train. Awash with extraordinary monuments, a visit to any of these cities takes you on a journey through the country's polyglot history, from the soaring Roman remains of Segovia, to the medieval defensive battlements of Ávila and the grand monuments, to religious enlightenment in Toledo.

If you're needing a break from city life, villages like Chinchón and those of the Sierra de Guadarrama or Sierra Pobre provide an antidote to the clamour. In the sierras, you can also leave behind the last outposts of civilisation and hike out into the wilderness and still be back in Madrid for a late dinner. Alcalá de Henares straddles the two experiences, with all the life and energy of an elegant university town grafted onto a place with the intimacy of a large village.

The royals who have always made Madrid their capital also understood that a country retreat was sometimes necessary from all the noise of the city. From a ledge in the mountains to the west of the city, the magnificence of San Lorenzo de El Escorial is one of the most extraordinary palace-monasteries in Spain. South of Madrid, Aranjuez is equally eye-catching, with a stately palace surrounded by monumental gardens that are the height of sophistication. And on any of the day trips covered in this chapter, you'll find restaurants where you can eat like a king.

Although you could easily stray further and make it back to Madrid by nightfall, you'd be rushing to do so. For this reason, we have restricted our coverage in this chapter to places that require no more than a two-hour round trip. We understand, however, that if you have more time, you may wish to stay overnight in cities such as Toledo, Segovia and Ávila with their many attractions – for this reason we've included a handful of sleeping options.

BEAUTIFUL CITIES

Toledo (p242) is a grandly austere city that once rivalled Madrid for the role of capital. Coming here is like stepping back into the Middle Ages, into a history when Christians, Muslims and Jews turned this into one of Spain's most enlightened cities. Ávila (p249), too, resonates with history, most notably in its imposing cathedral and encircling medieval walls. The Unesco World Heritage–listed old city of Segovia (p245) has an entirely different, light-filled charm as it surveys the surrounding mountains from its hill-top perch. The exceptional *alcázar* (Muslim-era fortress) and Roman-era aqueduct are its signature sights, but it's also a place where eating is an art form.

ROYAL PLAYGROUNDS

The imposing 16th-century monastery and palace complex of San Lorenzo de El Escorial (p252) guards the gateway to Madrid from the northwest and is a terrific excursion. Nearby the Valle de los Caídos (p253) is a curious monument to General Francisco Franco's delusions of grandeur – not royalty, but he would have liked to have been. Graceful Aranjuez (p254) is home to a magnificent palace and expansive gardens, and now serves as a fine retreat from the noise and bustle of Madrid just as it did for Spanish royalty down through the ages.

FIESTAS & FESTIVALS

It's worth planning a trip to coincide with some of the extravagant fiestas going on in the towns around Madrid:

- Semana Santa (Easter week) – Elaborate, sombre processions by pointy-hatted penitents fill Toledo, Ávila and Chinchón for one of the year's holiest festivals.
- Corpus Christi, Toledo (June) – Several days of festivities culminate in a solemn procession.
- Fiesta Mayor, Chinchón (12-18 August) – The town's splendid plaza is turned into a bullring each morning.
- Santa Teresa, Ávila (around 15 October) – Held in honour of Saint Teresa, this festival sees the town indulge in days of celebrations and processions.

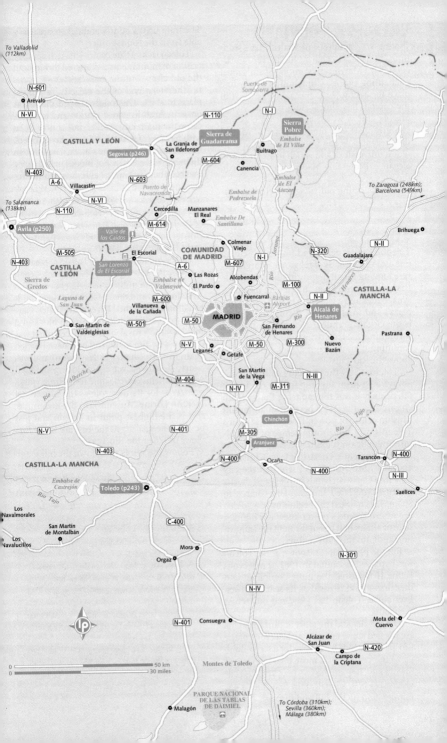

VILLAGES & MOUNTAINS

Chinchón (p255), southeast of Madrid, has a stunning, ramshackle charm; its uneven, porticoed Plaza Mayor ranks among Spain's most enchanting plazas. Chinchón is also a fine place for eating. Alcalá de Henares (p256), east of the capital, has almost outgrown its village origins, but is worth as much time as you can give it. It was the birthplace of Miguel de Cervantes, is still home to one of Spain's oldest universities and is rich in architectural elegance. Protecting Madrid from the north, the Sierra de Guadarrama (p256) and Sierra Pobre (p257) shelter charming old villages, including Manzanares El Real (p256) and Buitrago (p257).

TOLEDO

Toledo is an imperial and imperious city, a one-time crossroads of religions, its architecture looking for all the world like the Middle East grafted onto Spanish soil with mosques, synagogues and a labyrinth of narrow streets, plazas and inner patios. Rising above it all is the Gothic grandeur of the cathedral and forbidding *alcázar*, which survey the surrounding country from a rocky ridge high above the Río Tajo.

'Toletum', as the Romans called it, was always a strategically important city. In the 6th century it was the capital of the Visigoth empire and after 711 it became an important Muslim centre of power. Under the Muslims Toledo was a flourishing centre of art, culture and religion, a multifaith city, which was home to peacefully coexisting Jews, Christians and Muslims. Alfonso VI wrestled the city back into Christian hands in 1085, and shortly after it was declared 'the seat of the Church' in Spain. This marked the beginning of a golden age where Toledo's power knew few limits, a state of affairs that lasted through the Inquisition and into the 16th century.

But too powerful for its own good, Toledo was bypassed as capital in 1561 as a nervous Felipe II favoured the more compliant and then-less-grand Madrid as its seat of power. Ever since, Toledo has glowered out across the plains.

The old city and the most important sights are stacked stone upon stone in a crook of the Río Tajo. The hills here make for a steep climb up to the centre; for a more relaxing view of the old city, hop on the Zoco Tren (☎ 925 23 22 10; adult/child €4/1.75), a small train that does a 45-minute loop up the hill and through Toledo.

The train leaves hourly and tickets are available from the tourist office.

Toledo lacks a true centre – its rich concentration of monuments is scattered throughout the old city – but the Plaza de Zocodover, at the northeastern end of the old city, is a good place to start. This oddly shaped plaza was once an Arab livestock market and later became the main city market, but is now lined with terrace cafés and filled with day-trippers. On the eastern side of the square, pass through the Arco de la Sangre (Gate of Blood), which once marked the city's walls, and down to the rewarding Museo de Santa Cruz (☎ 925 22 10 36; Calle de Cervantes 3; admission free; ☼ 10am-6.30pm Mon-Sat, 10am-2pm Sun), a splendid early 16th-century pastiche of Gothic and Spanish Renaissance styles, fine cloisters and a number of El Greco paintings, including *La Asunción de la Virgen*.

Up the hill to the south is Toledo's signature fortress, the four-spired Alcázar, which began life as a Roman military base, later became an Arab fortress and then a Christian one rebuilt by Alfonso VI in the 11th century. Later, Carlos V converted the harsh square block of a building into a royal visitors palace until it was damaged by fire in 1710. The palace burned again in 1810 (thanks to Napoleon) and was nearly destroyed yet again during the civil war. It remains closed while restoration works prepare it for its new role as the Museo del Ejército (Army Museum). In the meantime, this is the highest point in Toledo and just beyond the *alcázar* to the east are some fine views out over the Río Tajo.

Follow the spires west down the hill to Catedral de Toledo (☎ 925 22 22 41; Plaza de Ayuntamiento; adult/child €6/free; ☼ 10.30am-6.30pm Mon-Sat, 2-6pm Sun), the spiritual home of Catholic Spain

TRANSPORT: TOLEDO *€4.67 ALSA Buses PLAZA ELIPTICA Ⓜ*

Distance from Madrid 68km
Direction Southwest
Car From Madrid, head south on the N-401 highway, which leads to Toledo. In town, follow the signs to the *centro urbano* (town centre). Driving time is 55 minutes.
Bus Bargas buses (€3.95) make the 75-minutes trip from Madrid's Estación Sur (ticket windows 43-46) to Toledo every half-hour.
Train Renfe's new high-speed AVANT rail link (☎ 902 240 202; www.renfe.es; one way/return €9/€16) is the best way to get to Toledo, with up to 20 trains daily. The trip takes 30 minutes.

BUS 5 - BUS STA ←→ PLAZA DE ZOCODOVER

TOLEDO

[handwritten] (R) HOTEL CARLOS V   D4
[handwritten] TRISTAMARA 1   +34 925 222100

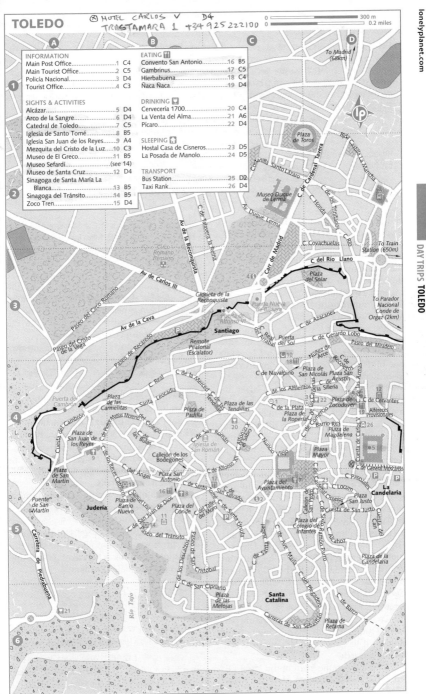

To Madrid (68km)

Plaza de Toros

To Train Station (650m)

To Parador Nacional Conde de Orgaz (2km)

243

EL GRECO IN TOLEDO

Few artists are as closely associated with a city as El Greco is with Toledo – many travellers come here for his paintings alone.

Born in Crete in 1541, Domenikos Theotokopoulos (El Greco; the Greek) moved to Venice in 1567 to be schooled as a Renaissance artist. Under the tutelage of masters, such as Tintoretto, he learned to express dramatic scenes with few colours, concentrating the observer's interest in the faces of his portraits and leaving the rest in relative obscurity, a characteristic that remained one of his hallmarks.

El Greco came to Spain in 1577 hoping to get a job decorating El Escorial, although Felipe II rejected him as a court artist. In Toledo, the painter managed to cultivate a healthy clientele and command good prices. His rather high opinion of himself and his work, however, did not endear him to all. He had to do without the patronage of the cathedral administrators, who were the first of many clients to haul him to court for his obscenely high fees. El Greco liked the high life and took rooms in a mansion on the Paseo del Tránsito, where he often hired musicians to accompany his meals.

As Toledo's fortunes declined, so did El Greco's personal finances, and although the works of his final years are among his best, he often found himself unable to pay the rent. He died in 1614, leaving his works scattered about the city.

and one of the largest and most opulent cathedrals in the world. An essentially Gothic creation with a few *mudéjar* (a Moorish architectural style) afterthoughts, it was built in the 13th century atop an earlier mosque. All the chapels and side rooms are worth peeking into, especially the Capilla de la Torre (Tower Chapel) in the northwestern corner and the Sacristía (Sacristy). The latter boasts a lovely vaulted ceiling and works by El Greco (see the boxed text, above), Rubens, Zubarán, Titian and Velázquez, while the Tower Chapel has one of the most extraordinary monstrances in existence, the 16th-century Custodia de Arfe. With 18kg of gold and 183kg of silver, this shimmering mass of metal has an astonishing 260 statuettes. Behind the main altar, the Transparente is a mesmerising piece of churrigueresque baroque. A lavish 18th-century embellishment, it also serves to remedy the lack of light in the cathedral.

Down the hill is a cluster of must-sees for El Greco fans, among them the wonderful Iglesia de Santo Tomé (☎ 925 25 60 98; www.santotome.org; Plaza del Conde; admission €1.90; ☉ 10am-6pm), which houses arguably El Greco's greatest work, *El Entierro del Conde de Orgaz* (The Burial of the Count of Orgaz). The painting tells the legend of the pious count's funeral in 1323, when St Augustine and St Steven appeared to lay the body in the tomb. Among the onlookers are El Greco himself and Cervantes. The Museo de El Greco (☎ 925 22 40 46; Calle Samuel Leví; admission €2.40; ☉ 10am-2pm & 4-6pm Tue-Sat, 10am-2pm Sun, until 9pm summer Tue-Sat) is nearby, with around two dozen of the master's minor works, although it, too, was closed for restoration at the time of research.

You're now in the heart of the judería (Toledo's old Jewish Quarter). Here, the Sinagoga

del Tránsito (☎ 925 22 36 65; Calle Samuel Leví; adult/child €2.40/1.20; ☉ 10am-2pm & 4-9pm Tue-Sat Mar-Nov, 10am-2pm & 4-6pm Tue-Sat Dec-Feb) should on no account be missed. Built in 1355 by special permission of Pedro I (construction of synagogues was by then prohibited in Christian Spain), the rich *mudéjar* decoration in the main prayer hall has been expertly restored. It's now the Museo Sefardí, which provides an insight into the history of Jewish culture in Spain.

A short way northwest, the Sinagoga de Santa María La Blanca (☎ 925 22 72 57; Calle de los Reyes Católicos 4; admission €1.90; ☉ 10am-6pm Nov-Mar, 10am-7pm Apr-Oct) is less grand but definitely worthwhile for its 29 horseshoe arches. Further along Calle de los Reyes Católicos is the imposing Iglesia San Juan de los Reyes (☎ 925 22 38 02; Plaza de San Juan de los Reyes; admission €1.90; ☉ 10am-6pm Oct-Mar, 10am-6.45pm Apr-Sep), a fine Franciscan monastery and church with tranquil cloisters and the chains of Christian prisoners liberated in Granada dangling from the walls.

For a glimpse of Muslim Toledo, head to the Mezquita del Cristo de la Luz (☎ 925 25 41 91; Cuesta de los Carmelitas Descalzas 10; admission €1.90; ☉ 10am-2pm & 3.30-6pm Oct-Mar, until 7pm Apr-Sep). During Muslim rule, there were 10 mosques in the city; this one, quite beautiful, is typical of its style and is the only one that remains.

INFORMATION

Policía Nacional (☎ 092; Plaza de la Ropería)

Main Post Office (☎ 925 49 04 21; Calle de la Plata 1; ☉ 8.30am-8.30pm Mon-Fri, 9.30am-2pm Sat)

Main Tourist Office (☎ 925 25 40 30; www.t-descubre.com; Plaza del Ayuntamiento; ☉ 10.30am-2.30pm Mon, 10.30am-2.30pm & 4.30-7pm Tue-Sun) Across from the cathedral.

Tourist Office (☎ 925 22 08 43; Carretera de Madrid; ⌚ 9am-6pm Mon-Fri, 9am-7pm Sat, 9am-3pm Sun) Outside the Puerta Nueva de Bisagra.

EATING

Of Toledo's specialities, *cuchifritos* (a potpourri of lamb, tomato and egg cooked in white wine with saffron) is especially good, while *carcamusa* (a pork dish) is also popular. Otherwise, it's good, hearty Castilian fare.

Hierbabuena (☎ 925 22 39 24; Calle de Navalpino 45; meals €35-40; ⌚ lunch & dinner Mon-Sat, lunch only Sun) Expensive but imaginatively classy, Hierbabuena is a dress-for-dinner restaurant serving food that's a cut above the usual traditional cooking with plenty of steaks, pâté and tasty meals.

Gambrinus (☎ 925 21 44 40; Calle de Santo Tomé; raciones €5-14, menú del día €9.50) As good for a meal as for beer and tapas, this place has pleasant outdoor tables and it does Tex-Mex if you're after something a little more spicy.

Ñaca Ñaca (Plaza de Zocodover; bocadillos €2.50-4; ⌚ 9am-11pm Mon-Thu, 9am-4am Fri, 9am-6am Sat, 11am-11pm Sun) This place is good for chunky *bocadillos* (filled rolls) deep into the night.

Convento San Antonio (☎ 925 22 40 47; Plaza San Antonio 1; ⌚ 11.15am-1.30pm & 4-6pm) The Franciscan nuns here sell their sweet speciality, *corazones de San Antonio* (San Antonio hearts) for €8 a box.

DRINKING

Cervecería 1700 (☎ 925 22 25 60; Plaza de las Tendillas 1; ⌚ 10am-11pm Mon-Sat) The tables of this relaxed beer bar spill out onto the cobblestones and it serves decent tapas to accompany your drink.

La Venta del Alma (☎ 925 25 42 45; Carretera de Piedrabuena 35; ⌚ 3.30pm-2am Sun-Thu, 3.30pm-6am Fri & Sat) Mild-mannered during the day, La Venta del Alma really gets going on Friday and Saturday. It's just outside the city; cross Puente de San Martín, turn left up the hill and it's 200m up on your left.

Pícaro (☎ 925 22 13 01; Calle de las Cadenas 6; ⌚ 4pm-2.30am Sun-Wed, 4pm-6am Thu-Sat) Pícaro is a popular café-*teatro* (theatre) serving an eclectic range of *copas* (drinks) and there's live music every Friday night. It really gets going after 2.30am on weekends.

SLEEPING

Toledo's charms can be diminished somewhat when it's overwhelmed by tour groups, so staying after dusk rewards those eager to experience the city when it returns to the locals and the streets take on a brooding, otherworldly air.

Hostal Casa de Cisneros (☎ 925 22 88 28; www.hostal -casa-de-cisneros.com; Calle del Cardinal Cisneros s/n; d Sun-Thu/Fri & Sat €60/75) Just across from the cathedral, this upmarket *hostal* is built on the site of an 11th-century Muslim palace, which is visible through the lobby floor. The rooms are decked out in stone and pretty wood beams and have renovated bathrooms.

La Posada de Manolo (☎ 925 28 22 50; www .laposadademanolo.com; Calle de Sixto Ramón Parro 8; s €42-50, d €72-85) This boutique hotel has themed each floor with furnishings and décor reflecting one of the 'three cultures' of Toledo. The views of the old city and cathedral from the rooftop terrace are stunning.

Parador Nacional Conde de Orgaz (☎ 925 22 18 50; www.parador.es; s/d from €115/160, d with views from €185) High above the southern bank of the Río Tajo, Toledo's parador boasts a classy interior and breathtaking views of the city.

SEGOVIA

Strewn with monuments and filled with life, this beautiful town was inscribed on Unesco's World Heritage List for its extraordinary Roman aqueduct, fine medieval monuments, fairytale *alcázar* and lovely setting amid the rolling hills of Castile.

Segovia has always had a whiff of legend about it. Perhaps it's because some city historians have claimed that Segovia was founded by Hercules or by the son of Noah. It may also have something to do with the fact that nowhere else in Spain has such a stunning monument to Roman grandeur survived in the heart of a vibrant modern city. Or maybe it's because art really has imitated life Segovia style – Walt Disney is said to have modelled Sleeping Beauty's Castle in California's Disneyland on Segovia's *alcázar*. Whatever it is, the effect is stunning with a city of warm terracotta and sandstone hues set against the backdrop of the often-snowcapped Sierra de Guadarrama.

The medieval walled city is in the far western corner of modern Segovia. The 11th-century walls stretch from the Roman aqueduct to the *alcázar* on the edge of town, encompassing just about everything worth seeing in a short visit. Two major plazas, the Plaza del Azoguejo near the aqueduct and the Plaza Mayor by the cathedral, are the nerve centres of the city. The

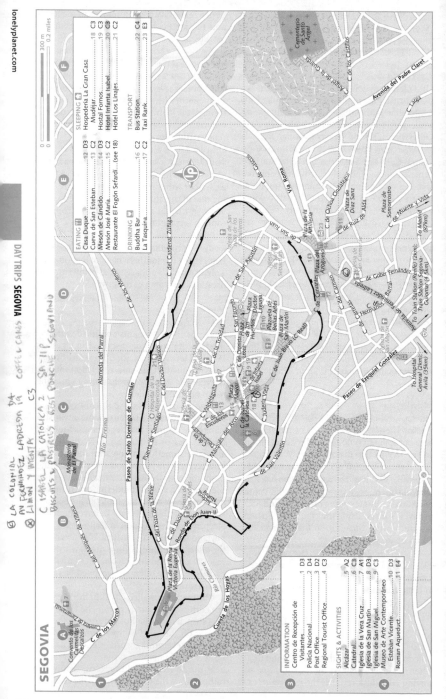

SEGOVIA

Ⓔ LA COLONIAL
AV FERNANDEZ LADREDA 14
BISCUITS & PASTRIES, BEST QUICHE SEGOVIANO

Ⓒ ISABEL LA CATOLICA 2   SA-110
ⓧ LIMON Y MENTA   C3

EATING 🍴
Casa Duque..........................12 D3
Cueva de San Esteban.............13 C2
Mesón de Cándido...................14 D3
Mesón José María.....................15 C2
Restaurante El Fogón Sefardí...(see 18)

DRINKING 🍷
Buddha Bar..........................16 C2
La Tasquina.........................17 C2

SLEEPING 🛏
Hospedería La Gran Casa............18 C3
Mudéjar.............................19 C3
Hostal Fornos.......................20 C3
Hotel Infanta Isabel................21 C2

TRANSPORT 🚌
Bus Station.........................22 C4
Taxi Rank...........................23 E3

INFORMATION
Centro de Recepción de
 Visitantes............................1 D3
Policía Nacional.......................2 D4
Post Office...........................3 D2
Regional Tourist Office...............4 C3

SIGHTS & ACTIVITIES
Alcázar...............................5 A2
Catedral..............................6 C3
Iglesia de la Vera Cruz...............7 A1
Iglesia de San Martín.................8 D3
Iglesia de San Miguel.................9 C3
Museo de Arte Contemporáneo........10 D3
Roman Aqueduct.......................11 E4

0   300 m
0   0.2 miles

246

lively commercial streets of Calle de Cervantes and Calle de Juan Bravo (together referred to as 'Calle Real') serve as the main artery connecting the two plazas.

Start your visit at the Roman aqueduct (El Acueducto), an 894m-long engineering wonder that looks like an enormous comb plunged into Segovia. It's 28m-high, has 163 arches and was built without a drop of mortar, just good old Roman know-how using more than 20,000 uneven granite blocks. It was most probably built around AD 50 to bring water to the Roman settlement from 18km away. The aqueduct's pristine condition is attributable to a major restoration project in the 1990s.

From the Plaza del Azoguejo, climb Calle Real into the ancient heart of Segovia, passing the sunny Plaza de San Martín, crowned with the lovely 13th-century Romanesque Iglesia de San Martín (☉ before & after Mass), with a *mudéjar* tower and arched gallery. The interior boasts a Flemish Gothic chapel. Well worth a brief detour is the Museo de Arte Contemporáneo Esteban Vicente (☎ 921 46 20 10; www.museoestebanvicente.es; Plazuela de las Bellas Artes; admission €2.40, free Thu; ☉ 11am-2pm & 4-7pm Tue & Wed, 11am-2pm & 4-8pm Thu & Fri, 11am-8pm Sat, 11am-3pm Sun), which showcases modern artworks in a 15th-century palace of Enrique IV, complete with Renaissance chapel and *mudéjar* ceiling.

Calle de Isabel la Católica leads to the shady, elongated Plaza Mayor, which is adorned by a fine pavilion. At the western end of the plaza the Catedral (☎ 921 46 22 05; Plaza Mayor; admission €3; ☉ 9.30am-5.30pm Oct-Mar, 9.30am-6.30pm Apr-Sep) towers over the plaza. Completed in 1577, 50 years after its Romanesque predecessor had been destroyed in the revolt of the Comuneros, the cathedral is one of the most homogenous Gothic churches in Spain. The austere, three-naved interior is delicate and refined, with a handful of side chapels, a fine choir stall and

THE DEVIL'S WORK

Although no-one really doubts that the Romans built the aqueduct, a local legend asserts that two millennia ago a young girl, tired of carrying water from the well, voiced a willingness to sell her soul to the devil if an easier solution could be found. No sooner said than done. The devil worked throughout the night, while the girl recanted and prayed to God for forgiveness. Hearing her prayers, God sent the sun into the sky earlier than usual, catching the devil unawares with only a single stone lacking to complete the structure. The girl's soul was saved, but it seems like she got her wish anyway. Perhaps God didn't have the heart to tear down the aqueduct.

stained-glass windows dating from the 1600s. You can visit the cloister and museum, with its fantastic collection of sacred art and 17th-century Belgian tapestries. The smaller Iglesia de San Miguel recedes humbly into the shadows by comparison to the cathedral, despite its historical significance – Isabel was crowned Queen of Castile in this small church.

From the Plaza Mayor head down Calle Marqués del Arco to reach the fortified alcázar (☎ 921 46 07 59; www.alcazardesegovia.com; Plaza de la Reina Victoria Eugenia; admission €4, tower €2, free 3rd Tue month for EU citizens; ☉ 10am-6pm Oct-Mar, 10am-7pm Apr-Sep), a fairytale castle perched dramatically on the western edge of Segovia. Fortified since Roman times, the site takes its name from the Arabic *al-qasr* (castle), but what you see today is a reconstruction of a 13th-century structure that burned to the ground in 1862. Inside is an interesting collection of armour and military gear, but even better are the 360-degree views from the *alcázar's* tower overlooking the hills and pastures of Castile.

From here you can make out one of Segovia's most interesting churches, the 12-sided

TRANSPORT: SEGOVIA

Distance from Madrid **90km**

Direction **Northwest**

Car From Madrid, take the A-6 motorway to the N-603 national highway, which will take you to the city centre. Driving time is 1¼ hours.

Bus Buses of La Sepulvedana (☎ 921 42 77 07; Paseo de Ezequiel González) leave every half-hour from Madrid's Paseo de la Florida bus stop and arrive in Segovia's central bus station ½ hours later. Tickets cost €5.87.

Train There are two options by train, both operated by Renfe (☎ 902 240 202; www.renfe.es). Up to nine normal trains run daily from Madrid to Segovia (two hours, one way €5.90), leaving you at the main train station 2.5km from the aqueduct. The faster option is the high-speed AVE (35 minutes, one way €9), which deposits you at the new Segovia-Guiomar station, 5km from the aqueduct.

Iglesia de la Vera Cruz (Church of the True Cross; ☎ 921 43 14 75; Carretera de Zamarramala; admission €1.75; ⊙ 10.30am-1.30pm & 3.30-7pm Tue-Sun Mar-Aug; 10.30am-1.30pm & 4-6pm Tue-Sun Sep-Feb), built in the 13th century following the floor plan of the Church of the Holy Sepulchre in Jerusalem. A relic of what was said to be the 'true cross' was once housed in the church. For great views of the town and countryside, hike uphill behind the church.

INFORMATION

Centro de Recepción de Visitantes (Tourist Office; ☎ 921 466 720; www.turismodesegovia.com; Plaza del Azoguejo 1; ⊙ 10am-7pm Sun-Fri, 10am-8pm Sat)

Policía Nacional (☎ 091; Paseo de Ezequiel González 22; ⊙ 24hr)

Post Office (☎ 921 461 616; Plaza Doctor Laguna 5; ⊙ 8.30am-8.30pm Mon-Fri, 9am-2pm Sat)

Regional Tourist Office (☎ 921 460 334, 902 203 030; www.turismocastillayleon.com; Plaza Mayor 10; ⊙ 9am-2pm & 5-8pm mid-Sep–June, 9am-8pm Sun-Thu, 9am-9pm Fri & Sat Jul–mid-Sep)

EATING

If you love your meat, you'll love Segovia. People come here from all over Spain for delicious *cochinillo asado* (roasted suckling pig) and *asado de cordero* (roasted lamb). Reservations are highly recommended, especially on weekends.

Casa Duque (☎ 921 46 24 87; www.restauranteduque.es; Calle de Cervantes 12; menú del día €21-39.50; ⊙ lunch & dinner daily) This place has been serving suckling pig (€19) since the 1890s and long ago mastered the art. For the uninitiated, try its *menú segoviano* (€31), which includes *cochinillo*, or the *menú gastronómico* (€39.50), which gives a taste of many local specialities. Downstairs is the informal *cueva* (cave), where you can get tapas and yummy *cazuelas* (stews).

Mesón de Cándido (☎ 921 42 59 11; www.mesondecandido.es; Plaza del Azoguejo 5; meals €30-40; ⊙ lunch & dinner daily) Set in a delightful 18th-century building in the shadow of the aqueduct, Mesón del Cándido is famous throughout Spain for its suckling pig and roast lamb.

Mesón José María (☎ 921 46 11 11; www.rtejosemaria.com, in Spanish; Calle del Cronista Lecea 11; meals €30-40; ⊙ lunch & dinner daily) Close to Plaza Mayor, this *mesón* offers great tapas in the bar and five dining rooms serving exquisite *cochinillo* (€21.35) and other local specialities.

Cueva de San Esteban (☎ 921 46 09 82; www.lacuevadesanesteban.com, in Spanish; Calle Valdeláguila 15; meals €35; ⊙ 11am-midnight) One of the only restaurants in Segovia not devoted to suckling pig, this popular spot focuses on seasonal dishes, with a few Galician treats and an excellent wine list.

Restaurante El Fogón Sefardí (☎ 921 46 62 50; www.lacasamudejar.com; Calle de Isabel La Católica 8; meals €30-40; ⊙ lunch & dinner daily) This place serves Sephardi cuisine in a restaurant with an intimate patio or a splendid dining hall with original, 15th-century *mudéjar* flourishes. There are also cheaper Sephardi tapas in the bar downstairs, as well as *cochinillo* in the main restaurant.

DRINKING

By night, head for Calle de Infanta Isabel, which is known locally as the 'Calle de los Bares' (Street of the Bars). This is the destination for serious drinking, cheap eating and merriment all around.

La Tasquina (☎ 921 461 954; Calle de Valdeláguila 3; ⊙ 9pm-late) Just off Plaza Mayor, this wine bar spills out onto the footpath and you can get good wines, *cavas* (sparkling wines) and cheeses.

Buddha Bar (Calle de los Escuderos; ⊙ 9pm-late) Located on another lively bar-filled street in the area, Buddha Bar has lounge music that can turn more towards house as the night wears on.

SLEEPING

You can get a taste of Segovia as a day trip from Madrid, but there are outstanding hotel choices if you'd like to linger longer.

Hospedería La Gran Casa Mudéjar (☎ 921 46 62 50; www.lacasamudejar.com; Calle de Infanta Isabel 8; d €60-160) Spread over two buildings, this place has been magnificently renovated, blending genuine, 15th-century *mudéjar* ceilings with modern amenities. In the newer wing, where the building dates from the 19th century, the rooms on the top floors have fine mountain views out over the rooftops of Segovia's old Jewish quarter.

Hostal Fornos (☎ 921 46 01 98; www.hostalfornos.com, in Spanish; Calle de Infanta Isabel 13; s €34-41, d €48-55) This tidy little hostel has a cheerful air thanks to its tasteful rooms, which have that fresh white-linen-and-wicker-chair look. Some are a bit larger than others, but the value is unimpeachable.

Hotel Los Linajes (☎ 921 46 04 75; www.hotelloslinajes
.com; Calle del Doctor Valesco 9; s €66-78, d €89-106) For
some of the best views in Segovia, Hotel Los
Linajes is exceptionally good. The rooms are
large, filled with character and all look out
onto the hills; many also have cathedral and/
or *alcázar* views.

Hotel Infanta Isabel (☎ 921 46 13 00; www
.hotelinfantaisabel.com; Plaza Mayor 12; s €64-128, d €83-128)
Sitting right on Plaza Mayor, this charming
hotel is a fine choice. The colonnaded building provides some hint to the hotel's interior,
where the large rooms have period furnishings
and plenty of character. Those with balconies
overlooking the Plaza Mayor are the best.

ÁVILA

The walled city of Ávila is one of Spain's most
spectacular skylines. This is also a deeply religious city of pilgrims and churches, a city
whose austere architecture and hearty cuisine
fortifies the inhabitants against the elements
in the same way that the walls have always
protected Ávila against the armies that buf-
feted the city down through the centuries.
As such Ávila is the essence of Castile, the
epitome of old Spain.

Medieval kingdoms battled over Ávila for
centuries and each ruler in his turn reinforced
the city until it reached its current, stunning
manifestation of eight monumental gates, 88
watchtowers and more than 2500 turrets (to
protect archers); the walls are illuminated to
magical effect at night. If you're here in winter
when an icy wind whistles in off the plains, it
can seem as if the walls were built to protect
the city from the harsh Castilian climate –
Ávila is one of the highest and windiest cities
in Spain and winters can be bitterly cold –
with the old city huddling behind the high
stone walls. Within the walls, Ávila can appear
as if caught in a time warp. Its many churches,
convents and high-walled palaces, all built of
sombre stone, date back to the city's golden
age, the 15th century, when the city's defining
figure, Santa Teresa (see boxed text, below), was
born. Shortly after her death in 1582, the city's
fortunes began a downward spiral that ended
in its economic ruin; Ávila has only recently
shaken off its slumber.

The Catedral (☎ 920 21 16 41; Plaza de la Catedral;
admission €4; ☼ 10am-7pm Mon-Fri, 10am-8pm Sat, noon-
6pm Sun Jun-Sep, shorter hours rest of year) is embedded
in the eastern wall of the old city. Although
the main façade hints at the cathedral's 12th-
century, Romanesque origins, the church was
finished 400 years later in a predominantly
Gothic style, making it the first Gothic church
in Spain. The grey, sombre façade betrays

IN THE FOOTSTEPS OF SANTA TERESA

Probably the most important woman in the history of the Catholic church in Spain, Santa Teresa spent most of her life in
Ávila. From the convent, plaza and gate that bear her name to the sweet *yemas de Santa Teresa* (yummy biscuits made
with egg yolk and supposedly invented by the saint) her trail seems to cover every inch of the city.

Teresa de Cepeda y Ahumada – a Catholic mystic and reformer – was born in Ávila on 28 March 1515, one of 10
children of a merchant family. Raised by Augustinian nuns after her mother's death, she joined the Carmelite order at
age 20. After her early, undistinguished years as a nun, she was shaken by a vision of Hell in 1560, which crystallised
her true vocation: she would reform her order.

With the help of many supporters Teresa founded convents of the Carmelitas Descalzas (Shoeless Carmelites) all over
Spain. She also co-opted San Juan de la Cruz (St John of the Cross) to begin a similar reform in the masculine order, a
task that earned him several stints of incarceration by the mainstream Carmelites. Santa Teresa's writings were first
published in 1588 and proved enormously popular, perhaps partly for their earthy style. She died in 1582 in Alba de
Tormes, where she is buried. She was canonised by Pope Gregory XV in 1622.

After a visit to the Convento de Santa Teresa (☎ 920 21 10 30; Plaza de la Santa; museum/relic room/church
€2/free/free; ☼ museum 10am-1.30pm & 3.30-5.30pm Nov-Mar, 10am-2pm & 4-7pm Tue-Sun Apr-Oct-7pm, relic
room 9.30am-1.30pm & 3.30-7.30pm Tue-Sun, church 8.45am-1.30pm & 3.30-9pm Tue-Sun), you can pop into the
nearby Iglesia de San Juan Bautista (☎ 920 21 11 27; Plaza de la Victoria; admission free; ☼ before & after Mass),
where she was baptised. The first convent she founded, Convento de San José (☎ 920 22 21 27; Calle del Duque de
Alba; admission €1.20; ☼ 10am-1.30pm & 3-6pm Nov-Mar, ☼ 10am-1.30pm & 4-7pm Apr-Oct), is here, too, and you
can visit its small museum packed with Teresa artefacts and memorabilia. To see a replica of her monastic cell, head to
the Monasterio de la Encarnación (☎ 920 21 12 12; Paseo de la Encarnación; admission €1.70; ☼ 9.30am-1.30pm
& 3.30-6pm Mon-Fri, 10am-1pm & 4-6pm Sat & Sun, closing time 1hr later May-Sep) outside the city walls where she
lived and worked for 27 years.

ÁVILA

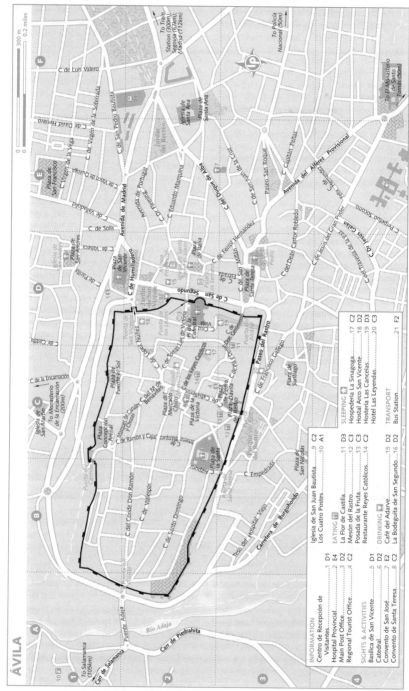

some unhappy 18th-century meddling in the main portal, but within are rich walnut choir stalls, a dazzling altar painting begun by Pedro de Berruguete showing the life of Jesus in 24 scenes and a long, narrow central nave that makes the soaring ceilings seem all the more majestic. The cloisters, sacristy and small museum are superb; the latter includes a painting by El Greco.

Among Ávila's highlights are splendid 12th-century walls (murallas; ☎ 920 21 13 87; admission €2.50/4), which rank among the world's best-preserved medieval defensive perimeters. At the time of writing, the two access points are at the Puerta del Alcázar (11am-6pm Tue-Sun Oct-Apr, 11am-8pm Tue-Sun May-Sep) and the Puerta de los Leales (Casa de las Carnicerías; 10am-6pm Tue-Sun Oct-Apr, 10am-8pm Tue-Sun May-Sep), which allow walks of 300m and 800m respectively; the same ticket allows you to climb both sections of the wall. By the time you read this, a third section of the wall from Puerta del Carmen to Puerta del Puente should have opened. The most impressive gates are the Puerta de San Vicente and Puerta del Alcázar, which are flanked by towers more than 20m high and stand on either side of the cathedral's apse. The last tickets are sold 45 minutes before closing time.

From close to the Plaza de la Catedral, the pedestrianised Calle de los Reyes Católicos, which is lined with shops and bars, runs down into the pretty Plaza del Mercado Chico. Southwest of the plaza, the Convento de Santa Teresa is even more beloved by locals and pilgrims than the cathedral because it was built on the site where Santa Teresa was born. This church was built in 1636 and today you can see its simple interior and the gold-smothered chapel that sits atop Teresa's former bedroom, though more interesting are the relics (including a piece of the saint's ring finger!) and the small museum about her life.

So much of Ávila's religious architecture is brooding and sombre, but the graceful Basílica de San Vicente (☎ 920 25 52 30; admission €1.20; 10am-1.30pm & 4-6pm) is a masterpiece of the subdued elegance of the Romanesque style. Work started in the 11th century, supposedly on the site where three martyrs – San Vicente and his sisters – were slaughtered by the Romans in the early 4th century. Their canopied sepulchre is an outstanding piece of Romanesque with nods to the Gothic.

Just northwest of the city on the road to Salamanca, Los Cuatro Postes affords the finest views of Ávila's walls; it marks the place where Santa Teresa and her brother were caught by their uncle as they tried to run away from home. They were hoping to achieve martyrdom at the hands of the Muslims.

INFORMATION

Centro de Recepción de Visitantes (Tourist Office; ☎ 902 102 121; www.avilaturismo.com; Avenida de Madrid 39; 10am-6pm Nov-Mar, 9am-8pm Apr-Oct)

Hospital Provincial (☎ 920 35 72 00; Calle de Jesús del Gran Poder 42; 24hr)

Main Post Office (☎ 920 31 35 06; Plaza de la Catedral 2; 8.30am-8.30pm Mon-Fri, 9.30am-2pm Sat)

Policía Nacional (☎ 091; Paseo San Roque 34; 24hr)

Regional Tourist Office (☎ 920 21 13 87; www .turismocastillayleon.com; Plaza de Pedro Dávila 4; 9am-2pm & 5-8pm mid-Sep–Jun, 9am-8pm Sun-Thu, 9am-9pm Fri & Sat Jul–mid-Sep) Run by the Castilla y León regional government.

EATING

Ávila is famous for its *chuleton de avileño* (T-bone-steak) and *judías del barco de Ávila* (white beans, usually with chorizo, in a thick sauce).

Mesón del Rastro (☎ 920 21 12 19; Plaza del Rastro 1; menú del día €20; lunch & dinner Thu-Sat, lunch only Sun-Wed) The dining room at Mesón del Rastro,

---

TRANSPORT: ÁVILA

Distance from Madrid 101km

Direction West

Car From Madrid, take the A-6 motorway northwest, then take the N-110 west. Driving time is around one hour; the toll costs €6.85.

Bus Up to nine buses run by Larrea/La Sepulvedana (☎ 902 222 282; www.lasepulvedana.es, in Spanish) connect Madrid's Estación Sur and Ávila (1hr 20 mins, €7.09) from Monday to Friday, with around five daily on weekends. Contact the bus station (☎ 920 25 65 05; Avenida de Madrid 2) for more information.

Train The company Renfe (☎ 902 240 202; www.renfe.es) has up to 30 trains to Ávila daily. The trip takes up to two hours (one way from €6.50), although the occasional train runs express, takes 1¼ hours and costs €8.40.

with its dark-wood beams, announces immediately that this is a bastion of Castilian cooking. Expect hearty, delicious mainstays, such as *chuleton de avileño* (€13), *judias del barco de Ávila* (€7) and *cordero asado* (roast lamb; €15).

Restaurante Reyes Católicos (☎ 920 25 56 27; Calle de los Reyes Católicos 6; meals €25-35, menú del día €16.90; ☽ lunch & dinner daily) Most *asadors* (restaurants serving roasted meats) in Ávila are old-school with dark, wood-panelled dining areas, whereas this slick, modern restaurant is a refreshing change. The cuisine offers a mix of traditional and fusion dishes. The restaurant has a range of set menus (€18 to €48) in addition to the *menú del día*; at lunchtime from Monday to Friday, don't be shy to ask for the latter even as it tries to steer you towards à la carte choices.

Posada de la Fruta (☎ 920 22 09 84; Plaza de Pedro Dávila 8; meals €10-18; ☽ lunch & dinner daily) Simple, informal meals can be had at the café-bar in a light-filled, covered courtyard, while the traditional *comedor* (dining room) serves *menús* (fixed-price meals) and à la carte dishes.

La Flor de Castilla (☎ 920 25 28 66; Calle de San Gerónimo; ☽ 10am-2pm & 5-8pm Mon-Sat) This is a fine place to buy the *yema de Santa Teresa*, a sticky ultrasweet biscuit made of egg yolk and sugar, which is said to have been invented by the saint.

DRINKING

La Bodeguita de San Segundo (☎ 920 22 59 17; www .vinoavila.com, in Spanish; Calle de San Segundo 19; ☽ 11am-midnight Thu-Tue) This gem of a wine and tapas bar is standing-room only most nights and more tranquil in the quieter afternoon hours. The setting in the 16th-century Casa de la Misericordia is superb and the wines here are excellent.

Café del Adarve (Calle de San Segundo 40; ☽ 5pm-late) About as lively as Ávila gets, Café del Adarve has quirky décor, weekend DJs and occasional live music during winter.

SLEEPING

Given that Ávila nights can be pretty quiet, the only real reason to linger after dark (or overnight) is to catch a glimpse of the city's walls lit up like in a fairytale.

Hospedería La Sinagoga (☎ 920 35 23 21; lasinagoga@ vodafone.es; Calle de los Reyes Católicos 22; s/d/tr from €53/74/106) This delightful little hotel incorpo-rates details from Ávila's main 15th-century synagogue with bright, spacious rooms. Rates for doubles can drop to as low as €42 on weekdays in winter.

Hostal Arco San Vicente (☎ 920 22 24 98; www .arcosanvicente.com; Calle de López Núñez 6; s €45-50, d €60-70) Another terrific option, this engaging *hostal* has lovely, brightly painted rooms and friendly owners. The location, just inside the city walls, is also a winner.

Hostería Las Cancelas (☎ 920 21 22 49, www.las cancelas.com; Calle de la Cruz Vieja 6; s/d/tr from €53/76/107; ☽ Feb-Dec) Tucked away behind the cathedral close to the Puerta del Alcázar, this place has large rooms with traditional furniture. The restaurant is equally good.

Hotel Las Leyendas (☎ 920 35 20 42; www.lasleyendas .es; Calle de Francisco Gallego 3; s €55-67, d €67-85) Occupying the house of 16th-century Ávila nobility, this intimate hotel is wonderful, with period touches (original wooden beams, exposed brickwork) wedded to modern amenities.

SAN LORENZO DE EL ESCORIAL

Home to the majestic monastery and palace complex of San Lorenzo de El Escorial (☎ 91 890 78 18; www.patrimonionacional.es; admission €8, free Wed for EU citizens, combined ticket with Valle de los Caídos €8.50; ☽ 10am-6pm Tue-Sun Apr-Sep, 10am-5pm Tue-Sun Oct-Mar), this one-time royal getaway rises up from the foothills of the mountains that shelter Madrid from the north and west. Although it attracts its fair share of foreign tourists, this prim little town is overflowing with quaint shops, restaurants and hotels (many of which close when things are quiet) that cater primarily to madrileños who are intent on escaping the city on weekends: the fresh, cool air, among other things, has been drawing city dwellers here since the complex was first built on the orders of King Felipe II in the 16th century. Admission to the basilica is free.

Several villages were razed to make way for the massive project, which included a monastic centre, a decadent royal palace and a mausoleum for Felipe's parents, Carlos I and Isabel. Architect Juan de Herrera oversaw the project.

The monastery's main entrance is to the west. Above the gateway a statue of St Lawrence stands watch, holding a symbolic gridiron, the instrument of his martyrdom (he was roasted alive on one). From here you'll first enter the

TRANSPORT: SAN LORENZO DE EL ESCORIAL

Distance from Madrid 59km

Direction Northwest

Car Take the A-6 motorway to the M-600 highway, then follow the signs to El Escorial. Driving time 40 minutes.

Bus Every 15 minutes (every half-hour on weekends), Herranz bus company (Map pp116–17; ☎ 91 896 90 28) runs a service (buses 661 and 664) to El Escorial from platform 30 of Madrid's Moncloa Intercambiador de Autobuses station. The one-hour trip costs €3.15.

Train A few dozen Renfe (☎ 902 240 202; www.renfe.es) C8 cercanía (local train network) trains make the one-hour trip (€2.45) daily from Madrid's Atocha or Chamartín stations to El Escorial.

Patio de los Reyes (Patio of the Kings), which houses the statues of the six kings of Judah.

Directly ahead lies the sombre basilica. As you enter, look up at the unusual flat vaulting by the choir stalls. Once inside the church proper, turn left to view Benvenuto Cellini's white Carrara marble statue of Christ crucified (1576).

You'll be led through rooms containing various treasures, including some tapestries and an El Greco painting – impressive as it is, it's a far cry from the artist's dream of decorating the whole complex – and then downstairs to the northeastern corner of the complex. You pass through the Museo de Arquitectura and the Museo de Pinturaf. The former tells (in Spanish) the story of how the complex was built, the latter contains a range of 16th- and 17th-century Italian, Spanish and Flemish art.

Head upstairs into a gallery around the eastern part of the complex known as the Palacio de Felipe II or Palacio de los Austrias. You'll then descend to the 17th-century Panteón de los Reyes (Crypt of the Kings), where almost all Spain's monarchs since Carlos I are interred. Backtracking a little, you'll find yourself in the Panteón de los Infantes (Crypt of the Princesses).

Stairs lead up from the Patio de los Evangelistas (Patio of the Gospels) to the Salas Capitulares (chapterhouses) in the southeastern corner of the monastery. These bright, airy rooms, whose ceilings are richly frescoed, contain a minor treasure chest of works by El Greco, Titian, Tintoretto, José de Ribera and Hieronymus Bosch (known as El Bosco to Spaniards).

Just south of the monastery is the Huerta de los Frailes (Friars Garden), which merits a stroll, while the Jardín del Príncipe, which leads down to the town of El Escorial (and the train station), contains the Casita del Príncipe, a little neo-Classical gem built under Carlos III for his heir, Carlos IV.

INFORMATION

Tourist Office (☎ 91 890 53 13; www.sanlorenzoturismo .org; Calle de Grimaldi 2; ⏰ 10am-6pm Mon-Fri, 10am-7pm Sat & Sun)

EATING

The tourist office's website has a list of restaurants and bars in town. These are two of our favourites.

La Cueva (☎ 91 890 15 16; www.mesonlacueva.com; Calle de San Antón 4; meals €35-40; ⏰ lunch & dinner Tue-Sun) Just a block back from the monastery complex, La Cueva has been around since 1768 and it shows in the heavy wooden beams and hearty, traditional Castilian cooking – roasted meats and steaks are the mainstays, with a few fish dishes.

La Fonda Genara (☎ 91 890 16 36; www.restaurante genara.com; Plaza de San Lorenzo 2; meals €35; ⏰ lunch & dinner daily) This is another bastion of traditional cooking, although here the décor is a little brighter. The kitchen is presided over by a father-son team, who make the odd concession to vegetarians.

VALLE DE LOS CAÍDOS

This extraordinary basilica and stone monument, the Valle de los Caídos (Valley of the Fallen; ☎ 91 890 55 44; www.patrimonionacional.es; Carretera 600; admission €5, combined ticket with El Escorial €8.50; ⏰ 10am-5pm Tue-Sat Oct-Mar, 10am-6pm Tue-Sat Apr-Sep), is built into the side of a mountain 15km north of San Lorenzo de El Escorial. Conceived in the grandiose imagination of the dictator Francisco Franco, it served as a memorial of the those who died during the Spanish Civil War (1936–39), though in reality it has always glorified Franco's side and was constructed by Franco's prisoners of war, many of whom died in the process. It has long been a pilgrimage site for the small reactionary rump of Franco supporters, who come here especially on November 20 – the anniversary of Franco's death – to reminisce about Franco's rule, complete with stiff-armed fascist salutes. Spain's Socialist government has plans to transform the site into a broader memorial.

The mammoth stone cross sits atop a bunker-like basilica dug into the mountainside in the middle of a pristine pine forest. Walking into the basilica, you enter into the heart of the mountain. Franco's body is interred by the altar, although given the unclear changes proposed for the site by the national government, no-one knows how long his body will remain there. Near the basilica are walking trails and a picnic area.

You can take a funicular (admission €2.50; ☒ 11am-4.30pm Tue-Sat Oct-Mar, 11am-5.30pm Tue-Sat Apr-Sep) up the mountain to the base of the cross, where, if the wind doesn't blow you away, you can enjoy great views of the surrounding sierra.

ARANJUEZ

Aranjuez was founded as a royal pleasure retreat, away from the riff-raff of Madrid, and it remains a place to escape the rigours of city life. The palace is opulent and its grandeur is amplified by its setting amid the greenery of lovely, expansive gardens.

The Palacio Real (☎ 91 892 15 32; www.patrimonionacional.es; child, senior & student/adult €2.50/5, EU citizens free Wed, gardens free; ☒ palace 10am-5.15pm Tue-Sun Oct-Mar, 10am-6.15pm Tue-Sun Apr-Sep, gardens 8am-6.30pm Tue-Sun Oct-Mar, 8am-8.30pm Tue-Sun Apr-Sep) started as one of Felipe II's modest summer palaces but took on a life of its own as a succession of royals, inspired by the palace at Versailles in France, lavished money upon it. By the 18th century, its 300-plus rooms had turned the palace into a sprawling, gracefully symmetrical complex filled with a cornucopia of ornamentation. Of all the rulers who spent time here, Carlos III and Isabel II left the greatest mark.

The obligatory guided tour (in Spanish) provides insight into the palace's art and history. And a stroll in the lush gardens takes you through a mix of local and exotic species, the product of seeds brought back by Spanish botanists and explorers from Spanish colonies all over the world. Within their shady perimeter, which stretches a few kilometres from the palace, you'll find the Casa de Marinos, which contains the Museo de Falúas (☎ 91 891 03 05; admission €2; ☒ 10am-5.15pm Oct-Mar, 10am-6.15pm Apr-Sep), a museum of royal pleasure boats from days gone by. If it has reopened after restoration, the Casa del Labrador (☎ 91 891 03 05; child, senior or student/adult €2.50/5) is also worth a visit. Further away, towards Chinchón, is the Jardín del Príncipe, an extension of the massive gardens. The Chiquitren (☎ 902 088 089; www.arantour.com; child/adult €3/5; ☒ 11am-5.30pm Tue-Sun Oct-Feb, 10am-8pm Tue-Sun Mar-Sep), a small tourist train, loops through town and stops at all the major sites.

INFORMATION

Tourist Office (☎ 91 891 04 27; www.aranjuez.es, in Spanish; Plaza de San Antonio 9; ☒ 10am-6.30pm Nov-Apr, 10am-8.30pm May-Oct)

EATING

Casa José (☎ 91 891 14 88; www.casajose.es; Calle de Abastos 32; meals €35-40; ☒ lunch & dinner Tue-Sat, lunch only Sun) The quietly elegant Casa José is the proud owner of a Michelin star and is packed on

THE STRAWBERRY TRAIN

You could take a normal train from Madrid to Aranjuez, but for romance it's hard to beat the *Tren de la Fresa* (Strawberry Train; ☎ 902 240 202, 902 228 822; adult/child return €24/16; ☻ late-March–mid-June). Begun in 1985 to commemorate the Madrid–Aranjuez route – Madrid's first and Spain's third rail line, which was inaugurated in the 1850s – the Strawberry Train is a throwback to the time when Spanish royalty would escape the summer heat and head for the royal palace at Aranjuez.

The journey begins at 10.05am on Saturday and Sunday between early April and late June when an antique Mikado 141F-2413 steam engine pulls out from Madrid's Atocha station, pulling behind it four passenger carriages that date from the early 20th century and have old-style front and back balconies. During the 50-minute journey, rail staff in period dress provide samples of local strawberries – one of the original train's purposes was to allow royalty to sample the summer strawberry crop from the Aranjuez orchards. Upon arrival in Aranjuez, your ticket fare includes a guided tour of the Palacio Real, Museo de Falúas and other Aranjuez sights, not to mention more strawberry samplings. The train leaves Aranjuez for Atocha at 6pm for the return journey.

Tickets can be purchased at any Renfe office or any travel agency that sells train tickets.

weekends with madrileños drawn by the beautifully prepared meats and local dishes with some surprising innovations.

El Rana Verde (☎ 91 891 13 25; www.aranjuez.com/ranaverde; Plaza Santiago Rusiñol; meals €25-35; ☻ lunch & dinner daily) The 'Green Frog' is a classic riverside restaurant whose speciality is frogs legs, but it does all sorts of local treats, including, of course, strawberries for dessert.

CHINCHÓN

Chinchón is just 45km from Madrid yet worlds apart. Although it has grown beyond its village confines, visiting its antique plaza is like stepping back into another era to a charming, ramshackle world. The heart of town is its unique, almost circular Plaza Mayor, which is lined with sagging, tiered balconies – it gets our vote as one of the most evocative plazas mayor in Spain. In summer the plaza is converted into a bullring (see boxed text, p240). It's also the stage for a popular passion play shown at Easter. Chinchón's other main attraction is made up of the traditional mesón-style restaurants scattered in and around the plaza, some with wonderful balcony tables.

There are a few other sights worth seeking out, particularly the 16th-century Iglesia de la Asunción that rises above the Plaza Mayor and the late-16th-century Renaissance Castillo de los Condes, which is about 1km south of Chinchón and which was abandoned in the 1700s; the tourist office has details of their irregular opening hours (usually weekends). But Chinchón's real charm lies in the Plaza Mayor and eating fine *cordero asado* (roast lamb).

INFORMATION

Tourist Office (☎ 91 893 53 23; www.ciudad-chinchon.com; Plaza Mayor 6; ☻ 10am-6pm Mon-Fri, 11am-3pm & 4-6pm Sat & Sun, longer hours summer) Small office but, staff are extremely helpful.

EATING

Café de la Iberia (☎ 91 894 08 47; www.cafedelaiberia.com; Plaza Mayor 17; meals €35-40; ☻ lunch & dinner Tue-Sun) This is definitely our favourite of the *mesones* (home-style restaurants) on the Plaza Mayor perimeter; it offers wonderful food served by attentive staff in an atmospheric dining area set around a light-filled internal courtyard or out on the balcony.

Mesón Cuevas del Vino (☎ 91 894 02 06; www.cuevasdelvino.com; Calle Benito Hortelano 13; meals €30-35, ☻ lunch & dinner Wed-Mon) From the huge goatskins filled with wine and the barrels covered in famous signatures, to the atmospheric caves underground, this is sure to be a memorable eating experience with delicious home-style cooking.

TRANSPORT: CHINCHÓN

Distance from Madrid 45km

Direction Southeast

Car Head out of Madrid on the N-IV motorway and exit onto the M-404, which winds its way to Chinchón.

Bus The La Veloz (Map pp126–7; ☎ 91 409 76 02) bus 337 leaves half-hourly to Chinchón. The buses leave from Avenida del Mediterráneo, 100m west of Plaza del Conde de Casal. The 50-minute ride costs €3.20.

ALCALÁ DE HENARES

So close to Madrid and just off an unappealing motorway, Alcalá de Henares is full of surprises with historical sandstone buildings seemingly at every turn. Throw in some sunny plazas and a legendary university, and Alcalá de Henares is a terrific place to go to escape the city.

The university (☎ 91 883 43 84; 6 free guided tours per day Mon-Fri, 11 per day Sat & Sun; ◯ 9am-9pm), founded in 1486 by Cardinal Cisneros, is one of the country's principal seats of learning. A guided tour gives a peek into the *mudéjar* chapel and the magnificent Paraninfo auditorium, where the King and Queen of Spain give out the prestigious Premio Cervantes literary award every year. The town is also dear to Spaniards because it is the birthplace of the country's literary figurehead, Miguel de Cervantes Saavedra (see p36). The site believed by many to be Cervantes' birthplace is recreated in the illuminating Museo Casa Natal de Miguel de Cervantes (☎ 91 889 96 54; www .museo-casa-natal-cervantes.org; Calle Mayor 48; admission free; ◯ 10am-6pm Tue-Sun Jun-Sep), which lies along the beautiful, colonnaded Calle de Mayor.

INFORMATION

Tourist Office (☎ 91 881 06 34; www.turismoalcala.com, in Spanish; Plaza de los Santos Niños; ◯ 10am-2pm & 5-7.30pm Jun-Sep, 10am-2pm & 4-6.30pm Oct-May)

EATING

El Ruedo (☎ 91 880 69 19; Calle de los Libreros 38; meals €20-25; ◯ 9am-11pm Thu-Tue) With a quiet patio for outdoor eating, this is a great place to get informal fare, such as salads and mixed plates.

Hostería del Estudiante (☎ 91 888 03 30; Calle de los Colegios 3; meals €30-35) Based in the parador, this charming restaurant has wonderful Castilian cooking and a classy ambience in a dining room decorated with artefacts from the city's illustrious history.

SIERRA DE GUADARRAMA

North of Madrid lies the Sierra de Guadarrama, a popular skiing destination and home of several charming towns. In Manzanares El Real you can explore the small 15th-century Castillo de los Mendoza (☎ 91 853 00 08; Manzanares El Real; admission incl guided tour €2; ◯ 10am-2pm & 3-6pm Tue-Sun Apr-Sep, 10am-5pm Tue-Sun Oct-Mar), a perfectly preserved storybook castle with round towers at its corners and a Gothic interior patio.

Cercedilla is a popular base for hikers and mountain bikers. There are several marked trails through the sierra, the main one known as the Cuerda Larga or Cuerda Castellana. This is a forest track that takes in 55 peaks between the Puerto de Somosierra in the north and Puerto de la Cruz Verde in the southwest. Get more information at the Centro de Información Valle de la Fuenfría. Small ski resorts, such as Valdesquí (☎ 91 570 12 24; Puerto de Cotos; lift tickets €25-34), welcome weekend skiers from the city.

INFORMATION

Ayuntamiento de Manzanares El Real (www.manzanares .org, in Spanish)

Centro de Información Valle de la Fuenfría (☎ 91 852 22 13; Carretera de las Dehesas; ◯ 10am-6pm) Located 2km outside Cercedilla on the M-614.

Navacerrada Tourist Information (☎ 902 882 328; www.puertonavacerrada.com, in Spanish)

TRANSPORT: ALCALÁ DE HENARES

Distance from Madrid 35km
Direction East
Car Head towards Zaragoza on the N-II highway. Driving time is 40 minutes.
Bus There are regular departures (every five to 15 minutes) from depots at the Avenida de América and Estación Sur. The trip takes about one hour (€1.55).
Train C1, C2 and C7 Renfe (☎ 902 240 202; www .renfe.es) *cercanía* trains make the 50-minute trip to Alcalá de Henares daily. The trip costs €1.15.

TRANSPORT: SIERRA DE GUADARRAMA

Distance from Madrid 50-70km
Direction North
Car Take the A-6 motorway to Cercedilla.
Bus Bus 724 runs to Manzanares El Real from Plaza de Castilla in Madrid (€2.75, 40 minutes). From Madrid's Intercambiador de Autobuses de Moncloa, bus 691 heads to Navacerrada (€2.75, one hour) and bus 684 runs to Cercedilla (€3.15, one hour).
Train From Chamartín station you can get to Puerto de Navacerrada (C8B *cercanía* line; €1.85, two hours with train change in Cercedilla, four daily) and Cercedilla (C2 *cercanía* line; €1.30, one hour 20 minutes, 15 daily).

DIY – GO FURTHER IN A DAY

Spain's ever-expanding network of super-fast AVE trains (Tren de Alta Velocidad España; known as *El Ave*) means that, for travellers short on time, many cities hundreds of kilometres from Madrid can now be visited as day trips from the capital, although we recommend longer stays if you have the time. For details, visit www.renfe.es.

The most obvious choice is Córdoba (one way from €46.20, less than two hours, up to 15 departures daily), a beautiful town of whitewashed patios, twisting old streets and the Mezquita de Córdoba, one of the architectural jewels in Andalucía's considerable crown. Córdoba lies 400km south of Madrid.

Other possibilities include Valladolid (one way from €31.20, one hour), which has a pretty Plaza Mayor and excellent museums, and Zaragoza (one way from €42.40, 1½ hrs) with its stunning architecture and incessant energy. Even Málaga (one way from €68, two hours), Sevilla (one way from €65.30, 2½ hours) and Barcelona (one way from €101.30, 2¾ hours) could be done in a day, although you'd have to be in an unconscionable rush. Although not yet covered by AVE, Salamanca (one way from €16.50, 2½ hours) is another possibility, but here you'd also be mad not to stay overnight, although it is possible with an early start.

All of these destinations are covered at length in Lonely Planet's *Spain* guide.

SIERRA POBRE

The 'Poor Sierra' is a toned-down version of its more refined western neighbour, the Sierra de Guadarrama. Popular with hikers and others looking for nature without quite so many creature comforts or crowds, the sleepy Sierra Pobre has yet to develop the tourism industry of its neighbours. And that's just why we like it.

Head first to Buitrago, the largest town in the area, where you can stroll along part of the old city walls. You can also take a peek into the 15th-century *mudéjar* and Romanesque Iglesia de Santa María del Castillo and into the small and unlikely Picasso Museum (☎ 91 868 00 56; Plaza Picasso; admission free; 11am-1.30pm & 4-6pm Wed-Mon), which contains a few works that the artist gave to his barber, Eugenio Arias.

Hamlets are scattered throughout the rest of the sierra; some, like Puebla de la Sierra and El Atazar, are pretty walks and are the starting point for winding hill trails.

TRANSPORT: SIERRA POBRE

Distance from Madrid **73km**
Direction **Northeast**
Car Take the N-I highway to Buitrago.
Bus The Continental Auto Company (☎ 91 745 63 00) has a dozen daily buses connecting Madrid's Plaza de la Castilla with Buitrago (€4.55, 1½ hours).

INFORMATION

Buitrago Tourist Office (☎ 91 868 16 15; 9am-3pm Jul-Sep)

EATING

El Arco (☎ 918 68 09 11; Calle Arco 6; mains €12-15; lunch only Fri-Sun mid-Sep–mid-Jun) The best restaurant in Buitrago, El Arco is known for its fresh, creative cuisine based on local ingredients and traditional Spanish dishes.

TRANSPORT

Getting to Madrid couldn't be easier with the city served by almost 100 airlines, excellent bus networks and trains that radiate into and out from the Spanish capital. The environmentally conscious also have an increasing number of options with the ongoing expansion of Spain's high-speed rail network – the early-2008 inauguration of the high-speed rail link between Madrid and Barcelona has brought Madrid that much closer to the rest of Europe.

Moving around the city is even simpler, with Madrid's extensive, modern metro system all you're likely to need. There are also plenty of buses, as well as reasonably priced taxis.

Flights, tours and rail tickets can be booked online at lonelyplanet.com.

AIR

Madrid's Barajas airport is Europe's fourth busiest hub, trailing only London-Heathrow, Paris Charles de Gaulle and Frankfurt, although it's rapidly closing in on the latter.

In addition to flights from the rest of Europe there are direct intercontinental flights from Asia, North and South America; some flights from North America involve a change at another major European hub en route.

Major low-cost airlines operating out of Madrid include easyJet, Air Berlin, Ryanair

THINGS CHANGE...

The information in this chapter is particularly vulnerable to change. Check directly with the airline or a travel agent to make sure you understand how a fare (and ticket you may buy) works and be aware of the security requirements for international travel. Shop carefully. The details given in this chapter should be regarded as pointers and are not a substitute for your own careful, up-to-date research.

and Vueling. These airlines work on a first-come, first-serve basis: the earlier you book a flight the less you pay. These no-frills airlines skip extras, such as in-flight meals (although you can buy snacks).

Domestic air travel can be expensive, but things are definitely changing. Iberia, Air Europa and Spanair, who once had a stranglehold over the market, now compete with many other international low-cost airlines on a limited number of domestic routes out of Madrid. Carriers and routes include easyJet (Oviedo, Fuerteventura, Ibiza, La Coruña and Lanzarote), Ryanair (Barcelona and Santander), Air Berlin (Palma de Mallorca) and Vueling (Barcelona, Canary Islands, Menorca, Santiago de Compostela and Jeréz).

CLIMATE CHANGE & TRAVEL

Climate change is a serious threat to the ecosystems that humans rely upon, and air travel is the fastest-growing contributor to the problem. Lonely Planet regards travel, overall, as a global benefit, but believes we all have a responsibility to limit our personal impact on global warming.

Flying & Climate Change

Pretty much every form of motor transport generates CO_2 (the main cause of human-induced climate change) but planes are far and away the worst offenders, not just because of the sheer distances they allow us to travel, but because they release greenhouse gases high into the atmosphere. The statistics are frightening: two people taking a return flight between Europe and the US will contribute as much to climate change as an average household's gas and electricity consumption over a whole year.

Carbon Offset Schemes

Climatecare.org and other websites use 'carbon calculators' that allow travellers to offset the greenhouse gases they are responsible for with contributions to energy-saving projects and other climate-friendly initiatives in the developing world – including projects in India, Honduras, Kazakhstan and Uganda.

Lonely Planet, together with Rough Guides and other concerned partners in the travel industry, supports the carbon offset scheme run by climatecare.org. Lonely Planet offsets all of its staff and author travel.

For more information check out our website: www.lonelyplanet.com.

Airlines

Increasingly airlines have abandoned their shopfront offices in Madrid so, in most cases, you'll have to go online, call the following numbers or contact a travel agent. The following are among the more popular airlines.

Aer Lingus (☎ 902 502 737; www.aerlingus.com)

Air Berlin (☎ 902 320 737; www.airberlin.com) German budget airline with flights to Madrid from around 20 cities across Western Europe.

Air Europa (☎ 902 401 501; www.aireuropa.com) Connects Madrid with Budapest, Milan, Prague, Paris, Rome, Warsaw and Venice, as well as destinations in Africa, the Caribbean, South America and dozens of Spanish airports.

Air France (☎ 902 207 090; www.airfrance.com)

Alitalia (☎ 902 100 323; www.alitalia.it)

American Airlines (☎ 902 115 570; www.aa.com) Flies to Madrid from New York and other US cities.

Austrian Airlines (☎ 902 257 000; www.aua.com)

British Airways (☎ 902 111 333; www.britishairways.com)

British Midlands (☎ 902 100 737; www.bmibaby.com) Connects Madrid to Birmingham and Manchester.

Cathay Pacific (☎ 91 296 04 16; www.cathaypacific.com) Flies Hong Kong–Madrid with connections throughout Asia.

Continental Airlines (☎ 900 961 266; www.continental.com) Daily flights to New York with connections to other US cities.

EasyJet (☎ 807 260 026; www.easyjet.com) Flies to Madrid from 18 European cities.

German Wings (☎ 91 625 97 04; www.germanwings.com) Flies to Madrid from Stuttgart.

Iberia (☎ 902 400 500; www.iberia.es)

KLM (☎ 902 222 747; www.klm.com)

Lufthansa (☎ 902 883 882; www.lufthansa.com)

Malev Hungarian Airlines (☎ 902 101 445; www.malev.hu)

MyAir.com (www.myair.com) Italian low-cost airline flying to Madrid from Bari and Milan.

Qatar Airways (☎ 902 627 070; www.qatarairways.com) Madrid–Doha and connections across the Middle East.

Royal Air Maroc (☎ 902 210 010; www.royalairmaroc.com)

Ryanair (☎ 807 220 032; www.ryanair.com) Flies to Madrid from 15 European airports.

Scandinavian SAS (☎ 802 112 117; www.flysas.es)

Spanair (☎ 902 131 415; www.spanair.com) Flights from dozens of destinations throughout Spain and Europe, as well as the US, Africa and Bangkok.

Swiss International Airlines (☎ 901 116 712; www.swiss.com)

TAP Air Portugal (☎ 901 116 718; www.flytap.com)

Thai Airways (☎ 91 782 05 21; www.thaiairways.com) Madrid–Bangkok with connections in Asia.

Transavia (☎ 902 010 105; www.transavia.com) Low-cost flights from Amsterdam to Madrid.

Turkish Airlines (☎ 902 111 235; www.turkishairlines.com)

Vueling (☎ 902 333 933; www.vueling.com) Spanish low-cost company with flights between Madrid and Amsterdam, Brussels, Lisbon, Valetta, Milan, Naples, Paris and Venice.

Airport

Madrid's Barajas airport (☎ 902 404 704; www.aena.es) lies 12km northeast of the city and every year more than 52 million passengers pass through here (double the number for 1998).

The airport's architecturally stunning Terminal 4 (T4) deals mainly with flights of Iberia and its partners (eg British Airways, American Airlines and Aer Lingus), while other intercontinental or non-Schengen European flights leave from T1. Spanair and Air Europa operate from both T1 and T2, depending on the destination. Air Berlin, Alitalia, Austrian Airlines, SAS and TAP Air Portugal also operate from T2. At the time of research only the tiny Lagun Air was operating out of T3. Iberia's Puente Aereo (air shuttle) between Madrid and Barcelona, which operates like a bus service with no advance booking necessary, operates from T4, while Spanair's equivalent

INTERNET AIR FARES

Most airlines, especially budget ones, encourage you to book on their websites. Other useful general sites to search for competitive fares include the following:

- www.atrapalo.com (in Spanish)
- www.cheaptickets.com
- www.despegar.com (in Spanish)
- www.ebookers.com
- www.expedia.com
- www.lowestfare.com
- www.opodo.com
- www.orbitz.com
- www.planesimple.co.uk
- www.rumbo.es (in Spanish)
- www.sta.com
- www.travel.com.au
- www.travelocity.com

GETTING INTO TOWN

Metro

The easiest way into town from the airport is line 8 of the metro (www.metromadrid.es, in Spanish; entrances in T2 and T4) to the Nuevos Ministerios transport interchange, which connects with lines 10 and 6 and the local overground *cercanías* (local trains serving suburbs and nearby towns). It operates from 6.05am to 2am. A single ticket costs €1 (10-ride Metrobús ticket €6.70); there's a €1 supplement if you're travelling from T4, including for those with a 10-ride ticket. The journey to Nuevos Ministerios takes around 15 minutes, around 25 minutes from T4.

Bus & Minibus

Alternatively from T1, T2 and T3 take bus 200 to/from the Intercambiador de Avenida de América (transport interchange on Avenida de América; Map p123). From T4 take bus 201, going to T4 take bus 204. The same ticket prices apply as for the metro. The first departures are at 5.20am. The last scheduled service from the airport is 11.30pm; buses leave every 12 to 15 minutes. There's also a free bus service connecting all four terminals.

AeroCITY (☎ 91 747 75 70; www.aerocity.com; Calle de Marzo 34) is a private minibus service that takes you door-to-door between central Madrid and the airport. Depending on the number of passengers (maximum of seven), the fare ranges from €5 to €17 per person. It operates 24 hours and you can book by phone or online.

Taxi

A taxi to the city centre will cost you around €25 in total (up to €35 from T4), depending on traffic and where you're going; in addition to what the meter says, you pay a €5.25 supplement. There are taxi ranks outside all four terminals.

service leaves from T3. For a full list of which airlines operate from which terminals visit www.esmadrid.com.

Although all airlines conduct check-in (*facturación*) at the airport's departure areas, some also allow check-in at the Nuevos Ministerios metro stop and transport interchange in Madrid itself – ask your airline. The service allows you to check your luggage in early, take the metro to the airport unburdened and avoid queues at the airport itself.

The T1 tourist office (☎ 91 305 86 56; 8am-8pm Mon-Sat, 9am-2pm Sun) is on the ground floor in the T1 area, while the T4 tourist office (☎ 902 100 007; 8am-8pm Mon-Sat, 9am-2pm Sun) is in the arrivals hall – both are run by the Comunidad de Madrid regional government. The Ayuntamiento (town hall) also runs an information booth (9.30am-8.30pm) in T4. There are ATMs and exchange booths in all terminals, and post offices (T1 8.30am-8.30pm Mon-Fri, 9.30am-1pm Sat, T4 8.30am-2.30pm Mon-Fri) in the arrivals lounges of T1 and T4. International car-rental companies have desks in the arrivals area of T1, T2 and T4.

There are three consignas (left-luggage offices; 24hr): one in T1 (near the bus stop and taxi stand); in T2 (near the metro entrance); and on the ground floor of T4. In either, you pay €3.60 for the first 24-hour period (or fraction thereof). Thereafter, it costs €4.64/4.13/3.61 per day in a big/medium/small locker. After

15 days the bag will be moved into storage (€1.85 plus a €37.08 transfer fee). For lost property in the airport, call ☎ 91 393 61 19 (T1) or ☎ 91 746 60 65 (T4).

Parking is available outside T1, T2 and T4. Rates are €1.95 per hour, up to €17.45 for 24 hours. Further away from the terminals and linked by a free shuttle bus is the Parking de Largas Estancias (Long-term Carpark; www.largaestancias.com; 1/2/5/10 days €10.20/20.40/48/74) if you plan to leave a vehicle for several days.

BICYCLE

Lots of people zip around town on *motos* (mopeds), but little has been done to encourage cyclists in Madrid and bike lanes are almost as rare as drivers who keep an eye out for cyclists.

You can transport your bicycle on the metro from 10am to 12.30pm and after 9pm Mondays to Fridays and all day on weekends and holidays. You can also take your bike aboard *cercanías* (local trains serving big cities, suburbs and nearby towns) from 10am onwards Monday to Friday and all day on weekends.

Bike Spain (p273) organises cycling tours of Madrid. It should also be your first stop for practical information and finding bike-friendly accommodation. The tourist office's Descubre Madrid (p273) programme of tours also includes cycling excursions.

Hire

There are plenty of places that hire bicycles. Recommended places:

Bike Spain (Map pp64–5; ☎ 91 559 06 53 www .bikespain.info; Plaza de la Villa 1, Calle del Codo; per half-/full day €10/15, Sat & Sun €25)

Karacol Sports (Map pp126–7; ☎ 91 539 96 33; www .karacol.es, in Spanish; Calle de Tortosa 8; per day €20; ⏰ 10.30am-3pm & 5-8pm Mon-Wed & Fri, 10.30am-3pm & 5-9.30pm Thu, 10.30am-2pm Sat; Ⓜ Atocha Renfe) Road bikes and mountain bikes. There's a refundable deposit of €50 and you need to leave an original document (passport, driving licence etc).

Trixi.com (Map pp64–5; ☎ 91 523 15 47; www.trixi.com; Calle de los Jardines 12; per 4/8/24 hr €8/12/15, helmet €2.50; ⏰ 10am-2pm & 4-8pm Mon-Fri, 10am-8pm Sat & Sun Mar-Oct, 10am-3pm daily Nov, Dec & Feb; Ⓜ Gran Vía)

Urban Movil (Map pp64–5; Calle Mayor 78; per hr/half-/full day €4.50/14/19)

BUS
Long Distance

Estación Sur de Autobuses (☎ 91 468 42 00; www .estaciondeautobuses.com, in Spanish; Calle de Méndez Álvaro 83; Ⓜ Méndez Álvaro), just south of the M-30 ring road, is the city's principal bus station. It serves most destinations to the south and many in other parts of the country. Most bus companies have a ticket office here, even if their buses depart from elsewhere.

The station operates a consigna (left-luggage office; ⏰ 6.30am-midnight) near where the buses exit the station. There are cafés, shops, exchange booths, a bank and a police post; there's also direct access to metro line 6.

Eurolines (www.eurolines.com), in conjunction with local carriers all over Europe, is the main international carrier connecting Spain to cities across Europe and Morocco from the Estación Sur. For information and tickets contact Eurolines Peninsular (☎ 902 405 040; www.eurolines .es). ALSA Internacional (☎ 902 422 242; www.alsa.es) is another international operator.

For domestic routes most services operate from the Estación Sur, although some services leave from other terminals around the city, including the Intercambiador de Autobuses de Moncloa (Map pp116–17) and the Intercambiador de Avenida de América (Map p123). Major companies:

ALSA (Map pp126–7; ☎ 902 422 242; www.alsa.es) A host of services throughout Spain. Most depart from Estación Sur but some buses headed north (including to Barcelona, Bilbao and Zaragoza) leave from the Intercambiador de Avenida de América.

AutoRes (☎ 902 020 052; www.auto-res.net) Services to Extremadura (eg Cáceres), Castilla y León (eg Salamanca and Zamora) and Valencia via Cuenca, as well as Lisbon, Portugal. All leave from the Estación Sur.

Herranz (Map pp116–17; ☎ 91 890 90 28; Intercambiador de Autobuses de Moncloa; Ⓜ Moncloa) Buses 661 and 664 to San Lorenzo de El Escorial from platform 30 at the Moncloa train station.

La Sepulvedana (Map pp126–7; ☎ 91 541 32 83, 91 559 89 55; www.lasepulvedana.es, in Spanish; Paseo de la Florida 11; Ⓜ Príncipe Pío) Buses to Segovia and La Granja de San Ildefonso.

La Veloz (Map pp126–7; ☎ 91 409 76 02; Avenida del Mediterráneo 49; Ⓜ Conde de Casal) Half-hourly buses (route 337) to Chinchón from 100m west of Plaza del Conde de Casal.

Madrid

Buses operated by Empresa Municipal de Transportes de Madrid (EMT; ☎ 902 507 850; www.emtmadrid .es) travel along most city routes regularly between about 6.30am and 11.30pm. Twenty-six night-bus *búhos* (owls) routes operate from midnight to 6am, with all routes originating in Plaza de la Cibeles. Fares for day and night trips are the same: €1 for a single trip, €6.70 for a 10-trip Metrobús ticket.

For details of the Madrid Visión sightseeing buses, see p273.

CAR & MOTORCYCLE

Madrid is 2622km from Berlin, 2245km from London, 1889km from Milan, 1836km from Paris, 1470km from Geneva, 690km from Barcelona and 610km from Lisbon. The A-1 heads north to Burgos and ultimately to Santander (for the UK ferry), the A-2 wends its way northeast to Barcelona and ultimately into France (as the AP-7), while the A-3 heads down to Valencia. The A-4 takes you south to Andalucía, while the A-5 and A-6 respectively take you west towards Portugal via Cáceres and northwest to Galicia. The A-42 goes south to Toledo.

The city is surrounded by two main ring roads, the outermost M-40 and the inner M-30; there are also two additional partial ring roads, the M-45 and the more-distant M-50. The R-5 and R-3 are two of a series of planned new toll roads built to ease the epic traffic jams as madrileños stream back from holidays and weekend getaways.

Coming from the UK you can put your car on a ferry from Portsmouth to Bilbao with P&O Ferries (www.poportsmouth.com) or from Plymouth to Santander with Brittany Ferries (www.brittany-ferries.com). From Bilbao or Santander you barrel south to the capital. Otherwise you can opt for a ferry to France or the Channel Tunnel car train, Eurotunnel (www.eurotunnel.com).

Vehicles must be roadworthy, registered and insured (third party at least). Also ask your insurer for a European Accident Statement form, which can simplify matters in the event of an accident. A European breakdown-assistance policy (eg AA Five Star Service or RAC Eurocover Motoring Assistance in the UK) is a good investment.

If you're here on a tourist visa, you only need your national driving licence, although it's wise to also carry an International Driving Permit (available from the automobile association in your home country); the same applies to drivers from EU countries regardless of how long you stay.

If you're a resident in Spain and come from a non-EU country, it depends on whether your government has a reciprocal rights agreement with Spain allowing you to drive. Visitors from some countries may need to sit their driving exams again. Check with your embassy.

Driving

The Spanish drive on the right-hand side. The grand roundabouts of the major thoroughfares sometimes require nerves of steel as people turn left from the right-hand lanes or right from the centre. The morning and evening rush hours frequently involve snarling traffic jams that are even possible in the wee hours of the morning, especially on weekends when the whole city seems to be behind the wheel or in a bar. The streets are dead between about 2pm and 4pm, when people are either eating or snoozing.

Hire

The big-name car-hire agencies have offices all over Madrid. Avis, Europcar, Hertz and National/Atesa have booths at the airport. Some also operate branches at Atocha and Chamartín train stations. If prices at the bigger agencies seem too high, try Auto Europe (www.auto-europe.com), which operates as a clearing house for the best deals by the major companies. The rental agencies' most central offices include the following:

Avis (Map pp110–11; ☎ 902 180 854; www.avis.es; Gran Vía 60; Ⓜ Santo Domingo or Plaza de España)

Europcar (Map pp110–11; ☎ 902 105 055; www.europcar.es; Calle de San Leonardo de Dios 8; Ⓜ Plaza de España)

Hertz (Map pp110–11; ☎ 902 402 405; www.hertz.es; Edificio de España, Plaza de España 18; Ⓜ Plaza de España)

Moto Alquiler (Map pp110–11; ☎ 91 542 06 57; motoalquiler@telefonica.net; Calle del Conde Duque 13; Ⓥ 8.30am-1.30pm & 5-8pm Mon-Fri; Ⓜ San Bernardo) Motorbike rental. Renting a Honda Sky 50 costs €26/120 per day/week with unlimited kilometres; a week consists of Monday to Friday. It also has Honda Lead 100 (€36/150), Honda CBF250 (€60/250) and Honda CBF500 (€85/335), and it will take a credit card imprint as a deposit. You'll need to bring your passport for identification purposes.

National/Atesa (Map pp110–11; ☎ 902 100 101; www.atesa.es; 1st fl, Gran Vía 80; Ⓜ Plaza de España)

Pepecar (Map pp116–17; ☎ 807 414 243; www.pepecar.com; underground parking area, Plaza de España; Ⓜ Plaza de España) Specialises in low-cost rentals. Bookings are best made over the internet.

Parking

Most of Madrid is divided up into clearly marked blue or green street-parking zones. In both areas parking meters apply from 9am to 8pm Monday to Friday and from 9am to 3pm on Saturday; the Saturday hours also apply daily in August. In the green areas you can park for a maximum of one hour (or keep putting money in the metre every hour) for €1.80. In the blue zones you can park for two hours for €2.55. There are also private parking stations all over central Madrid.

You'll see local cars parked in the most unlikely of places, but following their example by parking in a designated no-parking area exposes you to the risk of being towed. Double-parking is similarly common and decidedly risky if you wander far from your vehicle as fines can reach €300. Should your car disappear, call the Grúa Municipal (city towing service; ☎ 91 787 72 92). Getting it back costs €138.70 plus whatever fine you've been given.

METRO & CERCANÍAS

Madrid's modern metro (☎ 902 444 403; www.metromadrid.es) is a fast, efficient and safe way to navigate Madrid, and generally easier than getting to grips with bus routes. There are 11 colour-coded lines in central Madrid, in addition to the modern southern suburban MetroSur system as well as lines heading east to the major population centres of Pozuelo and Boadilla del Monte. The metro operates from 6.05am to 2am. In theory most trains are air-conditioned in summer, but that doesn't mean it always works.

Colour maps showing the main central Madrid metro system are available from any metro station; the MetroSur is unlikely to be of interest to visitors.

The metro covers 284km (with 282 stations), making it Europe's second-largest metro system, after London. To give you an idea of its scale and popularity, passengers make around 650 million metro rides in Madrid annually.

The short-range *cercanías* regional trains operated by Renfe (☎ 902 240 202; www.renfe.es), the national railway, go as far afield as El Escorial, Alcalá de Henares, Aranjuez and other points in the Comunidad de Madrid. Tickets range between €1.15 and €3.80 depending on how far you're travelling. In Madrid itself they're handy for making a quick, north–south hop between Chamartín and Atocha train stations (with stops at Nuevos Ministerios and in front of the Biblioteca Nacional on Paseo de los Recoletos only). Another line links Chamartín, Atocha and Príncipe Pío stations.

Major infrastructure works are currently underway which, when completed, will connect Atocha train station with Sol, Nuevos Ministerios (for connections to the airport), and Charmartín, making it a whole lot easier when arriving, passing through or leaving Madrid. Like most major works in Madrid, when they finish is anyone's guess.

Tickets

Unless you're only passing through en route to elsewhere, you should buy a Metrobús ticket valid for 10 rides (bus and metro) for €6.70; single-journey tickets cost €1. Tickets can be purchased at stations from manned booths or machines in the metro stations, as well as most *estancos* (tobacconists) and newspaper kiosks. Metrobús tickets are not valid on *cercanías* services.

Monthly or season passes *(abonos)* only make sense if you're staying long term and use local transport frequently. You'll need to get a *carnet* (ID card) from metro stations or tobacconists – take a passport-sized photo and your passport. A monthly ticket for central Madrid (Zona A) costs €42.10.

An Abono Transporte Turístico (Tourist Ticket; per 1/2/7 days €4/7.20/20.80) is also possible.

The fine for being caught without a ticket on public transport is €20 – in addition to the price of the ticket, of course.

TAXI

You can pick up a taxi at ranks throughout town or simply flag one down. Flag fall is €1.95 from 6am to 10pm daily, €2.15 from 10pm to 6am Sunday to Friday and €2.95 from 10pm Saturday to 6am Sunday; make sure the driver turns the meter on. You pay €0.92 per kilometre (€1.06 between 10pm and 6am). Several supplementary charges, usually posted inside the taxi, apply; these include €5.25 to/from the airport; €2.75 from taxi ranks at train and bus stations, €2.75 to/from the Parque Ferial Juan Carlos I; and €6.50 on New Year's Eve and Christmas Eve from 10pm to 6am. There's no charge for luggage.

Among the 24-hour taxi services are Radio-Taxi (☎ 91 405 55 00, 91 445 90 08, 91 447 51 80) and Tele-Taxi (☎ 91 371 21 31, 902 501 130).

Radio-Teléfono Taxi (☎ 91 547 82 00, 91 547 86 00; www.radiotelefono-taxi.com) runs taxis for people with a disability in addition to normal services. Generally if you call any taxi company and ask for a 'eurotaxi' you should be sent one adapted for wheelchair users.

A green light on the roof means the taxi is *libre* (available). Usually a sign to this effect is also placed in the lower passenger side of the windscreen.

Tipping taxi drivers is not common practice, although most travellers round fares up to the nearest euro or two.

TRAIN

Spain's rail network is one of Europe's best, with Madrid well-connected to cities and towns across Spain. A handful of international trains also serves the city.

For information on travelling from the UK contact Rail Europe (☎ 08448 484 064; www.raileurope.co.uk).

For travel within Spain, information (including timetables) is available from your nearest train station or travel agent, or from the operator of the rail network, Renfe (☎ 902 240 202; www.renfe.es).

There are different types of service, but remember that saving a couple of hours on a faster train can mean a big hike in the fare. Most trains have *preferente* (1st class) and *turista* (2nd class) and have dining cars.

High-speed Tren de Alta Velocidad Española (AVE) services connect Madrid with Seville (via Córdoba), Valladolid (via Segovia), Toledo, Málaga and Barcelona (via Zaragoza). AVE trains can reach speeds of 350km/h.

Train Stations

Two train stations serve the city. Note that many trains call in at either one or the other (but only sometimes both), so check when buying tickets. At Atocha train station (Map pp84–5; M Atocha Renfe), south of the city centre, there's an information and ticket centre for long-distance services (including the high-speed AVE) in the station (the part now serving as a tropical garden). In the same area are luggage lockers available from 6.30am to 10.20pm. Full timetables for long-distance trains are also posted outside the ticket office. Another information office (7am-11pm) near platforms 9 and 10 (look for the 'Atención al Cliente' sign) deals with regional and *cercanías* trains, and property lost on these trains. Tickets for regional trains can be bought at a separate counter.

In Chamartín train station (Map p123; M Chamartín) information and tickets are available at the Centro de Viajes (7am-11pm) between platforms 7 and 10. Exchange booths and ATMs are scattered about the station. Lockers are located outside the main station building (take the exit opposite platform 18) and are available between 7am and 11pm.

DIRECTORY

BUSINESS HOURS

Standard working hours are Monday to Friday from 8am or 9am to 2pm and then again from 3pm or 4pm for another three hours.

Banks open from 8.30am to 2pm Monday to Friday; some branches also open 4pm to 7pm on Thursday and/or 9am to 1pm on Saturday.

The Central Post Office opens from 8.30am to 9.30pm Monday to Friday and 8.30am to 2pm Saturday; many suburban post offices open from 8.30am to 8.30pm but many smaller ones only open from 8am to 2pm Monday to Friday.

Opening hours for shops are covered on p132, while restaurant times are on p158.

CHILDREN

For madrileños (and Spaniards in general), going out to eat or sipping a beer on a late summer evening at a *terraza* (open-air café or bar) rarely means leaving kids with minders. Locals take their kids out all the time and don't worry too much about keeping them up late, at least in summer. That, of course, doesn't apply to late-night revelling, when Madrid's army of willing grandparents are called into baby-sitting action.

Madrid has plenty of child-friendly sights and activities. Most churches and museums probably aren't among them, but the Museo de Cera (Wax Museum; p112) usually works for kids old enough to recognise the famous figures.

If your boy's a typical boy, he'll most likely love the Museo del Ferrocarril (p129) and the Museo Naval (p97), the railway and navy museums respectively. A trip to the Estadio Santiago Bernabéu (p122) to see Real Madrid and some of the greatest names in football or to stand on the hallowed turf is also a must for those who love their sport.

Riding to the top of the Faro (p119) or high above Madrid in the Teleférico (p119) can also score points. The Parque del Buen Retiro (p98) has ample space to run around or you can rent a boat; on weekends and holidays you may catch some marionette theatre or see jugglers. Check it out at www.titirilandia.com (in Spanish).

Not especially typical of Madrid, but fun nonetheless, are the amusement parks such as the Parque de Atracciones (p128) or Warner Brothers Movie World (p128), outside the city. For some animal fun, try Faunia (p129) or the Zoo Aquarium de Madrid (p128).

In the hot summer months you'll doubtless be rewarded by squeals of delight if you take the bairns to one of the city's municipal pools (p219). For something a little more exhilarating, try the Parque de Nieve (Ski Park) at Madrid Xanadú (p219) for year-round skiing. Other possibilities for something a little bit different:

Centro Cultural de la Villa (Map pp102–3; ☎ 91 480 03 00; www.esmadrid.com/ccvilla/; Plaza de Colón; Ⓜ Colón or Serrano) Occasionally has children's theatre.

Escuela Popular de Musica y Danza (Map pp116–17; ☎ 91 447 56 82; www.populardemusica.com, in Spanish; Calle de Trafalgar 22; Ⓜ Bilbao) Classes in music (instruments and appreciation) and dance for kids.

Espacio Flamenco (p269) Beginners and intermediate courses in flamenco dancing for kids; two hours a week costs €50 per month.

Laydown Rest Club (p171) One of Madrid's coolest club-restaurants serves brunch from 12.30pm to 6pm on Saturdays and Sundays, tells a different children's story every week and invites the kids to run around barefoot 'like they do at home'.

La Escalera de Jacob (p209) Children's theatre Saturdays and Sundays at 5.30pm.

Parque Secreto (Map pp116–17; ☎ 91 593 14 80; www .parquesecreto.com, in Spanish; Plaza del Conde del Valle Suchil 3; admission per 30min from €2.50; ⏰ 5-9pm Mon-Fri, 11.30am-2pm & 4.30-9pm Sat & Sun) With 800 sq metres of indoor playgrounds (labyrinths, floating castles, pits filled with plastic balls, toboggans etc) for kids from 0 to 11 years, this place will keep them occupied for hours while you rest in the cafeteria.

For great ideas and general advice on travelling with children, grab Lonely Planet's *Travel with Children*, by Maureen Wheeler and Cathy Lanigan.

Baby-sitting

There's no real tradition in Spain of professional baby-sitting services – most Spaniards have *abuelos* (grandparents) or other extended

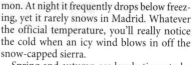
family at the ready. That said, some midrange and most top-end hotels in Madrid can organise baby-sitting. Or you can try to line something up through www.canguroencasa .com (in Spanish; *canguro* or 'kangaroo' also means baby-sitter in Spanish), although it's based around baby-sitters advertising their services rather than functioning as a centralised booking service; baby-sitters who speak English and other languages are highlighted.

CLIMATE

For Spaniards who don't live in Madrid, the capital's weather is a source of amusement. It has, they say, a climate of extremes, as summed up by the phrase *nueve meses de invierno y tres de infierno* (nine months of winter and three of hell). To a certain extent they're right: the *meseta* (high inland plateau) where the city is located indeed ensures scorching summers and bitterly cold winters. But Madrid's climate is not without its staunch supporters, among them Hemingway (who described Madrid's climate as the best in Spain) and fashion designer Agatha Ruiz de la Prada (who told us that 'it's a climate that can make you feel quite euphoric'). Personally, we love the absence of humidity, the piercing blue skies for much of winter, and the hot, dry summer days.

July is the hottest month, with August running a close second. Average highs hover above 30°C, but the maximum is frequently in excess of 35°C and sometimes nudges 40°C. When a heat wave sweeps through, it can get uncomfortable and at 4am you can still be gasping for air, but it's rare that the heat gets too oppressive for more than a couple of weeks a year. Air-conditioning in your room is, at such times, a godsend. Bringing some relief, and rare humidity, apocalyptic summer storms sometimes drench Madrid in summer.

The coldest months are January and February, when daily average highs are less than 10°C, although as high as 15°C is not uncom-mon. At night it frequently drops below freezing, yet it rarely snows in Madrid. Whatever the official temperature, you'll really notice the cold when an icy wind blows in off the snow-capped sierra.

Spring and autumn are lovely times to be in Madrid. In theory, it's also the period with the heaviest rainfall; more than 50mm can be quite common in October, and March can be unpredictable. In Spain they say *cuando en marzo mayea, en mayo marzea*. In other words, if you get nice, warm dry days in March (weather more typical of May), you'll be wiping that grin off your face in May, when the wet spells you missed earlier catch up with you! Never short of a saying, Spaniards say of April, *mes de abril, aguas mil* – it rains a lot in this spring month.

COURSES

Madrid is a good place to base yourself for learning Spanish or flamenco. If you're interested in shorter-term cooking courses, turn to p158, while wine appreciation courses are covered on p185.

Spanish Classes

Madrid is jammed with language schools of all possible categories, as eager to teach foreigners Spanish as locals other languages.

Non-EU citizens who want to study at a university or language school in Spain should, in theory, have a study visa. These visas can be obtained from your nearest Spanish embassy or consulate. You'll normally require confirmation of your enrolment, payment of fees and proof of adequate funds to support yourself before a visa is issued. This type of visa is renewable within Spain but, again, only with confirmation of ongoing enrolment and proof that you're able to support yourself.

Some language schools worth investigating include the following:

Academia Inhispania (Map pp64–5; ☎ 91 521 22 31; www.inhispania.com; Calle de la Montera 10-12; Ⓜ Sol) Intensive four-week courses start at €510.

Academia Madrid Plus (Map pp64–5; ☎ 91 548 11 16; www.madridplus.es; 6th fl, Calle del Arenal 21; Ⓜ Ópera) Four-week (30-hour) courses begin at €270.

Acento Español (Map pp64–5; ☎ 91 521 36 76; www .acentoespanol.com; Calle Mayor 4; Ⓜ Sol) Four-week courses start at €475.

Babylon Idiomas (Map pp84–5; ☎ 91 532 44 80; www .babylon-idiomas.com; Plaza de Santa Ana 1; Ⓜ Sol,

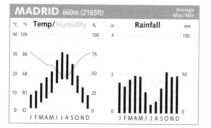

MADRID 660m (2165ft)

Sevilla or Antón Martín) Intensive 20-/30-hour per week courses cost €155/235 per week.

International House (Map pp116–17; ☎ 91 319 72 24; www.ihmadrid.es; Calle de Zurbano 8; Ⓜ Alonso Martínez) Intensive courses start at around €385 for two weeks. Staff can organise accommodation with local families.

Mosaic International Institute (Map p123; ☎ 91 535 74 06; www.mosaicinternationalinstitute.org/EN/; Calle del Comandante Zorita 4; Ⓜ Cuatro Caminos or Nuevos Ministerios) A range of courses. Intensive classes (20 hours a week) cost €590 a month

Universidad Complutense (Map pp58–9; ☎ 91 394 53 36; www.ucm.es/info/cextran/Index.htm; Secretaria de los Cursos para Extranjeros, Facultadole Filologia [Edificio A] Universidad Complutense, Cuidad Universitaria, 28040 Madrid; Ⓜ Cuidad Universitaria) You can try a range of language and cultural courses throughout the year. An intensive semester course of 150 contact hours costs €445.

Flamenco

There are plenty of places where you can learn to dance *sevillanas* or strum the guitar like the greats.

El Flamenco Vive (Map pp64–5; ☎ 91 547 39 17; www .elflamencovive.com; Calle del Conde de Lemos 7; ◷ 10.30am-2pm & 5-9pm Mon-Sat; Ⓜ Ópera) Guitar lessons for €25 per hour.

Espacio Flamenco (Map pp76–7; ☎ 91 298 19 55; http://espacio.deflamenco.com/escuelai.html; Calle de Ribera de Curtidores 26; ◷ 11am-2pm & 5.30-8.30pm Mon-Fri, 11am-2.30pm Sat & Sun; Ⓜ Puerta de Toledo) Intensive or longer courses in guitar, dancing and singing for €50 to €100 per month.

Fundación Conservatorio Casa Patas (Map pp76–7; ☎ 91 429 84 71; www.conservatorioflamenco.com, in Spanish; Calle de Cañizares 10; Ⓜ Antón Martín or Tirso de Molina) Every conceivable type of flamenco instruction (€40 to €136 per month, plus around €30 joining fee), including dance, guitar, singing and much more. It's upstairs from the Casa Patas flamenco *tablao*.

Academia Amor de Dios (Map pp76–7; ☎ 91 360 04 34; www.amordedios.com, in Spanish; 1st fl, Calle de Santa Isabel 5; Ⓜ Antón Martín) The best-known course for flamenco dancing (and probably the hardest to get into), although it's more for budding professionals than casual visitors.

Other Courses

Cultural centres around Madrid offer courses in just about anything, while a handful of places teach music and dance.

Centro Cultural de Lavapiés (Map pp76–7; ☎ 91 467 30 39; Calle del Olivar 46; ◷ 9am-2pm & 4-9pm Mon-Fri; Ⓜ Lavapiés) A range of (mostly Spanish-language) courses spanning ceramics, photography, t'ai chi, guitar, reflexology and more.

Escuela Popular de Musica y Danza (Map pp116–17; ☎ 91 447 56 82; www.populardemusica.com, in Spanish; Calle de Trafalgar 22; Ⓜ Bilbao) Classes in music, dance and drama.

Kabokla (p209) Samba and capoeira classes in this fine Brazilian live music venue.

CUSTOMS REGULATIONS

People entering Spain from outside the EU are allowed to bring in duty-free one bottle of spirits, one bottle of wine, 50mL of perfume and 200 cigarettes. There are no duty-free allowances for travel between EU countries. For duty-paid items bought at normal shops in one EU country and taken into another, the allowances are 90L of wine, 10L of spirits, unlimited quantities of perfume and 800 cigarettes. For more information on obtaining VAT refunds, see the boxed text, p135.

DISCOUNT CARDS

The International Student Identity Card (ISIC; see www.isic.org) and the Euro<26 card (www.euro26.org), for youth under 26 years, are available from most national student organisations and can gain you discounted access to sights.

If you intend to do some intensive sightseeing and travelling on public transport, it might be worth looking at the Madrid Card (☎ 902 877 996; www.madridcard.com). It includes free entry to more than 40 museums in and around Madrid (including the Museo del Prado, Museo Thyssen-Bornemisza, Centro de Arte Reina Sofía, the Estadio Santiago Bernabéu and Palacio Real) and free Descubre Madrid (p273) walking tours, as well as discounts on public transport, the Madrid Visión tourist bus, and in certain shops and restaurants. The ticket is available for one/two/three days (€42/55/68). There's also a cheaper version (€28/32/36), which just covers cultural sights.

The Madrid Card can be bought online, over the phone (☎ 91 360 47 72, 902 088 908), or in person at the tourist offices on Plaza Mayor and in Calle del Duque de Medinaceli (see p276), at Fortunata – La Tienda de Madrid (p134), and in some tobacconists and hotels; a list of major sales outlets appears on the website.

ELECTRICITY

The electric current in Madrid is 220V, 50Hz, as in the rest of continental Europe. Several countries outside Europe (such as the USA and Canada) use 110V, 60Hz, which means that it's safest to use a transformer. Plugs have two round pins, as in the rest of continental Europe.

EMBASSIES

Most countries have an embassy or consulate in Madrid. The following contact details were correct at the time of research, although a number of embassies (including Australia, Canada and the UK) have announced plans to move to the new skyscrapers at the northern end of the Paseo de la Castellana when they're completed. Check their websites, or www.esmadrid.com, for the most recent information.

Australia (Map p123; ☎ 91 353 66 00; www.spain .embassy.gov.au; 2nd fl, Plaza del Descubridor Diego de Ordás 3; Ⓜ Ríos Rosas)

Canada (Map pp102–3; ☎ 91 423 32 50; www.canada -es.org; Calle de Núñez de Balboa 35; Ⓜ Velázquez)

France (Map pp102–3; ☎ 91 423 89 00; www.amba france-es.org; Calle de Salustiano Olózaga 9; Ⓜ Retiro)

Germany (Map pp116–17; ☎ 91 557 90 00; www.madrid .diplo.de; Calle de Fortuny 8; Ⓜ Rubén Dario)

Ireland (Map pp102–3; ☎ 91 436 40 93; embajada@ irlanda.es; 4th fl, Paseo de la Castellana 46; Ⓜ Rubén Dario)

New Zealand (Map p123; ☎ 91 523 02 26; www.nz embassy.com; 3rd fl, Calle de Pinar 7; Ⓜ Gregorio Marañón)

UK consulate-general (Map pp110–11; ☎ 91 524 97 00; Paseo de los Recoletos 7/9; Ⓜ Banco de España); embassy (Map pp116–17; ☎ 91 524 97 00; www.ukinspain.com; Calle de Fernando el Santo 16; Ⓜ Colón)

USA (Map pp102–3; ☎ 91 587 22 00; www.embusa.es; Calle de Serrano 75; Ⓜ Núñez de Balboa)

EMERGENCY

For practical information on keeping your wits about you in Madrid, see p274. To report thefts or other crime-related matters, your best bet is the Servicio de Atención al Turista Extranjero (Foreign Tourist Assistance Service; Map p64–5; ☎ 91 548 85 37, 91 548 80 08; satemadrid@munimadrid.es; Calle de Leganitos 19; 🕑 9am-10pm; Ⓜ Plaza de España or Santo Domingo), which is housed in the central police station or comisaría of the National Police. Here you'll find specially trained officers working alongside representatives from

the tourism ministry. They can also assist in cancelling credit cards, as well as contacting your embassy or your family.

Ambulance (☎ 061)

EU standard emergency number (☎ 112)

Fire brigade (Bomberos; ☎ 080)

Local police (Policía Municipal; ☎ 092)

Military police (Guardia Civil; ☎ 062)

National police (Policía Nacional; ☎ 091)

Teléfono de la víctima (Hotline for victims of racial or sexual violence; ☎ 902 180 995)

HOLIDAYS

When a holiday falls close to a weekend, madrileños like to make a *puente* (bridge) and take the intervening day off. On the odd occasion when a couple of holidays fall close, they make an *acueducto* (aqueduct)! For madrileños the main holiday periods are during summer (July and especially August), Christmas–New Year and Easter. August can be a peculiar time as locals make their annual migration to the beach and the city they leave behind falls quiet and grinds to a halt – this is a bad time to be trying to do business, although the change is less pronounced than it used to be.

For more information on the city's colourful festivals and other events, turn to p16.

Public Holidays

Madrid's 14 public holidays are as follows:

Año Nuevo (New Year's Day) 1 January – see p16.

Reyes (Epiphany or Three Kings' Day) 6 January – see p16.

Jueves Santo (Holy Thursday) March/April – see p16.

Viernes Santo (Good Friday) March/April – see p16.

Labour Day (Fiesta del Trabajo) 1 May.

Fiesta de la Comunidad de Madrid 2 May – see p16.

Fiestas de San Isidro Labrador 15 May – see p16.

La Asunción (Feast of the Assumption) 15 August.

Día de la Hispanidad (Spanish National Day) 12 October – a fairly sober occasion with a military parade along the Paseo de la Castellana.

Todos los Santos (All Saints' Day) 1 November.

Día de la Virgen de la Almudena 9 November – see p16.

Día de la Constitución (Constitution Day) 6 December.

La Inmaculada Concepción (Feast of the Immaculate Conception) 8 December.

Navidad (Christmas) 25 December – see p16.

INTERNET ACCESS

If you're toting a laptop, almost all midrange and top-end hotels have either wi-fi or cable ADSL in-room connections; even some of the better hotels can run out of cables for the latter so ask for one as soon as you arrive. For everyone else, there are plenty of internet cafés around town.

Internet Cafés

Madrid is full of internet cafés. Some offer student rates, while most have deals on cards for several hours' use at much-reduced rates. In addition to the following handful of options, the Ayuntamiento's Centro de Turismo de Madrid (p276) on the Plaza Mayor offers free internet for up to 15 minutes.

BBiGG (Map pp64–5; ☎ 91 531 23 64; Calle Mayor 1; per 1/5 hr €2.50/3; ☺ 9.30am-midnight; Ⓜ Sol) A massive internet centre in the heart of town, with separate sections for Skype, internet and games.

Café Comercial (Map pp110–11; ☎ 91 521 56 55; Glorieta de Bilbao 7; per 50 mins €1; ☺ 7.30am-midnight Mon, 7.30am-1am Tue-Thu, 7.30am-2am Fri, 8.30am-2am Sat, 9am-midnight Sun) Ⓜ Bilbao) Surf the net in one of Madrid's grandest old cafés (p193).

Drop & Drag (Map pp110–11; ☎ 91 532 93 72; Calle de Augusto Figueroa 7; per hr €2; ☺ noon-1am Mon-Fri, 3pm-midnight Sat & Sun; Ⓜ Chueca) Handy if you're in Chueca.

La Bolsa de Minutos (Map pp84–5; ☎ 91 532 26 22; Calle de Espoz y Mina 17; per hr €2; ☺ 9.30am-midnight daily; Ⓜ Sol or Antón Martín)

MAPS

The maps in this book should be more than enough for most travellers. Long-termers seeking comprehensive map books and atlases are spoiled for choice. A good one is Almax's *Callejero de Madrid*, scaled at 1:12,000. The same publisher produces *Atlas de Madrid*, which covers Madrid and the surrounding municipalities. You could also try the super-detailed *Guía Urbana*. Michelin's *Madrid* (No 42) map is also excellent and far less cumbersome to carry around.

For something far less detailed, any of the tourist offices have maps of central Madrid. Alternatively, head to the Paseo del Prado at the northern end towards the Plaza de la Cibeles where, at the large standing maps that look like advertising posts, you can insert €1.20 and receive a reasonable city map.

If you're looking for a specific address, check out www.qdq.com and click on *Callejeros Fotográficos*, type in the street name and number and you'll get a photo of the building you're looking for and its map location.

MEDICAL SERVICES

All foreigners have the same right as Spaniards to emergency medical treatment in a public hospital. European Union (EU) citizens are entitled to the full range of healthcare services in public hospitals free of charge, but you'll need to present your European Health Insurance Card (EHIC); inquire at your national health service before leaving home. Even if you have no insurance, you'll be treated in an emergency, with costs in the public system ranging from free to €112. Non-EU citizens have to pay for anything other than emergency treatment – a good reason to have a travel insurance policy.

Your embassy should be able to refer you to doctors who speak your language. If you have a specific health complaint, obtain the necessary information and referrals for treatment before leaving home.

WI-FI ACCESS

There's an ever expanding network of wi-fi hotspots around town if you can't wait to get back to your hotel to get online. The most obvious places are the airport and some cafés, although free wi-fi hotspots are still pretty thin on the ground; exceptions include the Plaza de Colón (Map pp102–3) and Isolée (p151). Chueca Wifi (www.chuecawifi.com) is a barrio initiative aimed at transforming Chueca into one big wi-fi hotspot and dozens of businesses have signed up; check out its website for more details. Otherwise, check out www.totalhotspots.com/directory/es for a list of businesses offering wi-fi access. We've also heard of plans to make Plaza Mayor a hotspot, but they're still only plans.

If you're going to be in town a little longer, monthly subscriptions and prepaid accounts are possible through Telefonica (www.telefonica.es), as well as private operators such as Ya.com (www.ya.com, in Spanish), Orange (www.orange.es, in Spanish) and Jazztel (www.jazztel.com, in Spanish). Vodafone (www.vodafone.es, in Spanish) also offers wireless internet connection that works throughout Spain via a USB modem (€19 to €39 per month) that plugs into your laptop. It's ideal if you'll be travelling around while in Spain.

Some useful numbers and addresses for travellers:

Anglo-American Medical Unit (Unidad Medica; Map pp102–3; ☎ 91 435 18 23; www.unidadmedica.com; Calle del Conde de Aranda 1; ☺ 9am-8pm Mon-Fri, emergencies 10am-1pm Sat; Ⓜ Retiro) A private clinic with a wide range of specialisations and where all doctors speak Spanish and English. Each consultation costs around €120.

Hospital General Gregorio Marañón (Map pp126–7; ☎ 91 586 80 00; www.hggm.es, in Spanish; Calle del Doctor Esquerdo 46; Ⓜ Sainz de Baranda) One of the city's main hospitals.

Pharmacies

For minor health problems, you can try your local *farmacia* (pharmacy), where pharmaceuticals tend to be sold more freely without prescription than in other countries, such as the USA, Australia or the UK.

At least one pharmacy is open 24 hours per day in each district of Madrid. They mostly operate on a rota and details appear daily in *El País* and other papers. Otherwise call ☎ 010. Most pharmacies have a list in their window indicating the location of nearby after-hours pharmacies. Pharmacies that always remain open include the following:

Farmacia del Globo (Map pp76–7; ☎ 91 369 20 00; Calle de Atocha 46; Ⓜ Antón Martín)

Farmacia Velázquez 70 (Map pp102–3; ☎ 91 575 60 28; Calle de Velázquez 70; Ⓜ Velázquez)

Farmacia Real Botica de la Reina Madre (Map pp64–5; ☎ 91 548 00 14; Calle Mayor 59; Ⓜ Ópera)

MONEY

As in most other EU nations, Spain uses the euro, which replaced the peseta in 2002. Although it's becoming rarer, you occasionally see prices listed in pesetas alongside the euro price; this is especially common with house prices.

Changing Money

You can change cash or travellers cheques in currencies of the developed world without problems at virtually any bank or bureau de change (usually indicated by the word *cambio*). Central Madrid also abounds with banks – most have ATMs.

Exchange offices are open for longer hours than banks but generally offer poorer rates. Also, keep a sharp eye open for commissions at bureaus de change.

Credit Cards

Major cards, such as Visa, MasterCard, Maestro, Cirrus and, to a lesser extent, Amex, are accepted throughout Spain. They can be used in many hotels, restaurants and shops; in doing so you'll need to show some form of photo ID (eg passport). Credit cards can also be used in ATMs displaying the appropriate sign (if there's no sign, don't risk it), or, if you have no PIN, you can obtain cash advances over the counter in many banks. Check charges with your bank.

If your card is lost, stolen or swallowed by an ATM, you can call the following numbers toll-free to have an immediate stop put on its use:

Amex (☎ 902 375 637)

Diners Club (☎ 91 211 43 00, 902 40 11 12)

MasterCard (☎ 900 971 231)

Visa (☎ 902 192 100)

Travellers Cheques

Does anyone still use travellers cheques? If you do, most banks and exchange offices will cash travellers cheques; get most of your cheques in fairly large denominations to save on per-cheque commission charges. It's vital to keep your initial receipt and a record of your cheque numbers and the ones you have used, separate from the cheques themselves. It can also be a good idea to keep handy the number for reporting lost or stolen cheques, even though, best case scenario, you won't need to use it.

NEWSPAPERS & MAGAZINES

There's a wide selection of national newspapers from around Europe (including most of the UK dailies) available at newspaper stands all over central Madrid. The *International Herald Tribune (IHT), Time*, the *Economist, Der Spiegel* and a host of other international magazines are also available. The *IHT* includes an eight-page supplement of articles from *El País* translated into English.

Madrid has an outstanding new bilingual magazine *Madriz* (www.madriz.com; €3) that covers all the latest trends and quirks of the city and also has some great feature articles. The free English-language monthly *InMadrid* is a handy newspaper-format publication with articles on the local scene and classifieds. Pick it up in some bars and pubs, language schools, consulates and some tourist offices.

Spanish Press

The main Spanish dailies are divided roughly along political lines, with the old-fashioned *ABC* (www.abc.es, in Spanish) representing the conservative right, *El País* (www.elpais .com) identified with the centre-left and *El Mundo* (www.elmundo.es, in Spanish) with the centre-right. Further to the right than all others is *La Razón* (www.larazon.es, in Spanish), while *El Público* (www.publico.es, in Spanish) is associated with the left. For a good spread of national and international news, *El País* is the pick of the bunch and also the largest-selling of the news dailies. It also contains an informative central section devoted to the goings-on in the Comunidad de Madrid. But the best-selling daily of all is *Marca* (www.marca.com, in Spanish), which is devoted exclusively to sport. Free morning dailies that you're likely to find outside metro stations and busy intersections in the morning are *ADN*, *20 Minutos*, *Metro* (which has one English-language page devoted to international celebrity gossip) and the sensationalist *Que!*. Of the magazines devoted to Spanish politics, *Tiempo* (www.tiempodehoy.com) is probably the pick.

ORGANISED TOURS

For organised culinary or tapas tours around Madrid, turn to p162. Otherwise, the following offer tours around the city and some outlying sights.

Bike Spain (Map pp64–5; ☎ 91 559 06 53 www .bikespain.info; Plaza de la Villa 1, Calle del Codo; tours €30; ⏱ 10am-2pm & 4-7pm Mon-Fri, 10am-2pm Sat & Sun; Ⓜ Ópera) English-language guided city tours by bicycle, by day or (on Friday) by night, plus longer expeditions to San Lorenzo de El Escorial (€75).

Descubre Madrid (Discover Madrid; ☎ 91 588 29 06; www.esmadrid.com/monograficos/DescubreMadridv2 /es/index.html; walking tours adult/child, student, under 25yr or senior €3.30/2.70, bus tours €6.45/5.05, bicycle tours €3.30/2.70 plus €6 bike rental) Conducts tours in both Spanish and English. Nineteen highly recommended guided tours. Organised by the Centro de Turismo de Madrid (Tourist Office; Map pp64–5; Plaza Mayor 27).

Letango Tours (Map pp76–7; ☎ 91 369 47 52; www .letango.com; 1st fl, Plaza de Tirso de Molina 12; weekday/ weekend €98/138; Ⓜ Tirso de Molina) Walking tours through Madrid with additional excursions to San Lorenzo El Escorial, Segovia and Toledo.

Madrid Bike Tours (☎ 680 581 782; www.madridbike tours.com; 4hr tour & picnic lunch per person €65) Londoner Mike Chandler offers a guided two-wheel tour of Madrid as well as tours further afield.

Madrid en Bicicleta (☎ 91 559 06 53; www.mtb-spain .com; day tour per person €18-25) Mountain bike tours in the mountains surrounding Madrid. It also runs the two-day Guadarrama Extreme (€265). Bookings can be made through Bike Spain (see above).

Madrid Original (☎ 91 521 04 49; www.madridoriginal .com; per hr per group Mon-Fri €65, Sat/Sun €95/125) Privately run tours (for up to 6 people) in English, Spanish or French by professional guides. Tours include the major museums, historical eras, Gran Vía, the Parque del Buen Retiro and tailor-made itineraries.

Madrid Visión (☎ 91 779 18 88, 91 765 10 16; www.madrid vision.es; adult 1-/2-day ticket €16/20.50, child 7-16yr & senior over 65yr 1-/2-day ticket €8.50/11, child under 7yr free; ⏱ 9.30am-midnight 21 Jun-20 Sep, 10am-5pm 21 Dec-20 Mar, 10am-6.30pm rest of year) Hop-on, hop-off open-topped buses that run every 10 to 20 minutes along two routes: Historical Madrid and Modern Madrid. Information, including maps, is available at tourist offices, most travel agencies and some hotels, and you can get tickets on the bus.

Pullmantur (Map pp64–5; ☎ 91 541 18 07; www.pullman tur-spain.com; Plaza de Oriente 8; Ⓜ Ópera) One of several private companies offering tours of Madrid and excursions beyond, including to San Lorenzo de El Escorial and the Valle de los Caídos, Toledo, Segovia and Ávila.

The Wellington Society (☎ 609 143 203; www.wellsoc .org; tours €50-85) A handful of quirky historical tours laced with anecdotes and led by the inimitable Stephen Drake-Jones. Possibilities include Bullfights, Hemingway's Madrid, Curiosities & Anecdotes of Old Madrid.

Urban Movil (Map pp64–5; ☎ 91 542 77 71, 687 535 443; www.urbanmovil.com; Calle Mayor 78; 1-/2-hr Segway tours €35/60; ⏱ 10am-8pm) Segway tours around Madrid. Prices include 10-minutes worth of training before you set out and it also organises bike tours.

POST

Correos (☎ 902 197 197; www.correos.es), the national postal service, has its main office (Map pp92–3; ☎ 91 396 27 33; Plaza de la Cibeles; ⏱ 8.30am-9.30pm Mon-Fri, 8.30am-2pm Sat; Ⓜ Banco de España) in the ornate Palacio de Comunicaciones.

Sellos (stamps) are sold at most *estancos* (tobacconists' shops with *Tabacos* in yellow letters on a maroon background), as well as post offices.

A postcard or letter weighing up to 20g costs €1.07 from Spain to other European countries, and €1.38 to the rest of the world. For a full list of prices for certified *(certificado)* and express post *(urgente)*, go to www .correos.es (in Spanish).

All Spanish addresses have five-digit post-codes; using postcodes will help your mail arrive quicker.

Lista de correos (poste restante) mail can be addressed to you anywhere that has a post office. It will be delivered to the main post office unless another is specified in the address. Take your passport when you pick up mail. A typical *lista de correos* address looks like this:

Your name
Lista de Correos
28014 Madrid
Spain

Delivery times are erratic but ordinary mail to other Western European countries can take up to a week; to North America up to 10 days; and to Australia or New Zealand anywhere between one and two weeks.

RADIO

The Spanish national network Radio Nacional de España (RNE) can be heard on RNE 1 (88.2 FM in Madrid) and has general interest and current affairs programmes. Spaniards also divide between those who listen to the left-leaning Cadena SER (105.4 FM or 810AM) and the conservative, right-wing COPE network (100.7 FM). Among the most listened-to music stations are 40 Principales (97.7 FM), Onda Cero (98 FM) and Kiss FM (102.7 FM).

You can pick up BBC World Service (www.bbc .co.uk/radio/) on, among others, 6195, 9410 and 15,485 kHz (short wave). Voice of America (VOA) can be found on a host of short-wave frequencies, including 6040, 9760 and 15,205 kHz.

RELOCATING

If you're moving to Madrid and looking for somewhere to live, try Room Madrid (Map pp110–11; ☎ 676 977 557; www.roommadrid.es; Calle de Conde Duque 7; ☼ 11am-2pm & 5-8pm Mon-Fri; Ⓜ Plaza de España), a booking service that arranges medium- to long-term accommodation. Within its portfolio is everything from apartments to shared flats. Though it can be a bit slow to answer (make contact well in advance of arriving in Madrid), it's generally reliable. Several real

estate and relocation companies specialise in helping foreign clients; try Solution Relocation Services (☎ 91 550 03 97; www.solucionmad.com) or Immo Madrid (☎ 91 766 06 61; www.immomadrid .com). Once you're living here, pick up a copy of *The Notebook Madrid – Settling & Living in Madrid*, a locally produced publication (€20) with loads of useful tips and contacts; in English and French, it can usually be found at Petra's International Bookshop (p132). Other good resources include www.expatica.com and European Vibe (Map pp116–17; ☎ 91 549 77 11; www .europeanvibe.com; Calle de Fernando El Católico 63; Ⓜ Moncloa), whose aim is to plug you into the local expat scene.

SAFETY

Madrid is a generally safe city, although you should, as in most European cities, be wary of pickpockets in the city centre, on the metro and around major tourist sights. Although you should be careful, don't be paranoid; remember that the overwhelming majority of travellers to Madrid rarely encounters any problems.

You need to be especially careful in the most heavily touristed parts of town, notably the Plaza Mayor and surrounding streets, the Puerta del Sol, El Rastro and the Museo del Prado. Tricks abound. They usually involve a team of two or more (sometimes one of them an attractive woman to distract male victims). While one attracts your attention, the other empties your pockets. Be wary of jostling on crowded buses and the metro and, as a general rule, dark, empty streets are to be avoided; luckily, Madrid's most lively nocturnal areas are generally busy with crowds having a good time.

More unsettling than dangerous, the central Madrid street of Calle de la Montera has long been the haunt of prostitutes, pimps and a fair share of shady characters, although the street has recently been pedestrianised, installed with CCTV cameras and a police station. The same applies to the Casa de Campo, although it, too, has been cleaned up a little. The Madrid barrio of Lavapiés is a gritty, multicultural melting pot. We love it, but it's not without its problems, with drug-related crime an occasional but persistent problem; it's probably best avoided if you're on your own at night.

Where possible, only keep strictly necessary things on your person. Never put anything in your back pocket; small day bags are best worn across your chest. Money belts or pouches worn *under* your clothing are also a good idea. The less you have in your pockets or exposed bags the less you stand to lose if you're done. As with any travel, you should always keep a photocopy of important documents separate from the originals and travel insurance against theft and loss is also highly recommended.

For information on who to contact should you find yourself in difficulties, turn to p270. The numbers for reporting lost or stolen credit cards are on p272.

TELEPHONE

To call Spain, dial the international access code (00 in most countries), followed by the code for Spain (34) and the full nine-digit number. The access code for international calls from Spain is 00. International reverse-charge (collect) calls *(una llamada a cobro revertido)* are simple:

Australia (☎ 900 99 00 61)

Canada (☎ 900 99 00 15)

France (☎ 900 99 00 33)

Germany (☎ 900 99 00 49)

Ireland (☎ 900 99 03 53)

New Zealand (☎ 900 99 00 64)

UK (BT ☎ 900 99 00 44, Mercury 900 99 09 44)

USA (AT&T ☎ 900 99 00 11, Sprint and various others 900 99 00 13, MCI 900 99 00 14)

You'll get straight through to an operator in the country you're calling. There are changes afoot, so try an '800' prefix to the above numbers instead of '900' if the latter doesn't work.

If for some reason the above information doesn't work for you, in most places you can get an English-speaking Spanish international operator on ☎ 1008 (for calls within Europe or for Morocco) or ☎ 1005 (for the rest of the world).

For international directory inquiries dial ☎ 11825. Be warned, a call to this number costs €2! Dial ☎ 1009 to speak to a domestic operator, including for a domestic reverse-charge (collect) call. For national directory inquiries dial ☎ 11818.

Mobile (cell) phone numbers start with 6. Numbers starting with 900 are national toll-free numbers, while those starting 901 to 905 come with varying conditions. A common one is 902, which is a national standard rate number, but which can only be dialled from within Spain. In a similar category are numbers starting with 800, 803, 806 and 807.

Mobile Phones

You can buy SIM cards and prepaid time in Spain for your mobile (cell) phone (provided you own a GSM, dual- or tri-band cellular phone). This only works if your national phone hasn't been code-blocked; check before leaving home. Only consider a full contract unless you plan to live in Spain for a while.

All the Spanish mobile phone companies (Telefónica's MoviStar, Orange, Vodafone and Amena) offer *prepagado* (prepaid) accounts for mobiles. The SIM card costs from €50, which includes some prepaid phone time. Phone outlets are scattered across the city. You can then top up in their shops or by buying cards in outlets, such as tobacconists *(estancos)* and newsstands.

You can rent a mobile phone through the Madrid-based OnSpanishTime.com (www.onspanish time.com/web). Delivery and pickup are done personally at a cost of US$12 (US$15 on weekends and holidays). The basic service costs US$8/49/100 per day/week/month for the phone. You pay a US$150 deposit and the whole operation is done over the internet.

Phonecards

The ubiquitous blue payphones are easy to use for international and domestic calls. They accept coins, *tarjetas telefónicas* (phonecards) issued by the national phone company Telefónica and, in some cases, credit cards. Phones in hotel rooms are more expensive than street payphones. The Telefónica phonecards are best for domestic calls.

For international calls you have two cut-price options. Most internet cafés recommended in this book (see p271) are Skype enabled, allowing you to call (with your Skype user id and password) for no more than the cost of your internet time. The other option is an international phonecard, which can be bought from *estancos*, some small convenience stores and newsstands in central Madrid. Most outlets display the call rates for each card. For calls to Australia or Western Europe, Euro Hours has a phonecard costing €6, for 600 minutes of call time (plus the cost of the local call) or more than 200 minutes calling a toll-free local number.

TIME

Like most of Western Europe, Spain (and hence Madrid) is one hour ahead of Greenwich Mean Time/Coordinated Universal Time (GMT/UTC) during winter, two hours during the daylight-saving period from the last Sunday in March to the last Sunday in October. Spaniards use the 24-hour clock for official business (timetables etc), but often in daily conversation switch to the 12-hour version.

TOILETS

Public toilets are almost nonexistent in Madrid and it's not really the done thing to go into a bar or café solely to use the toilet; ordering a quick coffee is a small price to pay for relieving the problem. Otherwise you can usually get away with it in a larger, crowded place where they can't really keep track of who's coming and going. Another option is the department stores of El Corte Inglés (p133) that are dotted around the city.

TOURIST INFORMATION
Ayuntamiento de Madrid

Madrid finally has a tourist office worthy of the city at the Ayuntamiento's Centro de Turismo de Madrid (Map pp64–5; ☎ 91 588 16 36; www.esmadrid .com; Plaza Mayor 27; ☒ 9.30am-8.30pm; Ⓜ Sol). Housed in the delightful Real Casa de Panadería on the north side of the Plaza Mayor, it allows free access to its outstanding website and city database, and offers free downloads of the metro map to your mobile; staff are helpful. It also runs a useful general information line (☎ 010; Spanish only) dealing with anything from transport to shows in Madrid (call ☎ 91 540 40 10 from outside Madrid). There's another tourist office (Map pp102–3; Plaza de Colón; ☒ 9.30am-8.30pm; Ⓜ Colón), which is accessible via the underground passage on the corner of Calle de Goya and the Paseo de la Castellana, while smaller, bright orange tourist information points can be found at the following:

Plaza de Cibeles (Map pp92–3; ☒ 9.30am-8.30pm; Ⓜ Banco de España)

Plaza del Callao (Map pp64–5; ☒ 9.30am-8.30pm; Ⓜ Callao)

Paseo del Arte (Map pp84–5; cnr Calle de Santa Isabel & Plaza del Emperador Carlos V; ☒ 9.30am-8.30pm; Ⓜ Atocha)

Barajas Airport, T4 (☒ 9.30am-8.30pm; Ⓜ Aeropuerto T4)

Comunidad de Madrid

The regional Comunidad de Madrid government runs the helpful Comunidad de Madrid Tourist Office (Map pp84–5; ☎ 902 100 007, 91 429 49 51; www .turismomadrid.es; Calle del Duque de Medinaceli 2; ☒ 8am-8pm Mon-Sat, 9am-2pm Sun; Ⓜ Banco de España) covering the city and surrounding region. It also has a telephone information service (☎ 012) and branches at the following places:

Atocha train station (☎ 91 528 46 30; ☒ 8am-8pm Mon-Sat, 9am-2pm Sun; Ⓜ Atocha Renfe)

Barajas airport (Aeropuerto de Barajas; ☎ 91 305 86 56; T1, ground fl & T4; ☒ 8am-8pm Mon-Sat, 9am-2pm Sun; Ⓜ Aeropuerto or Aeropuerto T4)

Chamartín train station (☎ 91 315 99 76; ☒ 8am-8pm Mon-Sat, 9am-2pm Sun; Ⓜ Chamartín)

TRAVELLERS WITH DISABILITIES

Although things are slowly changing, Madrid remains something of an obstacle course for disabled travellers. Your first stop for more information on accessibility for travellers should be the Madrid tourist office website section known as Accessible Madrid (www.esmadrid .com), where you can download a calendar of guided tours for travellers with a disability, as well as a list of wheelchair-friendly hotels, restaurants and museums; among the latter are the Museo del Prado (p90), Museo Thyssen-Bornemisza (p95) and the Centro de Arte Reina Sofía (p82), although few museums have guides in Braille or allow visually impaired people to touch objects. The Ayuntamiento's programme of guided tours includes tours for blind, deaf and wheelchair travellers, as well as travellers with an intellectual disability. Such tours run once or twice a month on Saturdays at noon or 6pm; check the website for full details. Audio loops for the hearing impaired in cinemas are almost nonexistent, although most Spanish television channels allow you to turn on subtitles.

When it comes to transport, metro lines built since the late 1990s generally have elevators for wheelchair access, but the older lines are generally ill equipped; the updated metro maps available from any metro station (or at www.metromadrid.es, in Spanish) show stations with wheelchair access. On board the metro the name of the next station is usually announced (if the broadcast system is working, which it doesn't always!).

The single-deck *piso bajo* (low floor) buses have no steps inside and in some cases have ramps that can be used by people in wheelchairs. In the long term, there are plans to make at least 50% of buses on all routes accessible to people with a disability. Radio-Teléfono Taxi (☎ 91 547 82 00, 91 547 86 00) runs taxis for people with a disability. Generally, if you call any taxi company and ask for a 'eurotaxi' you should be sent one adapted for wheelchair users.

One attraction specifically for visually impaired travellers and Spaniards is the Museo Tiflológico (Museum for the Blind; Map p123; ☎ 91 589 42 00; http://museo.once.es/; Calle de la Coruña 18; admission free; 🕙 10am-2pm & 5-8pm Tue-Fri, 10am-2pm Sat; Ⓜ Estrecho). Run by the National Organisation for the Blind (ONCE; see below), its exhibits (all of which may be touched) include paintings, sculptures and tapestries, as well as more than 40 scale models of world monuments, including Madrid's Palacio Real and Cibeles fountain, as well as La Alhambra in Granada and the aqueduct in Segovia. It also provides leaflets in Braille and audio guides to the museum.

Further Information

The Spanish association for the blind, ONCE (Organización Nacional de Ciegos Españoles; Map pp110–11; ☎ 91 577 37 56, 91 522 50 00; www.once.es; Calle de Prim 3; Ⓜ Chueca or Colón), publishes a series of guides in Braille, although not every year.

Hearing-impaired travellers can contact the Comunidad de Madrid's Federation for the Deaf, Fesorcam (Federación de Personas Sordas de la Comunidad de Madrid; Map pp126–7; ☎ 91 725 37 57, 91 726 38 43; www.fesorcam.org, in Spanish; Calle de Ferrer del Río 33; Ⓜ Diego de León).

Travellers with an intellectual disability may wish to contact FEAPS Madrid (Map pp126–7; Federación de Organizaciones en Favor de Personas con Discapacidad Intelectual; ☎ 91 501 83 35; www.feapsmadrid.org, in Spanish; Avenida de la Ciudad de Barcelona 108; Ⓜ Menéndez Pelayo).

Outside Spain, national associations that can offer (sometimes including Madrid-specific) advice:

Access-able Travel Source (☎ 303-232 2979; www.access-able.com; PO Box 1796, Wheatridge, CO, USA)

Accessible Travel & Leisure (☎ 0145 272 9739; www.accessibletravel.co.uk) Claims to be the biggest UK travel agent dealing with travel for the disabled. The company encourages the disabled to travel independently.

Holiday Care (☎ 0845 124 9971; www.holidaycare.org.uk; The Hawkins Ste, Enham Place, Enham Alamein, Andover SP11 6JS, UK)

Mobility International USA (☎ 541-343 1284; www.miusa.org; 132 East Broadway, Ste 343, Eugene, Oregon 97401, USA)

Royal Association for Disability & Rehabilitation (RADAR; ☎ 020-7250 3222; www.radar.org.uk; 12 City Forum, 250 City Rd, London, EC1V 8AF, UK) Publishes a useful guide called *Holidays & Travel Abroad: A Guide for Disabled People*

Society for Accessible Travel and Hospitality (☎ 212-447 7284; www.sath.org; 347 5th Ave, Ste 610, New York, NY 10016, USA)

VISAS

Spain is one of 24 member countries of the Schengen Convention, under which EU member countries (except the UK and Ireland) plus Iceland and Norway have abolished checks at common borders. Legal residents of one Schengen country do not require a visa for another Schengen country. Citizens of the UK, Ireland and Switzerland are also exempt. Nationals of the 10 countries that entered the EU in May 2004 (Cyprus, Czech Republic, Estonia, Hungary, Latvia, Lithuania, Malta, Poland, Slovak Republic and Slovenia) don't need visas for tourist visits or even to take up residence in Spain, but won't have the full work rights enjoyed by other EU citizens until 2011. Nationals of many other countries, including Australia, Canada, Israel, Japan, New Zealand and the USA, do not require visas for tourist visits of up to 90 days. All non-EU nationals entering Spain for any reason other than tourism (such as study or work) should contact a Spanish consulate, as they may need a specific visa.

If you're a citizen of a non-Schengen country not mentioned in this section, check with a Spanish consulate about whether you need a visa. The standard tourist visa issued by Spanish consulates (and usually valid for all Schengen countries unless conditions are attached) is valid for up to 90 days and is not renewable inside Spain.

WOMEN TRAVELLERS

Women travellers have no special reason to fear Madrid as serious harassment of women travellers is rare and seldom extends beyond stares, occasional catcalls and unnecessary comments that you find in most Western European cities. Think twice about walking alone down empty city streets at night.

In the extremely rare event that you are the victim of sexual violence, contact the police (p270), while the Asociación de Asistencia a Mujeres Violadas (Association for Assistance to Raped Women; Map pp126–7; ☎ 91 574 01 10; Calle de O'Donnell 42; ◷ 10am–2pm & 4-7pm Mon-Thu, 10am-4pm Fri; Ⓜ O'Donnell) offers advice and help to rape victims; staff speak only limited English. You could also call the hotline for victims of sexual violence at ☎ 902 180 995.

WORK

Nationals of EU countries, Iceland, Norway and Switzerland are able to work in Spain without a visa, but for stays of more than three months they should apply for a *tarjeta de residencia* (residence card).

Virtually everyone else seeking to work in Spain is supposed to obtain, from a Spanish consulate in their country of residence, a work permit and, if they plan to stay more than 90 days, a residence visa. These procedures are well nigh impossible unless you have a job contract lined up before you begin them (or unless you're married to a Spaniard). Many people do, however, work without tangling with the bureaucracy.

Perhaps the easiest source of work for foreigners is teaching English (or another foreign language), but, even with full qualifications, non-EU citizens will find permanent positions scarce. Most of the larger, more reputable schools will hire only non-EU citizens who already have work and/or residence permits, but their attitude becomes more flexible if demand for teachers is high and you have particularly good qualifications. In the case of EU citizens, employers will generally help you through the bureaucratic minefield.

Madrid is loaded with 'cowboy outfits' that pay badly and often aren't overly concerned about quality. Still, the only way you'll find out is by hunting around. Schools are listed under *Academias de Idiomas* in the *Páginas Amarillas (Yellow Pages)*.

Sources of information on possible teaching work include foreign cultural centres (the British Council, Alliance Française etc), foreign-language bookshops and university notice boards. Many language schools have notice boards where you may find work opportunities, or where you can advertise your own services. Cultural institutes you may want to try include the following.

Alliance Française (Map pp64–5; ☎ 91 435 15 32; www .alliancefrancaisemadrid.net, in Spanish; Cuesta de Santo Domingo 13; Ⓜ Santo Domingo)

British Council (Map pp116–17; ☎ 91 337 35 00; www .britishcouncil.es; Paseo del General Martínez Campos 31; Ⓜ Iglesia)

Goethe Institut (Map pp116–17; ☎ 91 391 39 44; www .goethe.de/madrid, in German or Spanish; Calle de Zurbarán 21; Ⓜ Colón)

Translating and interpreting could be an option if you are fluent in Spanish and have a language that's in demand.

Another option might be au pair work, organised before you come to Spain. A useful guide is *The Au Pair and Nanny's Guide to Working Abroad*, by Susan Griffith and Sharon Legg. Susan Griffith has also written *Work Your Way Around the World* and *Teaching English Abroad*.

Doing Business

Madrid has, in the past decade, imposed itself as the financial as well as political capital of Spain, much to the chagrin of eternal rival Barcelona, which was once considered the country's economic motor. The kind of comparison people used to draw between the two cities and Rome and Milan (respectively the political and financial capitals of Italy) increasingly seems misplaced.

Much of Madrid's business activity takes place in the northern half of the city centre, on and around the Paseo de la Castellana. The biggest trade fairs are held in the complex of the Feria de Madrid, east of the city near the airport.

People looking to expand their business into Spain should contact their own country's trade department (such as the DTI in the UK). The commercial department of the Spanish embassy in your own country should also have information – at least on negotiating the country's epic red tape. The trade office of your embassy may be able to help.

The Cámara Oficial de Comercio e Industria de Madrid (City Chamber of Commerce; ☎ 91 538 35 00; www .camaramadrid.es; Calle de Ribera del Loira 56-58; Ⓜ Campo des las Naciones) offers advisory services on most aspects of doing or setting up business in Madrid, as well as video-conferencing facilities and an accessible business database. The chamber has an office (☎ 91 305 88 07) in terminal T1 (arrivals hall) at Barajas airport with fax, phone and photocopy facilities, and a small meeting area.

Exhibitions & Conferences

The Oficina de Congresos de Madrid (Madrid Convention Bureau; Map pp64–5; ☎ 91 480 24 05; Patronato de Turismo office, Plaza Mayor 27; Ⓜ Sol) publishes the *Guía de Congresos e Incentivos* (also in a CD-ROM version), in Spanish and English, which can be helpful for those interested in organising meetings or conventions.

Madrid's main trade-fair centre is the Feria de Madrid (IFEMA; ☎ 902 221 515; www.ifema.es, in Spanish; Parque Ferial Juan Carlos I; Ⓜ Campo de las Naciones) in Campo de las Naciones, one metro stop from the airport. It hosts events throughout the year. Another important trade-fair centre is the Palacio de Congresos y Exposiciones (Map p123; ☎ 91 337 81 00; www.pcm.tourspain.es; Paseo de la Castellana 99; Ⓜ Santiago Bernabéu). The auditorium can seat 2000 people and there are smaller meeting rooms, with technical support and secretarial services.

You can review the month's upcoming trade fairs in the free *EsMadrid.com* booklet available at tourist offices.

LANGUAGE

Español (Spanish), often referred to as *castellano* (Castilian) to distinguish it from other regional languages spoken in Spain, is the language of Madrid. The conservative Real Academia Española, located near the Prado, watches over Cervantes' tongue with deadly solemnity and issues the country's version of the *Oxford English Dictionary*, the weighty *Diccionario de la Lengua Española*.

While you'll find an increasing number of madrileños, especially younger people and hotel and restaurant employees, who speak some English, don't count on it. Those of you who learn a little Spanish will be amply rewarded as Spaniards always appreciate the effort, no matter how basic your mastery of the language. Madrileños tend to talk at high volume and high velocity. Although the Spanish you learned at school will be fine for most situations, you may start to flounder once the locals revert to local *cheli* (slang).

If you want to learn more Spanish than we've included here, pick up a copy of Lonely Planet's comprehensive but user-friendly *Spanish Phrasebook* or the more compact *Fast Talk Spanish*.

SOCIAL
Meeting People
Hello.
¡Hola!
Goodbye.
¡Adiós!
Please.
Por favor.
Thank you.
(Muchas) Gracias.
Yes.
Sí.
No.
No.
Excuse me.
Perdón.
Sorry.
¡Perdón!/¡Perdóneme!
Do you speak English?
¿Habla inglés?
Does anyone speak English?
¿Hay alguien que hable inglés?
Do you understand?
¿Me entiende?
Yes, I understand.
Sí, entiendo.
No, I don't understand.
No, no entiendo.
Pardon?; What?
¿Cómo?

Could you please ...?
¿Puede ... por favor?

speak more slowly	hablar más despacio
repeat that	repetir
write it down	escribirlo

Going Out
What's there to do in the evenings?
¿Qué se puede hacer por las noches?
Is there a local entertainment guide?
¿Hay una guía del ocio de la zona?

What's on ...?
¿Qué hay…?

locally	en la zona
this weekend	este fin de semana
today	hoy
tonight	esta noche

Where are the ...?
¿Dónde hay ...?

places to eat	lugares para comer
nightclubs	discotecas
pubs	pubs
gay venues	lugares gay

PRACTICAL
Question Words

Who?	¿Quién? (sg)
	¿Quiénes? (pl)
What?	¿Qué?
Which?	¿Cuál? (sg)
	¿Cuáles? (pl)
When?	¿Cuándo?
Where?	¿Dónde?

How?	¿Cómo?
How much?	¿Cuánto?
How many?	¿Cuántos?
How much is it?	¿Cuánto cuesta?
Why?	¿Por qué?

Numbers & Amounts

0	cero
1	una/uno
2	dos
3	tres
4	cuatro
5	cinco
6	seis
7	siete
8	ocho
9	nueve
10	diez
11	once
12	doce
13	trece
14	catorce
15	quince
16	dieciséis
17	diecisiete
18	dieciocho
19	diecinueve
20	veinte
21	veintiuno
22	veintidós
30	treinta
31	treinta y uno
32	treinta y dos
40	cuarenta
50	cincuenta
60	sesenta
70	setenta
80	ochenta
90	noventa
100	cien
1000	mil
2000	dos mil

Days

Monday	lunes
Tuesday	martes
Wednesday	miércoles
Thursday	jueves
Friday	viernes
Saturday	sábado
Sunday	domingo

Banking

I'd like to change some money.
Me gustaría cambiar dinero.

I'd like to change a travellers cheque.
Me gustaría cobrar un cheque de viaje.

Where's the nearest ...?
¿Dónde está ... más cercano?

ATM	el cajero automático
foreign exchange office	la oficina de cambio

Do you accept ...?
¿Aceptan ...?

credit cards	tarjetas de crédito
debit cards	tarjetas de débito
travellers cheques	cheques de viaje

Post

Where's the post office?
¿Dónde está Correos?

I want to send a/an ...
Quería enviar ...

fax	un fax
parcel	un paquete
postcard	una postal

I want to buy a/an ...
Quería comprar ...

aerogramme	un aerograma
envelope	un sobre
stamp/stamps	un sello/sellos

Phones & Internet

I want to buy a phone card.
Quería comprar una tarjeta telefónica.

I want to make a ...
Quería hacer ...

call (to ...)	una llamada a ...
reverse-charge/ collect call	una llamada a cobro revertido

Where can I find a/an ...?
¿Dónde se puede encontrar un ...?
I'd like a/an ...
Quería un ...

adaptor plug	adaptador
charger for my phone	cargador para mi teléfono
mobile/cell phone for hire	móvil para alquilar
prepaid mobile/ cell phone	móvil de prepago
SIM card for your network	tarjeta SIM para su red

Where's the local internet cafe?
¿Dónde hay un ciber (café) cercano?

I'd like to ...
Quería ...

get internet access	conectarme (a internet)
check my email	revisar mi correo electrónico

Transport

What time does the ... leave?
¿A qué hora sale el ...?

bus	autobús
bus (intercity)	autocar
plane	avión
train	tren

What time's the ... bus?
¿A qué hora sale el ... autocar/autobús?

first	primer
last	último
next	próximo

Is this taxi free?
¿Está libre este taxi?
Please put the meter on.
Por favor, ponga el taxímetro.
How much is it to ...?
¿Cuánto cuesta ir a ...?
Please take me (to this address).
Por favor, lléveme (a esta dirección).

FOOD

breakfast	desayuno
lunch	comida
dinner	cena
snack	tentempié

Can you recommend a ...?
¿Puede recomendar un ...?

bar	bar
cafe	café
coffee bar	cafetería
restaurant	restaurante

A table for ..., please.
Una mesa para ..., por favor.
Is service/cover charge included in the bill?
¿Está incluido el servicio en la cuenta?
Do you have a menu in English?
¿Tienen un menu en inglés?
I'm a vegetarian.
Soy vegetariano/a. (m/f)
Do you have any vegetarian dishes?
¿Tienen algún plato vegetariano?
I'm allergic to peanuts.
Soy alérgico/a a los cacahuetes. (m/f)

What is today's special?
¿Cuál es el plato del día?
What would you recommend?
¿Qué recomienda?
I'd like the set lunch, please.
Quería el menú del día, por favor.
The bill, please.
La cuenta, por favor.
Good health/Cheers!
¡Salud!
Thank you, that was delicious.
Muchas gracias, estaba buenísimo.

For more detailed information on food and dining out, see p156.

EMERGENCIES

Help!
¡Socorro!
It's an emergency!
¡Es una emergencia!
Could you help me please?
¿Me puede ayudar, por favor?
Where's the police station?
¿Dónde está la comisaría?
Where are the toilets?
¿Dónde están los servicios?

Call ...!
¡Llame a ...!

the police	la policía
a doctor	un médico
an ambulance	una ambulancia

HEALTH

Where's the nearest ...?
¿Dónde está ... más cercano?

(night) chemist	la farmacia (de guardia)
doctor	el médico
hospital	el hospital

I need a doctor (who speaks English).
Necesito un doctor (que hable inglés).

I have (a/an) ...
Tengo ...

diarrhoea	diarrea
fever	fiebre
headache	dolor de cabeza
pain	dolor

I'm allergic to ...
Soy alérgico/a a ... (m/f)

antibiotics	los antibióticos
peanuts	los cacahuetes

GLOSSARY

abierto – open
abono – season pass
acueducto – aqueduct
aduana – customs
albergue juvenil – youth hostel; not to be confused with *hostal*
alcalde – mayor
alcázar – Muslim-era fortress
Almoravid – Islamic Berbers who founded an empire in North Africa that spread over much of Spain in the 11th century and laid siege to Madrid in 1110
apartado de correos – post-office box
auto-da-fé – elaborate execution ceremony staged by the Inquisition
autonomía – autonomous community or region; Spain's 50 *provincias* are grouped into 17 of these
autopista – motorway (with tolls)
AVE – Tren de Alta Velocidad Española; high-speed train
Ayuntamiento – city or town hall; city or town council
asador – restaurant specialising in roasted meats

bailaores – flamenco dancers
baño completo – full bathroom, with a toilet, shower and/or bath, and washbasin
barrio – district, quarter (of a town or city)
biblioteca – library
billete – ticket (see also *entrada*)
bodega – literally, 'cellar' (especially a wine cellar); also means a winery or a traditional wine bar likely to serve wine from the barrel
bomberos – fire brigade
bota – leather wine or sherry bottle
botellón – literally 'big bottle'; young adolescents partying outdoors
buzón – postbox

cajero automático – automated teller machine (ATM)
calle – street
callejón – lane
cama – bed
cambio – change; currency exchange
cantaor/cantaora – flamenco singer (male/female)
capilla – chapel
Carnaval – carnival; a period of fancy-dress parades and merrymaking, usually ending on the Tuesday 47 days before Easter Sunday
carnet – identity card or driving licence
carretera – highway
casa de comidas – the most basic restaurants specialising in simple, cheap Spanish cooking; aimed at workers on their lunch breaks, they're often only open for lunch Monday to Friday
casco – literally, 'helmet'; often used to refer to the old part of a city
castillo – castle

castizo – literally 'pure'; refers to people and things distinctly from Madrid
catedral – cathedral
centro de salud – health centre
cercanías – local trains serving big cities, suburbs and nearby towns; local train network
cerrado – closed
certificado – registered mail
cervecería – bar where the focus is on beer
chato – glass
churrigueresque – ornate style of Baroque architecture named after the brothers Alberto and José Churriguera
comedor – dining room
comunidad – fixed charge for maintenance of rental accommodation
Comunidad de Madrid – Madrid province
condones – condoms; also called *preservativos*
consejo – council
consigna – a left-luggage office or lockers
coro – choirstall
Correos – post office
corrida (de toros) – bullfight
Cortes – national parliament
cuesta – lane (usually on a hill)
cutre – basic or rough-and-ready

día del espectador – cut-price ticket day at cinemas
diapositiva – slide film
discoteca – nightclub
documento nacional de identidad (DNI) – national identity card
ducha – shower
duende – an indefinable word that captures the passionate essence of flamenco

embajada – embassy
entrada – entrance; ticket for a performance
estación de autobuses – bus station
estanco – tobacconist shop

farmacia – pharmacy
faro – lighthouse
feria – fair; can refer to trade fairs as well as city, town or village fairs, bullfights or festivals lasting days or weeks
ferrocarril – railway
fiesta – festival, public holiday or party
fin de semana – weekend
flamenco – traditional Spanish musical form involving any or all of guitarist, singer and dancer and sometimes accompanying musicians
fútbol – football (soccer)

gasóleo – diesel
gasolina – petrol (a *gasolinera* is a petrol station)
gatos – literally 'cats'; colloquial name for madrileños
gitanos – the Roma people (formerly known as the Gypsies)
glorieta – big roundabout
guiri – foreigner

habitaciones libres – rooms available

habitación doble – twin room

horno de asador – restaurant with a wood-burning roasting oven

hostal – hostel; not to be confused with *albergue juvenil*

iglesia – church

infanta – princess

infante – prince

interprovincial – national (call)

IVA – impuesto sobre el valor añadido (value-added tax)

judería – Jewish quarter

largo recorrido – long-distance train

lavabo – washbasin; a polite term for toilet

lavandería – laundrette

librería – bookshop

lista de correos – poste restante

llamada a cobro revertido – reverse-charges (collect) call

locutorio – telephone centre

luz – electricity

macarras – Madrid's rough but usually likable lads

madrileño – a person from Madrid

marcha – action, life, 'the scene'

marisquería – seafood eatery

media raciones – a serving of tapas, somewhere between the size of tapas and raciones

menú del día – fixed-price meal available at lunchtime, sometimes evening, too; often just called a *menú*

mercado – market

meseta – the high tableland of central Spain

metropolitana – local (call)

mezquita – mosque

monasterio – monastery

morería – former Islamic quarter in town

moro – 'Moor' or Muslim, usually in medieval context

moto – moped or motorcycle

movida madrileña – the halcyon days of the post-Franco years when the city plunged into an excess of nightlife, drugs and cultural expression

mozarab – Christians who lived in Muslim-ruled Spain; also style of architecture

mudéjar – Muslim living under Christian rule in medieval Spain, also refers to their style of architecture

muralla – city wall

museo – museum

objetos perdidos – lost-and-found office

oficina de turismo – tourist office

Páginas Amarillas – *Yellow Pages* phone directory

panteón – pantheon (monument to a famous dead person)

parador – state-owned hotel in a historic building

pensión – guesthouse

peques – children; little ones

pijo/pija – male/female yuppie (can also mean snob, beautiful people)

piscina – swimming pool

plateresco – plateresque; ornate architectural style popular in Spain during the 16th century

plaza mayor – main plaza; square

preservativos – condoms; also *condones*

provincial – (call) within the same province

pueblo – village

puente – bridge

puerta – door or gate

RACE – Real Automóvil Club de España; Royal Automobile Club of Spain

ración – meal-sized serve of tapas

rastro – flea market, car-boot (trunk) sale; El Rastro is Madrid's (and Europe's) largest flea market

ronda – ring road

salida – exit or departure

Semana Santa – Holy Week; the week leading up to Easter Sunday

servicios – toilets

sierra – mountain range

sinagoga – synagogue

sol – sun

sombra – shade

tabernas – taverns

taifa – small Muslim kingdom in medieval Spain

tapas – bar snacks traditionally served on a saucer or lid ('tapa' literally means a lid)

taquilla – ticket window/office

tarde – afternoon

tarjeta de crédito – credit card

tarjeta de residencia – residence card

tarjeta telefónica – phonecard

tasca – tapas bar

temporada alta/media/baja – high, mid- or low season

terraza – terrace; usually means outdoor tables of a café, bar or restaurant; can also mean rooftop open-air place

tetería – teahouse, usually in Middle Eastern style with low seats and round low tables

tienda – shop or tent

torero – bullfighter or matador

toro – bull

torreón – tower

turismo – means both tourism and saloon car

urgencia – first-aid station

villa – town

vinoteca – wine bar

zarzuela – form of Spanish dance and music, usually satirical

zona de movida – an area of town where lively bars and discos are clustered

BEHIND THE SCENES

THIS BOOK

The 1st and 2nd editions of Madrid were written by Damien Simonis. For the 3rd edition he was joined by Sarah Andrews. The 4th and this edition were written by Anthony Ham. This guidebook was commissioned in Lonely Planet's London office, and produced by the following:

Commissioning Editor Clifton Wilkinson

Coordinating Editor Martine Power

Coordinating Cartographer Ross Butler

Coordinating Layout Designer Margie Jung

Managing Editor Brigitte Ellemor

Managing Cartographer Mark Griffiths

Managing Layout Designer Adam McCrow

Assisting Editors Sarah Bailey, Kristin Odijk

Assisting Cartographers Malisa Plesa, James Regan, Peter Shields, Bonnie Wintle

Cover Designer Pepi Bluck

Language Content Coordinator Quentin Frayne

Project Manager Chris Love

Thanks to David Connolly, Jennifer Garrett, Mark Germanchis, Lauren Hunt, Paul Iacono, Yvonne Kirk, Lisa Knights, John Mazzocchi, Trent Paton, Michael Ruff, Sally Schafer, Celia Wood

Cover photographs Detail of Casa de la Panadería (Plaza Mayor), Patrick Escudero/HoaQui/EyeDea/Headpress (top); Bar Antigua Botega Ángel de Sierra (Plaza de Chueca), Gunnar Knechtel/Laif (bottom).

Internal photographs p12 (#2 bottom) Bildarchiv Monheim GmbH/Alamy; p148 (middle) Michelle Chaplow/Alamy; p147 (middle right) dk/Alamy; p10 (#3) Kevin Foy/Alamy; p145 (bottom) Anthony Ham; p4 (#2) imagebroker/Alamy; p1 Gunnar Knechtel/Laif; p146 (middle) M@rcel/Alamy; p9 (#6) Alberto Paredes/Alamy; p12 (#1 bottom) Reuters/Picture Media; p11 (#2 bottom) Martin Thomas/Alamy. All other photographs by Lonely Planet Images: p147 (middle left) Richard Cummins; p3, p4 (#1), p5 (#4), p6 (#1), p6 (#3), p7 (#3), p8 (#1), p9 (#4), p9 (#5), p11 (#1 top), p11 (#2 top), p11 (#3 top), p144 (middle left), p145 (middle), p146 (bottom) Krzysztof Dydynski; p4 (#3) Christopher Groenhout; p11 (#1 bottom) Diego Lezama; p5 (#6), p7 (#2), p9 (#7), p141, p147 (bottom) Guy Moberly; p148 (bottom) Martin Moos; p5 (#5), p7 (#1), p8 (#3), p10 (#1), p10 (#2), p12 (#1 top) Richard Nebesky; p6 (#2) Witold Skrypczak; p8 (#2) Dallas Stribley; p2 David Tomlinson.

All images are copyright of the photographer unless otherwise indicated. Many of the images in this guide are available for licensing from Lonely Planet Images: www .lonelyplanetimages.com.

THANKS
ANTHONY HAM

Special thanks to Juan Manuel Herrero, Agatha Ruiz de la Prada, Oriol Balaguer, Carlos Baute, Manolo Osuna,

THE LONELY PLANET STORY

Fresh from an epic journey across Europe, Asia and Australia in 1972, Tony and Maureen Wheeler sat at their kitchen table stapling together notes. The first Lonely Planet guidebook, *Across Asia on the Cheap*, was born.

Travellers snapped up the guides. Inspired by their success, the Wheelers began publishing books to Southeast Asia, India and beyond. Demand was prodigious, and the Wheelers expanded the business rapidly to keep up. Over the years, Lonely Planet extended its coverage to every country and into the virtual world via lonelyplanet.com and the Thorn Tree message board.

As Lonely Planet became a globally loved brand, Tony and Maureen received several offers for the company. But it wasn't until 2007 that they found a partner whom they trusted to remain true to the company's principles of travelling widely, treading lightly and giving sustainably. In October of that year, BBC Worldwide acquired a 75% share in the company, pledging to uphold Lonely Planet's commitment to independent travel, trustworthy advice and editorial independence.

Today, Lonely Planet has offices in Melbourne, London and Oakland, with over 500 staff members and 300 authors. Tony and Maureen are still actively involved with Lonely Planet. They're travelling more often than ever, and they're devoting their spare time to charitable projects. And the company is still driven by the philosophy of *Across Asia on the Cheap*: 'All you've got to do is decide to go and the hardest part is over. So go!'

SEND US YOUR FEEDBACK

We love to hear from travellers – your comments keep us on our toes and help make our books better. Our well-travelled team reads every word on what you loved or loathed about this book. Although we cannot reply individually to postal submissions, we always guarantee that your feedback goes straight to the appropriate authors, in time for the next edition. Each person who sends us information is thanked in the next edition – and the most useful submissions are rewarded with a free book.

To send us your updates – and find out about Lonely Planet events, newsletters and travel news – visit our award-winning website: www.lonelyplanet.com/contact.

Note: We may edit, reproduce and incorporate your comments in Lonely Planet products such as guidebooks, websites and digital products, so let us know if you don't want your comments reproduced or your name acknowledged. For a copy of our privacy policy visit www.lonelyplanet.com/privacy.

Fernando at Café Comercial, Carolina Fernández and James Nicol. A big thank you to Clifton Wilkinson and Martine Power, my editors at Lonely Planet, who were a dream to work with and whose wisdom and patience made the book so much better. Thanks also to Ross Butler and Sarah Bai-ley. Many thanks to my wonderful family back in Australia and my special cast of madrileño friends, among them Dolores, Raul, Jota (in exile), Eva and Nacho. I couldn't have written this book without my wife, Marina – *eres un encanto y lo mejor de Madrid*. And to the most special person in the world, Carlota, who was born a madrileña just before I began research for this book – *cariño*, may all your dreams come true in this wonderful city.

OUR READERS

Many thanks to the travellers who used the last edition and wrote to us with helpful hints, useful advice and interesting anecdotes:

Leo Alvarado, Carlos Del Amo, Martin Ariaans, Mikael Asmussen, Elisa Åström, Sally Beer, Sarah Briggs, D Burke, Alexander Clarke, Bjorn Clasen, Bronwyn Cousins, Rachel Cowood, David Crowley, Elissa Davies-Colley, Andrew Dier, Yiannis Fanourakis, Linda Finch, Chris Fowler, Jamie Fyffe, Muriel Goldberg, Paul Henchliffe, Karsten Klint Jensen, Anders Jeppsson, Chris Jones, Natasha Josephidou, Anu Laakso, Jack Ljunggren, Rosolind Lowson, Luiz Marques, Kev Mccready, Thomas Mcguire, Sarah Morris, Richard Nosworthy, Lynne Parker, Eric Paya, Emma Ródenas Picardat, Craig Reeder, Paul Roberts, Oscar Sierra, Beverly Smrha, Keren Tuch, Barbara Watt, Dirk De Wilde, Katharina Wojczenko, Hilary Wootton, Manuele Zunelli

Notes

INDEX

000 map pages
000 photographs

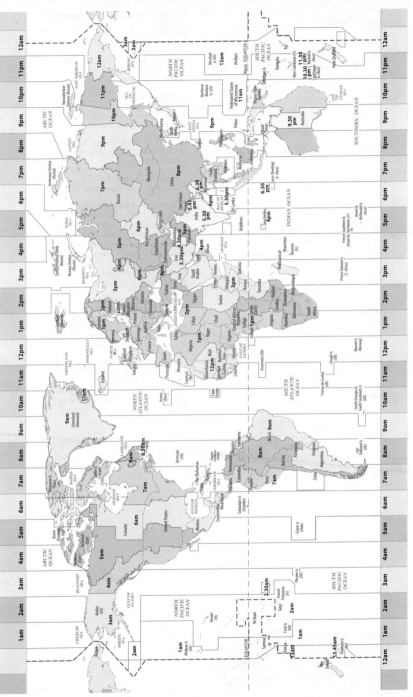

299

MAP LEGEND

ROUTES

..............Tollway
..............Freeway
..............Primary
..............Secondary
..............Tertiary
..............Lane
..............Under Construction
..............One-Way Street

..............Mall/Steps
..............Tunnel
..............Pedestrian Overpass
..............Walking Tour
..............Walking Tour Detour
..............Walking Trail
..............Walking Path
..............Track

TRANSPORT

..............Metro
..............Bus Route

..............Rail
..............Cable Car, Funicular

HYDROGRAPHY

..............River, Creek
..............Water

BOUNDARIES

..............Ancient Wall
..............Cliff

..............Regional, Suburb

AREA FEATURES

..............Airport
..............Area of Interest
..............Building
..............Campus
..............Cemetery, Christian
..............Forest

..............Land
..............Pedestrian Area
..............Market
..............Park
..............Rocks
..............Sports

POPULATION

● ....Large City
○ ....Small City

● ....Medium City
○ ....Town, Village

SYMBOLS

Information
🛈 ....Bank, ATM
..............Embassy/Consulate
✚ ....Hospital, Medical
🛈 ....Information
@ ....Internet Facilities
..............Police Station
..............Post Office, GPO
..............Telephone

Sights
..............Castle, Fortress
..............Christian Site
..............Islamic Site
..............Jewish Site
..............Monument
..............Museum, Gallery
● ....Point of Interest

..............Ruin

Shopping
..............Shopping

Eating
..............Eating

Entertainment
..............Entertainment

Drinking
..............Drinking
..............Café

Nightlife
..............Nightlife
..............Music

Arts
..............Arts

Sports & Activities
..............Pool

Sleeping
..............Sleeping

Transport
..............Airport, Airfield
..............Bus Station
..............Parking Area
..............Petrol Station
..............Taxi Rank

Geographic
..............Lookout
▲ ....Mountain, Volcano
..............National Park
) (..............Pass, Canyon
..............Picnic Area
→ ....River Flow
..............Waterfall

Published by Lonely Planet Publications Pty Ltd
ABN 36 005 607 983

Australia Head Office,
Locked Bag 1, Footscray, Victoria 3011,
☎ 03 8379 8000, fax 03 8379 8111,
talk2us@lonelyplanet.com.au

USA 150 Linden St,
Oakland, CA 94607,
☎ 510 250 6400, toll free 800 275 8555,
fax 510 893 8572, info@lonelyplanet.com

UK 2nd fl, 186 City Rd, London, EC1V 2NT,
☎ 020 7106 2100, fax 020 7106 2101,
go@lonelyplanet.co.uk

© Lonely Planet 2008
Photographs © As listed (p285) 2008

Printed by Hang Tai Printing Company, China.